Web–Based Learning Solutions for Communities of Practice:
Developing Virtual Environments for Social and Pedagogical Advancement

Nikos Karacapilidis
University of Patras, Greece

INFORMATION SCIENCE REFERENCE

Hershey · New York

Director of Editorial Content:	Kristin Klinger
Senior Managing Editor:	Jamie Snavely
Managing Editor:	Jeff Ash
Assistant Managing Editor:	Michael Brehm
Publishing Assistant:	Sean Woznicki
Typesetter:	Jeff Ash
Cover Design:	Lisa Tosheff
Printed at:	Yurchak Printing Inc.

Published in the United States of America by
Information Science Reference (an imprint of IGI Global)
701 E. Chocolate Avenue
Hershey PA 17033
Tel: 717-533-8845
Fax: 717-533-8661
E-mail: cust@igi-global.com
Web site: http://www.igi-global.com/reference

Library of Congress Cataloging-in-Publication Data

Web-based learning solutions for communities of practice : developing virtual environments for social and pedagogical advancement / Nikos Karacapilidis, editor.
     p. cm.

Includes bibliographical references and index.
Summary: " "This book provides readers with an up-to-date research manual in developing innovative and effective learning systems using web-based technologies"--Provided by publisher.

ISBN 978-1-60566-711-9 (hardcover) -- ISBN 978-1-60566-712-6 (ebook) 1. Web-based instruction. 2. Internet in education. 3. Social learning. I. Karacapilidis, Nikos.

LB1044.87.W43559 2010
371.33'44678--dc22
                          2009007737

British Cataloguing in Publication Data
A Cataloguing in Publication record for this book is available from the British Library.

Advances in Web-based Learning Series (AWBL)

ISBN: Pending

Editor-in-Chief: Nikos Karacapilidis, University of Patras, Greece

Web-Based Education and Pedagogical Technologies: Solutions for Learning Applications

Liliane Esnault; EM Lyon, France

IGI Publishing • copyright 2007 • 300+ pp •H/C (ISBN: 978-1-59904-525-2) • US $99.95 (our price)

The rapid development and expansion of Web-based technologies has vast potential implications for the processes of teaching and learning world-wide. Technological advancements of Web-based applications strike at the base of the education spectrum; however, the scope of experimentation and discussion on this topic has continuously been narrow. Web-Based Education and Pedagogical Technologies: Solutions for Learning Applications provides cutting-edge research on such topics as network learning, e-learning, managing Web-based learning and teaching technologies, and building Web-based learning communities. This innovative book provides researchers, practitioners, and decision makers in the field of education with essential, up-to-date research in designing more effective learning systems and scenarios using Web-based technologies.

The Advances in Web-based Learning (AWBL) Book Series aims at providing an in-depth coverage and understanding of diverse issues related to the application of web-based technologies for facilitating and augmenting learning in contemporary organizational settings. The issues covered address the technical, pedagogical, cognitive, social, cultural and managerial perspectives of the Web-based Learning research domain. The Advances in Web-based Learning (AWBL) Book Series endeavors to broaden the overall body of knowledge regarding the above issues, thus assisting researchers, educators and practitioners to devise innovative Web-based Learning solutions. Much attention will be also given to the identification and thorough exploration of good practices in developing, integrating, delivering and evaluating the impact of Web-based Learning solutions. The series intends to supply a stage for emerging research in the critical areas of web-based learning to further expand to importance of comprehensive publications on these topics of global importance.

Hershey • New York

Order online at www.igi-global.com or call 717-533-8845 x10 –
Mon-Fri 8:30 am - 5:00 pm (est) or fax 24 hours a day 717-533-8661

Editorial Advisory Board

Jan Frick, *Stavanger University College, Norway*
Martin Gaedke, *Universität Karlsruhe, Germany*
Cesar Garita, *University of Amsterdam, The Netherlands*
George Ghinea, *Brunel University, UK*
Danièle Herrin, *Univeristé de Montpellier, Montpellier, France*
Ikuo Kitagaki, *Hiroshima University, Japan*
VP Kochikar, *Infosys Technologies, India*
Andy Koronios, *University of South Australia, Australia*

List of Reviewers

Aida Boukottaya, *University of Fribourg, Switzerland*
Amaury Daele, *University of Fribourg, Switzerland*
Sandy El Helou, *École Polytechnique Fédérale de Lausanne, Switzerland*
George Gkotsis, *University of Patras, Greece*
Markos Hatzitaskos, *University of Patras, Greece*
Vasilis Kallistros, *Research Academic Computer Technology Institute, Greece*
Nikos Karousos, *Research Academic Computer Technology Institute, Greece*
Stéphane Sire, *École Polytechnique Fédérale de Lausanne, Switzerland*
Eleftheria Tomadaki, *Knowledge Media Institute, The Open University, UK*
Nikos Tsianos, *National & Kapodistrian University of Athens, Greece*
Manolis Tzagarakis, *Research Academic Computer Technology Institute, Greece*

Table of Contents

Detailed Table of Contents

Chapter 1

Evelyn Gullett, Universitas 21 Global, Germany

This chapter reports on a qualitative study that examined the depth of e-feedback given by online facilitators on case study and discussion board assignments, how that feedback contributed to the learner's social learning, development and growth, and how quality e-feedback influences the virtual social learning environment. This study identified seven criteria of feedback depth tied to social learning that serve online university communities of practice as a tool towards a base standard of e-feedback that encourages social learning and development of each learner.

Chapter 2 ·

Aida Boukottaya, University of Fribourg, Switzerland
Bernadette Charlier, University of Fribourg, Switzerland
Micaël Paquier, EPFL, Switzerland
Loïc Merz, EPFL, Switzerland
Stéphane Sire, EPFL, Switzerland
Christine Vanoirbeek, EPFL, Switzerland

Virtual communities of practice are gaining importance as a means of sharing and exchanging knowledge. In such environments, information reuse is of major concern. This chapter outlines the importance of structuring documents in order to facilitate the reuse of their content. The authors show how explicit structure representation facilitates the understanding of the original documents and helps considerably in automating the reuse process. Besides, they describe two tools: one performing automatic structure transformation using matching techniques and another one performing structure and instances evolution in a transparent and automatic manner.

This chapter presents the motivation and incentives behind the email-based eLogbook interface, developed in the framework of the PALETTE European research project. eLogbook is a Web-based collaborative environment designed for communities of practice, which enables users to manage joint activities, share related assets and get contextual awareness. As discussed, the purpose of this lightweight interface is twofold. First, it eases eLogbook access when using smart phones or PDA. Second, it eases eLogbook acceptance for community members hesitating to learn an additional Web environment.

This chapter investigates a tool integration perspective to support knowledge management and exchange between Web-based and traditional collaborative environments. In particular, it deals with the integration between a tool supporting collaborative argumentation and learning in Web-based communities of practices, and a sense making tool acting as a personal and collective knowledge management system in traditional collaborative environments. The results of a case study, in which the tools integration has been applied within a real community of practice, are presented. Also, the main results from the tools integration, which aims at leveraging communities of practice to a truly collaborative environment with no communication boundaries, are discussed.

Chapter 5

Distance learning institutions need to find a way to transplant the benefits of conventional tutoring practices into the development of digital content that is conducive to students' learning needs. Therein lie two great challenges: promote real distance learning effectively and, at the same time, try to accommodate the ability of students to learn via collaboration. This chapter's authors have proposed the development of learner's open-and-distance-learning courses as both a theoretical model and an applied methodology to be one of their key priorities, and describe how this concept co-evolves with Web mining and institutional infrastructures to address the needs of emergent communities of practice within their university.

The purpose of this chapter is to show how storytelling can be used as an effective pedagogical model for enhancing learning in a community of practice (CoP) using Web-based learning tools. CoPs provide opportunities for learning by sharing knowledge and experience. In such settings, storytelling can make the knowledge and experience sharing discourses more engaging. However, crafting engaging stories remains a challenge. The chapter reports on the movement oriented design (MOD) paradigm, which provides a framework for creating effective story plots using principles of good storytelling. As claimed, storytelling can be introduced as a mode of discourse in CoPs using existing text and multimedia authoring systems. However, creating new Web 2.0 tools for story development using the MOD paradigm will allow almost anyone to create engaging educational stories and use these in a CoP.

Chapter 7

Focusing on the particularities of online communities of practice (CoPs), and the tools they use for facilitating or enhancing collaboration among their members, this chapter introduces a framework for mining knowledge that is hidden in such settings. The authors' motivation stems from the criticism that contemporary tools receive regarding lack of active participation and limited engagement in their use, which is partially due to the inability of identifying and exploiting a set of important relationships among community members and the associated collaboration-related assets. The overall approach described in this chapter elaborates and integrates issues from data mining and social networking. The proposed framework enables CoPs members to rank the contributions of their peers towards identifying meaningful relationships, as well as valuable information about roles and competences. First, the characteristics of the overall collaboration setting are modeled and a set of associated metrics is proposed. Next, to reveal unnoticed knowledge residing within CoPs, a data mining technique that groups users into clusters and applies advanced social networking analysis on them is proposed.

Chapter 8

This chapter presents qualitative and quantitative data from a naturalistic insight into the use of two online synchronous communication tools, FM for videoconference and Hexagon for ambient awareness, to support an extended event in a working online community. As claimed by the authors, a complex mix of planned and opportunistic interactions requires a new set of working synchronous tools, managing the trade-off between awareness and disruption. Switching between foreground and background 'meeting activity' remains a very big challenge.

Nikos Tsianos, National & Kapodistrian University of Athens, Greece
Zacharias Lekkas, National & Kapodistrian University of Athens, Greece
Panagiotis Germanakos, University of Cyprus, Cyprus
Constantinos Mourlas, National & Kapodistrian University of Athens, Greece

The knowledge management paradigm of communities of practice can be efficiently realized in Web-based environments, especially if one considers the extended social networks that have proliferated within the Internet. In terms of increasing performance through the exchange of knowledge and shared learning, individual characteristics, such as learners' preferences that relate to group working, may be of high importance. These preferences have been summarized in cognitive and learning styles typologies, as well as emotional characteristics which define implications that could serve as personalization guidelines for designing collaborative learning environments. This chapter discusses the theoretical assumptions of two distinct families of learning style models, cognitive personality and information processing styles, and the role of affection and emotion, in order to explore the possibilities of personalization at the group level of communities of practice.

Manolis Tzagarakis, Research Academic Computer Technology Institute, Greece
Nikos Karousos, Research Academic Computer Technology Institute, Greece
Giorgos Gkotsis, Research Academic Computer Technology Institute, Greece
Vasilis Kallistros, Research Academic Computer Technology Institute, Greece
Spyros Christodoulou, Research Academic Computer Technology Institute, Greece
Christos Mettouris, Research Academic Computer Technology Institute, Greece
Panagiotis Kyriakou, Research Academic Computer Technology Institute, Greece
Dora Nousia, Research Academic Computer Technology Institute, Greece

As argued by this chapter's authors, current tools aiming at supporting argumentative collaboration provide either means to successfully tame wicked problems or advanced reasoning mechanisms to facilitate decision making creating a gap in today's landscape of systems supporting argumentative collaboration. The consequences of this gap are in particular severe for communities of practice when they have to employ tools from both sides to support their collaboration needs. The authors claim that a key factor in bridging this gap is viewing argumentative collaboration as an emergent phenomenon. Proper support of the emergent aspects of argumentative collaboration would benefit systems supporting argumentative collaboration as this would enable those systems to support the evolution of the entire collaboration at different levels. The authors also describe how such an approach has been implemented in CoPe_it!, an innovative Web-based argumentative collaboration support system.

In this chapter, the concept of an organizational knowledge circulation management system of e-learning is presented. Aiming at convincing their university's faculty about the benefits of e-learning by providing them with hands-on experience in online education, the authors have developed a mentoring system module and a learning design repository based on technological and pedagogical aspects, and evaluated the system in two case studies. The chapter also describes important functions and evaluation aspects of new information technology system of e-learning.

Chapter 12

This chapter explores the use of Web-based technologies incorporating communities of practice and social networks to enhance the learning experience in hybrid and distance classes. Research suggests that using a variety of technologies and methods to reach people with different learning styles improves overall learning in a class delivery though different methods are more effective in traditional vs. online classes. Moreover, using new, emerging Web-based technologies, including both Web 1.0 and Web 2.0 software, further enhances the engagement and value of the learning experience in these classes. This chapter examines the methods and technologies that can be potentially used to create excellence learning environments in traditional hybrid and online classes.

Chapter 13

Students experiencing an online educational community for the first time experience adjustment in the role of learner. Findings from a study of adjustment to online learning from the instructor's point of view validate five main areas of adjustment identified in previous research: technology, instructor role, modes of interaction, self-identity and course design. Using a confirmatory research model, instructors from two open and distance institutions were interviewed. Data confirmed that instructors also perceive adjustment in the five areas of online experience identified by students. In addition, student adjustment in these five areas can be understood in light of core dimensions of learner role requirements in an online community of inquiry. Instructor comments provide understanding of the experience of online learners, including the challenges, interventions and resolutions that present themselves as unique incidents. Recommendations for the support and facilitation of adjustment are also made.

    Hannu Salmi, University of Helsinki, Finland
    Sofoklis Sotiriou, Ellinogermaniki Agogi Foundation, Greece
    Franz Bogner, University of Bayreuth, Germany

This chapter presents an implementation of Augmented Reality technology in science education. While this technology up to now mainly was used by very special users such as the military and high-tech companies, it gradually converts into wider educational use. Specific research programs applied this technology with a specific focus on selected learning scenarios by a close co-operation of formal education and informal learning. As discussed in detail in this chapter, empirical effects related to intrinsic motivation and cognitive learning of students were encouraging.

Selected Readings

    Lakshmi Goel, University of Houston, USA
    Elham Mousavidin, University of Houston, USA

This chapter provides a framework which suggests that KM success can be achieved by designing sustainable communities of practice. Communities of practice have proven to have significant economic and practical implications on organizational practices. A growing body of literature in KM recognizes the importance of communities that foster collaborative learning in organizations and almost all KMS have a 'network' component that facilitates connecting people in communities of practice. Evidence has shown that communities have been a key element in KMS of many companies including Xerox PARC, British Petroleum Co., Shell Oil Company, Halliburton, IBM, Proctor and Gamble, and Hewlett Packard.

    Juan Pablo Soto, University of Castilla - La Mancha, Spain
    Aurora Vizcaíno, University of Castilla - La Mancha, Spain
    Javier Portillo-Rodríguez, University of Castilla - La Mancha, Spain
    Mario Piattini, University of Castilla - La Mancha, Spain

This chapter proposes a multi-agent architecture and a trust model with which to foster the reuse of information in organizations which use knowledge bases or knowledge management systems. The architecture and the model have been designed with the goal of giving support to communities of practice. However, members of these communities are currently often geographically distributed, and less trust therefore exists among members than in traditional local communities. To address this issue, the chapter proposes a trust model, which can be used to calculate what piece of knowledge is more trustworthy.

This chapter starts by hypothesizing that virtual communities of practice (VCoPs) are valuable to business schools and universities because they contribute to the emerging paradigms of just-in-time, action-based informal learning. It presents a real case study of a VCoP called Virtual eBMS that was built by applying participative observation. The chapter provides a process-oriented model of Virtual eBMS that is composed of four main elements: the people participating in the community, the processes and the purpose of the community in terms of the value created for the business school, and the technology enabling the interactions between the community members. From a technological point of view, the community is supported by an integrated Web learning and knowledge management platform, described in terms of the main knowledge processes triggered and the correspondent technologies supporting the actions.

The chapter examines the IntelCities Community of Practice (CoP) supporting the development of the organization's e-learning platform, knowledge management system (KMS) and digital library. It begins by outlining the IntelCities CoP and goes on to set out the integrated model of electronically enhanced government (eGov) services developed by the CoP to meet the related front-end needs, middleware requirements and back-office commitments. The chapter goes on to examine the information technology adopted by the CoP to develop the IntelCities e-learning platform, KMS and digital library as a set of semantically interoperable eGov services supporting the crime, safety and security initiatives of socially-inclusive and participatory urban regeneration programs.

This chapter introduces the experience of the Argentine IT Professionals Forum (ITPF) that enriches the definition of processes involving the tasks of e-government. The ITPF has become a cross-agency network that involves all the IT professionals of the public administration. It was created in 2002 as a response to the institutional crisis in Argentina in order to solve problems associated with the IT areas. The most important contribution of the ITPF is the basis for the back office as an interesting management model, theoretically known as "communities of practice" and networks, which have become core organizational tools as far as carrying out difficult innovation processes, such as the development of free software, cross-agency applications, and interoperability.

This chapter offers interesting insights for the implementation of communities of practice, which are being viewed as a tool for knowledge management and improvement of competitiveness in organizations. The reflection made on the challenges of the creation of these communities clarifies possible uncertainties or incoherencies that could appear after reading the applicability of these communities on a practical level. It also analyzes the various documented real experiences, which can contribute to better understand concepts such as design, cultivation of communities, promotion of communities, organic communities, etc.

Preface

For more than ten years, communities of practice (CoPs) have been recognized as effective environments to support learning among professionals, organizations and educational institutions. Collaborative learning is inherent in such communities, in that their members learn from each other by making their knowledge and practices explicit, sharing them with their peers, and reflecting on them. Web-based technologies could support the development of virtual CoPs. Consequently, more and more CoPs use virtual environments to support their activities. However, despite the rapidly increasing potential offered by technologies (including Web-based platforms, wireless communications, mobile devices and extensive use of multimedia contents), recent research underlines the lack of adequate scaffolding in the form of both technical supports and usage of the technology to address the diversity of CoPs' requirements.

This volume of Advances in Web-based Learning (AWBL) Book Series, entitled *Web-Based Learning Solutions for Communities of Practice: Developing Virtual Environments for Social and Pedagogical Advancement*, reports on recent approaches that aim at aiding CoPs members to express, represent and share practices, debate and reflect about the practices and about the life of the CoP, develop, reify and exploit knowledge inside and outside of the CoP, and facilitate engagement, participation and learning. Such approaches elaborate and build on various concepts that are related to the information, knowledge management and collaboration services required. Particular emphasis is given to the design, implementation and evaluation of the related solutions. The value and main contribution of the book lies in the joint exploration of diverse technological, social and pedagogical issues towards designing, implementing and testing e-learning solutions for CoPs, while paying equal attention to the issues of individual and organizational learning.

Chapter 1, "The Impact of Quality E-Feedback as an Element of Social Learning Theory Applied in the Context of E-Learning Communities of Practice" by Evelyn Gullett, Universitas 21 Global (Germany), reports on a qualitative study that examined the depth of e-feedback given by online facilitators on case study and discussion board assignments, how that feedback contributed to the learner's social learning, development and growth, and how quality e-feedback influences the virtual social learning environment. This study identified seven criteria of feedback depth tied to social learning that serve online university communities of practice as a tool towards a base standard of e-feedback that encourages social learning and development of each learner.

Chapter 2, "A Document Reuse Tool for Communities of Practice" by Aida Boukottaya, University of Fribourg (Switzerland), Bernadette Charlier, University of Fribourg (Switzerland), Micaël Paquier, École Polytechnique Fédérale de Lausanne – EPFL (Switzerland), Loïc Merz, École Polytechnique Fédérale de Lausanne – EPFL (Switzerland), Stéphane Sire, École Polytechnique Fédérale de Lausanne – EPFL (Switzerland), and Christine Vanoirbeek, École Polytechnique Fédérale de Lausanne – EPFL (Switzerland), outlines the importance of structuring documents in order to facilitate the reuse of their content. The authors show how explicit structure representation facilitates the understanding of the original documents and helps considerably in automating the reuse process. Besides, they describe two tools: one performing automatic structure transformation using matching techniques and another one performing structure and instances evolution in a transparent and automatic manner.

Chapter 3, "Tackling Acceptability Issues in Communities of Practice by Providing a Lightweight Email-based Interface to Social Software" by Chiu Man Yu, Denis Gillet, Sandy El Helou, and Christophe Salzmann, École Polytechnique Fédérale de Lausanne - EPFL (Switzerland), presents the motivation and incentives behind the email-based eLogbook interface, developed in the framework of the PALETTE European research project. eLogbook is a Web-based collaborative environment designed for communities of practice, which enables users to manage joint activities, share related assets and get contextual awareness. As discussed, the purpose of this lightweight interface is twofold. First, it eases eLogbook access when using smart phones or PDA. Second, it eases eLogbook acceptance for community members hesitating to learn an additional Web environment.

Chapter 4, "Supporting Communities of Practice by Advancing Knowledge Management between Hybrid Collaborative Environments", by Anna De Liddo, Open University (UK), and Grazia Concilio, Politecnico di Milano (Italy), investigates a tool integration perspective to support knowledge management and exchange between Web-based and traditional collaborative environments. In particular, it deals with the integration between a tool supporting collaborative argumentation and learning in Web-based communities of practices, and a sense making tool acting as a personal and collective knowledge management system in traditional collaborative environments. The results of a case study, in which the tools integration has been applied within a real community of practice, are presented. Also, the main results from the tools integration, which aims at leveraging communities of practice to a truly collaborative environment with no communication boundaries, are discussed.

Chapter 5, "Using Graphs in Developing Educational Material" by Thanassis Hadzilacos, Open University of Cyprus (Cyprus) & Research Academic Computer Technology Institute (Greece), Dimitris Kalles, Hellenic Open University (Greece), Dionysis Karaiskakis, Hellenic Open University (Greece), and Maria Pouliopoulou, Research Academic Computer Technology Institute (Greece), proposes the development of learner's open-and-distance-learning courses as both a theoretical model and an applied methodology to be one of the key priorities of distance learning institutions. The authors describe how this concept co-evolves with Web mining and institutional infrastructures to address the needs of emergent communities of practice. As the authors argue, distance learning institutions need to find a way to transplant the benefits of conventional tutoring practices into the development of digital content that is conducive to students' learning needs. Therein lie two great challenges: promote real distance learning effectively and, at the same time, try to accommodate the ability of students to learn via collaboration.

Chapter 6, "Using Storytelling as the Pedagogical Model for Web-Based Learning in Communities of Practice" by Nalin Sharda, Victoria University (Australia), shows how storytelling can be used as an effective pedagogical model for enhancing learning in a community of practice (CoP) using Web-based learning tools. CoPs provide opportunities for learning by sharing knowledge and experience. In such settings, storytelling can make the knowledge and experience sharing discourses more engaging. However, crafting engaging stories remains a challenge. The chapter reports on the movement oriented design (MOD) paradigm, which provides a framework for creating effective story plots using principles of good storytelling. As claimed, storytelling can be introduced as a mode of discourse in CoPs using existing text and multimedia authoring systems. However, creating new Web 2.0 tools for story development using the MOD paradigm will allow almost anyone to create engaging educational stories and use these in a CoP.

Chapter 7, "Mining Unnoticed Knowledge in Collaboration Support Systems" by George Gkotsis, Research Academic Computer Technology Institute (Greece) and Nikos Tsirakis, University of Patras

(Greece) - by focusing on the particularities of online communities of practice (CoPs) and the tools they use for facilitating or enhancing collaboration among their members - introduces a framework for mining knowledge that is hidden in such settings. The authors' motivation stems from the criticism that contemporary tools receive regarding lack of active participation and limited engagement in their use, which is partially due to the inability of identifying and exploiting a set of important relationships among community members and the associated collaboration-related assets. The overall approach described in this chapter elaborates and integrates issues from data mining and social networking. The proposed framework enables CoPs members to rank the contributions of their peers towards identifying meaningful relationships, as well as valuable information about roles and competences. First, the characteristics of the overall collaboration setting are modeled and a set of associated metrics is proposed. Next, to reveal unnoticed knowledge residing within CoPs, a data mining technique that groups users into clusters and applies advanced social networking analysis on them is proposed.

Chapter 8, "Live Virtual Technologies to Support Extended Events in Online Communities of Practice" by Eleftheria Tomadaki, Peter Scott and Kevin Quick, Open University (UK), presents qualitative and quantitative data from a naturalistic insight into the use of two online synchronous communication tools, FM for videoconference and Hexagon for ambient awareness, to support an extended event in a working online community. As claimed by the authors, a complex mix of planned and opportunistic interactions requires a new set of working synchronous tools, managing the trade-off between awareness and disruption. Switching between foreground and background 'meeting activity' remains a very big challenge.

Chapter 9, "Individual Learning and Emotional Characteristics in Web-based Communities of Practice" by Nikos Tsianos, National & Kapodistrian University of Athens (Greece), Zacharias Lekkas, National & Kapodistrian University of Athens (Greece), Panagiotis Germanakos, University of Cyprus (Cyprus), and Constantinos Mourlas, National & Kapodistrian University of Athens (Greece), argues that the knowledge management paradigm of communities of practice can be efficiently realized in Web-based environments, especially if one considers the extended social networks that have proliferated within the Internet. In terms of increasing performance through the exchange of knowledge and shared learning, individual characteristics, such as learners' preferences that relate to group working, may be of high importance. These preferences have been summarized in cognitive and learning styles typologies, as well as emotional characteristics which define implications that could serve as personalization guidelines for designing collaborative learning environments. The chapter discusses the theoretical assumptions of two distinct families of learning style models, cognitive personality and information processing styles, and the role of affection and emotion, in order to explore the possibilities of personalization at the group level of communities of practice.

Chapter 10, "From 'Collecting' to 'Deciding': Facilitating the Emergence of Decisions in Argumentative Collaboration" by Manolis Tzagarakis, Nikos Karousos, George Gkotsis, Vasilis Kallistros, Spyros Christodoulou, Christos Mettouris, Panagiotis Kyriakou, and Dora Nousia, Research Academic Computer Technology Institute (Greece), elaborate argumentative collaboration issues in the context of communities of practice. As argued by the authors, current tools aiming at supporting argumentative collaboration provide either means to successfully tame wicked problems or advanced reasoning mechanisms to facilitate decision making creating a gap in today's landscape of systems supporting argumentative collaboration. The consequences of this gap are in particular severe for communities of practice when they have to employ tools from both sides to support their collaboration needs. The authors claim that a key factor in bridging this gap is viewing argumentative collaboration as an emergent phenomenon. Proper support of the emergent aspects of argumentative collaboration would benefit systems supporting argumentative collaboration as this would enable those systems to support the evolution of the entire collaboration at different levels. The authors also describe how such an approach has been implemented in CoPe_it!, an innovative Web-based argumentative collaboration support system.

Chapter 11, "An Organizational Knowledge Circulation Management System for Universities" by Toshie Ninomiya, Fumihiko Anma, and Toshio Okamoto, The University of Electro-Communications (Japan), deals with the concept of an organizational knowledge circulation management system of e-learning. Aiming at convincing their university's faculty about the benefits of e-learning by providing them with hands-on experience in online education, the authors have developed a mentoring system module and a learning design repository based on technological and pedagogical aspects, and evaluated the system in two case studies. The chapter also describes important functions and evaluation aspects of new information technology system of e-learning.

Chapter 12, "Using Web-Based Technologies and Communities of Practice for Transformative Hybrid & Distance Education" by Nory Jones and Omar Khan, The Maine Business School, University of Maine (USA), explores the use of Web-based technologies incorporating communities of practice and social networks to enhance the learning experience in hybrid and distance classes. Research suggests that using a variety of technologies and methods to reach people with different learning styles improves overall learning in a class delivery though different methods are more effective in traditional vs. online classes. Moreover, using new, emerging Web-based technologies, including both Web 1.0 and Web 2.0 software, further enhances the engagement and value of the learning experience in these classes. This chapter examines the methods and technologies that can be potentially used to create excellence learning environments in traditional hybrid and online classes.

Chapter 13, "The Role of Learner in an Online Community of Inquiry: Instructor Support for First-time Online Learners" by Martha Cleveland-Innes, Athabasca University (Canada), and Randy Garrison, The University of Calgary (Canada), presents findings from a study of adjustment to online learning from the instructor's point of view. These findings validate five main areas of adjustment identified in previous research: technology, instructor role, modes of interaction, self-identity and course design. Using a confirmatory research model, instructors from two open and distance institutions were interviewed. Data confirmed that instructors also perceive adjustment in the five areas of online experience identified by students. In addition, student adjustment in these five areas can be understood in light of core dimensions of learner role requirements in an online community of inquiry. Instructor comments provide understanding of the experience of online learners, including the challenges, interventions and resolutions that present themselves as unique incidents. Recommendations for the support and facilitation of adjustment are also given.

Chapter 14, "Visualising the Invisible in Science Centres and Science Museums: Augmented Reality Technology Application and Science Teaching" by Hannu Salmi, University of Helsinki (Finland), Sofoklis Sotiriou, Ellinogermaniki Agogi Foundation (Greece), and Franz Bogner, University of Bayreuth (Germany), presents an implementation of augmented reality technology in science education. While this technology up to now mainly was used by very special users such as the military and high-tech companies, it gradually converts into wider educational use. Specific research programs applied this technology with a specific focus on selected learning scenarios by a close co-operation of formal education and informal learning. As discussed in detail in this chapter, empirical effects related to intrinsic motivation and cognitive learning of students were encouraging.

In addition to the above, this volume includes six chapters (Chapters 15-20), considered as *selected readings,* which aim to provide supplementary related information in support of the book's concepts, principles and results. These chapters increase the appeal of this book as a one-stop reference source on Web-based learning solutions for communities of practice.

Advances reported in this book are expected to augment current learning-related practices in diverse CoPs' contexts, including organizations, academia and Web-based communities. The book is also expected to advance research being conducted in the field of technology-enhanced learning by assigning equal importance to its underlying technological, social and pedagogical dimensions. *Web-Based Learning Solutions for Communities of Practice: Developing Virtual Environments for Social and Pedagogical Advancement* is valuable to people from both academia and industry (teachers, researchers, professionals or practitioners in the field of e-learning). It covers a large number of topics concerning the appropriate information, knowledge management and collaboration services to be offered in order to facilitate collaboration and augment learning in diverse communities' contexts. By also paying attention to the social dimension of technology-enhanced learning, the book is of particular importance to researchers and supporters of the so-called social software.

Nikos Karacapilidis
Editor-in-Chief
Advances in Web-Based Learning Book Series

Chapter 1

The Impact of Quality E-Feedback as an Element of Social Learning Theory Applied in the Context of E-Learning Communities of Practice

Evelyn Gullett
Universitas 21 Global, Germany

ABSTRACT

This chapter discusses the preliminary study of meaningful quality e-feedback as an element of social learning theory applied in the online learning environment, or a Web-based community of practice. This qualitative study compared the depth of e-feedback given by online facilitators on case study and discussion board assignments, how that feedback contributed to the learner's social learning, development and growth, and how quality e-feedback influences the virtual social learning environment. This study identified seven criteria of feedback depth tied to social learning that serve online university communities of practice as a tool towards a base standard of e-feedback that encourages social learning and development of each learner.

INTRODUCTION

Overall, it has been observed that higher educational organizations are "becoming increasingly business-like" (Holmes, George, McElwee, Gerard, 1995). With the continuous powerful growth of online university and corporate programs reaching global customers, it is just as crucial for those e-learning establishments to include not only service quality assessments for which they are held accountable (Kerlin, 2000), but to also include continuous good practices or quality and improvement mechanisms to help e-facilitators to maintain the highest quality standard consistently when lecturing, teaching, guiding, administering and supporting the online learner. Giving meaningful and quality e-feedback as an element of social learning to the student in online communities of practice is an essential part of this endeavor.

DOI: 10.4018/978-1-60566-711-9.ch001

This chapter discusses the preliminary study of meaningful quality e-feedback as an element of Social Learning Theory applied in the environment of online communities of practice. Specifically, the study will compare and contrast the depth of feedback given by various professors for online assignments such as Discussion Board postings and Case Studies, for example, and how they contributed to the students' social learning experience. Moreover, this study will undertake the effort to understand feedback and its importance as a social learning theory in e-learning, and how it may influence virtual communication and the overall learning environment of this online community of practice, or online classroom and its members.

This study will assume to identify criteria of feedback depth tied to social learning that will serve online Communities of Practice (such as online universities and corporate training programs) as a tool to achieve a base standard for consistent quality behavior. This is not only crucial for accreditation purposes for universities offering online learning programs, but also to remain a high rigor of quality management and assessment of their online educational programs; thus, making them more competitive. Encouraging consistent quality feedback as a social learning theory element to be applied as part of an activity among scholars and practitioners in the e-learning Community of Practice will enhance the overall learning outcome of the student and add to the rigor and quality of the educational program as a whole.

BACKGROUND

Social Learning Theory

As researched by Albert Bandura, Jean Piaget and Lev Vygotsky, teaching and learning are highly social activities and are key elements in the process of learning and development (Kim, Y., & Baylor,

A., 2006). Bandura's social learning theory focuses on the individual's observation and modeled behavior, attitudes and emotional reactions (1977). An individual is most likely to adopt the modeled behavior if the following criteria are met. He or she finds the outcomes of the modeled behavior meaningful, the person observed is similar to him or her, the model is admired, and the behavior is perceived to be of functional significance. "Social learning theory explains human behavior in terms of continuous reciprocal interaction between cognitive, behavioral, an environmental influences" (Bandura, n.d.).

Similarly, Vygotsky also highlights the significance of social learning. His social development theory discusses the fundamental influence social interaction has on the cognitive development of the human being. Vygotsky (1978) states that "every function in the child's cultural development appears twice: first, on the social level, and later, on the individual level; first, between people (interpsychological) and then inside the child (intrapsychological). This applies equally to voluntary attention, to logical memory, and to the formation of concepts. All the higher functions originate as actual relationships between individuals." (p. 57).

An additional feature of Vygotsky's theoretical framework is his suggestion of the "zone of proximal development". Once children interact socially, they will reach a certain level of development that will influence their cognitive development. Full maturation is thus dependent upon social interaction. An individual's potential level of development can be continuously developed "through problem solving under adult guidance or in collaboration with more capable peers" (Vygotsky, p. 86, 1978). In other words, students are able to achieve more with the help and feedback of e-facilitators than on their own.

The social learning theory embraces various theories of learning to include cognitive, humanistic and behaviorist. In the 19th century, behavior was included in the study of the mind and how people acquire knowledge. Aristotle believed that individuals come to know through their senses (Hergenhahn, 1988), and according to Plato, by making connections in their daily observation of physical objects (Caffarella & Merriam, 1999).

Thinking individuals will translate and interpret their experienced sensation of an event and give meaning to that event (Grippin & Peters, 1984). In other words, to make sense of external stimuli, a person uses his or her mental processes by categorizing his or her experiences, which is the cognitive approach to learning. This is closely tied to the humanist theory of learning in that individual growth is emphasized on the idea of unlimited potential for growth and development based on their perceived experiences (Rogers, 1983, Maslow, 1970).

Thorndike, Tolman, Guthrie, Hull, and Skinner (Ormond, 1995) held three basic assumptions about the behaviorist learning process. First, behavioral change is triggered by learning. Second, behavior, as well as what one learns, is triggered by external stimuli of the person's environment. Third, the proximity of occurrence for these two events and the frequency of reinforcement of these events are crucial elements when explaining the learning process of the individual (Grippin & Peters, 1984). Combining cognitivist and behaviorist orientations, the social learning theory suggests that individuals learn from observing others (Caffarella & Merriam, 1999).

Being engaged in conversation and activities with others is the element that develops an individual (Vygotsky, et al., 1978). While different types of performance feedback has various outcomes on the learner's self-efficacy (Schunk & Lilly, 1984), logical and educational feedback is an essential and effective element towards the growth of social learning, social and cognitive development in a collaborative environment, of which online communities of practice are a part of.

Feedback

For the purpose of this chapter, feedback is defined as giving and sharing information in the form of guidance and support as an integral element to foster improvement, development, and understanding of material learned and applied.

According to Merriam-Websters Online Dictionary, feedback is "the transmission of evaluative or corrective information about an action, event, or process to the original or controlling source" (2008). Feedback can also be defined as the receiving of information about past behavior, as being delivered in the present, and as possibly being of influence of future behavior (Seashore, et al., 1999). Feedback can also be seen as a systems concept as it is an ongoing process of which at least two individuals must be a part.

Studies have shown (Krause, K., Hartley, R., James, R., & McInnis, C. 2005; Hounsell, D., 2003) that the depth and amount of feedback to students varied from course to course and instructor to instructor. Inconsistent feedback also led students to feel uncertain and confused. Related studies (Hounsell, D., McCune, V., Hounsell, J., & Litjens, J., 2008) indicate that students do perceive differing levels of quality in their feedback and are able to identify inconsistency in feedback by different facilitators. The type of feedback requested by students also varied. A pre-requisite for a successful teaching and learning environment in higher education (in both traditional and online settings) is the importance of having feedback standards in place (Hounsell et. al, 2008). Some of these standards include checklists, reports on teaching quality, and indicators of effective assessment. Others have found that influential and mutual feedback between peers, which has its focus on development rather than evaluation, is the most important feature during assessment (Smyth, K., 2004; Eisen, M.J., 2001).

In an online learning community of practice, a facilitator providing continuous, clear and constructive feedback will influence the environment, which will ultimately influence the way the students socially develop and cognitively grow. Constructive feedback is an element of the humanistic approach of social learning. It gives the e-learner an opportunity to review, contrast and compare the work he or she has delivered (particularly in writing assignments), make a connection and seize the opportunity towards unlimited potential in the application of knowledge. As an element of the social learning theory, e-feedback can therefore be seen as a feature of social presence as well as interpersonal communication in an online community of practice, all of which influence the cognitive and social development of the student. Being modeled by the online facilitator, quality e-feedback produces a collaborative atmosphere of social learning within a virtual community of practice, such as an online class room.

ISSUES, CONTROVERSIES, AND PROBLEMS

Rationale for Quality e-Feedback as an Element of Social Learning Theory

The depth and interest in meaningful e-feedback grew from my experience as an e-facilitator and Faculty Manager (some of which I held in an adjunct capacity) for five different universities. Some of the online universities which I taught at had different requirements for feedback on assignments. As most of the e-universities or online programs did not set feedback standards; it led me to feel that it was not placed at the same level of importance as being present in online discussions.

Interesting enough, I observed that students began sending me emails to thank me for taking the time to give them such indepth and constructive feedback on their assignments. Moreover, students commented on how much they have learned from the feedback, and how they can apply it in the future not only to improve their academic work, but also in their workplace. To my surprise, I learned from some of the students that this was the first time they have received such meaningful feedback.

Furthermore, in my position as a Faculty Manager, I observed that e-facilitators were giving various degrees of feedback to students. I was surprised to learn that there was neither consistency nor standards applied when giving feedback to students, and that the quality of e-feedback did not appear to be a priority at the time. I then wondered how the various degrees of e-feedback affected the students' learning outcome and how e-feedback was related to social learning in a virtual community of practice as a whole. How could this be assessed and measured? What could be put in place to consistently maintain the highest quality of e-feedback as a social learning tool in an online community of practice?

In my capacity as a full-time professor and Faculty Manager, I became aware of a pressing need for consistent quality e-feedback and its ties to social learning in a virtual community of practice, such as the online classroom. I also became conscious of the fact that providing students with quality e-feedback may be equally important as the presence of the e-facilitator in online discussions, especially when a solid quality learning outcome is concerned. Implementing the social learning theory element of quality e-feedback may just be a wonderful quality improvement tool that will place accountability and responsibility on both the e-professor/e-facilitator and the e-educational institution and organization, or virtual community of practice, towards meeting the new demands of quality made by its customers.

Context of the Study

U21Global is a joint venture between a consortium of Universitas 21 and Manipal Education, which delivers a number of online learning graduate programs. The U21 member universities participating in U21Global are The U21 member universities participating in U21Global are the University of Virginia, Tecnológico De Monterrey, University of Birmingham, The University of Edinburgh, University of Glasgow, The University of Nottingham, University College Dublin, Lund University, The University of Melbourne, The University of Queensland, National University of Singapore, The University of Hong Kong, Shanghai Jiao Tong University, Fudan University, Korea University, University of Delhi and Waseda University.

Unlike traditional universities, the representation of international learner presence at U21G is nearly 100%, making cross-cultural approaches to virtual teams an important pedagogical issue. With all courses being conducted entirely online and with more than 3,000 enrolled students from more than 60 countries which include China, India, the United Arab Emirates, New Zealand, Australia, Germany, England, North and South America, the need to cater for different cultures in each class, or virtual community of practice, is evident. This is ensured by employing professors from all over the globe to develop the online course content in a cross-culturally sympathetic manner (as opposed to a mono-cultural approach) and also by ensuring that professors from all over the globe facilitate the classes. On average, students in this Executive MBA program are 35 years of age with 10 years of work experience.

Focus of the Study and Methodologies

The data in this empirical analysis is derived from observations by the author of email communication between students and the e-facilitator, as well as performance feedback given by the e-facilitator to the student on case assignments and discussion board performance.

The qualitative content analysis allowed the distillation of a large amount of raw data into distinct categories or themes. On average, classes consisted of 40 students and the duration of the subject spanned 12 weeks. For the purpose of this study, a focused review and analysis was carried out on e-feedback to Organizational Behavior students on case and discussion board assignments from four facilitators for performance duration of four weeks. In addition, an analysis of email correspondence between students and facilitators in 10 Organisational Behavior classes was conducted, specifically reviewing for indicators on how the facilitator's feedback has impacted the student's social learning, growth and development in this online community of practice. Coding sampling units were defined syntactically by using words, sentences, or paragraphs of the data/texts (email, facilitator feedback to student).

Table 1. Facilitator 1 feedback

Criteria	e-Feedback Provided
Demonstrated the ability to communicate according to the normal conventions with respect to language usage, grammar and referencing.	Well-referenced throughout and well-written
Demonstrated the ability to identify, select and use essential readings.	Good use of readings and showing clear understanding of the case
Included relevant supportive qualitative and/or quantitative data, which were presented in a clear and integrated way.	Evidence of extended reading – and you have integrated them well
Analyzed critically the issues using appropriate concepts and methods.	Good analysis of the case presented
The key elements of the topic were outlined and clearly justified.	You let yourself down with Answer 4 – too short.
Conclusions were developed clearly, logically and concisely.	---------

Table 2. Facilitator 2 feedback

Criteria	e-Feedback Provided
Demonstrated the ability to communicate according to the normal conventions with respect to language usage, grammar and referencing.	You write well, but this is a professional paper and making a list is not the same as a scholarly indepth analysis of the case.
Demonstrated the ability to identify, select and use essential readings.	You had a golden opportunity to use the Sources of Power literature, the 10 Questions technique, the Root Cause analysis and other models, but you did not use them.
Included relevant supportive qualitative and/or quantitative data, which were presented in a clear and integrated way.	You did not mention much to support your thinking.
Analyzed critically the issues using appropriate concepts and methods.	You did not apply any models from the course.
The key elements of the topic were outlined and clearly justified.	You did not list the key aspects of the case.
Conclusions were developed clearly, logically and concisely.	You gave your opinion but you did not support it with any relevant literature.

SOLUTIONS AND RECOMMENDATIONS

Results and Analysis

Case Study e-Feedback

A part of this study compared and contrasted the clarity and depth of e-feedback for case studies and discussion board contributions given by four e-facilitators in the subject of Organisational Behavior. Facilitators were required to provide feedback according to a pre-determined set of criteria.

Some qualitative examples illustrating the degree of difference in feedback for case studies are shown in Tables 1 and 2.

Facilitator 3 wrote the following paragraph of e-feedback.

"I like what you have written on this Assignment 3.8, I just would like to see more of it. I tend to grade somewhat on level of effort, and the amount of discussion a student puts into their work. I am looking for more comments, more analysis, and more effort. Be sure to use a format which enables you to examine and analyze the questions there were presented in the unit. In summary: more input = more points. You earned 70 points on this assignment. Some additional thoughts: 1) Overall, I would encourage you to make more comments/ discussion/analysis in developing your answers and case analysis. 2) I really would have liked to see more references, an effort to expand your knowledge with that research—the Internet is a superb source that I would have liked to have seen you use more. 3) I would have liked to have seen you develop a good more comprehensive summary or conclusion for this assignment--I believe it helps review and confirm your learning, to demonstrate you really know what you are talking about in your paper."*

Discussion Board Feedback

This part of the study compared and contrasted the clarity and depth of e-feedback given on discussion board contributions during a four-week period in the subject of Organisational Behavior. On the giving of feedback, facilitators did not receive any feedback guidelines or criteria beforehand. Qualitative examples illustrating the degree of difference in feedback for discussion board contributions include the following:Facilitator 1:

"You need to involve yourself more in the class by adding to the discussion, responding to posts

Table 3. Facilitator 4 feedback

Criteria	e-Feedback Provided
Demonstrated the ability to communicate according to the normal conventions with respect to language usage, grammar and referencing.	Satisfactory: You did a good job here, factual and straightforward.
Demonstrated the ability to identify, select and use essential readings.	Satisfactory: It is clear that you read and understood the case and the subject content of the course, although you need to pay attention to the "guidelines for writing a case analysis".
Included relevant supportive qualitative and/or quantitative data, which were presented in a clear and integrated way.	Satisfactory: You did a good job creating matrixes to present some of your data, although I would have preferred them as Exhibit attachments to the actual analysis write-up.
Analyzed critically the issues using appropriate concepts and methods.	Satisfactory: • Nice Matrix for Gap Analysis • Great job listing problem statements • Nice job looking at the uncertainty factor • Nice Matrix on Objectives and their priorities • Good job listing an action plan, which are your solutions generated. • However, I did miss your IMPLEMENTATION recommendation, which is a part of the four-step process "Plan to implement solutions".
The key elements of the topic were outlined and clearly justified.	Unsatisfactory: In regards to your format, I would like for you to write your analysis in text flow. You may include some matrixes as exhibits, but you need to write it out. Further, as outlined in the "Guidelines for writing a case analysis", you need to always include an executive summary, an introduction, and then the main body of your analysis, a set of recommendations, and a conclusion. I also want to point out that, while there may be a lot of issues/gaps, you need to make a decision and decide on perhaps two or three (perhaps it is only one issue that could potentially affect many elements) MOST CRUCIAL to address. In reality, you could not address all eight problems you have identified. You make a decision here and then focus your entire analysis on those gaps in detail. In your set of recommendations/proposing of solutions, for example, you need to discuss pros and cons to each alternative. This will make your analysis much richer in content.
Conclusions were developed clearly, logically and concisely.	Unsatisfactory: Here I refer back to assessment criteria #5 where I discuss recommendations. Following a clear presentation with sub-headers will not only help you organize your content, but also generate a sequential flow to your work that will help with the clear and logical development of your product and ensure that concluding remarks are present.

from fellow classmates, asking questions. Help push the conversation along. Although your posts are well-written and show clear understanding, they do not add to the debate—more activity is needed along with more participation."

"You need to make many, many more postings to earn a good grade. The top students submitted over 70 responses and you submitted fewer than six."

"I appreciated your input to the discussion board, but would like to encourage you to participate a little more and to respond more frequently to others in the discussions. I tend to grade on two criteria— the quality of the postings and the level of effort I see from my students in responding to others in the discussion. I saw you posted four discussion items and replied to 14 others. Just for your information, the averages in the course were five individual contributions and 38 responses to others."

"Focus on reading peers' posts and engaging in discussions to include more quality posts by adding knowledge. You are doing a good job in some of your posts giving us your original thoughts. I would like to see you engaging more with your peers by responding to their posts and adding knowledge. If you disagree or agree, tell us why; probe further. Great conversations and quality content, as well as quantity (frequency of engaging with your peers) CONSISTENTLY is what I look for. Your contributions overall were weak during the grading time frame. Thank you for your reflective post. I will look for consistency of quality and frequency of your engagement for the reminding eight weeks to come. Thanks for your efforts."

These qualitative results confirm some of the literature findings on feedback that it does vary in depth, clarity and the degree of being constructive towards learning for the student. This is further confirmed by the findings outlined in the section below, as there is a strong indication of e-feedback influencing the level of social learning as well as the influence on social development and growth for the student.

Impact of Quality e-Feedback on Student Personal Growth and Development

This study also looked at email correspondence of 10 online Organizational Behavior classes to specifically observe if there were any signs indicating that the type and degree of e-feedback given to students by their facilitator had an impact on social learning, personal growth and development.

After reading through the email correspondence, there were numerous emails addressed to the facilitator regarding to his or her e-feedback. The following seven categories emerged (some qualitative samples of student responses are given for each):

1. Appreciation and Gratitude for e-Feedback
   - Thanks for your feedback to us on the case analysis.
   - Thank you very much for your time and feedback on my case.
   - I am deeply touched by your neatly organized feedback on my case analysis. I have read your feedback not less than 10 times. I have never expected that any guide tutor would give me such a long a reply as you did for my performance. I thank you for your conscientious work and what you did was beyond your responsibility.
   - Thank you very much for the case feedback and grading. It is much more comprehensive.
2. High Value Ascribed to eFeedback
   - Thank you very much for this very valuablepiece of advice.
   - Thanks once again for the valuable guidance.
   - Thanks for your valuable feedback. I will remember to make my analysis more complete in future
3. Aid to Learning and Improvement
   - This feedback will certainly help me in improving my skill in answering case studies.
   - I shall take your feedback and correct myself as I progress in my course
   - There has been great learning indeed.
4. Request for Continual e-Feedback
   - I look forward to some illuminating feedback, enlightening me to the quality of my performance as I proceed.
   - Kindly let me know so as to improve in the future – HOW TO improve further.
   - May I seek your feedback as to whether my recent discussions are in line with the course content and expectations?

5. Empowerment to Request for More Guidance
   ◦ Could you please guide me?
   ◦ I want to understand from you what went wrong and request your guidance to improve my score immediately.
   ◦ I ask for your kind advice on my troubles that I have due to a sudden change of work environment.
6. Increase in Self-Confidence
   ◦ I would like to take a moment and express my sincere appreciation on what I am learning. Professor inputs have aligned my knowledge, enhanced professional working, now I felt more confident.
   ◦ Seeing your feedback on my DB performance, I feel relaxed.
   ◦ Professor inputs have aligned my knowledge, enhanced professional working, now I felt more confident.
7. Inconsistency in e-Feedback Quality across Different Modules
   ◦ Thank you for the feedback. This being my 6th module, I must say you are the first professor to take the time to provide useful and constructive feedback. Thank you, it is much appreciated!
   ◦ I am deeply touched by your neatly organized feedback on my case analysis. I have read your feedback not less than 10 times. I have never expected that any guide tutor would give me so long a reply as you did to my performance.
   ◦ I thank you for your conscientious work and what you did beyond your responsibility if compared to other courses I have taken.

In a study by Roberts (1996), geology students indicated that their preference was for detailed feedback. Similarly, Rice, M., Mousley, I., & Davis, R. (1994) found that detailed comments were most helpful to students when asked about their opinions on feedback in general. Another study by Stevenson, K., Sander, P., & Naylor, P. (1996) also showed that students desired detailed comments on their work. It is apparent that the student comments on facilitator e-feedback confirm with the literature.

It is evident from this data that e-feedback given in an online learning environment does vary in depth and thus quality. Some of the facilitators give more guidance, clarity and educational feedback to the student than others. Moreover, the study confirmed that different types of performance feedback have various effects on the learners' self-efficacy (Schunk & Lilly, 1984). In addition, the student reactions to feedback obviously indicate that comprehensive and informative e-feedback facilitate "cognitive growth in peer collaborations" (Kim, Y., Baylor, A.L., 2006).

Characteristics of Quality e-Feedback as an Element of Social Learning

Considering the different degrees of feedback provided to the students along with the identified categories as far as the impact of feedback is concerned, it is evident that an e-feedback model must include certain considerations in order to provide an effective and quality social learning environment in online university, or web-based community of practice. In order to design e-feedback effectively in an online learning environment, the following multiple criteria need to be considered simultaneously:

- Feedback should always be **positive and constructive.**
- Consider feedback **style** (guiding, supporting, improving, informative vs. motivational).

- Feedback must be **useful** and **formative.**
- Give detailed comments on **good** work and work that needs improvement.
- Consider your **level** of feedback (general or context specific).
- Know **where** to focus the feedback when giving it— it varies from student to student (for example form or content issues).
- Give **timely** feedback (immediately vs. delayed); consider feedback a time for reflection for students prior to the next assignment.
- Consider learner **characteristics** (learning styles, motivational skills, personality).
- Consider learner work and life **experiences.**
- Consider students' **perception** of your feedback and how it will affect their learning experience.
- Remember that the clarity of feedback is also **tied** to clarity of assessment and expectations.
- Bear in mind the possibility of **misinterpretation** as English may not be the first language for global students.

FUTURE TRENDS

Further studies may enhance the understanding of e-feedback in general and add to the knowledge of e-feedback as an element of social learning and development in various communities of practice. A study on treating the impact of e-feedback as a holistic one may give insight to the correlation of (1) Training and development for e-facilitators (2) Quality assessment tool linked to e-facilitators annual performance appraisal, and (3) Tying e-feedback to continuous quality improvement efforts university-/organization-wide.

Another study may look at involving students in generating feedback on their own work by providing self-reflection and self-criticism. This may add to the collaborative aspect of social learning in the community of practice and also possibly compel both students and facilitators to give quality feedback. One could also investigate how online students feel about feedback given by creating a questionnaire that specifically measures items such as e-feedback clarity, did it help them improve, and has it motivated the student to improve, for example. Finally, one could explore self-criticism on the part of the facilitator on how well e-feedback was given.

CONCLUSION

This chapter has drawn from data of an online community of practice, an Organizational Behavior course and specifically examined the quality of e-feedback to students and how this feedback has impacted learners' social learning and development.

Data was gathered by comparing and contrasting feedback of four professors each facilitating an online Organisational Behavior course, along with examining student emails to the facilitator on how feedback has impacted their learning. The findings gave a compelling picture of the learners' perception of the impact of e-feedback given and how they experience e-feedback as indicated by the seven e-feedback categories identified:

Appreciation and Gratitude for e-Feedback, Aid to Learning and Improvement, High Value Ascribed to e-Feedback, Request for Continual e-Feedback, Empowerment to Request for More Guidance, Increase in Self-Confidence, and Inconsistency in e-Feedback Quality across Different Modules.

Furthermore, some of the findings provide valuable confirmation of results from other studies mentioned in the literature. This chapter provides a significant advance in understanding that the depth and quality of feedback given by the facilitator is an integral piece of the whole social learning experience of the student within a virtual community of practice and does not stand separately in a vacuum. It was apparent that the "characteristics of quality e-feedback as element of social learning theory" are a robust model in any community of practice. These characteristics set the tone for a social learning environment by encouraging students and the facilitator to give and take clear and formative feedback when engaging collaboratively. Finally, there is evidence that quality e-feedback as an element of social learning contributes to the building of trust between students and facilitator, a vital ingredient to any community of practice.

REFERENCES

Bandura, A. (1977). *Social learning theory*. New York: General Learning Press. Bandura, A. (n.d.). *Social learning theory*.

Eisen, M. J. (2001). Peer-based professional development viewed through the lens of transformative learning. *Holistic Nursing Practice, 16*(1), 30–42.

Grippin, P., & Peters, S. (1984). *Learning theory and learning outcomes*. Landham, MD: University Press of America.

Hergenhahn, B. R. (1988). *An introduction to theories of learning* (3rd ed.). Englewood Cliffs, NJ: Prentice Hall.

Holmes, G., & McElwee, G. (1995). Total quality management in higher education how to approach human resource management. *Total Quality Management, 7*(6), 5.

Hounsell, D. (2003). Student feedback, learning and development. In M. Slowey & D. Watson (Eds.), *Higher education and the lifecourse* (pp. 67-78). Buckingham, UK: SRHE and Open University Press.

Hounsell, D., McCune, V., Hounsell, J., & Litjens, J. (2008). The quality of guidance and feedback to students. *Higher Education Research & Development, 27*(1), 55–67. doi:10.1080/07294360701658765

Kerlin, C. A. (2000). *Measuring student satisfaction with the service processes of selected student educational support services at Everett Community College* (Doctoral dissertation, Oregon State University).

Kim, Y., & Baylor, A. (2006). A social-cognitive framework for pedagogical agents as learning companions. *ETR & D, 54*(6), 569–596. doi:10.1007/s11423-006-0637-3

Krause, K., Hartley, R., James, R., & McInnis, C. (2005). *The first year experience in Australian universities: Findings from a decade of national studies*.

Maslow, A. H. (1970). *Motivation and personality* (2nd ed.). New York: Harper-Collins.

Merriam, S. B., & Caffarella, R. S. (1999). *Learning in adulthood*. San Francisco: Jossey-Bass.

Ormrod, J. E. (1995). *Human learning* (2nd ed.). Englewood Cliffs, NJ: Merrill.

Rice, M., Mousley, I., & Davis, R. (1994). Improving student feedback in distance education: A research report. In T. Evans & D. Murphy (Eds.), *Research in distance education 3: Revised papers from the third research in distance education conference*. Geelong, Australia: Deakin University Press.

Roberts, D. (1996). Feedback on assignments. *Distance Education, 17*(1), 95–116. doi:10.1080/0158791960170107

Rogers, C. R. (1983). *Freedom to learn for the 80s*. Columbus, OH: Merrill.

Schunk, D. H., & Lilly, M. W. (1984). Sex differences in self-efficacy and attributions: Influence of performance feedback. *The Journal of Early Adolescence, 4,* 203–213. doi:10.1177/0272431684043004

Seashore, N. C., Whitfield-Seashore, E., & Weinberg, G. M. (1999). *What did you say? The art of giving and receiving Feedback*.Columbia, MD: Bingham House Books.

Smyth, K. (2004). The benefits of students learning about critical evaluation rather than being summatively judged. *Assessment & Evaluation in Higher Education, 29*(3), 370–378. doi:10.1080/0260293042000197609

Stevenson, K., Sander, P., & Naylor, P. (1996). Student perceptions of the tutor's role in distance learning . *Open Learning, 11*(1), 22–30. doi:10.1080/0268051960110103

Vygotsky, L. S. (1978). *Mind in society*. Cambridge, MA: Harvard University Press.

Vygotsky, L. S. (n.d.). *Social development theory*.

Webster Dictionary. (2008). *Feedback*.

Chapter 2
A Document Reuse Tool for Communities of Practice

Aida Boukottaya
University of Fribourg, Switzerland

Bernadette Charlier
University of Fribourg, Switzerland

Micaël Paquier
EPFL, Switzerland

Loïc Merz
EPFL, Switzerland

Stéphane Sire
EPFL, Switzerland

Christine Vanoirbeek
EPFL, Switzerland

ABSTRACT

Virtual communities of practice are gaining importance as mean of sharing and exchanging knowledge. In such environments, information reuse is of major concern. In this paper, the authors outline the importance of structuring documents in order to facilitate the reuse of their content. They show how explicit structure representation facilitates the understanding of the original documents and helps considerably in automating the reuse process. The authors propose two main tools: the first performs automatic structure transformation using matching techniques and the second performs structure and instances evolution in a transparent and an automatic manner.

INTRODUCTION

Communities of Practice (CoPs) are becoming more important as a mean of sharing information within and between organizations. A **Community of Practice** emerges from a common desire to work together; it can be defined as a network of people that identifies issues, shares approaches, methodologies, documents, experiences, and makes the results avail-

DOI: 10.4018/978-1-60566-711-9.ch002

able to others (Wenger, 1998). With the rise of the Internet, virtual **CoP**s are gaining importance as a new model for virtual collaboration and learning. In virtual **CoP**s, the common space is provided by a suite of collaborative and communicative environments, ranging from simple mailers, forum, discussion lists, and audiovisual conferences to more advanced collaborative work environments that enable information and knowledge exchange and sharing.

In this context, the process of capturing and sharing a community's collective expertise is of major concern. Burk (1999) describes such process as a cyclic one composed by four basic steps: *find/ create*, *organize*, *share*, and *use/reuse*. The "find/ create" step concerns the creation of knowledge/ information gained through research and/or industry experiences, expertise, publications, etc. The goal of the two next steps in the cycle, "organize" and "share", is to first filter and organise expertise (e.g., creating different categories of knowledge related to specific purposes, linking such knowledge with available resources, etc). Second, the expertise has to be shared for wide availability, making use of the Internet and other techniques of information sharing. The final phase of the cycle, "use/reuse," enables shared expertise to be used and reused in order to minimize information overload and maximize content usability, which decreases time, effort and cost. The results are then captured as part of learned lessons and new expertise is created which enable the cycle to begin again. Using and reusing expertise could be achieved by several manners including both informal contacts (phone, meetings, etc), access to reports, documents, practices, and other forms of communication, including demonstrations, and training sessions.

In this paper, we essentially focus on *document reuse* within CoPs. As in Levy (1993), we identified at least two kinds of **document reuse**: (1) by *replication*: from a single document, several presentations can be produced; and (2) by *extraction*: portions of a document can be taken

from one document and moved to another (generally performed by means of the now popular "Cut&Paste" command). Since documents reflect in general authors' vision and "understanding" of the Universe, **document reuse** requires access to the intentions and interpretations underlying the original document. The capability of reuse suggests then the understanding of authors' representation of the Universe in terms of concepts and semantic relationships among them. Such representations only exist "in the mind" of authors and usually are not made explicit in the document itself. Branting & Lester (1996) describe **document reuse** process as a tedious and costly (in term of time and effort) process. In fact, given a set of goals to be accomplished by the new document and a library of existing documents, document reuse process involves three main steps: (1) finding the reusable documents (or fragments of document) that satisfy current goals; (2) comparing the goals of the retrieved documents and/or fragments and the current goals in order to ensure the compatibility of the two; (3) adapting them as needed i.e., remove incompatible parts that not satisfy current goals (excision) and add new materials (augmentation). Moreover, when reuse requires crossing system and application boundaries, several problems arise due to the heterogeneities of such systems. One response to these problems is to *structure documents* by using Markup Languages such as XML (World Wide Web Consortium, 2008). The advent of **structured documents** on one hand leveraged a promising consensus on the encoding syntax for machine processable information and this resolves several issues, such as parsing and character encoding recognition. On the other hand, mark-up is also used for identifying meaningful parts of a document, and thus makes authors intentions more explicit.

In our work, we essentially address the second kind of reuse (extraction). We consider documents as an effective mean for storing explicit knowledge, and study the additional benefits of using explicit structure. This work have been done in the framework of Palette project (http://palette.ercim. org/) aiming to provide **communities of practice** with a set of services concerning information production, exchange and reuse; reification of explicit and tacit knowledge about practices and advanced collaboration.

The outline of the rest of the paper is the following: Section 2 gives an overview of the benefits of **structuring** documents and presents solutions to easily produce such documents. Section 3 describes proposed solutions and tools for automating the reuse process.

STRUCTURED DOCUMENT PRODUCTION

Why Structuring Documents?

The goal of this section is to show the benefits of **structuring** documents. **Structured document** refers to a document conforming to a pre-defined grammar or schema that describes the permissible document components and their logical organization (Abiteboul, Buneman, & Suciu, 2000). XML is the mark-up language for presenting information as structured documents. The design of XML was driven by the idea to have a generic language for representing data in a self describing way. The latter is achieved by **structuring** the contents using tags. Every XML application defines its own tags which are described in a DTD or more recently using an XML Schema (World Wide Web Consortium, 2001). The document structure can be utilized to facilitate several issues such as document authoring, document publishing, document querying and browsing, etc. Recent research has shown that during the authoring process of documents as much as half of the time is spent on formatting. A basic principle of **structured documents** is to separate the structure from its presentation, this shields authors from formatting tasks allowing them to only worry about the content. The writing of documents can then be guided

by prompting the required structural parts, and by interactively validating the resulting structure. Another advantage of the structure is that the authoring tool may help the user with powerful commands. According to structure, the tool can automatically update cross-references, and establish a table of content or an index (Furuta, Quint, & André, 1988), (Brown & Cole, 1992).

Based on structure, it is easy to achieve replication. Different layout formats such as Word (Doc/RTF), HTML (for Web sites), PDF (Printed documentation), WML (for wireless devices) could be generated automatically. This greatly facilitates the publishing of structured documents and saves efforts (reuse by replication). **Structuring** documents clearly facilitates their later processing. In fact, producing a class of documents that conforms to a unique grammar typically enhances the specification of appropriate processing operations on documents belonging to a given class, since processing is uniformly defined for a set of documents and not for individual document.

Re-thinking Document Structure

However the benefit behind **structuring** documents, the production of such documents is a long and complex process that generally requires some specific languages mastery and programming skills. The first task is typically to define a document model and to produce its related instance(s). The second task is to convert such document to XHTML (or any other presentation language) for publication and delivery purposes using a transformation language such as XSLT. This process is long, complex and requires being familiar with XML family languages as well as existing editors (such as XMLSpy, etc.). In many cases authors prefer to take another, very different and simpler approach: they write directly Web documents ready for publication, thus missing the benefits of structuring documents. Another obstacle to produce **structured documents** is the difficulty of their reuse and **evolution** which require structure transformation attained typically by writing scripts and code. In order to motivate CoPs to produce structured document, a specific focus is given to provide them with an easy and automatic means to first produce and then reuse structured documents without dealing with syntax problems. This section describes provided solutions to produce structured documents, next section focuses on reuse issues through the presentation of DocReuse tool (http://docreuse.epfl.ch/).

In the context of the Palette project, we try to combine the advantages of two approaches: a rigorous document structure, but a simple production and reuse process. The idea is to provide CoPs members with a graphical user interface and allow authors to interact with familiar representations of documents presented as templates. This approach, called **template**-driven editing, is used by many HTML editors (Dreamweaver, FrontPage, etc.). In most cases the **template**s are predefined to describe a series of common used documents. The notion of **template** in our work is intended to guide an editing tool for building **structured documents** that follow a predefined model (describing the document logical structure). Some variants of the document **template** production have been described in the literature, as in Haake, Lukosch, & Schummer (2005) where it is applied in the context of literature teaching with a special type of wiki. These wiki based variants require users to learn special wiki languages to produce structured documents. The introduction of document **template**s in this context is only possible through the introduction of new wiki language extensions to describe the templates, which also augments the learning curve for users that wish to edit or evolve the templates. In our work we propose editors for multimedia content and try to encompass the whole reuse process.

To address these issues, an editing tool and a language were developed in the context of the Palette project. The tool (Amaya web editor: http://www.w3c.org/Amaya) makes editing templates and instances easier and simpler. The language,

called XTiger (Extensible **Template**s for Interactive Guided Edition of Resources: http://www.w3.org/Amaya/Templates/XTiger-spec.html), allows semantic XHTML and document structure to be clearly described. Amaya uses descriptions expressed in XTiger language to help authors to produce valid instances. The XTiger language describes a generic structure under the form of a template. A **template** is a document with some fixed contents and "holes" where the user can insert information. A **template** defines the skeleton of the document. It declares components that are specific to the kind of document. By filling the template, the user produces in a transparent manner a class of structured documents (so-called instances) that share the same characteristics. The XTiger language offers more advanced features such as typing and type references as in XML schema language which facilitates a modular construction of document, by sharing reusable pieces of structure. More technical details and examples of templates could be found at http://www.w3.org/Amaya/Templates/.

Making Existing Resources Structured

In our work we mainly propose solutions to automatically reuse and make evolving **structured documents** (see next section). Through CoPs interviews and synthesis (available in the context of Palette project), we noticed that although CoP members are motivated to produce **structured documents**, they also express the need to reuse existing resources in (semi) automatic manner. Much of the available CoPs' data that we focus on (e.g., contact information, course scheduling, publications, meeting minutes, etc.) already reside in HTML pages, and the challenge is to entice users to make the effort of structuring the available data. For this we develop *the **template**-driven structuring tool*.

The key idea underlying the tool is to address a scenario where the data comes *before* the

Figure 1: The Template-driven structuring tool interface

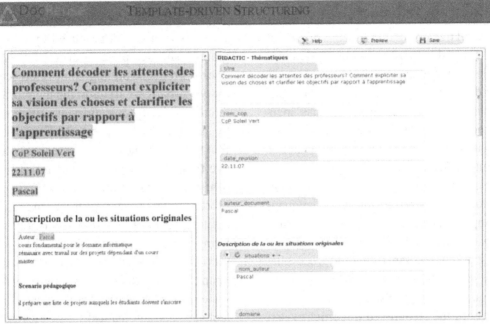

structure (**template**). In order to entice people to structure their data, we offer to CoP members a set of predefined templates to which they can map their data easily. Given a HTML file and a template, the user is able to drag and drop content from the HTML file to instantiate the template. The **template** appears as a form that defines the skeleton of the document. Once the template is filled, a structured instance (XHTML instance) is produced. The produced instance follows the structure described in the template. Moreover, the system allows the user to keep track of his **structuring** activities. In fact, the user can upload several templates. Documents to be structured are associated to each template to become structured instances. The **structuring** can be done in several steps and in a collaborative manner thus facilitating the **structuring** of huge HTML documents and enhancing collaborative work between CoP members. Graphical highlights are used to indicate already structured parts of the document.

Figure 1 represents a **template** as visualized in the *template-driven **structuring** tool*. The lat-

ter **template** traduces the structural organization of CoP group meetings. To produce structured instances, CoPs members have just to upload their existing HTML files and drag and drop their content to fill the template. An online demo of the tool is available from http://docreuse.epfl. ch:8080/

DOCREUSE: A TOOL FOR STRUCTURED DOCUMENT REUSE

A very important aspect of structured mark-ups is that the documents are software and system independent, which enables interchange between different environments. However, dealing with **structured documents**, constrained by a model (described via a DTD, a schema, or a **template**) has also some drawbacks. Reusing structured documents within users' environments raises a number of fundamental problems to transform or to adapt their intrinsic structure. Structure transformation is typically attained by writing translators which are often manually encoded on a case-by-case basis using specific transformation languages such as XSLT (World Wide Web Consortium, 1999). The process of transformation and thus of reuse is generally divided in three main phases (Kuikka, 1996). The first one aims at understanding the source and target schemas' structures. The goal of the second phase is to discover schemas' mappings by means of inter-schema correspondences, capturing input and output constraints imposed on the documents. In the third phase discovered mappings are translated into an appropriate sequence of operations in a given transformation language over the input document, to produce the required output document (which requires non-trivial programming skills). The transformation process has long been known to be extremely laborious and error-prone at several levels.

The aim of the **structured document reuse** tool "DocReuse" is to allow existing documents initially structured for a given purpose to be restructured for use in a different context, thus improving reusability and information sharing between **communities of practice**. DocReuse tool is composed of two services: (1) *Automatic matching and transformation*: takes as input two templates (source and target), a set of source instances and produces automatically structured target instances. The goal is to enable CoP members to transform structured documents in a transparent and automatic manner. The automatic transformation is based on a mapping file produced automatically by the system. (2) *Template-driven evolution*: ensures the automatic adaptation and validity of instances when templates evolve. Moreover, it enables CoP members to modify the **template** without knowing XTiger syntax.

Motivating Examples

Here we present motivating examples that show how the manual reuse process is difficult. Figure 2 depicts two examples of **template**s (used by two different CoP groups) that describe the bib-

liography used by CoP groups in order to support their activities.

Example 1: One **CoP** group (using template 1) wants to use data produced by another CoP group (using template 2) in order to enrich his already produced bibliographic references. Since the two groups are **structuring** their data in a different manner (publications are either classified by author or by category), the first group needs first to identify the correspondences between the two **template**s then to restructure each instance of template 2 which is a time consuming process. Moreover, this kind of restructuring requires the mastery of the XSLT transformation language. Using the automatic **matching** and transformation service, a CoP user needs just to upload the two templates and instances he wants to transform, the system identifies the similarities between the two templates and automatically generates transformation script as well as transformed instances.

Example 2: Let us now consider the **CoP** group working with the template 1. Let's imagine that after a certain time; they want to make the template evolve by splitting the author name into two sub-elements First Name and Last Name. Performing the suggested change leads to the invalidity of the related instances. To remain valid according to the new change, each author name instance (in each article and each book) should be removed and two sub-elements First Name and Last Name should be created, paying attention to keeping their content corresponding to the original author name. Manually modifying the instances will be time consuming. Moreover, if the user is not familiar with the XTiger language (which is the case of the majority of **CoP** members) the task will be infeasible. Using the **template** driven **evolution** service, a CoP member has just to select the author name, to choose an operation "Split" and to select the instances he want to make evolve, the system will automatically generate a new template and new valid instances.

Figure 2: Examples of templates

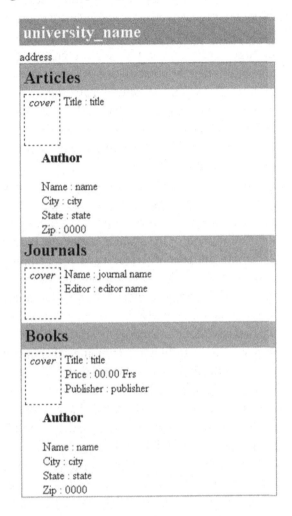

Automatic Matching and Transformation Service

As seen in the beginning of this section, a serious obstacle for translating directly between two **structured documents** is that a mapping between both templates needs to be carefully specified by a human expert. Manual mapping is known to be a time consuming and error-prone process. One response to this problem is *schema matching*. Schema **matching** is the task of semi-automatically finding correspondences between two heterogeneous schemas. Several applications relying on schema matching have arisen and have been widely studied by the database, AI communities and more recently document engineering community (Rahm & Bernstein, 2001), (Cali, Calvanese, Giacomo, & Lenzerini, 2002), (Popa, Velegrakis, Miller, Hernandez, & Fagin, 2002). However, these works generally deal with relational schemas. Little research has been dedicated to XML structures **matching**. Boukottaya (2004) and Boukottaya & Vanoirbeek (2005) establish a state of the art of available XML structures **matching** techniques.

In our work, the goal is to identify the parts to be transformed in the reusable documents and to describe how to place their content in appropriate context within the target template. The result is a set of mappings (correspondences) relating facts from the source documents with the target template by encapsulating all necessary information to transform source documents into instances of the target template. In order to achieve this goal, we adopt a multi-criteria matching process. Each criterion will be represented by a service. These services are extensible. As new criterion becomes available, a new service is created. Examples of services include: (1) *Label matching:* measures the similarities between entities based on the meaning inferred from their names (e.g. author and writer are synonyms). This service uses **CoP**s specific vocabularies (thesauri), local dictionaries (that define the common set of abbreviations, acronyms, and commonly used substring/short hand notations for a given CoP) as well as CoPs ontologies; (2) *Constraint matching:* relates entities based on their respective constraints. Such constraints include the use of Datatypes, occurrence constraints, etc. and (3) *Structural matching:* relates entities based on the similarity of the structural context in which they appear. For this templates are modelled as trees (treated as a collection of paths). This has two advantages: (1) a match between two paths can be defined as long as there are some matching nodes along the paths; and (2) a match between two nodes can be defined irrespective of where they occur in the tree as long as there is at least a partial match between their paths.

We have designed an algorithm to combine all the above criteria and produce a mapping result that clearly defines source and target mapped entities, required transformation operations, and conditions under which the mapping can be executed. Boukottaya (2004) summarizes an evaluation study of the proposed algorithm. The algorithm was evaluated in term of precision, recall, F-measure and overall using real world application: bibliographic date description. Globally it gives good result and only presents some limitations in some cases where complex matches are required. The proposed structural matching technique is based on

the notion of node context. We define three kinds of contexts for a given node: the ancestor context, the child context and the leaf context. We show through a comparative study with other matching algorithms that the combination of these contexts highly improves the structural matching.

Experience suggests that fully automated schema matching is infeasible, especially for complex matches that involve complex transformation operations. For this, we designed an efficient user interface where the templates (source and target) are represented as trees and a set of mapping operations have been made available to the user to modify the system mappings. Figure 3 depicts the user interface used for mapping validation. Once the user validates the mapping, the system generates automatically the appropriate transformation scripts (XSLT programs). For this, we first have defined a model for structuring mapping results according to a mapping schema that describes the five dimensions of a mapping result: entity, cardinality, structural, transformation and constraint dimensions. Second we have designed an algorithm that generates automatically XSLT scripts based on the above mapping structure. For each matching node pair, the algorithm traverses the target template tree in a depth-first manner and generates progressively transformation rules. **Template**s, produced mapping results as well as the transformation scripts are stored. When new instances are available, the transformation process is done automatically without re-applying the entire matching process.

Template-Driven Evolution

In a **community of practice** context, templates continuously evolve to reflect a change in the practices, to adhere to new users' requirements, to correct initial design errors, to allow expansion of the template scope over time or to simply allow for incremental maintenance. However, **template**s updates have a major consequence: documents being valid for the original template are no more

Figure 3: The validation mapping interface

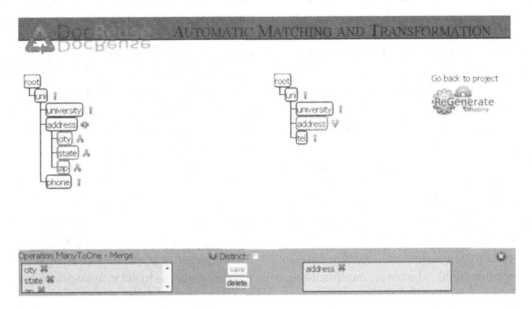

guaranteed to meet the constraints described by the evolved **template**. These documents should be *adapted*, *restructured* and *revalidated* against the new template. The validity is a crucial issue since the template is often relevantly exploited in several applications such as querying, transforming and document retrieval. The manual restructuring and validation is difficult, time consuming (especially when it concerns a large number of documents). and requires generally specific skills. Moreover, the observation of CoP members performing manual adaptation shows that this operation frequently results in introducing errors and inconsistencies. We develop the **template**-driven **evolution** service to answer two needs (1) evolving a **template** without knowing the XTiger syntax; (2) transform in an automatic manner the instances to remain valid.

The need for schema **evolution** is not a new problem and much effort has been done toward automating such process. Many traditional database projects have focused on the schema **evolution** issues, where the main goal is to develop mechanisms to change not only the schema but also the underlying objects (Bretl et al., 1989), (Lerner,

1996), (Claypool, Jin, & Rundensteiner, 1998). More recently, several works have been dedicated to XML structure/data **evolution**. XML schema evolution has been investigated for schemas expressed by DTDs in (Kramer & Rundensteiner, 2001), where a set of DTDs evolution operations have been proposed and their semantics have been discussed in detail. Issues related to the impact of such operations on existing instances have not been addressed. More recent work focused on the **evolution** of XML schemas. In a 2006 article, Guerrini, Mesiti, & Rossi proposed a set of evolution primitives dealing with more specific XML schema features (Typing, Type restriction/extension, etc.). They focus on detecting the document parts potentially invalidated by the schema changes. Revalidation and transformation issues are not addressed.

In our work, we adopt the same model as in Guerrini et al. (2006) in order to represent XTiger statements and provide a theoretical way to describe **evolution** primitives. However, the latter model as well as the **evolution** primitives have been modified in order to fit the specification of XTiger. In addition to this, the proposed primitives have been negotiated with **CoP** members to answer their specific needs. The basic idea is to keep track of the updates made to the **template** in a *mapping* file, and to identify the portions of the template that require a revalidation because of these updates. From the mapping file, a transformation script is generated automatically and the document portions affected by those updates can then be identified and adapted in an automatic manner. For this, we first propose a taxonomy of atomic **evolution** primitives.

As in Guerrini et al. (2006) we consider three categories of atomic evolution primitives: *insertion*, *modification*, and *deletion*. These primitives are applied to types and elements (as defined in the XTiger specification). Moreover, modifications can be further classified in three sub-categories: structural, re-labelling, and migration modifications. Structural modifications allow to modify the type of an element and its constraints (e.g. cardinality constraints). Re-labelling modifications allow to change the name of an element/ type. Migration modifications cover two cases, first moving a sub-element from an element to another one and second transforming a local type/ element to a global type/element (and vice versa). In order to ensure that the modified **template** remains well formed and valid according to the XTiger specifications, applicability conditions are enforced on each primitive.

Moreover, we propose high level primitives in order to express more complex updates. A high level primitive is represented as a sequence of atomic primitives that can be executed as a single operation. These primitives have been introduced to facilitate the template **evolution** task for **CoP** members and to describe more common sequence of atomic primitives. Examples of high level primitives include: *Aggregator primitives*: they mainly include primitives for inserting, moving, changing whole substructures rather than a single element at a time; *Merge/split primitives*: Elements values are not always represented at the same level of atomicity. For example the author name

in the template of figure 2 is represented using an element of type string. However, as described in the motivating example 2, for a given reason a new design choice could be to separate the author name into a First-Name and a Last-name. For such cases, instead of removing the elements and inserting new ones without any guarantee that the content will be preserved, we define two operations Merge and Split to perform this task and ensure that the content will be preserved.

Figure 4 depicts the template driven evolution service interface. Two categories of evolution primitives are presented: primitives applied to template elements and the ones applied to types. The template is graphically presented using the form metaphor as in the template-driven structuring tool. The user has just to select the template element/type he wants to modify, only applicable evolution primitives can then be applied. The template is updated (new XTiger code is generated in a transparent manner). Instances are then automatically transformed.

SUMMARY

Communities of practice are social networks of relationships that provide information, knowledge, and a space where people interact for mutual benefit. This paper studies document content reuse problem within CoPs. Faced with the diversity of documents formats, content and goals, a critical step in document reuse is to make such documents self-explaining. The main idea is that by enriching original documents with an explicit logical structure, we can assist authors in the reuse process. This is done by proposing a template-driven editing approach in order to produce structured documents.

In order to reuse such documents, two services are proposed: the first one determines similarities between two templates (source and target) using matching techniques and then generates automatically a transformation script able to re-

Figure 4: Template-driven evolution interface

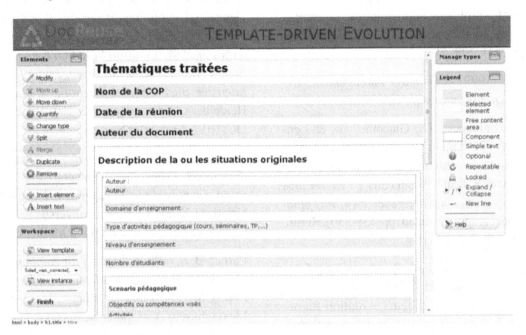

structure source instances to produce target ones. The second one enables CoP members to make a template and its related instances evolving in a complete transparent manner. Both services are available in a demo version and are tested within real CoPs in the context of the Palette project. In the future, interoperability issues between DocReuse and other Palette services such as information retrieval and knowledge management services is under investigation in order to provide CoP members with a complete and compatible set of tools for capturing and sharing a community's collective expertise.

REFERENCES

Abiteboul, S., Buneman, P., & Suciu, D. (2000). *Data on the Web: From relations to semistructured data and XML*. San Francisco: Morgan Kaufmann Publishers.

Boukottaya, A. (2004). *Schema matching for structured document transformations* (Doctoral dissertation). Lausanne, Switzerland: École Polytechnique Fédérale de Lausanne.

Boukottaya, A., & Vanoirbeek, C. (2005). Schema matching for transforming structured documents. In *Proceedings of the 2005 ACM symposium on Document engineering*, Bristol, United Kingdom (pp. 101-110). New York: ACM Press.

Branting, I. K., & Lester, J. C. (1996). Justification structures for document reuse. In I. Smith & B. Faltings (Eds.), *Proceedings of the Third European Workshop on Case-Based Reasoning*, Lausanne, Switzerland (pp. 76-90). Berlin, Germany: Springer-Verlag.

Bretl, R., Maier, D., Otis, A., Penney, J., Schuchardt, B., Stein, J., et al. (1989). The Gem-Stone data management system. In W. Kim & F. Lochovsky (Eds.), *Object-oriented concepts, databases and applications* (pp. 283-308). New York: ACM Press.

Brown, H., & Cole, F. C. (1992). Editing structured documents: Problems and solutions. *Electronic Publishing -- Origination . Dissemination and Design, 5*(4), 209–216.

Burk, M. (1999). *Knowledge management: Everyone benefits by sharing information.*

Cali, A., Calvanese, D., Giacomo, G., & Lenzerini, M. (2002). On the expressive power of data integration systems. In S. Spaccapietra, S. T. March, & Y. Kambayashi (Eds.), *Proceedings of 21st International Conference on Conceptual Modeling*, Tampere, Finland (pp. 338-350). Berlin, Germany: Springer-Verlag.

Claypool, K. T., Jin, J., & Rundensteiner, E. A. (1998). OQL SERF: An ODMG implementation of the template-based schema evolution framework. In S. A. MacKay & J. H. Johnson (Eds.), *Proceedings of the 1998 conference of the Centre for Advanced Studies on Collaborative research*, Toronto, Canada (pp. 108-122). Armonk, NY: IBM Press.

Furuta, R., Quint, V., & André, J. (1988). Interactively editing structured documents. *Electronic Publishing -- Origination, Dissemination and Design, 1*(1), 19-44.

Guerrini, G., Mesiti, M., & Rossi, D. (2006). *XML schema evolution* (Tech. Rep.). Genova, Italy: Universita di Genova.

Haake, A., Lukosch, S., & Schummer, T. (2005). Wiki-templates: Adding structure support to Wikis on demand. In *Proceedings of the 2005 international symposium on Wikis*, New York, USA (pp. 41-51). New York: ACM Press.

Kramer, D. K., & Rundensteiner, E. A. (2001). Xem: XML evolution management. In K. Aberer & L. Liu (Eds.), *Proceedings of the Eleventh International Workshop on Research Issues in Data Engineering: Document Management for Data Intensive Business and Scientific Applications*, Heidelberg, Germany (pp. 103-110). Washington, DC: IEEE Computer Society.

Kuikka, E. (1996). *Transformation of structured documents. Processing of structured documents using a syntax-directed approach* (Doctoral dissertation). Kuopio, Finland: University of Kuopio, Computer Science and Applied Mathematics.

Lerner, B. S. (1996). *A model for compound type changes encountered in schema evolution* (Tech. Rep. UM-CS-96-044). Amherst: University of Massachusetts, Computer Science Department.

Levy, D. M. (1993). Document reuse and document systems. *Electronic publishing, 6*(4), 339-348.

Popa, L., Velegrakis, Y., Miller, R. J., Hernandez, M. A., & Fagin, R. (2002). Translating Web data. In P. A. Bernstein, Y. E. Loannidis, R. Ramakrishnan, & D. Papadias, *Proceedings of the International Conference of Very Large Databases*, Hong Kong, China (pp. 598-609). Very Large Data Base Endowment Inc.

Rahm, E., & Bernstein, P. A. (2001). *On matching schemas automatically* (Tech. Rep. 1/2001). Leipzig, Germany: University of Leipzig, Department of Computer Science.

Wenger, E. (1998). *Communities of practice: Learning, meaning and identity*. UK: Cambridge University Press.

World Wide Web Consortium. (1999). *XSL transformations (XSLT) version 1.0* (W3C recommendation).

World Wide Web Consortium. (2001). *XML schema part 0: Primer* (W3C recommendation).

World Wide Web Consortium. (2008). *Extensible markup language (XML) 1.0 (fifth edition)* (W3C recommendation).

Chapter 3
Tackling Acceptability Issues in Communities of Practice by Providing a Lightweight Email–Based Interface to Social Software

Chiu Man Yu
École Polytechnique Fédérale de Lausanne (EPFL), Switzerland

Denis Gillet
École Polytechnique Fédérale de Lausanne (EPFL), Switzerland

Sandy El Helou
École Polytechnique Fédérale de Lausanne (EPFL), Switzerland

Christophe Salzmann
École Polytechnique Fédérale de Lausanne (EPFL), Switzerland

ABSTRACT

In the framework of the PALETTE European research project, the Swiss federal Institute of Technology in Lausanne (EPFL) is designing and experimenting with eLogbook, a Web-based collaborative environment designed for communities of practice. It enables users to manage joint activities, share related assets and get contextual awareness. In addition to the original Web-based access, an email-based eLogbook interface is developed. The purpose of this lightweight interface is twofold. First, it eases eLogbook access when using smart phones or PDA. Second, it eases eLogbook acceptance for community members hesitating to learn an additional Web environment. Thanks to the proposed interface, members of a community can benefit from the ease of use of an email client combined with the power of an activity and asset management system without burden. The Web-based eLogbook access can be kept for supporting further community evolutions, when participation becomes more regular and activities become more complex. This chapter presents the motivation, the design and the incentives of the email-based eLogbook interface.

DOI: 10.4018/978-1-60566-711-9.ch003

INTRODUCTION

eLogbook (http://eLogbook.epfl.ch) is a Web-Based **collaborative environment** particularly adapted to the needs of **communities of practice** (CoPs). It is developed at the Swiss Federal Institute of Technology in Lausanne (EPFL). It relies on three fundamental entities: *Actors*, *Activities* and *Assets*. An actor is any entity capable of initiating an event within the eLogbook workspace. An **asset** is any kind of resource (e.g. text documents and images) shared between community actors. An **activity** is the formalization of a common objective to be achieved by a group of actors. In eLogbook, the term *"space"* is used instead of *"activity"*, and these two terms are considered to be equivalent. *Events* related to these three entities are governed by *Protocols*. eLogbook supports management of invitations, roles, and deliverables for the activities; and supports access rights management for the assets. It provides personalized and context-sensitive awareness information crucial in collaborative environments (Gillet, El Helou, & et al., 2007; El Helou, Gillet, & et al., 2007). The features of eLogbook are useful to any kinds of CoPs (Rekik, Gillet, & et al., 2007).

The eLogbook is a general-purpose activity-oriented **collaboration space** that can be customized by users to serve as a task management tool as well as an asset management system allowing the collaboration around shared artifacts. Moreover, awareness services of different types are provided by eLogbook, because awareness is crucial in collaborative environments.

The original interface of eLogbook environment relies on Web 2.0 technologies for enabling effective Web-based user interaction. It can be considered as a flexible and adaptive Web-based collaborative activity and asset management system or service that could easily be adopted by communities of practice.

The main Web **interface** of eLogbook is called Context-Sensitive View. Awareness cues are embedded in the view for providing contextual information to users. Communities of practices expressed the need to work in a user-friendly environment that can serve simultaneously as a task and asset management system, a **social network**, and a discussion platform. The context-sensitive view was designed as a response to this need. In fact, this view consists of a central element, surrounded by three main regions, respectively dedicated to activities, assets and actors. The central element can be either an asset, an actor or an activity. Selecting an entity to become the context or the central element causes a change in the surrounding areas to display related entities, their relation with it and the eventual related actions that a user can perform on it. Consequently, just by changing the type of the focal point from an activity to an actor or an asset, the interface can serve different purposes, keeping however the same overall skeleton layout and structure. Awareness "cues" of different types are seamlessly incorporated in every area through the use of symbolic icons, colors and the manipulation of the layout order in which information is displayed. Figure 1 illustrates an example where a specific activity is chosen as the focal element. In this case, the assets posted in this activity, the actors participating in it and the other activities related to it, are displayed.

As pointed out by de Moor in (de Moor & van den Heuvel, 2004) and confirmed in the framework of the Palette project (http://palette.ercim.org) through a participatory design approach (Daele, Erpicum, & et al., 2006), it is difficult for a community to select and adopt new environments and services for enhancing their practice without inducing disturbances. For the communities that have been using email as the main communication tool, email-based interface environment may be more acceptable than Web-based one. It is desirable to enable communities to choose their suitable environments. Therefore, there is a need for solutions that facilitate the introduction of advanced collaboration services in CoPs. Our assertion is that, by providing an email-based

Figure 1. Web-based GUI of eLogbook.

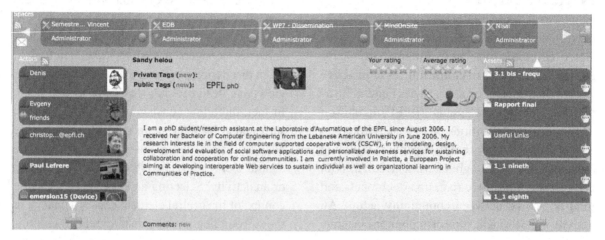

interface to eLogbook, its further adoption can be strengthened and further evolutions of **CoPs** can be better supported. To validate this assertion, an email-based interface has been designed as described in the next section. Its **acceptability** is currently investigated in the framework of the Palette project with pilot CoPs.

The **email**-based eLogbook **interface** enables users to manage their activities, assets, and awareness by sending emails directly to eLogbook and to receive requested information. Additionally, users can trace occurring events by receiving automatic notification emails from eLogbook. The advantages of providing an email-based interface to eLogbook are the following:

- To use the email-based interface, the users' devices only need to have email client installed. It is very common for desktop PCs, pocket PCs and even smart-phones to integrate built-in email clients.
- The communication cost induced by using an email-based interface is cheaper than the Web-based one. This is still an important factor for mobile users.
- The users can store emails on their devices. Afterwards, they can manage joint activities, share related assets and get

contextual awareness without connecting to the Internet. The email-based eLogbook interface provides offline information management and relies on standard email synchronization solutions.

- The users can send and check emails at a time of their choosing.
- As pull scheme, email access is intrinsically context-oriented.

The rest of this paper is structured as follows. Section 2 describes work related to email-based collaborative environments. Section 3 introduces the specifications of the email-based eLogbook interface. Section 4 explains how the email-based interface facilitates eLogbook acceptance. Section 5 ends with concluding remarks.

RELATED WORK

Email systems are widely deployed in workflow, task and activity management systems (Dredze, Lau, & Kushmerick, 2006; Kushmerick & Lau, 2005; Siu, Iverson, & Tang, 2006; Tailby, Dean, & et al., 2006; Whittaker, Bellotti, & Gwiydka, 2006). Workflow systems specify and monitor evolution of business processes. Email usually does not require real-time interactions. It is a convenient means for offline communication between users and systems. *Lynx* (Vélez & Vélez, 2006) is an email extension for workflow systems based on Web Services. It provides a Web service through which a workflow application can interact with human partners via an email-based forms interface without requiring a specialized client. Its server side is composed of a BPEL execution engine, an outgoing email Web service and other partner Web services, as well as an incoming email gateway. The client side is composed of a standard email client application and an XForms player component. *Taskmaster* (Belotti, Ducheneaut, & et al., 2003) is an email-based task management system. It uses an email system that can embed task management information directly in the email inbox. The information includes warning bars (which show task deadlines), action clusters, and task-specific contact lists. This solution enables management of emails and tasks in single application.

EDI (Electronic Data Interchange) systems are used in commercial organizations for trading partners to exchange information with each other. (Bergeron & Raymond, 1992) has identified the advantages of EDI systems. The systems have been using email as a means of exchanging messages. Each trading partner needs to provide an email address for EDI messages, and an email address for personal communications related to EDI. Typically, the MIME encapsulation specification would be used to enclose the EDI data within the email message. The trading partners would need to agree upon an encryption method for secure email.

EMAIL-BASED INTERFACE OF eLOGBOOK

The email-based **interface** of eLogbook allows service invocations and information requests via email. The users are authenticated by their registered email address that is hence required to send requests. The requests must follow a number of predefined rules to be interpreted by eLogbook properly.

First, this section presents the system flow for the email-based interface of eLogbook. Second, it states the syntax of the email requests. Third, it describes how notification mechanisms can be controlled via email and how particular information can be requested. Finally, it presents how two kinds of eLogbook actions can be triggered via email.

System Flow for the Email-Based Interface of eLogbook

Figure 2 shows the system flow for the email-based interface of eLogbook. The email address for accessing eLogbook is *action.elogbook@epfl.ch*.

Every time eLogbook receives an email from a user, it handles the request according to the following steps:

- Step 1: *Sender Identification*. In this step, a check on whether the email sender is indeed a registered eLogbook user is performed. If this is the case, step 2 is initiated. Otherwise, the email is ignored.
- Step 2: *Email Dissemination & Action Identification*. The content of the email is parsed (subject and body), and the action to be performed is identified. In cases of ambiguous requests, an error message is sent back to the user.
- Step 3: *Protocol Checking*. A check is performed in this step to make sure that the sender is allowed to perform the requested action based on the access rights s-he has been granted over the entities involved. For example, if the user wishes to create a sub-space of another already existing space, s-he must have administrative rights over the latter.
- Step 4: *Confirmation Request*. If the sender is allowed to perform the requested action,

Figure 2. System flow for the email-based interface of eLogbook.

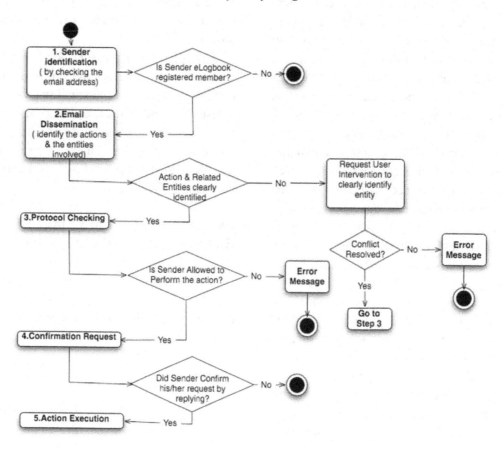

then an email is sent back for requesting a confirmation. This step is important for two reasons. First, it is used for security purpose in order to make sure that the corresponding eLogbook user was indeed the one who actually sent the request. Second, it ensures that the user indeed wishes to perform the action based on what s he had sent and how it was interpreted by eLogbook. Each confirmation request has an expiration time, e.g., 24 hours from the sending of the confirmation request.

- Step 5: *Action Execution.* If the user confirms by replying to the email from eLogbook, then the requested action would be executed.

Syntax of Emails

The lightweight email-based interface of eLogbook allows users to write email in simple syntax to request for actions or information. Figure 3 shows the syntax of the request email from a user, and that of the confirmation email from eLogbook.

A request **email** contains four parts. The *email recipient* states the email address of the eLogbook server. The *email sender* states the email address of the requester. The *email subject* states the type of requested action, e.g., "create new space". The *email attachment* is used for attaching file for "create new asset" action. The *email body* states the information related to the requested action. It is formatted in plain text such that any actor can compose its request email using simple text

Figure 3. Syntax of a request email.

```
    Email recipient: <eLogbook email address>
    Email sender: <actor email address>
    Email subject: <type of action>
    Email attachment: <File>
    Email body:
    'Name: <string>'
    'Description: <string>'
    'Public tags: <strings>'
    'Private tags: <strings>'
    'Public role: <string>' or 'Public right: <string>'
    'Relation: <type of relation>'
  'DESTINATION: <NAME OF SPACE OR USER>'
```

editor. In addition, plain text format is compatible with all email clients.

The *command tags* used in the email are in the format '*<command string>*'. Currently there are seven command tags for defining names, descriptions, tags, roles and relations of space/ asset/deliverable (refer to Figure 3). Among them, only the *Name* field is compulsory for all actions (except "disable/enable all notifications"); other fields are optional.

The confirmation email is sent by the eLogbook server to the sender in order to authenticate her/ his identities (Figure 4). The actor needs to reply to the confirmation email to invoke the action stated in the email subject. The detailed action information is also listed in the email body. The confirmation email contains a unique *reference number* for each particular action request. The eLogbook server also generates and stores a

hash value of the email for integrity check. The email contains an access link for the actors to access their new space/asset/deliverable through the Web interface after confirmation or at a later stage if s-he deems it appropriate.Currently the email-based interface can be used for the following functions:

1. Request information,
2. Tune default notification mechanism,
3. Trigger administrative actions, and
4. Trigger operational actions, e.g., creation of spaces, assets and deliverables.

Requesting Information and Tuning Default Notification Mechanism

By default, an eLogbook user can be notified of several events via email, e.g., the reminder of the

Figure 4. Syntax of a confirmation email.

```
    Email recipient: <actor email address>
    Email sender: <eLogbook email address>
    Email subject: Confirmation of the <type of action> action
    Email body:
    <information of the requesting action>
    'Reference: <reference number>'
  ACCESS LINK: <URL>
```

submission or validation of deadlines, and the invitation to join a new space. The user can completely or partially disable the default eLogbook notification mechanism through the Web-based or the email-based eLogbook interface. In the latter case, the email subject and body are interpreted in order to invocate the user's requested action.

- If the email subject is set to "disable all notifications", then the user will stop receiving all sorts of eLogbook notifications. An email with the subject "enable all notifications" induces the opposite action.
- If the email subject is set to "disable notifications", then the body of the email contains the name of activities, assets and actors, in the format illustrated below. The requested action is to disable all notifications related to one of the activities, assets and actors listed in the email.
- At any point in time, the user can "ping" eLogbook to get information related to a specific actor, space or asset by setting the subject of the email in the form: "get info <entity_type>: <entity_name>" where the entity_type can be space, actor or asset, and the entity_name can consist of the name of a space, an actor or an asset. This feature is mostly suitable for people who prefer "pull" rather than "push" notifications means. eLogbook responds by sending to the user a report of the executed actions related to the stated entity since the last time the user visited the eLogbook site or requested related notifications via email.

Triggering Administrative and Operational Actions

eLogbook users can trigger two kinds of actions. First, *administrative actions* are related to administrating and structuring the activities of the community by defining common objectives, scheduling deliverables and managing the roles assigned to the community members. Second, *operational actions* enclose all other kind of non-organizational collaborative actions such as posting an asset in a space, linking, tagging and/ rating an actor, a space or an asset.

By simply sending an email to eLogbook (*action.elogbook@epfl.ch*), members can invocate operational as well as organizational actions. Examples on how activities, assets and deliverables are created are given below in order to illustrate the interactions between eLogbook and users via email.

Creating a Space

Setting the subject of the email to "create new space" creates a space with its default administrator being the sender of the email. The body of the email should contain the *name of the space*, optionally the space description and the following fields:

- *Public/Private tags*: Public tags will be shown to all the people who can see the space; private or personal ones are only visible to their creators.
- *A public role*: If the email sender sets this field to "yes", then the space is made public with default rights granted to everyone (allowing them to perform all non-organizational actions). The administrator can decide not to rely on default rights but define a new set of rights. This can be done via email as well. If the email sender sets the field to "no" or does not mention it at all, then the space is kept secret except for members who will be explicitly invited by the space initiator.
- A relation to another already existing space: The sender can define a relation between this space and an already existing one. The most frequently used unidirectional relation type is "sub-space of".

Figure 5. Body of the email for creating a new space.

```
'Name: TelCop07'
'Description: Workshop TelCoP07'
'Public tags: email, usability'
'Public role:yes'
'Relation:"sub-space of" "Palette"
```

Figure 5 shows the body of an email example for creating a space. The actor "Sandy helou" wants to create a space called "TelCoP07" which is a sub-space of "Palette". The email states two public tags, "email" and "usability", for the space. After the actor sends the email and before performing the requested action, eLogbook sends a confirmation email to the actor "Sandy helou", as shown on the Figure 6. Once confirmed, eLogbook runs the action requested, and the new sub-space called "TelCoP07" for the existing space "Palette" will be created. Figure 9 shows the new activity in the Web-based eLogbook interface.

Creating an Asset

Setting the subject of the email to "create new asset" creates an asset with its owner being the sender of the email. In the body of the email should contain the *name of the asset*, and optionally the asset description and the following fields:

- *Public/Private tags*: Public tags will be shown to all the people who can see the asset; private or personal ones are only visible to their creator.
- *A public role*: If the email sender defines this field, then the asset is made public. The field can have three possible values: "owner", "editor" or "reader". If this field is skipped, the asset is kept secret except for members who will be explicitly granted access rights over the asset.
- A relation to another already existing asset: Any sort of predefined or user-defined semantic link can be used such as "reply to", "complements", "in favor", "against". For unidirectional links, the "of" preposition

Figure 6. Body of the confirmation email.

```
Confirm the following information:

'Name: TelCop07'
'Description: Workshop TelCoP07'
'Public tags: email, usability'
'Public role:yes'
'Relation:"sub-space of" "Palette" '

'Reference: 12'
Access link: http://elogbook.epfl.ch/context/actor/42

Please, confirm this action by REPLYING to this email. Otherwise, the action
will be ignored.
```

Figure 7. Body of the email of creating a new asset.

```
'Name: TelCop07 paper v1'
'Description: This is the first version'
'Public right: reader'
'Public tags: to revise'
'Private tags: change chapter1, read conclusion'
'Destination:"TelCoP07" editor'

TelCop_V1.d...KB) (19.0 KB)
```

may be used.

- A *destination* field: If the user includes this field in the email body then access rights are granted to the stated entities which can be activities or particular actors. If an entity mentioned corresponds to a space, then the asset is automatically posted in the space. If it contains an actor's username or email, then access right over the asset is granted to the actor.

Figure 7 shows the body of an email for creating a new asset. The actor "Sandy helou" wants to create an asset called "TelCoP07 paper v1" for the space "TelCoP07". The email states two private tags, "change chapter1" and "read conclusion", for the asset. The asset is stored in the email as an attachment. After the actor sends the email and before the requested action is performed, eLogbook sends a confirmation email to the actor "Sandy helou" (similar to the one we have seen in Figure 6). Once confirmed, eLogbook runs the action requested, and an asset called "TelCoP07 paper v1" is created. Figure 9 shows the created asset in eLogbook.

Creating a Deliverable

Setting the subject of the email to "create new deliverable" creates a deliverable inside a space. In the body of the email should contain the *name of the deliverable* as well as *the name of the space* in which the former should be posted. Optionally the deliverable description and the following fields can be appended:

- *Public/Private tags*: Public tags will be shown to all the people who can see the deliverable; private and personal ones are only visible to their creator.
- A relation to another already existing deliverable: It is mostly used to define the order of deliverables submission with a space (using "precedes" or "exceeds").

Figure 8 shows the body of an email of creating new deliverable. The actor "Sandy helou" wants to create a deliverable called "del07-07" for the space "TelCoP07". Figure 9 shows the created deliverable in eLogbook after the email request.

Figure 8. Body of the email for creating a new deliverable.

```
'Name: del07-07'
'Space name: TelCoP07'
'Description: This is the deliverable for the 7 July'
```

Figure 9. Screenshots of new space, asset and deliverable created in eLogbook.

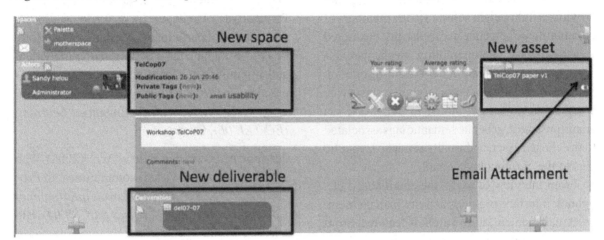

HOW THE EMAIL-BASED INTERFACE FACILITATES ELOGBOOK ACCEPTANCE

In this section, we describe a use case scenario to illustrate how the email-based interface is used by eLogbook users.

Alice, Bob and Carol are members of a CoP. In real life, they are colleagues of a trading company. In working days, they need to visit a number of wholesales and retail companies in different countries to collect goods information. Usually they divide their jobs such that each one is responsible to visit a different country. Since they travel frequently, for the sake of convenience, they use Blackberry smart-phone to allow them to send and receive email anytime. They have been using eLogbook to mange their activities and documents.

In one working day, Alice has just visited a wholesales company in Thailand, and collected some information of agricultural products. She wants to share the information to Bob and Carol. She documents the information and saves it as a word file. Since the data transmission cost of her Blackberry is based on data size, instead of using Web-based eLogbook, Alice prefers to use the lightweight email-based eLogbook interface.

She uses the email interface to create an asset attached with the word file in an eLogbook space where Alice, Bob and Carol are members. After successful creation of the asset, both Bob and Carol receive a notification email through their Blackberry. Being aware of the new asset created by Alice, they can go to eLogbook to browse the asset and download the word file.

CONCLUSIONS AND FUTURE WORK

The email-based eLogbook interface enables users to manage their activities, assets and awareness through email. It provides an alternative lightweight non-Web interface to ease eLogbook access when using smart phones or PDA and to facilitate eLogbook acceptance for community members hesitating to learn an additional Web environment. It also has other advantages over Web-based access, such as low communication cost and offline information management.

The user-friendliness, security and efficiency of the email-based eLogbook interface will be further investigated. In addition, the comparative acceptability of the Web-based and email-based systems for communities of practice users will be assessed.

The email-based eLogbook interface not only provides a lightweight solution to the members of communities of practice, it can also be considered as a high-level interoperability mechanism for other services that can benefit from eLogbook features. For example, a semantic analysis service could request an asset stored in eLogbook via email, process it, generate semantic tags associated to the chosen asset, and finally send the semantic tags to the eLogbook via email.

From the view of users, the email-based eLogbook interface provides activity management, asset management, and awareness features. From the view of other services, the email-based eLogbook interface provides workflow support for collaboration. Therefore, this interface integrates the features of legacy email-based systems to support both CoP users and services.

ACKNOWLEDGMENT

We thank Amagoia Madina Berastegui and Yassin Rekik for their contributions to this paper.

This work has been partially funded by the European Union through it s Sixth RTD Framework Programme in Information Society Technologies (Palette Integrated Project).

REFERENCES

Belotti, V., Ducheneaut, N., Howard, M., & Smith, I. (2003). Taking email to task: The design and evaluation of a task management centered email tool. In *Proceedings of the SIGCHI Conference on Human Factors in Computing Systems* (pp. 345-352).

Bergeron, F., & Raymond, L. (1992). The advantages of electronic data interchange. *SIGMIS Database, 23*(4), 19–31. doi:10.1145/146553.146556

Daele, A., Erpicum, M., Esnault, L., Pironet, F., Platteaux, H., Vandeput, E., & Wiele, N. (2006). An example of participatory design methodology in a project which aims at developing individual and organisational learning in communities of practice. In *Proceedings of the first European Conference on Technology Enhanced Learning (EC-TEL'06)*, Greece.

de Moor, A., & van den Heuvel, W. J. (2004). Web service selection in virtual communities. In *Proceedings of the 37th Annual Hawaii International Conference on System Sciences (HICSS'04)*, Big Island, Hawaii.

Dredze, M., Lau, T., & Kushmerick, N. (2006). Automatically classifying emails into activities. In *Proceedings of the 11th International Conference on Intelligent User Interfaces*, Australia.

El Helou, S., Gillet, D., Salzmann, C., & Rekik, Y. (2007). Feed-oriented awareness services for eLogbook mobile users. In *Proceedings of the 2nd International Conference on Interactive Mobile and Computer aided Learning (IMCL 2007)*, Jordan.

Gillet, D., El Helou, S., Rekik, Y., & Salzmann, C. (2007). Context-sensitive awareness services for communities of practice. In *Proceedings of the 12th International Conference on Human-Computer Interaction (HCI2007)*, Beijing.

Kushmerick, N., & Lau, T. (2005). Automated email activity management: An unsupervised learning approach. In *Proceedings of the 10th International Conference on Intelligent User Interfaces* (pp. 67-74).

Rekik, Y., Gillet, D., El Helou, S., & Salzmann, C. (2007). The eLogBook framework: Sustaining interaction, collaboration, and learning in laboratory-oriented CoPs. *The International Journal of Web-Based Learning and Teaching, 2*(3).

Siu, N., Iverson, L., & Tang, A. (2006). Going with the flow: Email awareness and task management. In *Proceedings of the 2006 20ᵗʰ Anniversary Conference on Computer Supported Cooperative Work* (pp. 441-450).

Tailby, R., Dean, R., Milnerm, B., & Smith, D. (2006). Email classification for automated service handling. In *Proceedings of the 2006 ACM Symposium on Applied Computing* (pp. 1073-1077).

Vélez, I. P., & Vélez, B. (2006). Lynx: An open architecture for catalyzing the deployment of interactive digital government workflow-based systems. In *Proceedings of the 2006 International Conference on Digital Government Research* (pp. 309-318).

Whittaker, S., Bellotti, V., & Gwiydka, J. (2006). Email in personal information management. *Communications of the ACM, 49*(1), 68–73. doi:10.1145/1107458.1107494

Chapter 4

Supporting Communities of Practice by Advancing Knowledge Management Between Hybrid Collaborative Environments

Anna De Liddo
Open University, UK

Grazia Concilio
Politecnico di Milano, Italy

ABSTRACT

In this chapter the authors investigate a tool integration perspective to support knowledge management and exchange between Web-based and traditional collaborative environments. In particular they discuss the integration between a tool (CoPe_it!) supporting collaborative argumentation and learning in Web-based communities of practices and a hypermedia and sense making tool (Compendium) acting as a personal and collective knowledge management (KM) system in traditional collaborative environments. The authors describe the tools and drive a comparative analysis of the two groupware by focusing on the general applicability of the tools integration for supporting communities of practices and, more generally, collaborative works. Moreover the authors present the results of a case study in which the tools integration has been applied within a real community of practice. Finally they discuss main results of the tools integration in order to leverage communities of practice to a truly collaborative environment with no communication boundaries.

Communities of Practice are increasingly demanding for new ways of working together. The introduction of disruptive Web 2.0 social networking and groupware tools with self-organising user communities, have radically changed the way in which people perform knowledge work. Information and knowledge are gathered and created in real world settings and then diffused on the web; while at the same time a growing amount of information and knowledge is made accessible by web services

DOI: 10.4018/978-1-60566-711-9.ch004

which extend the concrete impact and influence that these information and knowledge exert on traditional social networks. Knowledge works are increasingly looking for new ways to manage and integrate knowledge created and exchanged within and between virtual and traditional environments. However the information and knowledge exchange between these hybrid collaborative environments is not codified, and there are not specific means or tools to blend between virtual and real world information, knowledge and communities.

In this chapter we investigate a tool integration perspective to support knowledge management and exchange between web-based and traditional collaborative environments. In particular we propose and discuss the integration between a tool (CoPe_it!) supporting collaborative argumentation and learning in web-based Communities of Practice and a hypermedia and sensemaking tool (Compendium) acting as a personal and collective Knowledge Management (KM) system in traditional collaborative environments. We focus on the general applicability of this integration for supporting Communities of Practice and, more generally, collaborative works. In particular we present results of a case study in which the tools integration has been tested and evaluated with a community of practice. A community of farmers in southern Italy has been engaged with the tools testing and evaluation. On the base of the case study results we finally discuss objectives and challenges to be addressed to support a transparent knowledge integration and exchange between hybrid (virtual vs traditional) collaborative environments.

In the first section we present the background issue and propose the concept of Hybrid Community of Practice (HCoP). Moreover we motivate and propose the integration of Compendium and Cope_it! in order to support knowledge works in Hybrid Community of Practice. In the second section we briefly present both tools showing their functionality, outlining their complementarities and identifying potential mutual benefits of their

integration (third section). In the third section we discuss possible technical solutions for the tools' integration and we describe the integration scenario that has been implemented. The fourth section is centered on the description of a real case study in which the integration project have been applied and tested to support a real community of practice. Results of the experimentation are described and discussed in the light of the evaluation results. Finally in the last section we discuss main results of the tools' integration in order to leverage Communities of Practice to a truly collaborative environment with no communication boundaries.

HYBRID COMMUNITIES OF PRACTICE (HCOP): BLENDING BETWEEN VIRTUAL AND TRADITIONAL COLLABORATIVE ENVIRONMENTS

Communities of Practice (CoP) naturally generate and act in real world settings like work contexts, leisure and family or familiar places (Lave & Wenger 1991). Contextual and contingent situations can bring people to discover common aims, desires, needs or problems and then trigger new unpredictable ways of collaboration towards shared objectives. Starting from these objectives people communicate and organize their actions towards common goals. In this process of community definition, specific roles, tasks, and expertise start emerging within the group (Wenger 1998). Eventually, the different roles are legitimated by social relationships of trust among the community members, forging the overall identity of the group as a whole (Brown & Duguid 2000).

This complex process of transition from a group towards a Community of Practice is determined by the simultaneous occurrence of personal actions, choices and attributions of value. This transition is strictly related to the individual knowledge of the community members (often tacit knowledge) and to the contextualization of this knowledge to different environments, situations and times (Lave & Wenger 1991).

Defining the prototypical transition from a group towards a CoP is, therefore, highly challenging; it is particularly sensitive to the environment and highly dependent on the specificities of involved actors which can be only temporarily involved in the community actions. What happens to this complex dynamics when we look at web-based environments and we refer i.e. to virtual Community of Practice (VCoP)?

We could assume that acting in virtual environments, like web-based environments, means acting with fixed and predetermined protocols for information exchange, language and communication roles, which represents a significant help to analyse the VCoP dynamics. In VCoP knowledge objects and communication rules are pre-structured and then we can monitor and control some of the social implications and influences that in traditional CoP would make the problem more complex. Despite this we cannot consider VCoP members as isolated entities with no social (external to the VCoP) life, environment and relationship, separated from their personal histories which indeed affect their actions and positions within the VCoP.

Then the question is: In the global village does it make sense to distinguish traditional (real-world) CoP and VCoP? We should rather start thinking about a hybrid version of CoP (HCoP) whose community members act and communicate in both virtual and traditional modes in a way that is continuously shifting from one mode to the other one (Kimble & Barlow 2000)?

HCoP can be conceived as CoP in which members shift between virtual and traditional spaces in order to accomplish complementary functions in an attempt to fulfill the same community objectives. HCoP members work on accomplishing tasks and objectives of the same community but they can contemporarily act in the virtual and physical space (or in only one of the two spaces

but defining a hybrid community of virtual/non virtual members). This hybrid environment of influence in which members accomplish their knowledge works needs to be assisted by tools that effectively support knowledge transfer between both spaces, so that knowledge can be exchanged and reused by the whole community (both in its virtual and physical component).

When we think about virtual and traditional collaborative spaces we mainly refer to the web and to real-world environments; we mainly refer to activities performed on-line and off-line. In this sense we can consider computer supported works as real-world activities when they are performed off-line. The focus is on communication modalities rather than on the specificities of the communication space: traditional spaces are spaces in which humans communicate by real-world means, whereas in virtual spaces humans (or agents) communicate by artificial means.

Knowledge works are increasingly looking for tools and environments able to manage and to integrate knowledge created and exchanged within and between virtual and traditional environments.

What integration method and tools should be envisioned and provided in order to take into account the influence and impact of hybrid knowledge in order to enlarge individuals and community networks?

Our aim is twofold: 1. enhancing virtual interaction networks by exploiting social relationships in traditional spaces and, vice versa, 2. enlarging the social and real-world networks by exploiting links and knowledge from virtual communities.

Knowledge from virtual community networks is a key feature in the real-world environment for CoP in order to make them able to leverage internal debates to a new way of communication: not only face-to-face but also remotely (i.e. distance and asynchronous interactions as they can be supported within virtual environments). At the same time knowledge from real-world communities is a key feature for VCoP (Kimble & Wright 2001) to exploit social networks of members (in real-world settings) in order to enlarge participation and attract new individuals into the VCoP.

To cater for this we propose the integration between CoPe_it!, a tool to support collaborative argumentation in VCoP, and Compendium, a hypermedia and sense making tool acting as a personal or collective knowledge management system in physical CoP.

CoPe_it! is the tool to gather knowledge from virtual communities. It helps VCoP in discussing and making collaborative decisions about common issues. On the other hand Compendium is the tool to gather and manage knowledge from real world collaborative environment. It helps traditional CoP: i. to gather and represent knowledge coming from face-to-face meetings taking trace of argumentative discussions about common issues; ii. to manage and reuse this knowledge in diverse environments making sense of them in a personal way (using compendium as a personal KM tool); iii. to manage and reuse this knowledge in diverse environments making sense of them in a CoP perspective (Using Compendium as a collective KM tool). The integration of these tools allows to exchange knowledge and to enlarge the field of discussion between web-based and real world environments, several advantages and potentials of this integration will be discussed in the following sections.

COMPENDIUM AND COPE_IT!: A BRIEF DESCRIPTION

In the following sub-paragraphs we briefly describe the tools object of the integration. Then we discuss peculiarities and similarities of the tools and motivate why these have been considered suitable for the integration project.

Compendium: A Hypermedia and Knowledge Management Tool for Individual and Collective Sensemaking

Compendium is the result of over 15 years of research and development. It is difficult to give one comprehensive definition of the software because different uses are already carried out and new uses are continuously envisaged emerging from the practice and creativity of the users.

From the analysis of the state of the art (Selvin & Sierhuis 1999) we can group the diverse Compendium uses in two main families: i. in-real-time and ii. post-hoc uses. This distinction mainly refers to the work the user needs to do on-the-fly or post-hoc (during and after the meeting).

In the first family we count Dialogue Mapping (DM) and Conversational Modeling (CM) techniques. These techniques require high moderation skills either on-the-fly (for DM) or both on the fly and post-hoc (for CM techniques).

The first is mainly adopted in face-to-face meetings and Compendium is used for arguments' visualization and meeting moderation: the moderator (possibly assisted by an experienced Compendium user in charge of the mapping) maps the meeting (captures and displays discussion) in order to reach shared understanding about a problem. The process consists of both an incremental negotiation of meanings and the micro-agreements about problem representation (Conklin 2005).

Conversational Modeling (CM) has a balance between users' skills in mapping and modeling and the work in and behind the meeting room. In order to apply this technique a Compendium user needs to prepare templates, devoted to model the meeting evolution and to structure the discussions, in order to help and drive the group to decide about and define design variables (criteria, alternatives, priorities, list of actions, etc). In this phase the user applies process modeling skills and he works behind the meeting room. In order to manage such meetings the CM practitioner needs to be experienced in meeting moderation and mapping, nevertheless the template driven moderation is a valuable support and makes the moderation work less dependent on the moderator skills.

Dialogue Mapping and Conversational Modeling are two techniques for collective sensemaking and these are 'real time techniques' for capturing meeting discussions and involving people in collective definitions and collaborative argumentation about problems.

In the second family, i.e. the post-hoc techniques, we count Knowledge Management oriented uses of Compendium. In these cases Compendium provides users with diverse features for managing knowledge, making sense of knowledge contents and using and reusing information in disparate knowledge works (hypermedia files and documents can be linked and enriched with comments, ideas, tags, etc).

KM oriented applications range from managing a PhD research (Selvin, & Buckingham Shum 2005) to political debates representation (Renton & Macintosh 2007; Ohl 2007). In these latter cases Compendium has been used as a Computer Supported Argument Visualization tool oriented to represent a debate, making it easily exportable and eventually open for public discussion on the web. The main objective is to enlarge participation and deliberation about public policies. In these case studies Compendium has been used for post-hoc analysis and representation (mainly mapping) of political arguments. Contents are first gathered by interviews and/or public forums and then structured into argument maps (mainly following an IBIS model of argument representation). A different attempt has been carried out in the Participatory Planning domain and considers the use of Compendium as a multimedia project memory. In this application a post-hoc analysis of videos, interviews, documents, graphs, photos, and other material has been conducted to map the memory of a participatory urban planning project (De Liddo & Buckingham Shum, 2007).

In all post-hoc applications the work on information structuring is committed to a knowledge manager who has to organize the contents according to specific objectives (i.e. how to trigger participation? What are the topics to focus on?, etc).

In the light of the examples reported above, Compendium can be defined as an hypermedia and knowledge management tool for individual and collective sensemaking. In the literature it is referred to not only as a software tool but as an approach to gather, structure, represent, and manage knowledge for individual or collaborative knowledge intensive works. In a Compendium approach knowledge objects (ideas, multimedia documents, artifacts, etc) are represented as nodes of a graph like structure; afterwards nodes are linked so as to organize contents and make-sense of individual and/or collective concepts and concerns.

Cope_it!: A Web-Based Tool for Collaborative Argumentation and Learning

CoPe_it! is a software developed in the context of a EU project, Palette (Pedagogically Sustained Adaptive Learning through the Exploitation of Tacit and Explicit Knowledge). Mainly it is a web-based tool supporting collaborative learning in VCoP (Kimble & Barlow 2000).

CoPe_it! has been designed according to what the research group describe as an incremental formalization approach (Karacapilidis & Tzagarakis 2007); it is based on the idea that different levels of formalization of the argumentation contents need to be provided in order to support collaborative decision making.

CoPe_it! supplies members of VCoP with different features in order to deal with argumentative discussions. The software supports i. definition of alternative solutions and ii. analysis and evaluation of the discussion contents in order to drive groups throughout decision making processes. CoPe_it! is more than a web tool for collaborative argumentation, it is rather a tool supporting learning processes in VCoP. It supports i. the first step of problem setting, ii. the definition of alternative solutions, iii. the discussion and negotiation of meanings, pros and cons of each alternative, and finally iv. the analysis of content and the definition of solutions priorities.

CoPe_it! offers basically three levels of formalization corresponding to different representations of argumentative discussions, each of them associated to one of the following views:

1. Desktop view: it consists in the lower level of formalization; the community members can add contents in the most user friendly way (in a Compendium like approach). This is an intuitive way of gathering contents from the users without forcing them with pre-defined communication rules.
2. Formal view: this view consists in a machine readable version of the previous one. Predefined algorithms of conversion are applied to the desktop view contents in order to convert them in a IBIS-model like argumentative discussion.
3. Forum view: this view represents contents in a temporal sequence showing contents and node types (statement, argument, document type, etc).

Future developments include the support for simultaneous posting from all the tree views. Another important improvement to be implemented concerns the possibility to define and negotiate with the community members the specific algorithm of conversion between the desktop view and the formal one. This opportunity will couple a tool for collaborative argumentation with a valuable support for decision-making.

CoPe_it! provides members of communities with a common workspace where they can post and share ideas, resources, and arguments in a way that makes sense to them. Community members are registered and have specific names, roles and privileges within the community. Each user is assigned his personal workspace and he can make it private and organize his/her own ideas and contents to be eventually shared with the group in a second moment.

Knowledge items can change during the discussion (free interchange between node types: idea, comment, and note) and they can be linked with personalized links (of specific thickness, colors, and labels). Nodes can be arranged and moved freely in the workspace, and they can also be clustered using adornments (colored rectangles used to group together nodes). Other interesting features are i. the possibility to open a new browser for searching information by Google and Wikipedia, ii. the possibility to define and manage a list of bookmarks.

This synthetic overview of CoPe_it! main features is not intended to be exhaustive and is the result of the testing of the most recent up-dating of the tool.

Why an Integration? Discussing Similarities and Peculiarity of the Tools

Although addressing different tasks, Compendium and CoPe_it! show high integration potentials mainly because, they share similar communication principles and visualization means. Starting from the analysis of peculiar features of the software, (see the following table) we want to make visible the complementarities of the tools.

Table 1 shows in light-grey features which are similar (or will be similar referring to the future planned versions of CoPe_it!) like: export and import formats, source code distribution policy, administrator rights (registration and download), visualization and structure of contents (supported file types, IBIS model of argumentation, tagging etc).

Dark-grey rows identify the features in which both systems complement each other. The first complementarity refers to the communication mode (on-line/off-line use). Since we are interested in knowledge exchange between virtual/

non-virtual spaces, candidate tools for the integration need to be complementary with regards to this feature.

Other key complementarities are: at distance synchronous and asynchronous collaborations; users' roles, rules and privileges; hypertext features; personalization and revision of contents and decision making support.

Table 1. Compendium and CoPe_it! main features

Main Features	Compendium	CoPe_it!
Export formats	It supports 5 formats: XML, Jpeg, Html - web-maps and web-outline, power export.	It will support XML files and Jpeg format (not yet delivered)
Import formats	It supports XML imports, images and image folders, Quest Map files, Flash- Meeting files	It will support XML files and Jpeg format (not yet delivered)
Free download/access	YES	YES
Source Code Distribution Policy	Open source	Source code is intended to be released
WEB-BASED	NO	YES
Software download	YES (you need to download Compendium in order to access the full functionality)	NO (you don't need to download any software)
Registration	Needed the first time for the software download.	Needed the first time to get the User ID and Password and to get the administrator acceptance
Members attributes	There are no roles, rules and privileges imposer to the members not even any administration control on contents	There are roles, rules and privilege within a community
At distance asynchronous collaboration	YES - only on local networks	YES (through the web)
At distance synchronous collaboration	NO (yes - only slow performances)	Supports synchronous collaboration, supports tagging, modification of contents is allowed to workspace moderators
Structure of contents	No contents structure are pre-imposed	Desktop view: flat; formal view: rules of communication and contents have a pre-defined structure
References: supported file types	drag+drop in any document, website, email, image	At the moment you can upload any kind of local file type, not yet any url on the web
Support IBIS model of argumentation	YES	YES Partially (it doesn't support 'question' nodes, each question is supposed to be addressed in a separate workspace)
Tagging	You can choose between default tags and assign your own keyword 'tags'	NOT YET (it intends to offer some tagging features)
Personalization and customization of icons, backgrounds, colors, links, etc	You can create your own palettes of icons, links types, colors	At the moment no personalization features are present. Some features are under consideration for future versions: e.g. links color)
Hypertext features: Transclusion	You can place/edit a given knowledge object in many different views (supports transclusions)	Does not support transclusions, objects of different workspaces cannot be copied or linked
Contents revisions	Allows continuous changing and reviewing of contents and their organization	Does not support contents modification and revision (just erasing or adding new contents)
Information overload	It supports maps with large numbers of nodes	Not suitable for large number of nodes (very slow)
Support Decision making	NO (yes, only when paired with human assisted techniques)	YES (Support automatic generated view for different purposes)

Table 2. Additional features that the integration can provide to CoPe_it!

Compendium --------------------> CoPe_it!	
Additional features	**Complementarities**
1. Enlarges the advantages of real time capturing and integration with different materials, information, documents and hybrid files so that the face-to-face meeting memory can be shared in and out the meeting group	Compendium complements Cope_it! offering real time capture of meeting
2. Provides CoP with a hypermedia environment in which community members can use, correlate and manage contents of different collaboration spaces (contents raised in different workspaces can be discussed and transcluded in new contexts)	Compendium complements Cope_it! offering transclusion features
3. Offers a KM tool in which community members can organize, structure and define information and resources also being off line on their machine, but always giving them the possibility at any time to publish content on the web and to share them with a list of community members or making it public for the whole VCoP	Compendium complements Cope_it! offering an off-line KM tools
4. Toward un Organizational Memory System	Exports Cope_it! discussions in an offline environment without any problem of information overload (Compendium support maps with thousands nodes) Allows to customize organization and archiving of knowledge objects in larger organizational databases (linking and referring discussion contents to any other off-line and private data sources)	Compendium complements Cope_it! supporting maps up to large number of nodes Compendium complements Cope_it! offering customization of knowledge object and hyper textual environment running on your machine

Table 3. Additional features that the integration can provide to Compendium

CoPe_it! --------------------> Compendium	
Additional features	**Complementarities**
1. Opens Compendium face to face meeting to a wider community on the www	CoPe_it! complements Compendium offering a web-based argumentation environment
2. Gives the possibility to trigger online discussions on specific topics (this is particularly useful in Public Policy cases)	CoPe_it! complements Compendium offering the possibility to modify and enrich Compendium maps directly on the web
3. Provides at distance Compendium users with an environment of asynchronous discussions that can easily be imported in their Compendium maps	CoPe_it! complements Compendium offering synchronous interaction for real time at distance discussions
4. Gives to Compendium based Project memory system the possibility to update results of at distance meeting and consultation forum on the web	CoPe_it! complements Compendium offering the possibility to import, in forms of Compendium maps, contents of at distance meeting and consultation forum
5. Offers support for Decision Making	CoPe_it! complements Compendium offering automatic analysis of Compendium maps, with customized algorithms

Starting from the software analysis and focusing on the complementary aspects, we can identify the main mutual advantages of the envisaged integration.

In Table 2 and 3 we analyze complementary features trying to link each of them to the relative additional feature it would provide both to *Compendium* and *CoPe_it!* users, in the case the integration is successfully implemented.

As better detailed in Table 2 *Compendium* complements *CoPe_it!* by offering real time capture of meetings, thus sharing face-to-face meetings results in and out the meeting group. Moreover *Compendium* complements *CoPe_it!* by offering an off-line knowledge management environment in which community members can organize, structure and define information and resources also being off line.

Community members can work on their machines while always having the possibility to publish afterword selected contents on the web. Moreover they can also choose to share these contents with a list of community members or to make it public for the whole VCoP.

In other terms by offering an off-line hypermedia knowledge management environment

Compendium allows CoP members to customize organization and archiving of knowledge objects in larger organizational databases (linking and referring discussion contents to any other off-line and private data sources). Moreover some specific Compendium functionalities (i.e. tranclusion, customizations of icons, links and canvas background etc) allow enriching information and knowledge gathered on-line in CoPe_it! workspaces. CoPe_it! maps can be merged and linked with off-line information and documents thus reusing them in new off-line context and workspaces.

In addition CoPe_it! complements Compendium offering a web-based argumentation environment thus opening up the access to Compendium maps to a wider community on the WWW. Moreover being a web-tool CoPe_it! provides Compendium users with an environments for at distance asynchronous interaction. Results of these interactions can then be imported in Compendium environments and reused off-line. Another important improvement offered by CoPe_it! is the support to decision making. Compendium maps can be automatically analyzed with customized algorithms. This feature is particularly promising if we think about the problem of information overload; in fact Compendium support maps with thousands nodes, in this case CoPe_it! can help to analyze and simplify Compendium maps by selecting relevant information.

POSSIBLE INTEGRATION SCENARIOS

In the previous section we gave evidence of the mutual advantages when integrating Compendium and CoPe_it! In the following we'll discuss the integration proposal describing three possible scenarios:

First scenario: Importing CoPe_it! workspaces in Compendium maps (from virtual to real world settings – from VCoP to CoP).

Second scenario: Importing Compendium maps in CoPe_it! workspaces (from real to virtual world settings – from CoP to VCoP).
Third scenario: both sides import.

In the first scenario the main goal is to enlarge to communities on the web discussions and collaborative knowledge works performed in real world communities. In order to make on and off line discussions completely complementary and to allow the on-line discussions to evolve together with the face-to-face process, we need to transfer into Compendium the contents gained in CoPe_it! workspaces. Contents can be imported in Compendium and then re-organized, linked and discussed within the same community or in different ones during ad-hoc face-to-face meetings.

The second scenario aims at:

- Importing Compendium Dialogue maps in order to discuss within the virtual communities the results of face-to face meetings;
- Importing single-user concept maps used as a reference for arguing something in the virtual discussion
- Importing Compendium templates and models in order to trigger, organize or moderate the discussion in new workspaces.

The third scenario is the bi-directional integration between both tools, and it exhibits the benefits gained by performing the two scenarios already described. An additional advantage is envisaged: the results of virtual meetings can be submitted to the discussion in traditional communities (scenario 1) and the results of face-to-face discussions can go back to virtual environments (scenario 2) closing the cycle and allowing further contributions from the virtual community. This possibility provides means for continuously validating and revising contents from virtual to real world settings and vice-versa.

For the envisaged scenarios diverse technical solutions are possible. In figure 1 three options for

Figure 1. Technical options for the proposed integration

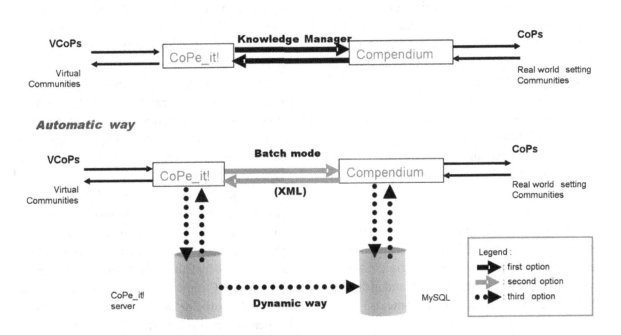

implementing the three scenarios are synthesized: one manual and two automatic options.

In the first option a knowledge manager is in charge of the knowledge integration and exchange between both systems. This option offers three positive opportunities: i. to select specific knowledge contents according to specific needs, ii. to control and avoid knowledge redundancies, and iii. to locate imported and exported maps in their original position (spatial positions in the two-dimensional canvas) that is crucial for contents' interpretation. On the other hand, this option enhances external influence on knowledge interchange (knowledge manager interpretation) and the time and effort required to be implemented.

In the second option the knowledge exchange is performed in batch mode, allowing XML export/import. This option has the advantages to be transparent and fast but it presents several theoretical and technical criticalities in the defini-

tion of conversion rules. Therefore efforts have to be devoted to:

- Defining conversion rules for contents export for CoPe_it! – Compendium objects: i.e. nodes types (each one with its features - title, descriptions, reference files, etc), links (with colors, thickness, texts labels, etc), adornments (with colors and titles), documents and reference objects (addressing compatibility and equivalence of document formats);
- Building a XML export/import readable in both systems (compare and integrate XML schemas, detect information and decide how and which ones of them can or have to be converted, etc).

In the third option the integration is obtained connecting Compendium and CoPe_it! databases. This option offers additional capabilities by allowing synchronous update of both Compendium and CoPe_it! spaces. In this scenario, virtual and traditional communities can work together in synchronicity on the same project or collaborative knowledge work, with different means but in a unique hybrid environment. This is a suitable environment for HCoP, hybrid Communities of Practice in which members can:

1. Shift continuously between virtual and real world environments
2. Simultaneously discuss, modify and produce knowledge objects in a whole hybrid space of collaboration.

This type of integration provides HCoP's members with a new collaboration space in which they have the opportunity to perform collaborative argumentation at various level and in diverse (virtual/non-virtual) groups and contexts.

The Integration Project

We implemented the third scenario and we allowed both sides import export of Compendium maps and CoPe_it! workspaces. This scenario has been realized relying on the second technical solution by allowing knowledge exchange in batch mode through XML export/import.

As previously discussed we had to establish specific conversion rules in particular for nodes types, links, documents and reference objects.

In the next figures we show the equivalence between CoPe_it!-Compendium icons. All CoPe_it! icons have an equivalent in Compendium environment. The icons are slightly different but they have an intuitive meaning (Figure 2). On the contrary some Compendium nodes, such as question nodes, list nodes, map nodes, decision nodes and pro and con nodes, have not an equivalent in CoPe_it! desktop view. Thereby we associated all these node types to a 'comment' node in CoPe_it! (Figure 3). This complicates the information transfer from Compendium to CoPe_it! and some

information are lost in the transfer. About the links labels and link colors, they are respected in information transer. Moreover the XML import/export has been designed so that nodes maintain the same XY coordinate on the video canvas.

Despite the described differences, results of application shows that Compendium and CoPe_it! integration allowed to create almost identical maps thus preventing misleading interpretation and minimizing the information lost in the information exchange process. In example Figure 4 represent the results of an import of a Compendium map in CoPe_it workspace.

As we see in the image, knowledge objects like statements, narratives, images, documents can be represented in the same position, with similar icons (exception made for the question icon, which is not supported by CoPe_it!). In essence, CoPe_it! makes some Compendium features available on line so that off-line and on line discussion can happen in a unique hypermedia discourse (Buckingham Shum 2007). In the following sections we will give an examples of how the two tools can be used to perform collaborative works in a real case study.

A CASE STUDY: TESTING COPE_IT!-COMPENDIUM INTEGRATION WITH A COMMUNITY OF FARMERS

A case study has been driven in the environmental planning field in order to test the integration performances and the users reactions to the use of CoPe_it!.

Compendium and CoPe_it! have been used by a community of farmers to discuss about issues concerning the organization of a new biological production. In particular Compendium maps describing some CoP meetings and activities have been imported in CoPe_it! workspaces in order to trigger on-line at distance discussion between CoP members. In the following sub paragraphs we first describe the case study and the CoP

Figure 2. CoPe_it! Compendium icons conversion

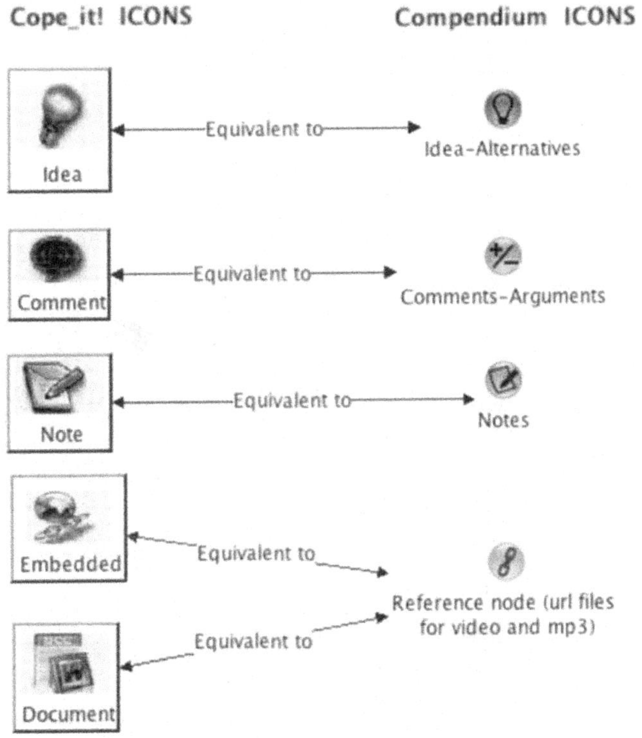

involved in the experimentation. Then results of the experimentation are presented and results of the evaluation discussed.

An Hybrid Community of Practice (HCoP): The Torre Guaceto Community

The case study of Torre Guaceto is not about a conventional environmental planning activity but concerns the activities performed by a community of farmers to enhance their biological production income. A planning team was in charge of helping this community of practice to build their past and present project history. Therefore, Compendium was used both to rebuild and represent the past history of the community and to capture and represent the new, ongoing activities. This case study aims at testing the combined use of Compendium and CoPe_it! to capture a deliberation

process in the ongoing phase and at testing new way to support an hypermedia discourse which happens in hybrid collaborative environments (on-line and off-line).

We chose this case study because it was still running; this gave us a good occasion to do some live testing directly involving the Torre Guaceto community members in real discussions. Furthermore this case involved a real farming Community of Practice, providing the opportunity to investigate CoP activities outside an institutional environment, where we could better appreciate the differences and difficulties of working with local communities, in their environments and with their communication protocols. As previously described Torre Guaceto case study is not a conventional planning case, it is built around a Community of Practice composed of heterogeneous groups of stakeholders (a community of farmers, NGOs, local agencies etc) that emerged

Figure 3. Compendium icons that have not equivalent in CoPe_it!

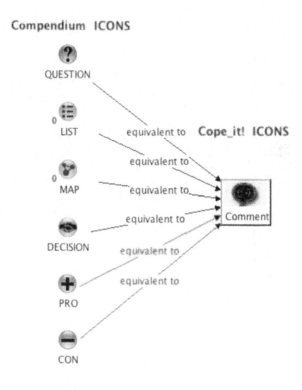

around the shared goal to enhance the biological production in a agricultural area in the south of Italy (Puglia region, Brindisi province) called Torre Guaceto. The main goal of the farmer group was to build a repository of best practices to be used to inform potential customers about the agricultural production and its biological value, then hopefully enhancing the sales of the Torre Guaceto local products. The main objective for the farmers' group was to increase the profit gained from the biological production. On the other hand other project partners were more concerned about the quality of the product and of the biological production in term of environmental protection. In particular several local agencies (such as Torre Guaceto Park Agency, Liberaterra, Slow Food.. etc) were involved in the project each one to accomplish different tasks, such as coordinating the activities, enabling the commercialization of products, implementing pilot cultivation projects etc. In this scenario the planning team was in charge

of helping the Torre Guaceto community of practice to build their past and present project history. Thereby the tools (Compendium and CoPe_it!) have been used both to rebuild and represent the past history of the community and to capture and represent the new on going activities.

Results of the Experimentation

Torre Guaceto case study has been designed to test the integration between CoPe_it! and Compendium. A group of four CoP members has been asked to discuss new challenges and open issues for the Torre Guaceto community to address in the near future. CoPe_it! has been used form the community members to conduct at distance discussions about results and challenges for the new biological production. Compendium maps that were used to represent organizational networks, face-to-face discussions and topic of past meetings have been imported in a CoPe_it! workspace to trigger the

Figure 4. Example of the integration of Compendium (top image) and CoPe_it! (bottom image)

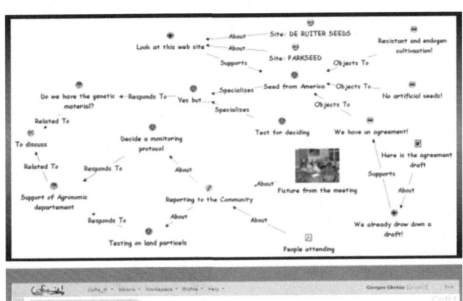

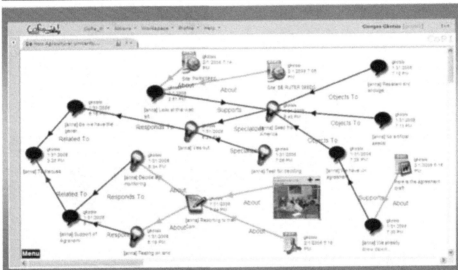

on line discussion. As we can see in Figure 5, nodes, pictures and images that were represented in Compendium maps (i.e. the representation of the organizations involved in the TG project, or claims raised from community members in previous face-to-face meetings) have been imported in CoPe_it! workspace and discussed from the community members at distance through CoPe_it! As Moderators of the on-line community we have also assisted farmers to directly engage in the use of the tool. After that an evaluation questionnaire has been distributed to the participants in order

to test CoPe_it! perceived usefulness and ease of use. Moreover general question on the tool has been made like: What would you use this tool for in your organization? What did you like dislike? How would you improve it?

Reactions have been favorable but they also show that the agricultural community of Torre Guaceto is probably not ready to use ICT tools as a mean to discuss and communicate CoP issues. As admitted from one of the participants they "prefer personal interaction and communication out of any structured protocol". Torre Guaceto is a small

Figure 5. CoPe_it! Workspace for On-line Discussion in TG Community

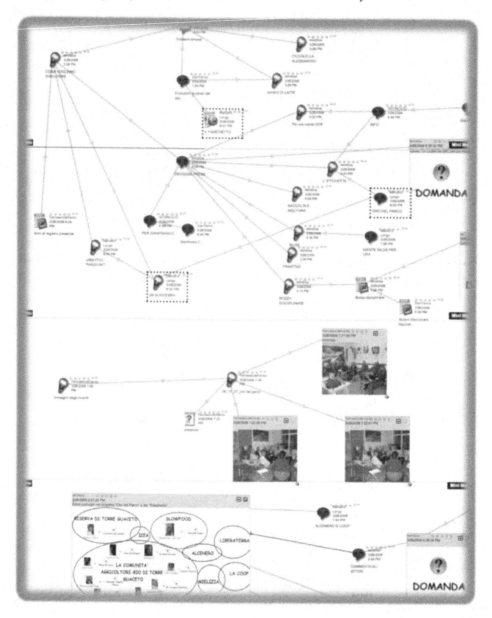

community of farmers which is used to work and discuss face-to-face. Moreover they are almost all from the same geographical area thereby they do not really need at-distance communication. These can be some of the reasons why the users claimed that they would "rather use the tool for sharing and exchanging data and information more than for discussing or taking decisions". One of the users suggested that a good way to enhance the on-line interaction performances can be involving the younger agriculturists, or the child of the farmers, in the testing and use of the tools. In any case all users agreed that virtual interaction could not be the only available communication way within the community. In fact as suggested from one of the farmer, "in the agricultural field a handshake and a eyes look are always the best way to communicate".

On the other hand evaluation results showed one big potential in using the tools as experiences repository, a hybrid environment where CoP members can collect and interchange documents of common interest, a place where they can share best practices and experiences. Instead of opening up the use of these technologies to the all CoP members, the farmers rather envisaged an asynchronous use of the tool which involves just the key actors, such as representative of the groups of interest and representatives of the local agencies.

However questionnaire results show that involved users appreciated the possibility to take trace and reconstruct the path of events, documents and claims raised within the group. They consider that this possibility, which is made available by the combined use of CoPe_it! and Compendium, help to understand the different positions expressed by the stakeholders and also the changing positions and the evolution of relationship inside the community. Users suggested using the tools to understand the results of the interaction process within the CoP and also between the group of farmer and the enlarged community.

CONCLUSION

In this chapter we showed the results of the project of integration between Compendium and CoPe_it! with the main aim in mind to enable a transparent and quasi-automatic integration of information and knowledge between hybrid collaborative environments (on-line and off-line). Results of the implementation show that the technical integration was successful, but some cultural boundaries make still difficult to exploit the use of these groupware technologies to their full potential. In fact, in the described case study we tested Compendium and CoPe_it with a community of farmers that, supported by a planning team, have engaged directly in the use of the tools. Results of the evaluation show that, despite some

interaction problems, the users recognized two main potential uses of the tools:

i.   Compendium and CoPe_it! as experiences repositories of the Community of Practice;
ii. Compendium and CoPe_it! as environments to monitor and reconstruct CoP members positions and interaction dynamics when performing collaborative works.

These advantages are made available by the integration project for interactions which happen both within virtual and traditional collaborative environments. The described integration allows to represent knowledge with a similar visual language and to make knowledge easily reusable in both collaborative environments.

Moreover the case study results show that the integration between Compendium and CoPe_it! supports environmental planning practices with effective tools to collect and manage knowledge about deliberation and then to communicate them to the community. The integration between Compendium and CoPe_it! shows how deliberation can be enlarged to a wider community on the web by coupling on-line and off-line consultation into a unique process of knowledge exchange and production. This unique process needs to handle and integrate knowledge coming from different collaborative environments (virtual and traditional), thus leveraging CoP to a truly collaborative environment with no communication boundaries. This is the environment in which HCoP perform. HCoP are an emerging kind of CoP where users are no longer constrained to a particular communication environment may it be virtual or real. HCoP is a novel approach to CoP providing users with diverse environments for collaboration in knowledge works. In this perspective, we have proposed the integration of Compendium and CoPe_it! as an example of an integration platform to perform virtual and traditional interactions in a unique hybrid collaboration environment.

REFERENCES

Brown, J. S., & Duguid, P. (2000). *The social life of information*. Boston: Harvard Business School Press.

Buckingham Shum, S. (2007). Hypermedia discourse: Contesting networks of ideas and arguments. In *Conceptual structures: Knowledge architectures for smart applications*, (LNAI 4604, pp. 29-44).

Conklin, J. (2005). *Dialogue mapping: Building shared understanding of wicked problems*. New York: John Wiley & Sons.

De Liddo, A., & Buckingham Shum, S. (2007). Capturing, mapping and integrating argumentation as project memory in participatory urban planning. In *Proceedings of the Workshop on Argumentation Support Systems for eParticipation, EU-IST DEMO-net Network of Excellence*, Berlin, Germany.

Karacapilidis, N., & Tzagarakis, M. (2007). Supporting incremental formalization in collaborative learning environments. In E. Duval, R. Klamma, & M. Wolpers (Eds.), *Proceedings of the 2nd European Conference on Technology Enhanced Learning (EC-TEL 2007)* (LNCS 4753, pp. 127-142). Berlin: Springer-Verlag.

Kimble, C., Hildreth, P., & Wright, P. (2001). Communities of practice: Going virtual. In Y. Malhotra (Ed.), *Knowledge management and business model innovation* (pp. 220-234). Hershey, PA: IGI Global.

Kimble, C., Li, F., & Barlow, A. (2000). *Effective virtual teams through communities of practice* (Paper No. 00/9). University of Strathclyde, Management Science Research.

Lave, J., & Wenger, E. (1991). *Situated learning. Legitimate peripheral participation*. UK: Cambridge University Press.

Ohl, R. (2007). *Compendium used to map Queensland public consultation*. Retrieved January 18, 2007 from http://news.kmi.open.ac.uk/rostra/news.php?r=55&t=2&id=26

Renton, A., & Macintosh, A. (2007). Computer supported argument maps as a policy memory. *The Information Society*, *23*(2), 125–133. doi:10.1080/01972240701209300

Selvin, A. M. & Sierhuis, M. (1999). Case studies of project compendium in different organizations. In *Proceedings of the Workshop on Computer-Supported Collaborative Argumentation for Learning Communities, CSCL '99*, Stanford, CA. Retrieved from http://d3e.open.ac.uk/cscl99/Selvin-CaseStudies/Selvin-CaseStudies-paper.html

Selvin, A. M., & Buckingham Shum, S. J. (2005). Hypermedia as a productivity tool for doctoral research. [Special Issue on Scholarly Hypermedia]. *New Review of Hypermedia and Multimedia*, *11*(1), 91–101. doi:10.1080/13614560500191303

Wenger, E. (1998). *Communities of practice: Learning, meaning and identity*. UK: Cambridge University Press.

Chapter 5
Using Graphs in Developing Educational Material

Thanasis Hadzilacos
Open University of Cyprus, Cyprus & Research Academic Computer Technology Institute, Greece

Dimitris Kalles
Hellenic Open University, Greece

Dionysis Karaiskakis
Hellenic Open University, Greece

Maria Pouliopoulou
Research Academic Computer Technology Institute, Greece

ABSTRACT

Distance learning institutions need to find a way to transplant the benefits of conventional tutoring practices into the development of digital content that is conducive to students' learning needs. Therein lie two great challenges: promote real distance learning effectively and, at the same time, try to accommodate the ability of students to learn via collaboration. The authors have proposed the development of learner's open-and-distance-learning (ODL) courses as both a theoretical model and an applied methodology to be one of their key priorities and describe how this concept co-evolves with Web mining and institutional infrastructures to address the needs of emergent communities of practice within their university, primarily of students and secondarily of tutors.

INTRODUCTION

Developing an educational experience for a learner has at least two cornerstones: the existence of educational material and the organization of activities with that material. For example, a textbook is a repository of educational material. Reading it chapter by chapter is an educational activity. Consulting selected book parts when trying to solve an exercise is a totally different activity.

Meaningful educational experiences are usually based on the organization of carefully designed activities on quality educational material. The shrewd organization and the careful design necessarily cover some aspects of resource planning, such as how much time the learner is supposed to dedicate to the activity or, what is the sequence of activities that will

DOI: 10.4018/978-1-60566-711-9.ch005

best attain the educational goal. They also cover conventional aspects of design, such as the target audience and, the combination of tools to attain the goal. Detailed planning of learning activities, apart from the significant effort needed by the course designer, reduces the control students have over their own learning (Evans & Lockwood, 1994). Learner support services (Simpson, 2000) were proposed to provide individualized advice, but usually at a significant cost, especially in large scale applications and in Open and Distance Learning (ODL). Also note that educational experiences can be turned into educational material themselves. For example, watching a fellow student carry out an experiment in chemistry certainly produces an educational experience.

Furthermore indirect collaboration (based on observation, for example) can also significantly enhance the learning experience. Social Navigation (Höök, Benyon & Munro, 2003) can be direct but also indirect based i.e. on the traces of others. Those are quite significant in ODL where learners are supposed to have control on planning and implementing their learning. Collaboration and what comes with it is also the core concept in Communities of Practice. However when we deal with dispersed communities of practice, such that are formed in distance learning, collaboration can only be supported by technological means.

In this contribution, we present a conceptual artefact, termed a **Learner's ODL course**, which, we claim, is a generic model that is suitable for accommodating the practices of the educational process, both solitary and collaborative, while still allowing room for developing new abstractions. Its real importance is in that it serves as a conceptual framework around which we attempt to integrate the technologies that are available to us, at any given time point.

We are careful to note that the educational process comprises of observable and explicitly initiated activities, as opposed to the learning process which is ad hoc and may or may not be a direct or indirect outcome of the educational process. After all, education does not necessarily result in measurable learning.

The rest of this paper is structured in five sections. We first briefly review the key stakeholders of the educational process in the context of Communities of Practice and Distance Learning. We then move to present a theoretical model of that process, outline its relation to learning design and argue why this model is a good springboard for the deployment of sophisticated data analysis applications (in the web mining context) that can spur the development of personalization services. We then discuss the practical issues of tool deployment and relate these issues to a large on-going application, before concluding by highlighting the context of an organization that is heavily investing in integrating its ICT infrastructures.

BACKGROUND: LONG DISTANCE EDUCATION AND COMMUNITIES OF PRACTICE

The educational system, at any level of specification, form or organization, cannot exist without teachers and students. Even in the case of delivery of courses through Learning Management Systems on the web, where students can have absolute control over the process, there has to be an instructor that will provide the educational material and will apply his teaching skills in creating it. Students can participate in groups, independently, from a distance or in a classroom. Any formation still includes both these necessary components.

All students have the same goal, to learn. A practical observation that we all have from personal experience is that although students work on their own when studying or solving exercises, they still interact with each other and exchange ideas and views on the process they follow or their approach in a given problem and their perception on the concepts that they are taught about. Such an interaction can affect their personal views and lead towards an attitude influenced and enhanced by their peers which is eventually what a community of practice is all about.

A Community of Practice (CoP) is "… a set of relations among persons, activity and world, over time and in relation with other tangential and overlapping CoPs" (Lave & Wenger, 1991).

This roughly refers to the situation that is formed between people in groups working for the same purpose, share common working practices, evolve them through interaction within their own members and other communities. A particular working culture is cultivated during the operation of the group and every newcomer is firstly introduced to the given situation, becomes a part of it and then offers his or her input that consequently adds on the existing methods and contributes to the aforementioned evolution.

An element that is basic for the definition of communities is the face-to-face interaction of their members. Due to the introduction of new technologies in an increasingly globalized workplace we can now speak about different forms of communities of practice, namely the distributed communities of practice and the virtual communities of practice that lack the characteristic of direct interaction. Although there have been many arguments about the validity of their differences (Lueg, 2000), we cannot ignore the practical observation that groups of people even in different parts of the world that are working on a project using the internet for their communication are forming their own communities of practice even though they may never interact in person and even if the formal definition of the CoP does not apply to them in an absolute manner. Daniel, Schwier & McCalla, (2003) are presenting in more detail the differences between the aforementioned groups and the characteristics that distinguish them from one another.

Long distance learners form a group that exhibits characteristics of both a distributed community and a virtual learning community. They have stable memberships, formalized and focused learning goals, high shared understanding (Daniel et al.,

2003). Although they cannot be placed with absolute certainty in one of the categories it is evident that they form a group with common interests and goals that each of its members can be significantly helped by the input of fellow students in regards to more practical views on the way they study, explore and solve problems. This last aspect is the *soft knowledge* (Kimble & Hildreth, 2005) that is a vital part of the knowledge that is gradually gained by the participation of an individual in a community of practice. 'It is the sort of knowledge that can not be easily articulated, although it can be understood even if it is not openly expressed.' (Kimble & Hildreth, 2005). On the contrary hard knowledge is the knowledge that can be easily structured and communicated.

In groups that work towards the same goal and frequent face-to-face interaction between participants is difficult to occur, it is also difficult for common practices to be observed and most importantly diffused. In order for long distance students to be able to experience that basic but informal part of the process of learning, which is their interaction and the sharing of common practices, they have to be provided with tools for their communication or better yet, a way to capture soft knowledge (Shipman & Marshall, 1999).

In long distance learning the educational material obtains a more significant role since it is the main resource for the learner's practice. A simple book cannot cover all the needs that a long distance learner has, because it is used as a component in the traditional delivery of education where students can attend lectures and form a structure of their study through the oral presentation of a subject and the clarifications that can be given in real time. Long distance learning educational material has to be structured in a way that can simulate, at least to some extent that experience and incorporate additional resources or written observations and guidelines. In a way it must present a more complete view of the educational process, even parts of it that are not easily or explicitly modeled in the traditional process.

And here is where new technologies come in the picture. The tools they offer are necessary for their communication, for the delivery of courses, for finding educational material. The ODL course we propose here can combine hard and soft knowledge in one piece and it is an alternative form of educational material based on new technologies that is ideal for use for long distance learners. The course itself offers concrete information, whilst the future plan is that in the background artificial intelligence techniques will capture the navigational patterns of users through the material, incorporating additional information such as the time they spent in each unit, repeated visits, non-visited material, in general a student's behavior of study in a course that offers more than just the directly related material. In a sense it is an effort to capture the practice of the community by identifying the learning patterns and not only the navigational evidence, just a plain sequence of visits. Although the users do not necessarily and consciously interact to exchange experiences and benefit by the direct observation of others, the instructor might discover (Karacapilidis & Tzagarakis, 2007) interesting nuggets of behavioral similarities by using the results returned by the AI techniques employed in the course. Such results can refer to how the students proceed through it and even yet how their online communication or other parameters may affect their patterns through time. Furthermore the patterns can reveal weaknesses and strengths of the original structure as well as the context that can assist to the improvement of the original design. The learners, without even realizing it, are offering valuable information about the way they are exploiting the material in the course and the instructor can use it in order for them to view an improved version of the course, based on their own unconscious usage of it.

From that viewpoint, it is not difficult to expect that every tutor group that collaborates on a subject will be able to elect one person from that group to attempt to post-process the tutors' collaboration results in order to extract useful abstracts that will allow the whole group to efficiently summarize their collaboration fruits. An infrastructure that allows the gathering and processing of navigational information is a rich source of input for any educational intelligence project; however, it is always up to a human entity to be eventually responsible for structuring the knowledge that resides in collaboration workspaces.

A LEARNER'S ODL COURSE AS A MODEL FOR THE EDUCATIONAL PROCESS

A graph-theoretic model of a Learner's ODL course is a computational model. It builds on top of some basic components which are elaborated below and it involves, at several points, activities of the stakeholders as described above.

A *learning object* is any piece of (multimedia) data or program whose purpose (intention) is to be used for learning. A learning object can be recursively defined as a set of learning objects. Examples of *learning objects* are the following: the text of Odyssey, MS Word, Sketchpad, a video lecture, a set of multiple choice questions, a Euclidean geometry high school textbook, an MS PowerPoint presentation of organic compounds.

A *learning task* is a task whose purpose is learning. Examples of learning tasks are the following: read, solve an exercise, write a program, practice a musical instrument, draw a picture, design a database, make a summary, think over, correct, argue for/against.

A *learning activity* is an ordered pair: (learning object, learning task). Examples of learning activities are the following:

- Write a program to add two numbers (learning task) using a C++ compiler (learning object)
- Write down (type to the computer) what you hear (the learning object is a digitized dictation) and then check the spelling errors

(in fact the learning object is the set {word processor, soundtrack, speller}).

A *learning environment* is a directed labeled multigraph (*LA, P*), where *LA* is a set (of vertices or, nodes) of learning activities and *P* is a bag (of edges) of labeled precedents. A multigraph is a "graph whose edges are unordered pairs of vertices, and the same pair of vertices can be connected by multiple edges" (Dictionary of Algorithms and Data Structures, National Institute of Standards and Technology (NIST), http://www.nist.gov/dads/). Examples of labeled edges are the following:

- From node LA5 to node LA15 "if you found LA5 very easy to do"
- From node LA5 to node LA100 "if you found LA5 very interesting"
- From node LA5 to node LA3 "if you did not manage to complete the task of LA5 satisfactorily"

A *reference node* is (a learning activity that is) connected to all other nodes via bidirectional (unlabeled) edges. Examples of *reference nodes* are the following:

- Dictionary (to look up a word or phrase)
- Calculator (to perform an arithmetic operation)
- On-line discussion (to communicate with a tutor or with fellow learners)

A *learning experience* (or, a *learning trip*) is a path (sequence of connected learning activities) on the learning environment graph.

A *learner's note* is a data structure attached to a specific node by a specific learner. A *learner's note* includes structured data fields (learner/user id, timestamp, access rights, etc.) and any (multimedia) data the learner chooses to attach (for example, files). Examples of *learner's notes* are the following:

- The list of adjectives asked for in example B1.
- A text that criticizes the effectiveness of the learning activity (node).
- A new soundtrack of the dictation (left by a student who found the pronunciation incomprehensible).
- A comparison or a synopsis of the past 10 notes left on the current learning activity (node).

A *learning environment communication system* is a communication system (such as email, discussion forum, etc.) with content consisting only of (pointers to) learner's notes. Examples of such content are the following:

- From a student to his teacher "Here is the list of adjectives asked for in LA5".
- From a student to all other students "I found LA12 particularly useful, you can look up my comments in the note attached".
- From a teacher to his students "Before attempting task LA112 read my note there".

A *learning activity control block* is a snapshot of the usage of all the above in the context of a particular learner. It is a data structure containing (at least) the following fields:

- learner/user id
- timestamp
- (pointer to) learning object
- (pointer to) learning task
- (pointer to) learner's note

A learning experience may well be a single-session path; for example, a learner dedicates a good solid hour to navigating the educational material along a particular line. A learning experience may also be a sequence of such paths; for example, we usually "remember" where we stopped studying (for a short or long break), and can resume from that point. A (metaphorically speaking) concatenation of such paths delivers a longer path that can still be a learning experience.

The graph-theoretic model also allows us to build in temporal information in the navigation paths. As a matter of fact, relative temporal information is inherently available in a path (sequence of node visits). Furthermore, the annotation of edges in terms of actual time spent in an activity before moving on to the next is a straightforward enhancement.

The detour ends here by noting that the above considerations simply suggest that, after we get the initial graph-theoretic model fixed, there exist a set of computational processes that will allow us to define arbitrarily complex layers of information based on the ground data. We elaborate on that in a following section.

DISCUSSION ON LEARNING DESIGN

The main purpose of the above schema is not to propose a new learning design and is certainly not intending to form a new specification. We are using the idea of a graph as the foundation of a learning environment and therefore we need to identify the modules that can be the nodes of the graph, given that a student will need certain resources and use certain material. We simply define the modularity of the material and the resources in accordance to the activities a learner will perform, so that we can clarify what the nodes in the graph will be.

There are no expected outcomes and objectives that necessarily have to be met and that will define the future progress of the course. Every activity is intended to offer specific gains to the student, but they are not explicitly measurable and the student is free to navigate and choose his own course of studies. That is exactly what we want to examine, how the user forms his path and not whether he can be successful or not in a predefined one where the structure determines the path. We are more concerned in pinning down the modules that a learner might need for a complete educational ex-

perience and we want to observe his walk through that graph. His path will reveal the usage of the resources and whether the proposed granularity, structure and assembly of different resources is used to its full extent and is assistive or whether the users' patterns reveal a different structure and a behavior that was not foreseen.

On a first look there is a similarity to the IMS learning design model and in specific to its conceptual model. In the IMS design information model (IMS Global Learning Consortium, 2003) website, the specification includes learning activities, a learning environment, learning objects but they are explicitly defined for a specific model. For example the environment in IMS is defined as "… a structured collection of learning objects, services, and sub-environments. The relationship between an activity and an environment can be derived from the linguistic description of the activities. …", whereas we consider it to be an underlying graph connecting learning activities. We can see a resemblance in the definition of learning activities and learning objects, however we use a more plain definition since we are not trying to capture a wide variety of pedagogical concepts. Our main focus is to the process followed by users and not the design we offer to them.

TOOL DEPLOYMENT ISSUES

We start by noting that the theoretical model can be in principle implemented using rudimentary technology, such as hyper-linked files of conventional office-type applications, where educational assets can be grouped together in repository-type worksheets. Assets can then be drawn to compile learning activities. Such tools offer relatively smooth short learning curves for data collection and web publishing too.

As an example, Figure 1 shows how MS Excel could be used to design a learning environment. A learning activity is composed by an asset and by a learning task (allowing, of course, for some

Figure 1: A snapshot of a learning environment in MS Excel

The divide-and-conquer approach ...	
Learning Task	**Learning Object**
read	2.3.1 The divide-and-conquer approach
	... the first two paragraphs
write	Think how you would apply the above principle to ....
read	2.3.1 The divide-and-conquer approach
	... the next paragraph
write	You might want to rethink your previous answer
	Think about the following details
exerc	How do you split in two a sequence that has an odd number of elements?
exerc	How do you decide that a sub-problem is "small enough"?
exerc	Is there an oprimal number of sequences?
read	2.1 Insertion sort
read	2.2 Analyzing algorithms
observe	Presentation by MIT OCW Algorithms Lecture 01
read	2.3.1 The divide-and-conquer approach
	... the next three paragraphs
programming	Write a program for mergesort (do not test it)
exerc	What kind of input do you think you need for testing?
WWW	See an applet that demonstrates the mergesort algorithm
WWW	See a collection of sorting algorithms
exerc	Can you argue which of the above algorithms are divide-n-conquer?

terseness in representation: when no task is shown for a text asset, the implicit task is "read"). Indentation can be used to designate priorities and preferences; this allows transitions between activities to be tagged (potentially) by attributes such as "was it interesting?".

After one settles on the issue of the implementation of the basic model, the issue of linkage with external resources must be addressed. Discussion rooms, and other related communication-oriented applications can be readily used to support the implementation of learner's notes and of a learning environment communication system. At that point, one can opt to start integrating different technology offerings (having, of course, to address the overhead of inter-application communication) or adopting a generic platform approach that will allow for customization to retro-fit the implementation of the model as well (Hampel & Keil-Slawik, 2001; Trindade, Carmo, & Bidarra, 2000). The latter approach can be more scalable (for example, portal offerings by commercial organizations) but the analysis to decide on such an investment may be too difficult to carry out effectively (hidden costs can surface quite easily and the steepness of the learning curve for developers

may be expensive to estimate) (Henry, 2004; Mc Lean, 2004; Smith, Rodgers, Walker, & Tansley, 2004). Note that a need for development may be inevitable with any platform if one attempts to implement some relatively sophisticated objects (for example, the learning activity control block of the graph theoretic model earlier presented), even at the entry level.

However, there also exist some in-between approaches; in these approaches one may decide to use building blocks based on generic digital object identification schemes, such as DOI (http://www.doi.org) and expect that third-party providers (for example, a university) will supply the naming space, and couple these identification schemes with generic object ensemble builders, such as Fedora (Lagoze, Payette, Shin & Wilper, 2006) or SCORM (ADL Technical Team, 2004), which accommodate a disciplined format of digital object creation and manipulation.

As a matter of fact this is exactly the development roadmap for LAMS (Learning Activity Management System, 2007), which expects that activities will be structured around a *lesson* plan and that the support tools to implement these activities will be increasingly supplied by third

Figure 2. A snapshot of an activity workflow in LAMS

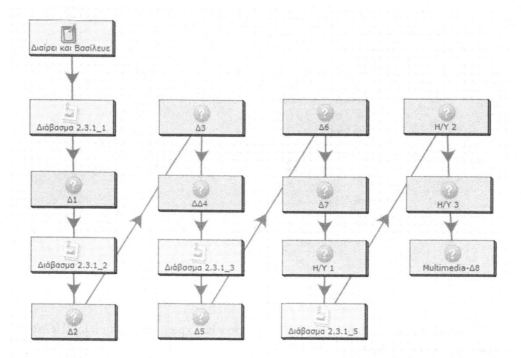

parties. Incidentally perhaps, LAMS also seems to be the closest implementation of our graph formalism concept and one that explicitly foresees the linkage of collaboration activities within the educational process; moreover it indeed structures activities as tasks to be done with some resources. See Figure 2 for an example, of how LAMS implements the workflow described in Figure 1 (but also note that, since LAMS does not yet fully support branching, the only graph node transitions available are the ones from one node to the next; i.e. a strictly sequential experience).

WEB MINING WITH A LEARNER'S ODL COURSE

Cliques and connected components are usually employed as a means of demonstrating graph properties that are related to localization; here, we use *localization* as a metaphor to show that

some *areas* of a graph may be very close neighbors in the sense that one has to venture explicitly outside this area through very specific paths. This is not a new concept and has been used in a very similar context in web site adaptation (Pierrakos, Paliouras, Papatheodorou, & Spyropoulos, 2003) Automatically improving the organization and presentation of web sites based on data mining usage logs is a burgeoning scientific field and one of the approaches is based on the PageGather algorithm (Perkowitz & Etzioni 2000). Therein, a clustering method, called *cluster mining*, is employed, which works on an input of user sessions, represented as sets of visited web pages (note the correspondence with learning experiences). PageGather then builds a graph by linking nodes (pages) with an edge whenever co-occurrence of these pages is detected across some user sessions. Page clusters (or, similar learning experiences) can then be defined using either cliques or connected components, with cliques considered to be more coherent and connected components considered to be faster to compute and easier to find.

There exist legitimate arguments about the computational cost of graph-based algorithms for inferring usage patterns (Pierrakos et al., 2003). However, if we can agree that our *a posteriori* analysis of the usage (by various users) of a Learner's ODL course will be used to improve its presentation and organization in a future version (thus, we do not focus on providing immediately customizable content), then these arguments are not related to our employing of the graph-based representation. Nevertheless, web usage mining is a complicated, of course, as it involves data pre-processing, pattern discovery and pattern analysis (Srivastava, Cooley, Deshpande, & Tan, 2000). Data used for these procedures can be related to *content* (the real data in the Web Pages), *structure* (data describing the organization of the content), *usage* (data describing the pattern of usage in web pages) and *user profile* (data providing demographic information) (Srivastava et al., 2000). Industrial reports (also based on anecdotal data) suggest that the data pre-processing can easily take up 80% to 95% of a project's time and resources (Edelstein, 2001).

The technical challenge is how to relate the relatively flat structure of web log files with the apparently deep structure of learning experiences (therein, we note again the introduction of cycles in experience paths). Our approach is to specify the course multi-graph in advance (*php* scripts interfacing to a *mySql* database were embedded in the course's *html* code). This approach is supported by the published experience in a similar project (Marquardt, Becker, & Ruiz, 2004), where the difficulties of developing a data pre-processing environment are set out for a case study in a distance learning educational domain.

A coarse example of these concepts is shown below. Figure 3 demonstrates the course multi-graph structure, as specified by the course designer (actually, it is a view of the multi-graph where, for the sake of conciseness, we have only included

learning activities). Figure 4 shows a learner's path during a single learning session in the course, with nodes being numbered according to the relative order of visit.

We also used a slight variant of the above mechanism to implement the note-passing mechanism between students and tutors (as described in Section 3). However, for this particular aspect of the Learner's ODL course, we are investigating the usefulness of open-source asynchronous discussion forum systems (and the extent to which they might accommodate the multi-graph specification as opposed to programming it from scratch).

The generalization of the above implementation to compute shared paths between collaborative (or non-) co-workers (students, tutors) is relatively easy. However, the visualization of those shared paths necessarily raises the issue of how to accommodate in the relatively limited estate of a computer screen the individual interactions of team members with the same material. While web usage mining applications are close to this problem, understanding which shared paths are meaningful and which are not will initially entail the close scrutiny by knowledgeable experts.

CONCLUSION

Like many other open universities, the Hellenic Open University (HOU) has gradually embarked on e-learning initiatives, spanning from virtual classrooms, to discussion forums and to the mass-scale development of complementary on-line material.

The HOU has lately completed a major transition to a common commercial portal platform and has initiated the installation and operation of an open-source digital asset management system as well as a commercial SCORM-compliant authoring tool. Deploying the newly-developed courses on that platform will allow for the production and sophisticated analysis of log files, according to the principles (and, mostly, to the ideas) outlined above. We are also experimenting with

Figure 3. A view of the course multi-graph

Figure 4. A visitor's path through the course

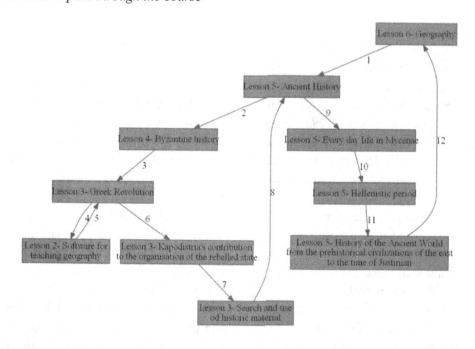

the possibility of developing path detection as a web-service to be provided by a third party at the course deployment level as opposed to on-line log file analysis.

The graph model was a necessary tool in our design approach because it helped model important aspects of the educational process and, then, seamlessly supported the semantic annotation of student activities while allowing us the convenience of knowing that graph-processing algorithms and software are available as a commodity.

Why did we *not* use a different model? Actually we did. The MS Excel example was our first implementation attempt at attracting fellow tutors to the didactical merits of explicitly stating learning tasks and expected time for related activities. Note that these very tutors may well be excellent when addressing an audience; it is their skills at developing distance learning material that we aim to further develop. So, the tabular Excel model was the easiest to communicate.

Thus, taking into account that we need to also address the needs of tutors with limited IT skills, the careful selection of tools for the initial compilation and development of learning activities is a key factor in our decisions. It turns out that we must really first lower the entry threshold for tutors in order to be able to realize benefits for the students. That threshold, in turn, has to do with both the development of content as well as the development of a collaborative conscience. The latter is necessary to reinforce the sense of belonging to an academic environment that our students (and, sometimes, our tutors) seem to desperately need and that our tutors may sometimes find difficult to re-invest in, since most of them are already part of a conventional environment.

In that sense, we believe that our key contribution is the bridging of design richness and implementation practicalities in the context of a very large scale project of distance learning digital educational material. We feel that similar situations will be common in the context of almost all organizations developing similar content.

ACKNOWLEDGMENT

Dionyssis Zafeiropoulos, Panagiota Mpekou and Spyros Papadakis have been instrumental in the set-up and functioning of the LAMS platform at our site. Ernie Ghiglione (of LAMS) provided several technical and development insights that have reinforced our commitment to the graph formalism for representing the activities of the educational process. The paper is an extended version of a paper that appeared in the Proceedings of the Workshop on Technology Enhanced Learning – Communities of Practice (Chania, Greece, September 2007). The paper also shares content with other works by some of the authors; however, the Communities of Practice view is unique to this paper.

REFERENCES

ADL Technical Team. (2004). *Sharable content object reference model (SCORM) 2004* (2nd ed.). Alexandria, VA: Advanced Distributed Learning.

Daniel, B., Schwier, R. A., & McCalla, G. (2003). Social Capital in virtual learning communities and distributed communities of practice. *Canadian Journal of Learning and Technology, 29*(3).

Edelstein, H. A. (2001, March 12). Pinning for gold in the Clickstream. *Information Week.*

Evans, T., & Lockwood, F. (1994). *Understanding learners in open and distance education.* London: Koggan Page Ltd.

Hampel, T., & Keil-Slawik, R. (2001, Summer). sTeam: Structuring information in team–distributed knowledge management in cooperative learning environments. *Journal of Educational Resources in Computing, 1*(2), 1–27. doi:10.1145/384055.384058

Henry, G. (2004, September). Connexions: An alternative approach to publishing. In *Proceedings of the European Conference on Digital Libraries*, Bath, UK.

Höök, K., Benyon, D., & Munro, A. (2003). *Designing information spaces: The social navigation approach*. London: Springer.

IMS Global Learning Consortium. (2003). *IMS learning design information model, revision: 20 January 2003*.

Karacapilidis, N., & Tzagarakis, M. (2007). supporting incremental formalization in collaborative learning environments. In *Proceedings of the EC-TEL 2007*, Crete, Greece (LNCS 4753, pp. 127-142).

Kimble, C., & Hildreth, P. (2005). *Communities of practice: Going one step too far?* EconWPA, Industrial Organization 0504008.

Lagoze, C., Payette, S., Shin, E., & Wilper, C. (2006). Fedora: An architecture for complex objects and their relationships. [special issue on Complex Objects]. *Journal of Digital Libraries*, 6(2), 124–138. doi:10.1007/s00799-005-0130-3

Lave, J., & Wenger, E. (1991). *Situated learning. Legitimate peripheral participation,* Cambridge: Cambridge University Press.

Learning Activity Management System. (2007). *Learning activity management system*.

Lueg, C. (2000, September). Where is the action in virtual communities of practice? In *Proceedings of the German Computer-Supported Cooperative Work Conference (D-CSCW), Workshop on Communication and Cooperation in Knowledge Communities*, Munich, Germany.

Marquardt, C. G., Becker, K., & Ruiz, D. D. (2004). A pre-processing tool for Web usage mining in the distance education domain. In *Proceedings of the International Database Engineering and Applications Symposium*.

Mc Lean, N. (2004, September). The ecology of repository services: A cosmic view. In *Proceedings of the European Conference on Digital Libraries*, Bath, UK.

Perkowitz, M., & Etzioni, O. (2000). Adaptive Web sites . *Communications of the ACM, 43*(8). doi:10.1145/345124.345171

Pierrakos, D., Paliouras, G., Papatheodorou, C., & Spyropoulos, C. D. (2003). Web usage mining as a tool for personalization: A survey. *User Modeling and User-Adapted Interaction, 14*(4).

Shipman, F. M. III, & Marshall, C. C. (1999). Formality considered harmful: Experiences, emerging themes, and directions on the use of formal representations in interactive systems. *Computer Supported Cooperative Work, 8*(4), 333–352. doi:10.1023/A:1008716330212

Simpson, O. (2000). *Supporting students in online open and distance education*. London: Koggan Page Ltd.

Smith, M., Rodgers, R., Walker, J., & Tansley, R. (2004, September). DSpace: A year in the life of an open source digital repository. In *Proceedings of the European Conference on Digital Libraries*, Bath, UK.

Srivastava, J., Cooley, R., Deshpande, M., & Tan, P.-N. (2000). Web usage mining: Discovery and applications of usage patterns from Web data. *SIGKDD Explorations, 1*(2).

Trindade, A. R., Carmo, H., & Bidarra, J. (2000). Current developments and best practice in open and distance learning. *International Review of Research in Open and Distance Learning, 1*(1).

Chapter 6
Using Storytelling as the Pedagogical Model for Web–Based Learning in Communities of Practice

Nalin Sharda
Victoria University, Australia

ABSTRACT

The purpose of this chapter is to show how storytelling can be used as an effective pedagogical model for enhancing learning in a community of practice (CoP) using Web-based tools. CoPs provide opportunities for learning by sharing knowledge and experience. Storytelling can make the knowledge and experience sharing discourses more engaging. However, crafting engaging stories remains a challenge. Movement oriented design (MOD) paradigm provides a framework for creating effective story plots using principles of good storytelling. Web-based tools are being used for enhancing interaction in CoPs, and now more responsive systems can be created by using Web 2.0 frameworks such as AJAX. Storytelling can be introduced as a mode of discourse in CoPs using existing text and multimedia authoring systems. However, by creating new Web 2.0 tools for story development using the MOD paradigm will allow almost anyone to create engaging educational stories and use these in a CoP.

INTRODUCTION

Storytelling is a powerful means for communicating experiences, ideas and knowledge; and it has been used since time immemorial. In most traditional societies people sat around a campfire and told stories. Knowledge has been communicated from one generation to the next through stories even before written scripts were invented. With

DOI: 10.4018/978-1-60566-711-9.ch006

modern technologies we can make storytelling a very powerful pedagogical tool; however, creating effective educational stories remains a challenge. This chapter addresses some of these challenges and shows the pathway to fulfill the potential of storytelling as a pedagogical model for web-based Communities of Practice (CoP).

The concept of CoP offers a new perspective on learning. Anthropologist Jean Lave and educationist Etienne Wenger coined this term while studying apprenticeship as a learning model. Wegner (2008) defines a CoP as follows: "Communities of practice are groups of people who share a concern or a passion for something they do and learn how to do it better as they interact regularly".

However, a CoP is not formed by people meeting just for a common interest, e.g. playing golf every Saturday. "Members of a community of practice are practitioners. They develop a shared repertoire of resources: experiences, stories, tools, ways of addressing recurring problems—in short a shared practice" (Wenger, 2008). And, storytelling can be used as the vehicle for sharing experiences in a CoP; however, we need to develop better web-based tools to make storytelling easier and more effective for CoPs.

Early web-based CoPs used static web pages and emails for communicating with each other. More recently, Web2.0 has provided new generation tools for collaborating and creating CoPs. Some of these new generation web tools are based on Blogs (web-logs) and RSS (Really Simple Syndication) systems (Wenger, White, Smith, & Rowe, 2005). To some extent Blogs embody some elements of storytelling, but not all Blogs tell stories well.

Some people are naturally good storytellers, while others are not. Thus, there is a need to provide models and tools that help in creating engaging stories. Movement Oriented Design (MOD) provides a methodology for creating educational stories that are emotionally engaging (Sharda, 2006). This emotional engagement makes the message of the story easier to learn and remember. And we can develop Web 2.0 tools that facilitate the creation of effective stories.

Articulating how to create effective educational stories for web-based communities of practice is the overall aim of this chapter, and its specific objectives include:

- To understand how storytelling can improve learning.
- To explore the role of storytelling in the CoP context.

- To explain what is Movement Oriented Design (MOD), and how it can be used to create effective educational stories.
- To investigate Web 2.0 platforms for creating tools for storytelling using MOD.
- To explore how to introduce storytelling as mode of interaction in a CoP.

STORYTELLING AS A PEDAGOGICAL MODEL

We need to create a new pedagogical model based on storytelling, because the traditional classroom-based teaching is unable to meet the demands of the modern world of ongoing learning in the workplace and community.

Egan (2004) confirms the efficacy of storytelling as an alternative approach to learning. He states that the teaching that relies on serial development of objectives, content, teaching methods and evaluation techniques leads to mechanistic education and lacks the essential ingredients required for deep learning. Egan focuses on children; however, as per Berne (1996) every adult has a child within, and winning the heart of this child is the most effective way to win the adult. Thus, storytelling can be used as an effective pedagogical model for children and adults alike.

Importance of Storytelling

Knowledge has been passed on from one generation to the next through storytelling for many millennia, because storytelling has a close connection with how the human brain works. As per anthropologist Levi-Strauss (1995) our brain uses a story oriented structure to absorb the events taking place in the life around us. Snippets of our life experiences are retained in the long-term memory as narratives.

Furthermore, even facts, ideas, theories are learnt more effectively if these are linked as a narrative (Heo, 2004). Another advantage of the narrative form is that we can reconstruct our experiences as new narratives in new contexts, and derive new meanings from them.

Storytelling is such a powerful means of communication because it can fulfill a basic need of all human beings, i.e. to have their emotions engaged and moved. As a corollary, only stories that can engage and move human emotions can succeed (Sharda, 2005).

Need for a New Pedagogy

A new pedagogy is required because the traditional pedagogy has proven to be ineffective at many levels. We are social beings and have learnt a lot from social interactions; however, the lecture oriented pedagogy does not recognize this fully. Wenger (1991) poses the rhetorical question:

Why is it then that we always think of learning in individualistic terms of acquisition of information? We associate it with lecturing teachers, with orderly classrooms, with didactic training sessions, or with lonely evenings of homework. We think of individual capabilities judged in standardized terms of intelligence. And we think of books, assuming that information exists on paper or in words, there to be acquired by individual minds?

We need to move away from such purely classroom and lecture oriented pedagogy and device a new pedagogical model. This new pedagogy has to provide the opportunity to all for learning on-demand, i.e. free from stringent time and location constraints. Some of the challenges that predicate the need for this new pedagogy included the following.

Most industries need to tackle increased competition in the modern globalised economy. Moreover, today technological advances take place at an unprecedented rate, and this demands ongoing retraining of staff and management. Developing, organizing and running formal courses is very expensive. If the employees have to be sent away to a training centre at another location, the cost of

transportation and accommodation, and the loss incurred due to their absence adds to excessive cost for retraining.

Increased competition in the industry also requires that employees become more creative and innovative. In today's business world, a company can gain competitive advantage over its rivals mainly by creating new innovative products, and by marketing these with innovative campaigns. Creativity and innovation require the ability to make connections between different domains of knowledge and experience (Stevens, 2007). And often, as we hear someone else's experience, we connect it with our problems and get new insights for solving the problem in some innovative manner.

These days no one has a job for life with one company, or in just one area of expertise. This demands that we all become lifelong learners. How should this lifelong learning take place, and be available when we want it and where we can afford to access it? How can we learn about the latest technology when the traditional teachers have not yet had the opportunity to learn it themselves, let alone create good course to teach the same?

Such questions have led to the development of communities of practice, i.e. groups formed to share knowledge and practical experiences in a specific domain of business or personal life.

Communities of Practice (CoP)

Even though the term Communities of Practice is a recent coinage, the idea is as old as humanity. In fact, it predates the development of formal models of learning. Even in the modern world people have been using informal communities of practice for sharing problems and devising solutions: around the cooler, in the dining hall, and over a cup of coffee.

Nickolas (2003) defines two types of CoPs: Self-Organizing and Sponsored. Self-organizing CoPs are started by a group of members interested in learning from each other in a specific domain. Knowledge transmission takes place when members share stories about their personal experiences.

Sponsored CoPs are mandated and supported by a preexisting organization, such as a private company, a government department, or a university. In this case the domain of interest is often predefined by the sponsoring body, and the prospective members themselves choose to join. Often some resources are provided by the sponsoring body, while the members organize other resources as and when required. As per Nickolas (2003), a sponsored CoP has three main objectives:

1. To enable colleagues to learn from one another through the sharing of issues, ideas, lessons learned, problems and their solutions, research findings and other relevant aspects of their mutual interest;
2. To more broadly share and better leverage the learning that occurs in the CoP with others;
3. To generate tangible, measurable, value-added benefits to the business.

One of the main benefits of forming a CoP is that its objectives are congruent with those of the new pedagogy required for on-demand and life-long learning. This new pedagogy is based not on prepared lectures but on sharing experiences; and there is no better way to share experiences than storytelling. However, the story must engage the audience's emotions to be memorable, and thus, effective in imparting memorable understanding.

For the story to be engaging and effective it must be told well by combining aspects of storytelling that make a story engrossing, while conveying the educational message embodied in the experience being related.

Aristotle gave the principles of good storytelling in his treatise called Poetics, around 2300 years ago (Aristotle, 1996). McKee (1998) has added

storytelling principles that are more modern in their approach and connotation, and can be applied to creating engaging educational stories as well (Sharda, 2006).

Some of the challenges faced by most people when creating a story for describing their experience are: not knowing where to start, how to proceed, how to end, what to include, and what to leave out of the story. Movement Oriented Design (MOD) is a framework for creating effective stories using principles of good storytelling to create an engaging narrative.

MOVEMENT ORIENTED DESIGN (MOD)

Movement Oriented Design (MOD) provides a methodology for crafting the plot and the narrative of a story starting with just the story concept. The terms story, plot and narrative refer to similar concepts, with some subtle differences in connotation. Succinct definitions of these terms are given in the following (Bateman, 2008):

- **Event** is a happening that takes place in a story. However, by itself a single event is not a story.
- **Story** is a collection of events, which together create a meaningful discourse.
- **Plot** is the way in which the events of a story are connected, to create the intended meaning. A given story has a main plot, and can have one or more sub-plots.
- **Narrative** is the sequence in which the events are revealed to the audience. A given story with a given plot and some sub-plots can be told with different narratives. Each narrative is likely to have a different emotional impact on the audience.

The focus of storytelling in a CoP context is to narrate personal experiences or events, such that the narration of the story keeps the audience

Figure 1. a) A Complete Story; b) A Story Unit; c) A Movements

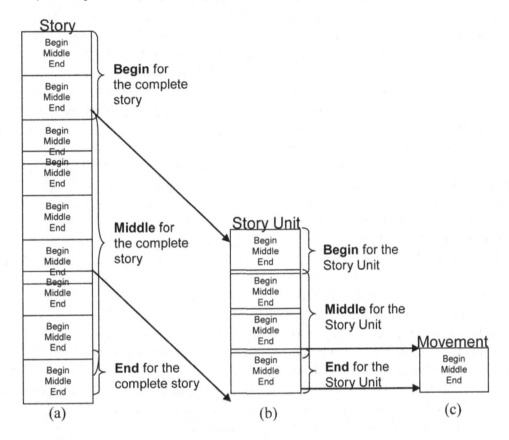

engrossed and, at the same time conveys the educational message that can be derived from these experiences.

Imparting knowledge as a series of facts and theories is generally boring, and can lead to loss of attention by the audience, as often happens in a classroom lecture. The MOD methodology is underpinned by the idea that any learning construct –lecture, presentation, seminar, or tutorial–can be viewed as a storytelling artifact (Sharda, 2006) and presented with a more impactful narrative.

MOD is based on the concept that every story must have a beginning, middle and an end, as predicated by Aristotle (1996). Furthermore, it uses the idea that stories are problem solving narratives, a concept introduced by the Dramatica theory of story design (Phillips & Huntley, 2001). As per this view, in any story the protagonist has

a problem to solve, and the events in the story are his/her attempts to solve this problem.

The core element of the MOD paradigm is a Movement; which can be defined as a micro story with its own Begin (a mnemonic for beginning), Middle and End components (Sharda, 2005), as shown in figure 1. A complete story is then a collection of Story Units, where each Story Unit is a sequence of Movements (Sharda, 2007).

Thus, the term Story refers to a complete story, the term Story Unit refers to a part story, and Movement refers to the smallest part of a story. The complete Story, as well as a Movement, is also a Story Units, in general. Each Story Unit must have clearly identifiable Begin, Middle and End components.

The purpose of dividing any story into three components –Begin, Middle and End– is to recognize clearly how to begin a story, what to present in the middle and how to end it, so as to create an effective narrative.

The purpose of a good Begin is to grab the listeners' attention, such that they want to find out more. Then the Middle can be used to deliver the message or knowledge, and the End should conclude the Story Unit and link it to the next, unless it is the very last one. When creating an educational story, if the author starts straightaway by relating facts and figures, the learners' interest often wanes. Therefore, getting the listeners emotionally engaged is of paramount importance, and a good Begin should do just that.

To produce a story that keeps the listeners engaged throughout the discourse, it must link the Story Units into an effectively plot and present the plot as an engaging narrative. Often the Middle occupies a major proportion of any Story Unit. To keep the audience engaged even through the middle of the story, the events presented in it should be linked in a cause and effect manner.

For MOD, it implies that as a Movement answers some questions raised in a previous Movement, it should raise some more questions, which are answered in the following Movement(s).

Therefore, developing a good narrative using MOD becomes a recursive process, where the entire story has its Begin (B), Middle (M) and End (E) components; and then each of these can be broken into their B, M, E components, till we find Movements, i.e. micro-stories that have B, M, and E components that are small enough to be implemented directly.

MOD Example

An example of the application of the MOD methodology is given here to clarify how an educational idea can be developed into a narrative. The objective of this example is to show how the process of selecting B, M, E components, and then expanding these into their own B, M, E components can be carried out systematically.

The MOD-based story development process is shown here up to three stages. In some story development projects this process may have to go deeper. The B, M, E components need to be expanded until Movements are discovered. The decision if there is the need to expand the B, M, E components any further, or otherwise, is a creative choice made by the author. In general, the author will stop further expansion when she can see (in the eye of her mind) how to instantiate each B, M, and E component of a Movement.

The purpose of this educational story being developed in this example is to explain the important aspects of electric current to high school students; this example is taken almost verbatim from the seminal MOD paper by Sharda (2005).

We begin by articulating the concept of electric current as a problem that needs to be solved. Next, we state the solution as a generic statement, and then expand it into its first level Begin (B1), Middle (M1), and End (E1) components. At this stage we express these (B, M, E) components only as statements, i.e. ideas about how these may be instantiated.

STAGE-1

Problem: What is Electric Current?**Solution:** Explain the meaning of electric current

B1 Demonstrate the importance of electric current

M1 Define and exemplify electric current

E1 What determines electric current strength?

In Stage-2 of the story development process, each of the Stage-1 story components (B1, M1 and E1) are expanded into their own B, M, E components. In Stage-2 story, the label B1,B2 stands for the Begin of the story unit B1, and the label M1,E2 stands for the End of the story unit M1.

STAGE-2

B1 Problem: Why is electric current important?**B1 Solution:** Explain the importance of electric current.

B1,B2 Many people die of electric shock.

B1,M2 Understand and respect electric current, not be afraid of it.

B1,E2 Electric current is useful for running appliances.**M1 Problem:** How is electric current defined?**M1 Solution:** Define and exemplify electric current.

M1,B2 Amperes = Coulombs / second.

M1,M2 It's like watching Coulombs as water in a river, and count how many go past in one second.

M1,E2 Demonstrate the effect of electric current through multimedia and multi-sensory experience.**E1 Problem:** What determines electric current strength?**E1 Solution:** Link to Ohm's Law. Explain alternating and direct current.

E1,B2 Current depends upon voltage and resistance.

E1,M2 Ohm's Law: I = V/R

E1,E2 Current can be direct or alternating.

The Stage-2 story is then expanded further using the B, M, E expansion recursively. In the Stage-3 story, only some of the story units from Stage-2 have been expanded. The remaining story units are left for the reader to expand themselves.

STAGE-3

B1 Problem: Why is electric current Important?**B1 Solution:** Explain the importance of electric current**B1, B2 Problem:** Cause and effect of electric shock**B1, B2 Solution:** Many people die of electric shock

B1,B2,B3 Video clip of a person getting a shock

B1,B2,M3 Explain the reason for the shock

B1,B2,E3 Ask, "So what is electric current?"**B1, M2 Problem:** How should we treat electric current?**B1, M2 Solution:** Understand and respect electric current, not be afraid of it.

B1,M2,B3 *(Left un-instantiated*

B1,M2,M3 *for the reader to*

B1,M2,E3 *try out some options)***B1, E2 Problem**: How do we use electric current?**B1, E2 Solution:** Electric current is useful for running appliances

B1,E2,B3 *(Left un-instantiated*

B1,E2,M3 *for the reader to)*

B1,E2,E3 *try out some options)***M1 Problem:** How is electric current defined?**M1 Solution:** Define, exemplify and inject electric current**M1, B2 Problem:** What are the units of electric current?**M1, B2 Solution:** Amperes = Coulombs / second

M1,B2,B3 *(Left un-instantiated*

M1,B2,M3 *for the reader to*

M1,B2,E3 *try out some options)***M1, M2 Problem:** How to visualize electric current**M1, M2 Solution:** Watching Coulombs go past

M1,M2,B3 Animation of Coulombs (blobs) going past.

M1,M2,M3 Update a counter

M1,M2,E3 Show Ampere value rises and falls as Coulombs go past at different speeds.**M1, E2 Problem:** How does electric current feel?**M1, E2 Solution:** Demonstrate the effect of currents with a sensory experience

M1,E2,B3 Ask the user to hold two probes interfaced to a constant low current generator.

M1,E2,M3 Increase current through the circuit. Display current in (mille) Amperes.

M1,E2,E3 Explain the physiological effect of current on the body.**E1 Problem:** How do we calculate electric current?**E1 Solution:** Link to Ohm's Law. Explain alternating and direct current.

E1,B2 Current depends upon voltage and resistance

E1,M2 Ohm's Law: V = IR

E1,E2 Current can be direct or alternating.

The Stages-3 story expansion is given here to show how the MOD process can be applied recursively to create a story plot, i.e. to deter-

Figure 2. Story Development Phases

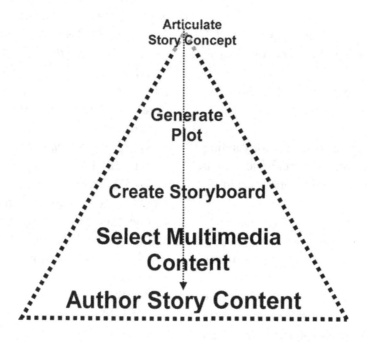

mine the events that should make up the story. However, any story unit can in instantiated in more ways than one, giving multiple story plots. Furthermore, any given story plot can have different narratives, i.e. the sequence in which these events are presented.

Thus, MOD provides a systematic process for brainstorming and creating one or more story plots based on a concept; thus one can explore various narrative options for the plot. As multiple story plots can be created for one story, we need to develop methodologies for testing their effectiveness to select the most effective plot before developing the final presentation. The development of a complete presentation is a rather expensive exercise and a waste of time and resources if the presentation does not have an engaging plot and narrative.

Therefore, before incurring the cost of authoring a complete story as a multimedia presentation it should be tested with prospective users to get their feedback on their experience with the various plots and their narrative options, to select the most effective one. However, this testing aspect is beyond the scope of this chapter.

MOD Based Story Development

MOD provides a systematic process to develop educational stories beginning with just a topic, or with a collection of experiences that one wishes to share in a CoP. Such a story can be viewed as comprising the experiences arranged as a narrative, where the experiences will convey the meaning, and the narrative will provide an envelope to delivery these experiences as an engaging story.

Story Development Phases

MOD-based story development can be broken into the following five main phases, shown in figure 2. The Story Concept is the apex of this triangular model, representing the high-level story idea that needs to be expanded step-by-step to author the story. This transformation of the Story Concept into a presentable story can be broken in to the following five phases (Sharda, 2007).

Phase 1: **Articulate Story Concept:** Start by articulating the story concept, and brainstorm and record various options for BME components, expanding these down to a level where the story units are close to being the Movements.

Phase 2: **Generation Plot:** Generate one or more Story Plots by choosing well-linked Movements.

Phase 3: **Create Storyboard:** Develop the Narrative as a Storyboard by representing Movements with iconic multimedia elements.

Phase 4: **Select Multimedia Content:** Select the required content including text, videos, images, graphics, and sounds.

Phase 5: **Authoring Story Content:** Author the story as a multimedia presentation by instantiating the story plot linked into a narrative with multimedia elements.

Creative input is required in each of the five phases articulated for story development. However, Phase-1 and Phase-2 are critical in getting the story right. Because, if the story plot is not engaging, no matter what flashy content and technical gizmos are used, the final product will be sub-optimal.

There are many systems and tools available for storyboarding, content storage, and authoring; however, presently, what is missing in the current crop of web-based tools is the ability to generate effective plots and narratives, given an idea or a set of concepts that need to be linked into a good story. Therefore, in the following the focus is on principles for developing good story plots.

Using McKee Principle for Story Plot Development

McKee (1998) has articulated the principles for creating emotionally moving story plots. While these principles have been given for creating fictional stories, they can also be used to create engaging educational stories (Sharda, 2007). An engaging story experience comes about by moving human emotions (Sharda, 2006), therefore we need to focus on creating emotional movement to make the story engaging.

McKee defines the concept of emotional charge as the level of built-up emotions. Positive Emotional Charge can be associated with feelings such as being happy, satisfied, and elated. In the context of an educational story this could imply a feeling of accomplishment on acquiring new knowledge, or realizing the connections between different areas, or discovering how to apply newly gained knowledge (Sharda, 2007).

Negative Emotional Charge can be associated with emotions such as anxiety due to the lack of knowledge about some new concept, or confusion, possibly in the face of contradictory facets encountered in some knowledge area.

To keep the listeners engaged, emotional charge must move up and down (McKee, 1998); this must happen even in an educational story (Sharda, 2006). This emotional movement is represented in figure 3 as the arrows pointing up and down alternately, as the transmission of knowledge advances going from left to right. The arrows representing Emotional Charge form a Narrative Envelope around the core knowledge, which helps to move the knowledge transmission agenda, by engaging the viewer's emotions.

To be able to move emotions incessantly, Mc-Kee suggests that a story should have five stages: Inciting Incident, Progressive Complications, Crisis, Climax, and Resolution. These concepts have been articulated originally for fictional stories; however some of these can be used for creating effective educational stories as well, as articulated in the following.

1. **Inciting Incident** is an event that gets the story going. It is often the main problem that needs to be solved. This construct is useful for finding good beginnings.

2. **Progressive Complications** are needed to keep the listeners emotionally engaged. To achieve this, every problem that gets solved should raise another. McKee (1998) describes it as the Law of Conflict: "... conflict is to storytelling what sound is to

Figure 3. Story Designed to move Emotional Charge

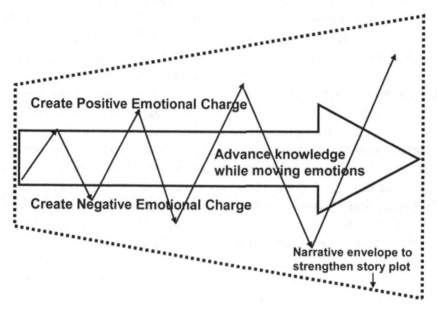

music. Both story and music are temporal arts, and the single most difficult task of the temporal artist is to hook our interest, hold our uninterrupted concentration...". Telling an educational story is also a temporal art; and to introduce progressive complications in any educational story the narrative should be organized such that the answer given to one problem should raise a new question. These progressive complications should happen especially in the middle part of the complete story, where attention tends to wane.

3. **Crisis** happens when the protagonist is surrounded by insurmountable problems, and in the **Climax** emotions explode. These two stages are not easy to include in an educational story; however, if one can find these constructs for an educational story it will become even more engrossing.

4. **Resolution** happens when all problems are solved. An educational story must have a resolution, i.e. towards the end, the story should answer all the questions raised therein. However, throughout the story, the resolution in one Story Units should link to the problem for the next Story Unit.

To make any educational story more effective we need to surround the educational content with a narrative envelop that makes the story engaging, as shown in figure 3. In other words, just presenting facts is not enough; elements of good storytelling must be added to communicate the educational message more effectively. Even though this narrative overhead will add to the 'volume' of the story, it will nonetheless make the educational content more understandable and memorable.

The Web, and in particular the Web 2.0 systems offer unprecedented opportunities for developing tools for collaboration that can help CoPs in making their interaction more effective. Listening to stories and then retelling these in new contexts is a very powerful means of learning in a CoP.

This process can be supported by a plethora of Web 2.0 tools available today. However, these tools do not use models of good storytelling as their underlying authoring metaphor. By developing tools that use MOD as the authoring model we can support the creation of more effective stories, and introduce storytelling as a model for interaction in CoPs.

DEVELOPING STORY AUTHORING TOOLS IN WEB 2.0

The past few years have seen large volumes of user-generated content on the Web giving an ideal platform for CoPs to share their experiences. Rich Internet Applications (RIAs) allow users to post and share multimedia information over the Web for free. In 2007 the Time magazine proclaimed "You" (the general computing public) as the "Person of the Year" (Glass, 2007). The reasons given for this choice included Web-based collaboration opportunities, because:

It's "about community and collaboration."

It's "about the many wresting power from the few."

It's "the beast with a billion eyes"!

However, Glass (2007) argues against this choice due to the misuse of the Web for frivolous and salacious activities. Despite rampant misuse of the Web, the fact remains that Web 2.0 tools such as Blogs, RSS and Wikis have changed the way we communicate and keep ourselves informed.

Current Web 2.0 Development Environments

The Web 2.0 environments that provide tools for building Rich Internet Applications include AJAX, Flash and XULRunner (Farrell & Nezlek, 2007).

Asynchronous JavaScript and XML (AJAX)

Asynchronous JavaScript and XML (AJAX) provides a highly responsive user experience due to the fact that it constantly loads small chunks of data in the background (Paulson, 2005). This aspect of AJAX makes it more responsive than the languages such as Hyper Text Markup Language (HTML) and Dynamic HTML (DHTML).

In an AJAX based application the client can download information – such as graphics and data– just once, and then these are updated incrementaly in real-time. This reduces the system response time appreciably (Backbase, 2008).

Advantages of AJAX

The asynchronous nature and other features of AJAX have made it a popular choice for building Rich Internet Applications. The main advantages of AJAX framework include the following:

1. Applications are more responsive as they don't experience full-page reloading delays.
2. It is based on open standards and widely used languages, namely JavaScript and XML; therefore it does not need plug-ins to run applications.
3. Applications provide users with rich functionality and operate with all Web-browsers and platforms.
4. It is being used widely to build Web 2.0 applications.

Challenges with AJAX

However, AJAX has got some drawbacks as well, these include:

1. It is a new technology, making the application development more expensive.

2. Some differences in JavaScript implementations exist across browsers, and require the applications to be rendered via alternative means.
3. It is cumbersome to run applications on older browsers that don't fully support modern AJAX features.
4. It doesn't reload the entire pages to update content; thus it is possible that search engines skip indexing of some important information.
5. AJAX can't be used for audio and video streaming, as neither HTML nor JavaScript have audio or video APIs.

Flash Environment

The Flash environment offers some features similar to those provided by AJAX. Graphical User Interface (GUI) developed for Flash have polished desktop-like look and feel, having been coded in XML-based markup languages such as OpenLaszlo Language (LZX) and Maximum Experience Markup Language (MXML). For displaying these images the server or the client renders the images using the Flash player, which is installed on most servers, and is available for free download in any case (Stearn, 2007).

XULRunner Framework

The XULRunner framework combines features of Web browsers and desktop-based RIAs (Stearn, 2007). XULRunner is highly flexible and can be adapted to work in different environments. It can work with data-intensive application by using custom components or with HTML and JavaScript-based applications.

XULRunner is written in C/C++, and works in the Mozilla framework, which itself is a set of components taken from the Cross Platform Component Object Model (XPCOM). XULRunner combines an application's components into a single reusable package building a robust, stable,

and cross-platform development environment (Stearn, 2007).

Selecting a Development Environment

In selecting the environment for developing the MOD based storytelling tools, we can short-list AJAX and Flash, as these are most widely used in the industry. XULRunner, though a good candidate, needs further industry support before it can be considered seriously. Some of its current shortcomings are articulated more fully by Stearn (2007).

Using Storytelling as Pedagogy in a Web-based CoP

To use storytelling as a new pedagogy, we need to develop a systematic methodology for its introduction in any CoP. In the following, we first reiterate the main objectives of CoPs, explore how CoPs are organized, how various web-based tools are used in these CoPs, and then articulate how MOD based storytelling can be introduced in a CoP.

Objectives for CoPs

While the detailed objectives of any CoP depend upon its specific purpose and domain in which it operates, the following can be considered as the overarching objectives of any CoP (Nickols, 2003).

1. Stimulate interaction
2. Foster learning
3. Create new knowledge
4. Identify and share best practices

CoP Membership and Roles

To achieve the above listed objectives, a CoP needs the following group of people with the listed responsibilities (Nickols, 2003). The role each of these people can play in introducing storytelling is also suggested in the following.

1. **A Champion** is required to engender enthusiasm for organizing meetings. The Champion leads the organization of events, and manages communications. Therefore, the champion should lead the introduction of storytelling as the new paradigm for interaction and organize the tools and systems required for telling, listening and retelling stories.

2. **Members** form the core of a CoP; they attend meetings to share information, insights and experiences. Participation by members in discussions often raises new issues; therefore they are expected to participate in meetings actively, to learn as well as to impart their knowledge to others. Storytelling can be new to some members, and they may need some training in creating engaging stories. MOD will help such members in creating effective stories and overcome any hesitation they may have in relating their experiences.

3. **A Facilitator** takes on the responsibility for keeping the communications going in meetings, makes any clarifications, encourages participation, ensures that all opinions are heard, and advances discussions while keeping them on topic. This can be applied to face-to-face as well as virtual meetings. Therefore, the facilitator will play a key role in introducing and encouraging storytelling as the new model of discourse.

4. **A Practice Leader** leads the CoP based on his or her competence in a given domain. Practice Leaders can change as the domain of interaction shifts. Getting a Practice Leader for advancing storytelling and all its facets in a CoP will facilitate the introduction of this new pedagogical model in a given CoP.

5. **A Sponsor** advances the cause of a CoP in an organization by providing time, funding and other resources. The Sponsor often guides the development of the mission statement and expected outcomes for the CoP. It will help if the sponsor is enthusiastic about introducing the storytelling paradigm to the CoP, and provides support with time, funding and the tools required to do the same.

Introducing Storytelling with New Technology

Introducing new technology is always a challenge in any workplace. Similarly, introducing a new communication and learning paradigm can challenge the way a CoP works.

While the development of new Web 2.0 tools was proposed earlier, it is important to note that the availability of such tools is not a prerequisite for introducing storytelling to the CoP. Existing systems such as MS Word and PowerPoint can be used to create textual or multimedia stories respectively. Other authoring systems are also available, some of these target the creation of videos and some the development of audio narrations.

For face-to-face meetings people can bring in their well developed stories, and relate these verbally or present them as multimedia presentations. Web-based tools will be particularly useful in virtual meetings. Initially, a simple information sharing system can be used; such as email or collaborative videoconferencing.

One of the problems in getting new Web tools is that the development of new practice is not always aligned with the direction taken by the technology providers (Wenger, White, Smith, & Rowe, 2005). Also, the solidarity shown by some members in a CoP can lead to resistance in introducing new innovative technology; though, ideally, it should encourage innovation.

A significant effort may be required to adopt a new tool, let alone develop it. Some members in a CoP may resist the introduction of a new tool, as it can shift the power structure, bring in new members, and may seem like a distraction from the core business of the community, at least for some time (Wenger, White, Smith, & Rowe, 2005).

However, bringing in a new practice and related tools to a community can enhance the engagement of members. Nonetheless, the following points should be considered in relation to the introduction of new practices and technology (Wenger, White, Smith, & Rowe, 2005):

1. Experience of the new members as they join the CoP, because their experience can bring out shortcomings and opportunities not noticed by long-standing members.
2. Experience and use of similar practice and technology in other environments.
3. Experience of other CoPs in adopting new practices and tools.
4. Sharing experience and observing each other when using existing tools.
5. Exploring how existing tools can be used in new innovative ways to enhance collaboration.

In general, exploring new technologies and practices should be encouraged in a CoP, as long as it does not distract the community from its objectives. Therefore, introducing storytelling using MOD to a CoP may be facilitated by running workshops that articulate the concepts underpinning storytelling and the MOD paradigm, and demonstrate how MOD can be used to create educational stories.

Story Creation Workshop

Crafting stories is a creative activity and collaboration with people coming from different viewpoints enhances creativity. Therefore, developing educational stories is best approached as a collaborative activity.

Workshops are a good interaction model for enhancing collaboration, and for engendering creativity and innovation in a group (Sharda, 2007). Running story development workshops in a CoP would offer many benefits, such as:

- Stimulating creativity
- Developing innovative ideas
- Provide time and space for this creative activity
- Learning the MOD methodology to create educational stories
- Enhancing collaboration with people from similar as well as diverse backgrounds

Creativity is "the ability to generate and use insight" (Stevens, 2007). Stuck in a routine, most people cannot use their creative potential to the fullest and their ability to innovate suffers.

Innovation takes place when even a small improvement to something that already exists enhances the way it works and can be used. Innovation does not imply the invention of something completely new. Innovation can be made to improve a product or even a process. Joyce Wycoff states that innovation as a "mental extreme sport" and that it requires "pulling unrelated things together" (Newhart & Wycoff, 2005). Consequently, story creation workshops will generate new innovative solutions as the members of a CoP consider a problem from different perspectives.

A number of workshop running techniques have been developed to enhance collaboration and creativity, such as the Design Consequences workshop technique (Reichelt, 2007). In most workshops, to get the best outcomes workshops should provide some 'personal time' and some 'shared time'. Personal time gives the opportunity to individual participants to contemplate, think, imagine, document and present their own ideas. Free-form documentation techniques, such a mind maps can be combined with structured story development techniques such as MOD for documenting the new ideas. Shared time is also important to be able to brainstorm ideas and provide feedback.

Narrative Development Workshop

The purpose of a Narrative Development Workshop is to develop the plot and the narrative of an educational story and share it with other participants to get feedback.

This narrative development workshop should begin by presenting the fundamental concepts of storytelling, the Movement Oriented Design paradigm, and the application of 'McKee Principles' for creating educational stories. Each participant should lead the development of the plot and narrative for one educational story. The workshop should proceed in the following steps (Sharda, 2007):

1. Members attend a seminar on good storytelling principles and Movement Oriented Design.
2. Each member selects a topic and builds a bag of creative ideas: some coming from self, and some more from other group members.
3. Classify ideas into groups: Positive, Negative, Complication, Crisis, Climax, Resolution, to use these for creating interesting narratives.
4. Use the MOD process to develop one or more story plots.
5. Select a plot and get feedback from other workshop participants, vis-à-vis the effectiveness of the plot in emotional engagement and educational content delivery.
6. Create story a narrative based on the plot, the feedback from the other members.

As the purpose of the feedback is to check if the story plot fulfills its educational purpose and has an engaging narrative, the feedback from other group members should address the following points (Sharda, 2007):

1. Does the plot flow smoothly?
2. Are the Begins, Middles, and Ends appropriate for each Movement?
3. Are there any Movements that need further expansion?
4. Are there any inconsistencies or holes in the message or the knowledge the story aims to convey?

This narrative development workshop would lay the foundations for introducing storytelling as a formal method for sharing experiences and transferring knowledge in a CoP.

CONCLUSION

In a CoP, learning takes place through sharing of knowledge and experience. This chapter has articulated how storytelling can be used as a model for interaction to enhance learning in a Community of Practice (CoP). The task of knowledge and experience sharing can be made more engaging by using storytelling as a model for interaction. Movement Oriented Design provides a systematic process and framework for creating effective story plots by using well recognized principles of good storytelling.

Many Web-based tools have been used for improving interaction in CoPs, which can be enhanced by developing new, more responsive tools in a Web 2.0 framework such as AJAX. To begin with, storytelling can be introduced in a CoP using existing text and multimedia authoring systems. Nonetheless, new Web 2.0 tools for storytelling tools should be developed using the MOD paradigm, so that almost anyone can create engaging educational stories and use these in a CoP context. Workshops should be used to introduce the concepts of storytelling and MOD to the members of the CoP.

REFERENCES

Aristotle. (1996). *Poetics* (M. Heath, Trans.). New York: Penguin Books.

Backbase. (2008). *AJAX in enterprise* [white paper].

Bateman, C. (2008). *Story, plot & narrative.*

Berne, E. (1996). *Games people play: The basic handbook of transactional analysis.* New York: Penguin Books.

Egan, K. (2004). *Teaching as story telling.* London, Canada: The Althouse Press.

Farrell, J., & Nezlek, G. S. (2007). Rich Internet applications the next stage of application development. In *Proceedings of the 29th International Conference on Information Technology Interfaces, ITI 2007* (pp. 413-418).

Glass, R. L. (2007). What's with this blog thing? *IEEE Software, 24*(5), 103–104. doi:10.1109/MS.2007.151

Heo, H. (2004). Story telling and retelling as narrative inquiry in cyber learning environments. In R. Atkinson, C. McBeath, D. Jonas-Dwyer, & R. Phillips (Eds.), *Beyond the comfort zone: Proceedings of the 21st ASCILITE Conference,* Perth, Australia (pp. 374-378).

Lévi-Strauss, C. (1995). *Myth and meaning: Cracking the code of culture.* New York: Schocken Books.

McKee, R. (1998). *Story: Substance, structure, style and the principles of screenwriting.* London: Methuen.

Newhart, R. L., & Joyce, C. (2005). Free radicals of innovation [videorecording]. Innovation Center, Star Thrower Distribution.

Nickols, F. (2003). *Communities of practice: An overview.*

Paulson, L. D. (2005). Building rich Web applications with AJAX. *IEEE Computer, 38*(10), 14–17.

Reichelt, L. (2007). *Design consequences: A fun workshop technique for brainstorming & consensus building.*

Sharda, N. (2005). Movement oriented design: A new paradigm for multimedia design. *International Journal of Lateral Computing, 1*(1), 7–14.

Sharda, N. (2006). Applying movement oriented design to create educational stories. *International Journal of Learning, 13*(12), 177–184.

Sharda, N. (2007). Authoring educational multimedia content using learning styles and story telling principles. In *Proceedings of the ACM Workshop on Educational Multimedia and Multimedia Education in conjunction with ACM Multimedia 2007,* Augsburg, Germany (pp. 93-102).

Stearn, B. (2007). XULRunner: A new approach for developing rich Internet applications. *IEEE Internet Computing, 11*(3), 67–73. doi:10.1109/MIC.2007.75

Stevens, C. D. (2007). *Coming to insight, eventually. Screenhub.*

Wenger, E. (2008). *Communities of practice, a brief introduction.*

Wenger, E., White, N., Smith, J., & Rowe, K. (2005). *Technology for communities, CEFRIO book chapter v 5.2.*

Chapter 7
Mining Unnoticed Knowledge in Collaboration Support Systems

George Gkotsis
University of Patras, Greece

Nikos Tsirakis
University of Patras, Greece

ABSTRACT

Numerous tools aiming at facilitating or enhancing collaboration among members of diverse communities have been already deployed and tested over the Web. Focusing on the particularities of online communities of practice (CoPs), this chapter introduces a framework for mining knowledge that is hidden in such settings. The authors' motivation stems from the criticism that contemporary tools receive regarding lack of active participation and limited engagement in their use, which is partially due to the inability of identifying and exploiting a set of important relationships among community members and the associated collaboration-related assets. The authors' overall approach elaborates and integrates issues from the data mining and the social networking disciplines. More specifically, the proposed framework enables CoPs members to rank the contributions of their peers towards identifying meaningful relationships, as well as valuable information about roles and competences. In the context of this chapter, the authors first model the characteristics of the overall collaboration setting and propose a set of associated metrics. Next, in order to reveal unnoticed knowledge which resides within CoPs, a data mining technique that groups users into clusters and applies advanced social networking analysis on them is proposed. Finally, the authors discuss the benefits of their approach and conclude with future work plans.

GETTING STARTED

As information diffusion is becoming enormous, contemporary knowledge workers are facing a series of problems. People are straggling when trying to

DOI: 10.4018/978-1-60566-711-9.ch007

filter relevant information, extract knowledge out of it, and apply specific practices on a problem under consideration. This phenomenon, broadly known as "information overload", has currently raised new, challenging, but not fully addressed issues. It is widely undisputed that one of the best means to keep a knowledge worker's competence high is through continuous learning (Rosenberg, 2001). In fact, most organizations already support learning activities through seminars and other traditional learning activities. Nevertheless, all of the above are not sufficient ("codified and transferred" learning (Robey, D., Khoo, H.M. and Powers, 2000); new methodologies, based on networked technology, have emerged to satisfy the gap between tacit and explicit knowledge. Collaborative environments - aiming at supporting collaboration among groups of people forming Communities of Practice (CoPs) - are believed to be one of the most promising solutions to promote what is commonly known as "collective intelligence" or "organizational memory" (Ackerman, 1998). The term CoP is used to define a group of people with "common disciplinary background, similar work activities and tools and shared stories, contexts and values" (Millen, Fontaine & Muller, 2002).

A comparison between online and traditional CoPs naturally results to several differences (Palloff & Pratt, 1999). Even though the goal of this work is not to study them thoroughly, some of them are intentionally mentioned. A traditional CoP often confronts time and space limitations and its members are assigned a specific role. Furthermore, entrance to a traditional CoP may require a more intentional motivation, while CoP members tend to self-organize through certain physical activities. On the other hand, online CoPs are more likely to define more "fluid" limitations. This can result to more "peripheral" members with less "visibility" (Zhang, Wei & Storck, 2001). Taking the above into consideration, several implications arise concerning online CoP contribution. In fact, usage analysis of online CoPs has shown that one of the greatest problems is the "fading back" and absence of members' identities (Haythornthwaite, Kazmer, Robins & Shoemaker, 2000).

Related with the above remarks, contemporary tools receive criticism regarding lack of active participation and limited engagement in their use, which is partially due to the inability of identifying and exploiting a set of important relationships among community members and the associated collaboration-related assets. In order to further investigate the aforementioned problem, we proceed to a thorough examination of environments provided to online CoPs. Aiming at keeping our subject of study as general as possible, we prescribe some commonly met characteristics. In order to sufficiently elaborate collaboration among CoP members, we prescribe a framework that elaborates and integrates issues from the Data Mining and the Social Networking disciplines. By applying such an interdisciplinary approach, our aim is to reveal meaningful relationships, as well as valuable information about the members' roles and competences, thus strengthening the community's integrity.

RELATED WORK

Contemporary approaches to online environments hosting a large group of users build on diverse user profiling mechanisms (Fink & Kobsa, 2001). These approaches usually distinguish between static (or user defined) and dynamic (a set of attributes updated by the system) user profiles. Dynamic attributes derive by tracking down user actions and aim at providing a more personalized environment. Personalization of the environment may include user interface adaptation by making most usable actions or information more easily accessible. Moreover, by taking into account a user's profile, these approaches aim at filtering information which generally resides in a big collection of documents. Information filtering is achieved by reading the content of these documents and combining its content with the user's profile. The main goal of these approaches is to provide individualized recommendations to users concerning the system items (Burke, 2002).

Social network analysis (SNA) is a tool that allows the examination of social relationships in a group of users and reveals hidden relationships (Wasserman & Faust, 1994). In fact, social network analysis has been a research area applied for several decades on organizations. In business, SNA can be a useful tool to reveal relationships and organizational structure beneath the ones formally defined. Those relationships are extracted by examining the communication level among employees, resulting to a related graph. The outcome of this graph analysis is likely to result to a flow chart that does not necessarily follow the formal organizational structure. Traditionally, those relationships are revealed by acquiring data manually either through questionnaires or interviews. SNA has been applied with success in business for decades and is regarded a useful tool to analyze how a corporate functions. This includes identifying employees that are "key players" in the communication flow of the company.

In recent years, a large number of web sites aiming at easing online communication forming virtual communities –not necessarily with a special goal or context- have been deployed. Popular web sites like friendster (http://www.friendster.com claimed to have 5 million users by 2003), facebook (http://www.facebook.com claims to have over 100 million users currently) and myspace (http://www.myspace.com has reached 100 million users on 2006) have attracted a vast number of users. In order to increase a user's network, contemporary systems are using "friend of friend" approach. This approach is based on the reasonable hypothesis that if two users share one or more common friends, those users are very likely to have some kind of connection or relationship between them as well.

From a more technological approach, on 2000 a technology was deployed called "Friend of Friend", which is an extension of Resource Description Framework (RDF), specified with Web Ontology Language (OWL). This solution has received great appraise and may be considered a part of the effort to enhance Web with more semantics (Semantic Web). It is worth noting that -within this context- Tim Berners Lee has coined up with the title Giant Global Graph as

the graph that unites both World Wide Web and Social Graph (Lee 2007). The past four years, research based on the above technology has been conducted (Paolillo 2004), (Mika, 2005). Research work mainly focuses on technological solutions that exploit the FOAF (http://www.foaf-project.org/) standard in order to create large organized information concerning users. For example, Flink (Mika, 2005) "is a presentation of the professional work and social connectivity of Semantic Web researchers". Through a set of components that mine information sources like FOAF profiles, web pages, publication archives (e.g. through Google or Google Scholar) the system is aiming at presenting over the web the community under investigation. It is worth noting that similar research concerning scientific research has been conducted by examining co-authorship or citations (Barabási, 2002).

From a more formal perspective, data mining can play an important role in the area of collaboration systems, in that it can provide advanced awareness about diverse community activities. Data mining in these systems can be defined as the effort to generate actionable models through automated analysis of their databases. Data mining can only be deployed successfully when it generates insights that are substantially deeper than what a simple view of data can give. Clustering is one of the basic data mining techniques (Han & Kamber, 2001), (Hand, Mannila & Smyth, 2000), on which numerous approaches have been proposed. Generally speaking, the goal of clustering is, given a dataset, to find "naturally" occurring groups within this dataset. With the rapid increase in web-traffic, understanding user behavior based on their interaction with a website is becoming more and more important for website owners. Clustering in correlation with personalization techniques of this information space has become a necessity. Web-based systems (including collaboration systems) can have mechanisms with multiple ways to report on events, conditions, errors and alerts. In addition, when we have to do with web-based collaboration systems, we can consider even the common log files about users' requests. The combination of this information and the use of data mining techniques can help us analyze users' activities in depth.

In summary, the need for extracting and analyzing relationships among users has been in play for a long time. It can be claimed that there are two different approaches that are rather supplementary to the topic of the present work. One discipline adopts traditional Social Network Analysis with sophisticated and complex techniques for gathering required knowledge. This approach is applied to *specific* organizations aiming at revealing issues like management or human resource vulnerabilities. The other discipline is making use of Semantic Web technologies, which includes a rather one-dimensional approach (FOAF) which may *scale* for the whole Social Graph.

Based on the above research, we present a web system that is been provided to an online Community of Practice and through the adoption of both Data Mining and Social Network Analysis techniques, we describe a related framework.

A NEW FRAMEWORK

In this section, we provide a brief description of the basic characteristics of a collaboration support system. Our approach may be applied to any software platform that supports collaboration through exchange of documents. We also propose a set of metrics that can be found useful to analyze diverse CoPs.

Description

The system we prescribe is a web application, where users are able to create workspaces. Workspace is a term coined to define an entity that resides under specific CoPs and can be perceived as a placeholder for various artifacts. For instance, each workspace may be identified by its specific is-

sue topic and users may contribute with questions, ideas and comments (or any other collaboration item). These user-contributed information units may be regarded as explicit documents. Users are able to rate each document to a scale from 1 to 5. Document rating is optional, but is a mechanism which will enable us to extract information concerning the CoP members' affinity.

Definitions:

- We define DocumentRate as a numerical to describe rating submitted on a document k created by user j and rated by user i.

$$DocumentRate_{ij}(k) \qquad (1)$$

- We define $Affinity_{ij}$ to describe user-user ranking from user i to user j within a workspace.

$$Affinity_{ij} = Avg(DocumentRate_{ij}(k)) \qquad (2)$$

where k is every document created by user j and has been rated by user i.

- We define $Relationship_{ij}$ to indicate the existence or not of a relationship between user i and user j.

$$Relationship_{ij} = \begin{cases} 1 & when \ A_{ij} \geq t \\ 0 & when \ A_{ij} \leq t \end{cases} \qquad (3)$$

where

$$A_{ij} = |\{DocumentRate_{ij}(k)\}| + |\{DocumentRate_{ji}(k)\}| \qquad (4)$$

and $DocumentRate \neq nullA$ is used to express the number of ratings exchanged between users i and j for every document k and t is a threshold which is parameterized according to the current needs of the community that we analyze. For these numericals, we notice the following properties:

- $Avg(DocumentRate_{ij}(k)) \equiv null$ if author $k \neq j$, or user i has not ranked document k.
- $Affinity_{ij} \neq Affinity_{ji}$ i,j (non-reflective affinity)

This means that there are cases, where the user affinity is not *reciprocal*. This remark is of great importance and will be taken into consideration later when the discussion concerning the adopted clustering technique will continue.

A Modeling Approach

As described above, we use a set of tools and metrics that can be found useful to extract information regarding a network of users forming a CoP (Wasserman & Faust, 1994), (Han & Kamber, 2001), (Hand, Mannila & Smyth, 2000), (Bock, 1989):

1. *Clusters:* are groups of entities (users in our occasion), in a way that objects in one cluster are very similar, while objects in different clusters are quite distinct. Each cluster can combine various plausible criteria (Bock, 1989). Sometimes there are some requirements about the objects in the cluster such as: a) to share the same or closely related properties; b) to show small mutual distances or dissimilarities; or c) to have "contacts" or "relations" with at least one other object in the cluster.
2. *Degree:* expresses the number of people a CoP member is connected to. Members with central role may be considered of major importance in the network hub, since they keep the CoP tightly connected.
3. *Betweenness:* While someone may be tightly connected with someone else, it might be the case that some CoP members express the CoP's integrity "better". People with high betweenness degree are considered to be obliging and may express a collective consensus effectively. So it can be expressed by the total number of shortest paths between pairs of members that pass through a member.

4. *Closeness:* We already described affinity as a measure to describe one member's opinion about another. Closeness is extracted from the above in order to describe an "overall" affinity, or else closeness regarding the rest of the CoP members. So the closeness of a member can be expressed by the total number of links that a member must go through in order to reach everyone else in the network.

Mining Hidden Knowledge

Collaboration support systems provide to users the opportunity to share and express their opinion about several issues. These systems are used by communities of users and each community has spaces where users can collaborate with each other. Each user can participate in several spaces of a selected community, where he can take actions such as read/write or make a comment or rank a given idea. All these actions turn out to be useful input data in order to characterize and model users. Thus, we can separate them into groups according to their relationship so as to give out some useful conclusions.

We aim at separating users into groups in order to provide them with better services such as recommendations. The most common technique for this purpose is clustering. Clustering can be defined as the process of organizing objects in a database into clusters/groups such that objects within the same cluster have a high degree of similarity, while objects belonging to different clusters have a high degree of dissimilarity (Anderberg, 1973), (Jain & Dubes, 1988), (Kaufman & Rousseeuw, 1990). Generally speaking, clustering methods about numerical data have been viewed in opposition to conceptual clustering methods developed in

Artificial Intelligence. More precisely, numerical techniques emphasize on the determination of homogeneous clusters according to some similarity measures, but provide low-level descriptions of clusters (Anderberg, 1973). Recently, there are works on clustering that focus on numerical data whose inherent geometric properties can be exploited to naturally define distance functions between data points, such as DBSCAN (Ester, Kriegel, Sander & Xu, 1996), BIRTH (Zhang, Ramakrishnan & Livny, 1996), C2P (Nanopoulos, Theodoridis & Manolopoulos, 2001), CURE (Guha, Rastogi & Shim, 1998), CHAMELEON (Karypis, Han & Kumar, 1999), WaveCluster (Sheikholeslami, Chatterjee & Zhang, 1998). However, data mining applications frequently involve many datasets that also consist of categorical attributes on which distance functions are not naturally defined.

Clustering

In our case, we have numerical data that characterize users. In order to cluster them, we have to form a clustering algorithm in these input data. As we have different users and different communities of users, it is desirable to find clusters of users by referring to a specific community each time, so as to result to some valuable conclusions. Referring to a specific community, we regard a cluster as the collection of users that have something in common by working on the same workspace and thus. For example, let SP1, SP2,..., SPk be the k spaces (from now on the term workspace and space should be treated as equal) used by a community A. We build an array X with size n x n (n is the number of users), where the cell Xij denotes the correlation between user i and user j.

First of all, we have to consider both cases for symmetric undirected and directed arrays of data depending on the analysis we want to make. In addition, we can use the affinity metric introduced in section 3.1, in order to build the array X.

So we have an array for each space in the community A. After the construction of these arrays, we build a unified array for the whole community by using the arrays of each space. More precisely, we may use the average of each cell, which is the most common way. This final array will have the relationships between users of the same community. Having this array as an input and applying an appropriate clustering algorithm into them, we can find hidden relationships and correlations between users of a community by observing the resulted clusters of users.

An interesting approach could be the use of all data arrays for all spaces and not the unified data array of a community. According to this idea, we can have more detailed views of users. This can be derived by applying a clustering procedure for each certain space. By clustering user data for a specific space, we can provide micro-clusters of users and give lower level clusters. After that, we can perform a macro-clustering procedure. This procedure can exploit user properties from micro-clusters and find higher level clusters in a history or time horizon. Based on this method, we can have - at the same time - both detailed and general views of users.

Depending on the kind of the analysis we want to make about the users of the system, we have to follow two different approaches about the nature of the arrays that we use, one concerning symmetric undirected arrays, and one concerning directed arrays. Both of them are described below.

Symmetric Undirected Arrays

In this case, we can use any known hierarchical algorithm for clustering where we use relevant distances. In hierarchical clustering, there is a partitioning procedure of objects into optimally homogeneous groups. It is based on empirical measures of similarity among the objects that have received increasing attention in several different fields (Johnson, 1967). There are two different categories of hierarchical algorithms: those that repeatedly merge two smaller clusters into a larger one, and those that split a larger cluster into smaller ones. As reported in (Ding & He, 2002), the MinMax linkage (Ding, He, Zha, Gu & Simon, 2001) is the best in agglomerative clustering and the average similarity is the best method in divisive clustering.

1. In MinMax given n data objects the pairwise similarity matrix $W=(w_{ij})$ (where w_{ij} is the similarity between i,j) we want to partition the data into two clusters C_1, C_2 using the min-max principle - minimize similarity between clusters and maximize similarity within a cluster. The similarity between C_1 and C_2 is defined as $s(C_1, C_2)$. Linkage l is the closeness or similarity measure between two clusters and helps in getting better results for clusters. It is defined as follows:

$$l_{\text{MinMax}} (C_1, C_2) = s(C_1, C_2)/s(C_1, C_1)s(C_2, C_2)$$

2. The average similarity is based on the min-max clustering principle. The purpose here is to choose the loosest cluster to split, or in other words the cluster with the smallest average similarity. The self-similarity of cluster C_k is $s(C_k, C_k)=s_{kk}$ which has to be maximized during clustering. The average self-similarity now is computed as $\bar{s}_{kk} = s_{kk} / n_k^2$ where $n_k = |C_k|$. When a cluster has large average self-similarity then its objects are more homogeneous.

Directed arrays

If we consider that there is a difference between the meaning of Xij and Xji, then we understand that the Euclidean distance between users does not exist and we have to focus on a directed graph of users. More precisely, we need a clustering technique for directed graph in order to optimize the separation of users into clusters. An array X may correspond to a community of spaces or to a space. The commonly used approach is to obtain the symmetric array X of data and then apply clustering to $\bar{X}$. In our case, we propose the framework of clustering by weighed cuts directly in X (Meila & Pentney, 2007). This framework unifies many different criteria used successfully on undirected graphs (like the normalization cut and the averaged cut) and directed graphs. It formulates clustering as an optimization problem where the objective is to minimize the weighted cut in the directed graph which can be equivalent to the problem of a symmetric matrix.

A different approach, that could probably lead to better (in a semantic sense) results would be to use the clustering algorithm presented in (Chakrabarti, Dom, Gibson, Kumar, Raghavan, Rajagopalan & Tomkins, 1998); to do that, we have to consider X as an adjacency matrix of an underlying graph, with nodes as the users. This algorithm inspired by the web search algorithm of (Kleinberg, 1999) can produce clusters, where in each cluster each user is characterized by two different scores. The first score (authority score) depicts the quality of the incoming links a user has, while the second score (hub score) depicts the quality of the outgoing links a user has. Hence, the first score can be used to depict how strong or weak author is a user and the second score can be used to depict how good or bad reviewer is this user. Users that have high authority scores are expected to have relevant ideas, whereas users with high hub scores are expected to have worked in spaces of relevant subject.

Social Network Analysis

The final scope of this analysis involves the mapping and measuring of the normally unnoticed relationships between users and, more specifically, between clusters of users. The presented metrics are largely regarded as a means of evaluating properties of particular interest. Even though it is not the goal of this paper to thoroughly study the different algorithmic and implementation approaches concerning social networking analysis, some of them will be mentioned. Closeness (Sabidussi, 1966) and betweenness (Freeman, 1977), (Anthonisse, 1971) are two measures of the centrality of vertex within a graph and can be computed with well established algorithms that are tightly coupled with common shortest path algorithms (e.g. graph traversal using Djikstra algorithm). From an implementation point of view, LEDA (Mehlhorn & Näher, 1999) is a general scope library which provides adequate support to extract the required computations.

As a second step of analysis, and after the clustering procedure, we have groups of users that have the same or closely related properties in different levels for each CoP. In particular, consider a partition of the CoP into C1, C2,..., Ck and that for a community Ci there is a division of members into the following set of clusters, $Cluster_{i_1}$ n, ..., $Cluster_{i_m}$ (let n_{i_1}, n_{i_2}, ..., n_{i_m} be the number of members in each cluster). Then, we can compute the values of each Social Network Analysis measures for every single community of practice by properly adjusting the various formulas taking into account the values of the parameters in each cluster. This type of analysis provides different results than the results of the previous step. After clustering, we can examine each cluster separately and then consider a sub-graph of the initial graph where we take into account only users that belong to this cluster. It is obvious that now the measures of the metrics are different, and we can extract different types of observations. For example a specific group of users within the same community considered to have high connectivity and thus may appear as a cluster is actually a "weak" cluster, where in reality only a part of this cluster is the "knot sum". For instance, we can find out users of the same cluster that already share some common characteristics, and were not communicating as expected. The system can make use of the outcome of our analysis and provide links or notifications to the users of the same cluster by

emphasizing the users with low communication flow and highlighting their activity.

Having these groups of users (clusters) we can also perform cluster analysis. This analysis can give a better understanding about the relations between users especially in this type of systems where we have multiple types of data. Also it can help detect outliers (objects from the data that have different distribution of values from the majority of other objects in the space), which may emerge as singletons or as small clusters far from the others. For a given intensity of communication or actions, clusters emphasize the various intensity levels. Cluster analysis also reveals useful information for interpretation. We can find how many groups are in the same community and each group can be inspected to reveal patterns of interest. In this phase, we can make specific analysis in each cluster and measure the metrics mentioned before. In this way, we can have different type of analysis. For instance, consider some users that belong to the same community and have a relationship, but their actions in this community are limited. In this case, clustering can assist by grouping them into the same cluster and evaluate the metrics just for them. Otherwise, we cannot have the opportunity to analyze just the users that share some common characteristics (like the users of this example) and their relationship would not be so easy to be revealed.

SUMMARY

A CoP may be regarded as a dynamic organization. Like any other network, there are some parts which may have crucial impact on its efficiency. The identification of a set of qualitative metrics that describe the above network can be useful to help members work more adequately and guarantee the CoP continuity. The framework we describe may be applied to a large number of systems designed to support collaboration and may help people identify information that was not obvious from every day use. More specifically, by identifying clusters of users within a community, it is possible to reveal intellectual, social or spiritual differences among community members and the way these users self-organize to smaller groups. The above remarks may either be proven of vital importance to assure the community's survivability, or may possibly expose the need to review the community's current structure and future. Furthermore, by applying social network analysis on clusters, it is possible to identify whether a social network is centralized or not. Establishment of de-centralized networks is considered a healthier network, since there are no single points of failure. In that manner, members that are found to have crucial impact on the group activity or collaboration may be notified and assume their corresponding duties and tasks, thus making sure that information is being propagated properly. Moreover, users that share common ideas and tend to rate other users' contribution similarly are brought together close, since our proposed framework reveals relationships that are yet to be promoted. In such a way, communication among members may be certified and collaboration can persist, even if some communication problems occur. Finally, one more issue that was taken under consideration and may be subject of exploitation is enlargement of legitimate peripheral participation (Lave & Wenger, 2001). By this term, we refer to the ability CoP has to attract newcomers and to accommodate their ability unfolding.

If we take under consideration all of the above scenarios of use, it is obvious that the estimated benefits from our proposed framework can provide great use to the members of the CoP. Analyzing user actions, identification of user relationships and extraction of several metrics regarding the communication level among CoP members is a promising technique in order to improve community productivity and awareness; members will have the chance to resolve issues faster and more efficiently and members' competencies will emerge in a more natural way. In this paper we describe a system that takes into account all of the

afore-mentioned operations. This assures that the CoP will advance faster and more securely, while its evolution remains under constant observation and examination. In that way, a community may be assured that its purpose is served more satisfyingly and its members' actions are clearly diffused.

CONCLUSION

In this paper, we presented a framework which can be applied to a wide range of software platforms aiming at facilitating collaboration among users. Our motivation stems from the fact that contemporary collaboration support environments suffer from low user engagement. Having described the basic characteristics of our prototype system, we focus on a model which combines techniques from both data mining and social network analysis disciplines. More precisely, we formulated two different clustering approaches in order to find the values of some interesting metrics. Moreover, we combined the outcomes of the proposed clustering methodology with social network metrics. The result of the above effort is to unfold meaningful knowledge which resides at a CoP. This knowledge may be used in a variety of ways, to enhance the system ability and allow users communicate (and thus collaborate) more effectively. It is our belief that the whole framework is both general and flexible.

It is necessary to underline that the exact tool that will be responsible to present the outcome of the analysis taking place in our framework is only functionally outlined and is yet to be fully described in later work. Future work plans include the conduction of experiments with real data from diverse CoPs using a particular collaboration support tool (namely CoPe_it! – http://copeit.cti. gr), and investigation of scenarios for a further exploitation of the proposed framework.

REFERENCES

Ackerman, M. S. (1998). Augmenting organizational memory: A field study of answer garden. [TOIS]. *ACM Transactions on Information Systems*, *16*(3), 203–224. doi:10.1145/290159.290160

Anderberg, M. R. (1973). *Cluster analysis for applications*. New York: Academic Press, Inc.

Anthonisse, J. M. (1971). *The rush in a directed graph* (Tech. Rep. BN 9/71). Amsterdam, The Netherlands: Stichting Mathematisch Centrum.

Barabási, A. L., Jeong, H., Néda, Z., Ravasz, E., Schubert, A., & Vicsek, T. (2002). Evolution of the social network of scientific collaborations. *Physica A*, *311*(3-4), 590–614. doi:10.1016/S0378-4371(02)00736-7

Berners-Lee, T. (2007). *Giant global graph*.

Bock, H. H. (1989). Probabilistic aspects in cluster analysis. In *Conceptual and numerical analysis of data*. Berlin, Germany: Springer-Verlag.

Burke, R. (2002). Hybrid recommender systems: Survey and experiments. *User Modeling and User-Adapted Interaction*, *12*(4), 331–370. doi:10.1023/A:1021240730564

Chakrabarti, S., Dom, B. E., Gibson, D., Kumar, R., Raghavan, P., Rajagopalan, S., & Tomkins, A. (1998). *Spectral filtering for resource discovery*. In *Proceedings of the ACM SIGIR workshop on Hypertext Information Retrieval on the Web*.

Ding, C., & He, X. *(2002)*. Cluster merging and splitting in hierarchical clustering algorithms. *In* Proceedings of the IEEE International Conference on Data Mining (ICDM'02).

Ding, C., He, X., Zha, H., Gu, M., & Simon, H. (2001). A min-max cut algorithm for graph partitioning and data clustering. In *Proceedings of the IEEE Int'l Conf. Data Mining* (pp. 107-114).

Ester, M., Kriegel, H., Sander, J., & Xu, X. (1996). A Density-Based Algorithm for Discovering Clusters in Large Spatial Databases with Noise. In *Proceedings of 2nd International Conference on KDD*.

Fink, J., & Kobsa, A. (2001). A review and analysis of commercial user modeling servers for personalization on the World Wide Web. *User Modeling and User-Adapted Interaction, Special Issue on Deployed User Modeling, 10*(3-4).

Freeman, L. C. (1977). A set of measures of centrality based on betweenness. *Sociometry*, *40*, 35–41. doi:10.2307/3033543

Guha, S., Rastogi, R., & Shim, K. (1998). CURE: An efficient clustering algorithm for large databases. In *Proceedings of ACM SIGMOD International Conference on Management of Data* (pp. 73-84). New York: ACM Press.

Han, J., & Kamber, M. (2001). *Data mining: Concepts and techniques*. San Francisco: Morgan Kaufmann Publishers.

Hand, D. J., Mannila, H., & Smyth, P. (2000). *Principles of data mining*. Cambridge, MA: MIT Press.

Haythornthwaite, C., Kazmer, M. M., Robins, J., & Shoemaker, S. (2000). Community development among distance learners: Temporal and technological dimensions. *Journal of Computer-Mediated Communication*, *6*(1), 1–26.

Jain, A. K., & Dubes, R. C. (1988). *Algorithms for clustering data*. Upper Saddle River, NJ: Prentice-Hall, Inc.

Johnson, S. C. (1967). Hierarchical clustering schemes. *Psychometrika*, *2*, 241–254. doi:10.1007/BF02289588

Karypis, G., Han, E. H., & Kumar, V. (1999). Chameleon: A hierarchical clustering algorithm using dynamic modeling. *IEEE Computer*, *32*, 68–75.

Kaufman, L., & Rousseeuw, P. J. (1990). *Finding groups in data*. New York: John Wiley & Sons.

Kleinberg, J. (1999). Authoritative sources in a hyperlinked environment. *Journal of the ACM, 46*(5), 604–632. doi:10.1145/324133.324140

Lave, J., & Wenger, E. (1991). *Situated learning: Legitimate peripheral participation*. Cambridge, UK: Cambridge University Press.

Mehlhorn, K., & Näher, S. (1999). *The LEDA platform of combinatorial and geometric computing*. Cambridge, UK: Cambridge University Press.

Meila, M., & Pentney, W. (2007). Clustering by weighted cuts in directed graphs. In *Proceedings of the SDM 07.*

Mika, P. (2005). Flink: Semantic Web technology for the extraction and analysis of social networks. *Journal of Web Semantics, 3*(2), 211–223. doi:10.1016/j.websem.2005.05.006

Millen, D. R., Fontaine, M. A., & Muller, M. J. (2002). Understanding the benefit and costs of communities of practice. *Communications of the ACM, 45*(4), 69–73. doi:10.1145/505248.505276

Nanopoulos, A., Theodoridis, Y., & Manolopoulos, Y. (2001). C2P: Clustering based on closest pairs. In *Proceedings of the 27th International Conference on Very Large Data Bases* (pp. 331-340).

Palloff, R. M., & Pratt, K. (1999). *Building learning communities in cyberspace*. San Francisco: Jossey-Bass Publishers.

Paolillo, J. C., & Wright, E. (2004). The challenges of FOAF characterization. In *Proceedings of the 1st Workshop on Friend of a Friend, Social Networking and the Semantic Web.*

Robey, D., Khoo, H. M., & Powers, C. (2000). Situated-learning in cross-functional virtual teams. *IEEE Transactions on Professional Communication, 43*(1), 51–66. doi:10.1109/47.826416

Rosenberg, M. J. (2001). *E-learning: Strategies for delivering knowledge in the digital age*. New York: McGraw-Hill.

Sabidussi, G. (1966). The centrality index of a graph. *Psychometrika, 31*, 581–603. doi:10.1007/BF02289527

Sheikholeslami, G., Chatterjee, S., & Zhang, A. (1998). WaveCluster - a multi-resolution clustering approach for very large spatial databases. In *Proceedings of the 24th VLDB conference* (pp. 428-439).

Wasserman, S., & Faust, K. (1994). *Social network analysis: Methods and applications*. Cambridge, UK: Cambridge University Press.

Zhang, T., Ramakrishnan, R., & Livny, M. (1996). BIRCH: An efficient data clustering method for very large databases. In *Proceedings of the 1996 ACM SIGMOD International Conference on Management of Data*, Montreal, Canada (pp. 103-114).

Zhang, W., & Storck, J. (2001). Peripheral members in online communities. In *Proceedings of the Americas Conference on Information Systems*, Boston, MA.

KEY TERMS AND DEFINITIONS

Community of Practice: refers to the process of social learning that occurs and shared social and cultural practices that emerge and evolve when people who have common goals interact as they strive towards those goals.

Clustering: clustering is an algorithmic concept where data points occur in bunches, rather than evenly spaced over their range. A data set which tends to bunch only in the middle is said to possess centrality. Data sets which bunch in several places do not possess centrality. What they do possess has not been very much studied, and there are no infallible methods for locating the describing more than one cluster in a data set (the problem is much worse when some of the clusters overlap)

Data Mining: is the process of autonomously extracting useful information or knowledge ("actionable assets") from large data stores or sets. Data mining can be performed on a variety of data stores, including the World Wide Web, relational databases, transactional databases, internal legacy systems, pdf documents, and data

Chapter 8

Live Virtual Technologies to Support Extended Events in Online Communities of Practice

Eleftheria Tomadaki
Knowledge Media Institute, The Open University, UK

Peter J. Scott
Knowledge Media Institute, The Open University, UK

Kevin A. Quick
Knowledge Media Institute, The Open University, UK

ABSTRACT

Online communities of practice often require support for collaboration over extended periods of time, in what are effectively very long meetings. While there are a wide range of support systems for 'foreground' interactions, such as phone calls and video meetings, and a similar range of tools for 'background' interactions, such as email and instant messaging, there is a lack in tools that exclusively cater for extended events without switching to different platforms. The current study presents qualitative and quantitative data from a naturalistic insight into the use of two online synchronous communication tools, FM for videoconference and Hexagon for ambient awareness, to support an extended event in a working online community. A complex mix of planned and opportunistic interactions require a new set of working synchronous tools, managing the trade-off between awareness and disruption. Switching between foreground and background 'meeting activity' remains a very big challenge.

INTRODUCTION

A wide variety of live communication tools are used by Technology-Enhanced Learning (TEL) communities of practice in order to meet and work virtually. These technologies generally provide a whole range of features, such as presence, availability and awareness, instant messaging, videoconferencing, ambient video awareness, collaborative tagging, social networking etc. Presence is an indispensable social software function, stimulating group awareness (Boyle & Greenberg, 2005; Chen & Gellersen, 1999) and the building of collective knowledge in online communities. Presence has evolved from just

DOI: 10.4018/978-1-60566-711-9.ch008

being 'online' or 'offline' to a range of preferences such as availability or geolocation. In instant messaging systems, a set of presence attributes may include time, context, availability, location, activity, state of mind and identity. Presence is currently plotted to geographical maps with tools, representing the individuals' presence with icons on maps. Geolocation can also be integrated in virtual learning environments and indicate presence and availability of contacts according to the courses a user may be enrolled on.

Along with presence, a great variety of tools supporting group interaction and location based social software applications make use of presence data for a wide variety of purposes, e.g. providing awareness of friends being in the vicinity or providing awareness of who is visiting online community sites, or recommending users with similar interests etc. Other social software features may involve activity awareness, indicating individual users' thoughts to a community, such as in Twitter, describing a current activity, a goal, or an achievement etc. Video presence is another feature increasingly found in desktop applications and can be integrated in ambient awareness tools, forming collaborative media spaces, or used in videoconferencing applications. It can be argued that collaborative spaces can be considered as a collective product and can be transformed through the use of technology (Dourish, P., 2006). Following Kreijns et al (2002) "social affordances encourage social interaction, which is responsible for establishing a social space". In Buxton (1992), *person space* is used to denote the sense of presence in videoconference participants who see each other's facial expressions and *task space* is used to denote copresence in task realisation.

Tasks and activities may be realised in the context of foreground or background attention (Buxton, 1992) and collaboration can be changed from a background activity to a foreground activity (Sire et al, 1999). Foreground presence indicates that users are interacting with the other users. In the context of background attention, social awareness

can run without any interactions, whilst being on the same shared space at the same time may cause the activity of meeting synchronously if needed (Sire et al, 1999), switching from background to foreground attention. However, when a background activity is switched into the foreground through a presence and collaboration tool in shared spaces, awareness changes and may be discussed along with issues of privacy interruption.

Online communities of practice need tools for social presence, group awareness and interaction that make their communication effective. Without such tools, the members of a community of practice lack the possibility to interact and construct knowledge collectively. Presence tools enhance the sense of community in a group, by making synchronous collaboration possible. Presence contributes to the social dimension in the collaboration of knowledge workers, and learning is not a lonely experience, but an activity that engages social skills together with the knowledge transfer. Collective activities can be improved when awareness tools are used in intense collaborative phases with community members working for a common task.

Interestingly, TEL communities of practice are usually supported by a range of tools providing ambient awareness for community building, instant messaging for quick opportunistic interactions and videoconferencing for pre-arranged meetings of an hour or so. However, these communities are often required to meet for days, in 'hot' collaborative phases. TEL community members can be engaged in 'extended' events, which can last many hours / days or even weeks or so and can include users 'dropping in' and 'out' of the workflow at many points. Most users may be involved in short, opportunistic interactions via text or video chat with other community members and may run applications on the background for community awareness for the rest of the time. A few other users may drop in the event for a short while to communicate with a specific person and then get back to their work. Extended events have an end when there was a communicative goal which was achieved.

Although there is still little research into synchronous tools supporting extended communicative events, a set of challenging questions derives from the choice of systems for online video communication. In this chapter, we focus on the following:

How can different synchronous tools support social presence and interaction patterns in online communities?

What are the parameters influencing the selection of the suitable application in extended meetings?

- Is the selection random, or opportunistic?
- How are the trade-offs between awareness and disruption in foreground and background communication channels managed?

Do we need to redesign synchronous tools or integrate existing tools to support extended online events?

The main objective of this study is to investigate the choice of tools employed by online communities in extended collaborative events, which require the use of a mixture of tools to support knowledge workers in their tasks and activities. This chapter discusses a case study of naturalistic interactions in an extended event held by an online community of practice in the context of collaborative proposal writing. We examine whether existing tools meet the users' requirements for such events and explore the possible need to redesign presence tools combining foreground and background communication channels, managing at the same time the trade-offs between awareness and privacy in shared media spaces. Even for the same event, it seems that users select a combination

of synchronous tools, depending on the context and nature of interaction. We discuss results from virtual ethnographic studies of two live online tools, FM for videoconferencing and Hexagon, initially designed for ambient video awareness, but evidently used successfully in a variety of contexts for extended meetings. In the extended meeting use, the FM and Hexagon participants all share the same project goals for a number of days, with a very specific outcome beyond any 'ambient' usage. We provide insights into the tools usage in one extended event and report on qualitative user feedback from questionnaires and interviews. It appears that the choice of the tool for extended meetings depends on a range of factors, such as event temporal duration (FM events with specific duration versus prolonged Hexagon events), communication purpose (make a quick decision, make a decision after longer discussions), social awareness need (reassurance that other community members are immediately contactable to help with questions or decision making) and interaction patterns between partners (audio/ video communication, private or public chat, file sharing, web tour etc.).

SYNCHRONOUS TOOLS TO SUPPORT EXTENDED EVENTS

A variety of synchronous and asynchronous tools may support online communities of practice. Email is currently the most popular computer-mediated communication form, running in the background, addressed to one or multiple receivers. Forums are another form of asynchronous communication intended for virtual communities. Synchronous communication involves the exchange of text chat messages, which can be done in parallel with other tasks (Isaacs et al, 2002), and ambient shared spaces, running in the background. Telephone and live videoconferencing are synchronous and considered as foreground communication channels (for a summary account of such online communication tools, see Weinberger & Mandl, 2003). All these tools can be used to support different kinds of concrete communicative events. However, none of these tools has been created with the view to support extended events. Communities of practice not only have formal meetings, but also work through an ambient presence, or via a combination of both. At the moment, not many applications can provide both formal and informal communication in virtual communities or assist in the switching between them. We discuss the use of videoconferencing and ambient video awareness over a detailed period of time by one technology-enhanced learning community (Scott et al, 2007b).

Video Meeting with FM

Videoconferencing was introduced with the first videophone by AT&T in the 60's and is now a well-established video-enhanced technology (Edigo C., 1988), with distinct eco-friendly benefits across various organisations, also saving traveling time and cost. Videoconferencing attendees usually participate in 'limited' events of a specific duration, with pre-agreed start and end times and a precise communicative goal, e.g. a teachers' meeting on students' progress reports. The FM tool (http://flashmeeting.open.ac.uk/) has been developed since June 2003 by the UK Open University as part of the FlashMeeting project. FM runs with the Adobe Flash player on the web-browser, requiring no additional software installation. A video meeting can last up to six hours and can include up to 25 attendees. The system generates a URL which can be clicked to gain access to the videoconference. The application provides a 'push-to-talk' audio system, allowing only one person to broadcast at any one time, while those who wish to talk, raise a symbolic hand and queue, waiting for their turn to come, or, alternatively, they can break in to a broadcast by using the 'interrupt' button. FM events can be recorded and syndicated. The FM system is currently used by

over 40 EU projects, several international school networks, and student and tutor communities worldwide. It initially aimed at producing a useful 'in house' communication and research tool but rapidly increased in usage throughout the world. Over 5,000 discrete events have been recorded in three years of experimental research.

Ambient Video Awareness with Hexagon

Ambient video awareness is a concept introduced in the 70's with NYNEX Portholes (Lee et al. 1997), supporting group awareness in distributed workers (Girgensohn et al, 1999), but there has been no major deployments of the technology that appear to have survived long-term (Scott et al, 2006). Issues of privacy, surveillance, reciprocity and gaze have been reported in previous literature as inhibiting factors regarding the use of the technology (Lee et al. 1997), while image filtering techniques have been previously used to alleviate privacy concerns (Gueddana & Roussel, 2006). Group awareness and availability checking is considered to be the major benefit in ambient video technologies (Boyle & Greenberg, 2005; Chen & Gellersen, 1999).

Hexagon is a simple applet running in a web page with the Adobe Flash browser plug-in, requiring no additional software installation. Hexagon users share live, personal webcam images, updated every 20 seconds on a grid of hexagons. Communication channels include group and private text chat and 'push-to-talk' audio. When two members are exchanging text messages, an animated envelope flies between the text chatting members. Hexagon provides a 'room-based' view of connected users. A webcam image appears as a hexagon, which can be moved around on the grid, and can be zoomed in and out. Users without a camera appear as a grey hexagon, while availability can also be expressed with individual status indicators. A range of communities have used the Hexagon technology at work or in learning and collaborative contexts for over three years. Workers situated in the same location use ambient cues to interact more effectively, e.g. to check their colleagues' availability. Students can interact with other students or tutors using the video for opportunistic learning interactions. The system was offered to various multinational enterprises, European research projects, UK-based organisations and educational institutes. The Hexagon server has hosted over 20 rooms since its launch. Most groups only meet in the context of specific events, with concrete communicative goals, after their initial trials. The tool is used on a daily basis by at least two of these communities for daily video presence and social networking and to enhance the sense of community for workers from remote locations, who interact with co-workers. The other communities may present some minor activity, such as summer school events and collaborative document authoring.

The Study

This study focuses on the research question of *how different tools can support social presence and interaction in online communities*, by discussing quantitative data logged on the Hexagon and FM servers. This data indicates the number and duration of user connections during one extended event in Hexagon, as well as visual representations of the user participation in broadcast and chat in time-limited events held via FM. A qualitative data analysis of synchronous chat in FM was conducted to refine the description of the meetings and measure social presence.

Qualitative feedback is used to provide insights into the research question of *what parameters affect the choice of tools for extended meetings*. A questionnaire circulated in September 2006 and completed by 20 members of one community, who have used Hexagon for at least 5 times and FM many more was supported by a set of 9 interviews. The interview feedback is used in this study to explore into issues regarding the choice of tools

supporting extended events, as well as views on the *trade-offs between awareness and privacy in foreground and background communication channels*.

The respondents' feedback, as well as their synchronous chat messages indicated that they used a rich mix of tools and technologies in support of their work and community engagement; email for asynchronous communication and file exchange, telephone for informal conversations, FM for formal meetings and Hexagon for ambient awareness and impromptu encounters. In this analysis, we will focus on the use of just these two tools as representing a primarily foreground communication channel and background channel respectively, to draw conclusions on whether *tools need to be redesigned or integrated in order to support extended events*.

The Community

We have selected to analyse a community which has held regular meetings for a long period of time and which includes members who use a range of online communication tools for their daily interaction regarding the writing of project deliverables and reports, or research proposals. This community was funded by the FP6 Network of Excellence Prolearn, which focused on innovative aspects of technology enhanced professional learning, with researchers from several European institutes in a variety of countries. The members used social presence and ambient awareness tools for events of varied duration, depending on the goals to be achieved. The co-authoring of a proposal for example might have taken weeks, while the organisation of an event could last a few hours.

The Prolearn community is composed of academics, researchers and PhD or post graduate students who have often used the FM tool for limited video meetings, while they have used Hexagon more rarely for longer events. During four years of activity on the FM server, the Pro-

Figure 1. Community events in the sample calendar year (Sep 2006 – Aug 2007)

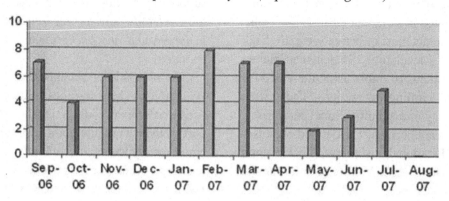

learn community booked 147 meetings including the word 'Prolearn' in their title, and many more events including other keywords related to the work-packages and deliverables' names, virtual seminars and interviews by over 30 bookers. A broader view of the community activity can be seen in Figure 1, showing the total number of events (61) hosted at the server each month during the calendar year (Sep 06 – Aug 07).

While the mean average is 5 meetings per month, February demonstrates the highest activity with 8 events attended. No meetings took place in August due to the summer break when the users tend to be on holiday, but the community continued conducting meetings from September 2007 onwards. The members regularly held a number of meetings every month, either moderated by one member, or peer-to-peer driven.

The community activities can include collaborative writing of reports, deliverables, proposals, organisation of conference events, seminars, summer schools, interviews and others. To undertake these activities, the members needed synchronous tools to satisfy the following communicative needs:

- One-to-one communication
- One-to-many communication
- Ambient awareness
- Interactive shared spaces (e.g. whiteboard)

- Text chat communication
- Audiovisual communication

The tools used by the community appear to support effectively arranged meetings or impromptu encounters in ambient spaces. However, it seems that there is still room for improvement in supporting effectively extended events, such as the writing of a project deliverable report or a research project proposal.

Anatomy of a Sample Extended Event

In this section, we synthesise findings from our analyses in a series of video meetings with FM and the use of ambient awareness with Hexagon in the context of one extended event of nearly one-month duration. These results give some insights into how tools are selected for extended events and how social presence and interaction are supported by different applications.

Members of the Prolearn community have formed sub-communities of (relatively) short duration around specific events. Here we consider one 'natural' extended event of such a sub-community in some detail. The event included 10 main participants from different European countries and lasted nearly a month with the main goal of writing a proposal for a European research grant. The

Figure 2. Arranged video meetings during the course of the extended event

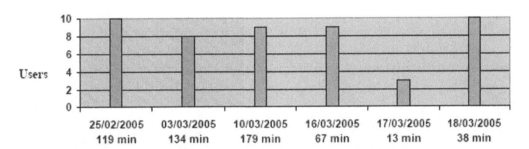

extended event started with a series of emails and an opening formal meeting held via FM on 25th February 2005 with 10 videoconferencing attendees and ended on the 23rd March with 2 simultaneous user connections in the Prolearn Hexagon room.

Arranged Meetings

This sub-community of members arranged a series of 6 FM events (Figure 2) with an overall duration of over 5 hours, while the mean average time of these events is nearly 53 min. The FM events were booked by two different users using in the title the name of the proposal. The first event was conducted at the start of this extended period 14:30 GMT on the 16th at which the use of the Hexagon system for a longer-period interaction was discussed. The first 3 FM events lasted more than 2 hours, as the participants had, at that point, many issues to resolve, such as task distribution. The fourth of these events was the shortest FM meeting of 13-minute duration and included 3 participants. While all other events were called 'meetings', the shortest one was called 'instantFM', denoting its limited duration. The final video meeting was held on Friday, 18th March, and lasted only 38 minutes, possibly because most issues were resolved by that time. The first and last events included the same 10 attendees.

In order to examine the interaction patterns in these meetings, we present visualisations of the user participation in the broadcast and text chat channels. The broadcast and text chat dominance of certain users is represented in the polar area diagrams in Figure 3. The meetings were usually moderated by one person, whilst everyone contributed their opinion in broadcast and text chat. The diagrams on the left hand side represent the air time taken by different users portrayed with different numbers (circumference = duration of broadcasts, while radius = turns taken). The diagrams on the right hand side show the text chat dominance again distributed to different users portrayed with different numbers (circumference = number of characters typed, while radius = number of messages sent) (Scott et al, 2007a). The community members participating in the events have been anonymised.

In four out of six of the following video meetings, the most dominant participant in the broadcast is the moderator who also booked the meetings and is the same person in all four events (event 1 – user 15, event 2 – user 7, event 3 – user 7 and event 6 – user 5). This community member distributes work amongst partners and makes sure that the meeting goals are met by discussing each of the proposed workpackages. The text chat is equally spread amongst all participants. Event 5 was booked by a different community member and the person who moderated the

Figure 3. The shapes of broadcast and chat dominance in the video meetings

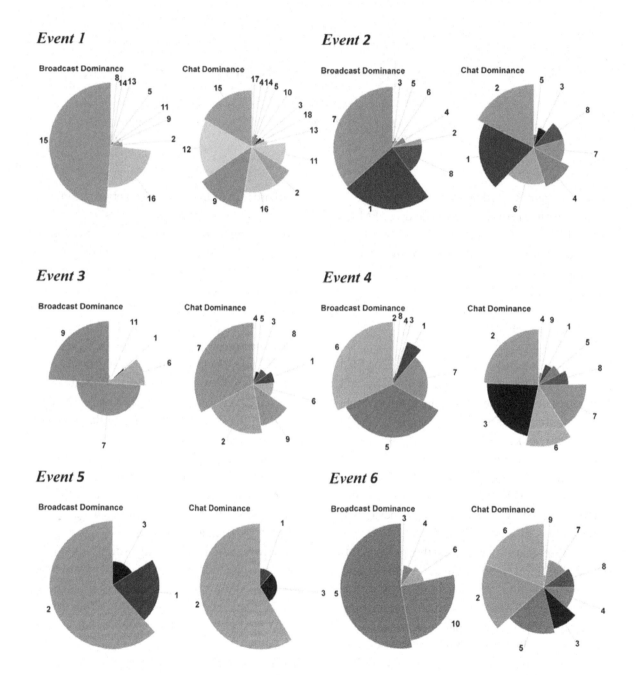

previous meetings did not participate. Interestingly, in event 5 the most dominant participant (user 2) in both text chat and broadcast is also the meeting booker.

The broadcast diagrams show that participation depends on the user role, e.g. moderator or participant. The moderator dominates the broadcast channel, by leading the discussion and answering questions. The other attendees present actual work in the text chat, asking or replying to questions and providing URLs to the rest of the group. A high number of broadcasts with shorter duration may indicate that users ask a question and then wait for an answer by the interlocutors. No lurkers were detected in this set of meetings, showing that everyone contributes in the process of knowledge exchange, although not all attendees share equal dominance in the communication channels. A high number of text chat messages and characters may represent members who prefer doing work using the background communication channels, or use the text chat due to the broadcast dominance of other characters, or in order not to interrupt them. It may simply be that other reasons (e.g. lack of webcam or microphone) are the only way to communicate their thoughts to the group..

While the broadcast is mostly dominated by a moderator who manages the discussion, the text chat appears to be more interactive as it is spread amongst the group. We have attempted to refine the description of the meetings, presenting a qualitative data analysis of the six FM text chat transcripts. Following Rourke et al (1999), we measure the *social presence density* in synchronous text chat held via the text chat communication channel. Six FM text chat transcripts totaling 5,782 words were analysed, applying the model presented in Rourke et al (1999). We identified the following:

- *Interactive* responses by posting messages to the chat referring either to other messages in the text chat or in other cases to the speaker in the video. These responses include interchanged segments referring to the following acts: *agree, ask, reply, refer to* and *compliment*.

- *Affective* responses, showing emotional presence with the *use of emoticons, jokes,* and *self disclosure* instances expressing emotion.

- *Cohesive* responses denoting group cohesion and a sense of community, including the words "we", "our", "us", expressions performing social tasks (phatics), vocatives (calling the participants with their names, and salutations.

Applying the model in Rourke et al (1999) on synchronous text chat data is challenging, as the model was originally designed based on asynchronous messages. Moreover, both tools discussed here provide text chat as a parallel communication channel to the audiovisual channel. In FM, the attention was switched to use the background communication channel, when users experienced slow connection problems, while it has been used as the main output channel for several participants who ask or reply to questions of the speaker in the video. We have thus adapted the model identifying in our set of data as *interactive responses*, the text chat instances that *reply to* what is asked in a previous text chat message but also in the video broadcast. Similarly, interactive responses include instances explicitly or implicitly *referring to* a previous text chat message, to a live video and audio broadcast or to the regularly updated video thumbnails of participants. Additionally, in several instances in the FM text chat, the participants were *referring to* the tool communication, commenting on the uses of ambient tools and which one to select to continue their communication during the following hours. Table 1 shows examples of FM text chat for each category of responses.

An agreement of 0.9 was reached in coding the FM data, between two anonymous annotators who were discussing their results during the process and agreed on conventions of annotating responsive references to text chat, as well as to broadcast.

Table 1. Interactive, affective and cohesive responses in the FM chat

Affective	Expression of emotion		":-)"
	Humour		"Silence is always worrying for us ;-)"
	Self disclosure		"I don't like closing the meeting like that"
Interactive	Asking questions		"What time?"
	Replying to	Questions asked in the text chat	"3.30"
		Questions asked in the video	"no problem"
	Referring to	Previous text chat message	"so this is all the data"
		Video	"I just got the document"
		Thumbnail	"It looks like you had an accident"
		Tool communication	"We will use Hexagon"
	Compliment		"Very good! This is important"
	Express agreement		"I agree"
Cohesive	Group sense		"We should write that down"
	Phatics		"Nice weather also"
	Salutations		"hi"
	Vocatives		"hi Peter"

Annotating FM text chat transcripts required also watching the video meeting to decide whether several text chat messages referred to something that was said in the broadcast or to the video thumbnails of participants. The coders agreed in most instances of affective and cohesive responses, as the identification of emoticons, phatics, salutations and group sense was straightforward, except for a few instances of self-disclosure.

The six FM transcripts are included in the same extended event and thus we consider them as one corpus of merged scripts. The *social presence density* is calculated according to the number of raw social presence instances detected for each sub-category of social presence indicators (Group, Humour, Phatic, Salutation, Vocatives, Agree, Ask, Compliment, Refer to, Reply, Emotion, Self disclosure) divided to the number of total words in all six transcripts. The total number of indicator's instances is the aggregate of instances for each subcategory in all six scripts and the total number of words is 5,782 words which is the total number of words of the corpus of the six FM transcripts:

$$\text{Social presence density} = \frac{\text{total num of indicator's instances}}{\text{total number of words}}$$

According to the method in Rourke et al (1999), as the values of the resulting numbers are very small, we multiplied the social presence density figure by 1,000, which represents a unit of incidents per 1,000 words. Figure 4 shows the categories and the number of raw instances of coded segments expressing cohesive, interactive and affective responses.

The instances expressing interactive responses of agreeing, asking and referring to are the most frequent, whilst cohesive responses such as addressing the group and affective responses such as emotional expressions were also frequent. The social presence indicators accompany the tasks and activities realised by the community. Usually participants ask and reply to questions related to the work load and task sharing, and agree on what has been accomplished in the writing and the future goals set in the meeting. The group is

Figure 4. Social presence density in the FM text chat

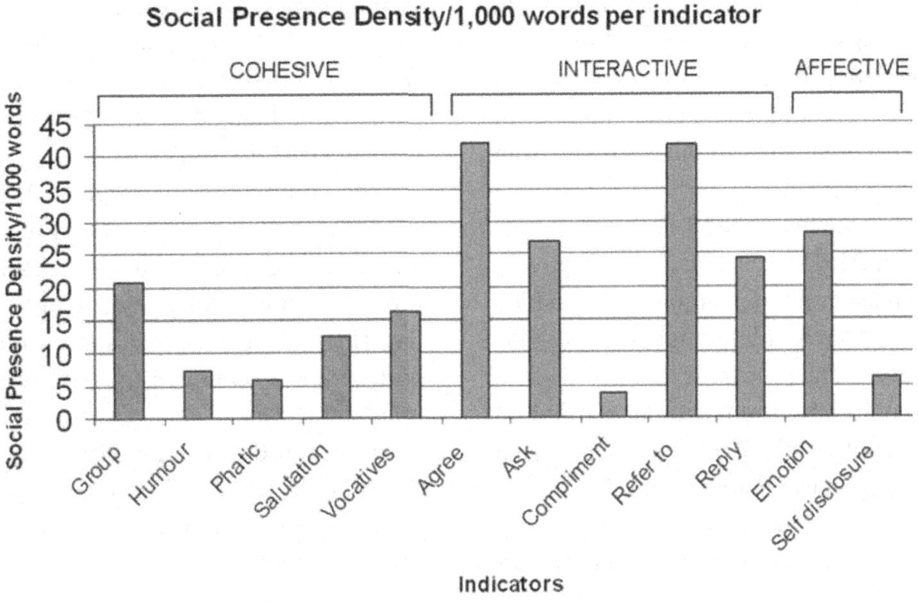

Social Presence Density/1,000 words per indicator

Indicators

addressed on several occasions when tasks are discussed. Emoticons are quite frequently used by most participants after a joke or to denote emotion towards a tight deadline.

The next step in the analysis was to calculate the aggregate social presence. If p_x is the social presence density of each indicator where $x=1,...,12$ then the aggregate social presence density results from the following equation:

$$\text{Aggregate social presence density} = p_1 + p_2 + ... + p_{12}$$

The aggregate social presence density of the six transcripts is *235.034*. This number is up to ten times higher than the number of social presence density found in studies of asynchronous text chat (Rourke et al, 1999). This is due to the nature of synchronous communication in text chat, which differs from text chat messages in an asynchronous forum. The synchronous text chat messages studied here are short in length, when compared to asynchronous messages in forums. The FM text chat runs in parallel with

the video communication channel, thus a high number of interactive responses are identified, as those instances may not only refer to something said in previous text chat messages, or in the live video or audio, but also to other media, such as an image thumbnail. Questions and replies also express interaction and are frequent as they can be asked and answered in a short time period; they are a medium of achieving intellectual goals, or making an important decision via the synchronous communication. The high number of affective responses, such as expressions of emotion and cohesive responses, for example addressing the group, indicates a sense of community.

Ambient Awareness

When the formal events stopped on the 18th March, users continued to communicate via Hexagon as the workflow required the 'bid document' to be finally 'tweaked' and finalised. At this stage, the community members selected neither to use FM anymore nor arrange meetings, switching in this way to ambient awareness. Interestingly, the community members were discussing the use of Hexagon and other ambient awareness tools in the FM meetings to decide on a tool that they could all use after the end of the arranged FM event. Figure 5 shows the maximum number of connected Hexagon users in this scenario from 14th-27th March 2005.

As shown in the figure, the 8-day working period from 16th-23rd March 2005, was effectively a single extended event for this community which peaked on 17th March with 11 simultaneous working connections. The event was initiated with an uninterrupted 40-hour room activity starting on Wednesday (16th March) of that week. On the first 3 days of Hexagon use, 3 foreground FM events took place, one informal amongst 3 individuals and the other two including the main participants

(the "stars" in Figure 5 represent the FM video meetings running in parallel with the Hexagon usage). It should be noted that the times in the figure are listed as the server time (GMT), while participants situated in different parts of Europe were in GMT +1 or +2.

The community interrogated for this study used Hexagon to display activity in sending text messages, and audio chats. After this intensive 2-day (40 hours long) engagement - the next day (Friday) represented some minor activity with people dropping in and out and a maximum number of 3 users connected at the same time. Interestingly, during the next two days - Saturday and Sunday, from 8.00-24.00, many more users connected to the room, reaching 10 simultaneous users on Sunday, indicating intensive weekend

Figure 5. Hexagon connected users during sample (14th - 27th March 2005)

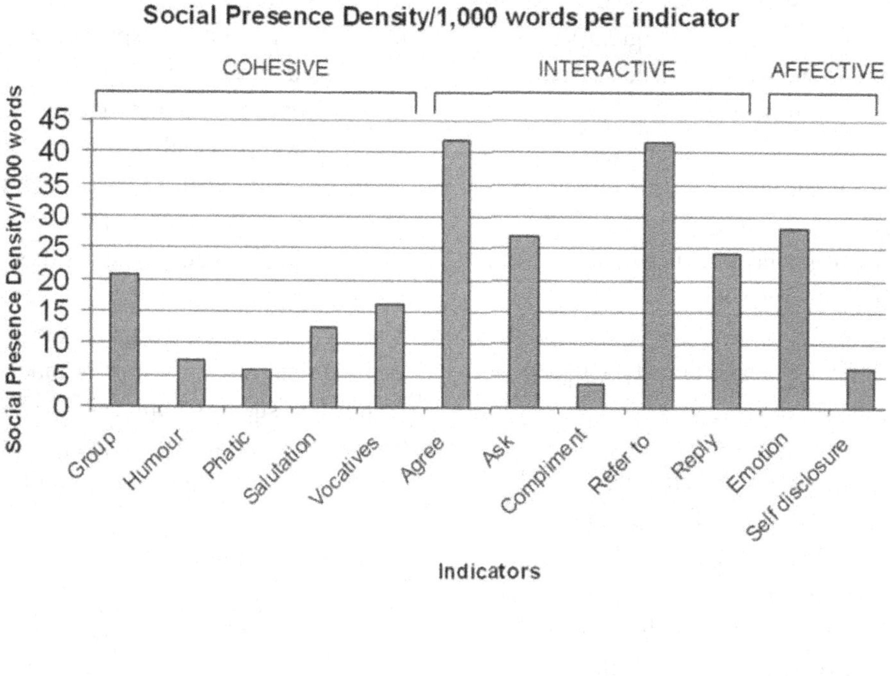

Social Presence Density/1,000 words per indicator

Figure. 6. A (Hexagon) grid of (8 participants)

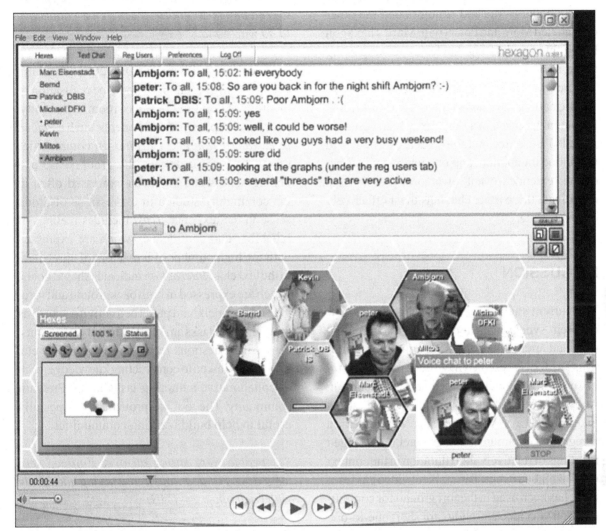

activity for this extended event. On Monday and Tuesday the room was 'empty' after 18.00. On the last day of the proposal work, 5 different users entered the room, with a maximum of 2 users connected simultaneously. Approximately 100 hours of overall room activity has been recorded during that period, including at least one connection. During that week, 12 different individuals were entering the room at different times, while 2 of them were in the room for a limited time and for a specific purpose, e.g. to help with part of the proposal or to provide technical facilitation.

In Figure 6, a Hexagon room screenshot during this period, shows eight participants at work in this community, communicating synchronously via private or group text chat, and audio chat, whilst participating in the concerted writing of the project proposal. The communication channels provided in Hexagon are used in different ways. While the video channel, which is continuously open, is used for group awareness, a piece of information relating to the overall proposal can be communicated via group chat, visible by everyone, and pairs of two can collaborate via audio chat. The Hexagon view displays two audio chats taking place at this time, one including users labeled Bernd and Ambjörn and the other one labeled Marc and Peter (with Marc's hexagon highlighted, indicating that he is speaking using audio at that moment).

The text chat area shows 7 group messages related to participants' tasks for the proposal writing. Hexagon was used in a rich mix, which certainly included other technologies such as email and telephone interaction, and one interesting aspect of the 'extended event' awareness was to help coordinate these other channels most effectively over this time.

DISCUSSION

The current study gives some insights into how different synchronous tools support social presence and interaction patterns in online communities. The tools presented have been proved useful in supporting social presence and interaction in working groups of short life for extended events in different ways. Video meetings were used as a foreground communication channel for arranged meetings of relatively short duration in the context of an extended event. The ambient video environment has been used in the foreground for communication via video and audio, for short one-to-one audio interactions or group messages, but most of the times it was running as an ambient presence in the background. While video meetings were a pre-arranged sub-event within the extended event, participants selected the ambient environment for opportunistic interactions, which allowed at the same time to be concentrated at their work and be able to communicate with peers for a short while, to ask or answer questions related to work. The work undertaken is seen by all respondents as a very valuable and positive experience.

"We used it to write collaboratively a proposal, we discussed the documents we were working on, told each other when to expect the new versions

of the portfolios, which meant that we didn't have to send things around, as much as we would have to do with e-mail" (AN)

According to Rovai's theory (2002), the sense of community is enhanced upon the realisation of the information flow in a classroom community, which is composed of components, such as *spirit*, *trust*, *interaction* and *learning*. In communities of practice, *spirit* defines the group sense and belongingness and has been expressed often in the community studied in expressions of group sense in the text chat. *Trust* includes feelings of reliability and confidence, which are expressed with the high number of indicators of agreement in the text chat. *Interaction* indicates shared goals, which are expressed in both background and foreground channels, and patterned activities, such as the delivery of tasks amongst different participants, answering questions related to deliverables etc. *Learning* is linked to constructing knowledge, such as collaborative authoring tasks in the Prolearn community. The tool has proven to be especially useful to help build working communities.

"... people were sitting all over Europe, were logged into Hexagon and were working intensively with each other ..." (MH)

It appears that community members select which tools to use in extended events, according to the goals to be achieved, for example if there is an agenda of specific tasks to be accomplished, arranged video meetings are more appropriate. Nevertheless, in the final and intensive phases of writing proposals, when all tasks were distributed and members had to complete the proposal, ambient video awareness was more suitable. While some participants were involved in one-to-one chats, others just used Hexagon as background awareness, not exchanging messages, but still able to read others' messages and have a view of their working community. In this way, the community was able to handle the intensive workflow of the proposal writing and discussion around it in an effective public forum, and manage their other work in the context of this community effort.

"... it helped just to know who was there in these final days of working hard to get it finished on time, it was really helpful to see who was there, say how is it going, do you need any help, are you OK with what's in this document etc. ... when it comes to the final stage when time is getting short and we have to interact in a very short time basis and synchronously sometimes, then it is really valuable" (AN)

It must be noted, however, background interactions can dynamically change the workflow when they become foreground activities and disrupt the user's attention. The selection of a communication tool relates also to the privacy concerns arising from its usage, such as being in control of what is being transmitted and minimise interruptions triggered by the 'main-channel' interactions. As there is a trade off between awareness and privacy, and between awareness and disturbance (Hudson & Smith, 1996), managing disruption in the 'backchannels' is quite challenging (Kellogg et al, 2006).

For me it is too intrusive, that's why I stopped using it after the starting try out, I don't really like to be captured on video without me being in control of what is being transmitted or not. (MW)

... that has to do with somebody's vision of how people are supposed to work. I have often the impression that as soon as you see someone looking not really busy, sitting at their desk, it looks like they're not working actually, so that might be one of the reasons why people would not feel comfortable if they are permanently on camera. (MH)

It seems that users have different privacy issues when it comes to video enhanced communication tools. These may relate to the temporal length of the event and to the communicative goal, expected to be achieved by the event. Events with an end and start and with a specific topic to be discussed, are less likely to make participants think for self presentation issues, as they are engaged in the social event.

If you use hexagon, you need a specific topic and a specific sort of time frame where you work intensively with each other... If you don't have anything specific to discuss, then you would rather send an e-mail or you would sort of use the phone (MH)

The interviewees' feedback indicates that an ambient video awareness environment, providing instant messaging and audio chatting, works well for extended meetings with a specific purpose and temporal duration, and when the communicative model is made obvious to the users beforehand.

We really told them Tuesday evening at 8 you will be online with this tool, with this passport and we will chat synchronously about this topic. This worked because they had a clear goal. (MC)

In the context of an extended event held by a community with common and specified goals, privacy issues did not occur. Participants reported that seeing their colleagues working via Hexagon denoted their availability, allowing the immediate communication with them if needed.

"It was very convenient to be in a Hexagon room and checking who's sitting in front of his desk and sort of ask him a question without needing to phone somebody up or sending him an e-mail" (MH)

The selection of tools may depend on parameters such as the event temporal duration, and the communicative goals expected to be fulfilled during its course. During an extended event, a range of trade-offs may take place, including formal and informal, explicit or ambient interactions in no specific order. There is a lack in appropriate synchronous tools to support such unusual patterns, avoiding at the same time the disruption of the workflow, by leveraging the use of foreground and background channels.

Finally, this study clearly indicates a need for a better model of how to effectively combine communication channels, such as multi-party videoconferencing, video presence, instant messaging and audio chat, that together may form an appropriate collaborative virtual space for community members, managing the challenging switch between foreground and background communication.

CONCLUSION

The concept of an extended event is introduced here as a challenging scenario which requires a set of tools to allow for multi-party, prolonged and multi-channeled communication. Online communities of practice often participate in such events driven by activities such as collaborative proposal writing. However, there are no platforms integrating the features that can effectively support the activities held in the context of these events. Due to the lack of such platforms, different tools are used in different phases of extended events.

The community studied uses the combination of the audiovisual channel as the foreground communication medium and the text chat channel as the background communication medium in pre-arranged meetings or opportunistic communicative events resulting from ambient awareness interactions. The audiovisual channel has been dominated by a moderator in arranged meetings and was also used for impromptu one-to-one interactions. The qualitative analysis of the text chat has shown that the community members used the

text chat channel effectively in interactions related to work as well as to denote social presence and enhance their group sense. The text chat favoured multi-party communication in both videoconference and video awareness applications, allowing everyone to communicate anytime without interrupting the speaker's flow.

The selection of synchronous tools is not random. It is identified by the needs of the group at different temporal points during the course of the event. The group meets in a pre-arranged setting with a moderator who ensures that work is delivered on time. Once tasks are assigned, all participants go back to work, running ambient awareness applications to be able to communicate with peers in case they need to ask a question or make a quick decision, but without interrupting their workflow for longer periods as they would in a videoconference. Every time the users have to decide what to select for their prolonged collaboration, whilst each time they may use a different tool or a combination of tools.

Awareness and disruption trade-offs were not a main issue in the current context of an extended event. This is due to the goal driven nature of the event, with shared tasks that need to be accomplished in a short time periods with group collaboration. The well-defined goals and duration of the collaboration can lower the barriers for acceptability of background communication systems. In extended events, users need to be in continuous contact either using pre-defined meetings or ambient awareness to collaborate with their colleagues or make a decision, without considering this sort of communication intrusive regarding their privacy.

The main inconvenience of using a set of tools to support extended events was that the users had to switch from one tool to another. When for example a videoconference event was reaching its end, participants were discussing the use of another tool to continue working together, not necessarily in the context of a set meeting. On other occasions, users were discussing the experience

Table 2. An integrated solution with features for any communication scenario

	Planned meetings	*Impromptu encounters*	*Extended events*
One-to-one communication	√	√	√
One-to-many communication	√	√	√
Ambient awareness	-	√	√
Interactive shared spaces	√	-	√
Text chat	√	√	√
Audiovisual communication	√	√	√

they previously had on Hexagon or other tools in the context of the extended events. Moreover, different tools offer different features. For example, multi-party communication and shared whiteboard do not feature in Hexagon, while FM cannot be employed for ambient awareness.

FUTURE TRENDS

Users learn how to use different synchronous tools in order to communicate and collaborate more effectively in extended events. In this perspective, a methodology depending on the community goals, tasks, activities and temporal duration of communication can be suggested for the selection of the appropriate application. Nevertheless, the effort made in being trained to use different tools and managing the switch from one application to another can be time-consuming.

The next step is to redesign tools which can support extended events in arranging video meetings with specific goals, as well as opportunistic interactions of multiple participants in one single platform. An integrated solution should include features to support scenarios of pre-arranged meetings, impromptu encounters as well as extended events.

ACKNOWLEDGMENT

This research is supported by the EU 6th Framework Network of Excellence in Professional Learning – Prolearn. The authors would like to acknowledge the contribution of Jon Linney to the design and implementation of the Hexagon and FM systems. We finally thank Michael Aristotelidis for his invaluable feedback regarding the text chat analysis.

REFERENCES

Boyle, M., & Greenberg, S. (2005). The language of privacy: Learning from video media space analysis and design. *Journal of ACM Transactions on Human Computer Interaction, 12*(2), 328–370. doi:10.1145/1067860.1067868

Buxton, W. (1992). Telepresence: Integrating shared task and person spaces. In R. Baecker (Ed.), *Readings in groupware and computer-supported cooperative work* (pp. 816-822). San Francisco: Morgan Kaufman.

Chen, D., & Gellersen, H. W. (1999). Recognition and reasoning in an awareness support system for generation of storyboard-like views of recent activity. In *Proceedings of the International SIG-GROUP Conference on Supporting Group Work*, Phoenix, AZ.

Dourish, P. (2006). Re-space-ing place: "Place" and "space" ten years on. In *Proceedings of the ACM conference on Computer-supported cooperative work*, Banff, Canada, Edigo, C. (1988). Videoconferencing as a technology to support group work: A review of its failure. In *Proceedings of the ACM conf. on Computer-Supported Cooperative Work*.

Girgensohn, A., Lee, A., & Turner, T. (1999). Being in public and reciprocity: Design for portholes and user preference. In [Amsterdam, The Netherlands: IOS Press.]. *Proceedings of the Human-Computer Interaction INTERACT, 99*, 458–465.

Gueddana, S., & Roussel, N. (2006). Pêle-Mêle, a video communication system supporting a variable degree of engagement. In *Proceedings of the ACM conference on Computer Supported cooperative work*, Banff, Alberta, Canada.

Hudson, S. E., & Smith, I. (1996). Techniques for addressing fundamental privacy and disruption tradeoffs in awareness support systems. In *Proceedings of the ACM Conference on Computer-Supported Cooperative Work*, Cambridge MA, USA.

Isaacs, E., Walendowski, A., Whittaker, S., Schiano, D. J., & Kamm, C. (2002). The character, functions and styles of instant messaging in the workplace. In *Proceedings of the ACM CSCW*, New Orleans, Louisiana, USA.

Kellogg, W., Erickson, T., Vetting Wolf, T., Leevy, S., Christensen, J., Sussman, J., & Bennett, W. E. (2006). Leveraging Digital bakchannels to enhance user experience in electronically mediated communication. In *Proceedings of the ACM CSCW*, Banff, Alberta, Canada.

Kreijns, K., Kirschner, P., & Jochems, W. (2002). The sociability of computer-supported collaborative learning environments. *Educational Technology & Society, 5*(1), 8–22.

Lee, A., Girgensohn, A., & Schlueter, K. (1997). NYNEX portholes: Initial user reactions and redesign implications. In *Proceedings of the International ACM SIGGROUP Conference on Supporting Group Work*, New York, (pp. 385-394).

Rourke, L., Anderson, T., Garrison, D. R., & Archer, W. (1999). Assessing social presence in asynchronous text-based computer conferencing. *The Journal of Distance Education / Revue de l'Education à Distance, 14*(2), 50-71.

Scott, P. J., Quick, K. A., Tomadaki, E., & Linney, J. (2006). Ambient video awareness: It's great, but i still don't want it. In E. Tomadaki & P. Scott (Eds.), *Proceedings of the innovative approaches for learning and knowledge sharing, EC-TEL Workshops* (pp. 207- 214).

Scott, P. J., Tomadaki, E., & Quick, K. A. (2007). Using live virtual technologies to support communities of practice: The impact of extended events. In *Proceedings of the EC-TEL Workshop on Technology-Enhanced Learning Communities of Practice*.

Scott, P. J., Tomadaki, E., & Quick, K. A.(2007). The shape of live online meetings. *International Journal of Technology, Knowledge and Society, 3*.

Sire, S., Chatty, S., Gaspard Boulinc, H., & Colin, F.-R. (1999). How can groupware preserve our coordination skills? Designing for direct collaboration. In A. Sasse * C. Johnson (Eds.), *Proceedings of the Human-Computer Interaction - INTERACT'99*. Amsterdam, The Netherlands: IOS Press.

Weinberger, A., & Mandl, H. (2003). *Computer-mediated knowledge communication* (Research Rep.). Institute for Empirical Pedagogy and Pedagogical Psychology, University of Munich.

Chapter 9
Individual Learning and Emotional Characteristics in Web–based Communities of Practice

Nikos Tsianos
National & Kapodistrian University of Athens, Greece

Zacharias Lekkas
National & Kapodistrian University of Athens, Greece

Panagiotis Germanakos
University of Cyprus, Cyprus

Constantinos Mourlas
National & Kapodistrian University of Athens, Greece

ABSTRACT

The knowledge management paradigm of communities of practice can be efficiently realized in Web-based environments, especially if one considers the extended social networks that have proliferated within the Internet. In terms of increasing performance through the exchange of knowledge and shared learning, individual characteristics, such as learners' preferences that relate to group working, may be of high importance. These preferences have been summarized in cognitive and learning styles typologies, as well as emotional characteristics which define implications that could serve as personalization guidelines for designing collaborative learning environments. This chapter discusses the theoretical assumptions of two distinct families of learning style models, cognitive personality and information processing styles (according to Curry's onion model), and the role of affection and emotion, in order to explore the possibilities of personalization at the group level of CoP.

DOI: 10.4018/978-1-60566-711-9.ch009

INTRODUCTION

Traditionally, the social aspect of learning from a psychometric point of view has been correlated to personality traits. For example, a widely used personality psychometric tool is the Myers Briggs Type Indicator (MBTI) classification of types (Myers-Briggs et al, 1998), that separates the way people perceive and learn in mutually exclusive preferences that involve (or not) social interaction (specifically, orientation to people: Feeling vs. Thinking types).

Moreover, major factor analysis approaches to personality (Feist and Feist, 2006) refer to extraverted and introverted persons, whose behavior is more or less socially oriented, with consequent effects to group dynamics. It must be stated that this extraversion-introversion scale is not the equivalent to MBTI extraverted/ introverted types, which are derived from the work of C.G. Jung and refer to the conceptualization of the outer world.

However, personality traits and their integration in an adaptive mechanism might seem rather vague in terms of quantifying and optimizing possible implications; still, the role of social interaction in learning has already been summarized in a number of cognitive and learning style theories, providing a useful personalization guideline for Web-based CoP designers.

The term Communities of Practice obviously emphasizes on collaborative learning processes that are conducted horizontally within groups of people. The three elements that comprise a Cop are (Wenger, 1998):

- Domain – the area of knowledge
- Community – the group of people
- Practice – body of knowledge, methods and tools

The concept of incorporating individual characteristics in the context of a Web-based environment could fit both in the Community and Practice elements, since:

- The usage of adaptive tools and methods (Practice element) can increase the level of comprehension by matching the learning material to the cognitive and emotional style of the learner, or by providing different types of knowledge resources to groups of participants with common cognitive and emotional characteristics.
- Collaborative learning processes can be optimized by assigning equally distributed different types of individuals in groups. Such an allocation would increase the number of problem solving approaches, since different types of learners approach problems in distinct ways (e.g. rely on others or work alone, theoretical vs. practical etc).

At the generic level of learning, Web-based environments need to integrate individual and group characteristics in order to facilitate effective learning for every single user. It has been argued that the distribution of learning material in ways that match learners' ways of processing information is of high importance, since it "can lead to new insights into the learning process" (Banner and Rayner, 2000). Regarding these individual differences, there have been many attempts to clarify cognitive and learning parameters that correlate to the effectiveness of learning procedures, often leading to comprehensive theories of learning or cognitive styles (Cassidy, 2004).

Amongst these theories, some deal with the most intrinsic individual cognitive characteristics, such as Riding's CSA (Rayner and Riding, 1997) or Witkin's Field Dependence (Witkin et al, 1977), whilst some also take into account group interrelationship characteristics, such as Kolb's Learning Style Inventory (Kolb and Kolb, 2005) or Felder/Silverman's Index of Learning Style (Felder and Silverman, 1988), regardless of their theoretical classification. As a result, the selection of the appropriate cognitive or learning style theory to be integrated in a Web-based application should be in accordance to the context or the goals of each environment, and of course the availability of between learners' interactions.

Communities of Practice are essentially based on participants' interactions and socializations (Wenger, 2004), which subsequently seem to favor personalization on the basis of a theory that emphasizes on the social aspect of learning. In any case, an effort to personalize the way an individual learns through a Web-based CoP environment could follow three distinct approaches:

a. By incorporating a theory such as Kolb's LSI, different types of learners that have a different approach in problem solving could be equally distributed in Web-based CoPs, in order to avoid the possibility of one-sided approaches to the building of knowledge. Thus, this leads to personalization at the group level, since the CoP Web-environment allocates users according to their profile.

b. By choosing a more individually focused theory (e.g. CSA), application designers could offer to users learning material that matches their cognitive preferences; at a second level, the exchange of similar material between same types of learners could be enhanced. It could also be hypothesized that interactions between same types may increase comprehension or performance, which is the case of i Help (Bull and McCalla, 2002).

c. By taking into consideration the affective and emotional attributes of all the community members in a way that a further adaptation to the individual characteristics and to the community behavioral style can be achieved. In order to make this possible, team dynamics and intra-group interaction principles must be examined, as well as the emotional intelligence and emotional regulation mechanisms of the individual must be analyzed and adapted to the whole.

The issue of personalizing content for each single user has already been under the scope of Adaptive Hypermedia research, and relevant functional applications have been developed (Papanikolaou et al, 2003; Gilbert and Han, 1999; Carver et al, 1999; Triantafillou et al, 2002), while the significance of cognitive/ learning styles, emotional mechanisms and intrinsic individual parameters in hypermedia environments constitutes a main research question (Germanakos et al, 2005; Graff, 2003, Lekkas et al, 2007). The authors have already conducted experiments that demonstrate that matching Web-based learning environment to a number of cognitive and emotional characteristics increases learning performance (Germanakos et al, 2007).

On the basis of Adaptive Hypermedia, cognitive/learning styles research and emotional processing mechanisms analysis, this paper examines how these theories describe distinct ways in which individuals could fit in collaborative working groups, setting a corresponding strategic context for personalized participation in Web-based CoPs.

One of the main challenges in Personalization research is alleviating users' orientation difficulties, as well as making appropriate selection of knowledge resources, since the vastness of the hyperspace has made information retrieval a rather complicated task. By personalizing Web-based content, taking into account emotional processing, we can avoid stressful instances and take full advantage of his / hers cognitive capacity at any time. We primarily aim to ground our hypothesis that personalizing Web content according to the participants' emotional characteristics (an individual's capability or incapability to control his / hers emotions and use anxiety in a constructing way), is of high significance in optimizing computer mediated learning processes.

Table 1. Classifications of Learning Style Theories according to Curry's onion model

Cognitive Personality Style	Information Processing Style	Instructional Preferences
Witkin's FD/FI	Kolb's LSI	Dunn & Dunn Model
Riding & Rayner's CSA	Honey & Mumford Model	
MBTI	Gardner's Multiple Intelligences	
Felder & Silverman ILS	McCarthy's 4MAT model	
	Gregorc's Learning Style Types	

THEORETICAL BACKGROUND

Learning Styles

The hypothesis that learning styles provide Web-CoP designers a useful tool for incorporating individual and group characteristics can be supported by the argument that as implied above learning styles are a link between cognition and personality (Sternberg and Grigorenko, 1997). It is a fact that it would be extremely ambitious to construct a model of users or groups that involve numerous personality and cognitive traits combined together, not to mention the psychometric challenges; therefore, learning style typologies could be the "next best thing". Learning styles, on the other hand, are widely varied, and some of them fail to exhibit satisfactory reliability and validity (Markham, 2004). However, as research often demonstrates, learning style is an important factor in computer mediated learning processes (Tsianos et al, 2006), though not always in an expected way (John and Boucouvalas, 2002; Redmond, 2004).

Curry's 3-layer onion model (Curry, 1983) classifies learning styles in a way that they are not mutually exclusive, but co-exist at different levels of learning processes. Specifically, moving from the inside to outside, the innermost layer is called *cognitive personality style*, and is the most stable trait. The middle layer is the *information processing style*, whilst the outermost consists of *instructional preferences* (see table 1).

Theories that fall into the inner layer are mostly related to cognition or traditional personality research, while more learner-centered approaches fit in the middle layer. The outer layer is more unstable, and it should be mentioned that according to Sadler and Riding (Sadler-Smith and Riding, 1999) it is affected by the inner layer. However, the Dunn & Dunn model that belongs to the layer of instructional preferences exhibits high reliability and validity, but its implications are not discussed here, since they are not easily related to Web environments.

Learning style theories are classified by Atkins, Moore and Sharpe (2001) on the basis of this onion model as shown in table 1.

In educational settings, all of these well-known theories have been tested; still, most hypermedia research focuses on theories that fit in the inner layer (with the exception of INSPIRE system (Papanikolaou et al, 2003). We believe that is strongly related to the fact that inner layer theories usually include scales of terms easily represented in hypermedia applications, such as preference for visual or verbal information, and structural organization of the presented content. On the other hand, middle layer theories provide a less cognition-based approach, since they focus on behavior and style in traditional learning environments, from a wider perspective.

Inner Layer Theories

Between theories that belong at the same layer, there are great similarities. At the inner layer, Witkin's construct of psychological differentia-

Table 2. Types of learners as defined by information processing style theories

Kolb's LSI	4MAT Model	Gregorc's Learning Styles	Honey & Mumford Model
Converger	Dynamic Learning	Concrete-Random	Pragmatist
Assimilator	Analytic Learning	Abstract-Sequential	Theorist
Accomodator	Common Sense Learning	Concrete-Sequential	Activist
Diverger	Imaginative Learning	Abstract-Random	Reflector

tion (Field Dependency vs. Field Independency) is strongly correlated with CSA's Wholist/Analyst Scale, since the latter is derived from the former (Sadler-Smith and Riding, 1999). Felder Silverman's ILS adds to CSA's two scales (Visual-Verbal, Wholist- Analyst) the similar to MBTI scales of Extraversion-Introversion and Sensing-Intuition.

It would seem that Felder Silverman's ILS could be a very inclusive theory, but it needs yet to provide further evidence for its theoretical and statistical grounding (Cassidy, 2004). The long history of MBTI certainly guarantees for its grounding and wide acceptance, but its extended questionnaire and personality rather than learning orientation are somehow impractical for Web settings.

In our opinion, though there are still reliability and validity issues to be resolved (Peterson and Deary, 2003), Riding & Rayner's CSA seems to be the appropriate representative of the *cognitive personality style* layer, and its individual and group implications will be further discussed.

Middle Layer Theories

With the exception of Gardner's Multiple Intelligences, all theories that have been classified in the middle layer of Curry's onion model, share common characteristics in the way they define types of learners (Kolb and Kolb, 2005; McCarthy, 1990; Gregorc 1982; Honey and Mumford, 1986) (see table 2).

Each horizontal row of Table 2 shows types of learners that share common characteristics,

according to their theoretical description. We should mention at this point that these similarities haven't been unnoticed by Gordon and Bull who have proposed a meta-model that combines multiple similar learning style models (Gordon and Bull, 2004), taking also under consideration theories that are not mentioned here.

These middle layer models directly refer to learners' attitude towards collaborating and working in groups; speaking in terms of personality theories, some types are people oriented and some are more logical (feeling vs. thinking). This is especially true for the case of Kolb's LSI, where convergers and assimilators are thinking types, while accommodators and divergers are feeling types, according to correlations with MBTI scores. We should clarify that these types (regardless of specific theory) are not absolutely stable, but one person can gradually change style; it is possible that a learner can alter his type as years go by. Moreover, belonging to a type doesn't necessary exclude the possibility that at instances a person can perceive information in any of these four styles, even though his persistence on a specific style is relatively stable (Sharp, 1997).

For the purpose of exploring the possible integration of middle layer learning styles into CoP environments, we believe that Kolb's LSI is the most appropriate representative of the aforementioned models, due to extended research on its implications and correlation with other psychometric constructs (such as the MBTI) (Kolb and Kolb, 2005). However, analogous considerations can be projected on other models that share the same theoretical assumptions.

Emotional Processing

Research on modelling affect and on interfaces adaptation based on affective factors has matured considerably over the past several years (Kort and Reilly, 2002), so that designers of educational products are now considering the inclusion of components that take affect into account. Emotions are considered to play a central role in guiding and regulating learning behaviour by modulating numerous cognitive and physiological activities. The purpose in our research is to improve learning performance and, most importantly, to personalize Web-content to users' needs and preferences, eradicating known difficulties that occur in traditional approaches. The emotional aspect of our model attempts to apply rules that help the system regulate user emotions on a Web-based learning environment, since we are attempting to measure and include emotional processing parameters, by constructing a theory that addresses emotion and is feasible in Web-learning environments.

In our study, we are interested in the way that individuals process their emotions and how they interact with other elements of their information-processing system. Emotional processing is a pluralistic construct which is comprised of two mechanisms: emotional arousal, which is the capacity of a human being to sense and experience specific emotional situations, and emotion regulation, which is the way in which an individual is perceiving and controlling his emotions. We focus on these two sub-processes because they are easily generalized, inclusive and provide some indirect measurement of general emotional mechanisms. These sub-processes manage a number of emotional factors like anxiety, boredom effects, anger, feelings of self efficacy, user satisfaction etc.

Emotional Arousal

Among these, our current research concerning emotional arousal emphasizes on anxiety, which is probably the most indicative, while other emotional factors are to be examined within the context of a further study. Anxiety is an unpleasant combination of emotions that includes fear, worry and uneasiness and is often accompanied by physical reactions such as high blood pressure, increased heart rate and other body signals like shortness of breath, nausea and increased sweating. The anxious person is not able to regulate his emotional state since he feels and expects danger all the time. The systems underlying anxiety are being studied and examined continuously and it has been found that their foundations lie in the more primitive regions of the brain. However, given the complexity of the human nature, anxiety is characterized as a difficult to be understood construct of emotions which is at a balance between nature and nurture and between higher perception and animal instinct (Kim and Gorman, 2005).

Barlow (2002) describes anxiety as a cognitive-affective process in which the individual has a sense of unpredictability, a feeling of uncertainty and a sense of lack of control over emotions, thoughts and events. This cognitive and affective situation is associated as well with physiological arousal and research has shown that an individual's perception is influenced in specific domains such as attentional span, memory, and performance in specific tasks. In relation to performance, the findings are controversial but there is a strong body of research which supports that anxiety is strongly correlated to performance and academic achievement. (Spielberger, 1972; Spielberger and Vagg, 1995)

Emotion Regulation

Accordingly, in order to measure emotion regulation, we are using the construct of emotion regulation. An effort to construct a model that predicts the role of emotion, in general, is beyond the scope of our research, due to the complexity and the numerous confounding variables that would make such an attempt rather impossible. However, there is a considerable amount of references concerning the role of emotion and its implications on academic performance (or achievement), in terms of efficient learning (Spielberger and Vagg, 1995). Emotional intelligence seems to be an adequate predictor of the aforementioned concepts, and is surely a grounded enough construct, already supported by academic literature (Goleman, 1995; Salovey and Mayer, 1990). Additional concepts that were used are the concepts of self-efficacy, emotional experience and emotional expression.

Self-efficacy is defined as people's beliefs about their capabilities to produce and perform. Self-efficacy beliefs determine how people feel, think, motivate themselves and behave. Such beliefs produce these diverse effects through four major processes. They include cognitive, motivational, affective and selection processes.

Emotional experience is the conceptualization of an emotion, the way in which the individual is dealing with it and how he perceives it.

Emotional expression is the way in which the individual is reacting after an emotion triggers. It is his behaviour after an affective stimulus. It can be argued that emotional expression is the representation of an emotion (Schunk, 1989). We created a questionnaire based on the aforementioned concepts of emotional intelligence, self-efficacy, emotional experience and emotional expression that we named emotion regulation. The questionnaire provides us with measures of the individual's ability to control his emotions and use them in a creative manner.

According the abovementioned theoretical approaches, it is evident that participants in CoPs differ in a variety of ways, at least as long as learning and problem solving are involved. Cognitive personality style theories demonstrate that different types of learning materials and objects in the information space should be used according to individuals' preferences, whilst information processing style theories show that each individual can be classified to a specific problem solving approach. Additionally, the moderating role of emotions seems to have an effect in participants'

interactions in such a setting. The next section proposes a way of integrating these considerations in on-line CoPs.

INDIVIDUAL CHARACTERISTICS CONSIDERATIONS FOR COPS

According to our rationale, there are two distinct ways to group users in CoP applications:

- Learners with common cognitive styles (as classified by Riding's CSA that we use in our paradigm) and emotional profiles (as can be extracted from the combination of emotional arousal and emotion regulation mechanisms), could be grouped together and collaborate in an environment that serves better their preferences- this is the case with i-Help that we mentioned above. Learners, in general, prefer to send information the way they receive it, and vice versa.

- In addition, each group of people should consist of practitioners of all different types of learners (according to LSI taxonomy that will be further discussed and their emotional attitude towards the learning procedure), in order to increase the variety of proposed problem solving approaches (with regards to social interaction) and to promote more efficient Knowledge Management practices.

These two ways of integrating cognitive and learning style typologies, and emotional and motivational attributes in Web-CoPs are not mutually exclusive: the first case refers mainly to the material used and its structure, whilst the second paradigm deals rather with group composition.

Table 3. Wholists/Analysts Characteristics

Wholists		Analysts	
View a situation and organize information as a whole	Organize material in loosely clustered wholes	View a situation as a collection of parts and often stress one or two aspects at a time	Organize information in clear-cut groupings (chunking down)
Proceed from the whole to the parts	Exhibit high assertiveness	Proceed from the parts to the whole	Exhibit low assertiveness

The Paradigm of CSA

The CSA taxonomy is consisted of two independent scales, Imager/ Verbal and Wholist/ Analyst. The Imager/ Verbal scale affects the way learning resources are presented, and is probably less important in terms of overall CoP grouping; it is important though in Web-content presentation. Within adaptive Web architectures, users who have been identified as Imagers or Verbals, could be presented with the corresponding learning resources (e.g. images or text).

The Wholist/ Analyst scale, though, is about organizing and structuring information (see table 3), and is consequently related to navigational patterns. It would make much sense that users with common navigational route and structural approach would work collaboratively more efficiently, the same way that matching teaching and learning style is expected to increase performance.

Otherwise, a radically differentiated approach on behalf of learners could hamper communication and the way tasks are perceived, since wholists move from the whole to the parts, while analysts follow the exact opposite route. Intermediate learners are expected to perform equally well in both structural settings.

Additionally, to the extent that the wholist/analyst scale coincides with Witkin's FD/FI scale, it can be argued that wholists are little more oriented towards other people, whilst analysts are more introverted. Moreover, wholists exhibit higher assertiveness than analysts.

Safe conclusions could be drawn only after this hypothesis is tested in a Web-CoP environment, and the aforementioned matchmaking is proven as important as the matching of teaching and learning style.

The Paradigm of LSI

On the contrary, the aforementioned middle layer theories (as represented by Kolb's LSI) describe learner types also in terms of collaboration. In other words, working in groups is perceived differently by each type; some types rely on others whilst some simply do not.

As in Riding's CSA (and the rest of the middle layer theories), Kolb's 4 types are drawn from two independent scales: Concrete Experience vs. Abstract Conceptualization, and Reflective Observation vs. Active Experimentation. People-oriented types are those that tend to Concrete Experience rather than Abstract Conceptualization, which in terms of personality theories are rather Feeling than Thinking.

More specifically, by focusing on group collaboration preferences according to Kolb's LSI [37], learners' characteristics are summarized in table 4.

As it is clearly defined by theory, diverger and accommodator's individual characteristics demonstrate a strong preference in group working, since collaboration may be a necessary prerequisite for maximizing learning performance. It also could be argued that the present modus operandi of Web-learning in general favors types of learners that prefer working alone (convergers and assimilators), than those who are people-oriented.

Implications for designers of CoP applications

Table 4. Learners' Characteristics in terms of group working preferences according to LSI

Divergers	Accommodators	Convergers	Assimilators
Are oriented towards people	Learn by teaching others	Prefer usually to work alone	Prefer working alone
Excel at brainstorimg and working in groups	Excel at influencing others	See group work as a waste of time	Will work in groups if assigned
Learn by sharing ideas and feelings	Rely on others for information in solving problems	Appear bossy and impersonal	Prefer the instructor reader to be an authority
Prefer the instructor/leader to be a motivator	Work well in groups		

can be summarized in the equal distribution of the different types of learners, and in further motivating convergers and assimilators to participate. For example, if for any reason a group consists only of these latter two types, then the CoP's functionality may be impaired.

A Combined Approach

Whether should an information processing style theory be chosen over a cognitive personality style theory (e.g. LSI vs. CSA), and which would that theory be, is still a matter of debate. Practical and convenience reasons, as much as reliability and validity scores, determine at some extent the final selection.

On the other hand, since these theories are not mutually exclusive, it is possible that they could be combined in a unified model that separates the practical implications of each theory according to the CoP element they relate to. Theories such as the CSA focus on the individual (practice methods and tools), while theories such as the LSI can be applied on group composition (community). Ideally, the concept of personalization in a Web-based CoP should address both these levels (see figure 1).

It should be clarified that the term "problem solving approaches" refers mainly to learners' preference (or not) to work with other people to promote efficient learning through practice, since this is of relatively higher importance in the

context of CoPs. Moreover, some people tend to "lead" others in collaborative learning processes, while some tend to "follow". Therefore, it is of importance to mix these types within a group.

This model demonstrates how cognitive and learning style theories may serve as well-defined guidelines for designers that are interested in expanding their center of attention to individual characteristics and their implications on group considerations, the same way that CoPs have changed the way Knowledge Management is conducted.

The Moderating Role of Emotions

Human emotions and qualities are developed through participation in social contexts (Vygotsky, 1985). This makes it possible for individuals to interact as feeling human beings and effective members of the various communities to which they belong. Through participation in the society or societies to which they belong, individuals learn more about human behaviour and develop an understanding of their role and function. People can become more effective participants through the interpretation given to these social interactions. Communities of Practice as a social setting are one location in which people may learn about their behaviour and emotions. This is in part due to the idea that effective learning and human relationships play a vital part in helping community members to achieve their learning objectives.

Figure 1. Unified approach to personalization in CoPs

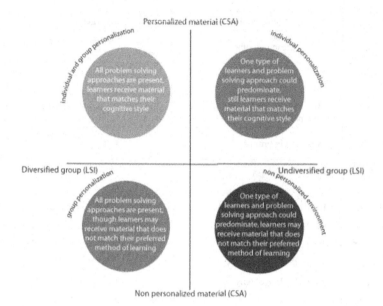

The competence of emotional awareness, defined as the ability to ``recognise one's emotions and their effects'' (Goleman, 1998) is ``our guide in fine-tuning on-the-job performance of every kind, managing our unruly feelings, keeping ourselves motivated, tuning in with accuracy to the feelings of those around us, and developing good work-related social skills, including those essential for leadership and teamwork'' (Goleman, 1998). If this competency is truly enhanced it could suggest that they are much more in control of their emotional states and possibly less inclined to be emotionally reactive.

Enhanced emotional awareness may help them to identify their attitudes and the main power relationships, and provide the means for them to understand and manage the group dynamics more effectively (Langley, 2000).

Another important issue is the feeling of safety that some individuals have to feel in order for them to function properly and perform their best within the boundaries of a team, group or community. This feeling of safety requires the existence of trust within the group and the lack of uncertainty

and anxiety. Teams that show high levels of trust and are provided with an environment which is perceived as safe and aesthetically appealing to the user, tend to perform better. It is strongly recommended that trust and safety should be of primary focus to the community culture and that behavior and other elements that promote trust and protection should be encouraged in teamwork (Erdem and Ozen, 2003).

Our proposal concerns the implementation of an interface that can appraise human emotion through the use of a set of parameters that can adapt according to the emotional condition of the user. An emotionally tense or unstable individual will be able to adjust the contents of a Webpage based to what he considers boring or entertaining and exciting etc. A certain emotional condition demands a personalization of equivalent proportions. The user will have the capability to respond emotionally either after being asked or after a question from the system. Another important aspect of a related system should be the ability to inform the database about the user preferences and inclinations.

At the interface level, the above notions would necessarily lead to the integration of an adaptive mechanism in CoPs supporting systems. A short practical overview of the personalization techniques that could be employed follows:

- First of all, users are required to build their profiles by the corresponding psychometric tests.
- Content selection and presentation is affected by each user's cognitive style (CSA). Navigation menus are either sequential or extensively hyperlinked (wholist or analytic mode of processing), while textual or imagery content predominates (verbal or imagery preference). This applies to the individual level of interacting with the interface.
- The assignment of users to each CoP is performed automatically by the system, ensuring that all types of problem solving approaches are included, as defined by the LSI.
- As it concerns the role of emotions, users should be able to provide emotional feedback to the system. Besides the inclusion of the corresponding psychometric tests, a self report measurement (i.e. a bar of anxiety) could serve as an indicator of emotional state, triggering the response of the adaptive mechanism of the system. The response is a) additional help, support and reinforcement and b) aesthetical enhancement of the interface.

The positive effect of the abovementioned personalization techniques (excluding the assignment on the basis of the LSI) in a hypermedia learning setting has been reported in previous work of the authors (Tsianos et al, 2008).

SUMMARY AND FUTURE WORK

The number and types of group interactions that learners are involved in a Community of Practice are strongly related to individual characteristics, which determine the degree of preference to group working, or at least common ways of structuring information.

Even if these social preferences are directly linked to personality factors, personality theories have far too complicated implications for CoP environments that focus on Knowledge Management, while theories that address low-level cognition processes are often too individualistic to consist a basis for user grouping.

Learning style theories and mechanisms that regulate emotions could be described as a much needed link between personality and cognition; still, one must not be too optimistic until issues of reliability and validity of psychometric instruments are resolved. Nevertheless, at theoretical level, these constructs provide useful insights for Knowledge Management applications that intend to explore the integration of learning methods of group working into Web-based CoPs.

As shown above, not all learning style theories address issues of group interaction at the same extent. Therefore, Web-CoPs designers that wish to incorporate individual learning characteristics should distinguish that each cognitive/learning style theory addresses issues of different elements of a CoP:

- *cognitive personality style* theories relate to the Practice element, since their implications may lead to a personalized approach to methods, tools and material.
- *information processing style* theories are relevant to the Community element, in the sense that different types of learners should be combined together in order to assure the occurrence of interactions at the level of shared learning and the building of coherent knowledge.

Subsequently, this leads to the need of experimentally evaluating the positive effects of a) matching content to practitioners according to their cognitive style (personality cognitive style models like CSA), and b) assigning to each group equally distributed different types of learners (information processing style, such as Kolb's LSI).

In any case, collaborative working is not a mere result of random real-time dynamics, but also the resultant of learner characteristics that individuals carry along, whatever the circumstance. Therefore, taking into account their preferences may promote efficient cooperation, or at least alleviate difficulties that occur from widely varied methods of learning between practitioners in CoPs.

More than a technologically driven determinism, personalization provides a very flexible platform for individual differences to be taken into account, and to assess their importance and role in cognitive processes. Still, there is the issue of which users' characteristics are to comprise the basis of personalization, since it is not yet clarified which cognitive science theories apply to human-computer interaction. The issue of Emotional processing is under research, since its role and effect on academic performance and learning is yet to be proven. There are indications though that taking emotions into account can help people to adjust easier into a group and find their role while at the same time cooperate with other group members with different emotional characteristics. Emotion regulation can be the motivational factor that humans need to activate their capabilities at a cognitive and a social level simultaneously.

REFERENCES

Atkins, H., Moore, D., Sharpe, S., & Hobbs, D. (2001). Learning style theory and computer mediated communication. In *Proceedings of the ED-MEDIA 2001 World Conference on Educational Multimedia, Hypermedia & Telecommunications*, Tampere, Finland (pp. 71-75).

Banner, G., & Rayner, S. (2000). Learning language and learning style: Principles, process and practice. *Language Learning Journal, 21*, 37–44. doi:10.1080/09571730085200091

Barlow, D. H. (2002). *Anxiety and its disorders: The nature and treatment of anxiety and panic* (2nd ed.). New York: The Guilford Press.

Bull, S., & McCalla, G. (2002). Modeling cognitive style in a peer help network. *Instructional Science, 30*(6). doi:10.1023/A:1020570928993

Carver, C. A., Howard, R. A., & Lane, W. D. (1999). Addressing different learning styles through course hypermedia. *IEEE Transactions on Education, 42*(1), 33–38. doi:10.1109/13.746332

Cassidy, S. (2004). Learning styles: An overview of theories, models, and measures. *Educational Psychology, 24*(4), 419–444. doi:10.1080/0144341042000228834

Curry, L. (1983). An organization of learning styles theory and constructs. In L. Curry (Ed.), *Learning style in continuing education* (pp. 115-131). Dalhousie University.

Erdem, F., & Ozen, J. (2003). Cognitive and affective dimensions of trust in developing team performance. *Team Performance Management: An International Journal, 9*, 131–135. doi:10.1108/13527590310493846

Feist, J., & Feist, G. J. (2006). *Theories of personality* (6th ed.). New York: McGraw-Hill.

Felder, R. M., & Silverman, L. K. (1988). Learning and teaching styles in engineering education. *English Education, 78*, 674–681.

Germanakos, P., Tsianos, N., Lekkas, Z., Mourlas, C., Belk, M., & Samaras, G. (2007). An adaptive Web system for integrating human factors in personalization of Web content. In *Proceedings of the 11th International Conference on User Modeling (UM 2007)*, Corfu, Greece.

Germanakos, P., Tsianos, N., Mourlas, C., & Samaras, G. (2005). New fundamental profiling characteristics for designing adaptive Web-based educational systems. In *Proceedings of the IADIS International Conference on Cognition and Exploratory Learning in Digital Age (CELDA 2005)*, Porto, Portugal (pp. 10-17).

Gilbert, J. E., & Han, C. Y. (1999). Arthur: Adapting instruction to accommodate learning style. In *Proceedings of the WebNet 99 World Conference on the WWW and Internet* (pp. 433-438).

Goleman, D. (1995). *Emotional intelligence: Why it can matter more than IQ*. New York: Bantam Books.

Goleman, D. (1998). *Working with emotional intelligence*. New York: Bantam.

Gordon, D., & Bull, G. (2004). The nexus explored: A generalised model of learning styles. In *Proceedings of the 15th International Conference of Society of Information Technology & Teacher Education*, Atlanta, Georgia, USA.

Graff, M. (2003). Learning from Web-based instructional systems and cognitive style. *British Journal of Educational Technology, 34*(4), 407–418. doi:10.1111/1467-8535.00338

Gregorc, A. F. (1982). *An adult's guide to style*. Maynard, MA: Gabriel Systems.

Honey, P., & Mumford, A. (1986). *A manual of learning styles*. Maidenhead, UK: Peter Honey.

John, D., & Boucouvalas, A. C. (2002). Multimedia tasks and user cognitive style. In *Proceedings of the International Symposium on CSNDSP 2002*.

Kim, J., & Gorman, J. (2005). The psychobiology of anxiety. *Clinical Neuroscience Research, 4*, 335–347. doi:10.1016/j.cnr.2005.03.008

Kolb, A. Y., & Kolb, D. A. (2005). *The Kolb learning style inventory – version 3.1 2005 technical specifications*. Experience Based Learning Systems Inc.

Kort, B., & Reilly, R. (2002). Analytical models of emotions, learning and relationships: Towards an affect-sensitive cognitive machine. In *Proceedings of the Conference on Virtual Worlds and Simulation (VWSim 2002)*.

Langley, A. (2000). Emotional intelligence - a new evaluation for management development? *Career Development International, 5*, 177–183. doi:10.1108/13620430010371937

Lekkas, Z., Tsianos, N., Germanakos, P., & Mourlas, C. (2007). Integrating cognitive and emotional parameters into designing adaptive hypermedia environments. In *Proceedings of the Second European Cognitive Science Conference (EuroCogSci '07)*, Delphi, Hellas, (pp. 705-709).

Markham, S. (2004). *Learning styles measurement: A cause for concern* (Tech. Rep.). Computing Educational Research Group.

McCarthy, B. (1990). Using the 4MAT system to bring learning styles to schools. *Educational Leadership, 48*(2), 31–37.

Myers-Briggs, I., McCaulley, M. H., Quenk, N. L., & Hammer, A. L. (1998). *MBTI manual (A guide to the development and use of the Myers Briggs type indicator)*. Mountain View, CA: Consulting Psychologists Press.

Papanikolaou, K. A., Grigoriadou, M., Kornilakis, H., & Magoulas, G. D. (2003). Personalising the interaction in a Web-based educational hypermedia system: The case of INSPIRE. *User Modeling and User-Adapted Interaction, 13*(3), 213–267. doi:10.1023/A:1024746731130

Peterson, E. R., Deary, I. J., & Austin, E. J. (2003). On the assessment of cognitive style: Four red herrings. *Personality and Individual Differences, 34*(5), 899–904. doi:10.1016/S0191-8869(02)00118-6

Rayner, S., & Riding, R. (1997). Towards a categorisation of cognitive styles and learning styles. *Educational Psychology, 17*(1&2), 5–27. doi:10.1080/0144341970170101

Redmond, J. A., Walsh, C., & Parkinson, A. (2003). Equilibrating instructional media for cognitive styles. In *Proceedings of the 8th annual conference on Innovation and technology in computer science*, Thessaloniki, Greece (pp. 55-59).

Sadler-Smith, E., & Riding, R. (1999). Cognitive style and instructional preferences. *Instructional Science, 27*(5), 355–371.

Salovey, P., & Mayer, J. D. (1990). Emotional intelligence. *Imagination, Cognition and Personality, 9*, 185–211.

Schunk, D. H. (1989). Self-efficacy and cognitive skill learning. In C. Ames & R. Ames (Eds.), *Research on motivation in education. Vol. 3: Goals and cognitions* (pp. 13-44). San Diego, CA: Academic Press.

Sharp, J. E. (1997). Applying Kolb learning style theory in the communication classroom. *Business Communication Quarterly, 60*(2), 129–134. doi:10.1177/108056999706000214

Spielberger, C. D. (1972). Conceptual and methodological issues in anxiety research. In C. D. Spielberger (Ed.), *Anxiety. Current trends in theory and research* (Vol. 2). New York: Academic Press.

Spielberger, C. D., & Vagg, P. R. (1995). Test anxiety: A transactional process model. In C. D. Spielberger & P. R. Vagg (Eds.), *Test anxiety: Theory, assessment, and treatment* (pp. 3-14). Washington, DC: Taylor & Francis.

Sternberg, R. J., & Grigorenko, E. L. (1997). Are cognitive styles still in style? *The American Psychologist, 52*(7), 700–712. doi:10.1037/0003-066X.52.7.700

Triantafillou, E., Pomportsis, A., & Georgiadou, E. (2002). AES-CS: Adaptive educational system based on cognitive styles. In *Proceedings of the AH2002 Workshop, Second International Conference on Adaptive Hypermedia and Adaptive Web-based Systems*, Spain.

Tsianos, N., Germanakos, P., & Mourlas, C. (2006). Assessing the importance of cognitive learning styles over performance in multimedia educational environments. In *Proceedings of the 2nd International Conference on Interdisciplinarity in Education (ICIE2006)*, Athens, Greece (pp. 123-130).

Tsianos, N., Lekkas, Z., Germanakos, P., Mourlas, C., & Samaras, G. (2008). User-centered profiling on the basis of cognitive and emotional characteristics: An empirical study. In *Proceedings of the 5th International Conference on Adaptive Hypermedia and Adaptive Web-based Systems (AH 2008)*, Hannover, Germany (LNCS 5149, pp. 214-223). Berlin, Germany: Springer-Verlag.

Vygotsky, L. S. (1985). *Vygotsky and the social formation of mind* (J. Wertsch, Ed.). Cambridge, MA: Harvard University Press.

Wenger, E. (1998). Communities of practice: Learning, meaning, and identity. Cambridge, UK: Cambridge University Press.

Wenger, E. (2004). Knowledge management as a doughnut: Shaping your knowledge strategy through communities of practice. *Ivey Business Journal Online*.

Witkin, H. A., Moore, C. A., Goodenough, D. R., & Cox, P. W. (1977). Field-dependent and field-independent cognitive styles and their implications. *Review of Educational Research, 47*, 1–64.

Chapter 10
From 'Collecting' to 'Deciding':
Facilitating the Emergence of Decisions in Argumentative Collaboration

Manolis Tzagarakis
Research Academic Computer Technology Institute, Greece

Nikos Karousos
Research Academic Computer Technology Institute, Greece

Giorgos Gkotsis
Research Academic Computer Technology Institute, Greece

Vasilis Kallistros
Research Academic Computer Technology Institute, Greece

Spyros Christodoulou
Research Academic Computer Technology Institute, Greece

Christos Mettouris
Research Academic Computer Technology Institute, Greece

Panagiotis Kyriakou
Research Academic Computer Technology Institute, Greece

Dora Nousia
Research Academic Computer Technology Institute, Greece

ABSTRACT

Current tools aiming at supporting argumentative collaboration either provide means to successfully tame wicked problems or offer advanced reasoning mechanisms to facilitate decision making creating a gap in today's landscape of systems supporting argumentative collaboration. The consequences of this gap are in particular severe for communities of practice when they have to employ tools from both sides

DOI: 10.4018/978-1-60566-711-9.ch010

to support their collaboration needs. The authors argue that a key factor in bridging this gap is viewing argumentative collaboration as an emergent phenomenon. Proper support of the emergent aspects of argumentative collaboration would benefit systems supporting argumentative collaboration as this would enable those systems to support the evolution of the entire collaboration at different levels. The authors describe how such approach has been implemented in CoPe_it! a prototype argumentative collaboration support system. In CoPe_it!, an incremental formalization approach facilitates the emergence of individual and loosely coupled resources into coherent knowledge structures and finally decisions.

INTRODUCTION

Argumentative collaboration can augment learning in formal as well as in informal group settings in many ways such as in explicating and sharing individual representations of the problem, maintaining consistency and focus on the overall process, thus increasing plausibility and accuracy, as well as to enhance the group's collective knowledge (Koschmann, 1999; Andriessen et al., 2003). Over the years, a variety of tools supporting argumentative collaboration have appeared; they usually facilitate argumentative discussions among members of a group and range from simple ones such as e-mail, chat and Web based forums to dialogue mapping and argumentative collaboration tools, reaching even into the realm of sophisticated conferencing and formal argumentation systems (Conklin et al., 2001; Karacapilidis & Papadias, 2001; Robinson & Volkov, 1997; Buckingham Shum et al., 1993)

Tools that facilitate argumentative discussion are of particular importance to Communities of Practice (CoPs); many CoPs have already integrated them into their processes. CoPs deal mostly with *wicked problems*, i.e. problems which are difficult to express, have no "correct solution" and exhibit a high degree of complexity (Conklin, 2005). A well known approach to address these kinds of problems is through discussing them among the group members aiming at collecting available alternatives, elaborating them further and finally deciding on the proper solution. Given the many different technologies for assisting the process of discussing and decision making, the selection of the proper one that fulfills a CoP's collaboration needs and successfully matches its processes is in general a critical success factor (de Moor & Aakhus, 2006).

However, in many cases, the basic building blocks for decision making, namely ideas and prospective alternative solutions do not exist beforehand and cannot be simply 'collected'. Ideas and prospective solutions usually do not arise spontaneously or instantly with clear conceptual boundaries. They are harvested as they gradually 'grow' out of existing resources that may even at first bear no indication of their potential. This lack of clearly identifiable alternatives and ideas may hinder groups in using sophisticated decision support systems that would fit their purposes such as (Karacapilidis & Papadias, 2001). These tools – which can play an active role during argumentative collaborations - require that alternative solutions have already crystallized and are clearly and unambiguously expressed within the system.

In general, argumentative collaboration support systems focus either on "taming" wicked problems in an attempt to harvest and justify alternatives or on supporting actively the decision making process. The consequences of this gap for CoPs (and groups in general) are rather severe: the group has to employ different tools during the same collaboration session, something that introduces problems and obstacles that ultimately harms the group's ability to address the problems at hand. One reason for this inflexibility of existing systems is their emphasis on providing rigid levels of formality.

In this chapter, we present how CoPe_it! – a Web-based tool to support argumentative collaboration (http://copeit.cti.gr) – attempts to bridge the aforementioned gap. In particular, CoPe_it! aims at reconsidering the notion of formality in argumentative collaboration systems. Within CoPe_it! formality is not considered a rigid property of the system, but rather an adaptable aspect of it. It builds on the assumption that argumentative collaboration environments are environments where *understanding occurs* through the emergence of the collaboration space. This emergence is characterized by small and incremental changes of the available items in the collaboration space that - although local in nature - when accumulated lead to global transformation of the collaboration space into something that is useful for the task at hand. In particular, CoPe_it! attempts to provide the framework to support the emergence of decisions in online collaborations. Within the CoPe_it! approach, the notion of emergence is conceived on two levels: *emergence within a shared collaboration space* where individual items are transformed into prospective solutions and *emergence between shared collaboration spaces* where the collaboration is transformed into a decision. In CoPe_it! these two forms of emergence are considered as related as *emergence between shared collaboration spaces is based on emergence within shared collaboration spaces*. To implement this framework, CoPe_it! introduces the notion of incremental formalization into argumentative collaboration research drawing upon approaches that have been well established in other related areas of research, such as hypertext (Marshall & Shipman, 1997; Shipman & McCall, 1994), knowledge management and CSCW (Cox & Greenberg, 2000). The rest of the chapter is organized as follows: first we outline the motivation and discuss the notion of emergence in argumentative collaboration. We then review existing systems with respect to their ability to support emergent structures and decision making and present the mechanisms provided by CoPe_it! to address the main concerns. The last section concludes the chapter and identifies issues for future work.

MOTIVATION

Two factors stimulate our work to reconsider the way, argumentative collaboration is currently supported by existing systems: the emphasis of these systems on formalization and the coming of the so-called Web 2.0 era.

Existing argumentative collaboration tools emphasize on formality, i.e. the provision of a fixed set of abstractions and rules, with well defined semantics, to which all participant actions must comply. Their main aim is to provide the tailored yet fixed vocabulary to articulate all involved considerations (ideas, positions etc) in a way that is close to the domain of use. By prescribing the possible discourse moves, not only a common understanding of the problem among participants can be achieved, but the fixed semantics makes it also possible to introduce active computational support. However, despite the apparent benefits, such prescribed methods received much criticism. In particular, the formal structures were the reason these systems were difficult to use, requiring great efforts from individuals (Grudin, 1996; Hurwitz and Mallery, 1995), and proved to be barriers rather than catalysts for collaboration, as they slow down the activities (Buckingham Shum, 1996). The formal structure imposed has been the leading cause for the failure of these systems for widespread adoption (Nam & Ackerman, 2007). This is consistent with similar observations in other fields such as knowledge-based systems, groupware systems, and software engineering tools (Shipman & Marshall, 1999). On the other, simpler online discussion tools, such as Web-based forums, gained phenomenal adoption precisely because of their lack of sophisticated formal structures, and their emphasis on "naturalness of interactions" (Nam & Ackerman, 2007).

A second motivation for rethinking argumentative collaboration tools is related to the advent of was has been termed as the Web 2.0 era (O'Reilly, 2005; Anderson, 2007). Although the term "Web 2.0" stills lacks a precise definition, and the discussion whether it constitutes simply a marketing hype or not is still ongoing, it nevertheless outlines a generation of applications that focus on taking full advantage of the networked nature of the Web (Ullrich, et al., 2008). Key ideas upon which these applications are built include user generated content, harnessing the power of crowds, data on an epic scale, architecture of participation, network effects and openness (Anderson, 2007). Although these ideas were to a great extent part of the initial vision of the Web (Berners-Lee, 1999), it's in Web 2.0 where these ideas are shifted at the center of interest of relevant applications. Fulfilling the initial vision, such move transforms the read-only web into a read-write medium, thus elevating it to the level of a platform. In this new environment, users are experiencing new ways of interactions and possibilities. In an attempt to avoid argumentation tools become a much smaller nice than they currently are, approaches to make them part of the Web 2.0 landscape have already begun to appear (Buckingham Shum, 2008; Debatepedia, 2008). In light of such developments, we focus on what lessons can be drawn from successful Web 2.0 ideas and how these can be successfully introduced into argumentative collaboration systems.

In the context of this work, the 2.0 concept of "harnessing the power of crowds" is of particular interest. Although argumentative collaboration systems are inherently collaborative, they have yet to embrace this power to an extent, Web 2.0 applications do. The "power of crowds" reveals in many Web 2.0 applications with their departure from application-driven formalization to user-driven formalization. In essence, these systems move away from prescribed forms of formalization and place structuring efforts into the hand of users. Semantics become emergent and not predefined (Buckingham Shum, 2008). Folksonomies are a characteristic example in this regard being able to produce - contrary to intuitive belief - high quality metadata (Zhang et al., 2006). What the experience from relevant Web 2.0 applications indicates is that prescriptive approaches are not the only

solution to the problem of meaningfully organize an information space. The examples indicate that opening up of the semantics layer and providing emergent structuring of the information space, is a very successful method for a wide range of collaborative work. Driven by this observation and recognizing the collaborative nature of argumentation, it is tempting to investigate the admission of such emergent semantics in argumentative collaboration systems as one promising solution to the problem of how to move away from fixed, prescribed methods.

EMERGENCE IN ARGUMENTATIVE COLLABORATION

Ideas do not arise well formed (Moran et al., 1997). In most situations of argumentative collaboration, ideas surface as the discussion proceeds. This is mainly due to the nature of the related resources and how they are brought in into the collaboration space.

In the course of argumentative collaboration, users bring in various resources in their effort to contribute to the issue being discussed. The term resources is used to denote any explicit claim, opinion, question or evidence that users contribute and assume to be valuable during the collaboration. In general, resources may be brought in into the discussion at any time may and may have many forms. For example, entire scientific articles (e.g. papers or books) may appear in the discussion and constitute resources, even if nevertheless only some part is in some way relevant to the issue being discussed. Alternatively, an entire set or such resources – as the result of a Web search - may be brought into the ongoing discussion. Even excerpts of texts – of unrestricted size ranging from a single sentence summarizing an opinion to lengthy essays – may appear. Due to the collaborative nature of the task, initially, the importance of every resource depends only on the subjective judgment of the user who admitted it into the discussion. This means that resources may at a later point be obsolete or characterized as unimportant by the group. Furthermore, resources may even change their role in the progress of the discussion and can be transformed from ideas to positions and vice versa. As the collaboration proceeds, more resources are available to the collaborating group.

Yet, as the number of resources increases, the complexity of the collaboration space becomes a serious problem. This complexity is characterized by the efforts required to keep track and follow all the events of the collaboration in order to understand the available resources and relate them to the issue being discussed. In such situations, users adopt practices similar to those of experienced analysts: they must understand how the resources add up, explore alternative explanations and interpretations, engaging in the process of "information triage" (Marshall & Shipman, 1997). The term "information triage" refers to the process of sorting the available resources, interact with them on the space in an attempt to interpret, recast, interrelate and organize them into larger structures to facilitate understanding and meet the needs of the task at hand..

The process of reorganizing existing resources proceeds in an incremental manner. Usually, each user conducts small changes to the collaboration space, affecting only a small part of the resources. While individual interactions have local consequences, they have a global impact on the understanding of the collaboration space as they accumulate over time. This results in transforming individual resources to something that is consequential for the task at hand and is referred to as sense-making (Cox & Greenberg, 2000). Hence, in argumentative collaboration sense-making does not happen automatically but rather *emerges naturally* as a consequence of the anticipated users interactions and modifications of the resources available in the collaborative space. In this context, the term emergence is used to denote the way semantics arises and forms from

relatively simple interactions such as changing the type and role of individual resources, relating and grouping the resources of the collaboration space. Research in CSCW has already outlined criteria with which collaborative environments can be characterized with respect to their ability to support emergence. These include (Edmonds et al., 1998): (a) arranging and spatial reasoning, (b) implicit structuring and (c) sketching.

As the shared collaboration space emerges towards sense-making, the entire collaboration emerges towards the decision to be made. Hence, a second level of emergence is in action. This form of emergence occurs only if the collaboration activity reached a state where sense-making has been achieved. The recognition of this kind of emergence gives the ability to reconsider the outcomes of the sense-making process in new contexts, such as the formal exploitation of collaboration items patterns, and the deployment of appropriate formal argumentation and reasoning mechanisms.

EXISTING SYSTEMS

Background Work

All existing argumentative collaboration systems provide means to support the kind of emergence outlined previously. Yet, they differ in the degree they support emergence and in particular whether they succeed in making the emergent semantics explicitly within the system (and thus system understandable) or not.

E-mail, chat and Web based forums are representatives of the most basic argumentative collaboration environments as they support only a limited form of emergent structures. In these systems, the processing of resources, such as their interrelation, grouping, summarization and interpretation with which emergence towards sense-making is achieved, occurs mainly in the mind of each individual and is not being able to

Figure 1. Support for emergence of various argumentative collaboration systems.

be represented within the system. This form of emergence is characterized as implicit. These systems allow only trivial discourse moves that include uploading of resources and their (implicit) association. Even in cases where explicit relationships between items are possible (e.g. by quoting a post), the semantic of this association is implicit. Nevertheless, Web-based forums may exhibit a slightly higher degree of explicit emergence, as they can deploy various visualization techniques; these techniques permit quasi-spatial placement and relationships between posts e.g. threaded view. Such implicit emergence is also witnessed in the majority of formal argumentation systems which attempt to provide advanced functionalities to actively support decision making such as Hermes. Although these systems provide means to explicitly structure the discourse based on prescribed rules, they nevertheless leave little or no room for alternative interpretation or the articulation of different types of relationships between existing items. Since such actions are not possible within these systems, they again must occur in the user's mind.

On the other hand, systems like Compendium

(Buckingham Shum et al., 1993) and PReSS (Cox & Greenberg, 2000) attempt to make emergence explicit i.e. emphasize on how understanding and sense-making "comes-out" by providing the necessary mechanisms with which knowledge structures can be created out of existing resources, and be represented within the system. Being within the system, these knowledge structures can then be shared between users. To support emergence of the collaboration space towards sense-making, these systems provide a rich set of mechanisms that permit the creation of arbitrary relationships between items with their semantics clearly articulated, spatial arrangement of the items, and changing the type and role of individual resources to better convey their meaning. Furthermore, they also provide mechanisms to build new resources by grouping, specializing or generalizing existing ones. Figure 1 shows how some existing systems can be classified when considering their mechanisms for supporting emergence towards sense-making.

When considering the aspect of how well they support decision making another picture can be drawn. In these situations, systems that exhibit a

Figure 2. Levels of supporting decision making in different argumentative collaboration systems.

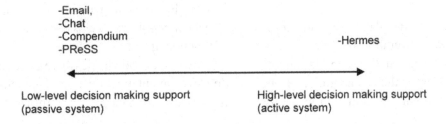

Figure 3. By adjusting the formality of CoPe_it! different intentions of the argumentative collaboration can be supported.

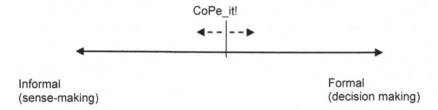

high degree of support for emergence provide very little or no support for decision making. On the contrary, some systems with rather low degree of supporting emergence exhibit advanced support for decision making (see Figure 2).

Both pictures above indicate a gap that exists in today's argumentative collaborative environments. Systems, that acknowledge the need to support emergence of individual resources into structures facilitating sense-making, neglect to take the next step to support the evolution of the process towards making the decision. When groups need both functionalities, only burdensome solutions can be provided. In these cases, technology proves to be an obstacle rather than a solution. CoPs, in general, face many times such situations; hence, in this context, bridging this gap will immensely benefit their ability to successfully address issues they encounter. The issue here is how the entire lifecycle of the argumentative collaboration within CoPs - namely from collecting and sharing resources to reaching a decision - can be supported.

ARGUMENTATIVE COLLABORATION WITH COPE_IT!

CoPe_it! is a Web-based tool that facilitates argumentative collaboration emphasizing on supporting emergent collaboration. It attempts to support the entire life-cycle of the collaboration: from collecting and exploiting information to taking

decisions. CoPe_it! permits semi-synchronous collaboration among group members. The term semi-synchronous denotes that synchronous as well as asynchronous collaboration is possible.

The approach of CoPe_it! builds upon the observation that environments aiming at supporting the emergence of sense-making provide more flexible means to build knowledge structures than environments aiming at decision making. In particular, they exhibit completely different levels of formality. By the term formality, we refer to the rules enforced by the system, to which all user actions must comply. In CoPe_it!, formality is not considered as a predefined and rigid property of the system, but rather as adaptable aspects that can be modified to meet the needs of the tasks at hand. Figure 3 illustrates the different objectives that can be supported by adjusting the level of formality. Decreasing the systems formality facilitates sense-making while increasing the system's formality facilitates decision making. Allowing formality to vary within the collaboration space, incremental formalization, i.e. a stepwise and controlled evolution from a mere collection of individual ideas and resources to the production of highly contextualized and interrelated knowledge artifacts, can be achieved (Shipman & McCall, 1994). In general, this evolution into a new collaboration level is associated with a set of functionalities.

CoPe_it! acknowledges three stages of evolution of argumentative collaboration, each of which is characterized by the prevalence of a particular set of operations. In CoPe_it!, a projection is a view on a particular collaboration space that provide the tailored support for each stage. Consequently, the same collaboration space can have three different projections.

A. **The collection and sharing stage.** This is the most informal setting supported by CoPe_it! where the tool functions simply as a web-based discussion place (such as a forum) or as common resource repository in which people can upload and share resources. The emphasis here is simply to express, gather and share knowledge items that the group may possess, making others aware of their existence. No advanced structuring is at this point necessary. Structuring of the collaboration space cannot be made explicit, hence no constraints exist on what and how a resource is related to another in the collaboration space. Relationships can only be established by quoting resources (posts) or by referencing them within the content of a resource (post).

B. **The synthesis stage.** While the previous one emphasizes on collecting and initial feedback on the collected items, this stage is mainly concerned with providing support for synthesizing existing items and support the emergence towards coherent knowledge structures that can act as building blocks for decision making purposes. The key aspect in this stage is that the emergent structures can be represented explicitly within the system. In this stage, gathering and collecting resources is also possible but do not constitute the main activities. The emphasis is how they relate to other resources and how they can be aggregated into larger structure. At this stage, sense-making means achieving the crystallization of the alternative solutions and explicitly represent them within the system.

C. **The decision stage.** This is the most formal setting supported by CoPe_it! as at this stage the alternative solutions of the synthesis stage can be further elaborated with active support of the system. In particular, the knowledge structures that emerged from the synthesis stage are transformed into the appropriate types, whose semantics are understandable by the system. Hence at this stage decision making is fully supported.

How argumentative collaboration evolves in the collection and decision stages has already been documented in previous work (Karacapilidis & Papadias, 2001) In the next sections we outline the mechanisms with which CoPe_it! supports the notion of emergence in the synthesis stage and describe how the entire collaboration space emerges from one stage into another. In CoPe_it! the later is also referred to as switching projections.

Emergence Within the Synthesis Stage

The projection supporting the synthesis stage provides a rich set of mechanisms with which the emergence of the available resources into coherent knowledge structures can be supported. In the next section we present and discuss these mechanisms in greater detail.

Knowledge Types

CoPe_it!'s projection aiming at the synthesis stage offers an open set of knowledge types with which the role of individual resources can be clarified. Currently, these include (a) notes, that are used to represent simple information content, the value of which has not yet been assessed by the community (the content of notes can be anything from text, images or video - a short title acts as the summary of the content), (b) comments used to annotate content and (c) ideas that constitute the main abstraction to explicate individual solutions.

Figure 4. Spatial metaphor of the collaboration space. Resources can be spatially arranged by anyone participating in the collaboration.

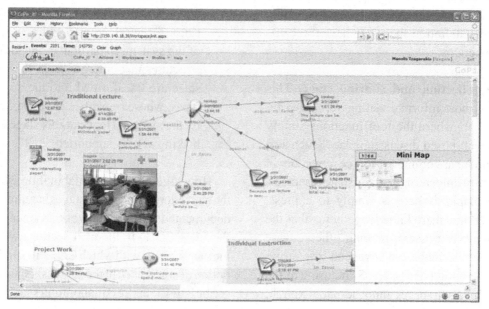

When resources are used in a collaboration space, a special icon indicates their knowledge type. The set of available knowledge types is not closed; when required, users can at any point in time define and use new set of types. Although all knowledge types have a number of specific attributes, all instances can receive arbitrary attribute-value pairs at any point during the collaboration.

Spatial Arrangement of Items in the Collaboration Space

CoPe_it! exploits a spatial metaphor for supporting the organization of the collaboration space (Marshall & Shipman, 1995). All the items on the collaboration space can be spatially arranged: they can be juxtaposed or piled up by anyone participating in the collaboration (see Figure 4). Such way of organizing the available items is in particular important for hatching tacit knowledge that resides latently in a collaboration space and has been pointed out as a key factor towards facilitating emergence (Edmonds et al., 1998).

Creating Relationships Between Resources

Between any two resources available on the collaboration space, relationships can be created. These relationships are visualized by directed lines, having customizable attributes such as title, width, color, etc. Visual cues are used to attach additional semantics to the relationship. For example, a relationship can be colored red or green to indicate that one resource is standing critically or favorably with respect to another. The thickness of the line representing the relationship may be used to indicate how strong a resource opposes or supports another (see Figure 5).

Abstraction Mechanisms

CoPe_it! includes means with which resources can be conceived at a higher level of abstraction allowing their transformation into artifacts useful for decision making tasks. These constitute important mechanisms to facilitate the piecemeal

Figure 5. Relationships between resources. Color and thickness of the relationships conveys meaning.

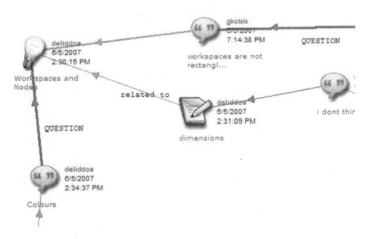

transformation of the available resources into knowledge structures. Within CoPe_it! these mechanisms include:

- Explicit transformation of resources. Individual resources can be transformed from one type to another without any constraint by anyone and at any point in time.
- Aggregation of resources. Resources can

be aggregated into larger structures and these structures can be treated as a single entity. Aggregated resources may be typed; they can be transformed into one of the available knowledge types and can take part in any structuring activity e.g. relating an aggregated entity with a note or another idea. For example, a set of aggregated resources can be cast into an idea, comment

Figure 6. Example of breaking-up a resource. The selected part of the content can be used as a separate entity within the workspace.

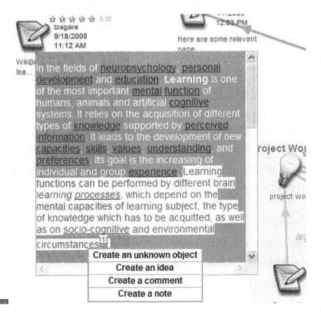

Figure 7. Instance of the collaboration stage at the synthesis stage.

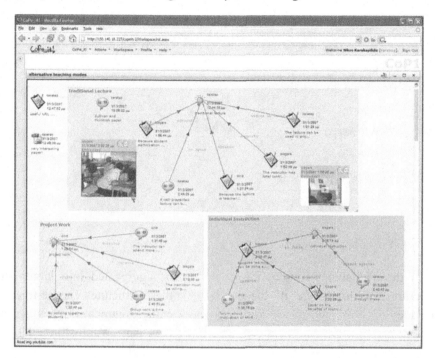

or note. Undoing of an aggregation is also possible. In these situations, the aggregation is dissolved and the constituent 'parts' appear as separate entities on the collaboration space.

- Breaking-up of resources. Individual resources may be broken up into smaller pieces in order to allow these smaller pieces to take part in relationships (see Figure 6). In particular, part of a resource's content may be selected and be treated as a separate knowledge type, in order to be more precise when using a resource in argumentative collaboration. During such break up, the relationship to the original resource is maintained as an attribute of the new instance, so that its origin can be traced back.

- Patterns of knowledge structures. Instances of interconnected knowledge items - of any type – can be designated as knowledge

type templates. These templates can then be used during the collaboration to create as types for new instances. This allows the definition and use of user-defined abstractions during the collaboration.

An instance of the projections with the abilities described above is shown in Figure 7. The figure shows the issue of "alternative teaching modes" being discussed. The argumentation has evolved to a stage where alternatives solutions have started to emerge. Alternatives to the issue at hand are indicated by the rectangles that enclose the structured items that have been jointly authored by the community members. Items that are placed within rectangles–without relationship to other items – imply that they are relevant to the particular alternative.

Table 1.

Projection of the Synthesis stage	Projection of the Decision stage
Collaboration space	Issue
Idea	Alternative
Relationship between comment/note and idea colored red	Position against the alternative
Relationship between comment/note and idea colored green	Position in-favor of the alternative
Relationship between comments/notes colored red	Position against the position
Relationship between comments/notes colored green	Position in-favor of the position
Thickness of relationships	Weight of the position

Emergence Towards Decision-Making

Once the collaboration space has been structured to the point where the semantics of individual items has been assessed and individual alternative solutions have taken shape advancing the entire collaboration to the decision phase is possible. This permits the community to elaborate the generated knowledge structures in new contexts characterized by the formal exploitation of collaboration items patterns, and the deployment of appropriate formal argumentation and reasoning mechanisms. In CoPe_it! such evolution is achieved by transform-

ing the projection supporting the synthesis stage into a new projection, suited for decision making purposes. The collaboration can then proceed within this new projection. Due to the projection's formal argumentation rules and use of reasoning mechanisms, the tool has at this point an active role in the collaboration and can –among others - identify current most discussed and 'winning' alternatives and positions that have been defeated.

The newly emerged projection for decision making employs an IBIS like formalism (Conklin & Begeman, 1989) and builds on the functionalities of previously developed argumentation system (Karacapilidis & Papadias, 2001).

Figure 8: An instance of a projection of the synthesis stage (left side) and its corresponding transformation into a projection of the decision making stage (right side).

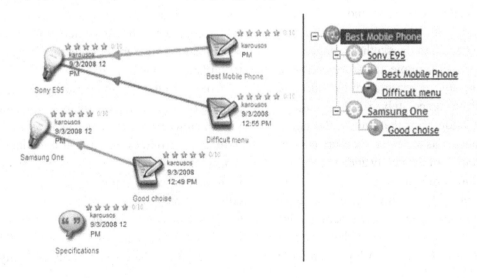

Transformation Rules

During the transformation of a projection, the knowledge structures that emerged out of the analysis stage are transformed into IBIS like structures of the decision stage and appear as such in the corresponding projection. Transformation rules determine how the transition will take place and take into consideration the type of knowledge items as well as the relationships between them. Visual attributes such as the color, direction and thickness of a relationship are also considered.

Transformation rules are not fixed, but can be modified in order to adapt to the needs of individual groups. The following table 1 gives an example of transformation rules, while figure 8 shows an instance of a projection of the synthesis stage and its corresponding transformation into a projection of the decision stage

Some resources present in the synthesis stage can be chosen to be simply ignored by the transformation mechanism. After completing this transformation the collaboration can continue at the decision stage where advanced functionalities supporting decision making are available.

Relationship between Projections

Although the collaboration can continue in the projection of the decision stage, the projection of the synthesis stage is still active and the collaboration can at any point in time leave the decision stage and fall back into the synthesis stage.

Furthermore, both projections are active in the sense that, any resource admitted into one projection will be immediately visible in the other. The transformation rules that guided the initial transformation, act as the filter to ensure consistent representation of the newly added resources in the destination projection.

For example, after a transformation took place and considering the transformation rules outlined previously, any newly added resource that is connected with a relationship colored red to an idea in the projection of the synthesis stage, will immediately appear in the projection of the decision stage as an position arguing against the respective alternative. Similar events occur in the projection for the synthesis stage, when resources are added in the projection for the decision stage. By this, consistency between the two projections can be ensured.

CONCLUSION

Current argumentative collaboration systems provide a fixed level of formality that is not flexible enough to support both sense-making and decision making activities. When CoPs (and groups of people in general) require support of both activities, then only burdensome solutions can be provided. In this chapter we have presented how CoPe_it! bridges this gap by reconsidering the notion of formality in argumentative collaboration systems. Its underlying framework permits the level of formality to vary and hence to provide the tailored support for both sense and decision making. In this regard, CoPe_it! is adopting practices found in successful Web 2.0 applications that seek to disengage from fixed, prescribed approaches to information organization. The framework considers argumentative collaboration as an emergent process, where the semantics of individual resources arises gradually. As the collaboration space emerges towards such sense-making, the entire collaboration emerges towards decision-making.

CoPe_it! attempts to support such emergent aspects of argumentative collaboration, and provides therefore a rich set of mechanisms to organize individual resources that appear in collaboration workspaces. This set of mechanisms enables the incremental formalization of the argumentative collaboration.

Preliminary evaluation of the tool in actual collaboration sessions of CoPs shows that the approach offered by CoPe_it! is not only well received by CoPs but that it also augments the CoP's ability to tackle data intensive and complex problems. Future work will focus on evaluating the synchronous collaboration features in situations of real CoPs. Moreover, future efforts will also concentrate on investigating additional mechanisms that facilitate the stepwise evolution of argumentation collaboration. In this regard the focus will be on awareness mechanisms and ways to support versioning of the collaboration space.

ACKNOWLEDGMENT

Research carried out in the context of this chapter has been partially funded by the EU PALETTE (Pedagogically Sustained Adaptive Learning through the Exploitation of Tacit and Explicit Knowledge) Integrated Project (IST FP6-2004, Contract Number 028038).

REFERENCES

Anderson, R. (2007). What is Web 2.0? Ideas, technologies and implications for education (Tech. Rep.). *JISC Technology and Standards Watch*.

Andriessen, J., Baker, M., & Suthers, D. (2003). Argumentation, computer support, and the educational context of confronting cognitions. In J. Andriessen, M. Baker, & D. Suthers (Eds.), *Arguing to learn: Confronting cognitions in computer-supported collaborative learning environments* (pp. 1-25). Amsterdam, The Netherlands: Kluwer.

Backingham Shum, S., MacLean, A., Forder, J., & Hammond, N. (1993). Summarising the evolution of design concepts within a design rationale framework. In *Adjunct Proceedings of the InterCHI'93: ACM/IFIP Conference on Human Factors in Computing Systems*, Amsterdam, The Netherlands (pp. 43-44).

Berners-Lee, T. (1999). *Weaving the Web*. London: Orion Business Books.

Buckingham Shum, S. (1996). Design argumentation as design rationale. In *The encyclopedia of computer science and technology* (pp. 95-128). New York: Marcel Dekker, Inc.

Buckingham Shum, S. (2008). Cohere: Towards Web 2.0 argumentation. In . *Proceedings of COMMA, 2008*, 97–108.

Conklin, J. (2005). Dialogue mapping: Building shared understanding of wicked problems. In *Wicked problems and social complexity*. New York: John Wiley & Sons.

Conklin, J., & Begeman, M. (1989). gIBIS: A tool for all reasons. *Journal of the American Society for Information Science American Society for Information Science, 40*(3), 200–213. doi:10.1002/(SICI)1097-4571(198905)40:3<200::AID-ASI11>3.0.CO;2-U

Conklin, J., Selvin, A., Shum, S. B., & Sierhuis, M. (2001). Facilitated hypertext for collective sensemaking: 15 years on from gIBIS. In *Proceedings of the Twelfth ACM Conference on Hypertext and Hypermedia*, Aarhus, Denmark (pp. 123-124).

Cox, D., & Greenberg, S. (2000). Supporting collaborative interpretation in distributed Groupware. In *Proceedings of the ACM Conference on Computer Supported Cooperative Work (CSCW '00)* (pp. 289-298).

de Moor, A., & Aakhus, M. (2006). Argumentation support: From technologies to tools. *Communications of the ACM, 49*(3), 93–98. doi:10.1145/1118178.1118182

Debatepedia. (n.d.).

Edmonds, E., Moran, T., & Do, E. (1998). Interactive systems for supporting the emergence of concepts and ideas. *SIGCHI Bulletin, 30*(1), 62–76. doi:10.1145/280571.280581

Grudin, J. (1996). Evaluating opportunities for design capture. In T. P. Moran & J. M. Carroll (Eds.), *Design rationale: Concepts, techniques and use*. Mahwah, NJ: Lawrence Erlbaum Associates.

Hurwitz, R., & Mallery, J. C. (1995). The open meeting: A Web-based system for conferencing and collaboration. In *Proceedings of the 4th International World Wide Web Conference*, Boston, MA.

Karacapilidis, N., & Papadias, D. (2001). Computer supported argumentation and collaborative decision making: The HERMES system. *Information Systems*, *26*(4), 259–277. doi:10.1016/S0306-4379(01)00020-5

Koschmann, T. D. (1999). Toward a dialogic theory of learning: Bakhtin's contribution to understanding learning in settings of collaboration. In C. M. Hoadley & J. Roschelle (Eds.), *Proceedings of the CSCL'99 Conference* (pp. 308-313). Mahwah, NJ: Lawrence Erlbaum Associates.

Marshall, C., & Shipman, F. (1995). Spatial hypertext: Designing for change. *Communications of the ACM*, *38*(8), 88–97. doi:10.1145/208344.208350

Marshall, C., & Shipman, F. (1997). Spatial hypertext and the practice of information triage. In *Proceedings of the 8th ACM Conference on Hypertext*, Southampton, UK (pp. 124-133).

Moran, T. P., Chiu, P., & van Melle, W. (1997). Pen-based interaction techniques for organizing material on an electronic whiteboard. In *Proceedings of the 10th Annual ACM Symposium on User interface Software and Technology UIST '97*, Banff, Alberta, Canada (pp. 45-54).

Nam, K., & Ackerman, M. S. (2007). Arkose: Reusing informal information from online discussions. In *Proceedings of the 2007 international ACM conference on Supporting Group Work*, Sanibel Island, Florida, USA.

O'Reilly, T. (2005). *What is Web 2.0: Design patterns and business models for the next generation of software*.

Robinson, W. N., & Volkov, S. (1997). A meta-model for restructuring stakeholder requirements. In *Proceedings of the 19th International Conference on Software Engineering*, Boston, MA (pp. 140-149). Washington, DC: IEEE Computer Society Press.

Shipman, F. M., & Marshall, C. C. (1999). Formality considered harmful: Experiences, emerging themes, and directions on the use of formal representations in interactive systems. *Computer Supported Cooperative Work*, *8*(4), 333–352. doi:10.1023/A:1008716330212

Shipman, F. M., & McCall, R. (1994). Supporting knowledge-base evolution with incremental formalization. In *Proceedings of the CHI'94 Conference*, Boston, MA (pp. 285-291).

Ullrich, C., Borau, K., Luo, H., Tan, X., Shen, L., & Shen, R. (2008). Why Web 2.0 is good for learning and for research: Principles and prototypes. In Proceeding of the 17th international Conference on World Wide Web, Beijing, China (pp. 705-714).

Zhang, L., Wu, X., & Yu, Y. (2006). Emergent semantics from folksonomies: A quantitative study. In *Journal on Data Semantics VI* (LNCS 4090, pp. 168-186). Berlin, Germany: Springer.

Chapter 11
An Organizational Knowledge Circulation Management System for Universities

Toshie Ninomiya
The University of Electro-Communications, Japan

Fumihiko Anma
The University of Electro-Communications, Japan

Toshio Okamoto
The University of Electro-Communications, Japan

ABSTRACT

In this chapter, the concept of an organizational knowledge circulation management system of e-learning is presented. The authors have developed a mentoring system module and a learning design repository based on technological and pedagogical aspects, and evaluated the system in two case studies. They also describe important functions and evaluation aspects of new information technology system of e-learning.

INTRODUCTION

Shifting to a knowledge based society requires a high level educational environment in which it is possible to continue learning not only for full-time students, but also for working students. E-Learning allows for realization of this type of educational environment: letting distributed students learn collaboratively by utilizing multimedia contents anytime and anywhere. At first, our university's practical activity is introduced, which offers high quality education with the consideration for learners' convenience (Allen & Seaman, 2004).

E-Learning outcomes have been judged to be equivalent or superior to face-to-face instruction at most institutes and it has the same educational effect on learners in instructors' opinions. However there are barriers to widespread adoption of e-Learning, especially by faculty (Allen & Seaman, 2006). For example it is an important concern for faculty that teaching online courses requires more time and effort than teaching face-to-face courses. Allen's survey indicated that there has been little increase in acceptance by faculty of the value and

DOI: 10.4018/978-1-60566-711-9.ch011

legitimacy provided by online education. On the other hand, data in Allen's survey shows that the faculty who are fully engaged in online education always acknowledge the value and legitimacy of online education.

Thus our practical purpose is to convince our university's faculty of the benefits of e-Learning by providing them with hands on experience in online education. Ways in which faculty can experience online education are:

1) Organizational collaboration
2) Facilities: e-Learning studio, e-Learning room, LMS
3) Developing system: authoring system, mentoring system
4) Faculty development: method of learning design

We have already established the center for research and developing e-Learning (CDEL) for activities in 1) and promoted it as a Good Practice Project for activities in 2) and 3) (Anma, Ninomiya & Okamoto, 2007; Ninomiya, Taira & Okamoto, 2007; Okamoto & Ninomiya, 2007). In this paper, we introduce development of mentoring system for activities in 3) and Learning Design Repository for activities in 4) (Okamoto, Nagata, Anma & Ninomiya, 2008).

Organizational Knowledge Circulation Management

Mission of the Center for Research and Developing e-Learning (CDEL)

The services provided and research conducted by the center for developing e-Learning are as follows:

Service

- provide e-Learning room, e-Learning studio, authoring system

- consult faculty about e-Learning
- management of contents' copy rights
- open seminars, forums, international conferences

Research

- develop/storage/re-use contents/tools/application for learning
- educational/technological research with international collaborators
- standardization in e-Learning (ISO/IEC-JTC1 SC36)
- educational improvement by ICT

The above services and research are based on the missions of CDEL shown in Fig.1. Using learning log data of CSCL in intelligent LMS, CDEL provides standards of academic ability and assures educational quality by conducting educational evaluation. In addition, CDEL contributes to faculty development by producing training in instructional design, learning design, contents developing and mentoring. As the result, improved faculty's ability allows to achieve a higher academic ability and educational quality. In this paper, we introduce new promotional activities based on the missions of CDEL, 1) developed mentoring system for supporting faculty from technological aspect, 2) developed Learning Design Repository based on pedagogical aspects.

Knowledge Circulation Management System

Based on technological and pedagogical aspects, we constructed parts of the modules of knowledge circulation management system shown in Fig.2. Creator and instructor constructed learning designs and practiced using learning design in the repository. These learning designs include learning contents and learning from learners' activities. The learners' activities are recorded in learning log DB. Learner activity integration system manages these

Figure 1. Mission of the center for research and developing e-Learning

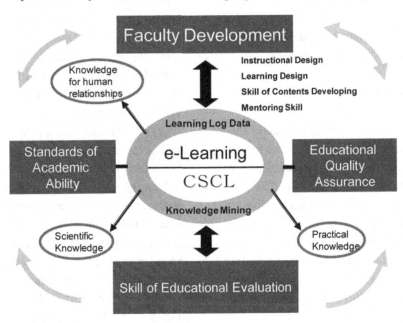

Figure 2. Knowledge circulation management system

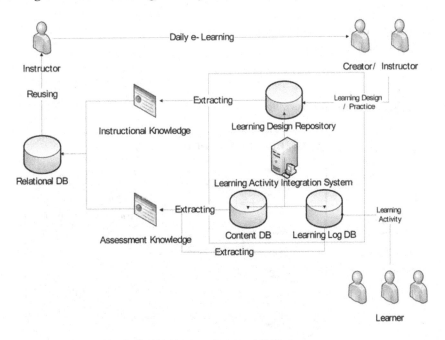

DBs as shown in Fig.2. Instructional knowledge is constructed by extracting information from learning design repository and assessment knowledge is constructed by extracting information from content DB and learning log DB. This knowledge stored in relational DB and is used by instructors in daily e-learning activities. At the current stage, the learning activity integration system does not have all of the modules implemented. However we have already developed several modules of knowledge circulation management system, in the next section we introduce these modules.

Mentoring System

It is difficult to sustain e-Learning activities. Thus regular mentoring for learners is important to keep their motivation to learn. However, to be able to give all learners advices on demand is costly in terms of time and effort required from lectures. Therefore automating mentoring activity is beneficial. Motivated by this we have developed auto-mentoring system. We define "auto-mentoring system for supporting lecturers" as a system in which it is possible to extract targets by learning from LMS log data and then sending mentoring messages automatically.

Architecture

The first version of our mentoring system supports learning activities in a course. In the next version

we plan to support learners in their courses by also answering their questions or pointing out their weak points. The outline of the first version of mentoring system is shown in Fig.3.

In the beginning, an instructor creates rules for learner classification and message construction. These rules are stored in a DB for further reuse (Fig. 3). Extracting target module matches leaning log data with production rules of learner classification module and extracts target learners who may need mentoring messages. Then sending message module creates appropriate messages for target learners and asks the instructor to verify them. In case instructor allows mentoring system to send messages to targets learners, sending message module then sends them to target learners. Learning activities of each learner are recorded in leaning log data base through LMS WebClass-RAPSODY. An example of how e-Karte learners go through this process is shown in Fig.4.

Figure 3. Architecture of mentoring system

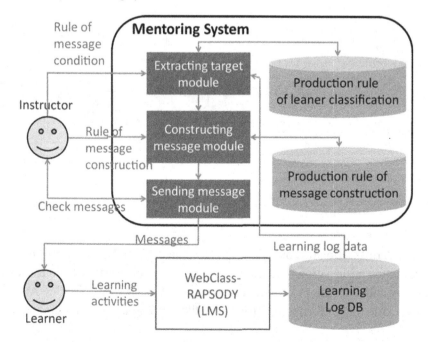

Figure 4. Example of e-Karte

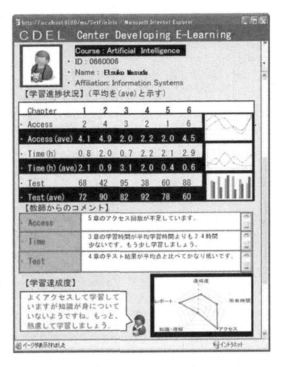

Default Production Rule for Learner Classification

The mentoring system has default production rules for learner classification and message construction. The default production rules are shown in Fig. 5.

An instructor should input only the number of weeks to open his/her contents (N) and standard learning time (minutes) of one content (X). Then learners are classified into six categories:

- **Delay 1:** total login number < 2*N AND total learning time < X*N min
- **Delay 2:** total login number < 2*N AND number of more than X min learning < N/2
- **Delay 3:** total learning time < X*N min AND number of more than X min learning < N/2
- **Excellent 1:** total login number < 2*N
- **Excellent 2:** total learning time < X*N min OR number of more than X min learning < N/2

- **Excellent 3:** NOT (total login number < 2*N OR total learning time < X*N min OR number of more than X min learning < N/2)

Learners in the status "Delay 1" did not perform learning activities at all, ones in "Delay 2" learn for a long period of time but only a few times, ones in "Delay 3" learn for a very short period of time, ones in "Excellent 1" learn only a few times, ones in "Excellent 2" learn for a short time a few times, and ones in "Excellent 3" learn very well.

It is possible to modify this default production rule through mentoring settings interface (Fig.6).

Default Production Rule for Message Construction

Constructing message module can create appropriate messages for learners, based on the learner's classification assigned by the extracting target

Figure 5. Process used to classify learner's status

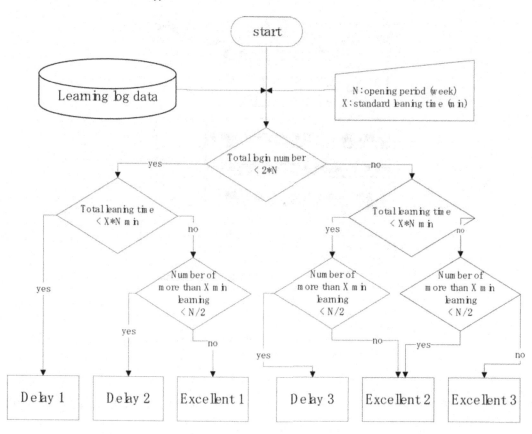

Figure 6. Interface for mentoring settings

module, and by utilizing default production rules as following:

IF learning status is "Delay 1" THEN message is "Your accessed system only a few times and your learning time is too little, so try to logging in frequently and learn for more than X minutes at once."

IF learning status is "Delay 2" THEN message is "Your accessed system only a few times. It is better to learn frequently during a shorter periods of time."

IF learning status is "Delay 3" THEN message is "Your learning time is short, so try to learn for more than X minutes each time."

IF learning status is "Excellent 1" THEN message is "You learn very well. Try to access system more frequently."

IF learning status is "Excellent 2" THEN message is "You learn very well. Try to learn for more than X minutes each time."

IF learning status is "Excellent 3" THEN message is "You learn very well. Keep up your learning pace."

After constructing messages, sending message module asks for the instructor's approval (Fig.7). After the instructor approves these messages, all messages will be sent to learners' e-mail addresses automatically.

CASE STUDY 1

We have used our system in a regular course for master students, results are shown in Table 1. Students can register for the course as learners through our LMS. However, they also need to formally register for the course to get credits through administration office within three weeks. Thus we compare the results of learning activities only for students who registered for the course formally. All learners attained excellent learning status by utilizing our mentoring system. However, it is not clear whether the system has an influence on learner's decision to formally resister for the course. It is necessary to study how to cope with this situation further.

Figure 7. Interface for message check

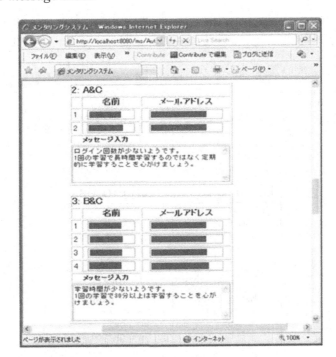

Table 1. Number and percentage of learners

	Registered through system (1)	Registered through administration office (2)	Delay in (2)	Excellent in (2)
2007(without mentoring system)	37	32	25%	75%
2008(with mentoring system)	29	17	0%	100%

Learning Design Repository

LICAP-LD Model

Okamoto proposed LICAP model for decision making in designing and evaluating CAI courseware in 1978 (Okamoto & Sato), and we redesigned it for constructing and evaluating e-learning contents as LICAP-LD model, which is a framework of PLAN, DO, ANALIZE and RE-CONSTRUCT used for constructing e-Learning contents. As shown in Fig.8, LICAP-LD model expresses learning design of e-Learning with four modules such as Learner characteristics module (L), Consequent Activities (CA), Learning design process (I: Instructional Process in LICAP model) and LD-analysis/evaluation module (P: Program Evaluation in LICAP model). We provided this model and an evaluation scale which support instructors in constructing, analyseing or evaluating learning designs.

Learning Activity Sequence

Our system includes LAMS 2.0 (LAMS (Learning Activity Management System) International, n.d.) based on IMS-Learning Design as a repository for learning activity sequences created by instructors. An example of learning activity sequences is shown in Fig.9, which is used as an experimental

Figure 8. LICAP-LD model

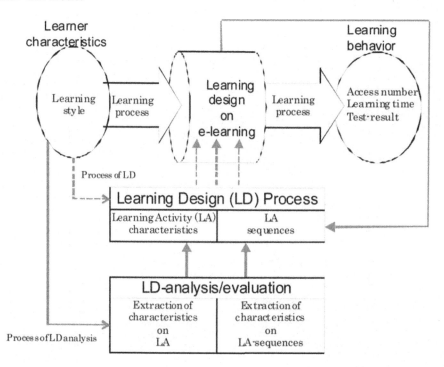

Figure 9. Learning Activity Sequence

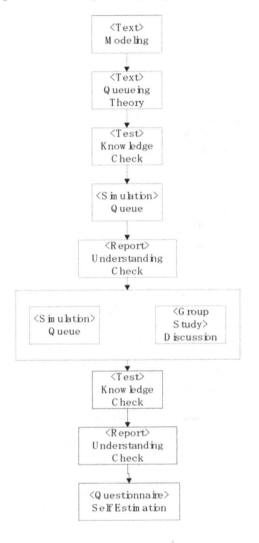

learning environment in order to estimate the effect of group study. A square represents a learning activity and several activities make up one sequence. There are many sequences in Learning Design Repository and instructor can reuse them.

Understanding Level Model

Goal oriented skill learning has been well received recently. It allows to see the effectiveness of learning for learners as well as for instructors (Fig.10a). However, many academic fields, especially new interdisciplinary fields, may not have explicit

goals. So we need an evaluation scale to show the effectiveness of learning for ill-structured knowledge (Fig.10b). To analyse educational effect of learning activity sequences, we have developed an understanding level model (Table 2). This model refers to "the Logical Categories of Learning and Communication" by G. Bateson (Bateson, 1942; Bateson, 1972; Bateson et al., 1956), which was constructed based on Russell's theory of Logical Types (Whitehead & Russell, 1910-13).

Fig.11 shows the ratio of topics (e.g. simulation, calculation, ratio of service, person, order) in classified reports with regards to the understanding levels. Basic topics like terms and calculations appear in low level reports, and general topics like simulation and person appear in high level reports, by utilizing text mining. Thus we consider that the understanding level model is appropriate evaluation scale for learning activity sequences.

CASE STUDY 2

Group Learning

We conducted a learning activity sequence experiment with 47 undergraduate students. Table 3 shows average understanding levels in this experiment. With the average understanding levels in Table 3, group study is shown to be the most effective learning activity in the sequence.

Number of Group Members

We have verified the theory of group dynamics (Lewin, 1935; Lewin, 1943) in a group study by reusing the learning design sequence shown in Fig.9. 47 Learners were divided into 10 two-member groups and 9 three-member groups. The average differences of understanding levels between individual and group learning are 0.5556 for two-member groups and 1.2609 for three-member groups. The effect of group dynamics in three-member groups is very clear

Figure 10. a)Structure of technique or skill, b)Ill-structured knowledge.

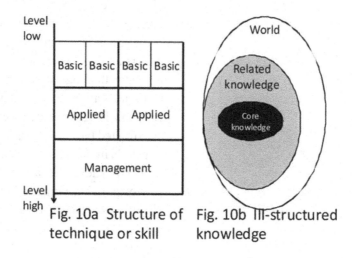

Fig. 10a Structure of technique or skill

Fig. 10b Ill-structured knowledge

Table 2. Understanding level model

Understanding level	Reaction model
1	s (stimulus) -> Knowledge -> r (reaction)
2	s1,s2,s3, ... -> Knowledge -> r1,r2,r3, ...
3	S1(s1,s2,s3, ...), S2(...), S3(...), ... -> Knowledge -> R1(r1,r2,r3, ...), R2(...), R3(...), ...
4	Meta concept of level 3

Figure 11. Ratio of including topics in the classified reports

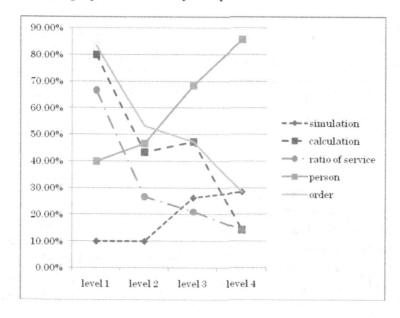

Table 3. Average understanding levels in a learning design sequence (Fig. 9)

Learning activity	Report 1	Report 2	Questionnaire
Understanding level	1.6087	2.5122	2.4474

Figure 12. Learning design case production by CBR

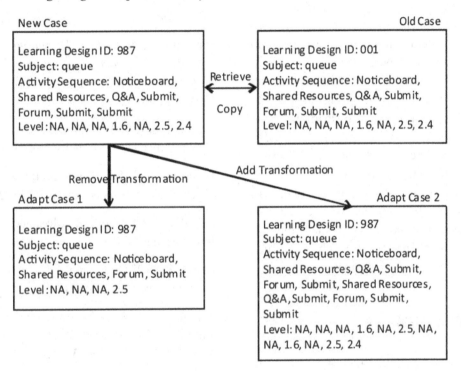

(t=2.8008, m=35.96, t(40,0.01)=2.423). So we set the number of group members in the sequence to three.

Self Estimation

Learners answered whether group learning was effective or not. Negative learners' group (difference=1.00) improved their understanding level more after group learning than for the positive one (difference=0.92). The discussions in negative groups may have different views and reach no conclusion, but it still has an effect on learners' understanding. We need to inspect how the context of discussion in group learning affects learners' understanding level in the future.

Learning Design Case Records

In Learning Design Repository of Fig. 2, there are many learning design case records utilizing our evaluation scale and understanding level model shown in Fig.12. When instructors request new case records, Learning Activity Integrate System in Fig.2 produces new cases by traditional case adaptation strategies (Fig.12).

CONCLUSION

Our practical goal is to convince our faculty of the value of e-learning by providing them with hands on experiences in effective online education. In this paper, a mentoring module of LMS and a leaning design repository (utilizing the proposed evaluation scale) was developed as to achieve our goal. The developed systems and tools are important components of knowledge circulated management system, which will be the core system for organizational collaboration in our university. Learning activity integration system has a learner classification function in a mentoring module and a case-based reasoning function in a learning design repository. The created data set, stored in DBs, will be used to make instructional knowledge and assessment knowledge in the near future. It will allow instructors to reuse the new knowledge for daily e-learning. Even though we are currently using these systems and tools separately, their effects on educational practice are high as indicated by the results shown in this paper.

ACKNOWLEDGMENT

This research was partially supported by the Ministry of Education, Science and Culture, Grant-in-Aid for Scientific Research (A), 20240069, 2008-2011 for technical parts, and Grant-in-Aid for Scientific Research (B), 18300298, 2006-2008 for pedagogical parts.

REFERENCES

Allen, I. E., & Seaman, J. (2004). *Entering the mainstream: The quality and extent of online education in the United States, 2003 and 2004.* Newburyport, MA: The Sloan Consortium.

Allen, I. E., & Seaman, J. (2006). *Online nation: Five years of growth in online learning.* Newburyport, MA: The Sloan Consortium.

Anma, F., Ninomiya, T., & Okamoto, T. (2007). A development of learning management system for interactive e-learning in higher education. In *Proceedings of the World Conference on E-Learning in Corporate, Government, Healthcare & Higher Education,* Quebec, Canada (pp. 1956-1963).

Bateson, G. (1942). *Social planning and the concept of deutero-learning: Conference on science, philosophy and religion, second symposium.* New York: Harper.

Bateson, G. (2000). *Step to an ecology of mind.* Chicago, IL: The University of Chicago Press.

Bateson, G. (1956). Toward a theory of schizophrenia. *Behavioral Science, 1,* 251–264.

LAMS (Learning Activity Management System) International. (n.d.).

Lewin, K. (1935). *A dynamic theory of personality.* New York: McGraw-Hill.

Lewin, K. (1943). Forces behind food habits and methods of change. *Bulletin of the National Research Council, 108,* 35–65.

Ninomiya, T., Taira, H., & Okamoto, T. (2007). A personalised learning environment architecture for e-learning. In *Proceedings of the 6th IASTED International Conference on Web-based Education,* Chamonix, France (pp. 517-521).

Okamoto, T., Nagata, N., Anma, F., & Ninomiya, T. (2008). The knowledge circulated-organisational management for e-learning practice. In *Proceedings of the IADIAS Multi Conference on Computer Science and Information Systems,* Amsterdam, The Netherlands (pp. 121-128).

Okamoto, T., & Ninomiya, T. (2007). Organisational knowledge management system for e-learning practice in universities. In *Proceedings of the 6th IASTED International Conference on Web-based Education*, Chamonix, France (pp. 528-536).

Okamoto, T., & Sato, K. (1978). A study of the decision making model on the design and evaluation for a CAI program. *Japan Journal of Educational Technology*, 3(1), 25–37.

Whitehead, A. N., & Russell, B. (1910-1913). *Principia mathematica, 3 vols* (2nd ed.). Cambridge, UK: Cambridge University Press.

Chapter 12
Using Web–Based Technologies and Communities of Practice for Transformative Hybrid and Distance Education

Nory Jones
University of Maine, USA

Omar J. Khan
University of Maine, USA

ABSTRACT

This chapter explores the use of Web-based technologies incorporating communities of practice and social networks to enhance the learning experience in hybrid and distance (online) classes. Research suggests that using a variety of technologies and methods to reach people with different learning styles improves overall learning in a class delivery though different methods are more effective in traditional vs. online classes. Moreover, using new, emerging Web-based technologies, including both Web 1.0 and Web 2.0 software, further enhances the engagement and value of the learning experience in these classes. This chapter examines the methods and technologies that can be potentially used to create excellence learning environments in traditional hybrid and online classes.

INTRODUCTION

Online education is assuming greater importance throughout higher education. As more non-traditional learners enter academics, especially at the graduate level, distance education becomes an important resource to enable them to achieve their academic goals given the demands of work and family. However, the challenge of creating a rich, contextual learning environment is often inhibited by technologies that impede collaboration, communication, and a true understanding of the material. This paper contributes to the existing literature by exploring the use of new, emerging technologies that incorporate communities of practice and social networks in order to enhance the distance learning experience. The study also contributes to understanding how to more effectively deliver quality education in all three types of classes: traditional, online and hybrid.

DOI: 10.4018/978-1-60566-711-9.ch012

THE TRADITIONAL CLASSROOM

A traditional class occurs in real time where the instructor and students meet in a physical location at specified times during a traditional time period such as a semester. The advantages of traditional classes include: personal attention, the ability to interact in a real-time environment, adapt to changing conditions or nature of the class and content, and the immediacy of responses and interactions among professors and students. The professors and students also have the opportunity to develop trust, rapport and relationships over the semester. Abstract and complex issues are easier to convey and explain in a face-to-face environment.

In contrast, the disadvantages include the inconvenience of time, travel, short, limited duration of the class, personality conflicts, and often, not enough time to digest and reflect on class presentations and discussions.

ONLINE DISTANCE CLASSES

Online education is often defined as involving the Internet and web-based technologies to deliver distance education. It can be delivered asynchronously, where the students and instructor do not communicate in real time, using web-based technologies such as asynchronous discussion forums, repositories, and e-mail. It can also be synchronous, where the students and instructor communicate in real time using web-based technologies such as chat rooms or teleconferencing over the Internet (Martinez, 2004).

The advantages of pure online classes include convenience, accessibility, the ability to spend time on course content and class discussions before responding. However, the disadvantages include a lack of rich, contextual cues from face-to-face interactions, potential feeling of separation from class, instructor, classmates, and difficulties in using technologies.

Distance education continues to proliferate both in higher education as well as in businesses, as the costs of travel and work pressures increase. According to the GAO (2007), enrollments in higher education distance classes have almost quadrupled since 1995. The Sloan Consortium reported that over 3.9 million students nationally took at least one online course in the fall, 2007 semester. This represented a 12% increase over 2006 statistics (Heck, 2009). Distance courses and programs in higher education represent a real avenue for growth, expanding opportunities for traditional and non-traditional students.

HYBRID CLASSES

A hybrid class is one where a professor offers a traditional class with regularly scheduled classes in a classroom with live students. However, the classroom doubles as a technology-enabled room which supports distance education. As budgets continue to shrink, administrators and faculty have recognized the value of providing hybrid classes to serve the traditional students as well as the non-traditional students.

Hybrid classes are also becoming popular in traditional classes as a form of supplementing the regular format. For example, in a study by Carnegie Mellon, they found a representative example of a statistics class where the professors created a web site with the class content and then held discussion sections after the students had studied the material. The results were positive, showing that the class took less overall time and the students had equivalent scores on the exams as in the traditional classroom (Timmer, 2009).

While hybrid classes are attractive because of their resource efficiencies, they also pose interesting challenges for the instructors who must design a dual delivery system. Most instructors will agree that it is more difficult to teach an online class because of the lack of face-to-face interactions, visual clues and the ability to easily converse and share knowledge and ideas.

USING WEB-BASED TECHNOLOGIES IN DISTANCE EDUCATION

A "build it and they will come" (Robinson, 1989) approach will not necessarily ensure success in distance or hybrid classes. Despite the technologies, motivating and engaging the students in a web-based virtual environment remains a major challenge. Brower (2003) suggests that one solution lies in creating virtual learning communities where the instructor takes the role of learning facilitator and students become engaged in the virtual discussion forums without the pressure of personality differences. This allows students and instructors to freely express their opinions and ideas. Chou (2003) also suggests that inter-activity with technologies enhances the learning experience. For example, on-demand whiteboards between online participants facilitates the exploration of concepts. A user-friendly interface to web-based tools that engage students in collaboration, problem-solving activities, and exploration can support virtual communities and is one effective solution for distance learning (Hedberg, 2003).

The above constitute examples of communities of practice (or CoP's) at work. In its broad definition, communities of practice are structured social networks constituted by individuals or organizations in pursuit of specific goals. They can, thus, be viewed as a subcategory of the broader term "social networks", which refers to the vast array of relationships formed between individuals and/or organizations.

Most classrooms today use a combination of Polycom for video-conferencing plus web-based applications including Skype, WebCT/Blackboard, NetMeeting, among other similar tools for one-way or two-way audio or video communications between the in-class professor and students and the distance students. Different bridging systems are used to connect the dispersed distance students into one virtual space where they can all communicate synchronously if desired. Some hybrid courses use the older synchronous one-way communication method where the lecture and class participation is filmed and either broadcast live to distance students or archived for later viewing by the distance students. Finally, some hybrid courses use the asynchronous method where the live classes are almost totally separate and the distance students simply view lecture documents or archived videos and communicate via asynchronous discussion forums or perhaps synchronous chats at pre-arranged times.

The next section discusses strategies for successful online course delivery.

STRATEGIES FOR SUCCESSFUL DISTANCE & HYBRID CLASSES

When designing a distance course, both learning factors and technology factors should be considered. While they are inter-related, we will discuss both aspects.

Learning Factors

According to Sharda et al. (2004), researchers have found three strategies to improve distance learning: "the cognitive domain, which focuses on intellectual content and problem solving; the affective domain, which focuses on learning emotions and values; and the psychomotor domain, which focuses on learning the characteristics of physical movement. (p.34)" The moral of this story is that people learn differently and respond to different types of technologies and instructional design. Other researchers have found that a high locus of control plus self-directed, motivated students were key factors in the cognitive domain. Student support was also important in providing the necessary technology or structural education

Table 1. GRSLSS Learning Styles

Learning Style	Description
Independent Learning	These students prefer independent study, self-paced instruction, and would prefer to work alone on course projects than with other students.
Dependent Learning	These students look to the teacher and their peers as a source of structure and guidance and prefer an authority figure to tell them what to do.
Competitive Learning	These students learn in order to perform better than their peers and to receive recognition for their academic accomplishments.
Collaborative Learning	These students acquire information by sharing and cooperating with teacher and peers. They prefer lectures with small group discussions and group projects.
Avoidant Learning	These students are not enthused about attending class or acquiring class content. They are typically uninterested and are sometimes overwhelmed by class activities.
Participant Learning	These students are interested in class activities and discussion, and are eager to do as much work as possible. They are keenly aware of and have a desire to meet teacher expectations.

and training needed to overcome perceived barriers (Roblyer et al, 2008). Students also need frequent, structured contact with the instructor (Schullo et al, 2009).

Another important factor in the design of the course is a high level of interactivity. Distance students need to feel connected and involved. Therefore, developing communities of practice represents one important part of course design. That is to say, clear objective-based communities among participants need to be developed in order for online delivery to be effective. Other strategies will also be discussed.

Impact of Learning Styles

The learning styles of students play a role in their success in a distance or traditional class. Significant research has shown that people have marked differences in their learning styles on two major dimensions: problem solving and decision making activities. While many different learning style models have been developed, the GRSLSS (Grasha-Reichmann Student Learning Style Scale) model is widely accepted (Diaz and Cartnal, 1999). Table 1 shows a summary of this model. The styles are not exclusive categories. Rather, student-preferred learning styles tend to span different categories, with just a few dominating.

Liu and Ginther (1999) found that academic achievement in distance education depends largely upon a match between the learning tasks and the student's learning styles. They found that students enrolled in distance courses tended to be older, to have independent learning styles, were more self directed, and often avoided collaborative or competitive situations. Diaz and Cartnal showed, however, that distance students were willing to participate in collaborative work if the instructor provided enough structure and guidance for those activities and the collaboration was motivated by attaining the rewards of the class.

In contrast, Valenta et al. (2001) found that traditional students tended to be more dependent learners, preferring more structure in the class and the assignments. They did react favorably to collaborative work with their motivation stemming from competition and a desire to meet the expectations of the instructor. Gee (1990) suggested that the independent learner was less reliant on interactions with others and was more successful in distance courses.

Technology Factors

An interesting, emerging model, called WisCom (Gunawardena et al., 2006), which stands for "Wisdom Communities", suggests that educators should focus on developing engaging communities of practice with existing technologies. They emphasize the human elements of mentoring, and developing trust, support, collaboration and communication as the keys to successful virtual communities in online environments.

Another model, called "Adventure Learning" by Doering (2006), contends that online learning can be enhanced via a hybrid model. Specifically, by combining real world projects with collaborative online learning with peers, teachers and subject experts, students become more engaged in the overall experience. This approach is supported by several researchers (Puntambekar 2006, Hedberg, 2006, Waddill et al., 2006, and Darabi, 2006) whose research all demonstrated that greater involvement with active, relevant projects enhances the online learning experience. Puntembekar also demonstrated that using web-based technologies can facilitate collaborative knowledge building, development of new ideas and constructs by bringing people with divergent views together.

COMMUNITIES OF PRACTICE IN DISTANCE LEARNING

With the exponential growth of internet use, the first collaborative technologies were termed Web 1.0. These included e-mail, video-conferencing, chat and discussion forums. CoP's began to develop on the web platform, engaged in the pursuit of common objectives (Wenger and Snyder, 2000). It became increasingly apparent that sponsorship and support of these communities, whose members regularly engaged in sharing and learning based on common interests, could significantly facilitate the transmission and spread of knowledge and improve organizational performance (Lesser and Storck, 2001).

In organizations, CoP's had been viewed as the best way to bring about the long-sought goal of creating a "learning organization" - getting

people to share their knowledge, and creating a pool of collective organizational intelligence. Research in distance learning has shown that a strong sense of community is crucial in the success of distance classes. In the case of web-based learning, the facilitator "creates" this community, but the extent to which CoP's develop is largely based on how the participants use this community (Johnson, 2001). Facilitation techniques need to be employed, which nurture the experience for those that may want to "tune out" of the experience. Creative solutions to this undesirable dynamic have included the use of blogs to retain student interest and active engagement (Dickey, 2004). Another important element in addition to trust and rapport is a shared sense of purpose in the learning community (Conrad, 2008). For example, students who work collaboratively on projects develop camaraderie and a sense of purpose in the achievement of their class goals.

This is further supported by the classic work on CoPs by Wenger (2009), who suggested that learning involves becoming part of a community, allowing people to share ideas and perspectives while working collaboratively on common tasks. These online learning communities allow people to actively seek and receive support and knowledge transfer to enhance the overall learning experience. However, CoPs in distance classes must also be nurtured to create environments of tolerance and respect in order to succeed. Participants in online classes also succeed when they have a high comfort level with the technologies required for use in the class. For example, using software like Blackboard/WebCT or searching the library's online databases for research must be user friendly and seamless in the course. The web "infrastructure" dimension that creates this user friendly, seamless experience is of particular significance to the success of web-based environments and learning platforms (Hung & Thanq, 2001). Unified structures that promote the ease of transmission of knowledge along CoPs have been shown to yield positive performance results in the web-based learning environment, as evidenced by the QSIA learning and knowledge sharing platform, for example (Rafaeli, et al, 2003).

Incorporating New Web 2.0 Technologies into Distance Learning

New, emerging Internet-based technologies, called Web 2.0 should also be considered for distance and hybrid classes. These include online social networks, blogs and wikis. As these have become more widespread across many different age cohorts, their use in distance classes should be considered among the many tools to incorporate.

Online social networks, such as Facebook, have become the de-facto communication tool among traditional college students. However, these networks are also being adopted by people in all generations and many socio-economic groups. The ability to easily communicate via instant messaging, images and the incorporation of video vehicles such as YouTube holds great promise in the virtual classroom. These new technologies and tools also have features that greatly facilitate work among students. These include shared calendars to coordinate work and scheduling, document editing, white board collaboration, and task management capabilities. Social desktops are new tools that offer a desktop area where many different applications (calendars, forums, messaging, etc.) can be accessed by collaborators in a unified manner. Even widely accepted distance educational technologies like Blackboard (WebCT) have now incorporated Web 2.0 features. For example, Blackboard 9.0 has added blogs and journals that students and professors can use to easily capture and share their reflections and knowledge (Redden, 2009). These updated distance technologies are also using the digital dashboard approach commonly found in the business world to make different applications easily available to students and professors.

Another value of incorporating social networking technologies involves the ability to engage the

students and increase their comfort level with the technologies and thus, with the course. According to the Technology Acceptance Model (TAM), user attitudes influence their acceptance and adoption of technologies (Lee et al., 2003). Therefore, by incorporating widely used and familiar technologies like Facebook into an online course, student can "hit the ground running" when they begin the course, feeling confident in their use of technology and the ability to communicate effectively with fellow students and the professor. Another interesting example of a social networking tool is Twitter - which serves a communication function similar to Facebook, and is also a widely used and accepted communication platform. According to Ritter (2008), "At Penn State, twitter has changed the culture on campus and has given us ways to connect across our university that we couldn't have imagined. We've used twitter to ask for help, work on projects, discuss topics during conferences, schedule impromptu lunches, and offer things for sale. We've planned meetings, found opportunities to collaborate and have become a much more connected, intelligent, communicative group that now includes people from several Penn State campuses, departments and academic colleges. We are IT professionals, professors, advisers, learning designers, and students. We have used twitter to build a community that now thrives at Penn State." Her statement clearly shows the value of a technology like this in an online class as well as across the campus.

Other Technologies

New, emerging technologies, such as "Second Life" represent potentially valuable tools to incorporate into a virtual classroom. For example, a Holocaust survivor used Second Life, with the help of her grand-daughter to share her memories, a powerful lesson in history (http://blog.wired.com/games/2009/01/video-holocaust.html). Similarly, widespread use of video platforms such as YouTube greatly enrich the educational experience, particularly in an online class where students appreciate the real examples and audio-visual experience.

Beldarrain (2006) encourages the use of new, emerging technologies like Blogs (Weblogs), wikis, and podcasts. Blogs encourage writing and reflection while wikis (central knowledge repositories like Wikipedia) encourage contributions to collective knowledge building. According to Wikpedia, "A podcast is a media file that is distributed by subscription (paid or unpaid) over the Internet using syndication feeds, for playback on mobile devices and personal computers" (http://en.wikipedia.org/wiki/Podcasting). These emerging technologies can be used to download audio or video files on a computer, creating new representations of ideas and communication. Bonk and Zhang (2006) extend this model by suggesting that these technologies support different learning styles. For example, podcasting would facilitate an audio-learning style while blogs or Communities of Practice / discussion forums could support an innovative, reflective learning style. Instant messaging, chat, online simulations, and portals represent other potential technologies to create active learning in online classes.

Virtual Teams in Distance Learning

While researchers have demonstrated the value of learning communities in distance classes, the reality and challenge still lie in the ability to achieve true communication among the students (Rigou et al, 2004). Collaborative interpretation allows students to engage each other via asynchronous communication of different ideas, perspectives, and knowledge (Sakai et al, 2004). Many of the technologies discussed focus on encouraging communication both synchronously or asynchronously.

Challenges of Hybrid Classes

In contrast to a live class, where theoretically everyone can contribute to a discussion or problem-solving session, the distance format often became bogged down. When students become very engaged and enthusiastic about the class and contribute to the discussion forums, the logistics of communication becomes overwhelming. With overlapping discussion postings and multiple threads occurring simultaneously, it becomes difficult to maintain coherence and teams can lose track of what the other teams are doing. Also, as CoP's thrive and the number of e-mails or discussion forum postings multiply, people often cannot find the information they need. This could be alleviated with a more organized system of e-mail folders. Technologies, such as G-Mail from Google (http://www.gmail.google.com) that allows effective searching within e-mail, may alleviate this problem in the future.

In addition, hybrid classes have the potential to create "us verses them" mentalities between the "live" and the distance students. By requiring everyone to communicate using all of the technologies, this helps to reduce the perceived differences among the students.

Value of Live Video-Conference Meetings

While asynchronous systems allow for exploration, collaboration, and discussion, many students have an 'Ah Ha!' experience during synchronous live video-conference meetings. Both systems can be incorporated within organically developed CoP's to enable effective distance learning. Videoconferencing greatly contributes to a shared understanding between students and instructors and among the students, thus significantly contributing to the learning experience. This is supported by Bernhard et al. (2006) in their study of collaborative learning in videoconferencing environments. They found that learners can create shared meaning and representations via the ability to elaborate and explain with both audio and visual aids. In other words, the ability to see, hear, and explain greatly facilitates learning of complex, theoretical, unstructured concepts. Therefore we believe that CoP's represent a vital component of a distance class, and a varied array of web technologies should be harnessed in order to create well functioning and interactive CoP's'.

LESSONS LEARNED

Hybrid, Traditional or Online Classes

As discussed in this chapter, course delivery makes a huge difference in how students become engaged and learn in the classroom. The lessons learned here are that instructors must design a course to take advantage of the strengths of the course delivery method as well as the learning styles of the students. For example, in a live traditional class, the instructor can engage the students with complex or controversial problems that require the rich, subtle face-to-face interactions that enhance the learning experience. In an online class, the instructor can take advantage of the vast amounts of information available on the web to encourage discovery of information and reflection via online discussion forums. An instructor can also explore new, emerging technologies such as Second Life to engage students in virtual hands-on simulations. An example would be a mechanical engineering class where students can work collaboratively to construct a new type of bridge in a simulated environment. Finally, the challenge of hybrid classes is how to develop a cohesive learning community between the traditional and the distance students. Lessons learned from this chapter involve the required use of technologies to develop virtual communities using a variety of technologies available, both synchronous and asynchronous.

Importance of Communities of Practice

A crucial component to a successful distance class is to establish a culture of participation and interaction among people who had had little or no personal contact. Communities of Practice that encourage respect and tolerance, while clearly communicating shared goals, help to create a vibrant online class. In addition, we believe that by challenging students and creating an intellectually stimulating, creative environment, where students explore areas of interest to them, a culture can be created to improve communication and motivation in the class., thus adding meaning and value to their own Community of Practice.

Importance of Live, Synchronous Communication

One of the most striking lessons from the literature is the immense value of bringing the students and professors together via video-conferencing technologies. The rapport and trust established at these meetings, where people met face-to-face (via video-conferencing technologies) has been found to be crucial to subsequent asynchronous communications. Live meetings create spontaneous innovation and knowledge discovery via knowledge sharing. The resulting idea generation, clarifications, and personal relationship development are crucial to meaningful knowledge sharing and collaborative work throughout the course.

Importance of New, Emerging Technologies

Instructors cannot forget the value of incorporating new, emerging technologies such as Facebook, You-tube, second life, wikis, and blogs among others, into the CoP's they wish to create. The adoption and diffusion of these relationship-oriented systems creates an added dimension of reality and camaraderie to the class.

CONCLUSION

Distance education represents a greatly needed vehicle for educational delivery, especially in higher education. Hybrid classes which mix traditional students in physical classrooms with distance students who participate via the Internet represent a wonderful use of scarce resources for college and universities. However, the "build it and they will come" approach will not work. Professors and administrators must recognize the challenges inherent in providing a quality education in a virtual environment as well as the difficulties in creating a unified class when people are in very different environments.

Using Communities of Practice to create collaborative work and engaged, meaningful student participation is essential to effective distance learning. Bringing students together via synchronous video-conferencing is required to build trust and develop relationships needed throughout the course. Finally, using newer Web 2.0 technologies represents the "icing on the cake" whereby students and professors can communicate in rich, engaging environments to make the class a real community where everyone feels included, valued, and expected to be part of a vibrant learning experience.

REFERENCES

Beldarrain, Y. (2006). Distance education trends: Integrating new technologies to foster student interaction and collaboration. *Distance Education, 27*(2), 139–153. doi:10.1080/01587910600789498

Bernhard, E., Fischer, F., & Mandl, H. (2006). Conceptual and socio-cognitive support for collaborative learning in videoconferencing environments. *Computers & Education, 47*, 298–315. doi:10.1016/j.compedu.2004.11.001

Bonk, C., & Zhang, K. (2006). Introducing the R2D2 model: Online learning for the diverse learners of this world. *Distance Education, 27*(2), 249–264. doi:10.1080/01587910600789670

Brower, H. H. (2003). On emulating classroom discussion in a distance-delivered OBHR course: Creating an on-line learning community. *Academy of Management Learning & Education, 2*(1), 22–37.

Chou, C. (2003). Interactivity and interactive functions in Web-based learning systems: A technical framework for designers. *British Journal of Educational Technology, 34*(3), 265–279. doi:10.1111/1467-8535.00326

Conrad, D. (2008). From community to community of practice: Exploring the connection of online learners to informal learning in the workplace. *American Journal of Distance Education, 22*(1), 3–23. doi:10.1080/08923640701713414

Darabi, A. A., Sikorski, E. G., & Harvey, R. B. (2006). Validated competencies for distance teaching. *Distance Education, 27*(1), 105–122. doi:10.1080/01587910600654809

Diaz, D., & Cartnal, R. (1999). Comparing student learning styles in an online distance learning class and an equivalent on-campus class. *College Teaching, 47*(4), 130–135.

Dickey, M. (2004). The impact of Web-logs (blogs) on student perceptions of isolation and alienation in a Web-based distance-learning environment. *Open Learning, 19*(3), 279–291. doi:10.1080/0268051042000280138

Doering, A. (2006). Adventure learning: Transformative hybrid online education. *Distance Education, 27*(2), 197–215. doi:10.1080/01587910600789571

GAO (United States Government Accountability Office). (2007). *HIGHER EDUCATION: Challenges in attracting international students to the united states and implications for global competitiveness*

Gee, D. (1990). *The impact of students' preferred learning style variables in a distance education course: A case study*. Portales, NM: Eastern New Mexico University. (ERIC Document Reproduction Service No. ED 358 836)

Gunawardena, C. N., Ortegano-Layne, L., Carabajal, K., Frechette, C., Lindemann, K., & Jennings, B. (2006). New model, new strategies: Instructional design for building online wisdom communities. *Distance Education, 27*(2), 217–232. doi:10.1080/01587910600789613

Heck, J. (2009). State, national universities see spike in distance-learning enrollment. *Dallas Business Journal*.

Hedberg, J. G. (2003). Ensuring quality e-learning: Creating engaging tasks. *Educational Media International, 40*(3), 175–187. doi:10.1080/0952398032000113095

Hedberg, J. G. (2006). E-learning futures? Speculations for a time yet to come. *Studies in Continuing Education, 28*(2), 171–183. doi:10.1080/01580370600751187

Hung, D., & Der-Thanq, C. (2001). Situated cognition, Vygotskian thought and learning from the communities of practice perspective: Implications for the design of Web-based e-learning. *Educational Media International, 38*(1), 3–12. doi:10.1080/09523980110037525

Johnson, C. (2001). A survey of current research on online communities of practice. *The Internet and Higher Education, 4*(1), 45–60. doi:10.1016/S1096-7516(01)00047-1

Lee, J. Cho., H., Gay, G., Davidosn, B., & Ingraffea, T. (2003). *Technology acceptance and social networking in distance education*.

Lesser, E., & Storck, J. (2001). Communities of practice and organizational performance. *IBM Systems Journal, 40*(4), 831–842.

Liu, Y., & Ginther, D. (1999). Cognitive styles and distance education. *Online Journal of Distance Learning Administration, 2*(3).

Martinez, R. (2004). Online education: Designing for the future in appraiser education. *The Appraisal Journal, 72*(3), 266–184.

Puntambekar, S. (2006). Analyzing collaborative interactions: Divergence, shared understanding and construction of knowledge. *Computers & Education, 47*, 332–351. doi:10.1016/j.compedu.2004.10.012

Rafaeli, S., Barak, M., Dan-Gur, Y., & Toch, E. (2004). QSIA – a Web-based environment for learning, assessing and knowledge sharing in communities. *Computers & Education, 43*(3), 273–289. doi:10.1016/j.compedu.2003.10.008

Redden, E. (2009). Blackboard 9.0. *Inside Higher Ed*.

Riedel, C. (2009). *Immersive gameplay: The future of education?*

Rigou, M., Sirmakessis, S., & Tsakalidas, A. (2004). Integrating personalization in e-learning communities. *Journal of Distance Learning Technologies, 2*(3), 47–58.

Ritter, S. (2008). *Social networking in higher education. Penn State World Campus*.

Robinson, P. (Director), & Kinsella, W. (Writer). (1989). *Field of dreams* [Motion picture]. USA: Gordon Company.

Roblyer, M. D., Davis, L., Mills, S. C., Marshall, J., & Pape, L. (2008). Toward practical procedures for predicting and promoting success in virtual school students'. *American Journal of Distance Education, 22*(2), 90–109. doi:10.1080/08923640802039040

Sakai, S., Mashita, N., Yoshimitsu, Y., Shingeno, H., & Okada, K. (2004). An efficient method of supporting interactions for an integrated learning system. *Journal of Distance Education Technologies, 2*(3), 1–10.

Schullo, S., Hilbelink, A., Venable, M., & Barron, A. (2009). Selecting a virtual classroom system: Elluminate live vs. macromedia breeze (Adobe Acrobat Connect Professional). *Journal of Online Learning and Teaching.*

Sharda, R., Romano, N., Lucca, J., Weiser, M., Scheets, G., Chung, J., & Sleezer, C. (2004). Foundation for the study of computer-supported collaborative learning requiring immersive presence. *Journal of Management Information Systems, 20*(4), 31–63.

Timmer, J. (2009). College courses: even "offline" classes are online now. *Science.*

Valenta, A., et al. (2001). Identifying Student Attitudes and Learning Styles in Distance Education. *Journal of Asynchronous Learning Networks, 5*(2).

Waddill, D. D., Milter, R., & Stinson, J. (2006). Innovative action-based e-learning strategies. In *Proceedings of the AHRD Scholar-Practitioner Track* (pp. 603-608).

Wenger, E. (2009). *Communities of practice.*

Wenger, E., & Snyder, W. (2000). Communities of practice: The organizational frontier. *Harvard Business Review, 78*(1), 139–145.

Wild, R. H., Griggs, K. A., & Li, E. Y. (2005). An architecture for distributed scenario building and evaluation. *Communications of the ACM, 48*(11), 80–86. doi:10.1145/1096000.1096009

Chapter 13

The Role of Learner in an Online Community of Inquiry
Instructor Support for First-time Online Learners

Martha Cleveland-Innes
Athabasca University, Canada

Randy Garrison
The University of Calgary, Canada

ABSTRACT

Students experiencing an online educational community for the first time experience adjustment in the role of learner. Findings from a study of adjustment to online learning from the instructor's point of view validate five main areas of adjustment identified in previous research: technology, instructor role, modes of interaction, self-identity and course design. Using a confirmatory research model, instructors from two open and distance institutions were interviewed. Data confirmed that instructors also perceive adjustment in the five areas of online experience identified by students. In addition, student adjustment in these five areas can be understood in light of core dimensions of learner role requirements in an online community of inquiry (Garrison, Anderson, and Archer, 2000). Instructor comments provide understanding of the experience of online learners, including the challenges, interventions and resolutions that present themselves as unique incidents. Recommendations for the support and facilitation of adjustment are made. Funding for this research was received from the Athabasca University Mission Critical Research Fund.

INTRODUCTION

The move to online delivery in post-secondary education institutions has increased exponentially over the last decade. Early concerns were raised about the extent to which students would embrace online education. However, recent evaluation of student enrolment in online courses indicates much willingness to engage; optimistic online enrolment projections are now a reality and there are implications that growth will continue. "Online enrolments continue to grow at rates faster than for the overall student body, and schools expect the rate of growth

DOI: 10.4018/978-1-60566-711-9.ch013

to further increase." (Allen & Seaman, 2004, Introduction, 3rd para.). Eighty-one percent of all institutions of higher education in the United States offer at least one fully online or blended course and 67% recognized online education as a critical long term strategy for their institution. In the United States enrolment of online learners grew to approximately 3.5 million, a 21 percent increase since 2002 (Allen & Seaman, 2007).

As growth continues, more and more students will experience online education. Students will require new skills to be competent online learners, and will modify behaviours from classroom learning to fit the online environment. The new skills include the ability to be socially and cognitively present (Garrison & Cleveland-Innes, 2005) by interacting with others, sharing experiences and demonstrating exploration, integration and application of content knowledge. This requires, in particular, the ability to overcome limitations in social and academic interaction precipitated by the lack of visual and verbal cues available in face-to-face learning. Otherwise, understanding content and constructing knowledge will be limited to what one can foster on one's own (Piccard, 1997; Rice; 1992).

The context then, of teaching and learning in online environments, is very different from long standing classroom structure in that it depends upon different technologies, unique communication processes, instructors operating from a distance, multimedia instructional materials within an involved course design and a new student identity (Collier, 2001). According to Wilson, et al. (2003), "there is also (sic) a need for better understanding of students' adaptation to online learning over time." Adaptation to the role of online learner can be understood by looking at the structure of the online pedagogical environment (Garrison, Anderson & Archer, 2000) and tenets of role theory (Blau & Goodman, 1995) and how role change occurs (Turner, 1990). The integration of new behaviours into one's role repertoire (Kopp, 2000) occurs in a context (Katz

& Kahn, 1978) and through an intricate process of role taking, role exploration and role making (Blau & Goodman, 1995). As such, the newness of the online environment will act as a catalyst for role adjustment for individual students moving online.

This paper replicates the study of adjustment identified by novice online students (Cleveland-Innes, Garrison & Kinsel, 2007), from the point of view of the instructor. Instructors from two open and distance institutions were interviewed regarding the online experience of teaching. Responses were coded and categorized according to five categories of adjustment identified in earlier research: interaction, instructor role, self-identity, course design, and technology. This data was then analyzed a second time to aligned with each of three online presences: cognitive, social and teaching presence. This data validates the earlier areas of adjustment, and gives a view to what instructors do that may support or hinder adjustment. Recommendations are made for incorporating actions or activity into design, direct instruction or facilitation in order to ease adjustment for learners new to the online environment.

Literature Review

Online Community of Inquiry

Learners experiencing an online educational community for the first time can explain the adjustment required for participation. Findings from a study of adjustment to online learning environments validate differences found in three presences in an online community of inquiry. Using pre- and post-questionnaires, students enrolled in entry-level courses in two graduate degree programs at Athabasca University, Canada, describe their adjustment to online learning (Cleveland-Innes, Garrison & Kinsel, 2007). Five areas of adjustment characterize the move toward competence in online learning: interaction, self-identity, instructor role, course design and technology.

Responses were analyzed in relation to the elements of cognitive, social and teaching presence, defined by Garrison, Anderson, and Archer (2000) as core dimensions of learner role requirements in an online community of inquiry.

The community of inquiry model, originally proposed by Garrison, Anderson and Archer (2000), served as the conceptual framework around which to study online learning and learner adjustment. The theoretical foundation of this framework is based upon the work of John Dewey (1938). At the core of Dewey's philosophy are collaboration, free intercourse, and the juxtaposition of the subjective and shared worlds. This is the essence of a community of inquiry. Consistent with his philosophy of pragmatism, Dewey (1933) viewed inquiry as a practical endeavour. Inquiry emerged from practice and shaped practice. Dewey's work on reflective thinking and inquiry provided the inspiration for operationalizing cognitive presence and purposeful learning in the community of inquiry framework (Garrison & Archer, 2000). The other elements of the community of inquiry model, social presence and teaching presence, were derived from other educational sources, but are consistent with Dewey's philosophy and the framework of a community of inquiry (Garrison & Anderson, 2003).

The community of inquiry framework has attracted considerable attention in higher education research. In particular, it has framed many studies of online learning. This speaks to both the importance of community in higher education as well as the usefulness of the framework and how the elements are operationalized. Moreover, the structural validity of the framework has been tested and confirmed through factor analysis (Arbaugh & Hwang, 2006; Garrison, Cleveland-Innes & Fung, 2004; Ice, Arbaugh, Diaz, Garrison, Richardson, Shea, & Swan, 2007). A review of the research using the framework and the identification of current research issues is provided by Garrison and Arbaugh (2007).

An online community of inquiry, replete with interaction opportunities in several places of 'presence' (Garrison & Anderson, 2003) provides a supportive context for the re-development of the role of learner. The relationship among these dimensions is depicted in Figure 1. These are the core elements in an educational experience and key to understanding role adjustment. Cognitive, social and teaching presences represent the primary dimensions of role in an educational context; it has a character of its own in an online environment. Changes in cognitive, social and teaching presence, as a result of a new context and communication medium, will necessitate role adjustments by the learners.

Cognitive presence is defined "as the extent to which learners are able to construct and confirm meaning through sustained reflection and discourse …" (Garrison, Anderson & Archer, 2001, p. 11). Role adjustment here reflects the nature of the communication medium: spontaneous, verbal communication is supplanted by a reflective, text-based medium. This represents a radical departure from classroom interaction. A more precise and recorded form of communication, the text-based medium has the potential to support deep and meaningful learning outcomes.

Social presence is defined as "the ability of participants to identify with the community (e.g., course of study), communicate purposefully in a trusting environment, and develop inter-personal relationships by way of projecting their individual personalities" (Garrison, in press). In addition to the general challenge of asynchronous written communication and its lack of non-verbal cues, is the challenge of group identity. An essential characteristic of online learning is open communication and group cohesion. Social presence provides the capacity to communicate and collaborate. This requires that members identify with the group or class (Rogers & Lea, 2005). Since the educational experience is a social transaction, special consideration must be given to the social interactions and climate. Interpersonal and emotional communication should build over time. Social presence represents a major role adjustment

Figure 1.

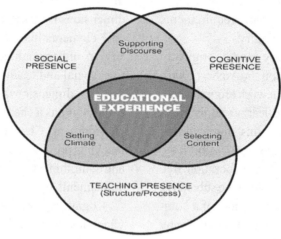

in moving from a real-time face-to-face classroom experience to a virtual community.

Teaching presence is defined as "the design, facilitation and direction of cognitive and social processes for the purpose of realizing personally meaningful and educationally worthwhile learning outcomes" (Anderson, Rourke, Garrison, and Archer, 2001). It is what binds all the elements together in a purposeful community of inquiry. The properties of the online community also necessitate significant design changes and role adjustment for the teacher. Teaching presence must recognize and utilize the unique features of the medium and structure and model appropriate learning activities. This translates into an experience and role that may not be at all familiar to the learner.

All three presences are required by instructor and student alike. The instructor holds the central authority and uses the opportunity to design, facilitate and instruct content, and to assist in the development of skill as a learner. Research indicates that adequate teaching presence is key to learner outcomes (Garrison & Cleveland-Innes, 2005; Murphy, 2004; Shea, Li, Swan & Pickett, 2005; Swan & Shih, 2005; Vaughn & Garrison,

2006; Wu & Hiltz, 2004) and that the learner is aware of the importance of the instructor in the development of a productive and satisfying learning experience (Cleveland-Innes, Garrison & Kinsel, 2007).

Role Adjustment

'Role' is used here as a sociological construct, defined as a collection of behavioral requirements associated with a certain social position in a group, organization or society (Kendall, Murray & Linden, 2000). At its most general level, role expectations are dictated by the social structure. Individuals who engage in the role are guided, through a process of socialization, to appropriate role performance. Socialization then refers to the "process by which people learn the characteristics of their group ... (and) the attitudes, values and actions thought appropriate for them" (Kanwar & Swenson, 2000, p. 397).

Under conditions of long-standing roles, individuals engage in 'role-taking' behavior, where observation and mimicry of role models allow those new to the role to 'practice' appropriate role behaviors. 'Role making' occurs as individuals construct aspects of the role with their own individual meanings and satisfying behaviors attached. This occurs under social conditions where such individual autonomy is allowed. It also occurs where role models are not readily available, and construction of the role is required.

Such is the case for becoming an online learner. An adjustment from the more generalized role of learner, the responsibilities and requirements of working online are not readily apparent to those new to the role. The transition to, and adjustment in, the role of online learner, is part of the current social climate in online learning. While maintaining the usual expectations and privileges attached to the role of learner, online learners add such things as:

- knowledge about, skill with and acceptance of the technology,
- new amounts and modes of communication with instructors, peers and administrators,
- increased levels of learner self-direction, and
- a new 'place' for learning in time (anytime, usually determined by the learner and their life circumstances) and space (anywhere, dependent upon equipment requirements).

An online community of inquiry is a distinct personal and public search for meaning and understanding. New roles are necessitated in an online community by the nature of the communication which compels students to assume greater responsibility for and control over their learning. As McLuhan observed, "each form of transport not only carries, but translates and transforms the sender, the receiver and the message" (McLuhan, 1995, p. 90). An asynchronous and collaborative learning community necessitates the adoption of personal responsibility and shared control. This goes to the heart of an online learning community and represents a significant shift from the information transmission of the lecture hall and the passive role of students. Thus, online learn-

ing communities demand role adjustments. This brings another need: to understand changes in responsibilities and roles.

Differences in the required activities of online learning, in comparison to classroom based face-to-face, result in new, required expectations and behaviors for learners. These new activities cluster into a pattern that is seen as the 'role' of online learner. The term role refers to the expected and generally accepted ways of behaving, acting and interacting (Knuttila, 2002). Taking on a role (e.g. teacher, mother, learner) involves learning what the expected behaviors are through a process of observation and trial and error attempts at the role (Collier, 2001). While the adoption and enactment of social role s is a standard, commonplace element of everyday experience, becoming an online learner has a unique characteristic. For many learners, role models for learning the required and expected activities are not present until one is already engaged in an online course (Garrison & Cleveland-Innes, 2003).

Role acquisition is part of individuation in the experience of working online. Each online learner engages in the experience of learning online and the process of role taking and role making occurs concurrently within the learning experience. From the perspective of the individual, learning online requires the development of competencies in the role of 'online learner'. As a new social role, the pathway to competence will occur over time as the role becomes prevalent and normalized. In this early stage, online communities will contribute to the socialization process for those engaging in this new role . The result is a new role and a new identity for learners.

Methodology

Sample

Instructors from online programs in two open and distance institutions were identified. One institution is located in Alberta, Canada and the other in

Catalonia, Spain. The institutions were chosen for their mandate to provide open, distance and online programs and courses. However, data from two institutions from two different geographic locations with different histories allows us to consider adjustment to online learning without the bias of culture or language. A convenience sample of online instructors working at these institutions, with varying amounts of experience, across a variety of subjects, was selected. Data collection stopped at thirty-nine (39) instructor interviews, twenty (20) from the institution in Canada and nineteen (19) from Spain, as it appeared no new insights were surfacing in the data.

Instructors from three separate programs participated. One program is a social science Master's Degree in Interdisciplinary Study. The two other programs are Master's Degrees in Education with a concentration in Distance Education. Both programs are offered entirely online on a learning platform of asynchronous communication. Courses ranged across multiple subject areas including philosophy, research methods and education technology. This variation of course was included to randomize any possible subject-matter effects that may influence results. All courses were delivered using a combination of print and electronic media and online conferencing. The online conferencing component provided the opportunity for student engagement and group interaction. Required conference participation was used for assessment in some courses while it remained a voluntary activity in others.

Data Collection

Three research assistants interviewed twenty-one Canadian instructors via telephone. As telephone interviews were inconvenient or unfeasible for Catalonia instructors, this group of respondents completed online questionnaires. Eighteen University of Catalonia instructors participated in the survey. Questions posed to Catalonia instructors were conceptually similar, but not worded identically to questions posed to Canadian instructors.

Interviews divided randomly between three interviewers for Athabasca sample. Interview process used semi-structured approach in that questions were used as guidelines and probing was allowed. This let interviewees speak off topic, going beyond the interview schedule at times. Interview data from OUC respondents was accepted at face value, as written by respondents.

Questions focused on instructional elements of design, facilitation and direct instruction as they relate to the three presences. References to student behaviour and adjustment to online environments were unintended findings that were analyzed as secondary findings.

Data Analysis

Five themes, identified from the grounded theory work provided in previous studies of first-time online students (Cleveland-Innes, Garrison & Kinsel, 20097). These themes are interaction, instructor role, self-identity, course design, and technology. Definitions of these constructs are outlined below. *Interaction:* Issues related to quality, quantity, and value of dialogue with other students and instructors. *InstructorRole*: Respondents commented on the activities of the instructor in the conference forums and the quantity, quality and timing of feedback. *Self-identity*: Respondents discussed learning style, personal needs, and increasing responsibility and *ownership* for learning. *Design*: Respondents commented on the effectiveness of course design and delivery and the availability of institutional support. *Technology*: Respondents pointed out technology issues that may affect *participation* in an online community, and slow adjustment to the role of online learner.

Identifiers were removed and interview transcripts saved based on a numerical scheme to retain confidentiality. Two interviewers imported transcripts to NVivo as rtf documents. A coding scheme was developed in NVivo based on a coding rubric previously created for coding online discussion transcripts. Inter-rater reliability was evaluated across coders. Inter-rater reliability ranged from 63% to 100% on initial coding. Discussion between coders regarding subjective meanings and code definitions resulted in almost perfect coding agreement.

Findings

The purpose of this study was to assess the instructor view of students in the role of online learner. Their responses to interview questions yielded one hundred and fifteen (115) pages of text. The data reflect varying aspects of the online learner experience, clustering around the emergent themes of interaction, instructor role, self-identity, course design, and technology. These themes are explored in relation to cognitive, social and teaching presence in the online environment. Sample comments from students, gathered in previous research, and instructor comments from this research are provided here. The complete data set is available from the authors. Numerical counts refer the amount of instructor reference to each area of adjustment in each category of presence in online communities.

Cognitive Presence

Table 1 provides sample comments from instructors regarding adjustments in cognitive presence in an online community of inquiry specific to each of the themes (numbers indicate the number of utterances identified under this code). Instructors identified unique student behaviours and the extent to which these vary. Instructors spoke much more about course design and interaction in relation to cognitive presence than they did about student identity, technology or instructor role .

Social Presence

Sample comments on adjustment in social presence in an online community of inquiry are shown in Table 2.

Teaching Presence

Table 3 includes sample comments from instructors and students regarding learner adjustment to a changed teaching presence from past experience in face-to-face learning environments.

All five components identified as areas of adjustment by the students were identified by instructors. Subsequent coding of presence in the online community of inquiry model was done. Across the three presences, instructor reference to areas of adjustment changed. *Interaction* was the discussed most often in relation to social presence (74 utterances coded to interaction/social presence). Interaction in relation to cognitive (38) and teaching presence (42) was demonstrated in roughly equal amounts. *Self-identity* for students is an issue for social (74) and teaching presence (52), but less so for cognitive presence (42). The *instructor role* was discussed almost solely in reference to teaching presence issues (116) of design, facilitation and direct instruction. Cognitive presence (18) and social presence (36) were offshoots and sub-textual requirements in the instructor discussion of their role . *Technology* is also sub-textual, peripheral to discussions of presence; "I think the technology is least important of all." Limited references were made to the technology and the three presences: cognitive presence (1), social presence (3) and teaching presence (5). *Course design* was described by these instructors with attention to all three areas, but an understandable predominance of attention to teaching presence: cognitive presence 16 times, social presence 14 times, and teaching presence 32 times.

Discussion

It is clear that adjustments are taking place for students engaging in online learning, and that students and instructors notice. Using the categories of adjustment from our previous work, and the community of inquiry model, a valuable taxonomy for organizing the character of this adjustment emerges. In each element of presence, the same five themes identified areas where change is taking place. Evident in instructor descriptions of the student experience is a unique orientation to

Table 1. Adjustment in Cognitive Presence

	Students' selected comments	**Instructors' selected comments**[1]
Interaction	At first, I hesitated in fear of saying something wrong (similar feelings in F2F situations as well). However, after receiving feedback from other colleagues, the online conference engagements became enjoyable and valuable from a learning outcome perspective.	I mean it is not just by default that, though I do try to word things for some of the conferences in such a way that they won't get enough, they won't get everything they need out of the lessons unless their fellow students share. (38)
Instructor Role	I have found that it is more difficult to be sure that you understand the material in the online learning because there is little discussion with the prof. The prof seems to set up the lecture and then let us talk amongst ourselves with no interaction to let us know if we are on the right track.	I would add clarity in the sense of being very, very aware of your interpretation of, of not only the course author's material but also how you understanding the student's posting. Because I found for example, little, there seemed to be instances where people were talking in this kind of assumptive way. Everybody is going to understand me in the way I am thinking...And it was kind of, I often had to step in and say, "Just a minute now, quick clarification, do you mean this or that?" And they would say, "Oh, I hadn't thought of that. And well, here's part of how I would always link it back to the course content...Here's how you are framed by Western thinking or whatever. You know what I mean, that you actually made this assumption and they started to become much more careful about the way they framed what they said. And one person actually emailed me and said, "You know I am getting a bit of a headache trying to do this." And I said, "Well, I am not forcing you to. I am encouraging you to and there is a difference." but you, there is always going to be the possibility that we will misunderstand each other without the visual clues...That the chance of that goes way up. So strategy with your words seems utterly important. And encouraging it with others is utterly important as well. (18)
Self-identity	I feel that I don't have as much to offer as others, either because I have had a more limited scope of learning or life experiences or because I can be intimidated by huge thoughts from bright people.	Certainly the fact that they are posting, some of them 20 and 30 posts a month, responding to each other and supporting each other would, you know, it is not a requirement, it is not a structured activity. It is something they do of their own volition. And I think if they weren't learning and weren't enjoying it they wouldn't be doing it. (42)
Course Design	Gaining equal participation and a common understanding in group work was a challenge. At the same time, it led to bonding between some group members. Group assignments early in the class helped to get us started quickly.	The final learning and application of the principles we've talked about in the lesson won't take place unless people take part in those conferences... They are crucial that way. (16)
Technology	I like asking questions, but I rarely do on-line. I like clarifying things, but I rarely do on-line. I like to participate in class, but I'm a slow typist, so I rarely do on-line.	They still made an effort to post at least once a week, you know, so it was an interesting dynamic that way anyway. So that, I would say that was the one case where it was hindering the course objectives. (1)

Table 2. Adjustment in Social Presence

	Students' selected comments	Instructors' selected comments[2]
Interaction	I did notice my emotional, social ability to communicate became easier and I felt more relaxed as the course progressed.	They also can use blogs or wikis to share with other students and teachers, their complains, problems, suggestions, doubts, etc. (74)
Instructor Role	The only aspect (once again) that I found challenging was that I didn't really feel that I got a sense of 'knowing' the instructor, nor did he really get to 'know' me.	I find these are teachers, they really jump in and share resources, programs, web sites, approaches. Often they'll even ask each other, they say, "Oh, you know, I have a situation like this." I am not sure what to do and they'll get like ten responses back. (36)
Self-identity	I find that I am much more open and interactive online than I am in person… I am not able to "hide in the corner" as I could in a live class.	After a bit of time, the social people, um, get an academic feel. You now, that starts to come through as they see where they fit. (74)
Course Design	I found the use of small working groups to be a positive way of getting people to interact with one another, allowing me to project myself as a "real" person. It may be tougher to do this in the context of the larger class (i.e. those in other working groups.) One does not have the same degree of back and forth "organizational" communication with these other people. I think I may be less of a three dimensional person to these other people.	Being able to conduct an online discussion is really an art and only some of the students know how to do that and the newer students can then learn form the more experienced. (14)
Technology	Not ever having learned how to type may also be a factor as I [consider it] to be a handicap the same way someone who has difficulty expressing themselves verbally would. (#37)	I think his intent in saying he felt it was a better forum in that his voice was still heard…electronically versus in the classroom the discussion bullies took over…but for him this was his opportunity to put, to have his voice heard where he wants it heard, when he wants it heard. (3)

five thematic areas, which together embody the experience of online learner.

This diagram also identifies challenges, intervention and resolution as a continuous process in the adjustment of students to online learning. Challenges are identified as those things students find difficult, uncomfortable or in any way problematic regarding the online learning environment. Interventions are any occurrence that ensued after the challenge, either deliberately or incidentally. Resolution refers to what the students describe as happening after. Instructor data has not yet been analyzed for these concepts; this will be reported in future discussions.

Cognitive Presence

Students and instructors identify he fear of being misunderstood or saying something wrong. Instructor responses to this lack of confidence include monitoring the light or absent posting, reassurance on postings, and private email to students. Instructors discussed the other end of this phenomenon as well; some groups of online students manage the group on their own, caring for reluctant members and supporting all members. In this case, the instructor role is diffused among students. The 'instructor of record' monitors activity and fills in any gaps of understanding or process noted. The online learners had reported an adjustment to assuming this greater responsibility for understanding of the material without direct instruction from the professors. Instructors noted

Table 3. Adjustment to Teaching Presence

	Students' selected comments	Instructors' selected comments[3]
Interaction	Once we were comfortable with his role as more of a guide and facilitator than an omni-present being, we were able to take more ownership for our role in the program and for our own investment in the course.	Because I leave the forums open they can come back to these discussions going on. So often in the discussion of the latter books people would make postings where they make connections between the previous six weeks. Its interesting how they would do that loop without my prompting. They were making these connections so that is an important part of leaving those open so they can go back. (42)
Instructor Role	I'm certain that [the professor] reviewed the discussion threads regularly but he seemed more like the virtual "fly on the wall" than an active participant.	I mean it is not just by default that, though I do try to word things for some of the conferences in such a way that they won't get enough, they won't get everything they need out of the lessons unless their fellow students share. (116)
Self-identity	I personally felt that a little more input and guidance from the instructor might have removed some anxiety and stimulated some interaction on my part.	The students would acknowledge to each other that something was very sobering and thank each other. That's, that's like, "Oh, right on!" You know, that typical thing that teachers feel when students have had an "A-ha" moment. And I find, to be honest, I find the ones when I wasn't responsible for that much more gratifying… It happened because of this organic thing that happens, you know, between each student in the class and the unique entity that is the group of students. (52)
Course Design	I think the instructor needs to be a very active participant at the beginning of the course. Everyone seems eager to talk to each other at the beginning (how many times did I log in on the first day to see if there was anything new?), and the instructor should tap into that by starting to focus that energy on the content.	But um but getting back to the notion of collaborative learning I mean, that could be, that could be happening in the discussions, but um, if it is it`s not happening by design, like they`re not designed with that in mind… It`s more the discussions are about sharing ideas um, so that…Yeah, so that collaborative learning if it`s happening, it`s incidental or accidental. (32)
Technology	Most emails sent by my instructor disappeared and I did not know what I had to do.	There's also issues of technical problems, where, for example, they can't even get into the discussion forum they're supposed to be in, to post at all. (5)

Figure 2.

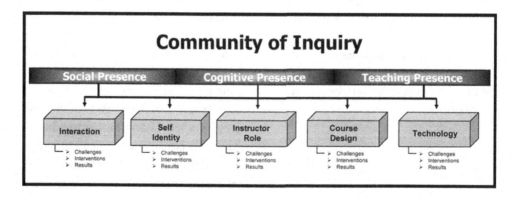

this is the case for some students, in some groups. In other groups, much more direct instruction and facilitation is required.

Social Presence

Instructors made reference to their role in the social group with the students, but only as it related to an effective role as instructor; appropriate social presence is a necessary but insufficient condition for teaching presence. Online learners expressed a need for time to feel comfortable communicating in a text-only environment and to adjust to expressing emotion and communicating openly without visual or other context cues. Instructors need to be sensitive and supportive in this regard. "I think if you do they do. You set the tone for what the comfort zone is in there, both in what you post and in how you post." Instructors provide opportunities for a student to engage each other in various ways; group project, joint presentations, special interest groups. Some students were happy to connect with one or a few other learners in a small group activity while others found this difficult to manage. Both instructors and students had stories to tell of group members who dominated the group. Instructors saw these 'leaders' as, at times, helpful to group development and learning, and at other times a hindrance.

Teaching Presence

The importance of teaching presence is demonstrated in differences noted across instructors. Evidence here affirms Garrison & Cleveland-Innes' (2005) premise that "teaching presence must be available, either from the facilitator or the other learners, in order to transition from social to cognitive presence." (p. 16). Without adequate support from the instructor, adjustment occurs without a clear point of reference to expectations. This lack may create a situation fails to sustain interest and engagement. This supports previous evidence that learners without guidance operate remotely: "without instructor's explicit guidance and 'teaching presence,' students were found to engage primarily in 'serial monologues'" (Pawan, et al., 2003, p. 119). Teaching presence supports sustained, beneficial academic interaction, movement within the presences of online community and, for first-time online learners, points of reference regarding expectations in the adjustment to the online environment.

Interaction

Interaction was seen as crucial means to relieve initial anxieties and to create group cohesion. Through communication, students come to learn that they are not alone with their fears and that others can offer valuable insights to assist them in overcoming obstacles. By sharing their opinions and experiences, students become familiarized with each other and develop mutual bonds that increase their motivation to learn. But group dynamics can differ with each course offering: one cohort may develop a strong learning community with vigorous exchanges, while another group may never gel and conversations may be stilted. When cohesion is strong, groups can take on a life of their own, requiring little effort on the part of instructors. But when cohesion is weak, coaxing students to interact is "kind of like dragging a sled over gravel…it's really hard work."

Student interactions also serve to broaden their understanding of subject matter and re-examine their positions. As different backgrounds and experiences come to bear on the subject, students are given an opportunity to consider matters from several perspectives. They may be forced to re-examine their own interpretations and positions in light of these new perspectives and refine their views as a consequence. "The experience they brought was extremely valuable and without that [student interactions] the course would simply not have been. Whatever value the course would have had it wouldn't have had it without that."

Comparisons between face-to-face and online interactions were made, with benefits and drawbacks ascribed to each. Classroom lectures can be immediately altered in response to non-verbal cues that may indicate students' interest (or lack of), confusion or emotional reactions. Picking up on these cues requires more vigilance on the part of online instructors, who must constantly look for clues that students may benefit from additional resources, may be struggling with concepts or emotionally reacting to content. However, online interactions allow learners to revisit and reflect on discussions and produce more in-depth analyses. By keeping conferences open after discussions have moved on to other areas allows students to revisit older lessons in light of their subsequent learning, assisting them to make connections and see larger themes. Online interactions were also considered to be preferable to face-to-face because students have more opportunity to participate. While "discussion bullies" may prevent others from speaking up in class, text-based formats allow everyone to express themselves, and to have more control over the timing and placement of their comments: "this was his opportunity to... have his voice heard where he wants it heard, when he wants it heard."

Instructor Role

Rather than experts who lecture their students, instructors generally saw themselves as active participants in the learning process. "Because I'm part and parcel of the discussion board as well, um, I am responding to individual uh, comments... And I'm also expecting students to take me on as well... And, and I've told them, you know, do not hesitate in challenging me...if I write something that is completely out to lunch, you know, as far as you're concerned, let's, let's get it on and discuss that. Because that's, that's part of the learning curve too."

However, comments must be delivered at appropriate time in order to facilitate dialogue. "I

try to avoid jumping into a discussion too soon. Because some students will, rightly or wrongly view me as the voice of authority. And I want to let them have their own, let them have their voices heard first before I jump in and completely derail it or ruin somebody else's thunder if you will." The timing of feedback is also an issue, as students demand a quick response to their questions and concerns.

Instructors' messages are carefully crafted to avoid misinterpretations, model appropriate behaviour and accomplish a variety of objectives. Questions are used to initiate discussions, stimulate additional dialogue and foster deeper processing. Debates may occasionally drift from their intended themes and require refocusing. Student participation is solicited and their subsequent efforts are acknowledged. Instructors may relate how course concepts have affected their professional practice and encourage students to apply subject matter to their own experiences. Additional resources may be offered to allow individual interests to be pursued.

Self-Identity

Students may initially be intimidated by the instructor's presence. To counter this apprehension, instructors attempt to humanize themselves by sharing personal and professional experiences, revealing personality traits, posting pictures or utilizing humor. They also encourage students to divulge personal details to allow the group to become acquainted and facilitate peer connections.

Students possess varying levels of learning experiences and confidence in their abilities and instructors must accommodate a broad spectrum of needs. Some students are accustomed to passive learning and are disoriented and anxious when they discover that they are now required to be active participants. Others may be intimidated by the learning tasks that they will be asked to perform. Instructors must be vigilant to detect students who may be uncomfortable or struggling: "constantly paying attention to when people seem to be putting barriers up for themselves…Paying attention to the types of cues that people are throwing out, if people are absent, you know, getting on and finding out why."

While instructors work to allay these fears, students take on some of this responsibility themselves as they tend to be very supportive of each other. More experienced students appear happy to provide resources, answer questions and offer advice to less experienced learners. "There's a tremendous generosity of spirit that as somebody who has um, more experience in a particular area or with certain kinds of students will often jump into a conversation and say, 'here you know, I have a url or I have a reference or my experience has been this or that' and they will share these with the other students... they'll go…to extraordinary lengths and actually look something up or find a resource for somebody and simply offer help."

In addition to the sharing of resources or experiences, students are also generally emotionally supportive to each other, displaying feelings of empathy and a "we're all in this together" type of mindset. Students' willingness to assist and support one another works to increase commitment and ownership of learning: "they 'embrace' the course: they actively participate, provide interesting references and websites, help their peers, and demonstrate interest and initiative."

Design

Instructors mention a number of design elements that assist with student role adjustment. Introductory social forums are a means to bring students together as a group and get to know each other. Subsequent conferences provide opportunities to engage with subject matter by sharing reactions, debating interpretations and applying concepts in practical contexts. "The final learning and application of the principles we've talked about in the lesson won't take place unless people take part in those conferences... They are crucial that way."

Student cafes offer students a place to discuss whatever they wish and assist in preventing off-topic discussions from disrupting academic debates. How activities are sequenced and communicated is also important, as is the need for flexibility to accommodate different interests and needs. Students need to know what they are expected to be doing at any given point in the course and how they are to be evaluated. To assist different learning styles and interests, flexibility can be achieved by adjusting time lines or by providing alternate tasks for evaluation purposes.

Technology

Technological breakdowns can hamper access and have a negative effect on both student and instructor participation. When students cannot access course materials or discussion boards they become frustrated and instructors must expend an inordinate amount of time and energy to rectify the situation. Motivation is affected, as students may decline to participate or consider abandoning their learning altogether. Motivation wanes for instructors as well as inboxes are inundated with student complaints and login issues interfere with discussion management.

The instructors made relatively few comments about the students adjusting to the technology. One instructor said "I've seen a positive evolution in the level of students in the use of ICT tools. As a consequence of this higher level, some parts of the subject are less important. Unfortunately the level is not homogeneous." Two issues are of note here. One is that instructors don't see themselves in a support role regarding the technology; the students who struggle are at the mercy of wider university supports, or their own resources, to adjust to the technology. Second, we can predict that, as the digital natives enter the adult cohort and participate in online education, the need for support will diminish. However, the technological expertise and competence will never be homogeneous, as noted by this instructor. This gap needs to remain on the radar screen to ensure equal opportunity for online presence.

These five thematic areas do not act in isolation. Technology use occurs within a particular course design and is more or less optimized by the role of the instructor. Moodle, for example, provides the opportunity to chat synchronously, create a blog, or hare resources; if the course design doesn't require it, or the instructor doesn't provide time to use it, students may or may not experience this technological opportunity. Interaction can be fostered or hindered by the instructor's ability to invite learners to participate, the learners' sense of competence regarding the presentation of ideas in print, the technological possibilities for interaction, and the design of the course in question. In other words, all five themes can be examined separately as they relate to online learning, but must be considered in a comprehensive relationship to each other if we are to illuminate the student experience online.

This is also the case as we examine all five themes in each area of presence. What emerges is a multidimensional perspective that must guide thinking as we design online courses to engage and support students as they adjust to, move into and become competent performing in the online community of inquiry. Technology, for example, has a unique role to play in each of cognitive, social and teaching presence. Social presence becomes possible as learners use the technology to present themselves as individuals through the written word or verbal language. This use of the technology overlaps with, but is unique from cognitive presence, where intellectual reasoning is presented as a portion of individual identity. Teaching presence, available to both students and instructors, emerges where the technology allows for presentation of material, directions from self to others and the interpretation of material.

CONCLUSION AND RECOMMENDATIONS

Course design in online environments is meant to be collaborative. The instructor suggesting that "collaborative learning, if it's happening, it's incidental or accidental" is reflecting lack of awareness about social learning. It is not by accident that students learn through interaction (Pascarella & Terenzini, 1991) and online learning environments run on interaction (Swan, in press). In fact, many instructors noted the importance of student conference activity, and interaction with each other, in the realization of the course objectives. While it may not be a design feature written in to the syllabus, it is an instructional design feature inherent in online communities of inquiry. Fostering safe climate and healthy community affords learning enhancement that is not incidental but critical. The instructor role of facilitation moves beyond facilitating specific learning objectives as stated in the syllabus, but to fostering community as well. Both students and instructors need greater awareness of constructivist processes, and the value of all interaction online.

The adjustment process to the requirements of online learning is not merely a matter of student satisfaction; there are practical and pedagogical implications as well. Much research demonstrates the authenticity of social, cognitive and teaching presence online (see, for example, Meyer, 2003; Shea, Pickett, & Pelz, 2004; Swan, 2003 and Swan, et al., 2008). These elements are unique to the medium and will require established role s for learners and instructors. "Balancing socio-emotional interaction, building group cohesion and facilitating and modeling respectful critical discourse are essential for productive inquiry" (Garrison, 2006, p. 7). The ability to do such things requires students move into the role of online learner; evidence here and elsewhere (Knuttila, 2002) supports the premise that students experience a dynamic adjustment to the role of online learner, made up of particular ways of behaving, acting and interacting. Students grapple with requirements, looking to their own reasoning, other students and the instructor for direction about the right things to do.

Instructors have the opportunity to support the creation of this new role through the elements of teaching presence: design, instruction and facilitation (Anderson, et al., 2001). Adjustments occur in all three areas of presence, and each presence is both constrained and enabled by course design, technology, the instructor, personal self identity and the interaction within the community. For instructors ".... there's a subtext in this course about paying attention to how they learn, how they emotionally respond" to being online.

Attention to these online elements in relation to the 'getting up to speed' or adjustment for learners, each time they join an online community, will smooth this move to competence. In order to become present in the important functionalities of an online community of inquiry, adjustment must occur. Without adjustment to competence as an online learner, the learning process may be hindered. Support for students to move to a place of comfort and sense of competence is of value.

Instructor comments provided additional insight on the comments of online learners describing adjustment to the online community of inquiry. The following recommendations for instructional design and delivery of online courses will ease the adjustment to the role of online learner participating in cognitive, social and teaching presence in an online community of inquiry.

1. Initiate dialogue early in the course to ease anxieties, assist with group cohesion, model appropriate online behaviours, and motivate students to participate.

2. Scale back instructor conference participation as students become accustomed to their role s. Summarize discussions at the end of conferences to acknowledge student efforts and indicate instructor involvement in the progression of learning.

3. Identify appropriate posting lengths and tone at the beginning of a course and model these appropriate behaviours throughout the course.

4. Provide supportive comments to acknowledge student posts and motivate them to continue participating.

5. Look for cues that students may be hesitant, intimidated or unsure of how to conduct themselves and encourage more experienced students to assist with their less experienced peers. Anxiety may be manifested in different ways, such as in a lack of participation, frustrated outbursts, admissions of confusion or fear.

6. Try to encourage group bonding and community development to increase students' ownership of learning and instil a shared sense of commitment to the endeavour. Examples include the use of introductory ice breakers, group activities, encouraging peer-peer support and rapport.

7. Encourage the sharing of personal and professional experiences to broaden learners' overall understanding of course material as multiple views provide a broader perspective.

8. Incorporate an element of flexibility in course design to accommodate different learning styles and needs.

9. Set up a chat room or student cafe for students to socialize outside of regular course confines.

10. Technological interruptions interrupt learning. Pilot-test changes to technology infrastructure to iron out glitches prior to implementation. Attempt to upgrade software and equipment in a manner that is the least disruptive to students, providing fail-safe measures, upgrading software during down times such as in the middle of the night.

11. Ensure that instructors and students are accustomed to educational technologies by providing initial practice conferences, instructor training and workshops.

Although not the topic of this discussion, changed practice implies role adjustment for the instructors as well as the learners. "I actually prefer online teaching because it can take time to think through responses to students, um, and you can do it on your own time, your own speed. So in other words, what's good for students is in terms of asynchronous is I think good for instructors as well." Professional development activities that focus on the affective components of course delivery will enable instructors to ease the adjustment of the learners to online learning as well as increase their own comfort level and effectiveness.

REFERENCES

Allen, I. E., & Seaman, J. (2004). *Entering the mainstream: The quality and extent of online education in the United States, 2003 and 2004.* Needham, MA: Sloan-C.

Anderson, T., Rourke, L., Garrison, D. R., & Archer, W. (2001). Assessing teaching presence in a computer conferencing context. *Journal of Asynchronous Learning Networks, 5*(2).

Arbaugh, J. B., & Hwang, A. (2006). Does "teaching presence" exist in online MBA courses? *The Internet and Higher Education, 9*(1), 9–21. doi:10.1016/j.iheduc.2005.12.001

Blau, J. R., & Goodman, N. (Eds.). (1995). *Social roles & social institutions.* New Brunswick, NJ: Transaction Publishers.

Cleveland-Innes, M., Garrison, R., & Kinsel, E. (2007). Role adjustment for learners in an online community of inquiry: Identifying the needs of novice online learners. *International Journal of Web-Based Learning and Teaching Technologies, 2*(1), 1–16.

Collier, P. (2001). A differentiated model of role identity acquisition. *Symbolic Interaction, 24*(2), 217–235. doi:10.1525/si.2001.24.2.217

Dewey, J. (1933). *How we think* (rev. ed.). Boston, MA: D.C. Heath.

Dewey, J. (1938). *Experience and education.* New York: Collier.

Garrison, D. R. (2006). *Online community of inquiry review: Understanding social, cognitive and teaching presence.* Paper presented at the Sloan Consortium Asynchronous Learning Network Invitational Workshop, Baltimore, MD.

Garrison, D. R., & Anderson, T. (2003). *E-learning in the 21ˢᵗ century: A framework for research and practice.* London: Routledge/Falmer.

Garrison, D. R., Anderson, T., & Archer, W. (2000). Critical inquiry in a text-based environment: Computer conferencing in higher education. *The Internet and Higher Education, 11*(2), 1–14.

Garrison, D. R., Anderson, T., & Archer, W. (2001). Critical thinking, cognitive presence and computer conferencing in distance education. *American Journal of Distance Education, 15*(1), 7–23.

Garrison, D. R., & Arbaugh, J. B. (2007). Researching the community of inquiry framework: Review, issues, and future directions. *The Internet and Higher Education, 10*(3), 157–172. doi:10.1016/j.iheduc.2007.04.001

Garrison, D. R., & Archer, W. (2000). *A transactional perspective on teaching-learning: A framework for adult and higher education.* Oxford, UK: Pergamon.

Garrison, D. R., & Cleveland-Innes, M. (2003). Critical factors in student satisfaction and success: Facilitating student role adjustment in online communities of inquiry. In J. Bourne & J. Moore (Eds.), *Elements of quality online education: Into the mainstream* (pp. 29-38). Needham, MA: Sloan-C.

Garrison, R., & Cleveland-Innes, M. (2005). Facilitating cognitive presence in online learning: Interaction is not enough. *American Journal of Distance Education, 19*(3), 133–148. doi:10.1207/s15389286ajde1903_2

Garrison, R., Cleveland-Innes, M., & Fung, T. (2004). Student role adjustment in online communities of inquiry: Model and instrument validation. *Journal of Asynchronous Learning Networks, 8*(2), 61-74.

Ice, P., Arbaugh, B., Diaz, S., Garrison, D. R., Richardson, J., Shea, P., & Swan, K. (2007). Community of inquiry framework: Validation and instrument development. In *Proceedings of the 13th Annual Sloan-C International Conference on Online Learning*, Orlando, FL.

Kanwar, M., & Swenson, D. (2000). *Canadian sociology*. IA: Kendall/Hunt Publishing Company.

Katz, D., & Kahn, R. (1978). *The social psychology of organizations*. New York: John Wiley & Sons.

Kendall, D., Murray, J., & Linden, R. (2000). *Sociology in our times*. (2nd ed.). Ontario, Canada: Nelson Thompson Learning.

Knuttila, M. (2002) *Introducing sociology: A critical perspective*. Don Mills, Ontario, Canada: Oxford University Press.

Kopp, S. F. (2000). The role of self-esteem. *LukeNotes, 4*(2).

McLuhan, M. (1995). *Understanding media: The extensions of man*. Cambridge, MA: The MIT Press.

Meyer, K. A. (2003). Face-to-face versus threaded discussions: The role of time and higher-order thinking. *Journal of Asynchronous Learning Networks, 7*(3), 55–65.

Murphy, E. (2004). Identifying and measuring ill-structured problem formulation and resolution in online asynchronous discussions. *Canadian Journal of Learning and Technology, 30*(1), 5–20.

Pascarella, E. T., & Terenzini, P. T. (2005). How college affects students: A third decade of research. San Francisco: Jossey-Bass.

Rogers, P., & Lea, M. (2005). Social presence in distributed group environments: The role of social identity. *Behaviour & Information Technology, 24*(2), 151–158. doi:10.1080/01449290410001723472

Shea, P., Li, C., Swan, K., & Pickett, A. (2005). Developing learning community in online asynchronous college courses: The role of teaching presence. *Journal of Asynchronous Learning Networks, 9*(4).

Shea, P., Pickett, A., & Pelz, W. (2004). Enhancing student satisfaction through faculty development: The importance of teaching presence. In *Elements of quality online education: Into the mainsteam*. Needham, MA: SCOLE.

Swan, K. (2003). Developing social presence in online discussions. In S. Naidu (Ed.), *Learning and teaching with technology: Principles and practices* (pp. 147-164). London: Kogan Page.

Swan, K. (in press). Teaching and learning in post-industrial distance education. In M. Cleveland-Innes & D. R. Garrison (Eds.), *An introduction to distance education: Understanding teaching and learning in a new era*. New York: Routledge.

Swan, K., & Shih, L.-F. (2005). On the nature and development of social presence in online course discussions. *Journal of Asynchronous Learning Networks*, *9*(3), 115–136.

Swan, K. P., Richardson, J. P., Ice, P., Garrison, R. D., Cleveland-Innes, M., & Arbaugh, J. B. (2008). Validating a measurement tool of presence in online communities of inquiry. *e-Mentor, 2*(24).

Turner, J. (1990). Role change. *Annual Review of Sociology*, *16*, 87–110. doi:10.1146/annurev.so.16.080190.000511

Vaughan, N., & Garrison, D. R. (2006). How blended learning can support a faculty development community of inquiry. *Journal of Asynchronous Learning Networks*, *10*(4), 139–152.

Wilson, D., Varnhagen, S., Krupa, E., Kasprzak, S., Hunting, V., & Taylor, A. (2003). Instructors' adaptation to online graduate education in health promotion: A qualitative study. *Journal of Distance Education*, *18*(2), 1–15.

Wu, D., & Hiltz, S. R. (2004). Predicting learning from asynchronous online discussions. *Journal of Asynchronous Learning Networks*, *8*(2), 139–152.

ENDNOTES

[1] The number of utterances in this cross-category is in brackets.

[2] The number of utterances in this cross-category is in brackets.

[3] The number of utterances in this cross-category is in brackets.

Chapter 14
Visualising the Invisible in Science Centres and Science Museums:
Augmented Reality (AR) Technology Application and Science Teaching

Hannu Salmi
University of Helsinki, Finland

Sofoklis Sotiriou
Ellinogermaniki Agogi Foundation, Greece

Franz Bogner
University of Bayreuth, Germany

ABSTRACT

This chapter presents an implementation of augmented reality (AR) technology in science education. While this technology up to now mainly was used by very special users such as the military and high-tech companies it gradually converts into wider educational use. Specific research programmes such as CONNECT and EXPLOAR applied this technology with a specific focus on selected learning scenarios by a close co-operation of formal education and informal learning. Empirical effects related to intrinsic motivation and cognitive learning of students (n: 308) were encouraging. The implementation of augmented reality in the context of the "Hot Air Balloon" exhibit at Heureka science centre in Finland unveiled encouraging results. While the high achievers again did best in the post-knowledge test, low achievers again were clearly catching up with the others. The difference to between the treatment and the control group was clear. It seems like that visualising a very theoretical scientific phenomenon increased the individual understanding substantially especially for those students who otherwise had severe difficulties. This is an essential result which needs further analysis. The "new educational model & paradigms" was monitored for 182 teachers. The main focus, however, pointed to a feed-back of in-service teachers and teacher students since they act as key players in the use and acceptance of any new educational technology or curriculum renewal. The main objectives were as follows: (i) From a teacher-controlled learning towards a pupil-orientated learning; (ii) connecting of ICT-AR with and between existing learning environments; and (iii) changes in roles and responsibilities of students and teachers.

DOI: 10.4018/978-1-60566-711-9.ch014

INTRODUCTION

Museums of the past sought artifacts, museums of the future will show facts

Otto Neurath
Museums of the future
Survey Graphic, 1933

Schools and the informal learning sector increasingly collaborate and provide an increasing value for lifelong learning combined as well as they contribute to the debate over values and utilities of digital resources. This debate includes an access to and a sharing of advanced tools, services and learning resources, whether it offers unique informal learning opportunities to visitors of science museums and science centers through its demonstration of a new method of interaction between a visitor and an exhibition. Over the last years digital media has increasingly entered the field of museums and science centers. Traditional media such as illustrated charts and audio guides together with interactive exhibits take the knowledge transfer to a complete new level of experience. The "Museums of the Future" of Neurath & Cohen (1973) focusing on facts rather on artifacts seems to come very close to this view. In their different ways, traditional science museums - with permanent collections, displayed in a historical context, and thematic exhibitions - and educational, interactive "science centres" are encouraging a more diverse range of people to explore the various fields of scientific knowledge - and their applications. Museums have an important role to play in facilitating lifelong learning, in terms of creative, cultural and intercultural activity beyond any merely vocational aspects. Lifelong learning, museums and digital technologies share many of the same attributes, with emphasis on learning from objects (rather than about objects) and on strategies from discovering information (rather than the information itself).

Since a few years, the number of virtual visitors to many museums' websites had already overtaken the number of physical visitors on-site (Hin, Subramaniam & Meng, 2005; ASTC 2009). These developments, both within the walls of the institution and outside, provide a number of challenges for educators and curators, at the heart of which lie the questions – what is distinctive about learning in science museums and science centres, and how might this change or evolve through the increasing use of digital technologies? These questions go to the heart of significant debates in this sector – how does learning in museums differ from or complement learning in schools? How can museums fulfil their potential to support lifelong learning? Should effort and money be spent primarily on the visitors who will enter the walls of the institution or those who will virtually explore the site through the web? What is the role of objects in the process of learning with digital technologies? How does the relationship between museum educator and learner change as technologies are developed?

Augmented Reality (AR) is about to join the described developments. With AR it is possible to combine real objects with virtual ones and to place suitable information into real surroundings. The possibility of AR to make convergence of education and entertainment is becoming more and more challenging as the technology optimises and expands to other areas. Natural or historical events and characters, reconstructed monuments or archaeological sites could be simulated and augmented to the real world. AR is a booming technology which attracts more and more attention from HCI (Human Computer Interaction) researchers and designers. This allows the creation of meaningful educational experiences. As these experiences are grounded in a substantive subject area of knowledge, they focus on the intellectual and emotional development of the viewer; therefore, AR learning environments have possession of both, educational and entertainment value.

The EXPLOAR service is the main outcome of the European CONNECT (www.ea.gr/ep/connect) which developed a personalized museum wearable system along with a long series of informal educational scenarios. The system was implemented in science centres in UK, Sweden, Greece and Finland (Sotiriou et al. 2007) which demonstrated the potential of such a system to offer unique experiences to the visitors. Similarly, the enrichment of the repertoire of learning opportunities as well as the blending helped to meet the challenge of "science for all", i.e., it provided science education opportunities tailored to diverse and heterogeneous populations of users. These populations vary both in their interest in learning science and in their abilities to learn science. In parallel it supports the provision of key skills to the future citizens and scientists (collaborative work, creativity, adaptability, intercultural communication).

The EXPLOAR service demonstrates a suitable example of an innovative approach involving visitors in extended episodes of playful learning. The EXPLOAR service specifically uses informal education as an opportunity to transcend from traditional museum visits, to a "feel and interact" user experience, by allowing a learning "anytime, anywhere", an openness to societal changes and at the same time a feeling culturally conscious. These pedagogical concepts and learning practices would address implementing a set of demonstrators (learning scenarios), employing advanced and highly interactive visualization technologies and also personalised ubiquitous learning paradigms in order to enhance the effectiveness and quality of the learning process. In this way, EXPLOAR demonstrates the potential of the AR technology to cover the emerging need of continuous update, innovate and development of new exhibits, new exhibitions, new educational materials, new programmes and methods to approach the visitors.

The CONNECT system provided the starting point to the EXPLAR approach. It consisted of an joint initiative of pedagogical, cognitive science and technological experts, museum educators and psychologists who searched for possibilities of using advanced technologies for educational purposes. The Virtual Science Thematic Park was It was developed as an active learning environment that functions in two distinct and equally important, from a pedagogical point of view, modes: the museum mode and the school mode. It allows for ubiquitous access to educational and scientific resources and incorporates all the innovative use of technology for educational purposes. The partnership has provided a variety of learning methods incorporating experimental, theoretical and multidisciplinary skills that will eventually may produce independent learners. The developed educational scenarios included field trips (virtual and conventional visits to science museums and parks) that are tangential to existing curricula, to pre- and post-visit curricular activi-

Figure 1. The EXPLOAR service offers unique opportunities to a science museum and a science centre visitor. A series of augmentations of physical phenomena, pictures, video and text are presented to the optical view of a user while explaining the physical laws and phenomena under investigation. The system also supports the work of the exhibition design and development team of a museum as it allows for enrichment of current exhibits with numerous applications and gadgets providing an easy way to update and to renovate each exhibition.

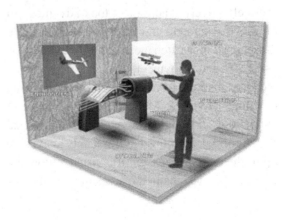

Figure 2. Visualizing the invisible: The CONNECT Science Thematic Park. The CONNECT experience may add to a visitor's view a series of augmentations, both, advanced or poor and simple. The advanced augmentations (E/M fields, molecular motions, microscopic view of the matter) were created by the CONNECT team. Through an authoring tool the museum educator or the teacher can upload additional simple content in order to create more personalized scenarios.

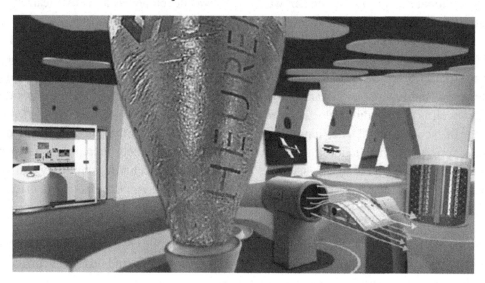

ties (including internet resources), to 'minds-on' experiments and models of different everyday coursework involving 'real' remotely controlled experiments. Altogether a "student-friendly" and engaging environment of thematic parks or museum are provided.

The working hypothesis of the CONNECT project was that the amendment of the traditional scientific methodology for experimentation with visualization applications and model building tools will help a learner to generally articulate mental models, to make better predictions and to reflect more effectively. The project took advantage of the fact that students enjoy tremendously visits to museums which often increases individual interest scores and enjoyment of science activities as well as constitute to valuable long-term learning outcomes (Ayres & Melear, 1998). The role of technology in bridging the gap between formal and informal learning environments may sum up to the delivery of scientific visualization and multimedia systems in the areas of virtual (VR)

and augmented reality (AR). The possibility of AR and VR to make convergence of education and entertainment is becoming more and more challenging as the technology is continuously optimised and expands to a wide area of applications. The CONNECT project has pushed the current boundaries further by providing a platform that integrates contextual information into classroom settings, by employing advanced, highly interactive visualization technologies embedded systems and wearable computing. Simultaneously it has introduced new activities and personalized learning paradigms that fluidly link the use of physical materials with digital technology in creative inquiry and inventive exploration.

The main technological innovation of CONNECT consisted in the development of an advanced learning environment, the Virtual Science Thematic Park (VSTP). It was supposed to act as a main "hub" of all available resources within the existing network of science parks, science museums and research centres. The VSTP serves

Figure 3. The general architecture of the CONNECT system.

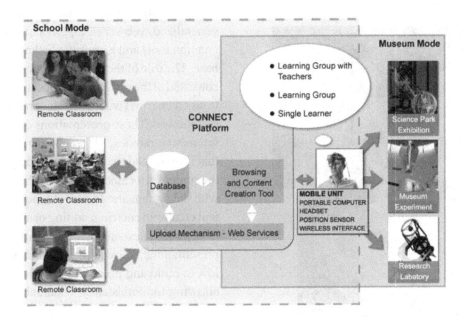

as distributor of information giving access to large databases, organizer of suitable didactical activities such as conventional or virtual exhibit visits or/and participation to live scientific experiments. Additionally it interconnects all the members of the network, by allowing for ubiquitous access to educational and scientific resources to students, teachers and users in general from all around Europe.

The Virtual Science Thematic Park provides support for single and multi-user (for groups as large as a school classroom) and it includes two major components (a) the mobile AR system which the visitor used during his/her real visit to a museum/science park and (b) the CONNECT platform which facilitated the virtual visits of a remote classroom to a museum/science park.

The Mobile AR System

The mobile AR system (figure 4) was designed to provide 3D graphics superimposed on the user's field of vision together with other multimedia information. Thus, it allowed to "extend" a real

exhibit with virtual objects. This is regarded as a particularly powerful tool for visualizing complex concepts in physics that are fundamental yet imperceptible (such as electric or magnetic fields, forces, etc). Furthermore, it allowed for remote classes to interact, either on-line or off-line, with a visit to a science museum/park. The mobile AR system consisted of several hardware devices, including: a wearable processing unit (heart of the system), personal display units (optical see-through glasses) to project/embed virtual 3-D objects onto the real exhibit environment, tracking sensors to determine the visitors' exact location and orientation (six degrees of freedom), video cameras for recording the students' learning activities and the exhibit augmentation, human interface devices (microphone and headphones for real-time interaction with the exhibit and the remote classroom) and the transmission module to the mainframe computer in order to stream the augmented view to the CONNECT platform.

Furthermore, the mobile AR system was supported by a multiplicity of software tools, such as recognition (tracing and identification) of individu-

Figure 4. The mobile AR system. © 2007 Heureka, Used with Permission.

als, groups and objects, a user friendly audio-visual interface to allow interaction with virtual objects and to interpret the learning scenario descriptions, natural language and speech interfaces for audio communication, reflexive learning systems (adaptable and customizable) for reviewing experiences, content design facilities, simulation and visualization aids. The purpose of the CONNECT platform.

Teachers could implement tools for facilitating a student's learning through managing third party objects. Thus, he/she made relevant instructional materials accessible in order to enhance the museum exhibits. The mediator within this networking was the platform of the Content Management System. Students were supported by an innovative learning using the AR system which contained objects and applications to be displayed during the real visit to the museum. Schools could communicate and observe museum visits, either real-time or recorded. Museums and Science centres were in charge to manage the specific exhibit augmentations.

The CONNECT platform was composed by several components, including specialized and generalized web-services, browsing and content creation tools and a multimedia knowledge database. The role of the content creator of the system consisted of the provision of educational presentations (scenarios) where different pathways could be followed. These presentations could consist of interactive movies, where the part of the movie that is presented to the student depends on where the student is located, on what his/her interactions with the system are. In order to facilitate the content creator in entering, editing or assembling and dissembling new-media objects into meaningful presentations, knowledge management tools allow to build and manage a knowledge database, allowing for persistency, coherence and data integrity. Archiving, cataloguing and indexing tools were employed for the creation of the knowledge repository contents.

The CONNECT platform maps the design artefacts into an object-oriented language code, supporting the mobile's AR system specifications and functionalities. The standards and the information that the mobile AR system uses to transact with the CONNECT platform specify the types of "data objects" which were stored in the database. These "objects" provided the communication and interaction of the CONNECT platform with the users of the mobile AR system. Furthermore, the developed system guaranteed the required efficiency in terms of access speed (for real-time scheduling of the application processes) and available bandwidth (for real-time video-audio communication between AR user and remote classroom).

Learning in Science Museums and Science Centres: Need for Interactivity and Learner Participation

Objects are the unique attributes of a museum, yet many museums and science centres apparently

Figure 5. The two modes of operation of the CONNECT system. The system supports both on-site learning and on-line learning giving access to a variety of resources and collections even to communities well beyond the wall of the science museum, who for geographical, social or historical reasons will never entered the hallowed halls.

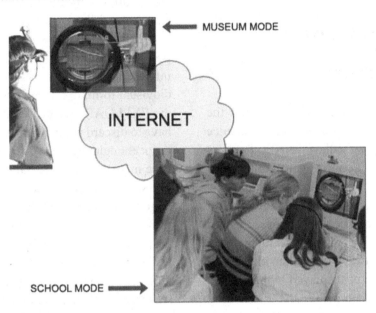

seek combination of objects and interactivity. Most of the learning issues were similar either mechanical or digital, either on-site or online. In any case, poor examples, of whatever type, do not substantially contribute to a learning potential of interactives. While many researchers and exhibit designers question the compatibility of objects and interactives, some key principles are emerging. Beyond the naive assumption that digital technologies are inevitably interactive, there are strident demands for clear learning objectives, for learner choice and initiative.

After interactivity, the goal of many museums is learner participation. This may involve a simple feedback (often digital voting), digital storage of images and ideas (for subsequent remote retrieval) or even contributing directly to the museum's own exhibits and interpretation. Digital technologies facilitate many kinds of collaboration – between museum and a learner, between different institutions and among a learner. Exciting examples include those between real and virtual learners

and of learners creating their own associations within and between collections. In many ways, the opposite of collaboration, digital technologies also facilitate personalisation. Freed from constraints, both physical and interpretative, of the curator and exhibition designer, any learner may appropriately use technologies to provide a dedicated and personal mentor. A new set of relationships is emerging, between objects, learners and digital technology, in which museums are, above all, places of exploration and discovery. In the museum of the future, distinctions between real and virtual, already blurred, will matter even less as both museums and learners better understand the processes of inquiry and of learning itself. The real key to future development is likely to be personalisation: of interpretation to significantly enhance social and intellectual inclusion; of technology to free both museums and learners from many of the current constraints; of learning to finally facilitate an escape from the deficit models so prevalent in educational institutions and release untold potential, as the individual learner is able to use technologies to exercise choice and to take responsibility for his/her own learning.

POTENTIAL IMPACT OF THE EXPLOAR SERVICE ON EXHIBIT DESIGN

Potential changes and improvements that the EXPLOAR service can produce for the science centres that participated to the CONNECT project became obvious in the course of the implementation of the trials. At the current exhibits the posters and labels occupy half of the available exhibit space, and while they certainly provide useful information, they require long stops for reading, take useful space away from other interesting objects which could be displayed in their stead, and are not nearly as compelling and entertaining as a human narrator (a museum guide) or a video documentary about the displayed phenomenon. The tracking data and the observation of the visitors also revealed that people (especially youngsters) do not spend sufficient time to read all of what is described in the posters to absorb the corresponding information. A great deal of the space occupied by the posters and text labels is therefore wasted, as most people don't take advantage of information provided in a textual form. The video stations, in many cases, complete the narration about the described phenomena and physical laws by showing animations, educational and explanatory videos. While the video stations provide compelling narrative segments, they are not always located next to the object or exhibit described, and therefore the visitor needs to spend some time locating the described objects in the surrounding space in order to associate the object to the corresponding narrative segment. The video stations detract attention from the actual objects on display, and are so much the center of attention for the exhibit that the displayed objects seem to be more of a

decoration around the video stations than being the actual exhibit.

The potential improvements to the exhibit layout offered by EXPLOAR system are summarized as follows:

There is no more need to have so many posters and text labels, as the corresponding information is provided in a more appealing audiovisual form, in a video documentary style by the EXPLOAR service. Typically most exhibits have to discard many interesting objects as there is not enough physical space available in the science museum or centre galleries for all objects. The space now made available by eliminating the large posters, can be used to display more exhibits, which are the true protagonists of the museum or the science centre. Figure 6 show how the posters at the exhibition area of EF in Athens can be replaced by more objects and phenomena to be seen and appreciated by the public, taking also into account that the visualizations could be different according to the profile of the visitor.

Visitors are better informed, as the information currently provided by the posters is mostly neglected by the public. The same information would instead become part of the overall narration provided by the EXPLOAR system, and it would be better absorbed and appreciated by the public.

The video kiosks are no longer be necessary because the same material would be presented by the EXPLOAR service. The exhibits would be again the center of attention for visitors, as the wearable's display allows both the real world and the augmented audiovisual information to be seen at the same time as part of the wearer's real surround view. This would again make more space available for additional objects to be displayed.

The fact that the EXPLOAR system presents audiovisual material together with the corresponding object, rather than separately in space and time, and within the same field of view of the visitor, thanks to the private-eye display, is also of great importance.

Figure 6. The EXPLOAR service offers unique opportunities to the exhibit design and development team of the science museums and centres as it gives them the opportunity to personalise the information available to each visitor according to his/her profile and interest and at the same time it eliminates the need for long explanatory texts, pictures and labels by offering visualization of the real physical phenomena.

BENEFITS FOR THE USERS: SCENARIOS OF USE

The EXPLOAR service aims to contribute towards this direction by:

- **Engage visitors of science museums and science centres in learning as constructive dialogue** rather than as a passive process of transmission.
- **Facilitate lifelong learning by providing a free-choice learning environment** that permits a plethora of pathways and possibilities.
- **Highlighting key trends in the adoption of digital technologies for learning** within and beyond the walls of museums.
- Providing pointers for potential future developments for curators and developers of digital technologies for museum learning.

Additionally the EXPLOAR service is raising the wider public's interest and awareness on science. As reflected in many surveys realized in the recent years there is a falling interest on behalf of the wider public concerning science, even if individuals in general have a positive perception of science. The main reason behind this attitude is the lack of attractiveness of science matters as well as the lack of relevance to the everyday life. The EXPLOAR service gives to the users a different insight in physical phenomena and physical laws. In this way they are able to observe and thus better understand the world they live, work, play, perform. As a result science is brought closer to the individuals. The way individuals experience science through the EXPLOAR service is expected to have a lasting positive impact on the general public attitude towards science in general. The aim of the EXPLOAR service is to demonstrate an innovative approach that involves visitors in extended episodes of playful learning. The EXPLOAR service offers a "feel and interact" user experience, allowing for learning "anytime, anywhere", open to societal changes and at the same time feeling culturally conscious. These pedagogical concepts and learning practices would address implementing a set of demonstrators (informal learning scenarios), employing advanced and highly interactive visualization technologies and also personalised ubiquitous learning paradigms in order to enhance the effectiveness and quality of the learning process. As the EXPLOAR service is expected to be used from a quite heterogeneous group of people (youngsters, adults, professionals, educators, school groups, families), the scenarios of use have to vary significantly in order to cover the different users needs and their objectives. These scenarios are the basic vehicles for the promotion and the dissemination of the service to the user communities.

Each scenario is accompanied with supportive material for the users in an effort to create a communication channel between the visitor and the museum after the visit. The material includes links to references and additional information from the specific field of interest or relative fields. The content and the proposed activities vary significantly taking into account the needs of the users. The content of the scenarios is presented in an open and modular way allowing for additions and improvements at any time, giving to the user the possibility to get involved according to her/his wish. The EXPLOAR scenarios have been implemented and validated in real conditions initially in two science centres in Greece and in Finland. During the implementation and validation phase of the project the developed scenarios have been also validated in the framework of specific events with the use of the EXPLOAR showcase mobile exhibit in additional science museums and centres (e.g. Deutches Museum, La Cite, CosmoCaixa, Technology Park of Thessaloniki). Some indicative examples are given below that will be tested during the market validation phase.

Figure 7. The EXPLOAR service aims to contribute to the access to and sharing of advanced tools, services and learning resources, by offering unique informal learning opportunities to the visitors of science museums and science centers through the demonstration of a new method of interaction between the visitor and the exhibition. The three main axes of the proposed intervention to the science museum visits and their interrelationship is presented schematically above.

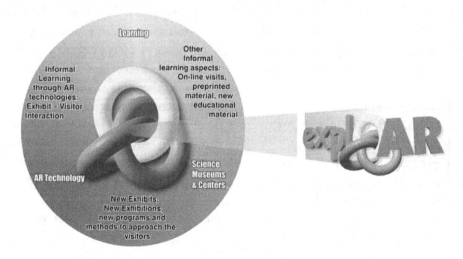

Scenarios for the General Public

In the science museums and science centres, the exhibits and the related phenomena are embedded in rich real world contexts where visitors can see and directly experience the real world's connections of these phenomena. The add-on of the EXPLOAR visit (compared to a conventional museum tour) is that the visitors with the support of the system will have in their disposal an additional wealth of information. The real exhibits are mixed in their optical view with the 3-D visual objects and representations that the AR system is producing and embedding into this augmented world through their glasses. By this way many "invisible" parameters in physical phenomena (e.g. forces, fields) will be visualised and presented in the eyes of the visitors augmented on the real experiments. For example, a visitor could investigate the question "why do planes fly?" In this case an Aerofoil exhibit could demonstrate the application of physical laws on an airplane wing and their effects on it. To "make the invisible visible," dynamic representations of air movement and the resultant forces can be created. It will also be possible to plot the wing's attack angles vs. lift force. Additionally the airflow could be represented with virtual lines moving towards the wing. These airflow lines could be superim-

posed on the top and the bottom of the real wing in the exhibit.

Scenarios for School Visits: Creating Links with the School Curriculum

Bearing in mind that around 40% of the visitors of the science museum are pupils with their teachers, a series of school subjects (from physics, chemistry, biology, geology, environmental education, to history and language learning) will be selected and presented in form of multidisciplinary educational scenarios. For example quite complex physical phenomena (e.g. visualization of the E/M waves emitted by the dipole, to observe this experiment will be able to observe the emission of electromagnetic waves by the dipole element, the oscillation of stored energy near the dipole and outgoing waves will be visualized through the augmented reality technique) which usually cause significant difficulties to students will be included. The 3-D visualization of a physical quantity (in this case a force acting on moving charged particles inside a real 3 dimensional magnetic field) which depends on two other independent quantities, is a vital concept in understanding the physical laws and their applications to real life situations. Figure

Figure 8.

Figure 9. (left) Real hands on experiment (right) Augmented Reality version of the same experiment wearing the device. The real exhibits are mixed in their optical view with the 3-D visual objects and representations that the system is producing and embedding into this augmented world through their glasses.

8 at the left shows a real experiment which is accompanied by explanatory text only. In the picture at the right the same experiment is shown to the student wearing the AR system with the addition of a virtual object which in this case is a 3-D hand, serving as "a rule of thumb" showing the geometric and physical connection of the three physical parameters involved (q, B, F). Depending upon orientation of the magnetic field (B) the electron beam is diverted upward or downward. For this change of direction the so-called "Lorentz Force" (F) is responsible. It affects all charged particles, which move in a magnetic field, thus also the negatively charged electrons. The force - and so the diversion - is larger, the stronger the magnetic field is and the faster the particle moves.

ADAPTING NEW CONTENT ON EXISTING EXHIBITS AND RENEWING THE EXHIBITION

The EXPLOAR service could support the work of the science museum design and development team to innovate the exhibition by adding new content to the optical view of the visitors when this is necessary.

The explanatory and additional materials currently accompany the exhibits are produced for general used and they are presented to all the different visitors categories. By introducing the EXPLOAR service the design team will have the chance to develop different content according to the needs of the visitors (families, school groups, experts, tourists) and in that way to make their visit more interesting and effective. The interaction with the exhibit and the learning objectives would be different since the available information is different. As the exhibit augmentations are easily updated, the information provided by the EXPLOAR service could not only present exhibit relations to everyday life but also current news on topical subjects. With this service curators would be able to present a larger variety and more connected material in an engaging manner within the limited physical space available for the exhibit. Furthermore, inexpensive changes and improvements of the exhibit are greatly supported by the EXPLOAR service. Altering the information provided by the service corresponds to a renewed exhibit with much less resources than a usual renovation.

Finally the museum team would have valuable information to their disposal regarding visitor's preferences and behaviour. Based on the amount

Figure 10. The drawing represents the area of an exhibition hall in a museum and specific data collected during a visit. The conical areas represent the area in which specific information is being available to the visitor for a specific exhibit. The EXPLOAR system is able to track the path of the visitor between the exhibit and to deliver a specific record about the timing and the interactions with the exhibits. In this way a total graph presenting the paths and the interactions with the exhibits for all visitors during a specific period of time can be produced offering excellent data for the evaluation of the design and the approach introduced by each exhibition.

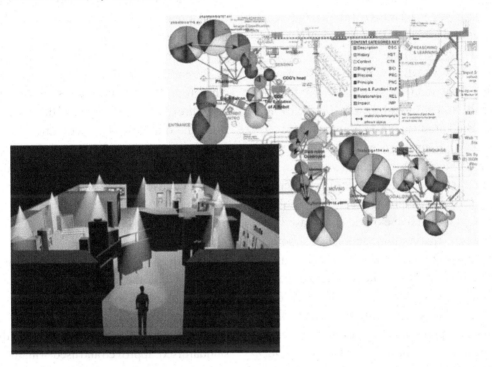

of data downloaded they could calculate the time spent on each exhibit, the trail that they followed, what exhibits provoked visitors to come back, etc. In this way the EXPLOAR service could be used as a supportive tool in the redesign of the exhibition, in the development of new materials and programmes, in the reallocation and the repositioning of specific exhibits.

TOWARDS AN OPEN LEARNING ENVIRONMENT (CLASSROOM AND SCIENCE CENTRE AS WELL) VIA AUGMENTED REALITY (AR)

Computer and communication technologies have profoundly altered our every-day lives. Since more than a decade, great promises for improving education arised, too. However, clear qualitative or quantitative results are still missing. *Making a Science of Education* demands a great deal of high-quality research by focussing on the utilisation and effects of the new technologies in both, school and informal learning environments as well. Only by careful monitoring students' learning outcomes we may narrow the numerous variable spectrum in order to specifically determine the effectiveness of different technologies and new learning methods. (Alberts, B. 2009, 15).

Ilomäki (2008, 33-37) has been mapping a list of teachers' problems when implementing ICT scenarios into educational practices. The author's focus was limited to a teacher's individual characteristic such as individual pedagogical conceptions and problems they experience while preparing the lessons as well. Very often, teachers with coherent ICT skills use more ICT solutions in their teaching and they do it in a more multi-faceted and student-oriented way (Moseley & al. 1999; Hakkarainen 2001; Kankaanranta & Puhakka 2008). Even more, meta-studies related to immersive learning environments seem to provide a clear evidence for a specific efficiency of this type of educational technology: "The more a virtual immersive experience is based on design strategies that combine actional, symbolic, and sensory factors, the greater the participant's suspension of disbelief that she or he is "inside" a digitally enhanced setting" (Dede 2009, 66). The immersive interfaces utilising the visual reasoning ability gives an opportunity to transfer educational experience from classroom to (other) real-world, open learning environments.

COMBINING REAL HANDS-ON LEARNING INTO VISUAL AND AUGMENTED REALITY

Hot Air Balloon is a classical science centre exhibit example provided in several institutes around the world, too. That was one of the reasons why it was chosen as a case within the described CONNECT/EXPLOAR learning scenario. The basic approach was to gain more educational value from the exhibit by using Augmented Reality –technology added to this classical exhibit. The main pedagogical goal was to *teach the skills of doing observations*. This was possible because by the AR-solutions certain invisible phenomenon could be done visible by animations and demonstrations. In this case the main phenomenon was temperature and molecule movement, i.e. Bolzmann constant.

Testing

Very often in the field, just paper-and-pencil tests are applied to monitor cognitive knowledge and achievement. However, science and technology has become more and more visual, and many of the skills trained and taught are not textual. Therefore, "there may be a mismatch between the structure of the knowledge and the structure of the print and oral language media traditionally used both impart and test that knowledge (Greenfield 2009, 71)". Consequently, testing in this study contained also non-text based tests.

Tests for the Students

First of all, we applied a visual reasoning ability -test, in detail, the VRA-Visual Reasoning Ability test published by Raven (2000). With regard to the virtual and visual nature of the topic, three major issues supported our choice: 1. the test is standardised, approved and used in many countries and cultures; 2. no translations are needed; and last but not least; 3. young people tend to like to administrate this type of test which they don't perceive as formal education type of task.

Secondly, for measuring the motivation (intrinsic, instrumental, and situation motivation) we administered two measures, the one of Deci & Ryan (1993) called IMI (Intrinsic Motivation Inventory) and the one of Salmi (1993; 2003) on our pre-test schedule. Thirdly, the cognitive knowledge based on 13 items was monitored on two different schedules, before and after the AR-intervention and science centre visit. Forth, we classified our participants with regard to their school grades given by their teachers in science, mathematics, and native language into three categories: A+ = Above average (25%), A = Average (50%); A- = Below average (25%).Finally, we

Figure 11. Raven Test. An example of the standardised test item. Raven 2000; Series 3.

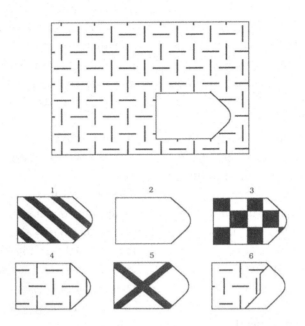

monitored the usability by applying the so called HCI-evaluation method which provides a specific feed-back with regard to the subjective feelings related to the technical usability, psychological usability, and the learning experience.

RESULTS AND DISCUSSION

Usability

A major character of any virtual and especially Augmented Reality technology lies in its' overwhelming effect as visual experience . Especially for a first time, user mostly find the tool effective and exiting, but may also feel frightened or physically unpleasant. A usability evaluation by a questionnaire and interviews (n: 78 students) revealed the following details:

The students experienced the *Combination of Real & Augmented reality* fascinating (mean 5,23; scale 1-7). However, the feed-back could have been even higher. The teenagers did not feel it "very cool".

The *Technical usability* did receive high scores (mean 8,44; scale 1-10). The best score (9,2) was by the item "dryness in eyes" and even the lowest "visual fatigue" was as high as 7,9.

The Psychological usability (mean 6.92; scale 1-10) was not as advantaged as the technical solutions. The lowest score (6.6) was received by the item *frustrating – satisfying*. Meanwhile the best feed-back was given to the item *terrible – wonderful* (7.2).

The overall results indicated that the students liked the experience and their situation motivation was positive to start the testing of the equipment. Especially the technological comfort was at least adequate.

In all the tests above the younger students (aged 11-13 y) gave clearly higher scores about the AR-effect than the older students (aged 14-15 y). The difference was in all aspect – Real & Augmented; Technical; Psychological - statistically significant ($p < .05$). No statistically significant gender differences were found. This is an important result because very often the high-tech or ICT-solutions are classified as male activities.

Knowledge Learning: Pre-test

High achieving students (who where above the average with their school grades, i.e. A+) unsurprisingly performed better in the pre-knowledge test (see the figure below) compared to average and below-average peers. Therefore, strong correlations applied.

The differences between the groups (A- ; Average; A +) were even clearer *inside the test group* as can be seen from the following figure:

The same trend was visible also *in the control group* as shown in the results in the next figure:

Knowledge Learning by AR-technology: Post-Test

Again, high achiever performed clearly best in the post-knowledge test, too (see figure below)

However, low achievers were *clearly catching up with* the others. The difference to their higher achieving peers decreased substantially.

The implementation of Augmented Reality in the context of the Hot Air Balloon exhibit unveiled similar results: While the high achiever again did best in the post-knowledge test, low achiever again were *clearly catching up with* the others. This was especially true for the girls who also managed well in the VRA-Visual Reasoning Ability test. It seems like that *visualising* very theoretical scientific phenomenon of molecule movement) increased the understanding substantially for pupils who otherwise had severe difficulties.

Knowledge Learning: Control Group without AR-Technology

The control group attended the science centre exhibition implementation with the same kind of pre- and post-lesson in the school. However, they studied the Hot Air Balloon content in the exhibition in the traditional way (with the text, label, and guide). The results were quite different from the AR-test group (see next figure) since low achievers were *not catching up with* the others.

The following figure confirms that gap between the low-achievers and the students with the higher school grades remained:

This is an essential result which needs further analysis. It seems evident that the use and application of the Augmented Reality might give certain advantaged for some of the less-than –average school-success students. Especially the girls were

Figure 12. School success vs. Knowledge learning pre-test [scale from 0 to 13]

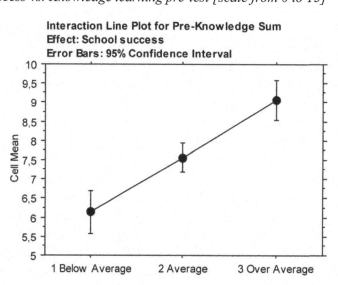

Figure 13.

Unpaired t-test for Pre-Knowledge Sum
Grouping Variable: School success
Hypothesized Difference = 0

	Mean Diff.	DF	t-Value	P-Value
1 Below Average, 2 Average	-1,121	158	-2,945	,0037
1 Below Average, 3 Over Average	-2,845	102	-6,428	<,0001
2 Average, 3 Over Average	-1,724	160	-4,350	<,0001

Figure 14.

Unpaired t-test for Pre-Knowledge Sum
Grouping Variable: School success
Hypothesized Difference = 0

	Mean Diff.	DF	t-Value	P-Value
1 Below Average, 2 Average	-2,172	56	-2,991	,0041
1 Below Average, 3 Over Average	-3,050	41	-3,943	,0003
2 Average, 3 Over Average	-,878	69	-1,681	,0974

Figure 15. **School success vs. Knowledge learning post-test (after AR-use) [scale from 0 to 13]**

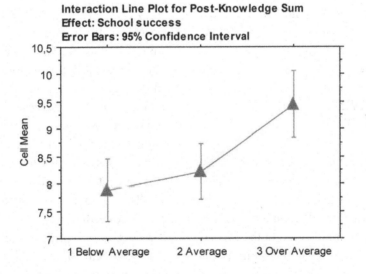

Figure 16.

Unpaired t-test for Post-Knowledge Sum
Grouping Variable: School success
Hypothesized Difference = 0

	Mean Diff.	DF	t-Value	P-Value
1 Below Average, 2 Average	-,345	150	-,823	,4119
1 Below Average, 3 Over Average	-1,567	95	-3,764	,0003
2 Average, 3 Over Average	-1,221	147	-2,826	,0054

Figure 17. School success vs. Knowledge learning post-test (control without AR) [scale from 0 to 13]

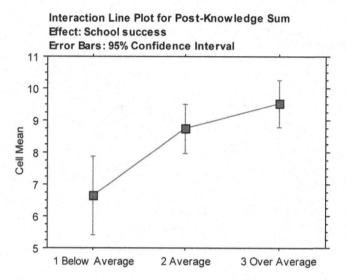

receiving better learning results. This is maybe related to the fact that they also managed well in the VRA-Visual Reasoning Ability test. It seems like that *visualising* very theoretical scientific phenomenon like the molecule movement made it much more understandable for students who otherwise had severe difficulties in understanding it.

TEACHER SURVEY AND EVALUATION

The recent *Rocard-report* [*Science education now: A renewed pedagogy for the future of Europe*] (2006) is describing the situation mostly in the pre-schools, primary and secondary schools while we also see the trends around the formal education. The role of informal learning is increasing in the modern societies – meaning the countries which are developing their societies by investing and creating opportunities for research, innovations, and education. The phenomenon is closely related to the growing impact of science and technology in our everyday lives. Lifelong learning needs new practical forms and the formal education can learn something from the

informal, open learning environments like the science centres.

The Rocard report specifically underlines the term *Inquiry-Based Science Education*. One of the weaknesses of school's science teaching has been that the studies and lessons at school are mainly deductive. There are some exceptions in some schools, but, historically the main trend in the European science teaching pedagogy has applied "Deductive approach". In this approach, the teacher presents the concepts, their logical – deductive – implications and gives examples of applications. This method is also referred to as 'top-down transmission".

"Hands-on learning" is the main pedagogical principle of the science centres. On opposite to "Deductive", it represents the "Inductive method". This classical "learning by doing" method is something that the science centres have been pioneering in Europe during the last decades. The multidiscipline contents of modern science centre exhibitions form a unique and reliable learning source for inductive, Inquiry-Based Science Education.

Similarly, the Rocard-report (p.7) requests new forms of teacher training, too: "Teachers are the key players in the renewal of science education. Among other methods, being part of the network allows them to improve the quality of their teaching and supports their motivation. – Networks can be used as an effective component of teachers' professional development, and they are complementary to more traditional forms of in-service teacher training and stimulate morale and motivation."

Background

The presentation of the "Hot Air Balloon" is a classical science centre exhibit in several institutes around the world. That was one of the reasons why it was chosen as a CONNECT-case for the research and development. The idea was to gain more educational value from the exhibit by using Augmented Reality –technology added to this classical exhibit.

The main pedagogical goal was to improve skills for individual observation. This was possible because by the AR-solutions certain invisible phenomenon could made visible by animations and demonstrations. In this case, the main phenomenon was the content of temperature and molecule movement. During the very first test of the Augmented Reality –equipment with the Hot Air Balloon seemed to work and give practical results, but at the same time, using the computer aided pre-lecture material (VSTP=Virtual Science Thematic Park) caused several difficulties.

Even teachers with clearly better than average knowledge and skills related to computers, ict, and e-learning had severe difficulties in using the pre- and post-learning solutions. After the pre-testing periods and teachers training workshop it became evident that the computer aided pre-lecture system (VSTP) was all too complicated to use for individual teachers – even for them with a long experience of ICT-pedagogy! The system had typical proto-type difficulties in reliability and usability. Therefore, an intensive training seminar

for teachers was offered in order to learn both, the technical use of the system and the application of relevant contents. These experiences, inputs and results were utilised in the final test runs.

TEACHER EVALUATION TOOL: THE ROLE OF ICT IN TEACHING AND LEARNING

As the pedagogical context for the development of AR-system the "NEW EDUCATIONAL MODEL OR PARADIGMS" (Hermant 2003) was used to receive the feed-back from the teachers. (Figure 18. below; original the EU-Minerva programme)

The teachers' (n:182) opinions and visions concerning the AR-technology were monitored by interviews and a tool called "New Educational Models or Paradigms", which is 1) describing the e-learning process by the terms *Role of ICT*, 2) showing the actual *Changes in learning environment*, and 3) defining *Innovative learning activities*.

The educators and teachers as well underlined the main characteristics of the model as following features and ranking order which differ clearly from their opinions about the ICT based education in the classroom setting.

Innovative Learning Approaches: *(i) Integration of other learning environments than the school; (ii) differentiated learning depending on different ways of perception; from teacher-controlled learning to pupil orientated learning; context-related knowledge*Role of ICT:

ICT as connection between learning environments; (ii) ICT as instruction tool; ICT as communication forum; ICT as mediaChanges in Learning Environments:

Technological innovation; (ii) new physical space; (iii) changes in roles and responsibilities of pupils; (iv) changes in roles and responsibilities of teachers

As the result of this inquiry, the pedagogical experts and teachers attending the process underlined as the main characteristics: innovative

Figure 18.

Unpaired t-test for Post-Knowledge Sum
Grouping Variable: School success
Hypothesized Difference = 0

	Mean Diff.	DF	t-Value	P-Value
1 Below Average, 2 Average	-2,095	54	-2,855	,0061
1 Below Average, 3 Over Average	-2,876	39	-4,453	<,0001
2 Average, 3 Over Average	-,780	67	-1,411	,1629

Figure 19.

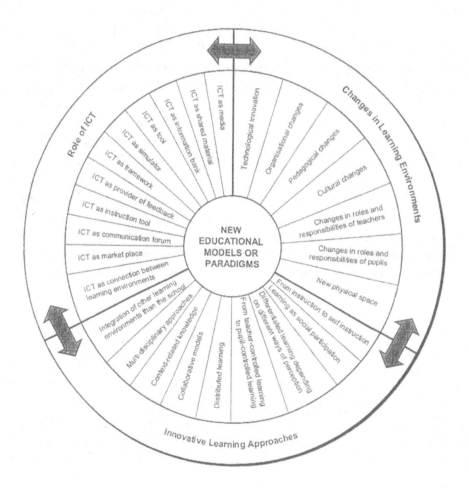

learning approaches, integration of other learning environments than the school, differentiated learning depending on different ways of perception. The main element was, however, moving from teacher-controlled learning to pupil orientated learning with context-related knowledge. It was also important that the teachers were no impressed about the technology itself but seeing ICT as connection between learning environment, an instruction tool. This can lead in best case– according the teachers' interviews – into changes in roles and responsibilities of pupils –and teachers.

Pre-Visit Stage: Teacher Feedback

The subject matter of the exhibit was part of the teaching of the school for all the teachers, and the timing did not cause any problems – mainly because in the school system of Finland the teachers are pedagogical experts who have the right and obligation to apply the curriculum and its timing during the school year. The teachers were informed about the opportunity to visit the exhibit in August when the school year started so they did not have difficulties scheduling the visit in October-November according their curriculum. – This process reflects also the ordinary visits to the science centre in Finland: the teachers make their plans normally 2-3 months before their visit to ensure the content of the visit to their ordinary school schema.

As the main objectives for the visit to the science centre *motivation* and *learning by doing* were mentioned. Specific content of the one single exhibit (Hot Air Balloon) was not so essential, but mentioned. Also the AR-technology was focus of visit for some teachers.

As supplementing reasons for a visit in a science centre the teachers mentioned a) the other exhibitions content as an entity and b) having an opportunity to utilise varying learning methods.

As a pre-visit activity the groups did use the computer aided (VSTP) lesson which lasted about one to two class periods (mainly more than one because of the technical complexity of starting the computer, connecting to platform, and getting instructions, and help for usability).

The help of the pre-visit –activities: all the teachers replied that the main effect of the VSTP-computer aided pre-lecture was for *the orientation for the visit* itself, and *the focus of the visit* to the Hot Air Balloon single exhibit. Of course the teachers mentioned also the cognitive learning effects, and but they did on see this time as the central objective of the project, but more the learning to learn –process.

Visit Stage: Teacher Feedback

All the teachers and classes had basically the same post ICT-learning activities (CONNECT-EXPLOAR platform) by repeating the main cognitive content of a specific topic. Most classes spent one to two class periods for a selected module. Teachers used a visit as an "integrative science learning" by forming links to other topics (such as Maths, English, and also visual arts lesson). Some teachers integrated the tests (knowledge, motivation, etc.) into their teaching by rating them as a support for their pupils' learning process.

The teachers did not totally agree that learning objectives they had set for the visit were fulfilled. The main reason was that the teachers expected the Hot Air Balloon experiment with the AR-equipment would have been longer than 20-30 minutes, because many other "demonstrations" at science centres last approximately 30-45 minutes. However, the teachers felt that the visit was clearly positive for the learning objectives especially learning to make observations.

The co-operative learning nature of the visit was found important by the teachers - although the very basic nature of the use of the AR-equipment is individual: only one person can use it at the same time. The reasons why the teachers felt that it was encouraging the students for co-operation related to the facts that a) they had prepared the visit together with at the classroom (typically two pupils per computer) and b) the students visited the exhibit in pairs discussing about the topic although only one student could use the equipment.

According the teachers, the students were using the AR-exhibit on their own, freely and by their on conditions. This is very natural because the AR-technique is based on self-centred orientation excluding the outer world or dominance by other people. It captures the user inside the intensive AR-world.

The teachers felt that the visit to the science centre was improving the attitudes of the students both towards the science in general and the specific subject matter.

Post-Visit Stage: Teacher Feedback

All the teachers and classes had basically the same post ICT-learning activities (CONNECT-EXPLOAR platform) by repeating the main cognitive content of a specific topic. Most classes spent one to two class periods for a selected module. Teachers used a visit as an "integrative science learning" by forming links to other topics (such as Maths, English, and also visual arts lesson). Some teachers integrated the tests (knowledge, motivation, etc.) into their teaching by rating them as a support for their pupils' learning process.

Half of the teachers were sceptical as their first experience about the cognitive learning results. However, there where not negative, but more curious to hear the research results. The other half of the teachers were convinced that the main principle of the phenomenon became clear for the pupils during the process.

For the subject matter, the most important element according the teachers was "learning by doing" and the opportunity to apply a method "to make observations". However, the teachers also replied that the AR-exhibit was only one part (lasting 10-15 min) of the whole science centre visit (lasting 3 hours 30 min) with many motivating elements. The teachers appreciated the entity: Pre-lecture + Visit + Post-lecture, because it gave back added-value for their work (while the teachers had invested a lot of their – especially mental – resources for the process).

All participating teachers felt that the new AR-technology provides better opportunities for learning and teaching. The limitations of the stage of the technology were clearly seen and recognised by the teachers. The technology was still on demonstration or proto-type level. Some teachers were comparing it to the period when the first pc-computers came to schools: ms-dos versions where demanding specific and often purely technical skills from the teacher who could not concentrate into the pedagogy and content topic. This was exactly the case of the AR-technology now, but it was fruitful to use. As the strongest side of the AR-solution the visualisation was named most often.

CONCLUSION

Open learning environments provide an holistic and integrated learning environment. There is an intention and a need as well to provide opportunities to lifelong learning and individual study: A learning environment is a place or a community where people can draw upon resources to make sense out of things and construct meaningful solutions to problems.

The main principles of planning open learning environment are based on learner's active learning and interaction. Learning is seen as an active process in network environment through information and communication technologies. Information technology can be an active part of the open learning environment or just a device to help in occasional learning situations. By using the modern technology possibilities arise to emphasis flexibility and mobility in study situations.

According the written and oral monitoring with the teachers and educators, the structural factors of an open learning environment related to combination of Augmented Reality, classroom, and hands-on exhibit can be categorised into four groups (see Sariola 1998; Salmi 2005; Ilola 2008; Maydas et. al 2009; Dede 2009): **(i)** Physical openness points out the accessible of facilities to be used for flexible teaching and learning situations. (ii) Didactic openness concentrates on the construction of a group experience. The learners should have enough opportunities for decision-making in their studies from the teacher, otherwise psychological and virtual aspects cannot be actualised. (iii) Psychological openness consists of a feeling of independence of space and time. This individual feeling, that a learner can influence own learning success substantially promotes motivation for learning. (iv) Virtual openness is made by using information and communication technology in teaching and learning process.

Open learning environments useable at school (and at home for informal learning!) need independence from platforms. They need scalability, multi-user capability, based on an open standard, in order to support a hypermedia structure which allows a working with free or inexpensive software, use client/server architecture, support communication via a network, integrate other interactive media and support working with real time applications. In summary, to support self-organised a learning within a computer mediated learning environment, three principles need discussion. Students specifically need to **(1)** create their own documents and construct links between documents **(2)** communicate with each other to **(3)** cooperate and collaborate on their work/learning. In order to create a appropriate combination of school classroom, exhibition and the web, science centres need to meet the challenge. This has been pointed out earlier in literature (Jones 2005; Salmi 2005; Piazzalunga & Barretto 2005; Ilola 2008), and it was also the main message of the feed-back of the teachers attending the CONNECT-EXPLOAR –Augmented Reality project. However, ICT based education needs content. To create learning objects with the structure of a pre-lecture – visit – post-lecture design with the specific help of ICT-methods, the combination of VSTP (Virtual Thematic Science Park) and AR-Augmented Reality approach at an exhibition will support a work in-between the classroom and exhibition also during the visit. The open learning environment consists typically of a combination of real physical environments and Augmented Reality ICT-based learning. This type of activities do need further research as new source of learning bridging the gap between formal education and informal learning. Latest signals show that AR-technology is moving from the high-tech and military solutions into everyday educational use with valid content.

REFERENCES

Alberts, B. (2009). Making a science of education. *Science*, *323*(2), 15. doi:10.1126/science.1169941

ASTC. (2008). *Sourcebook of statistics & analysis*. Washington, DC: Association of Science-Technology Centers (ASTC).

Connect. (2005). *Designing the classroom of tomorrow by using advanced technologies to connect formal and informal learning. The implementation guide*. Ellinogermaniki Agogi. EPINOIA S.A.

Connect. (2006). *D2.1* (Pedagogical report).

Dede, C. (2009). Immersive interfaces for engagement and learning. *Science*, *323*, 66–68. doi:10.1126/science.1167311

Greenfield, P. M. (2009). Technology and informal education: What Is taught, what is learned. *Science*, *323*, 69–72. doi:10.1126/science.1167190

Hermant, C. (2003). *Does mastery of ICT really improve pupil performance?* eLearning Programme, Directorate General for Education and Culture, European Commission.

Hin, L., Subramaniam, R., & Meng, D. (2005). Use of log analysis and text mining for simple knowledge extraction. In L. Tan & R. Subramaniam (Eds.), *E-learning and virtual science centre* (pp. 347-365). Hershey, PA: Information Science Publishing.

Ilola, L. (2008). *The effects of ICT on school: Teacher's and students' perspectives* (Ser. B. 314). Finland: Turun yliopisto.

Ilola, L., Lakkala, M., & Paavola, S. (2006). Case studies of learning objects used in school settings. *Learning, Media and Technology, 31*(3), 249–267. doi:10.1080/17439880600893291

INI-GraphicsNet. (2006). *Augmented reality. New fields of application through innovative technologies*. The International of Institutions for Advanced Education, Training and R&D in Computer Graphics technology, system and applications.

IST. (2006). *Technology-enchanced learning* [leaflet].

Jones, B. (2005). Establishing identification in virtual science museums: Creating connections and community. In L. Tan & R. Subramaniam (Eds.), *E-learning and virtual science centre* (pp. 1-27). Hershey, PA: Information Science Publishing.

Mayadas, A. (2009). Online education today. *Science, 323*, 85–88. doi:10.1126/science.1168874

Neurath, M., & Cohen, R. (1973). *Empiricism and sociology: The life and work of Otto Neurath*. Boston, MA: Reidel.

Pan, Z., Cheok, A., Yang, H., Zhu, J., & Shi, J. (2006). Virtual reality and mixed reality for virtual learning environments. *Computers & Graphics, 30*(1), 20–28. doi:10.1016/j.cag.2005.10.004

Piazzalunga, R., & Barretto, S. (2005). Challenges in virtual environment design: An architectural approach to virtual spaces. In L. Tan & R. Subramaniam (Eds.), *E-learning and virtual science centre* (pp. 251-271). Hershey, PA: Information Science Centre Publishing.

Raven, J., Raven, J. C., & Court, J. H. (2003). *Manual for Raven's progressive matrices and vocabulary scales*. Oxford, UK: OPP Limited.

Rocard-report. (2006). *Science education now: A renewed pedagogy for the future of Europe*. European Commission, Directorate-General for Research, Information and Communication Unit. Brussels.

Salmi, H. (2005). Open learning environments: Combining Web-based virtual and hands-on science centre learning. In L. Tan & R. Subramaniam (Eds.), *E-learning and virtual science centre* (pp. 327-344). Hershey, PA: Information Science Publishing.

Sariola, J. (1998). The planning of an open learning environment and didactic media choice in teacher education. In T. Nummi, A. Rönkä, & J. Sariola (Eds.), *Virtuality and digital nomadism: An introduction to the LIVE project (1997-2000)*. Finland: MediaEducation Centre. Department of Teacher Education. University of Helsinki. Media Education Publications 6.

Sotiriou, S., et al. (2007). *Proceedings of the Symposium Designing the Science Laboratory for the School of Tomorrow. Advantaged technologies in education*, Athens, Greece. Ellinogermaniki Agogi.

Wolf, K. D. (1995). The implementation of an open learning environment under World Wide Web. In H. Maurer (Ed.), *Educational multimedia and hypermedia, 1995. Proceedings of EdMedia 95*. Charlottsville, VA: Advancement of Computing in Education (AACE).

Selected Readings

Chapter 15
A Proposed Framework for Designing Sustainable Communities for Knowledge Management Systems

Lakshmi Goel
University of Houston, USA

Elham Mousavidin
University of Houston, USA

ABSTRACT

Despite considerable academic and practitioner interest in knowledge management, success of knowledge management systems is elusive. This chapter provides a framework which suggests that KM success can be achieved by designing sustainable communities of practice. Communities of practice have proven to have significant economic and practical implications on organizational practices. A growing body of literature in KM recognizes the importance of communities that foster collaborative learning in organizations and almost all KMS have a 'network' component that facilitates connecting people in communities of practice. Evidence has shown that communities have been a key element in KMS of many companies including Xerox PARC, British Petroleum Co., Shell Oil Company, Halliburton, IBM, Proctor and Gamble, and Hewlett Packard.

INTRODUCTION

Despite considerable academic and practitioner interest in knowledge management (KM), success of knowledge management systems (KMS) is elusive (Akhavan et al., 2005; Hammer et al., 2004). There is a considerable body of literature that has studied factors for KMS success. Jennex and Olfman (2005) provide a review of KMS success literature and propose a comprehensive framework for evaluation of KMS success. In this chapter, our goal is to contribute to this line of research by identifying how these success factors may be achieved. Specifically, we restrict our scope of inquiry to a certain type of knowledge management systems; those that are designed to support communities of practice (CoP).

Prior literature that has sought to identify important factors in KM success has adopted either the individual level of analysis (e.g., Bock et al., 2005; Kankanhalli et al., 2005), the organizational level of analysis (e.g., Brown & Duguid, 2000), or the technological level of analysis (e.g., Markus et al., 2002). We propose an approach that incorporates research on individuals, organizations, and the technology pertaining to knowledge management to suggest a set of design principles for sustainable communities of practice. Communities of practice have proven to have significant economic and practical implications on organizational practice (Brown & Duguid, 1999, 2000). A growing body of literature in knowledge management recognizes the importance of communities that foster collaborative learning in organizations and almost all knowledge management systems have a 'network' component that facilitates connecting people in communities of practice. Evidence has shown that community has been a key element in knowledge management systems of many companies including Xerox PARC, British Petroleum Co., Shell Oil Company, Halliburton,

IBM, Proctor and Gamble, and Hewlett Packard (Brown & Gray, 1995; Cohen, 2006; Cross et al., 2006; McDermott, 1999a,1999b).

Attributes of communities of practice, which we believe determine the success or failure of KM initiatives, have been thus far under-researched. KM can benefit from literature in virtual communities that looks at what properties of a community make it sustainable. These properties can then be viewed as a blueprint of what a community needs to have to achieve its function of fostering collaboration and hence, generating knowledge. In sum, this research is intended to help practitioners arrive at how best to design communities in KMS in order to achieve KM success.

KMS success models provide a strategic level process approach to achieving success. KMS success factors provide a means for evaluation of KMS success. Our goal is to suggest how these success factors could be achieved at an operational level. We draw on Jennex and Olfman's (2005b, 2006) work to arrive at a list of eight success factors that are applicable to our conceptualization of a KMS that supports CoPs. Table 1 below provides a list of these factors.

This chapter is structured as follows. In the next section we present a review of literature in knowledge management, KM success, and communities of practice. The literature helps provide the theoretical basis for our research. Our research methodology section follows the literature review.

Table 1. KMS success factors adopted from Jennex and Olfman (2005b, 2006)

Success Factor	Description
SF1	Identification of users, sources, knowledge, and links
SF2	Clear articulation of knowledge structure
SF3	Motivation and commitment of users
SF4	Senior management support
SF5	Measures for assessment of appropriate use
SF6	Clear goal and purpose
SF7	Support for easy knowledge use
SF8	Designing work processes to incorporate knowledge capture and use

We elaborate on the process and method for arriving at our design recommendations, and discuss each recommendation in detail. We next provide a discussion, and conclude with our suggestions for future research.

LITERATURE REVIEW

The primary goal of this research is to contribute to literature in KM success. We provide a brief review of literature in knowledge management and knowledge management success to summarize the state of current research. We then focus on the literature in communities of practice, which we use to augment research on KM success.

Knowledge Management and Knowledge Management Systems

Managing knowledge is a focal task for organizations today. Appreciating the importance of knowledge as a core capability or resource (Alavi & Leidner, 2001; Grant, 1996) has underscored the need for managing it strategically. Though the effort to manage what a company 'knows' is not a recent phenomenon, new technology and greater awareness fueled by a competitive business landscape has resulted in substantive attention paid to KM (Prusak, 2001).

Knowledge can be conceptualized in different ways. It can be seen as embedded in practices (Orlikowski, 2002) or processes (Epple & Argote, 1996), or as a separate entity or object (Schultze & Stabell, 2004). Another view of knowledge is that which is embedded in people's heads and is a *"fluid mix of framed experience, values, contextual information and expert insight that provide a framework for evaluation and incorporating new experiences and information"* (Davenport & Prusak, 1997, p. 5). This type of knowledge is referred to as tacit. While explicit knowledge is easily codified, stored, and transferred, by the use of technology (such as knowledge repositories, document control systems, or databases) tacit knowledge is 'stickier' (Hippel, 1994). Tacit knowledge, as conceptualized by Polanyi (1958) refers to knowing-how or embodied knowledge[1], and is the characteristic of an 'expert'[2] who can perform a task without deliberation of the principles or rules involved (Ryle, 1949/1984). This goes beyond a mere technical or physical knowhow (Dretske, 1991) as it is highly contextual. Employees of a certain culture may have tacit knowledge about practices that employees of other cultures do not. Being able to deliberately leverage such tacit knowledge is hypothesized to generate value and be a key differentiator for an organization (Alavi & Leidner, 1999, 2001; Grant, 1996). It is tacit knowledge that resides in employees' heads, which is vital for problem solving and organizational learning (Davenport & Prusak, 1997). Due to the uneven distribution of expertise, the task of managing tacit knowledge is especially essential in today's dynamic and global business landscape. In the context of large, geographically distributed, multi-cultural firms where employees do not have the opportunity to interact face-to-face, communication and transfer of knowledge becomes even more challenging (Lapre & Van Wassenhove, 2003). Therefore, designing systems that facilitate tacit knowledge management is important. The focus of many design articles is on information or content management, which deals with explicit knowledge. In this paper, we focus on managing tacit knowledge.

We conceptualize knowledge management systems (KMS) as systems designed specifically with the intent to manage organizational knowledge, in line with Jennex and Olfman's (2005b) infrastructure/generic approach to KM, by connecting people. In this approach, KMS are primarily designed to support communities of practice. We elaborate on this further in the subsequent sections.

Knowledge Management Success

KMS success has been defined in many ways. Jennex and Olfman (2004, 2005b) provide an integrated framework of KM success factors identified by previous authors. We adopt a definition of KMS success as proposed by Jennex (2005) as being able to reuse knowledge to improve organizational effectiveness by providing the required knowledge to those that need it when it is needed.

The attempt to manage knowledge is not always successful. IDC[3] estimated an expenditure of $12.7 billion on KM in 2005. However, approximately 70 percent of KM initiatives are deemed unsuccessful (Akhavan et al., 2005; Hammer et al., 2004). Stories such as the struggle of General Motors (GM) and NUMMI[4] in the initial stages of their initiatives for learning and knowledge transfer highlight the challenges (Inkpen, 2005). Though significant research in MIS is directed toward how to successfully implement information systems in general, KM presents unique challenges that are more complex than what models such as technology acceptance (TAM) (Davis, 1989) and task technology fit (TTF) (Goodhue & Thompson, 1995) can explain. Issues such as employees' reluctance to share knowledge, coordination of knowledge management efforts, and adoption of the right model for knowledge creation, management, and transfer, present unique difficulties for KM system success (Jennex & Olfman, 2005a; Jennex et al., 2007).

Most research on factors of KM success can be seen to fall within one of three categories. First, using the individual as the unit of analysis, employee reluctance to share knowledge has been studied using frameworks such as identity theory (e.g., Constant et al., 1994), social-cognitive theory (e.g., Constant et al., 1994), social exchange theory (e.g., Kankanhalli et al., 2005), and the theory of reasoned behavior (e.g., Bock et al., 2005). Power has also been discussed as an important factor (Gordon & Grant, 2005; Porra & Goel, 2006). Findings indicate mixed results where employees

want to share for reasons of 'showing-off' (Constant et al., 1994), altruism (Constant et al., 1994), or feeling of social obligation while employees are reluctant to share knowledge for reasons of fear of loss of hegemony (Shin, 2004), and costs (such as time and effort) (Butler, 2001) involved. Motivation (Ardichvili, 2003), and extrinsic reward structures (Shin, 2004; Yeu Wah et al., 2007) as predictors of knowledge sharing have also been studied.

Second, employing an organizational unit of analysis, management of KM activities has been examined. In particular, research in knowledge transfer (Argote & Ingram, 2000), organizational culture and norms (Constant et al., 1994; Faraj & Wasko, Forthcoming; Hart & Warne, 2006; Usoro & Kuofie, 2006), and senior and middle management support (Brown & Duguid, 2000) have been studied. Here, KM success is related to favorable organizational factors for knowledge sharing.

Third, using the system as the unit of analysis, technical characteristics of KMS such as repository structure, directory capabilities, and collaboration tools have been investigated (King, 2006; Markus, 2001; Markus et al., 2002). Hence, KM success is explained by theories such as task-technology fit (TTF) (Goodhue & Thompson, 1995), which focus on choosing the right technology.

This paper investigates KMS from a perspective that incorporates the individual, organizational, and system units of analysis by using the lens of communities of practice (Brown & Duguid, 1999; Lave & Wenger, 1991; Wenger, 1998).

Communities of Practice

Communities of practice have been used by many to study KM practices (for example, see Cheuk, 2006; Koeglreiter et al., 2006); however, this perspective has not been applied to designing KMS per se (an exception is Stein, 2006 who proposes a descriptive model of the functions and structure of a successful CoP). Knowledge management systems are not particularly complex or technically different from other information systems (Alavi & Leidner, 1999). The difference between knowledge management systems and other systems such as group decision support systems (GDSS), electronic meeting systems (EMS), and expert systems lies not primarily in the technology, but in the purpose for their use. GDSS focus on connecting a particular group of employees for the goal of solving particular problems, or arriving at a decision. EMS focuses on facilitating meetings and collaborative work among a certain group of people. Expert systems are typically rule-based, where the knowledge of an expert/s (where experts are identified by the organization) is captured in the system's knowledge base, and then queried by users. The goal of KMS, as we conceptualize them, is to connect all employees in an organization at all times. Unlike in expert systems, the roles of knowledge producers (experts) and consumers (users) are flexible. Groups are not dictated by organizational structures, but emerge ad-hoc as communities of employees with common interests and problems. Interaction within these communities may yield solutions to specific problems, but it is the interaction for the purpose of tacit knowledge exchange that is the goal of the system.

Since the central problem of KM is the creation and transfer of tacit knowledge, it is necessary to look at what facilitates these processes. Experiences and contextual insights have been traditionally transferred through methods such as story-telling (Brown & Duguid, 2000), sense-making (Brown & Duguid, 1999), or through conversations in informal social networks. Communities of practice are informal networks of like-minded individuals, where the process of learning and transfer of tacit knowledge is essentially social, involving a deepening process of participation (Lave & Wenger, 1991). Research shows that in the absence of decisive first-hand knowledge, an individual looks at successful decisions made by other like-minded, similarly-situated people (Nidumolu &

Subramani, 2001) as filters or guides to identify potentially good choices (Hill et al., 1995). Prior case studies have shown that even for individuals armed with extensive know-what (explicit knowledge), collective know-how (tacit knowledge) can be highly significant (Brown & Duguid, 1999; Orr, 1989). KM practitioners and researchers recognize the importance of communities that foster collaborative learning in organizations (Pan & Leidner, 2003) and almost all knowledge management systems have a 'network' component that facilitates connecting people in communities of practice (Faraj & Wasko, Forthcoming). The community perspective of knowledge management, which acknowledges the importance of informal networks and emphasizes collaboration, started in the late 1990s (Cross et al., 2006). Evidence has shown that communities have been a key element in knowledge management systems of many companies including Xerox PARC, British Petroleum Co., Shell Oil Company, Halliburton, IBM, Proctor and Gamble, and Hewlett Packard (Brown & Gray, 1995; Cohen, 2006; Cross et al., 2006; McDermott, 1999a, 1999b). Most of the companies that used IBM's first Web-based knowledge management system organized their activities around communities, an element that IBM had not deliberately implemented in the system initially (McDermott, 1999b).

While studying design characteristics of communities, defining what is meant by a community and its sustainability is important. In attempting to do so, we refer to prior IS literature on virtual communities, since we consider communities in knowledge management systems as virtual. The term 'virtual' has been used here to distinguish these communities from real-life communities with face-to-face interaction. Borrowing from biology, virtual community sustainability has been regarded as the 'intrinsic longevity' of the membership (e.g., Butler, 2001; Porra & Parks, 2005). Hence research has been devoted to studying how members can be encouraged to stay in a community. The concept of a 'community' has received much attention and there are different ideas as to what brings about a 'sense of community' (Blanchard & Markus, 2004). Reasons such as support (Blanchard & Markus, 2004), recognition (Blanchard & Markus, 2004), intimacy (Blanchard & Markus, 2004) and obligation (Wasko & Faraj, 2000), have all been studied as motivators of staying in a community. It has been acknowledged that in organizations tacit knowledge is shared in ad-hoc, informal settings (Brown & Duguid, 2000) that may not be replicable (such as brainstorming sessions, or when new hires approach veterans for specific advice). While the composition of members might change in a community, the community still serves the purpose as a platform for knowledge management. The existing literature does not reflect this functional aspect of communities. Therefore, we define a community as a platform for knowledge creation and exchange, and sustainability as how successful a community is in achieving its function of facilitating knowledge generation and exchange. This research attempts to draw on relevant literature and apply it to an organizational KM context in order to suggest how sustainable communities can be designed. Hence, the output of this chapter is design recommendations or guidelines for communities of practice that are the central part of KMSs.

One view of organizing CoPs is that the design structure should be emergent rather than imposed (Barab et al., 2003). However, it has been recognized that too little structure can also yield negative benefits, and a 'minimalist design' or a tentative platform for a community is needed (Wenger, 1998). Hence, while it is not recommended to have tightly controlled formal designs in place, informal structures and basic guidelines that allow flexibility, diversity, autonomy, creativity, and scalability are necessary (Wenger, 1998).

RESEARCH METHODOLOGY AND ANALYSIS

In this section, we first elaborate on our method for arriving at design guidelines for sustainable communities in KMS. We next present our design recommendations each preceded by supporting literature. These are followed by examples in prior research, which evidence the recommendations.

Method

We conducted an extensive search in literature using engines such as Google Scholar and Social Sciences Index using key words such as knowledge, knowledge management, knowledge management system, knowledge management system success, communities, virtual communities, and communities of practice. Keeping in line with our research objective, we narrowed the results to papers that were relevant to the design of communities in the context of knowledge management. We support each proposed design guideline with results from prior studies, both qualitative and quantitative. The qualitative data includes quotes from case studies in knowledge management and virtual communities. Data from quantitative research mainly includes their supported hypotheses. The data immediately follows each design recommendation. The goal of using data from previous research was solely for clarification and better understanding, as well as demonstrating that the importance of these issues has been acknowledged explicitly by other researchers. Though the evidence was implicitly or explicitly observed in different papers, the related design guidelines were not the primary focus of these studies. One of our key contributions is thus the synthesis of the findings across the different studies and bringing to the forefront the importance of the design guidelines.

Design Recommendations

A community of practice is defined by the commonality of an interest shared by its members. Members of the community form communal bonds, construct collective identities through communicative action (Blanchard & Markus, 2004; Donath, 1999; Postmes et al., 2000), and reach common understanding (Habermas, 1984), thus generating collaborative knowledge. The concept of a community boundary is hence important and delineates what a community is about, and what it is not. In organizations, it is especially important to make sure a community is 'specialized' or focused on a particular topic in order to maximize the signal[5] to noise ratio and minimize the costs of obtaining relevant information[6]. Thus:

Each community in a KMS should have a central focus which should be maintained throughout the life of the community by ensuring that all posts are relevant to the community's focus.

As will be discussed in the ensuing recommendations, a community manager, or a segmentation strategy, could play a key role in ensuring a topical focus. Jones and Rafaeli (2000) and Jones et al. (2004) conclude that in order for a virtual community to be sustainable, it has to have a topical focus because otherwise members might experience information overload, which is not tolerable by their cognition capacity. They add that:

It logically follows that beyond a particular communication processing-load, the behavioural stress zones encountered will make group communication unsustainable. (Jones & Rafaeli 2000, p. 219)

Overall, the empirical findings support the assertion that individual information-overload coping strategies have an observable impact on mass interaction discourse dynamics. Evidence was found [that] users are more likely to end active participation as the overloading of mass interaction increases. (Jones et al. 2004, p. 206)

Two complementary concepts discussed in literature are those of information overload (Rogers & Agarwala-Rogers, 1975) and critical mass (Licklider & Taylor, 1968; Markus, 1987). Critical mass refers to the required group size threshold for a sustainable community (Bieber et al., 2002). Information overload results from a higher number of messages, or messages that are not sufficiently organized in a sensible, linked structure, which makes it difficult for individuals to process. While critical mass indicates that a community that is too small will fail, information overload suggests that one that is too big will also fail. Hence, there is a maximum limit to the size of a community beyond which a low signal to noise ratio (Malhotra et al., 1997) and an upper bound on an individual's cognitive processing limits (Jones, 1997) will render it unsuccessful. This topic was the focus of studies conducted specifically on membership limits of communities (e.g., Jones & Rafaeli, 2000). While the limit is context dependent and varies with the nature of the community, a manager could determine an approximate threshold for when information overload or topical deviation occurs. When a community grows too large, a segmentation strategy can be employed to create an interrelated space (Jones & Rafaeli, 2000). Hence:

There should be a maximum limit set for the membership in the community in a KMS, beyond which the community should be split into interrelated sub-communities each with a central focus or topic.

Jones and Rafaeli (2000) provide examples of communities such as Amazon or Excite, in which a segmentation strategy has been used to keep the communities focused and prevent information overload.

Segmentation strategy' refers here to any systematic method used to split discourse spaces with the aim of creating a system of interrelated virtual publics. As studies of usage show (e.g., Butler, 1999), virtual publics are not 'scalable.' Therefore, a 'mega virtual public' cannot be sustained. Rather, virtual metropolises emerge from the creation of a series of related virtual publics, via the appropriate segmentation of discourse in different related cyberspaces. In turn, the resulting system of interconnected virtual publics encourages the expansion of user populations, while reducing the likelihood of overloaded virtual public discourse. (p. 221)

Moderation has been studied in virtual community literature (Markus, 2001). Human intervention is considered necessary for tasks such as maintaining community focus, preventing 'trolling' or 'flaming' (Malhotra et al., 1997), encouraging participation (Preece et al., 2003), and sanitizing data (Markus, 2001). Even though trolling and flaming are unlikely in organizational settings, moderation is required for the other reasons. Since moderators (often referred to as community or knowledge managers) are usually employees with regular duties, it is important that their work for the KM effort be recognized and that they are allowed to devote time to the community as part of their job (Davenport et al., 1998; Silva et al., 2006). Hence:

Each community should have at least one community manager with the authority and resources to manage and act for the benefit of the community.

The following remarks demonstrate the importance of the role of a community manager and the resources (e.g., people and time) that are available to him or her.

Knowledge managers have content leads that evaluate external knowledge resources and establish

pointers to the new resources for specific domains. The searches are synthesized to allow higher level of reuse. Knowledge researchers strongly support sharing and reuse of knowledge probes: 'The first thing I do is go check that database to make sure that no one hasn't already pulled that information before I go and start a whole new search.' (Sherif & Xing 2006, p. 538)

One person per project is in charge of posting project deliverables onto the repository ... On a weekly basis the knowledge manager goes in and makes sure it has been categorized correctly and the document has been zipped. He just makes sure it has been submitted according to all the standards and guidelines. (Sherif & Xing 2006, p. 536)

As seen in the following, lack of sufficient resources such as time can adversely affect the quality of community manager's job.

With the amount of time available to produce high quality and sanitized knowledge for dissemination ... It's not even just writing it ... I'm on the review committee and that's where a lot of time is as I've got to review every document ... The delay in implementing this second knowledge dissemination plan was due to ... the lack of resources to provide high quality, sanitized knowledge for consumption by customers. (Markus, 2001, p. 80)

Research on information overload posits that information should be organized hierarchically in order to place new information in the correct context quickly. Also, costs of obtaining new knowledge are lower when messages are simple and contextually relevant (Jones et al., 2004). Blogs, wikis, and net forums use chronological and topical organizing successfully to map information. Site maps on websites provide a graphical view of how information is arranged, reducing the time and effort required to access it while also providing an overall picture of the Web site. More recent work on the semantic Web enables tagging knowledge objects with keywords pertaining to the context and relevance of the topic (Daconta et al., 2003). Using descriptive tags enables searching and archiving information in a way that is most applicable to the topic. Semantic Web technologies make a static hierarchical representation extraneous. However, to make searches efficient, there needs to be standardization in the tags used to describe the same types of objects. The standards, while imposing a common structure, should also allow flexibility to reflect unique contextual information in the knowledge object (Geroimenko & Chen, 2003). Site maps can be used to provide community-specific keywords that can be used to tag and search for community related topics. The importance of site maps in knowledge management systems has been suggested in prior research (e.g., Jennex & Olfman, 2000, 2005). This leads to the following design recommendations:

Each community in a KMS should have a site map showing how knowledge is arranged and accessible in the community.

All posts in the community should be categorizable according to the site map.

Here is a description of the importance of a well-designed site map (or an equivalent).

We've got to put tags on that content in a way that it's retrievable, in a way that makes sense as to how we do business. When you've done a particular type of project, creating [a] particular set of deliverables to a particular type of client, then you want to be able to hand this next person a path or a navigational metaphor or structure so that they can find what they are looking for and [if it]..is meaningful to them they can reuse it with a slight change. (Sherif & Xing 2006, p. 536)

You cannot just willy-nilly grab content and throw it into a big pot and then hope that it can be reused. Obviously, you've got to put tags on that

content in a way that it is retrievable. You have to be able to provide the knowledge contributor with the analog on the front end, so that they can categorize and catalog their knowledge in a way that makes it meaningful for the person who is now coming and going to repeat it all. (Sherif & Xing 2006, p. 536)

Costs in terms of effort and time can also be reduced by maintaining a community home page which provides a quick overview of things such as the latest news related to the community topic, latest posts and replies. An effective and efficient search function is important in order for members to be able to locate relevant information quickly, which also could reduce the amount of effort made (Markus, 2001). Hence:

The home page for the community should be fresh and dynamic, presenting all new relevant information for the community in a concise and easy-to-read manner.

The KMS should support an efficient and effective search function.

The following statements elaborate on these guidelines.

You go to this site that has the method and you click on the phases and read about the phases, you read about stages, and it shows what work products and what deliverables come out of those activities and stages. You can click on that and it will bring up the best examples of those deliverables and work products. (Sherif & Xing 2006, p. 537).

Say you have someone on the ExxonMobil team, and they need to keep up with what's going on with ExxonMobil, so we set up a search term for them and we tie it into our Dow Jones service that we use and everyday, Dow Jones uses that search term that we put in there and dumps these articles about ExxonMobil into a profiling container so the team member can use it. They don't have to go to Dow Jones, they don't have to look through 50 different articles, they go right here and they see right here, here's the 10 articles that came in today about ExxonMobil. (Sherif & Xing 2006, p. 537)

A core capability of the tool the team was provided was the ability to reference-link entries and apply multiple keywords, and then use powerful search capabilities to identify similar entries. (Markus 2001, p. 80).

Version control system for documents can be used to keep track of dates of multiple submissions of the same document. In addition to automatic checking, members can be encouraged by community managers to periodically review their submissions to the KMS and make sure that they are current and delete the obsolete, inconsistent entries (Damodaran & Olphert, 2000; Kohlhase & Anghelache, 2004).

Accuracy and currency of the information should be maintained by using tools such as version control systems, as well as by encouraging members to review their submissions.

The importance of the ability to revisit and revise posts and to keep the information accurate and up-to-date is seen below.

...the database author might know that the answer could be made more general in order to answer more questions. This might involve abstracting both the question and the answer. Occasionally, the author would feel it necessary to correct incorrect, incomplete, or incoherent answers. (Markus 2001, p. 76)

The following shows how version control functionality benefits users of a web-based virtual learning environment for students.

Although this approach for providing group awareness is very simple, feedback from users of the BSCW system indicates that information such as 'A uploaded a new version of document X', or 'B has read document Y' is often very useful for group members in coordinating their work and gaining an overview of what has happened since they last logged in. (Appelt & Mambrey 1999, p. 1710)

Social network theory (Granovetter, 1973) and social identity theory (Tajfel & Turner, 1986) have been used to explain knowledge exchange and interactions in communities. According to social identity theory and theories of collective action, gaining self esteem and recognition for their expertise, and enhancing their reputation (Wasko & Faraj, 2005) motivate members to participate in communities (Donath, 1999; Douglas & McGarty, 2001; Postmes et al., 2000). 'Old-timers' in communities are frequently those whose advice is valued due to their track record in the community. Social network theory looks at relationships between members (Chae et al., 2005; Garton & Haythornthwaite, 1997; Wasko & Faraj, 2004; Wellman, 1996; Wellman & Guila, 1997; Wellman et al., 1996) and the normative structure of content and form in a group (Postmes et al., 2000; Wellman, 1996). While weak ties provide more opportunities for new knowledge (Hansen, 1999; Wellman, 1996), on-line strong ties provide more confidence in the information and reinforce real-life relationships (Wellman, 1996). With social network analysis (Wellman, 1996), a well connected member with a high social capital can be identified as a good information resource (Wasko & Faraj, 2005).

Technology should support multiple ways to connect people (Garton an&d Haythornthwaite, 1997) who need the information to those who have it. Social technologies such as online networking sites (e.g., Facebook, MySpace) and virtual worlds (e.g., Second Life) can be used to support collaboration (Goel & Mousavidin, 2007). Expert directries are often an integral part of KMS and serve as transactive memory systems to identify 'who knows what' in the organization (Argote & Ingram, 2000). If an employee knows exactly who to ask a particular question from, he/she should be able to contact the expert directly, and in the absence of the knowledge, the member can rely on the community to help arrive at an answer. Since members in a KMS can belong to multiple communities, these features apply to the entire system. This discussion leads to the following design recommendations:

The KMS should have the facility to maintain member profiles that indicate the number of posts, other member links, replies, and usage history of a member.

Members should be able to connect to other members directly through tools such as instant messaging as well as indirectly through forums and directories.

The user profile contains compulsory and optional information that a member provides upon registration. If a member of the community publishes a contribution or asks a question, the contributor's name is shown as a hyperlink. By clicking on this hyperlink, one obtains the user profile of the corresponding member. The extent of information other members see on the user profile depends on the level of anonymity the member has chosen. (Leimeister et al. 2005, p. 110)

In the remark below, Barab et al. (2003) discuss the importance of profiles in a community of practice called ILF[7].

In fact, the ILF encourages its members to create and edit their member profiles so other ILF members can learn more about one another. This enables ILF members to control how they are perceived by others within the community, and ideally, these profiles help ILF members to decide

who they want to communicate with and how they might interpret statements or attitudes of others. (Barab et al., 2003, p. 248)

Though social identity theory discourages anonymity, literature in MIS (especially in research on group decision support systems) has found anonymity to aid participation. However, an employee's trust in the content obtained from a KMS would be weaker if it were anonymous (Donath, 1999). Making authorship explicit adds legitimacy to the information. Literature in philosophy also discusses the importance of credentials in reliability on others for information (Hardwig, 1991). In addition, this makes the author responsible for making sure that the information he/she puts up is not erroneous. Investigating different levels of anonymity (such as using nicknames or real names) would be an interesting line of enquiry, as well.

Submissions to a KMS should not be anonymous.

The following statement supports this guideline.

An interesting metric developed by the specialists to assess data quality was their use of incident authorship as an indicator of quality. Each incident that is entered is automatically assigned a unique number, which includes a code identifying the particular specialist who entered it ... You tend to evaluate information differently from different people. So if you see 40 items from a search you go to the incidents of those folks you've gotten good information from in the past ... I know that Arthur has a reputation for writing shorts novels as resolutions. I mean, he's a wonderful source of information ... So when I get an incident from him, I'm very comfortable with that information. Whereas, some of the other people in the department will put in one or two sentence resolutions. And it tends to make it a little vaguer and more difficult to be confident about. (Markus 2001, p. 68, 69)

Participation in a community needs to be encouraged (Cross et al., 2006; Davenport et al., 1998; Prandelli et al. 2006). Reluctance on behalf of employees to participate is a primary reason for the failure of KM efforts (Ardichvili, 2003; Alavi & Leidner, 1999). Specifically, perceived loss of power (Constant et al., 1994), fear of criticism and unintentionally misleading members (Ardichvili, 2003), and costs involved in terms of time and effort (Markus, 2001) are primary reasons why employees do not participate. While appropriate design of a system can help minimize the aforementioned costs (Bieber et al., 2002), the organization needs to make efforts to alleviate the other factors. Engendering an organizational culture which encourages pro-social behavior and knowledge sharing has been suggested in prior literature (Constant et al., 1994; Huber, 2001). At a community level, the moderator or community manager can play a vital role in increasing the level of participation. In particular, the community manager needs to ensure that knowledge is transferred from producers (experts) to consumers (users) (Markus, 2001; Cross et al., 2006) by ensuring that questions are answered and new knowledge is posted. These functions of a community manager maintain the value and usefulness of the community to its members (Preece et al., 2003). Hence:

A community manager should ensure that queries are answered.

Some of the responsibilities of community managers (Sysops, in this case) are shown in the statement below.

System operators (Sysops) were appointed to monitor the discussions in the forums, track requests and make sure they were answered. Sysops would try to get answers in 24 hours; if not they would contact people directly and ask them to respond. Additionally, they were to give positive feedback to those who did respond. Since there were likely to be cultural difference and sensitivities, Sysops were to monitor the content of messages ... Three translators were hired and Sysops would decide which messages were to be translated into English with technical replies to be translated back to the originator's own language. The goal for completion of translation was 48 hours. (Markus 2001, p. 85)

A community manager should encourage experts to contribute tacit knowledge (experiences, ideas, etc.) to the community.

Some techniques for encouraging participation were observed by Jones and Rafaeli.

Where sustained interactive discourse is a goal, various techniques can be used to gain critical mass. Administrators can seed discussions by systematically encouraging a group of key individuals to contribute. Economic incentives can be given and where a number of related virtual publics already exist, group segmentation can be used to gain instant critical mass for new virtual publics. (Jones & Rafaeli 2000, p. 221)

In addition to voluntarily accessing the system for information, a KMS can be made a central repository for electronically storable information such as required documents, templates, and forms. Since knowledge sharing cannot be forced and extrinsic rewards may not work (Huber, 2001; Kankanhalli et al., 2005), making the KMS an obligatory passage point[8] (Callon, 1986) for explicit knowledge required for daily work would encourage employees who otherwise would not access the system, or make use of it. Most employees either do not think of using the KMS for posting such information, or may not want to spend the time and effort required to do so. More importantly, there should be a consistent format used for information posted. A community manager plays a key role in ensuring this consistency. Hence:

A community manager should encourage the posting of standardized documents, templates, forms, and other electronically storable information in a consistent manner.

The following shows some consequences of inconsistent postings.

We had to overhaul the [knowledge repository] after three years because nobody was following a consistent style [of classifying documents] ... [P]eople were building their case bases with different parameter settings, so it became like a soup of knowledge, and nobody could find anything. (Markus 2001, p. 81)

We summarize the design guidelines and highlight our contributions in the following section.

DISCUSSION AND FUTURE RESEARCH

The design recommendations derived from theory and past research are summarized in Table 2. In broad terms, the recommendations can be seen to fall into four categories: technological, membership, content, and organizational. To achieve our objective, we study KMS from a perspective that incorporates technical, individual, as well as organizational level literature. These are reflected in the technological, membership, and organizational categories. We tie our recommendations to prior research by suggesting how each of them could be used to achieve a particular success factor. In Table 2, each recommendation is followed by success factor(s) from Table 1 which we believe to be applicable.

Employing the lens of communities of practice allowed us to add a fourth level of analysis, that of a community. The guidelines regarding the content of KM communities address this level. In practice, most KMS incorporate communities as part of their architecture. By drawing on literature on virtual communities, we add to research in KMS by proposing design guidelines for the content and management of such communities. These categories are not mutually exclusive. For example, membership profiles need the corresponding technological features to support them. Also, the list is not intended to be exhaustive. Further research studying actual participatory behavior in KMS would help determine if there are other design characteristics that facilitate community participation.

Prior research in IS has not systematically studied design guidelines for knowledge management communities. While the design features discussed have been implemented in current KM practices, they have emerged more from a process of trial-and-error; not grounded in research. Organizations are spending considerable resources, both in terms of time and money, on knowledge management efforts, not all of which are successful. Results from this study could help managers concerned with KM increase their chances of success by designing sustainable communities.

Using a community of practice as a lens unifies the fragmented literature in knowledge management which, thus far, has studied the phenomenon separately at the individual, organizational, or system level. A shift of perspective of community sustainability from one that retains more members to one that serves as an effective and efficient platform for knowledge management also stimulates new lines of inquiry.

We looked at existing research on knowledge management and virtual communities, synthesized the literature, and applied it in the context of organizational KMS. Our goal was to conceptually identify guidelines for successful design of communities in KMS which can be used by practitioners who wish to implement KMS. Hence, these guidelines are intended as a blueprint to

Table 2. Summary of design recommendations for sustainable communities of practice in knowledge management systems

Design Guidelines	Success Factor
I. Technological features	
1. Site map	SF1, SF2, SF7
2. Search features	SF7
3. Document version control systems	SF1, SF2, SF7
II. Membership features	
1. Non-anonymity	SF1
2. Maintaining usage statistics and profiles	SF1, SF5
3. Connectivity between members – Directories, Forums, IM capabilities	SF1
III. Content features	
1. Making it an obligatory passage point (OPP) for documents, templates, forms etc.	SF3, SF8
2. Home page to represent community – fresh, dynamic	SF7
3. Content on the home page for summary of new relevant topics, news, and highlights	SF2, SF7
4. Moderation to ensure topical focus and relevance	SF2, SF3, SF5, SF6, SF7
5. Moderation to ensure questions are answered	SF3, SF5
6. Moderation to encourage 'experts' to contribute	SF3
7. Moderation to ensure currency of documents	SF3, SF5, SF7
8. Splitting into sub-communities, if size grows	SF3, SF5, SF6, SF7
IV. Organizational functions	
1. Creating and supporting role of moderator/community manager	SF3, SF4

design KMS communities. Furthermore, they can also be used as an evaluative tool for existing KMS. Future research would add value by evaluating and testing these recommendations in a representative setting through possibly an action research. An exploratory case study of existing KMS that implement these features would also provide validity. Each recommendation could be the subject of a separate study. For example, the role of a knowledge manager or the design of the search features could constitute substantial research agendas.

This chapter has the limitations associated with a conceptual study. It needs to be validated by empirical research. The suggestions presented for future research are intended to be a guide for a research program in this area. We draw on literature in virtual communities to inform us about the nature of communities in knowledge management systems. However, the design of these communities is contingent upon organizational factors such as organization culture, norms, practices, and structure. Hence, these guidelines may not be universally applicable but need to be tailored to the specific context and requirements. This research is intended to be a starting point for an inquiry on the topic.

REFERENCES

Akhavan, P., Jafari, M., & Fathian, M. (2005). Exploring failure-factors of implementing knowledge management systems in organizations. *Journal of Knowledge Management Practice.*

Alavi, M., & Leidner, D. E. (1999). Knowledge management systems: Issues, challenges, and benefits. *Communications of the AIS, 1*(7).

Alavi, M., & Leidner, D. (2001). Review: Knowledge management and knowledge management systems: Conceptual foundations and research issues. *MIS Quarterly, 25*(1), 107-136.

Appelt, W., & Mambrey, P. (1999), Experiences with the BSCW Shared Workspace System as the Backbone of a Virtual Learning Environment for Students. *In Proceedings of ED Media '99.'* Charlottesville, (pp. 1710-1715).

Ardichvili, A. (2003). Motivation and barriers to participation in virtual knowledge-sharing communities of practice. *Journal of Knowledge Management, 7*(1), 64-77.

Argote, L., & Ingram, P. (2000). Knowledge transfer: A basis for competitive advantage in firms. *Organizational Behavior and Human Decision Processes, 82*(1), 150-169.

Balasubramanian, S., & Mahajan, V. (2001). The economic leverage of the virtual community. *International Journal of Electronic Commerce, 5*(3), 103-138.

Barab, S. A., MaKinster, J. G., & Scheckler, R. (2003). Designing system dualities: Characterizing a web-supported professional development community. *The Information Society, 19,* 237-256.

Bieber, M., D., Engelbart, D., Furuta, R., Hiltz, S. R., Noll, J., Preece, J. et al.(2002). Toward virtual community knowledge evolution. *Journal of Management Information Systems, 18*(4), 11-35.

Blanchard, A. L., & Markus, M. L. (2004). The experienced 'sense' of a virtual community: Characteristics and processes. *Database for Advances in Information Systems, 35*(1), 65-79.

Bock, G. W., Zmud, R. W., Kim, Y. G., & Lee, J. N. (2005). Behavioral intention formation in knowledge sharing: Examining the roles of extrinsic motivators, social-psychological forces, and organizational climate. *MIS Quarterly, 29*(1), 87-111.

Brown, J. S. & Gray, E. S. (1995). The people are the company. *FastCompany.* Retrieved from http://www.fastcompany.com/online/01/people.html

Brown, J. S. & Duguid, P. (1999). Organizing knowledge. *The society for organizational learning, 1*(2), 28-44.

Brown, J. S. & Duguid, P. (2000). Balancing act: How to capture knowledge without killing it. *Harvard Business Review, 73-80.*

Butler, B. (1999) *The dynamics of electronic communities.* Unpublished PhD dissertation, Graduate School of Industrial Administration, Carnegie Mellon University.

Butler, B. S. (2001). Membership size, communication activity and sustainability: A resource-based model of online social structures. *Information Systems Research, 12*(4), 346-362.

Callon, M. (1986). Some elements of a sociology of translation: Domestication of the scallops and the fishermen of St. Brieuc Bay. In J. Law (Ed.), *Power, action and belief* (pp. 196-233). London: Routledge & Kegan Paul.

Chae, B., Koch, H., Paradice, D., & Huy, V. (2005). Exploring knowledge management using network theories: Questions, paradoxes and prospects. *Journal of Computer Information Systems 45*(4), 62-74.

Cheuk, B. W. (2006). Using social networking analysis to facilitate knowledge sharing in the British Council. *International Journal of Knowledge Management, 2*(4), 67-76.

Cohen, D. (2006). What's your return on knowledge? *Harvard Business Review, 84*(12), 28-28.

Constant, D., Keisler, S., & Sproull, L. (1994). What's mine is ours, or is it? A study of attitudes about information sharing. *Information Systems Research, 5*(4), 400-421.

Cross, R., Laseter, T., Parker, A., & Velasquez, G. (2006). Using social network analysis to improve communities of practice. *California Management Review, 49*(1), 32-60.

Daconta, M., Orbst, L., & Smith, K. (2003). *The semantic web.* Indianapolis: Wiley Publishing.

Damodaran, L., & Olphert, W. (2000). Barriers and facilitators to the use of knowledge management systems. *Behavior and Information Technology, 19*(6), 405-413.

Davenport, T. H., De Long, D. W., & Beers, M. C. (1997). *Building successful knowledge management projects.* Center for Business Innovation Working Paper, Ernst and Young.

Davenport T. H., De Long, D. W., & Beers, M. C. (1998). Successful knowledge management projects. *MIT Sloan Management Review, 39*(2), 43-57.

Davenport, T. H., & Prusak, L. (1997). *Working knowledge: How organizations manage what they know.* Cambridge, MA: Harvard Business School Press.

Davis, F. D. (1989). Perceived usefulness, perceived ease of use, and user acceptance of information technology. *MIS Quarterly, 13*(3), 319-341.

Donath, J. S. (1999). Identity and deception in the virtual community. In M. A. S. a. P. Kollock (Ed.), *Communities in cyberspace* (pp. 29-59).. London, Routledge.

Douglas, K. M., & McGarty, C. (2001). Identifiability and self-presentation: Computer-mediated communication and intergroup interaction. *British Journal of Social Psychology, 40*, 399-416.

Dretske, F. (1991). *Explaining behavior: Reasons in a world of causes.* Cambridge, MA: MIT Press.

Epple, D. & Argote, L. (1996). An empirical investigation of the microstructure of knowledge acquisition and transfer through learning by doing. *Operations Research, 44*(1), 77-86.

Faraj, S., & Wasko, M. M. (Forthcoming). The web of knowledge: An investigation of knowledge exchange in networks of practice. AMR.

Garton, L., Haythornthwaite, C., & Wellman, B. (1997). Studying online social networks. *Journal of Computer-Mediated Communication, 3*(1), 75-105.

Geroimenko, V. & Chen, C. (2003). *Visualizing the semantic web.* London: Springer.

Goel, L. & Mousavidin, E. (2007). vCRM: Virtual customer relationship management. forthcoming in DATABASE Special Issue on Virtual Worlds, November 2007.

Goodhue, D. L. & Thompson, R. L. (1995). Task-technology fit and individual performance. *MIS Quarterly, 19*(2), 213-236.

Gordon, R. & Grant, D. (2005). Knowledge management or management of knowledge? Why people interested in knowledge management need to consider foucault and the construct of power. *Journal of Critical Postmodern Organization Science, 3*(2), 27-38.

Granovetter, M. (1973). The strength of weak ties. *American Journal of Sociology, 78*, 1360-1380.

Grant, R. M. (1996). Toward a knowledge-based theory of the firm. *Strategic Management Journal 17(Winter Special Issue)*, 109-122.

Habermas, J. (1984). *The theory of communicative action.* Boston: Beacon Press.

Hammer, M., Leonard, D., & Davenport, T. H. (2004). Why don't we know more about knowledge? *MIT Sloan Management Review, 45*(4), 14-18.

Hansen, M. T. (1999). The search-transfer problem: The role of weak ties in sharing knowledge across organizational subunits. *ASQ, 44*, 82-111.

Hardwig, J. (1991). The role of trust in knowledge. *The Journal of Philosophy, 88*(12), 693-708.

Hart, D., & Warne, L. (2006). Comparing cultural and political perspectives of data, information, and knowledge sharing in organisations. *International Journal of Knowledge Management, 2*(2), 1-15.

Hill, W., Stead, L., Rosenstein, M., & Furnas, G. (1995). Recommending and evaluating choices in a virtual community of use. *SIGCHI Conference on Human factors in Computing systems,* Denver, Colorado.

Hippel, E. V. (1994). Sticky information and the locus of problem solving: Implications for innovation. *Management Science, 40*(4), 429-440.

Huber, G. (2001). Transfer of knowledge in knowledge management systems: unexplored issues and suggested studies. *European Journal of Information Systems (EJIS), 10*, 72-79.

Husted, K., & Michailova, S. (2002). Diagnosing and fighting knowledge-sharing hostility. *Organizational Dyanmics, 31*(1), 60-73.

Inkpen, A. C. (2005). *Learning through alliances: General motors and NUMMI. California Management Review, 47(4), 114-136.*

Jarvenpaa, S. L., & Staples, D. S. (2000). The Use of Collaborative Electronic Media for Information Sharing: An Exploratory Study of Determinants. Journal of Strategic Information Systems 9(2/3): 129-154.

Jennex, M.E. (2005a). What is knowledge management? *International Journal of Knowledge Management, 1*(4), i-iv.

Jennex, M. & Olfman, L. (2000). Development recommendations for knowledge management/organizational memory systems. In *Proceedings of the Information Systems Development Conference.*

Jennex, M., & Olfman, L. (2004). Assessing Knowledge Management success/Effectiveness Models. *Proceedings of the 37th Hawaii International Conference on System Sciences.*

Jennex, M., &Olfman, L. (2005b). Assessing knowledge management success. *International Journal of Knowledge Management, 1*(2), 33-49.

Jennex, M.E., & Olfman, L. (2006). A model of knowledge management success. *International Journal of Knowledge Management, 2*(3), 51-68.

Jennex, M., Smolnik, S. & Croasdell, D. (2007). Knowledge management success. *International Journal of Knowledge Management, 3*(2), i-vi.

Jones, Q. (1997). Virtual-communities, virtual settlements and cyber archeology: A theoretical outline. *Journal of Computer Mediated Communication, 3*(3).

Jones, Q., & Rafaeli, S. (2000). Time to split, virtually: 'Discourse architecture' and 'community building' create vibrant virtual publics. *Electronic Markets, 10*(4), 214-223.

Jones, Q., Ravid, G., & Rafaeli, S. (2004). Information overload and the message dynamics of online interaction spaces: A theoretical model and empirical exploration. *Information Systems Research, 15*(2), 194-210.

Kankanhalli, A., Tan, B. C. Y., & Kwok-Kei, W. (2005). Contributing knowledge to electronic knowledge repositories: An empirical investigation. *MIS Quarterly, 29*(1), 113-143.

King, W. R. (2006). The critical role of information processing in creating an effective knowledge organization. *Journal of Database Management, 17*(1), 1-15.

Koeglreiter, G., Smith, R., & Torlina, L. (2006). The role of informal groups in organisational knowledge work: Understanding an emerging community of practice. *International Journal of Knowledge Management, 2*(1), 6-23.

Kohlhase, M., & Anghelache, R. (2004). Towards collaborative content management and version control for structured mathematical knowledge. *In Proceedings Mathematical Knowledge Management: 2nd International Conference, MKM 2003*, Bertinoro, Italy,.

Lapre, M. A., & Van Wassenhove, L. N. (2003). Managing learning curves in factories by creating and transferring knowledge. *California Management Review, 46*(1), 53-71.

Lave, J., & Wenger, E. (1991). *Situated learning. Legitimate peripheral participation.* Cambridge: Cambridge University Press.

Leimeister, J. M., Ebner, W., & Krcmar, H. (2005). Design, implementation, and evaluation of trust-supporting components in virtual communities for patients. *Journal of Management Information Systems, 21*(4), 101-135.

Licklider, J., & Taylor, R. (1968). The computer as a communication device. *Sci. Tech.*

Lippman, S. A., & Rumelt, R. P. (1982). Uncertain imitability: An analysis of interfirm differences in efficiency under competition. *Bell Journal of Economics, 13*, 418-438.

Malhotra, A., Gosain, S., & Hars, A. (1997). Evolution of a virtual community: Understanding design issues through a longitudinal study. *International Conference on Information Systems (ICIS), AIS.*

Markus, L. M. (1987). Towards a critical mass theory of interactive media: Universal access, interdependence and diffusion. *Comm. Res., 14*, 491-511.

Markus, L. M. (2001). Towards a theory of knowledge reuse: Types of knowledge reuse situations and factors in reuse success. *Journal of Management Information Systems, 18*(1), 57-94.

Markus, L. M., Majchrzak, A., & Gasser, L. (2002). A design theory for systems that support emergent knowledge processes. *MIS Quarterly, 26*(3), 179-212.

McDermott, R. (1999a). How to get the most out of human networks: Nurturing three-dimensional communities of practice. *Knowledge Management Review, 2*(5), 26-29.

McDermott, R. (1999b). Why information inspired but cannot deliver knowledge management. *California Management Review, 41*(4), 103-117.

Nidumolu, S. R., Subramani, M., & Aldrich, A. (2001). Situated learning and the situated knowledge web: Exploring the ground beneath knowledge management. *Journal of Management Information Systems (JMIS), 18*(1), 115-150.

Nonaka, I. (1994). A dynamic theory of organizational knowledge creation. *Organization Science, 5*(1), 14-37.

Orlikowski, W. J. (2002). Knowing in practice: Enacting a collective capability in distributed organizing. *Organization Science, 13*(3), 249-273.

Orr, J. E. (1989). Sharing knowledge, celebrating identity: War stories and community memory among service technicians. In D.S. Middleton, & D. Edwards (Eds.), *Collective remembering: memory in society.* Newbury Park, CA: Sage Publications.

Pan, S. L., & Leidner, D. E. (2003). Bridging communities of practice with information technology in the pursuit of global knowledge sharing. *Journal of Strategic Information Systems, 12*, 71-88.

Polanyi, M. (1958). *Personal knowledge, towards a post-critical philosophy.* Chicago, IL: University of Chicago Press.

Porra, J., & Goel, L. (2006, November 18-21). Importance of Power in the Implementation Process of a Successful KMS: A Case Study. *In 37th Annual Meeting of the Decision Sciences Institute,* San Antonio, TX..

Porra, J., & Parks, M.S. (2006). Sustaining virtual communities: Suggestions from the colonial model. *Information Systems and e-Business Management, 4*(4), 309-341.

Postmes, T., Spears, R., & Lea, M. (2000). The formation of group norms in computer-mediated communication. *Human Communication Research, 26*(3), 341-371.

Prandelli, E., Verona, G. & Raccagni, D. (2006). Diffusion of web-based product innovation. *California Management Review, 48*(4), 109-135.

Preece, J., Nonnecke, B., & Andrews, D. (2003). The top five reasons for lurking: improving community experiences for everyone. *Computers in Human Behavior* In Press.

Prusak, L. (2001). Where did knowledge management come from? *IBM Systems Journal, 40*(4), 1002-1007.

Rogers, E. M., & Agarwala-Rogers, R. (1975). Organizational communication. G. L. Hanneman, & W. J. McEwen, (Eds.), Communication behaviour (pp. 218–236). Reading, MA: Addision Wesley.

Ryle, G. (1949/1984). T*he concept of mind.* Chicago, IL: University of Chicago Press.

Sherif, K., & Xing, B. (2006). Adaptive processes for knowledge creation in complex systems: the case of a global IT consulting firm, *Information and Management, 43*(4), 530 - 540

Silva, L., Mousavidin, E., & Goel, L. (2006). Weblogging: Implementing Communities of Practice. *In Social Inclusion: Societal and Organizational Implications for Information Systems: IFIP TC8 WG 8.2,* Limirick, Ireland.

Schultze, U., & Leidner, D. (2002). Studying knowledge management in information systems research: Discourses and theoretical assumptions. *MISQ, 26*(3), 213-242.

Schultze, U., & Stabell, C. (2004). Knowing what you don't know? Discourses and contradictions in knowledge management research. *Journal of Management Studies, 41*(4), 549–573.

Shin, M. (2004). A framework for evaluating economics of knowledge management systems. *Information & Management, 42*, 179-196.

Stein, E. W (2006). A qualitative study of the characteristics of a community of practice for knowledge management and its success factors *International Journal of Knowledge Management, 1*(4), 1-24

Tajfel, H., & Turner, J. C. (1986). The *social* identity theory of intergroup behavior. In S.Worchel & W. G.Austin (Eds.), *Psychology of intergroup relations* (pp. 7–24). Chicago: Nelson-Hall.

Usoro, A., & Kuofie, M. H. S (2006). Conceptualisation of cultural dimensions as a major influence on knowledge sharing. *International Journal of Knowledge Management, 2*(2), 16-25.

Wasko, M. M., &Faraj, S. (2000). 'It is what one does:' Why people participate and help others in electronic communities of practice. *JSIS, 9*(2/3), 155-173.

Wasko, M. M., & Faraj, S. (2005). Why should I share? Examining knowledge contribution in networks of practice. *MIS Quarterly, 29*(1), 35-57.

Wasko, M. M., Faraj, S., & Teigland, R. (2004). Collective action and knowledge contribution in electronic networks of practice. *JAIS, 5*(11-12), 493-513.

Wellman, B. (1996). For a Social Network Analysis of Computer Networks: A Sociological Perspective on Collaborative Work and Virtual Community. *SIGCPR/SIGMIS*, Denver, Colorado.

Wellman, B., & Gulia, M. (1997). *Net surfers don't ride alone: Virtual communities as communities. Communities and cyberspace.* New York: Routledge.

Wellman, B., Salaff, J., Dimitrova, D. Garton, L, Gulia, M., & Haythornthwaite, C. (1996). Computer networks as social networks: Collaborative work, telework, and virtual community. *Annual Review of Sociology, 22*, 213-238.

Wenger, E. (1998). *Communities of practice: Learning, meaning, and identity.* Cambridge: Cambridge University Press.

Yue Wah, C., Menkhoff, T., Loh, B., & Evers, H. D. (2007). Social capital and knowledge sharing in knowledge-based organizations: An empirical study. *International Journal of Knowledge Management,* 3(1), 29-38.

ENDNOTES

1. as opposed to theoretical knowledge
2. We adopt a broad definition of expertise. New hires can have tacit knowledge about certain technologies that more senior employees do not.
3. http://www.findarticles.com/p/articles/mi_m0NEW/is_2001_June_5/ai_75318288
4. California-based joint venture of GM and Toyota.
5. Signal is considered as relevant discussion.
6. In organizations, KMS typically consist of communities formed around functional areas or projects. For example, an engineering firm's KMS might have communities for piping, electrical engineering, structural and architectural design, process control, procurement, and for each client account.
7. Inquiry Learning Forum (ILF) is a "Web-based professional development system designed to support a community of practice (CoP) of in-service and preservice mathematics and science teachers who are creating, reflecting upon, sharing, and improving inquiry-based pedagogical practices" (Barab et al. 2003, p. 237).
8. An obligatory passage point would require employees use the system to access explicit work-related information. Using the system for explicit knowledge would make employees aware of the system and encourage them to refer to the KMS for tacit knowledge.

This work was previously published in International Journal of Knowledge Management, Vol. 4, Issue 3, edited by M. Jennex, pp. 82-100, copyright 2008 by IGI Publishing (an imprint of IGI Global).

Chapter 16
An Agent System to Manage Knowledge in CoPs

Juan Pablo Soto
University of Castilla - La Mancha, Spain

Aurora Vizcaíno
University of Castilla - La Mancha, Spain

Javier Portillo-Rodríguez
University of Castilla - La Mancha, Spain

Mario Piattini
University of Castilla - La Mancha, Spain

ABSTRACT

This paper proposes a multi-agent architecture and a trust model with which to foster the reuse of information in organizations which use knowledge bases or knowledge management systems. The architecture and the model have been designed with the goal of giving support to communities of practices which are a means of sharing knowledge. However, members of these communities are currently often geographically distributed, and less trust therefore exists among members than in traditional co-localized communities of practice. This situation has led us to propose our trust model, which can be used to calculate what piece of knowledge is more trustworthy. The architecture's artificial agents will use this model to recommend the most appropriate knowledge to the community's members.

INTRODUCTION

The need to support knowledge processes in organizations has always existed. However, its importance has definitely increased in the last few years. Recently, the concept of knowledge management suggests a paradox since compared with traditional production factors knowledge is so complex, scattered and hidden that it is rather complicated to manage it.

On the other hand, traditional Knowledge Management Systems (KMS) have received certain criticism as they are often implanted in companies overloading employees with extra work; for instance, employees have to introduce information into the KMS and worry about updating this information. As a result of this, these systems are sometimes not greatly used by the employees since the knowledge that these systems have is often not valuable or on other occasions the knowledge sources do not provide the confidence necessary for employees to reuse the information. Reusing information and not reinventing the wheel are frequently heard arguments. For this purpose, companies create both social and technical networks in order to stimulate knowledge exchange. An essential ingredient of knowledge sharing information in organizations is that of "community of practice", by which we mean groups of people with a common interest where each member contributes knowledge about a common domain (Wenger, 1998). The ability of a community of practice to create a friendly environment for individuals with similar interests and problems in which they can discuss a common subject matter encourages the transfer and creation of new knowledge. Many companies report that such communities help reduce problems caused by lack of communication, and save time by "working smarter" (Wenger et al, 2002). In addition, communities of practice provide their members with the confidence to share information with each other. Moreover, individuals are frequently more likely to use knowledge built by their community team members than that created by members outside their group (Desouza et al, 2006). For these reasons, we consider the modelling of communities of practice into KMS as an adequate method by which to provide these systems with a certain degree of control to measure the confidence and quality of information provided by each member of the community.

In order to carry this out, we have designed a multi-agent architecture in which agents try to emulate human behaviour in communities of practice with the goal of fostering the use and exchange of information where intelligent agents suggest "trustworthy knowledge" to the employees and foster the knowledge flow between them.

The remainder of this work is organized as follows. The next section focuses on community of practice then in section 3 two important concepts related to our work are described: agents and trust. In Section 4 the trust model is presented. Later in section 5 the multi-agent architecture proposed to manage trustworthy KMS is described. In Section 6 a prototype developed to evaluate our architecture is explained in order to illustrate how it could be used. Section 7 describes a preliminary experiment carry out to test this prototype. Section 8 outlined related work and finally, conclusions are presented in Section 9.

COMMUNITIES OF PRACTICE

Intellectual capital and knowledge management are currently growing since knowledge is a critical factor for an organization's competitive advantage (Kautz, 2004). This growth determines organizations' performance by studying how well they manage their most critical knowledge. However, to manage this critical knowledge it has to be known what knowledge is, and although there is no consensus about a knowledge concept (Kakabadse, et al, 2001), there are several definitions of knowledge as in (Ackoff, 1989) and (Davenport et al, 1998). In our case, knowledge is going to be understood as in (Ackoff, 1989), that is, as an appropriate collection of information, such that its intent is to be useful. In order to manage knowledge an important instrument are communities (Gebert et al., 2004; Malhotra, 2000). A community can be defined as a group of socially interacting persons who are mutually tied to one another and regularly meet at a common place (Hillery, 1955). The development of Internet and groupware technologies led to a new kind of community "virtual communities" where members can or not meet one another face to face and they may exchange words and ideas through the mediation of computers networks (Geib et al., 2004).

This type of communities can be divided regarding their objectives and scope into socially-oriented, commercially-oriented and professionally-oriented. We focus our research on the last one which consists of company employees who communicate and share information to support their professional tasks. An special case of professionally-oriented communities are the "Communities of Practice" (CoPs) defined by Wenger et al. (2002) as groups of people who share a concern, a set of problems, or a passion about a topic, and who deepen their knowledge and expertise in this area by interacting on an ongoing basis.

Regarding a knowledge point of view CoPs share values, beliefs, languages, and ways of doing things many companies report that CoPs help reduce problems due to lack of communication, and save time by "working smarter" (Wenger, 2002). Millen et al. (2002) discuss the costs and benefits of CoPs in a study of seven large, geographically dispersed organizations. The study indicates benefits on individual, community and organizational level, like increased access to experts and information resources, increased idea generation and better problem solving, to indications of more successfully executed projects and product innovations. Moreover, individuals are frequently more likely to use knowledge built by their community team members than that created by members outside their group (Desouza et al, 2006), that is, they are more likely to share knowledge with people they trust. However, since in current CoPs people are usually geographically dispersed they do not have a face to face communication and this situation could be a problem since the level of trust between members can decrease and in consequence there could be a lower level of sharing knowledge.

On the other hand, even though CoPs are a focus of knowledge sharing hardly ever there is any quality control of the knowledge generated in the community. Our proposal is to use agent's technology to foster knowledge exchange at communities of practice and to evaluate the suitability of knowledge shared.

AGENTS AND TRUST

Because of the importance of knowledge management, tools to support some of the tasks related to knowledge management have been developed. Different techniques are used to implement these tools. One of them, which is providing to be quite useful, is that of intelligent agents (van-Elst et al, 2003). Software agent technology can monitor and coordinate events, meetings and disseminate information (Balasubramanian et al, 2001). Furthermore, agents are proactive; this means they act automatically when it is necessary. The autonomous behavior of the agents is critical to the goal of this research since agents help to reduce the amount of work that employees have to perform, for instance searching information in a knowledge base. On the other hand one of the main advantages of the agent paradigm is that it constitutes a natural metaphor for systems with purposeful interacting agents, and this abstraction is close to the human way of thinking about their own activities (Wooldridge & Ciancarini, 2001). This foundation has led to an increasing interest in social aspects such as motivation, leadership, culture or trust (Fuentes et al, 2004). Our research is related to this last concept of "trust" since artificial agents can be made more robust, resilient and effective by providing them with trust reasoning capabilities.

For agents to function effectively in a community, they must ensure that their interactions with the other agents are trustworthy. For this reason it is important that each agent is able to identify trustworthy partners with which they should interact and untrustworthy correspondents with which they should avoid interaction. The stability of a community depends on the right balance of trust and distrust.

In literature we found several trust and reputation mechanisms that have been proposed to be used in different domains such as e-commerce (Zacharia et al, 1999), peer-to-peer computing (Wang & Vassileva, 2003), recommender systems (Schafer et al, 1999), etc. In next section we describe the trust model that we propose to be used in our multi-agent architecture.

TRUST MODEL

One of our aims is to provide a trust model based on real world social properties of trust in Communities of Practice (CoPs). An interesting fact is that members of a community are frequently more likely to use knowledge built by their community team members than those created by members outside their group (Desouza et al, 2006). This factor occurs because people trust more in the information offered by a member of their community than in that supplied by a person who does not belong to that community. Of course, the fact of belonging to the same community of practice already implies that these people have similar interests and perhaps the same level of knowledge about a topic. Consequently, the level of trust within a community is often higher than that which exists outside the community. As a result of this, as is claimed in (Desouza et al, 2006), knowledge reuse tends to be restricted within groups. Therefore, people, in real life in general and in companies in particular, prefer to exchange knowledge with "trustworthy people" by which we mean people they trust. For these reasons we consider the implementation of a mechanism in charge of measuring and controlling the confidence level in a community in which

the members share information to be of great importance.

Most previous trust models calculate trust by using the users' previous experience with other users but when there is no previous experience, for instance, when a new user arrives to a community, these models cannot calculate a reliable trust value. We propose calculating trust by using four factors that can be stressed depending on the circumstances. These factors are:

- *Position*: employees often consider information that comes from a boss as being more reliable than that which comes from another employee in the same (or a lower) position as him/her (Wasserman & Glaskiewics, 1994). However, this is not a universal truth and depends on the situation. For instance in a collaborative learning setting collaboration is more likely to occur between people of a similar status than between a boss and his/her employee or between a teacher and pupils (Dillenbourg, 1999). In an enterprise this position can be established in different ways by, for instance, using an organizational diagram or classifying the employees according to the knowledge that a person has, as can be seen in Allen's proposal in (Allen, 1984), which distinguishes between:
  - Technological gatekeepers, defined as those actors who have a high level of knowledge interconnectedness with other local firms and also with extra-community sources of knowledge. These basically act by channeling new knowledge into the community and diffusing it locally.
  - External stars, which are highly interconnected with external sources of knowledge but have hardly any interaction with other local firms.

Such different positions inevitably influence the way in which knowledge is acquired, diffused and eventually transformed within the local area. Because of this, as will later be explained, this factor will be calculated in our research by taking into account a weight that can strengthen this factor to a greater or to a lesser degree.

- *Expertise*: This term can be briefly defined as the skill or knowledge that a person who knows a great deal about a specific thing has. This is an important factor since people often trust experts more than novice employees. In addition, "individual" level knowledge is embedded in the skills and competencies of the researchers, experts, and professionals working in the organization (Nonaka & Takeuchi, 1995). The level of expertise that a person has in a company or in a CoP could be calculated from his/her CV or by considering the amount of time that a person has been working on a topic. This is data that most companies are presumed to have.

- *Previous experience*: This is a critical factor in rating a trust value since, as was mentioned in the definitions of trust and reputation, previous experience is the key value through which to obtain a precise trust value. However, when previous experience is scarce or it does not exist humans use other factors to decide whether or not to trust in a person or a knowledge source. One of these factors is intuition.

- *Intuition*: This is a subjective factor which, according to our study of the state of the art, has not been considered in previous trust models. However, this concept is very important because when people do not have any previous experience they often use their "intuition" to decide whether or not they are going to trust something. Other authors have called this issue "indirect reputation or prior-derived reputation" (Mui et al, 2002). In human societies, each of us probably has different prior beliefs about the trustworthiness of strangers we meet. Sexual or racial discrimination might be a consequence of

such prior belief (Mui et al, 2002). We have tried to model intuition according to the similarity between personal profiles: the greater the similarity between one person and another, the greater the level of trust in this person as a result of intuition.

By taking all these factors into account, we have defined our own model with which to rate trust in CoPs, and this is summarized in Figure 1.

The main goal of this model is to rate the level of confidence in an information source or in a provider of knowledge in a CoP.

As the model will be used in virtual communities where people are usually distributed in different locations we have implemented a multi-agent architecture in which each software agent acts on behalf of a person and each agent uses this trust model to analyze which person or piece of knowledge is more trustworthy.

As the number of interactions that an agent will have with other agents in the community will be low in comparison with other scenarios such as auctions we cannot use trust models which need a lot of interactions to obtain a reliable trust value; it is more important to obtain a reliable initial trust value and it is for this reason that we use position, expertise and intuition.

Figure 1. Trust Model

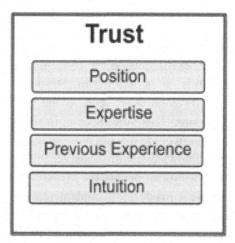

As observed in Figure 1, we use four factors to obtain a trust value, but how do we use these factors? We have classified these four factors into two groups: objective factors (position and expertise) and subjective factors (intuition and previous experience). The former are given by the company or community and the latter depend on the agent itself and the agent's experience in time. There are four different ways of using these factors, which depend upon the agent's situation (see Figure 2).

- If the agent has no previous experience, for instance because it is a new user in the community, then the agent will use its intuition and the position and expertise of other agents to discover which other agents it can trust.

- When the agent has previous experience obtained through interactions with other agents but this previous experience is low (low number of interactions), the agent calculates the trust value by considering the intuition value and the previous experience value. For instance, if an agent A has a high experience value for agent B because it interacted with B successfully several times but agent A has a low intuition value for agent B (profiles are not very similar), then agent A reduces the value obtained through experience. In this case the agent does not use position and expertise factors (objec-

tive factors) because the agent has its own experience and this experience is adjusted with its intuition which is subjective and more personalized.

- When the agent has enough previous experience to consider that the trust value obtained is reliable, then the agent only considers this value.

MULTI-AGENT ARCHITECTURE

In order to give support to CoPs, we have designed a multi-agent architecture that uses the trust model explained in previous section with the goal of recommending trustworthy knowledge in CoPs and therefore fostering the reuse of information generated in these communities. Therefore, we can say that the goals of this architecture are:

- Assists members in identifying trustworthy entities.
- Gives artificial agents the ability to reason about the trustworthiness of other agents or about a knowledge source.
- Encourages knowledge exchange between the community members.
- Provides the confidence necessary to foster the usage of information and knowledge of the community.

Taking these facts into account, we propose a multi-agent architecture which is composed of two levels (see Figure 3): a reactive level and a Deliberative-Social level. The reactive level is considered by other authors as a typical level that a multi-agent system must have (Ushida et al, 1998)(Ushida, 1998). A deliberative level is often also considered as a typical level but a social level is not frequently considered in an explicit way, despite the fact that these systems (multi-agent systems) are composed of several individuals, interactions between them and plans constructed by them. The social level is only

Figure 2. Using the trust model

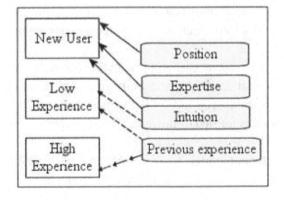

Figure 3. General architecture

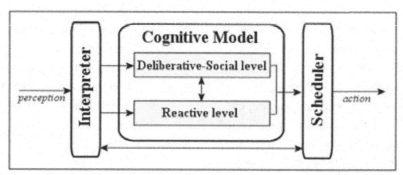

considered in those systems that try to simulate social behaviour or those that represent a more generic architecture which has been prepared to represent this or other behaviour. Since we wish to emulate human feelings such as trust, reputation and even intuition we have added a social part that considers the social aspects of a community which takes into account the opinions and behaviour of each of the members of that community. Other previous works have also added a social level. For instance, in (Imbert & de Antonio, 2005) (Imbert, 2005) the authors emulate human emotions such as fear, thirst or bravery but they use an architecture which is made up of three levels: reactive, deliberative and social. In our case the deliberative and the social level are not separate levels because we realised that plans created in the deliberative part involve social interactions so we considered that in our case it would be more efficient to define a level composed of two parts (Deliberative-Social level) instead of considering two separated levels.

- **Reactive level:** This is the agent's capacity to perceive changes in its environment and to respond to these changes at the precise moment at which they happen. It is in this level when an agent will execute the request of another agent without any type of reasoning.
- **Deliberative-Social level:** The agent has a type of behaviour which is orientated towards objectives, that is, it takes the initia-

tive in order to plan its performance with the purpose of attaining its goals. In this level the agent would use the information that it receives from the environment, and from its beliefs and intuitions, to decide which is the best plan of action to follow in order to fulfil its objectives. In this level we have individual goals which refer to the deliberative part and social goals or cooperative goals which refer to the social part.

Two further important components of our architecture are the *Interpreter* and the *Scheduler*. The former is used to perceive the changes that take place and to decide which level must take the initiative depending on the event that the agent perceives. The scheduler indicates how the actions should be scheduled and executed.

Each of the levels of our architecture is described in the following subsections.

Reactive Level

This level must respond at the precise moment at which an event has been perceived (see Figure 4).

For instance when an agent is consulted about its position within the organization or when a user wishes to send the system simple answers. This level is formed of the following modules:

Internal model: As an agent represents a person in a CoP this model stores the user's features,

Figure 4. Reactive level

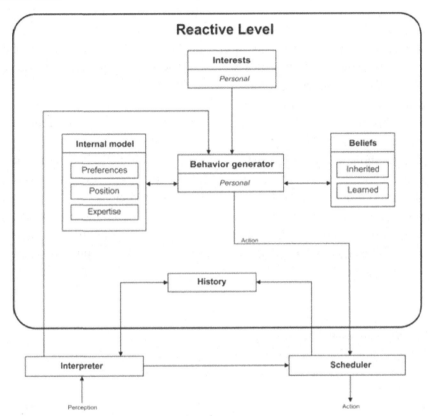

these features will be consulted by other agents in order to calculate trust values. Therefore, this module stores the following parts in the user profile:

- *Expertise*. This term has been explained in the Trust Model in section 4.
- *Preferences*. In this part we try to represent user preferences by using, for example, the Felder-Silverman test which tell us whether the agent is representing a visual user (one who prefers visual representations of presented information-pictures, diagrams, flow charts,…), a verbal user (who prefers written and spoken explanations) or another kind of user that the Felder-Silverman model supports (Felder & Silverman, 1988; Felder, 1996).
- *Position*. Explained in the Trust Model section.

Behaviour generator: This component is necessary for the development of this architecture since it has to select the agent's behaviour. This behaviour is defined on the basis of the agent's beliefs.

Interests: These are individual interests which represent the user's needs.

History: This component stores the interactions of the agents with the environment.

Beliefs: The beliefs module is composed of inherited beliefs and lessons learned from the agent itself. Inherited beliefs are the organization's beliefs that the agent receives. Examples of this might be an organizational diagram of the enterprise or the philosophy of the company or community. Lessons learned are the lessons that the agent obtains while it interacts with the environment. This interaction can be used to establish parameters in order to know what the agent can trust (agents or knowledge sources).

Deliberative-Social Level

In this level the agent's behaviour is based on goals, that is, the agent has several defined goals and it tries to achieve these goals by scheduling plans. Due to the fact that we are trying to represent human behaviour in CoPs, it is necessary to bear in mind that this human behaviour must benefit the whole community. Therefore, the agent has to deliberate about its individual goals but it must also act by taking community goals and the community's profit into account. That is why we have considered a social and a deliberative part. The former tries to achieve social goals (community goals) and the latter is more focused upon achieving individual goals.

In this level the agent obtains information about the environment and, by taking into account its interests and intuitions, it decides which plan is the best to achieve its goals (see Figure 5).

The components of the Deliberative-Social architecture are:

Interests: This component represents community interests. These interests are created when the community comes into being. There are some interests that all communities may share such as:
- Maintaining a constant collaboration of community members.
- Identifying and maintaining experts in the community

Figure 5. Deliberative-social level

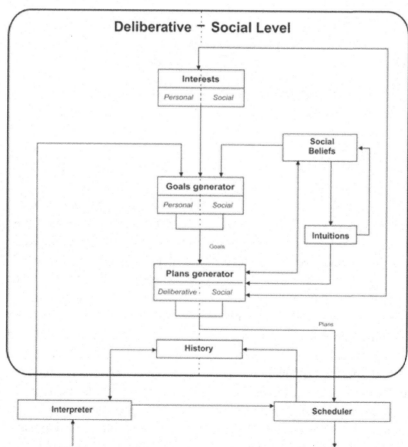

- Keeping community knowledge updated
- Maintaining a trustworthy environment in which community members share trustworthy knowledge.

There are also Personal Interests which influence the whole community such as sharing suitable knowledge.

Beliefs: This module represents a view that the agent has of the environment. In our case these beliefs are composed of the idea that the agent has of the communities and their members. For instance, in this module there is information about the community's topics, in which areas other members are working, etc.

Goals Generator: Depending on the state of the agent this module must decide what the most important goal to be achieved is.

Plans Generator: This module is in charge of evaluating how a goal can be attained and which plans are most convenient if this goal is to be achieved. We should recall that plans are a specification of the actions that an agent may carry out in order to attain its goals.

Intuitions: Intuitions are beliefs that have not been verified but which an agent thinks may be true. According to Mui et al. (2002)(Mui, 2002) intuition has not yet been modelled by agent systems. In this work we have tried to adapt this concept by comparing the agents' profiles (as we mentioned in Section 4) to obtain an initial value of intuition that can be used to form a belief about an agent when the intuition is proved be true. This is another important feature taken into account to calculate a trust value, since when an agent has little o null interaction with another; the agent will use this value to have a value of trust as it was previously explained.

History: This component stores the interactions of the agents with the environment.

In the following section, we will describe a prototype developed to validate our architecture.

PROTOTYPE

In order to test our architecture we have developed a prototype system into which people can introduce documents and where these documents can also be consulted by other people. The goal of this prototype is to allow software agents to help employees to discover the information that may be useful to them thus decreasing the overload of information that employees often have and strengthening the use of knowledge bases in enterprises. In addition, we try to avoid the situation of employees storing valueless information in the knowledge base.

One feature of this system is that when a person searches for knowledge in a community, and after having used the knowledge obtained, that person then has to evaluate the knowledge in order to indicate whether:

- The knowledge was useful.
- How it was related to the topic of the search (for instance a lot, not too much, not at all).

To design this prototype we have designed a *User Agent* and a *Manager Agent*. The former is used to represent each person that may consult or introduce knowledge in a knowledge base. Therefore, the *User Agent* can assume three types of behavior or roles similar to the tasks that a person may carry out in a knowledge base. The User Agent plays one role or another depending upon whether the person that it represents carries out one of the following actions:

- The person contributes new knowledge to the communities in which s/he is registered. In this case the User Agent plays the role of **Provider**.

- The person uses knowledge previously stored in the community. Then, the User Agent will be considered as a **Consumer**.
- The person helps other users to achieve their goals, for instance by giving an evaluation of certain knowledge. In this case the role is of a **Partner**. So, Figure 6 shows that in community 1 there are two User Agents playing the role of Partner, one User Agent playing the role of Consumer and another being a Provider.

The second type of agent within a community is called the *Manager Agent* (represented in black in Figure 6) which must manage and control its community.

The prototype provides the options of using community documents and when the documents are used, reputation values can be modified. An user can also propose new topics in the community, etc.

In order to make it easier to search for documents in a community, users can choose one topic from those which are available in the community and the user agent will try to find documents about this topic.

The general idea is to consider those documents which came from trustworthy knowledge sources according to the user's opinion or needs. In order to discover which knowledge sources are trustworthy the user agents will use the trust model. Depending on the context, this trust model can be used in different ways. We are going to consider how the trust model is applied in different situations. First, when agents have previous experience this means that user agents have previously interacted with a knowledge source and they have some feedback (trust values in our case) about it. The second scenario is a more complicated situation in which the agents have no previous experience and therefore do not have trust values for other user agents.

The way in which we apply these factors in the different contexts is as follows:

1. If the agent has no previous experience, for instance, because it is representing a new user in the community, and its user wants to search for documents relating to a topic T, the user agent follows these steps:
   1.1. The user agent makes a request to the other members of the community in order to discover which user agents

Figure 6. Communities of agents

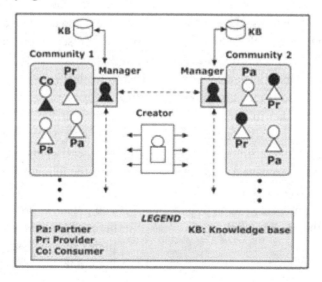

have documents about topic T.

1.2. The user agent stores the id (identification) in a list of those agents which have documents about T.

1.3. For each agent grouping in the list, the user agent calculates a trust value by using the position, expertise and intuition factors. For instance, the user agent might obtain a list with 10 agents that match the request and for each of these agents, the user agent will obtain information about their positions (to discover, for instance, if the agent represents a boss or a newcomer), their levels of expertise in the community area, in our case there are five possible levels (from novice to expert), and their intuition values in relation to the agent that has made the request (with five values from "totally different" to "totally equals"). In this case the intuition level is calculated by comparing user profiles, that is, if the user agent compares two profiles with very similar characteristics, this means that users, represented by user agents, work in the same area, have similar expertise level,..., etc and consequently the trust value will increase because the user agent "senses" that working with this user will be a successful interaction. So, the user agent's list might contain an agent that represents a newcomer user with a high level of expertise and with similar preferences, or a boss with different preferences and a medium level of expertise in the area concerned. Once the agent has obtained all these values, it calculates a general trust value per agent by combining the different factors, obtaining the lowest value when the agent, for instance, represents a rookie newcomer with a profile which is totally different

to that of the requester, and obtaining the highest value when the agent represents a boss with a high level of experience and who has a very similar profile to the agent which is making the request.

1.4. The user agent shows the results which are sorted by trust values, that is, the first documents on the list come from the most trustworthy knowledge sources (in this case the most trustworthy agent with the highest trust values). There are other possibilities, depending on user preferences. The user can choose to sort the list by using level of experience, position or level of intuition. At each request the user will receive a list and from each list the user will obtain information about each factor by the use of star icons and shield icons. For instance, as we can see in Figure 7, the results of the request (sorted by reputation) show a large amount of results, and the first one on the list has five stars in the reputation level and four shields in the position level.

2. If there is a small amount of previous experience and this previous experience is not sufficient for the agent to discover whether the other user agent is trustworthy or not then we combine previous experience with the other three factors. So in this context the user agent follows the following steps when looking for documents about a topic T:

2.1. The user agent makes a request to the members of the community in order to discover which user agents have documents about topic T.

2.2. For each agent (in the requested group) that our agent has previously interacted with, it uses the four factors (position, intuition, expertise and previous experience) to calculate a trust value by using (1).

Figure 7. Showing and sorting results

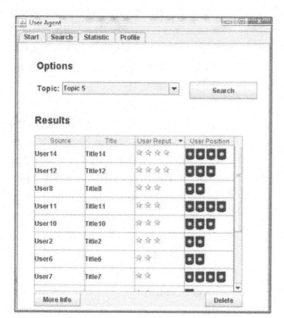

$$\mathbf{T}_{ij} = w_e * E_j + w_p * P_j + w_i * I_{ij} + (\sum_{j=1}^{n} QC_{ij})/n$$

(1)

where E_j is the value of expertise which is calculated according to the degree of experience that the person upon whose behalf the agent acts has in a domain. In this case the domain of the community which the agent wishes to join.

P_j is the value assigned to a person's position. This position is defined in the agent's internal model of the reactive architecture described in Section 4.1.

I_{ij} denotes the intuition value that agent i has in agent j which is calculated by comparing each user's profile.

In addition, previous experience should also be calculated. When an agent i consults information from another agent j, the agent i should evaluate how useful this information was. This value is called QC_{ij} (Quality of j's Contribu-

tion in the opinion of i). To attain the average value of an agent's contribution, we calculate the sum of all the values assigned to these contributions and we divide it between their total. In the expression n represents the total number of evaluated contributions. Finally, w_e, w_p and w_i are weights with which the trust value can be adjusted according to the degree of knowledge that one agent has about another.

2.3. For each agent in the group (the results group) that the agent has no previous experience it calculate a trust value as we mentioned in 1.3.

2.4. The user agent shows the results, which are sorted by trust or quality values as in the previous situation.

3. If the user agent has enough previous experience (this is considered when an agent has interacted many times with another. This number of interactions depends on a threshold that can be adjusted to each domain) then the user agent calculates the trust value by only using the previous experience factor. In this case we only consider this factor (experience) because this is the principal factor that humans usually consider when they have to trust somebody/something. That's why this concept is the base of all trust models described in literature as it will be explained in section 7. In this context the user agent follows the following steps when looking for documents about a topic T:

3.1. The user agent follows step 2.1

3.2. For each agent in the group (the results group) the user agent calculates a trust value by using the previous experience factor that is, by using (2) which is the last part of formula (1),

$$(\sum_{j=1}^{n} QC_{ij})/n$$

(2)

3.3. The user agent follows step 2.3.

3.4. The user agent shows the results which are sorted by trust or quality values.

These are three possible scenarios that illustrate how the trust model is used. When a person inserts a document in the community, s/he inserts the document and a quality value for that document. If another person uses that document, after using that document, the person who requested it must evaluate its quality. The User Agent compares the value given by the owner with the value given by the consumer to discover whether the two users have the same opinion about the document. If this is so then the previous experience value for the other user increases and if the opposite is true then the previous experience value is decreased. That is, if a user A thinks that a document D has a quality value of 8 and another user B, after using D, thinks that the document has a quality value of 2, the trust value that user B has for user A is decreased. This manner of rating trust helps to detect a problem which is increasing in companies or communities in which employees introduce not valuable information because they are rewarded if they contribute with knowledge in the community. Thus, if a person introduces documents that are not related to the community with the aim of obtaining rewards, the situation can be detected, because when the other person evaluate those documents or information, the rate of them will be low and the value of previous experience of this person became very low. Therefore, the community agent can detect that there is a "fraudulent" member in the community.

In a previous version of the prototype, when a person introduced a document in the system, s/he did not indicate the quality value of it. In this case the previous experience was calculated only in base to the rate that agent gave. We have introduced this change because we have a reference value for each document that can be used to compare quality values that different users have given to the same document and detect if there are "fraudulent members" and also can be used to sort documents when we have not enough information, at least we will have a quality value given by the person who introduced the document in the community.

The three situations must be applied to each user agent depending on the situation. If a user agent makes a request to search for documents it will receive answers from different user agents and, depending upon the situation between the requester and the other agents, the requester must apply one of the three situation steps and not only one situation for all the agents that have answered. This is shown in Figure 8 where agent *A* makes a request to search for documents about topic T and agents *X, Y, Z* answer because they have documents about T. In this case agent *A* applies situation 1 to agent *X* because agent *X* is not a known agent, and situation 3 to agents *Y* and *Z* because it has already interacted with both agents on previous occasions.

Figure 8. Mechanism through which to obtain trustworthy documents by using the model

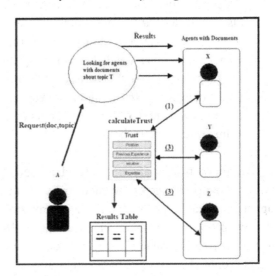

EVALUATION OF THE PROTOTYPE

Once the prototype has been finished we have evaluated it. To do this, different approaches can be followed, from a multi-agent point of view or from a social one. First of all we have focused on the former and we are testing the most suitable number of agents advisable for a community. Therefore, several simulations have been performed. As result of them we found that:

- The maximum number of agents supported by the Community Manager Agent when it receives User Agents' evaluations is approximately 800. When we tried to work with 1000 agents for instance, the messages were not managed conveniently. However, we could see that the Manager Agent could support a high number of petitions, at least, using simpler behavior.
- On the other hand, if we have around 10 User Agents launched, they need about 20 o more interactions to know all agents of the community. If a User Agent has between 10 and 20 interactions with other members it is likely that it interacts with 90% of members of its community, which means that the agent is going to know almost all the members of the community. Therefore, after several trials we detected that the most suitable number of agents for one community was around 10 agents and they needed a average of 20 interactions to know (to have a contact with) all the members of the community, which is quite convenient in order to obtain its own value of reputation about other agent.

All these results are being used to detect whether the exchange of messages between the agents is suitable, and to see if the information that we propose to be taken into account to obtain a trustworthy value of the reputation of each agent is enough, or if more parameters should be considered. Once this validation is finished we need to carry out further research to answer one important and tricky question, which is how the usage of this prototype affects the performance of a community.

RELATED WORK

This research can be compared with other proposals that use agents and trust in knowledge exchange. With regard to trust, in models such as eBay (1995)(ebay, 1995) and Amazon (1996) (Amazon, 1996), which were proposed to resolve specific situations in online commerce, the ratings are stored centrally and the reputation value is computed as the sum of those ratings over six months. Thus, reputation in these models is a single global value. However, these models are too simple (in terms of their trust values and the way in which they are aggregated) to be applied in open multi-agent systems. For instance, in (Zacharia et al, 1999)(Zacharia, 1999) the authors present the Sporas model, a reputation mechanism for loosely connected online communities where, among other features, new users start with a minimum reputation value, the reputation value of a user never falls below the reputation of a new user and users with very high reputation values experience much smaller rating changes after each update. The problem with this approach is that when somebody has a high reputation value it is difficult to change this reputation, or the system needs a high amount of interactions. A further approach of the Sporas authors is Histos which is a more personalized system than Sporas and is orientated towards highly connected online communities. In (Sabater & Sierra, 2002)(Sabater, 2002) the authors present another reputation model called REGRET in which the reputation values depend on time: the most recent rates are more important than previous rates. Carbó et al (2003) (Carbó, 2003) presents the AFRAS model, which is based on Sporas but uses fuzzy logic. The authors present a complex computing reputation mechanism which handles reputation as a fuzzy set while decision making is inspired in a cognitive human-like approach. In (Abdul-Rahman & Hailes, 2000)(Abdul-Rahman, 2000) the authors propose a model which allows agents to decide which agents' opinions they trust more and to propose a protocol based on recommendations. This model is based on a reputation or word-of-mouth mechanism. The main problem with this approach is that every agent must maintain rather complex data structures which represent a kind of global knowledge about the whole network.

Barber and Kim (2004) present a multi-agent belief revision algorithm based on belief networks (Barber, 2004). In their model the agent is able to evaluate incoming information, to generate a consistent knowledge base, and to avoid fraudulent information from unreliable or deceptive information sources or agents. This work has a similar goal to ours. However, the means of attaining it are different. In Barber and Kim's case they define reputation as a probability measure, since the information source is assigned a reputation

value of between 0 and 1. Moreover, every time a source sends knowledge, that source should indicate the certainty factor that the source has of that knowledge. In our case, the focus is very different since it is the receiver who evaluates the relevance of a piece of knowledge rather than the provider as in Barber and Kim's proposal. Some of these trust and reputation models are summarized in Table 1.

In (Huynh et al, 2004)(Huynh, 2004) the authors present a trust and reputation model which integrates a number of information sources in order to produce a comprehensive assessment of an agent's likely performance. In this case the model uses four parameters to calculate trust values: interaction trust, role-based trust, witness reputation and certified reputation. We use certified reputation when an agent wishes to join a new community and uses a trust value obtained in other communities, but in our case this certified reputation is made up of the four previously explained factors and is not only a single factor.

Also, works such as (Guizzardi et al, 2004) (Guizzardi, 2004) use the term 'Community' to

Table 1. Other trust and reputation models

Model	Authors	Reputation Management	Features
ebay	-	Global values	Simple values obtained through interactions
Sporas	Zacharia	Global values	Reduces changes when reputation is very high Most recent reputation values are the most important
Histos	Zacharia	Pair wise ratings in the system as a directed graph	Divides Reputation into three dimensions: Individual, Social and Ontological
Regret	Sabater and Sierra	Decentralized values	Most recent reputation values are the most important Presents a witness reputation component
Afras	Carbó and Molina	Decentralized values	Based on BDI agents Based on Sporas model but using fuzzy logic Compares and combines fuzzy sets
Fire	T. Dong Huynh and Nicholas R. Jennings	Decentralized values	Four main components: interaction trust, role-based trust, witness reputation, and certified reputation

support knowledge management but it is not used a specific trust model for communities.

The main differences between these reputation models (summarized in Table1) and our approach are that these models need an initial number of interactions to obtain a good reputation value and it is not possible to use them to discover whether or not a new user can be trusted. A further difference is that our approach is orientated towards collaboration between users in CoPs. Other approaches are more orientated towards competition, and most of them are tested in auctions.

CONCLUSION

Communities of practice have the potential to improve organizational performance and facilitate community work. Because of this we consider it important to model people's behavior within communities with the purpose of imitating the exchange of information that are produced in those communities. Therefore, we are attempting to encourage the sharing of information in organizations by using CoPs and knowledge bases. To do this we have designed a multi-agent three-layer architecture where the artificial agents use similar parameters to those of humans in order to evaluate knowledge and knowledge sources. These factors are: reputation, expertise, position, previous experience and even intuitions.

This approach implies several advantages for organizations as it permits them to identify the expertise of their employees and to measure the quality of their contributions. Therefore, it is expected a greater exchange and reuse of knowledge.

In addition, this work has illustrated how the architecture can be used to implement a prototype. The main functionalities of the prototype are:

- Controlling those employees who try to introduce valueless knowledge with the goal of obtaining some profit such as points,

incentives, rewards, etc.
- Providing the most suitable knowledge for the employee's queries according to the employee features and needs.
- Detecting the expertise of the employees within an organization.

All these advantages provide organizations with a better control of their knowledge repositories which will have more trustworthy knowledge and it is consequently expected that employees will feel more willing to use it.

ACKNOWLEDGMENT

This work is partially supported by the MELISA (PAC08-0142-3315) and MECENAS (PBI06-0024) project, Junta de Comunidades de Castilla-La Mancha, Consejería de Educación y Ciencia, both in Spain. It is also supported by the ESFINGE project (TIN2006-15175-C05-05) Ministerio de Educación y Ciencia (Dirección General de Investigación)/ Fondos Europeos de Desarrollo Regional (FEDER) in Spain and CONACYT (México) under Grant of the scholarship 206147 provided to the first author.

REFERENCES

Abdul-Rahman, A. and Hailes, S., (2000), "Supporting Trust in Virtual Communities". Proceedings of the 33rd Hawaii International Conference on Systems Sciences (HICSS'00), Vol. 6.

Ackoff, R., (1989), "From Data to Wisdom". Journal of Applies Systems Analysis. Vol. 16, pp. 3-9.

Allen, T., (1984), "Managing the Flow of Technology: Technology Transfer and the Dissemination of Technological Information within the R&D Organization", Cambridge, MA: MIT Press.

Amazon (1996). "URL: http://www.amazon.com".

Balasubramanian, S., Brennan, R., Norrie, D., (2001), "An Architecture for Metamorphic Control of Holonic Manufacturing Systems". Computers in Industry, Vol. 46(1), pp. 13-31.

Barber, K. and Kim, J., (2004), "Belief Revision Process Based on Trust: Simulation Experiments". 4th Workshop on Deception, Fraud and Trust in Agent Societies, Montreal Canada, pp. 1-12.

Carbó, J., Molina, M., Dávila, J., (2003), "Trust Management through Fuzzy Reputation". International Journal of Cooperative Information Systems. Vol. 12(1), pp. 135-155.

Davenport, P., (1998), "Working Knowledge: How Organizations Manage What They Know". Boston, MA, Project Management Institute, Harvard Business School Press.

Desouza, K., Awazu, Y., Baloh, P., (2006), "Managing Knowledge in Global Software Development Efforts: Issues and Practices". IEEE Software, pp. 30-37.

Dillenbourg, P., (1999), "Introduction: What Do You Mean By 'Collaborative Learning'?." Collaborative Learning Cognitive and Computational Approaches. Dillenbourg (Ed.). Elsevier Science.

eBay (1995). "URL: http://www.ebay.com".

Felder, R. and Silverman L, (1988), "Learning and Teaching Styles in Engineering Education". Engineering Education. Vol. 78(7), pp. 674-681.

Felder, R. M. (1996). "Matters of Style". ASEE Prism. Vol. 6(4), pp. 18-23.

Fuentes, R., Gómez-Sanz, J., Pavón, J. (2004). "A Social Framework for Multi-agent Systems Validation and Verification". Wang, S. et al Eds. ER Workshops, Springer Verlag, LNCS 3289, pp. 458-469.

Gebert, H., Geib, M., Kolbe, L., Brenner, W., (2003), "Knowledge-enabled Customer Relationship Management - Integrating Customer Relationship Management and Knowledge Management Concepts". Journal of Knowledge Management. Vol. 7(5), pp. 107-123.

Geib, M., Braun, C., Kolbe, L., Brenner, W., (2004). Measuring the Utilization of Collaboration Technology for Knowledge Development and Exchange in Virtual Communities. 37th Hawaii International Conference on System Sciences 2004 (HICSS-37), Big Island, Hawaii, IEEE Computer Society, Vol. 1, pp. 1-10.

Guizzardi, R., Perini, A., Dignum, V., (2004), «Providing Knowledge Management Support to Communities of Practice through Agent-Oriented Analysis». Proceedings of the 4th International Conference on Knowledge Management (I-KNOW), Granz, Austria.

Hillery, G., (1955), «Definitions of Community: Areas of Agreement», Rural Sociology, Vol. 20, pp. 118-125.

Huynh, T., Jennings, N., Shadbolt, N., (2004), «FIRE: An Integrated Trust and Reputation Model for Open Multi-agent Systems». Proceedings of the 16th European Conference on Artificial Intelligence (ECAI).

Imbert, R., and de Antonio, A., (2005), «When emotion does not mean loss of control». Lecture Notes in Computer Science, T. Panayiotopoulos, J. Gratch, R. Aylett, D. Ballin, P. Olivier, and T. Rist (Eds.), Springer-Verlag, London, pp.152-165.

Kakabadse, N., Kouzmin, A., Kakabadse, A., (2001), «From Tacit Knowledge to Knowledge Management: Leveraging Invisible Assets». Journal of Knowledge and Process Management, Vol. 8(3), pp. 137-154.

Kautz, H. (2004), «Knowledge Mapping: A Technique for Identifying Knowledge Flows in Software Organizations», EuroSPI, pp. 126-137.

Malhotra, Y. (2000), «Knowledge Management and Virtual Organizations», IDEA Group publishing, Hershey.

Millen, D., Fontaine, M., Muller, M., (2002), "Understanding the benefits and costs of communities of practice". Communications of the ACM., Vol. 45(4), pp. 69-73.

Mui, L., Halberstadt, A., Mohtashemi, M., (2002), "Notions of Reputation in Multi-Agents Systems: A Review". International Conference on Autonomous Agents and Multi-Agents Systems (AAMAS), pp. 280-287.

Nonaka, I. and Takeuchi, H., (1995), "The Knowledge Creation Company: How Japanese Companies Create the Dynamics of Innovation", Oxford University Press.

Sabater, J. and Sierra, C., (2002), "Social RE-GRET, a Reputation Model based on social relations", Proceedings of the Fifth International Conference on Autonomous Agents. Vol. 3(1), pp. 44-56.

Schafer, B. J., Konstan, A., J., Riedl, J. (1999). "Recommender Systems in E-Commerce", 1st ACM Conference on Electronic Conference (EC), pp. 158-166.

Ushida, H., Hirayama, Y., Nakajima, H., (1998), "Emotion Model for Life like Agent and its Evaluation". Proceedings of the Fifteenth National Conference on Artificial Intelligence and Tenth Innovative Applications of Artificial Intelligence Conference (AAAI/IAAI), Madison, Wisconsin, USA, pp. 8-37.

van-Elst, L., Dignum, V., Abecker, A., (2003), "Agent-Mediated Knowledge Management". International Simposium AMKM, Stanford, CA, USA, Springer, pp. 1-30.

Wang, Y., Vassileva, J., (2003), "Trust and Reputation Model in Peer-to-Peer Networks". Proceedings of the 3rd International Conference on Peer-to-Peer Computing.

Wasserman, S. and Glaskiewics, J., (1994), "Advances in Social Networks Analysis". Sage Publications.

Wenger, E., (1998), "Communities of Practice: Learning Meaning, and Identity". Cambridge U.K., Cambridge University Press.

Wenger, E., McDermott, R., Snyder, W., (2002), "Cultivating Communities of Practice", Harvard Business School Press.

Wooldridge, M., Ciancarini, P., (2001), Agent-Oriented Software Engineering: The State of the Art.

Zacharia, G., Moukas, A., Maes, P. (1999). "Collaborative Reputation Mechanisms in Electronic Marketplaces". In 32nd Annual Hawaii International Conference on System Science (HICSS-32).

This work was previously published in International Journal of Cognitive Informatics and Natural Intelligence, Vol. 3, Issue 1, edited by Y. Wang, pp. 75-94, copyright 2009 by IGI Publishing (an imprint of IGI Global).

Chapter 17
A Process–Oriented and Technology–Based Model of Virtual Communities of Practices:
Evidence from a Case Study in Higher Education

Giustina Secundo
University of Salento, Italy

Gianluca Elia
University of Salento, Italy

Cesare Taurino
University of Salento, Italy

ABSTRACT

This paper hypothesizes that Virtual Community of Practices (VCoPs) are valuable to Business Schools and Universities because they contribute to the emerging paradigms of just-in-time, action based and informal learning. It presents a real case study of a VCoPs called "Virtual eBMS", that was built by applying the participative observation (Yin, 1994). In particular, the paper provides a process-oriented model of the "Virtual eBMS", that is composed by four main elements: The People participating in the community, the Processes and the Purpose of the community in terms of value created for the Business School, and the Technology enabling the interactions between the community members. Indeed, from a technological point of view, the community is supported by an integrated Web Learning and Knowledge Management platform, described in terms of the main knowledge processes triggered and the correspondent technologies supporting the actions. Finally, the work presents some preliminary results and the value created through the use of the "Virtual eBMS".

INTRODUCTION

The rapid, discontinuous and non linear changes of today's economy, their qualitative and quantitative leaps (flux), the technological revolution, the collapse of time and space, and the increase of complexity are affecting not only the business environment, but also the education. If the new tasks is to educate students for highly dispersed, flexible, unstable organizations, with great emphasis on value reinventing processes, the educational community must increasingly address issues of identifying, understanding and articulating information, experience and knowledge (Baets & Van der Linden, 2003). New styles of learning approaches characterized by efficiency, just in time delivery, solution orientation, knowledge applications and anywhere access based on learning process internet based are arising (Maureer & Sapper, 2001).

The paradigms shifts in management educations require that students are not simply passive recipients of expertise but rather co-creators of their Just in Time and action learning. Learning is more characterised by interpretation, experimentation, problem solving than description and analysis. It's a journey through the world in which individuals live, and through networks of self-knowledge and self-development (Baets & Van der Linden, 2003). Hence the learning environment should be considered as a place where different stakeholders (program heads, faculty, executives, director, corporate action learning sponsors, advisory board) and students mutually engage in developing new understanding, approaches and unbounded sets of perspectives.

These conditions trigger a rethink of the traditional Business Schools and Universities models: new organizational forms based on Virtual Communities of Practices (VCoPs) are strongly recommended. There is no doubt that the concept of VCoPs is relevant in order to discuss learning approaches in Higher Education. Wenger's approach gives us the possibility to analyse learning

as a social practice that goes on at the micro-social level, largely through engagement in the tasks at hand (Lave & Wenger, 1991).

Starting from the above considerations, this work is aimed at:

- Defining an integrated VCoPs model supporting all the knowledge management cycle in a business school;
- Integrating Knowledge Management organizational and technological aspects in a VCoPs model for a Business School;
- Defining an integrated Web Learning and Knowledge Management (KM) system aimed at enhance learning opportunities both in daily researcher's practices and in student's learning experience.

In order to address these points, at first we reviewed the CoPs literature to demonstrate that VCoPs are relevant organizational model for emerging learning approach in business schools, then we propose an integrative model of VCoPs named *"Virtual eBMS"*, as a result of an empirical study of a higher education community, the e-Business Management Section (eBMS) of Scuola Superiore ISUFI – University of Salento (Italy). Finally some results will be presented in terms of value created by the "Virtual eBMS" Community for Higher Education.

VCOPS AS ORGANIZATIONAL MODEL SUPPORTING BUSINESS SCHOOLS

Existing Literature on VCoPs

For the purpose of our work the operational definition for Community of practices (CoPs) is *"Groups of individuals who participate in a collection of activities, share knowledge and expertise, and function as an interdependent network over an extended period of time with the shared goal of furthering their 'practice' or doing their work better."(Allen, Evans, & Ure, 2005).*

CoPs typically involved people who where located in the same vicinity; to overcome the typical problems of the dispersion it is necessary to take advantage of the Internet technologies. As a consequence, a new typology of communities emerges: the *Virtual Communities of Practices (VCoPs)*. A VCoPs can be seen as a *distributed community of practice*, which refers to a group of geographically distributed individuals who are informally bound together by shared expertise and shared interests or work. Such individuals depend on information and communication technologies to connect to each other (Daniel, Schwier, & Mc-Calla, 2003).

Moreover, when adding "virtuality" to the concept of CoPs we mean, following the Cohen and Prusak's definition (Cohen & Prusak, 2001), any work carried out over a distance of time and space, usually with the aid of electronic communication. Indeed, VCoPs are fostered by a blend of hardware and software that allow people to communicate easily, immediately, universally, and inexpensively. But, virtuality represents a great challenge for the knowledge creation processes, because technology can not completely substitute face-to-face interactions. In this sense virtual communities will supplement, not supplant, traditional communities. Another meaningful way to con

Before presenting the model of VCoPs that we propose in this work, we will discuss about some rising approaches in teaching and learning methodologies in Business Schools, by also providing a set of conditions which are common in the context of Business Schools and that we think they can be applied also in VCoPs.

Emerging Approaches in Learning Methodologies in Business Schools

Emerging trends in teaching and learning approach in Business Schools sustain that learning occurs in informal exchanges and is largely based on constructivism paradigms (Kowch & Schwier, 1997). Constructivism paradigm provides a new way of looking the learning process, because it asserts that learners construct knowledge as they interact with the world, strive to make sense of their experiences, and seek meaning. The *teacher's centered approach* is substituted by the *learner centered approach* in which individuals are engaged in developing knowledge and cognitive models through a process of co-participation with others members in a shared learning community acting on a geographically dispersed basis. Learners become builders of facts in constructing contents of knowledge, rather than passive recipients of knowledge from the instructor. Consequently, learners should be engaged in active, constructive, authentic and cooperative learning (Jonassen, Davidson, Collins, Campbell, & Hag, 1995).

Constructivists (Duffy & Jonassen, 1992, Barrows & Tamblyn, 1980) believe that the following four conditions must be met for learning to occur in Business Schools. We affirm that these conditions are met in VCoPs:

- *Learning must be embedded in complex, realistic, and relevant environments increasing the interaction among learners.* The National Research Council emphasizes the importance of community in learning environments and upholds that learning environments should be a combination of learner-centered, knowledge-centered, assessment-centered, and community-centered environments (Bransford, Brown, & Cocking, 1999). VCoPs provide opportunities for learners and researchers to interact with others, engaging learners in learning activities with peers. VCoPs members generate an increased information flow and new ideas through interaction. These methods include: asking and answering questions, chatting with experts, problem solving, resource and information sharing, connecting with other VCoPs, creating sub-communities around special interest topics, and sharing best practices. These increases in information and ideas are powerful tools that benefit VCoPs members and business schools.

- *Social negotiation must be provided for as an integral part of learning:* other research has also reinforced the idea that knowledge accrues through social interaction and cultural experience, and that learning and social negotiation are inseparable practices. Learning theorists indicate that people learn by co-constructing their knowledge with the help of experts and peers in a situated context. They assert that by doing so, people are elevated to new planes of knowledge and awareness (Cole & Engestrom, 1993; Driscoll, 2000; Lave & Wenger, 1991; Leont'ev, 1981; Luria, 1976; Rogoff & Wertsch, 1984; Salomon & Perkins, 1998; Scribner, 1985; Vygotsky, 1987). As VCoP members interact and learn from each other, they meet these social and cultural expectations.

- *Learners must be encouraged to own their learning and basing on his/her existing knowledge.* Ownership as it relates to learning means that people are aware of what knowledge they need and are involved in satisfying those needs (Driscoll, 2000). Therefore, learners must take control of their own learning by seeking for answers to their questions and solutions to their problems. This is exactly what happens in informal learning exchanges – individuals decide they need to know something to do their work while they are doing their work and take steps to learn it (Brandenburg & Binder, 1999; Sorohan, 1993; Weintraub; 1995). Individuals often join CoPs to search for knowledge they lack or to share knowledge they have. Members of CoPs help one another discover knowledge and solve problems by taking responsibility for their own and other's Knowledge.

- *Learning should be just-in-time and should provide context-specific solutions to problems.* VCoPs members can access needed resources at any time and from any place. The ability to identify solutions to problems right when they are needed most increases learners' performance capabilities. Recent developments in the design of web based tools for communication and problem solving suggest new way of delivering courses, based on collaborative and skills-based learning. In the process of getting and giving answers to solve problems, CoPs members learn how to acquire what they need to know and do. Thus, members of CoPs become aware of their learning processes as they learn, they became self directed learners. In this way, learners are self motivated – motivated through the wish to do a job more effectively and achieve greater recognition for it, alongside the capacity to have more influence in work situation.

In summary, VCoPs enable an efficient and effective process of learning through the sharing of knowledge with a wide range of members, and they enhance action learning process which is widely recognized in the literature as essential for managerial competency development (Gibb, 1997, Gorman et al., 1997, Deakins & Freel, 1998).

RESEARCH DESIGN

Research Questions

Starting from the above consideration, in our work we address the following questions:

- Can we define an integrated VCoPs model that will support all the knowledge management cycle in a Business School?
- In which way the Knowledge management organizational and technological aspects are integrated in a VCoPs?

- Is it possible to define an integrated Web Learning and KM platform enhancing learning opportunities both in daily researcher's work practices and in student's learning experience?

For answering to these questions, we propose an integrative conceptualization of VCoPs model, supported by the organizational learning processes, as an innovative way to apply KM to Higher Education. The model named *"Virtual eBMS"* is the result of an empirical study of a Higher Education community, the e-Business Management Section (eBMS) of Scuola Superiore ISUFI – University of Salento (Italy).

The eBMS is a cross-disciplinary Business School for international young talents, aimed at creating human capital and knowledge assets, by integrating advanced education, research and technology transfer focusing on digital innovation and business transformation. Currently, the eBMS leads a capacity building program to bridge the "Digital Divide" in Southern Mediterranean Countries and it's strongly involved into joint research and education programs with top level, national and international, academic and industrial organizations. Through the advanced education programs, the School aims to create business leaders capable to identify and exploit the distinctive potential of the new Information and Communication Technologies (ICTs) for reconfiguring traditional business contexts, which we refer as the *ICT-driven Business Innovation Leadership* (Romano et al., 2001), the eBMS brand consolidated over those seven years of experiences. Some Education activities (Executive programs and the International Master in e-Business Management) are organized in mobility between Italy and the Southern Mediterranean Countries and are devoted to people graduated in Business, Engineering or computer science coming form Italy, Morocco, Tunisia, Jordan and other Southern Mediterranean Countries. The close relationship between Italy and other countries has been recognized as the critical success factors in order to assure students a deep understanding of the business reality of their origin countries and for developing a CoPs interacting on virtual basis.

Research Method

For the study, we applied a participative observation (Yin, 1994), because we observed the community, while taking part in it, from November 1999 till September 2006. According to the methodology chosen, researchers actively participated in the eBMS meetings of the group of facilitators that initiated the community research, in the activities and learning processes.

In the first phase of the research the focus of our data collection was on the expectations of the members for developing a community model, and in a later phase on aspects that were learned from belonging to the community, as well as on the value created by the community. Individuals who were either involved or familiar with the initiative were identified and interviewed using a semi-structured questionnaire. The rationale for conducting these types of interviews was to draw rich, contextual details which could not have been elicited via closed ended survey instruments. These interviewees included management staff, core groups members, who represented the leadership of the community, community members and teaching staff who where not directly part of the community but were the intended recipients of outputs generated by the community. In particular, 8 researchers, 5 executive staff, 30 students, eBMS Director and 6 Laboratory's Coordinators and 10 teaching staff were involved. The involvement of such a wide variety of stakeholders allowed data to be obtained from multiple levels and perspectives. In addition, archival data, memos, e-mail, concept papers and web site was collected to triangulate the responses given by the interviewees.

DEVELOPING A VCOPS MODEL IN HIGHER EDUCATION: THE "VIRTUAL EBMS" COMMUNITY CASE

According the methodology chosen, we developed the model of VCoPs, as the output of the experiences of the eBMS launched in 1999. We named our community the "Virtual eBMS" community. For the purpose of our study, we define the *"Virtual eBMS" Community as a web based integrated learning environment, in which thinking, studying and acting are strongly correlated to reinforce and improve the effectiveness of the knowledge creation processes, through action learning projects, to invent new ICT-based Business Configurations.*

The model explains the KM processes (i.e. Knowledge Creation, Knowledge Organisation, Knowledge Application, Knowledge Sharing) as they happen in a VCoPs, and it is supported by an integrated Web Learning and KM platform creating participation, structuring the learning environment, in which diverse working and learning activities take place simultaneously. The holistic model of the "Virtual eBMS" community is composed of 3 main elements: *The People*, i.e. the participants taking part in the community as organizational assets and embodiers of knowledge; *The processes*, i.e. the eBMS set of roles, relationships, knowledge and learning flows;

the Purpose i.e. the output of the community in terms of value created by the community for Higher Education. All the elements showed in Fig. 1, lays at different levels, but that interact bi-directionally and continuously, enabling the community people (INPUT) to benefit from a variety of value (OUTPUT).

The totality of the members belonging to the "Virtual eBMS" community can be described according the typology shown in (Tab. 1).

Primary Aim

The primary aim of the "Virtual eBMS" community is to "sponsor" the continuous development of its people' managerial competencies (mainly postgraduate students and researchers) through their participation in research activities strongly integrated with Higher Education programs. By *managerial competencies* we adopt the following definition: a bundling of strategic resources and intellectual technologies underlying managerial roles and practices, and processes to understand, connect and exploit them in a uniquely competitive way (Baets & Van der Linden, 2003). Managerial competencies in eBMS are based on the *Global Business Capabilities* defined as the capacity to lead organizational change in the changing environment of the Digital Economy (Andrews &Tyson, 2004).

Figure 1. The "Virtual eBMS" Community Model

People	*Processes: Community characteristics*	*Purpose*
Staff; Student; Lecturer; Partner; Testimonial; Alumni; Visitor.	*Primary aim*	*Value for Higher Education processes.*
	Value Proposition	
	Primary values	
	Knowledge Sources	
	Knowledge management cycle	
	Governance structure	
Technology		
Virtual eBMS system		

Table 1. People of the "Virtual eBMS" community

Members typology	Profile
Staff	Researcher, professors and administrative staff of the institution
Student	Students attending the advanced education activities of the institution
Lecturer	Researchers or professors from other institutions
Partner	People of industries or universities involved in joint activities
Testimonial	Outstanding people invited for conferences, talks and meetings
Alumni	People that attended with success educational program of the institution
Visitor	People that occasionally visit the community

Value Proposition

The "Virtual eBMS" value proposition is to enhance intellectual capital creation. Intellectual Capital could be framed into three interdependent elements: human, social, and structural capital (Seeman et al., 2000). Human capital is defined as knowledge, skills and attitudes created in people (*Global Business Capabilities*). Social Capital reflects the ability of groups to collaborate and to work together and is a function of trust. Structural capital is usually defined as buildings, software, processes, patents, organization's image and values, information system, databases.

Primary Values

The "Virtual eBMS" primary values are the following:

- *Information and Communication Technologies (ICTs)* make individuals and organizations distinctively competitive in every field. ICTs change the way people live and work, as well as the way companies and institutions organize themselves and interact with each other.
  Knowledge should be created through a *cross-disciplinary approach*, supported by experiential laboratories, where participants think, work and learn together how to invent new ICT-based business configurations.

- *Diversity* means richness. The eBMS strongly encourage a multicultural environment based on mutual respect and trust because innovation springs from comparison and exchange of different experiences, passions and emotions.
- *"Mediterraneity"* is a synonym of culture and dialogue. The eBMS is in the core of the Mediterranean area and it would like to be a bridge to promote innovation in Southern Mediterranean Countries.
- *Public and private Partnerships* with national and international Centers of Excellence, represent a strategic lever to assure competence growth and the internationalization of higher education and research activities.
- *New business models and organizational practices* should be developed to seize the opportunities deriving from the Internet Economy.

Knowledge Sources

The Knowledge sources in the "Virtual eBMS" can be organized around domains – specialized areas of knowledge, subject areas, disciplines, frequently used information and similar characteristic knowledge. The following domains shown in Tab. 2 (both general purpose and specific context) have been considered for developing the eBMS knowledge base, according to the education and research activities.

Table 2. Knowledge domains for the eBMS knowledge base

Knowledge category	Knowledge Domain
General Purpose	New Competitive Macro-Environment
	Business Management
	Internet Business Management
	Business Innovation Leadership
	ICT Management
Specific context	e-Tourism
	e-Agrifood
	Aerospace
	Territorial Marketing

Knowledge Management Cycle

The Knowledge Management cycle in the "Virtual eBMS" Community is divided in: Knowledge sharing, knowledge creation and Knowledge organization. *The knowledge sharing* retrieves knowledge from the organisational memory and makes it accessible to the users. Individuals, teams and laboratories often share ideas, opinions, knowledge and expertise in meetings held in face-to-face format or virtually. The *knowledge organisation* stage takes the nuggets of knowledge and classifies them and adds them to the organisational memory. Much of this knowledge can be represented in electronic form as expert systems. This is where even tacit, intangible knowledge assets are transformed to tangible one. The "Virtual eBMS" approach to *knowledge creation* is based on a self-organizing kind of learning, derived from direct experience, as it is exposed in Kolb's theory of experiential learning, that is the best learning model framed according the principles of Constructivism approach. According to Kolb (1984), the knowledge creation process are expressed in terms of:

- *Concrete Experience:* learners are involved in an active exploration of experience used

to test out ideas and assumptions rather than to obtain practice passively.

- *Reflective Observation:* Learners must selectively reflect on their experience in a critical way rather than take experience for granted and assume that the experience on its own is sufficient.
- *Abstract Conceptualization:* Learners create theories to explain one's observations.
- *Active Experimentation:* Learners use theories to solve problems and make decisions.

Governance Structure

The "Virtual eBMS" Governance Structure is a mid level control from leaders and coordinators. In the "Virtual eBMS", community coordinators are well respected member of the community: the Director, the Executive Staff and the eBMS Laboratories' coordinators. Their role is to keep the community alive, connecting members with each other, helping the community to focus on important issues, and bringing new ideas when the community start to loose energy. Moreover, the community coordinators maintain, organize and distribute the central knowledge to the other members.

An Integrated Process and Technology Oriented Description of the "Virtual eBMS" Community

Following the "Virtual eBMS" community requirements, we designed and developed the technological system, the "Virtual eBMS" system, as an integrated and completely web-based platform providing Web Learning and Knowledge Management (KM) services and developed ad-hoc to support the "Virtual eBMS" learning community, both from the organizational and the technological point of view. The system allows the definition of a dynamic Virtual Learning Environment in which to build rich and effective learning experiences (Romano et al., 2001) for all the members of the community, supporting the constructivist approach to learning.

The system has been designed and developed at eBMS in partnership with IBM Italy eKnowledge Factory, under a two years project founded by the Italian Ministry of University and Research. In 2006 the project got the "2006 Brandon Hall Excellence in Learning Award", since it was recognized as one of the three worldwide best projects in learning technology. Such complex system was created by integrating different market products and some components developed ad hoc: at the base of the KM and the Web Learning system integration process there is the use of open source technology.

From the technological point of view, the *Knowledge Management component* of the platform is made up of the following systems: a cross-functional component providing a set of user management and personalisation services, a document management system, a workflow management system, a web content management system, a project management system, a set of community services (chat, mail, forum, agenda, bookmark, questionnaire, blackboard, newsletter, e-Library), a recommendation system (that suggests to the final user, according to his/her profile, both documents, experts and other members of

the community with the same interests), a search engine (for basic search, taxonomy navigation, graphical search and advanced search), and a Web Mining System. The *Web Learning component* of "Virtual eBMS" system is composed by a Learning Management System (LMS), a Learning Content Management System (LCMS), a Content Delivery System (CDS), a set of audio/video collaboration tools and by an "ad hoc" developed layer that implements the Problem Based Learning approach.

More in details, the Web Learning component is used for the development and the delivery of curricula related to Technology Management, Business Management and Internet Business Management domains, for Master and PhD Students as well as for Enterprises Executives and Managers. Indeed, from the final users perspective, in addition to the traditional and structured offering of learning content, the Web Learning component of the "Virtual eBMS" allows learners both to freely access to a structured knowledge base and therefore to self-organize their learning patterns, and to follow recommended learning paths suggested by the system according to their interests or competences.

The taxonomy-based organization of the learning materials, on the base of a dynamic and extensible "ad-hoc" competence taxonomy, allows the learners to quickly search and get small pieces of self-consistent learning objects. Such learning objects can be easily organized into customized learning patterns and delivered on demand to the user, according to her/his profile and knowledge needs, giving flexible access to the learning materials (Damiani et al., 2002).

In the following table (Table 3) an integrated process and technology oriented view of the Virtual eBMS systems is offered. For each community process and actions (*Knowledge organisation, knowledge creation, knowledge apply and knowledge sharing*) are given the correspondent main functionalities of the "Virtual eBMS" system, grouped in content management systems, content delivery systems, and learning management systems functionalities.

The main strength points of the "Virtual eBMS" can be referred especially to the Web Learning component, and they are:

- a systemic architecture integrating a LMS, a LCMS, an authoring tool, streaming audio/video collaborative tools, and a project management tool;

Table 3. A process / technology oriented view of the "Virtual eBMS" Community

	VIRTUAL EBMS COMMUNITY SYSTEMS FUNCTIONALITIES		
COMMUNITY PROCESSESS AND ACTIONS	**Content management System**	**Content Delivery System**	**Learning Management System**
KNOWLEDGE ORGANISATION O1. Storing community knowledge O2. Know who is in the community and the domain of expertise O3. Developing Knowledge maps O4. Quickly and systematically find the right information	Creation and management of knowledge objects, metadata management, document search and retrieval. Automatic indexing of unstructured content, automatic categorization to a taxonomy and automatic creation of taxonomies to provide content in context. E-library, document management , search (full text, taxonomies, knowledge map, recommendation).	Free search of leaning resources: full-text and taxonomy search of learning resources (Knowledge Objects, SCORM Objects, Learning Modules, Learning Plans), both from mentors (back-office area) and from learners (front-office-area)	Deliverable submission by learners, deliverable approval/reject by mentors. Course Tracking: SCORM Objects on-line/off-line tracking. In the off-line mode: course download and attend, synchronization with the e-Learning system
KNOWLEDGE CREATION C1. Situating learning into daily work practices C2. Proving just in time learning C3. Providing content specific solutions to problems C4. Create competences according to the personal profile	Creation and management of tests. Textual and graphic report on learner activities and results, as well as on the usage of resources and learning material. Skill gap Analysis: analysis of learner competence-gap based on self-assessment.	Competences management through a three-level competences taxonomy. *Learning module management:* creation and management of learning modules, by assembling multimedia presentations, Web resources, knowledge objects, SCORM objects, virtual events.	Creation and management of learning plans by assembling learning modules, glossary management, multimedia presentation management.
KNOWLEDGE APPLY A1. Debriefing after attending seminars or important meeting with geographically dispersed partners. A2. Documenting knowledge into manuals, deliverables, papers, diagrams. A3. Having access to specialised libraries. A4. Access to on line repository of files.	A relational or object-oriented repository of content and activities, which allows granular storage content, with descriptive and category metadata to facilitate retrieval. Management of individuals, competencies, expertise, temporary and permanent groups/ communities.	Enrolment Requests: learners can send a request of enrolment to their mentors for learning modules and learning plans Management of resources and facilities for training, meetings, etc.	Assessment of competence acquisition through tests (automatic) and/or deliverables (by mentors). Learning catalogue available for: Knowledge Objects, SCORM Objects, Learning Modules, Learning Plans.
KNOWLEDGE SHARING S1. Stimulate Dialogue S2. Embed Know-how Sharing into work practices S3. Mentoring, coaching and other forms of action learning S4. Running internal seminars led by experts S5. Virtual meeting	One to one communications tools (chat, e-mail); one to many communication tools (forum, questionnaires) One to all communications tools (news, bookmark, blackboard)	Support and Feedback: support to learning activities of learners by tutors/ facilitators.	*Pedagogical Relations Management:* creation and management of pedagogical relations with which to create some logical and propedeutic links between learning content.

- an ad hoc developed software layer, integrated in the overall architecture, ensuring the delivery of learning curricula according to the Problem Based Learning (PBL) methodology.
- a cross-disciplinary competence taxonomy integrated to the KM taxonomy and organized around the Business Management, Technology Management and Internet Business Management domains;
- an integrated Knowledge Base made up of multimedia learning objects (compliant to the SCORM standard), external knowledge resources (i.e. web links) and knowledge objects extracted from the knowledge management repository;
- a recommendation system that suggests PBL curricula according to the knowledge workers' competence profile, interests and skill gaps;
- a search engine that supports both taxonomy-based and problem-oriented searches.

PRELIMINARY RESULTS AND DISCUSSION

VCoPs enable an efficient and effective process of Knowledge creation through the sharing of knowledge with a wide range of members and enhance a learner centered approach to management education which is widely recognized in the literature as essential for action learning. The *"Virtual eBMS"* community model supports the interconnectivity allowing access of different cultural environment, provide linkages to reference materials, resource people on a global scale, provide feedback from staff, learners, alumni, experts and industry partners, improving responsiveness by monitoring and incorporating lessons learned from the experiences of colleagues, student evaluations, and corporate or other constituent input.

In seven years of experimentation of the "Virtual eBMS" community, almost 100 young talented people have been selected between 350 applicants in 7 Master editions, since 1999. 29% of Master students participated to the community, coming from Morocco (80%), Albania (6%), Libya (1%), Palestine (5%), Jordan (7%) and Spain (1%). More than 450 mentors, and speakers mostly coming from Europe, North-America, and Japan, and testimonials have been involved in learning activities, advanced seminars and Summer Schools and remained in contact through the community. Daily, about 40 researcher and 60 students share knowledge within the community. All these people (*Human capital*) contributed to aliment and sustain the "Virtual eBMS" community.

The people belonging to the "Virtual eBMS" community have also contributed to develop the eBMS *structural capital* – what is usually defined as software, processes, patents, organization's brand and values, information system, databases, research projects – as a result of a complex activity in carrying out several projects awarded on competitive base. These act at the same time as enabling factors (since structural capital is generated for matching projects' requirements) and as catalysts of the learning-in-action environment of the School. The projects' development, then, reinforces the dynamics of interactive learning which constitute the core mission of the eBMS.

The *social capital* of eBMS is based on trust and commitment of the strong partnership worldwide contributing to aliment the eBMS education and research activities.

We would like to conclude this paper by describing the primary benefits the people receive participating in the "Virtual eBMS" community. In a series of questions, we asked members of the Community to explain the main benefits; almost everyone responded in terms of value created by the community. Table 4 presents the results of the responses (*Nature of value added*) with the *attributes that create value*. We think that these results can be generalized to the other "Virtual Community" within Higher Education Environment.

Table 4. The valued added by the "Virtual eBMS" Community

Nature of Value Added	Attributes that create Value
Higher quality of knowledge creation	– Reflection process that occur at the end of a virtual meeting consolidates learning – Leveraging of previous research and proposal efforts – Diversity in membership and less emphasis on hierarchical status increase the probability of group think
Greater capacity to deal with unstructured problem	– Research activities occur under a set of super ordinate goals rather than task goal – Knowledge leaders are allowed to emerge on the basis of issues rather than by assignments to a team or roles within a teams
More effective knowledge sharing among research laboratories	– Voluntary participation implies higher motivation that turn leads to faster, deeper internalization of learning – Long term relationships increase trust
More effective knowledge delivery	– Self paced and not sequential, independent learning via resource-based and technology enhanced activities: many methods of learning, many media, varied resources, self-test, formative evaluation, critical thinking – Lecturer are just facilitator for students experimenting new knowledge
More effective improved individual development and learning	– Active learning as part of a group is more effective than learning alone – Learners' choice are competency-based – The opportunity to learn engaging in practice is embodied in processes that the community developed – Support collaborative projects among different research laboratories
Course design	– Offer flexible, multidisciplinary and non sequential learning – Stimulate and engage learners via well crafted learning issues – Interdisciplinary curriculum design and development facilitated by navigating across laboratories

Future developments steps of the work will consist in the identification of measurements systems to evaluate the development and the renewal of the community.

REFERENCES

Allen, S., Evans, S., & Ure, D. (2005). Virtual communities of practices: Vehicles for organisational learning and improved job performance. *International Journal of Learning Technology, 1*(3), 252-272.

Andrews, N., & Tyson, L. D. (2004). *The upwardly global MBA*. Retrieved from http://www.strategy-business.com

Baets, W., & Van der Linden, G. (2003). *Virtual corporate universities: A matrix of knowledge and learning for the new digital dawn*. Kluwer Academic Publisher.

Barrows, H. S., & Tamblyn, R. M. (1980). *Problem-based learning: An approach to medical education*. New York: Springer Publishing Co.

Brandenburg, D. C., & Binder, C.V. (1999). Emerging trends in human performance interventions. In H. D. Stolovitch & E. J. Keeps (Eds.), *Handbook of human performance technology: Improving individual and organizational performance worldwide (pp. 843866)*. San Francisco: Jossey-Bass.

Bransford, J., Brown, A. L., & Cocking, R. R. (Eds.). (1999). *How people learn*. Washington, DC: National Academy Press.

Cohen, D., & Prusak, L. (2001). *In good company: How social capital makes organizations work.* Boston: Harvard Business School Press.

Cole, M., & Engestrom, Y. (1993). A cultural-historical approach to distributed cognition. In G. Salomon (Ed.), *Distributed cognitions: Psychological and educational considerations.* New York: Cambridge University Press.

Damiani, E., Corallo, A., Elia, G., & Ceravolo, P. (2002). *Standard per i learning objects: Interoperabilità ed integrazione nella didattica a distanza.* Convegno internazionale: eLearning. Una sfida per l'Universita: Strategie metodi prospettive.

Daniel, B., Schwier, R. A., & McCalla, G. (2003). Social capital in virtual learning communities and distributed communities of practice. *Canadian Journal of Learning and Technology, 29*(3), 113-139.

Deakins, D., & Freel, M. (1998). Entrepreneurial learning and the growth process in SMEs. *Learning Organisation*, pp. 144-155.

Driscoll, M. P. (2000). *Psychology of learning for instruction.* Boston: Allyn & Bacon.

Duffy, T., & Jonassen, D. H. (1992). Constructivism: New implications for instructional technology. In T. Duffy & D. H. Jonassen (Eds.), *Constructivism and the technology of instruction: A conversation.* Hillsdale, NJ: Erlbaum.

Gibb, A. (1997). Small firms training and competitiveness: Building up the small business as a learning organisation. *International Small Business Journal, 3*, 13-29.

Gorman, G., Hanlon, D., & King, W. (1997). Some research perspectives on entrepreneurship education, enterprise education and education for small business management: A ten year literature review. *International Small Business Journal, 3*, 56-77.

Jonassen, D., Davidson, M., Collins, M., Campbell, J., & Hag, B. (1995). Constructivism and computer-mediated communication in distance education. *American Journal of Distance Education, 9*(2), 7-26.

Kolb, A. (1984). *Experiential learning: Experience as the source of learning and development.* Boston: McBer & Company.

Kowch, E. G., & Schwier, R. A. (1997). *Characteristics of technology-based virtual learning communities.* Retrieved September 27, 2003, from http://www.usak.ca/education/coursework/802papers/communities/community

Lave, J., & Wenger, E. (1991). *Situated learning: Legitimate peripheral participation.* New York: Cambridge University Press.

Leont'ev, A. N. (1981). The problem of activity in psychology. In J. V. Wertsch (Eds.), *The concept of activity in soviet psychology (pp. 37-71).* Armonk, NY: Sharpe.

Lesser, E., & Prusak, L. (2000). Communities of practices social capital and organisational knowledge. In E. Lesser, M. Fontaine, & J. Slusher(Eds.), *Knowledge and communities.* Butterworth-Heinemann.

Luria, A. R. (1976). *Cognitive development: Its cultural and social foundations.* Cambridge, MA: Harvard University Press.

Rogoff, B., & Wertsch, J. (1984). *Children's learning in the zone of proximal development.* San Francisco: Jossey-Bass.

Romano, A., Elia, V., & Passiante, G. (2001). *Creating business innovation leadership: An ongoing experiment. The E-Business Management School at ISUFI.* Naples, Italy: Edizioni Scientifiche Italiane.

Salomon, G., & Perkins, D. N. (1998). Individual and social aspects of learning. In P. D. Pearson & A. Iran-Nejad (Eds.), *Review of research in education* (Vol. 23, pp. 1-24). Washington, DC: American Educational Research Association.

Scribner, S. (1985). Vygotsky's uses of history. In J. V. Wertsch (Eds.), *Culture, communication, and cognition: Vygotskian perspectives* (pp. 119-145). Cambridge, United Kingdom: Cambridge University Press.

Sorohan, E. G. (1993). We do; therefore we learn. *Training and Development, 47*(10), 47-55.

Vygotsky, L. S. (Ed.). (1987). *The collected works of Vygotsky.* New York: Plenum Press.

Weintraub, R. (1995). Transforming mental models through formal and informal learning: A guide for workplace educators. In S. Chawla & J. Renesch (Eds.), *Learning organizations: Developing cultures for tomorrow's workplace (pp.* 417-429). Portland, OR: Productivity Press.

Yin, R. K. (1994). *Case study research: Design and methods.* CA: Sage.

This work was previously published in International Journal of Web-Based Learning and Teaching Technologies, Vol. 3, Issue 1, edited by L. Esnault, pp. 90-102, copyright 2008 by IGI Publishing (an imprint of IGI Global).

Chapter 18
The IntelCities Community of Practice:
The eGov Services Model for Socially Inclusive and Participatory Urban Regeneration Programs

Mark Deakin[1]
Napier University, Scotland, UK

ABSTRACT

The chapter examines the IntelCities Community of Practice (CoP) supporting the development of the organization's e-Learning platform, knowledge management system (KMS) and digital library for eGov services. It begins by outlining the IntelCities CoP and goes on to set out the integrated model of electronically enhanced government (eGov) services developed by the CoP to meet the front-end needs, middleware requirements and back-office commitments of the IntelCities e-Learning platform, KMS and digital library. The chapter goes on to examine the information technology (IT) adopted by the CoP to develop the IntelCities e-Learning platform, KMS and digital library as a set of semantically-interoperable eGov services supporting the crime, safety and security initiatives of socially-inclusive and participatory urban regeneration programs.

INTRODUCTION

The notion of the intelligent city as the provider of electronically-enhanced services has become popular over the past decade or so (Graham and Marvin, 1996; Mitchell, 2000). In response to this growing interest in the notion of intelligent cities,

researchers have begun to explore the possibilities of using CoPs as a means of getting beyond current 'state-of-the-art' solutions and use the potential such organizations offer to develop integrated models of e-government (eGov) services (Curwell, et.al, 2005; Lombardi and Curwell, 2005). This chapter shall report on the outcomes of one such exploration and review the attempt made by a consortium of leading European cities to use the intelligence that CoPs offer as the organizational means by which to get beyond current state-of-the-art solutions. The CoP in question is that developed under the IntelCities Project[1] and which is known as the IntelCities CoP. The chapter shall report on the development of the IntelCities CoP under the leadership of Manchester and Siena. It shall explore the value of using CoPs as the organizational means by which to secure the intelligence - humans and artificial - that cities need to develop integrated models of eGov services. Integrated models of eGov services seen as being of particular value for the reason they meet the e-learning needs, knowledge transfer requirements and capacity building commitments of Europe's policy on socially-inclusive and participatory urban regeneration programs.

THE INTELCITIES COMMUNITY OF PRACTICE

The IntelCities CoP is made up of research institutes, information, communication and technology (ICT) companies and cities, all collaborating with one another and reaching consensus on how to develop integrated models of eGov services. Made up of researchers, computer engineers, informational managers and service providers, the IntelCities CoP has worked to develop an integrated model of eGov services and support the actions taken by cities to host them on platforms (in this instance something known as the eCity platform) with sufficient intelligence to meet the e-learning needs, knowledge transfer requirements and capacity building commitments of socially-inclusive and participatory urban regeneration programs (Deakin and Allwinkle, 2006).

As an exercise in CoP development, the organization is particularly successful for the reason the intelligence it has sought to embed in cities and integrate within their platforms of eGov services,

is inter-organizational, networked, virtual and managed as part of a highly-distributed web-based learning environment. If we quickly review the legacy of CoPs in organizational studies, the value of developing such a learning environment should become clear. For as the literature indicates, CoPs are an emergent property of organizations and the challenges they pose for those seeking to exploit their potential in such learning environments is considerable.

Literature on CoPs

The literature on CoPs reveals many different kinds of situated practices, all of them displaying quite varied processes of learning and knowledge generation, gathered around distinct forms of social interaction. In this respect, Wenger's (1998, 2000) studies of CoPs is of the ways that insurance claim processors and other such occupational groups learn to be effective in their job. Orr (1996) also studies the importance of CoPs amongst photocopier repair technicians. Osterlund (1996) studies are of CoPs as learning organizations that cut across craft, occupational and professional divisions and which transfer knowledge between them. The collective representation of CoPs in the literature suggests such organizations have the characteristics displayed in Table 1.

Taking this representation of CoPs as a starting point for their examination, Amin and Roberts (2008) suggest there are four distinct types of inter-organizational learning and knowledge transfer. These being: craft, professional, creative and virtual.[2] As Amin and Roberts (2008) go on to point out, until recently it has been assumed that virtual organizations cannot be considered as a CoP, promoting learning and transferring knowledge on its own terms. Although, as they go on to stress, as it becomes easier to communicate with 'distant others' in real time and in increasingly rich ways, there is interest in understanding how such learning environments can be used to manage knowledge. The resulting proliferation of online

Table 1. Key characteristics of a community of practice. Source: Compiled from Wenger (1998)

Sustained mutual relationships
Shared ways of engaging in doing things together
The rapid flow of information and propagation of innovation
Absence of introductory preambles, as if conversations and interactions were merely the continuation of an ongoing process
Very quick setup of a problem to be discussed
Substantial overlap in participants' descriptions of who belongs
Knowing what others know, what they can do, and how they can contribute to an enterprise
Mutually defining identities
The ability to assess the appropriateness of actions and products
Specific tools, representations, and other artefacts
Local lore, shared stories, inside jokes, knowing laughter
Jargon and shortcuts to communication as well as the ease of producing new ones
Certain styles recognised as displaying membership
A shared discourse reflecting a certain perspective on the world

communities associated with such developments in turn suggesting that interest is now centering on how the knowledge dynamics of virtual CoPs differ from those organizations which are dependant on social familiarity and direct engagement (Ellis et.al., 2004; Johnson, 2001).

Two Types of Online Interaction

As Amin and Roberts (2008) acknowledge, there are now two types of online interaction that merit close attention as spaces where CoPs engage in learning and get involved in knowledge generation. Firstly, innovation-seeking projects that can involve a large number of participants and secondly, relatively closed interest groups which

face specific problems and are consciously organized as platforms needed for learning about and gaining a knowledge of, how to build the capacity required to include 'distant others' as participants in such projects.

As they say: open source software groups provide a good example of the first CoP. Typically, they involve short-lived projects that make source code freely available to technical experts who are motivated by the challenge of solving a difficult programming problem. Successful projects of this kind are those guided by shared notions of the problem, defined by a core group of highly motivated experts, who associate with one another to learn about the subject and transfer the knowledge generated to distant others.

More recently, however, we have seen a rapid rise in the development of the second type of CoP. These are established explicitly by professionals, experts, or lay people to advance knowledge. Typically, they involve experts interested in developing and exchanging best practice, or lay people wishing to learn about and transfer knowledge about and build capacity for such electronically-mediated communication. Here a CoP is seen to emerge once the technologies for the virtual organization is available and success is seen to emerge from the ability such platforms have to transfer knowledge. Furthermore, it is also stressed that with these CoPs the technology which is available to support the development of virtual learning organizations, has to be managed. As Josefsson (2005) points out, such virtual learning organizations are successfully managed in accordance with a 'netiquette', where semantically-rich language is used to develop a culture of engagement replete with humor, empathy, kindness, tact, and support. This way virtual learning organizations are seen to replicate the rich texture of social interaction normally associated with CoPs marked by high levels of inter-personal trust and reciprocity, or collaborations built around strong professional or occupational ties.

Defining Features of the IntelCities CoP

Made up of both open source software groups, experts and lay people, the IntelCities CoP is unique in the sense its network provides an example of a virtual organization set up to manage the learning needs and knowledge requirements of a technological platform. That virtual organization set up under the name of the IntelCities Project and as a platform which:

- Offers the means to meet the learning needs, knowledge transfer requirements and capacity building commitments of its integrated eGov services model.
- Meet them in a manner that is socially inclusive and participatory in the way the platform of integrated eGov services under development allows users to learn about the availability of such services, how to access them and the opportunities they offer everyone to become engaged with and get involved in meeting the knowledge transfer requirements and capacity building commitments of their urban regeneration programmes.

There are three features that define the IntelCities CoP and which give it meaning and a sense of purpose. These are: the shared enterprise, the technology and online services. The shared enterprise relates to the work undertaken by all members of the IntelCities CoP to develop an integrated model of eGov services. The technology refers to the open source software underlying the development of the eCity platform upon which the integrated model of eGov services rests and that supports online access to the socially-inclusive and participatory urban regeneration programmes this provides. These defining features of the IntelCities CoP align with nine of the characteristics highlighted by Amin and Roberts (2008) and set out previously in Table 1.

Table 2 underlines the importance of these as characteristics and adds another six that have been exploited by the network to develop a virtual learning organization capable of bridging the gap which exists between the Type 1 and 2 (innovation-seeking and knowledge generating) classifications of virtual CoPs offered by Amin and Roberts (2008). What follows should like to suggest the extra characteristics are those needed to span the divide between what are in crude terms, the technical and social requirements of the IntelCities CoP.

In line with current definition of CoPs as shared enterprises, the additional features clearly highlight these particular qualities and reflect their importance, but in addition to this they underline

Table 2. Defining characteristics of the IntelCities CoP

sustained mutual relationships
shared ways of engaging in doing things together
the rapid flow of information and propagation of innovation
absence of introductory preambles, as if conversations and interactions were merely the continuation of an ongoing process
very quick setup of a problem to be discussed
substantial overlap in participants' descriptions of who belongs
knowing what others know, what they can do, and how they can contribute to an enterprise
a shared discourse reflecting a certain perspective on the world
shared enterprise between research institutes, ICT companies and cities
joint venture commitment to product development
support for the use of ICTs as a means to bridge the digital divide
shared commitment to social-inclusion and participatory urban regeneration programmes to bride such divisions and lose the gap between the information-rich and poor
support for the modernisation of local government service provision using technological platforms
consensus-based decision making, consultative and deliberative in nature

the technical rational and social purpose of the virtual organization in question. This suggests that in developing integrated eGov service models it is not possible for intelligent cities to develop as either Type 1 or 2 CoPs and this is because the shared enterprise and joint venture characteristics such virtual learning organizations share, means they have to be technical and social in equal measures.

The following examination of the IntelCities CoP shall to a large extent, reflect this position. It shall begin by examining the integrated model of eGov services and IT underlying the eCity platform developed as an intelligent solution to the virtual organization's learning needs and knowledge transfer requirements. The examination shall then reflect on the search for intelligent city solution in terms of the step-wise logic adopted to meet the challenge the learning needs and knowledge transfer requirements of virtual organizations pose. From here the e-Learning platform, knowledge management system and digital library developed for such purposes shall be outlined. Having done this, attention shall turn to the innovative features of this platform, management system and library and the semantically-interoperable qualities of the learning, knowledge and repository services this offers shall be reviewed. From here the examination turns attention towards a review of how the learning, knowledge management and digital library services now available as eGov services are integrated into the eCity platform and made available over the web.

This turns attention to what is termed the eTopia demonstrator developed to illustrate the functionality of the semantically-rich eGov services in question. This term is borrowed from Mitchell's (2000) account of intelligent cities as e-topias and as organizations that are: 'SMART', lean, mean, green software systems, driven by networked communities which are virtual (see, Deakin and Allwinkle, 2007; Deakin, 2007). Those organizational characteristics which the author would add are built on the learning needs,

knowledge management requirements and digital libraries of electronically-enhanced government services that are available on the eCity platform as a pool of integrated eGov services.

THE INTEGRATED MODEL OF EGOV SERVICES

Figure 1 outlines the integrated eGov services model developed by the CoP. At the front-end there are a range of eGov services under development, highlighted as social inclusion, participation and regeneration and shown in terms of the middleware integrating them between the front-end presentation tier and back-office core interoperability and infrastructure service layer of the eCity platform. This also illustrates the services located in the back-office and the relationship this develops between the organization's e-Learning platform, KMS and digital library. This shows that it is the middleware of the eCity platform which integrates the front-end delivery of government services to citizens with the back-office business functions. Figure 1 also shows that it is the middleware which in turn provides the opportunity for the e-Learning platform, KMS and digital library making up the back office functions, to do the same and become an integral part of the eCity platform, supporting the pool of eGov services which are available for citizens to access at the front-end. This integration of the e-Learning platform, KMS and digital library into the middleware and use of it as the eCity platform supporting the presentation of eGov services to citizens at the front-end, is the challenge the IntelCities CoP has set out to meet and sought a solution for.

THE IT UNDERLYING THE INTELLIGENT CITY SOLUTION

The main challenge for the IntelCities CoP has been that of finding a solution which has the intel-

Figure 1. Integrated eGov services model

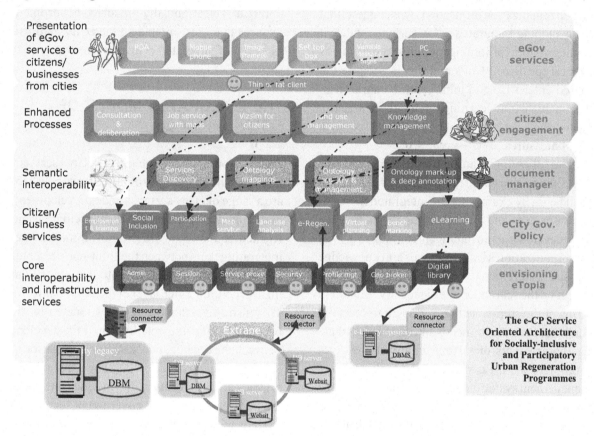

ligence cities need for the information technology (IT) underpinning the presentation of eGov services to be extensible, flexible and also have the capacity to carry existing local government legacy systems. The Services Oriented Architecture (SOA) of the enterprise-wide business model adopted as the joint venture vehicle for such an 'intelligent solution' meets this challenge by offering the IntelCities CoP a distributed, web-based and extendable access system. This intelligence in turn offers cities the opportunity to build a web services enabled platform of eGov services, with XML IT utilisation and SOAP communication.

An important element in the initial system design relates to the use of the Unique Modelling Language (UML) and Rational Unified Process (RUP) methodology used for developing the integrated model of electronically-enhanced government (eGov) services. This allows for the development of complex 'N-tiered' systems and the possibility of cities hosting eGov services on e-Learning platforms, KM systems and digital libraries utilising the intelligence such IT offers. This has the advantage of offering a homogenous platform solution supporting the development of specific service applications meeting the e-learning needs, knowledge transfer requirements and capacity building commitments of the IntelCities CoP. It also manages to do this while leaving open the possibility of sharing services developed by other organizations not yet integrated into the eGov services model and eCity platform supporting this particular organization's e-learning needs, knowledge transfer requirements and capacity building commitments.

THE SEARCH FOR AN INTELLIGENT SOLUTION

The search for an intelligent solution to the e-Learning needs and KM requirements of the eCity platform has progressed by applying a stepwise logic to the challenge it poses the IntelCities CoP. This has taken the following form:

- A survey of user learning needs.
- Analysis of the knowledge requirements
- Review of learning and knowledge services leading city portals provide.
- Benchmarking of existing e-learning platforms against the user's knowledge transfer and capacity building requirements
- Selecting the e-learning platform able to meet these requirements and develop as a KM system supported by a digital library.
- Integrating the aforesaid into the IntelCities middleware as a platform of eGov services delivered to citizens at the front-end.

Following this step-wise logic has meant focusing attention on the underlying pedagogical issues, the competencies, skills and training requirements of IntelCities. The next step involved a review of the learning services leading city portals offer as legacy systems and benchmarking of the e-learning platforms these systems are based upon against the knowledge transfer and capacity building requirements of the IntelCities CoP. Here the learning services of five leading city portals were reviewed. These included the learning services provided on the city portals of: Edinburgh, Dublin, Glasgow (Drumchapel), Helsinki (Arabianranta and Munala) and Reykjavic (Garoabaer). The review found:

- The said city portals provide learning services for citizens.
- These portals provide citizens with a community grid for learning.

- Much of the data available to the community is informative, telling citizens about learning opportunities in their neighborhoods' and providing links to the service providers.
- While being used by up to 10% of the population and offering free email and storage, most of the services provided by the city portals are insufficiently engaging for citizens to use them as grids for communities to base development of their learning partnerships with cities on.

As legacy systems, the review found these e-learning platforms were insufficient to meet the knowledge transfer requirements of the IntelCities and needed to represent the point of departure for the CoP. However, on a more positive note, the review made clear the focus of the IntelCities e-Learning platform should be the needs of the citizen, their knowledge requirements and the technology adopted to deliver this ought to break with the tradition of existing city portals, be more socially-inclusive and offer greater opportunity for communities to participate in their development. With this in mind, the examination went on to benchmark the e-learning systems which existing portals are based on and examine them against the knowledge transfer and capacity building requirements that they set.

THE E-LEARNING PLATFORM

Figure 2 illustrates the results of this benchmarking exercise, presenting the average percentage scores of tools provided by 67 commercial e-learning platforms and compares these against the industry standard (Web CT) & European Dynamics' OSS eOWL system. This benchmarking exercise has in turn produced an OSS (Open Source Standards) approach to e-Learning, where the exercise is driven by a small e and a capital 'L'. This has opened up the opportunity to get beyond the tendency for city learning

Table 3. Results of the e-learning platform benchmarking exercise. Source: Deakin et.al (2004)

Learner tools	Commercial platforms[1]	WebCT[2]	IntelCities platform[2]
Communication Tools	57%	71%	86%
Learning Tools	62%	60%	60%
Learner Involvement Tools	64%	75%	100%
Administration Tools	79%	75%	100%
Course Delivery Tools	72%	80%	100%
Course Design	56%	83%	83%
Hardware/Software	70%	80%	63%
Pricing/Licensing	80%	40%	100%

[1] *Indicates average percentage of learner tools covered by the 67 commercial e-Learning platforms surveyed.*
[2] *Highlights the percentage of functionality of individual learning tool covered by services available on WebCT and European Dynamics' OSS (e-OWL) platform*

portals to merely provide links to resources held elsewhere and provided the means to customise an e-Learning platform capable of meeting the particular knowledge transfer requirements of the IntelCities CoP.

The Learning Management System

The Learning Management System (LMS) developed for such purposes lies at the centre of the platform. This management system provides the common ground between course tutors, trainers and learners, a virtual space where they can co-operate with one another by sharing experiences and offering personal and confidential advice on the available courses, content and communication tools. It is designed as a set of modules in which tutors can create content, administer the resulting course and create assessments for learners, while learners are able to work with that related material. The services offered by the LMS are underpinned by a set of repositories holding information on personal data of registered members, learner's profiles, material available to support the structured course of studies and other unstructured data also available to learners.

The system architecture rests on three levels, each supported by a dedicated administrator: the platform administrator, and the course coordinators, tutors and trainers. Here the administrator is responsible for managing the directory of members registered to a course (this provides the interface between the course provider and the learner), whilst the tutor/trainer will be the course content creator, and the coordinator is responsible for distributing the course(s) to the learner and the services supporting the relating studies. This is supported by core services that provide the learning content, communication, collaboration, assessment and administration of the IntelCities courses (i.e. the learning materials, skill packages and training exercises used for developing socially-inclusive and participatory urban regeneration programmes) which are available to the CoP (see Figure 2).

The E-Learning Materials and Courses

The e-learning materials are made up of three IntelCities courses. The first short course is

Figure 2. Sample of learning material for the Level 1 (lesson 3) eCitizenship course. Source: http://elrn. eurodyn.com/edos/elearning/welcome.do

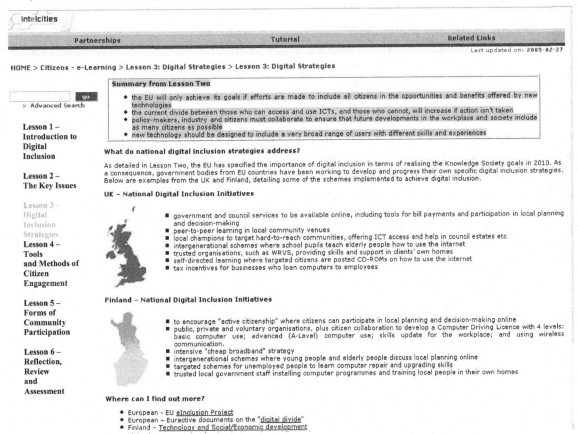

aimed at members of the public with an interest in becoming more involved in civic life via the use of new technologies. The second course targets administrators within the public sector: those responsible for meeting citizens' expectations, in terms of access to electronically-enhanced eGov services. The third is aimed at policy-makers and strategists within city administrations who want to make their cities leading examples of the digitally-inclusive knowledge society. Together, these three courses make up the CoPs eCitizenship module. Under this heading, the course materials tackle the same core concepts: digital inclusion; citizens' expectations and the means by which cities can meet the needs of their e-ready citizens, whilst enabling access for those currently excluded

from the knowledge management systems and digital technologies underlying the public's use of online services. The pitch and tone vary accordingly across the suite of materials, yet each progresses the learner towards an understanding of the tools and methods currently available for cities to use to engage citizens as members of an online community.

Whilst the short course on digital inclusion provides as set of 'taster' sessions on citizens' engagement with digital technologies, no prior experience of ICTs is needed as a prerequisite for the learning. It is designed to be open to everyone and provide universal access as a bottom line for the learning experiences to follow. Level 2 is targeted at citizens with different levels of experiential learning and, therefore, abilities. Those collaborating on the development of learning materials for Levels 2 have developed three representative e-service users, each with different levels of familiarity with ICTs. The novice user is characterised as a citizen with little experience in using computers or the internet, but an interest in learning how to find information and pay bills online. The semi-skilled, or intermediate level user is a citizen with regular access to a computer and average to-good ICT skills. At this level of ICT ability, the citizen is interested in locating detailed, up to- date information online and in submitting comments and feedback to the City. The advanced user has frequent access to ICTs and is highly skilled and confident in their ability to interact using the internet. This user wants maximum benefit from new technologies and is keen to interact with the City via services such as online debates and e-petitions.

These three characterisations serve to elicit the relationship between citizens' ICT skills and competencies and the e-services they expect their cities to provide. Figure 3 summarises this relationship. The left-hand column details the expectations of novice ICT users, the challenges these represent and action cities can take in response to them. With little access to ICTs, such as home PCs or 3G mobile phones, the novice ICT user has little confidence in the e-services under development and the potential benefits they offer. In terms of their priorities, citizens at this level prioritise the accessibility of new online services. The challenge cities are faced with is that of meeting these very basic requirements without alienating those which have higher skill levels.

As Figure 3 indicates, citizens with minimal ICT skills are unable to make use of cutting-edge, interactive technologies. Digitally-excluded citizens, often amongst the most socially deprived, risk being further alienated for the reason they lack the skills to progress in the workplace and are not members of the online communities, where citizens and their cities consult with one another and meet to deliberate on issues of public concern. By investing in community-based training initiatives and online user support, cities ensure that citizens with little-or-no-ICT experience are offered the chance to develop their skills, be included and participate in more complex interactive online activities.

Figure 3. Citizens' skills and competencies. Source: Campbell and Deakin (2005)

	information	transaction	consultation
what citizens expect	accessible secure reliable efficient quick user-friendly engaging minimum user effort	up-to-date seamless responsive comprehensive high quality	intuitive personalised self-service interoperable increased transparency & accountability democratic engagement active citizenship
the challenges facing cities	encouraging to new users citizen-friendly language must be easy to use secure and private accessible by all citizens can develop their ICT skills	meeting set response times maintaining continuity introducing electronic case handling interactive services at appropriate technical levels	cost-effective/ cutting edge technology citizens as customers encouraging citizens to engage as an online community empowering citizens to improve the quality of online services
how cities can respond to these challenges	enable access from a range of devices personalised information life-cycle approach clear security and privacy statements training and support available online and in community venues	thematic entry points news/ update pages content management systems evaluated pilot projects large-scale e-case handling choice of feedback mechanisms	procuring technology based on performance requirements participating in international networks publicly-available benchmarking results providing resources to maximise deliberation

citizens' skills and competencies →

Figure 3 identifies citizens at the lowest skill level as seeking engagement at an informational level. Citizens who have progressed beyond basic ICT skills are referred to as seeking engagement at a transactional level. The semi-skilled, or intermediate level, user has better access to ICTs than the novice and is already comfortable accessing basic information and making bill payments online. It also identifies the intermediate user's expectations: for up to-date information of a high quality and the seamless transition between different online services and websites.

As with the novice user, the user at this level requires services that are pitched at the appropriate skill level, again presenting the city with the challenge of meeting the needs of a diverse society. At this 'transactional' level, citizens are interested in establishing online communication with the City and, in order to engage these users and encourage repeated use of these services, cities are required to respond within set times. Electronic case handling is listed in Figure 3 as one method of managing the information flow and building citizens' trust in e-services, as are content management systems to ensure continuity across a range of web pages and services.

Citizens with advanced ICT skills and regular access pose an addition set of challenges to their cities, given their expectations of personalised and intuitive services like those offered in e-commerce. However, citizens at this level of ability are also able to make use of the more complex technologies cities can offer to encourage online consultative and deliberative participation. By engaging increasing numbers of citizens in online dialogue, city administrations harness the knowledge and experiences of local people in order to improve the quality of services they provide.

The Level 3 set of lessons examines the skill bases and competencies of a user who has just such abilities, who expects their city to provide personalised and intuitive services and to make use of the more complex technologies cities can offer to encourage online consultation and deliberative participation. Level 3 provides a set of lessons on how cities can use the skills and competencies their citizens have to make use of these complex technologies and become leading examples of the IntelCities CoP. Two inter-active video lessons have also been produced to support this set of lessons.

The Pedagogy

The pedagogy of the course materials is grounded in the transformational logic of situational learning, very much action-orientated and problem-based in the sense the platform's knowledge transfer capacity is framed in 'structured query language' (SQL) protocols. This can be classified as follows:

- For the basic level of learning and this respective user of the ICTs, it is instructional, providing an outline of the material needed to be informed about them and develop the literacy required for any such communication.

- With the intermediate level of user, the pedagogy is again instructional, but the emphasis here is on the social context of the eCity platform and sets out the skill bases, competencies and training needed for citizens to use the services and engage with others by carrying out online transactions, or by consulting with others as members of a community.

- The pedagogy of the advanced learner is constructivist. Drawing upon the learning of the previous level, this course uses this knowledge as a platform for citizens to use as a means of intervening in decision-making processes, engaging in consultations and deliberating with others to influence the level of government service provision. Here, users of the eCity platform learn how to actively participate as members of an online community that seeks to democratise decision-making and develop the degree of reciprocity which is needed to build trust between citizens and the organizations governing the delivery of services.

Having established the user requirements and found an e-Learning platform to carry them, attention has turned to the development of this into a KM system and digital library supporting the activities of the IntelCities CoP. Developed as back-office functions, attention has subsequently been given to integrating the KM system and digital library into the IntelCities middleware and delivering the resulting pool of eGov services to citizens wanting to learn about them.

THE KNOWLEDGE MANAGEMENT SYSTEM AND DIGITAL LIBRARY

The KMS is organised and grouped according to the requirements of a pre-specified, but evolving, eGov services ontology. The overriding objective of the IntelCities CoP is to provide an e-Learning platform that allows access to a KMS and which is both accessible and usable. This objective has been met by developing the KM system's Document Manager (DM). The DM developed has built the capacity to perform Ontology-based Annotation in Semantic Web for the easy creation, application and use of semantic data. This is particularly important where learners require the KMS to perform a deep and semantically-rich annotation of materials.

The digital library is the electronic repository storing the information available for extraction by the KMS. The rationale for developing the digital library as part of the KM system lies with the potential the DM has to function as a service capable of:

- Capturing, storing, indexing and (re)distributing the learning materials, skill packages and training manuals.

- Extending this to include the formal semantics (metadata, knowledge) for the retrieval and extraction of the said materials, packages and manuals available to support the integrated modelling of eGov services.
- Offering access to the extensive range of products stored as knowledge objects in the digital library and available for extraction by those managing the development of the middleware as a platform for pooling the said eGov services together and extending delivery of them to citizens as front-end users.

SEMANTICALLY-INTEROPERABLE EGOV. SERVICES

Utilising the Semantic Web paradigm, the e-Learning platform is capable of delivering data to its users in a way that enables a more effective 'query-minded' discovery, integration and reuse of the knowledge which can be accessed from the digital library. Through the platform's utilisation of Semantic Web technologies, data uploaded by the KMS (as information available from the system's DM) presents knowledge products corresponding not only to documents (web pages, images, audio clips, etc. as the internet currently does), but more pre-defined objects, such as people, places, organizations and events deposited in the digital library.

Using a pre-defined ontology of this type, the DM allows multiple relations between objects to be created. Currently none of the e-learning platforms forming the basis of the CoP's S.W.O.T. analysis offer such services. Until now it has only been common to see references to the possible convergence of e-learning platforms, KMS and digital libraries. This platform and system gets beyond the call for the convergence of such technologies and begins to integrate eGov services with the ICTs available to achieve this. Perhaps most importantly of all, the outcome of all this is an e-Learning platform, KMS and digital library with the embedded intelligence cities need to deliver semantically interoperable eGov services and meet this requirement as a standard measure of the socially-inclusive and participatory urban regeneration programmes the IntelCities CoP has a particular interest in.

INTEGRATION INTO THE ECITY PLATFORM

Figure 4 illustrates how the IntelCities CoP proposes the integration of the e-Learning platform, KMS and digital library should take place and shows the workflow supporting this. This shows the workflow as having its basis in the digital library and KMS of the e-Learning platform. It also shows the workflow between the courses held on the said platform and KMS. Here the system's DM is shown to semantically annotate the learning materials, skill packages and train-

ing manuals supporting the courses held on the platform and mark them up in line with the index and classification of the eGov services ontology evolving to manage the knowledge drawn from the digital library.

These back-office functions in turn lead to the creation of the citizen engagement matrix, designed as a semantically-rich grid, allowing communities to be inclusive and actively participate (via consultative and deliberative operations) in the development of the middleware as applications which this platform of eGov services delivers to the front-end. These developments provide the knowledge management toolkit. This term is preferred to "e-Learning platform" because this best captures the contribution the tools: the electronic repository, document manager, semantic annotation and mark-up system, make to the type of knowledge management and digital library services currently found on city portals.

While it is recognised this journey from the front-end eGov services to the middleware and

Figure 4. Integration into the eCity platform

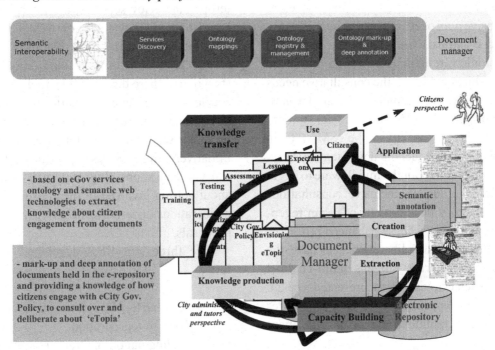

towards the back-office functions, represents a significant detour, it is undertaken because the path taken does mark a significant step forward. Not only in terms of the additional learning services that existing city portals are now able to offer, but in 'squaring of the circle' and providing a platform with the intelligence - KMS and digital library - to integrate the front, middle and back-office sections of their organization as a virtual CoP. As a virtual CoP that in this instance is based on standards which are interoperable across a growing pool of extensible eGov services and have the capacity to support socially-inclusive and participatory urban regeneration programs.

THE 'ETOPIA' DEMONSTRATOR

At present this integration is mainly technical, concerning the software developments needed to host such services and meet with the semantics of the platform's e-learning needs, knowledge transfer requirements and capacity building commitments. This currently takes the form of an 'eTopia' demonstrator, showing in session-managed logic how the eCity platform accesses the extensive pool of eGov services located in the back-office and uses the intelligence embedded in the middleware to deliver Level 3 (advanced e-Citizenship) courses on the consultative needs and deliberative requirements of such developments. This provides a 'real time' demonstration' of the platform's capacity to be 'SMART' in developing both the technical and semantically-rich content required for the middleware to begin supporting the socially-inclusive consultations and participatory deliberations of urban regeneration programmes. These enhanced processes of consultation and deliberation also have the advantage of offering citizens multi-channel access to such eGov services, presented to them as socially-inclusive and participatory urban regeneration programmes designed to bring about

improvements in the quality of life (Deakin and Allwinkle, 2007). This goes a long way to:

- Uncover the business logic needed to base the intelligence-driven (re)organization of cities on and standards required to benchmark the performance of the platform against.
- Provide the performance-based measures needed to assess whether any plans cities posses to develop eGov services (over the platform) have the embedded intelligence (the learning, knowledge-based competencies and skills) required to support such actions.
- Also provide the means to evaluate if such planned developments build the (intellectual) capacity – learning, knowledge-based competencies and skills – needed to support such actions.

TESTING THE ETOPIA DEMONSTRATOR

In addition to developing the semantically-interoperable eGov services, the IntelCities' CoP has also sought to evaluate how well they perform as components of the eCity platform. This has meant developing three 'eTopia demonstrator' storylines, where the typical learners referred to previously, use the eCity platform to query the development of urban regeneration programmes by either searching for information on a given initiative, gaining accessing to possible online transactions supporting any such actions, or about getting involved in the consultations and deliberations underlying the governance of such proposals.

The three storylines developed scenarios for:

- Accessing local services in neighbourhoods subject to regeneration.
- Carrying out online transactions related to the use of land.

- Consultations and deliberations about the safety and security issues underlying the governance of urban regeneration programmes.

The storylines aim to fulfil three requirements: first to continue the loosely structured scenarios used to demonstrate the significance of the citizen-led learning agenda developed under the alpha version of the eCity platform; secondly, to integrate this into the back-office business logic of the beta version testing of the eCity platform and thirdly, to establish whether the interoperability resulting from the vertical and horizontal integration of the services is beneficial because it enables urban regeneration programmes to work better in meeting citizens' expectations. The following shall summarise the scenario-based testing of the third and "advanced" level of eCitizenship held on the e-Learning platform and accessed via the KMS.

The exercise began by introducing an 'integrated eGov services scenario' in which two people, Mark and Sarah, are keen to discover what governance services the eCity platform offers for them to learn about how it is possible to become actively involved in initiatives promoted by cities to tackle problems associated with crime in their neighbourhood. The material demonstrates the ways in which Mark and Sarah can use the eCity platform (vis-à-vis, e-Learning platform and KMS) to not only learn about what they can do to tackle crime, but gain a knowledge of how the community's participation in such initiatives can lead to the development of safe and secure neighbourhoods.

The integrated eGov services scenario:

Both Mark and Sarah feel their family and work commitments have prevented them from becoming more involved with local groups in the past. However, both are keen on home computing and have broadband connections to the internet. Mark feels that the City's website should provide information on crime rates and proposes that he and Sarah should logon and initiate a search to see how much they can learn about crime prevention initiatives online. They both want to know what their local administration is currently doing to address neighbourhood issues across the city and to submit their comments on past and present initiatives. They also feel it would be valuable to see what local groups are doing to tackle crime and whether any operate in their neighbourhood. They are also keen to discover how they, as citizens, can use the platform of services available on the city's information portal to ensure the urban regeneration programmes affecting their neighbourhoods are effective in tackling crime and making the areas safe and secure.

The steps Mark and Sarah can take to use the eCity platform as the means to begin tackling the problems they encounter are set out below, and in Table 4.

As Mark's work frequently takes him to one of the country's larger cities and he has been impressed by local initiatives to address neighbourhood issues, such as a 'Neighbourhood scheme involving local residents'; he's also interested in comparing the crime rates in his neighbourhood with those in other cities and finding which crime-prevention schemes seem to work best.

The information flowchart demonstrates how the eCity platform helps Mark and Sarah to query the developments they have a particular interest in and use this to find the information they need. They are able to access a wide range of data sets from their local administration, such as policy documents and strategies but, most importantly, they are able exploit the potential to use this information to interact with other like minded people as part of a larger group. In this aim, Mark and Sarah can develop a web page and host it on City's learning platform, setting out their concerns about crime and encouraging others to join them as members of an online community discussing how the City

Table 4. Step-wise logic of the service discovery

Step 1: use the city's website view information on current neighbourhood policies, strategies and targets;
Step 2: use the website to access a list of current public consultations;
Step 3: use the search tools to learn about any local online crime prevention and environmental clean-up groups, run either by local people or by the City;
Step 4: use the neighbourhood reporting service on the interactive maps to report problems such as abandoned cars, graffiti and fly tipping ;
Step 5: set up a web page for local people interested in tackling crime, security and environmental problems;
Step 6: post comments on the City's discussion boards;
Step 7: See how the City compares to other cities on issues like crime and pollution;
Step 8: submit a formal e-petition, setting out an agenda for tackling these types of neighbourhood issues.

Table 5. Benefits of the eCity platform

- accessing information from a wide range of City departments and databases at any time of day or night, from any location;
- locating relevant information in a quick, hassle-free way and interesting way;
- user-friendly search facilities which offer clearly signposted routes to relevant information;
- the opportunity to personalise web space hosted by the City, in order to engage other local groups or individuals;
- the ability to add useful features to personalised spaces, such as mailing list sign-ups and links to other pages;
- providing a range of starting points and options to either continue or end the search at various points;
- allowing users to consider how the information they obtain affects them, easily contribute their comments/ feedback and actively promote change.

should tackle neighbourhood safety and security issues. As an online community they are also able to compare their City's agenda for tackling crime with those of other administrations and learn about good practice examples from elsewhere. These materials can in turn be used to shape the community's online discussions and enable Mark and Sarah to submit a formal e-petition to those responsible for leading the development of such initiatives. The "one-stop shop" approach of the eCity platform offers them a range of benefits, such as shown in Table 5.

Meeting Citizens' Expectations

The results of this testing exercise are encouraging. Figure 5 demonstrates the responses of the group

in quesiton. As this shows, all found the scenarios, steps and information flow to be understandable, in terms of the vocabulary used and also easy to follow. One attendee commented, "I found the material quite open, easy to understand. It made me think more about how I would go about things in the future." As Table 6 also illustrates, most of those participating in the testing exercise found the demonstration to be offer a useful representation of how to learn about the eCity platform's on-line services and use the information this uploads to transfer knowledge about how communities of like minded people can ensure the safety and security measures of urban regeneration programmes work in their interests.

Figure 5. Information flow of the testing scenario

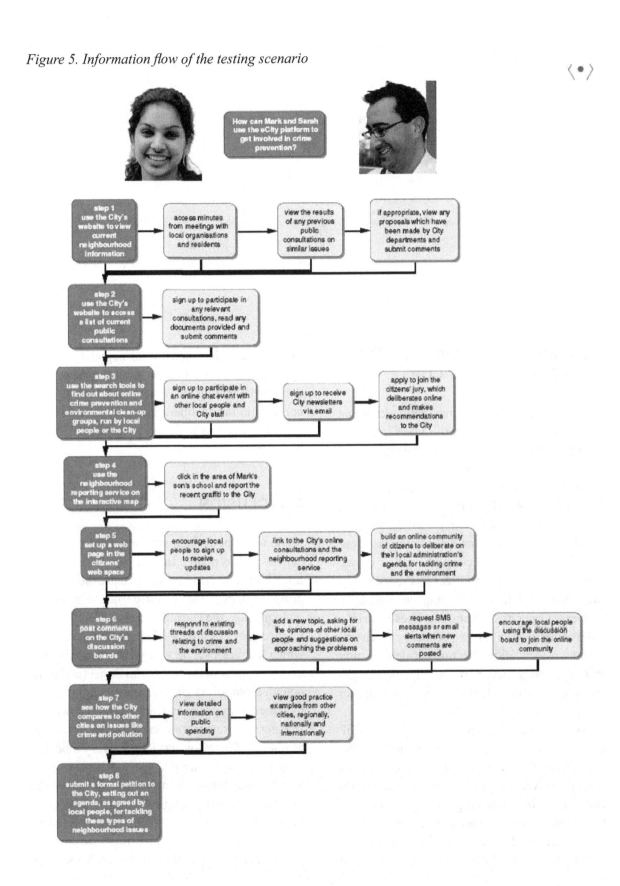

Table 6. Feedback responses to the scenario

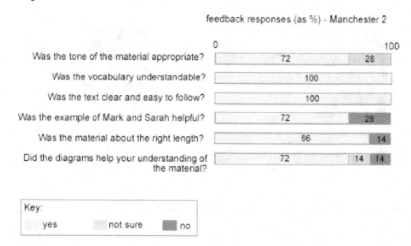

SUSTAINING THE DEVELOPMENT OF THE INTELCITIES COP

Table 7 illustrates the research, networking and consorted actions that underlie IntelCities CoP and which have used to sustain the development of this particular virtual learning organization. As can be seen, much of this Research and Technical Development (R&TD) is multi-scalar in nature, covering a range of international, national and regional knowledge domains. The funding for these activities has been and currently still is drawn from EC and UK-based R&TD Programmes. These R&TD actions are complemented by a number of Capacity Building exercises at various scales of intervention. As can be seen, such virtual learning organizations are not self-determining entities and only survive by sourcing the budgets available to finance their development as either research, or capacity building exercises.

As a shared enterprise, the IntelCities CoP operates a match (joint venture) funding business model and draws upon the income this generates to fund the R&TD activities underlying the integration of the e-Learning platform, KMS and digital library's into the middleware of the eGov. Services model. Exploitation of the middleware is organized through and sustained by research

institutes and ICT companies negotiating local agreements with cities on how they can best deploy this intelligence as a means to govern the consultation and deliberation services of socially-inclusive and participatory urban regeneration programs.

CONCLUSION

Made up of both open source software groups, experts and lay people, this chapter has argued the IntelCities CoP is unique in the sense the network provides an example of a virtual organization set up to manage the learning needs and knowledge requirements of a technological platform. That which has been set up as a virtual organization under the name of the IntelCities Project and technological platform that in turn develops the means by which to meet the learning needs, knowledge transfer requirements and capacity building commitments of its eGov services delivery model.

The examination has suggested there are three features that define the Intelcities CoP and which give it a sense of meaning and purpose. These are: the shared enterprise, the technology and online services. The shared enterprise relates to the work undertaken by all members of the IntelCities CoP

Table 7. R&TD, network and concerted action projects

R&TD, Network and Concerted Action projects 1997-2002	R&TD	2003+	Scale	Fund
BEQUEST	IntelCities	LUDA	International	EC E&C
INTELCITY		SusComm	National	UK ESRC
	Capacity Building			
		Deliver	Trans-national	EC Structural
		eBusiness	Inter-regional	EC Inter-reg
		URBan	Regional	EC Structural

to develop an integrated model of eGov services. It has gone on to underline the importance of these as characteristics of the IntelCities CoP and in this aim has added another six qualities that have been exploited by the network to develop a virtual learning organization which is capable of bridging the gap which exists between the type 1 and 2 classifications offered by Amin and Roberts (2008). This has been done in the interests of illustrating how the IntelCity CoP spans the divide between what are in crude terms representative of the technical and social components of virtual organizations. The additional features referred to clearly highlight these qualities and reflect there importance, but in addition to this they also serve to underscore the technical rational and social purpose of the virtual organization in question. This suggests that in developing integrated eGov service models it is not possible for intelligent cities to develop as either type 1 or 2 CoPs because the shared enterprise and joint venture characteristics of such virtual learning organizations means they have to be both technical and social.

The examination has also reported on the intelligent solutions cities are seeking out as a means to meet their e-learning needs, knowledge transfer requirements and capacity building commitments. Having gone on to discuss the technical solutions adopted to integrate the eGov services model with the legacy systems operated by cities involved in this enterprise, attention has turned

to the SOA adopted as the business model for the eCity platform. From here the paper has gone on to outline the 'intelligent' solution cities are developing as e-learning platforms for managing the knowledge transfer requirements and capacity building commitments of such organizations.

As has been shown, these developments are valuable because they provide the means to address the criticisms of the learning services currently available on city portals and offer the opportunity for the emerging technologies of the e-Learning platform, KMS and digital libraries, to meet the learning needs, knowledge transfer requirements and capacity building commitments of the IntelCities CoP. This it has been suggested, marks a significant step forward in the development of learning services and offers the opportunity for platforms of this type to develop as a KMS supported by digital libraries. In view of this, the chapter has suggested that if the full significance of these technically-innovations is to be realised, then this integration needs to progress and requires the e-Learning platform, KM system and digital library developed for such purposes, to not only be interoperable across the IntelCities middleware, but all the eGov services which are available to citizens at the front-end. The way in which the IntelCities CoP proposes to achieve this is particularly innovative because the organization offers a strategy to consolidate the underlying learning aspirations of city portals, but as particular types of eGov services that have previously remained beyond the reach of the platforms developed for such purposes. That is to say, out with the grasp of previous attempts which have been made by such organizations to develop a knowledge-base capable of delivering the consultation and deliberation services key to all this.

REFERENCES

Amin, A., & Roberts, J. (2008). Knowing in action: beyond communities of practice. *Research Policy, 37*, 353–369.

Campbell, F., & Deakin, M. (2005). Cities as leading examples of digitally-inclusive knowledge societies: the e-citizenship course, representative users, pedagogy and engagement matrix. In M. Osborne & B. Wilson (Eds.), *Making Knowledge Work*. Stirling: Stirling University.

Curwell, S., Deakin, M., Cooper, I., Paskaleva-Shapira, K., Ravetz, J., & Babicki, D. (2005). Citizens expectations of information cities: implications for urban planning and design. *Building Research and Information, 22*(1), 55-66.

Deakin, M. (2007). e-Topia, SUD and ICTs: taking the digitally-inclusive urban regeneration thesis full circle. *Journal of Urban Technology, 14*(3), 131-139.

Deakin, M & Allwinkle, S. (2007). e-Topia, SUD and ICTs: the post-human nature, embedded intelligence, cyborg-self and agency of digitally-inclusive regeneration platforms. *International Journal of the Humanities, 5*(2),199-208.

Deakin, M. & Allwinkle, S. (2007). Urban regeneration and sustainable communities: the role of networks, innovation and creativity in building successful partnerships. *Journal of Urban Technology, 14*(1), 77-91.

Deakin, M. & Allwinkle, S. (2006). The IntelCities community of practice: the e-learning platform, knowledge management system and digital library for semantically-interoperable e-governance services, *International Journal of Knowledge, Culture and Change Management, 6*(3),155-162.

Deakin, M., Van Isacker, K. & Wong. A. (2004) *Review of the IntelCities Knowledge Capture Requirements Using a S.W.O.T. Analysis.* Edinburgh: Napier University.

Ellis, D., Oldridge, R., & Vasconcelos, A. (2004) Community and Virtual Community. *Annual Review of Information Sciences and Technology, 38*, 146–186.

Graham, S. and Marvin, S. (1996). *Telecommunications and the City.* London: Routledge.

Johnson, C. (2001). A survey of current research on online communities of practice. *Internet and Higher Education, 4*, 45–60.

Josefsson, U. (2005). Coping with illness online: the case of patients online communities. *The Information Society, 21*, 143–153.

Lombardi, P. and Curwell. S. (2005). INTELCITY Scenarios for the City of the Future. In D. Miller & D. Patassini (Eds.), *Beyond Benefit Cost Analysis.* Aldershot: Ashgate.

Mitchell. W. (2000). *e-Topia: Urban Life, Jim But Not as You Know It.* Cambridge Massachusetts: MIT Press.

Orr, J. (1996). Talking About Machines: *An Ethnography of a Modern Job.* New York: IRL Press (an imprint of Cornell University Press).

Wenger, E., (1998). *Communities of Practice: Learning, Meaning, and Identity.* Cambridge: Cambridge University Press.

Wenger, E., (2000). Communities of practice and social learning systems, *Organization, 7*(2), 225–246.

KEY TERMS

Capacity Building: Refers to assistance which is provided to organizations which have a need to develop a certain skill or competence, or a general upgrading of performance ability. Most capacity is built by societies themselves, sometimes in the public, sometimes in the non-governmental and sometimes in the private sector. They are activities which strengthen the knowledge, abilities, skills and behaviour of individuals and improve institutional structures and processes such that an organization can efficiently meet its mission and goals in a sustainable way.

Community of Practice: Groups of people who share a concern or a passion for something they do and learn how to do it better as they regularly interact with one another as knowing subjects.

Digital Library: A library in which collections are stored in digital formats (as opposed to print, microform, or other media) and is accessible by computers. The digital content may be stored locally, or accessed remotely via computer networks. The terms is diffuse enough to be applied to a wide range of collections and organizations, but, to be considered a digital library, an online collection of information must be managed by and made accessible to a community of users. Some web sites can be considered digital libraries, but they may not offer such functionality.

E-Government Services: Internet technologies that act as a platform for exchanging information, providing services and transacting with citizens, businesses, and other arms of government. Such e-Government services include:

- Pushing information over the Internet, e.g: regulatory services, general holidays, public hearing schedules, issue briefs, notifications, etc.
- Two-way communications between the agency and the citizen, a business, or another government agency. In this model, users can engage in dialogue with agencies and post problems, comments, or requests to the agency.
- Conducting transactions, e.g: lodging tax returns, applying for services and grants.
- Governance, e.g: online polling, voting, and campaigning.

The most important anticipated benefits of e-government include improved efficiency, convenience, and better accessibility of public services.

E-Learning: A general term used to refer to a form of learning in which the instructor and student are separated by space or time where the gap between the two is bridged through the use of online technologies. The term is used interchangeably in a wide variety of contexts and can be used to define a specific mode to attend a course or programmes of study where learners rarely, if ever, attend face-to-face contact, or rely upon such direct support.

Knowledge Transfer: The practical problem of transferring knowledge from one part of the organization to another (or all other) parts of the organization. It seeks to organize, create, capture or distribute knowledge and ensure its availability for future users. It is considered to be more than just a communication problem and more complex because:

- Knowledge resides in organizational members, tools, tasks, and their sub-networks.
- Much of the knowledge organizations have is tacit or hard to articulate in direct communication.

Middleware: The enabling technology. It functions as a piece of software that connects two or more applications, allowing them to exchange data. It is computer software that connects software components or applications. The software consists of a set of enabling services that allow multiple processes running on one or more machines to interact across a network. This technology evolved to provide for interoperability in support of the move to coherent distributed architectures, which are used most often to support and simplify complex, distributed applications. It is especially integral to modern information technology based on XML, SOAP, Web services, and service-oriented architecture.

Open Source Software: Computer software for which the human-readable source code is made available under a copyright license, or arrangement This permits users to use, change, and improve the software, and to redistribute it in modified or unmodified form. It is often developed in a public, collaborative manner.

Semantic-Interoperability: The ability of two or more systems or components to exchange or harmonize cognate subject vocabularies and/or knowledge organization schemes to be used for the purpose of effective and efficient resource discovery without significant loss of lexical or connotative meaning and without special effort by the user.

Virtual Organization: A collection of individuals, companies or organizations who have agreed to work together and use the ICTs as the main tools to enable, maintain and sustain member relationships in distributed work environments.

ENDNOTES

[1] See http://www.intelcitiesproject.com.

[2] While the title of the article by Amin and Roberts (2008) goes under the curious name of "beyond communities of practice", they use the phrase to suggest the need to "get beyond" the "undifferentiated" use of the term and requirement for more "contextualised" studies of the type set out in this chapter.

Chapter 19
The Argentine IT Professionals Forum:
Building the Basis for the Back Office through Communities of Practice

Ester Kaufman

Facultad Latinoamericana de Ciencias Sociales (FLACSO), Argentina

ABSTRACT

This chapter introduces the experience of the Argentine IT Professionals Forum (ITPF) that enriches the definition of processes involving the tasks of e-government. The ITPF has become a cross-agency network that involves all the IT professionals of the public administration. It was created in 2002 as a response to the institutional crisis in Argentina in order to solve problems associated with the IT areas. The most important contribution of the ITPF is the basis for the back office as an interesting management model, theoretically known as "communities of practice" (CoPs) and networks, which have become core organizational tools as far as carrying out difficult innovation processes, such as the development of free software, cross-agency applications, and interoperability. However, traditional government structures have found it hard to deal with this kind of processes. Among the specific tasks involved, it is worthwhile mentioning the development of suitable software, the creation of cross-agency consensus, the generation of institutional networks, and so forth.

INTRODUCTION

The experience of the Argentine IT Professionals Forum (ITPF[2]) enriches the definition of processes involving the tasks of e-government. The ITPF has become a cross-agency network that involves all the IT professionals of the public administration (in Argentina it is called Foro de Responsables Informáticos[3]). It was created in 2002 as a response to the institutional crisis in Argentina in order to solve problems associated with the IT areas. The most important contribution of the ITPF is the basis for the back office as an interesting management model. The components of this model are theoretically known as "communities of practice" (CoPs) and "networks," which have become core organizational tools as far as carrying out difficult innovation processes, such as the development of free software, cross-agency applications, and interoperability. However, traditional government structures have found it hard to deal with this kind of processes, such as the setup of the back office. Among the specific tasks involved, it is worthwhile mentioning the development of suitable software, the creation of cross-agency consensus, the generation of institutional networks, and so forth. The new institutional forms are based on knowledge management (KM) related to ongoing learning and innovation within organizational environments. These new models were incorporated into e-government plans in order to solve the problems of the integration of technological, institutional, and cultural systems. Nowadays, such models are at the core of knowledge theories and are being used in real e-government experiences.

To consider the ITPF experience and the usefulness of the CoPs in the development of e-government (including back-office plans), I will deal with the following items: the background, including definitions and theoretical approaches; the context in which the ITPF took place; and the technological models at the time and the current problems they have been generating. Then I will describe the different periods of the ITDF and other experiences (future and emerging trends), and finally I will lay out the conclusion of those experiences.

BACKGROUND

Much research to date has focused on the front office—on the use and take-up of electronic public services by citizens and businesses. However, no systematic research has dealt with the way public agencies are using ICT to reorganize in order to change the relationship between the front and back offices. Bearing this in mind, I would like to discuss, in detail, a striking experience of the ITPF within the Argentine central government. Its most important contributions are the following:

1. The creation of the basis for the back office, consisting of cross-integration among IT areas at the national government level, as the first step toward further development.
2. The implementation of a management model that guarantees this back office. This model is based on KM techniques that take up institutional forms such as networks and CoPs.
3. The design of new perspectives, differentiated from those in force in the '90s (new public management [NPM] and the technological model).
4. The awareness of the huge task involved in solving the basic problems generated by the approaches of the past decade.

In the following sections I will develop these contributions, taking into account the models and underlying views.

The Basis for the E-Government Back Office

The tasks involved in this basis take place prior to the development of back offices for specific services to citizens and businesses, such as driving licenses, passports, and payment of taxes. These tasks consist of organizing the information systems in such a way that they enable the government to share the data. They include, for example, the following:

1. How to use standards for feeding people's names to the systems
2. How to recognize state employees

3. How to locate files
4. How to agree on shared software developed by specific IT public areas (in case the proprietary software is not available, is unsuitable, or is too expensive)

In its final report (Danish Technological Institute, 2004), the European Commission takes these tasks for granted in defining the back office. According to them:

the "back office" is a term relative to the front office which in this context is a user interface to an online service. The back office receives and processes the information which the user of a service enters in order to produce and deliver the desired service. This may be done completely manually, fully automatically or by any combination of both. In some cases such a service is produced by one unit or back-office, in other cases several back-offices of the same service supplier agency or of different agencies, at the same government level or at different levels may be involved. (p. 16)

In developing countries, such as Argentina, the above-mentioned previous tasks do not take place due to the institutional weakness of the governments as well as their lack of technical rationality (Weber, 1992). Therefore, lines of action should be set up for the development of the back office. For that reason, I would like to describe a successful experience that would be useful as far as showing the lines of action to be taken.

New Management Models Underlying the ITPF Experience: Networks and CoPs

In order to understand the management model developed by the ITPF, it is essential to define and differentiate networks and CoPs, considering that this forum is a mixture of both forms. A community of practice is a group of peers with a common sense of purpose who agree to work together to share information, share a common repertoire of resources, build knowledge, develop expertise, and solve problems. CoPs are characterized by the willing participation of members and their ongoing interaction in developing a chosen area of practice and competencies. Identity and autonomy are essential to enhance CoPs.

On the other hand, networks allow a mutually negotiated specialization: They are made of heterogeneous agents whose cognitive activity is to exchange knowledge. They interact together through informal and formal meetings, and the recruitment rule is mutual trust" (Cohendet, Creplet, & Dupouët, 2001, p. 6).

The CoPs describe groups of people who share a concern or a passion for something they do and who interact regularly to learn how to do it better[4] (Lave & Wenger, 1991). On entering these types of communities, every new member learns from the veteran members participating in certain activities related to the practice performed by the community. Thus, their participation progresses from the periphery until it reaches a full integration (Falivene, Silva, & Gurmendi, 2003).

The fact that the ITPF has functioned alongside traditional structures is also an enriching experience. It gives strength to new institutional models empowering e-government plans through the ICT networks tissue, which constitutes an essential feature of the information society.

Contexts and Models in the Last Decade: New Outlooks

Globalization has meant for many countries the inability to function in an autonomous way. This effect has been even more startling in developing countries such as Argentina. In the last decade, the government model responsible for this lack of autonomy was a limited version of NPM.[5]

NPM in Argentina was applied only to privatizations and downsizing in public agencies. Less attention was given to the training and recruitment of professionals by public agencies. Instead, recruitment was organized mainly around political cronyism. Because of this, the government did not count on specialized professionals to carry out its policies. Neither did it develop sound methods for enhancing the quality of its human resources, a key strategy to implement the e-government agenda. In Argentina, bureaucracies usually lack any behaviour toward Weberian "technical rationalities." The state is trapped by political interests and sluggish routines.

With regard to state personnel, every administration appoints its own public officials. The result of this chronic practice is that once a new administration takes power—bringing along a new set of appointees—the former members usually keep their jobs but are highly mistrusted. This is a recurring cycle in public administrations.

Every new administration announces its own e-government project that is seldom fulfilled.

The above-mentioned scenario makes it difficult to develop a sustainable e-government plan because deep restructuring is called for in order to achieve a step-by-step integration of the public sector. Ironically, this limited NPM seemed to be working by the mid-'90s, fed by an overabundance of foreign funding (by multilateral organizations) and political oversight with regard to the public debt that was being accrued. Parts of those funds were allotted to the purchase of ICT for government use.

It was in this context that a technological model of e-government was set up as a supposed emulation of American politics. This model was supported on the still-current belief that the incorporation of ICT was mainly an IT issue rather than a public-policies issue. The reliance of the government on a technological model meant profits for some businesses as well as for some public officials who allowed the random purchase of technology at high costs. This only improved the efficiency of a few isolated areas of the public administration such as tax collection. The government has not yet grasped the potential of ICT to offer better performance in order to help develop the information society.

Up to the present, the Argentine administrations have only applied general formulas suggested by international organizations that have been repeated automatically by government officials and consulting agencies. These formulas present a straightforward and mechanical view of development in four consecutive and cumulative stages:

1. Informative stage
2. Interactive stage
3. Transactional stage
4. Integrational stage

However, no logic can guarantee this lineal development. Considering the self-centeredness that characterizes many third-world administrations, the above process is unthinkable except for tax collection and e-procurement. Otherwise, many third-world administrations have no interest in sharing information or interchanging different points of view with fellow citizens or users. That is to say, Stages 2 through 4 never take place, which goes to show that e-government policies are not carried out seriously. Had they been taken seriously, a reengineering of structures and processes together with cultural changes would have been taken into account.[6] In contrast with first-world governments, the Argentine administrations did not understand these complex processes. E-government policies were limited to the purchase and installation of technology and the setting up of sloppy informational Web sites. These isolated courses of action brought about a negative connotation concerning the potential of e-government. Argentine citizens were under the impression that such policies had been motivated by shady businesses, which meant a profit for government officials. In some cases, these suspicions were proved true (Herzog, 2002).

Even if no corruption was involved, officials used e-government as a purely technological model. Considered as such, some basic concepts associated with this model are as follows:

1. The assumption that technology acquisition automatically implies positive effects
2. The fact that it is a self-centered model, which generates incomplete institutional information without any degree of participation from nongovernmental actors
3. E-government is considered a matter that belongs to IT professionals, not an issue concerning the generation of public policies.
4. The implementation of e-government consists of building portals featuring some official information (informative model), a little technology, and some governmental internal electronic procedures, all overlapping the existing bureaucratic structure.

The Awareness of the Basic Problems of the Technological Model

Bruce Rocheleau (1997) points out the failures of a related model applied to the reinvention policies launched by Al Gore in the United States. This author emphasizes that sharing information is made difficult in an organization in spite of advances in the ability to share. Politicians have resorted to the Internet as a way of providing easy access to information. This ability of technology to solve problems has raised a false optimism in the political spectrum given that there is more hope than empirical proof.

Rocheleau (1997) suggests the need to examine information-system failures more closely in order to draw lessons on how to improve their performance. These difficulties could be traced to what I call "the basis of the back office."

Rocheleau (1997) identified some basic problems of this model and their possible causes. Among them, he mentioned inadequate training, caused by lack of investment, low priority, and poor quality of training; poor quality of data caused by inadequate oversight, lack of technical controls, and organizational resistance; and obstacles to sharing data caused by interoper-

ability problems, database incompatibilities, and organizational obstacles.

Since its inception in 2002, the ITPF has tried to solve some of the kinds of problems mentioned by Rocheleau. The following list of proposals was devised in one of its first meetings:

1. Availability of IT application systems such as keeping track of files, human-resource management, income and expenditure control, patrimony, and training
2. Use of standards to classify goods and services
3. Design of basic outlines to develop government Web sites
4. Development of techniques to improve interoperability, and the definition of standard and metadata schemes
5. Improvement and optimization of agencies' connectivity and the use of the Internet through safety tools
6. Compilation of strategic issues to generate specific training

THE ITPF: FUNCTIONING, STRENGTHS, AND CHALLENGES

Functioning of the ITPF

In order to set up the present ITPF, created at the beginning of 2002, representatives of over 100 national public agencies were invited to participate. Ninety organizations and 200 technicians are now involved in different processes within the forum. This methodology was developed in Argentina by the Latin American School of Social Sciences (FLACSO).The KM applied consists of articulating several work meetings where the accomplished tasks are agreed upon and new actors incorporated. The meetings may be plenary, thematic, or group meetings. They are mainly face-to-face gatherings.

The global structure of the activities depends on a core group open to all members of the ITPF led by the ITPF coordinator. Their purpose is to develop a strategic viewpoint of ITPF, and plan the meetings according to the topics already agreed upon by the whole group in previous meetings.

Participants of the plenary meetings are professionals in the IT areas within the national government, although over time professionals from other local governments as well as from the academic sector have joined in. The average turnout was 100 people with monthly meetings throughout 2002 and 2003. Lately, the meetings have been less frequent due to the widespread growth of the virtual forum.

The plenary meetings are divided into three stages:

1. Presentation and consensus of the tasks accomplished by the core group and by the work groups and new lines of action
2. Work performed in workshops, where new ideas and proposals are discussed openly
3. Conclusion with a shared presentation of the subjects addressed in the workshops and action plans. At this point, new work groups are set up, and the existing ones may be modified. Should a relevant topic require discussing in depth, external specialists are called in to present experiences and existing papers at a special plenary meeting.

Goals are established in each meeting in order to connect one meeting with the next. These goals are written up in a record of proceedings. Taken together, these documents allow the members to trace the steady quality of the interchange, the building of a balance of information among the different actors, a prospective analysis, as well as the history of the process. Likewise, the collective conceptualizations enable the upgrading of the level of understanding and the monitoring of tasks, advances, or setbacks.

The work groups are fully dedicated to the development of leading issues for the back office of an electronic government, including, for example, the following:

1. **Free Software Group:** It performs discussion and legislative support activities on draft laws dealing with that subject. It relays the existing developments in the state as an input for its own work on software development.
2. **Cross-Agencies Applications Group:** It focuses on the need to incorporate IT processes into the ordinary administrative ones in different areas within the state, such as human resources, files, hospital administration, and financial administration. Its line of action is to identify best practices, coordinating their transfer, and to generate upgraded applications.
3. **Interoperability Group:** The aim of this group is to create a framework of technological standards and data structure that enable the users to interchange information. Interoperability is the ability of a system or a product to work with other systems or products without special effort on the part of the user.

ITPF Strengths and Challenges

These strengths are to be found in the following:

1. In the steady attendance of its members, considering that the initiatives are generated by the permanent or quasi-permanent staff
2. In the certainty that the work that has been produced will be implemented given that the practitioners who present the innovations coincide with the ones who implement them

3. In the legitimacy of its productions due to the general consensus regarding their suitability

4. In its transparency and responsibility as a result of periodic and steady collective control of the initiatives, processes, and products

The challenges the ITPF has to confront are as follows:

1. Its continuity beyond changes in government

2. The need for greater resources considering the extraordinary growth of its activities, especially for the development of free software

3. The channeling of foreign funding destined to information technologies for their use and control via the forum

4. The use of the virtual ITPF as its own efficient means

THE IMPORTANCE OF THE ITPF

The ITPF has become a key actor in the development of the first stages of e-government initiatives by putting into operation the basic platform that could solve such problems as interoperability, cross-agency applications, and the development of suitable software, among others.[7]

The work performed by the ITPF suggests solutions to problems regarding the basic conditions that would ensure the enforcement of an elementary e-government and that would enable upgrading in order to make up networks of different levels (local, state, national, international) and origins (public or private), that is to say, the creation of "back networks."[8,9]

By elementary e-government, I mean one that starts the creation of the missing basic platform of the back office in order to interconnect several government agencies. These agencies offer a front office where services will be integrated cohesively according to the customers' needs. This process will eventually lead to a "one-stop shop" enabling access to services that will be grouped together and classified by subject. The development of the back office must lead up to reorganization as well as a redefinition of processes and structures. Further, it must also contemplate changing organizational cultures. This basic platform of the back office should also be the basis for a progressive technological development that could establish sensible criteria for purchasing hardware and software. Likewise, this technological development could pave the way for the creation of suitable software to ensure better services and to protect confidential government data.

For the time being, this concept of the basic platform of the back office is carried out only by the ITPF. The forum has provided prompt responses in contrast to the lack of action on the part of the authorities responsible for e-government politics. After President Menem's second term in office, the relationship between ICT and the government went on a discouraging downward path. The miracle recipes of the '90s never materialized, unjustly discrediting the potential of ICT and hence putting at risk the placement of our country with respect to the new economy. E-government policies suffered likewise.

This loss of credibility mirrored the descent of the IT National Office[10] (ITNO) in government hierarchies. Having been an undersecretariat (during Menem's administration), it became a lower ranking office (Dirección Nacional) deprived of power to regulate ICT activities within the state.

This is the context in which the ITPF developed.

DEVELOPMENT OF THE ITPF

I deal with the ITPF experience separating it in two steps. The first started with the creation of the

ITPF (during the 2002 crisis) and finished when President Kirchner took office in May 2003. The second step deals with overcoming the crisis, and the relationship between ITPF and the new authorities and teams. I also deal with other similar international experiences. Finally, I arrive at the conclusions centered on the liaison between the traditional and emerging institutions.

In order to describe the above-mentioned sequences, I go back to the ITPF's inception.

Step One: The Crisis. Setting up the ITPF[11]

The ITPF came about in response to the institutional crisis that started in Argentina in December 2001. The forum designed within the public-management undersecretariat as an inter-institutional network, cutting across bureaucratic management tiers linked to the ITNO to solve problems associated with these fields.

In the past, experts from international organizations, such as the World Bank, the Inter-American Development Bank, and consulting companies, were sought after for the design and implementation of technological policies. However, these experiences failed due to the lack of contact between these agencies and the local staff who would have developed the knowledge gained by these experiences. When the crisis set in, the default was declared by the authorities, generating isolation from the international framework. Therefore, the government was left without economic resources to keep up expenditures related to outsourced consultants. As a result, the local IT staff started to assemble the ITPF invited by the ITNO.

Other forums were created as a result of the above-mentioned crisis. Indeed, during the crisis, government policies were focused on overcoming bureaucratic limitations. One of the most important government directives was informality. Different public sectors were called to create CoPs and networks. This gave rise to forums through

which organizational knowledge could be accessed to generate competencies and in this way overcome the crisis. Thus, cross-agency forums were created with reference to the following activities: human resources, file management, documentation centers, IT areas, budget management, statistics, international cooperation units, and so forth.

Finally, technology enabled the government to overcome the communication problem through the use of e-mail, thus solving inconveniences such as the lack of paper or ink for printers (crucial at the time). ICT provided a solution for these shortages in an informal way, ensuring an adequate number of functioning computers, something that could not be taken for granted at the time.[12] This issue is related to the IT area, as well as the supply of software programs. However, considering that it is next to impossible to afford proprietary software licenses, IT experts have continually faced the challenge of creating new applications.

The above-mentioned situations involve almost all the information pertaining to the state. With this in mind, the ITPF tackles these tasks in a highly motivated way, thus enhancing its members' self-esteem. The result has been that this forum is already providing effective answers to core IT questions that politicians had not been able to confront.

As already mentioned, the ITPF has outperformed other forums in the sense that it has acquired a quasi-autonomous profile due to the ability of its members to face constant innovation.[13]

I should mention that these forums were originally created having in mind training objectives at zero cost. This goal was perfectly accomplished by the ITPF using the KM model, which relies on the challenge of learning by doing and sharing experiences, thus transforming them into a common asset. This practice, never before applied in the booming '90s, turned out to be vital in the absence of other training resources. The only available source of expertise at the time was the knowledge developed throughout decades by the ITPF members.

Step Two: Overcoming the Crisis

As of 2003, the different groups have widened the scope of their tasks. This came about because the ITPF members became familiar with the KM tools. Another reason for this positive result was the stability that the Kirchner administration has achieved. Thus, the groups have been able to envision long-term core activities.[14]

Up to the present, an important activity has been the creation of the Web Space Group that deals with the ITPF Web site, where the interaction between the members is enhanced through virtual support.

Besides this, it is worthwhile noticing the development of the Free Software Group. It created three subgroups:

1. **Training Group:** It organizes training based on an inter-sectorial cooperative-practices model. A training scheme was developed in LINUX for three learning levels on which different organizations have been contributing complementary resources (tutors, classrooms, and computers).[15]
2. **Software Licenses Group:** It works on two items: the incorporation of free software developed outside the state, and state developments and internal transferences among public organizations.[16]
3. **Interstate Knowledge Network:** It is constantly being upgraded on the ITPF Web site, where successful public free-software experiences can be accessed. A support desk is under way thanks to the voluntary and anonymous help of the ITPF members.[17]

The other work groups continue improving their lines of action.[18]

The development of the ITPF can be seen as contrasting with bureaucratic structures that so far have failed to provide an integration proposal for a back office.

I will try go over the following issues in the light of the strained relationship between the network and stiff bureaucratic structures.

With regard to the network's range of action in the face of political institutional power that continues to manage institutions in the traditional hierarchical way, it can be declared that the relationship between traditional hierarchical institutions and the ITPF was the main concern in the first period of the process.

The beginning of this process signaled the change from a negative view toward informal working relationships. The resulting benefits started to be seen inasmuch as these informal relationships decreased bureaucratic drawbacks, such as the following:

1. Lack of shared effort and a tendency toward fragmentation
2. Reduced capacity to integrate innovation
3. Censorship related to such innovation
4. Self-centeredness

The forums brought "fresh air" into bureaucratic behaviours

The ITPF's range of action was wide from the very beginning. The national authorities overlooked IT areas (ITNO), thus leaving this field open for the ITPF to operate in. It can then be concluded that the government did not delegate to the ITPF the responsibility of handling IT policies in a legal fashion. The ensuing problem was that the available tools managed by the ITPF were applied in a random way. If the back office tasks are understood as standard practices that implement an interoperable system, the lack of general rules brings about a difficult problem to solve. However, little by little, this situation has been changing as the institutions gain stability and the crisis diminishes. During 2003, President Kirchner achieved a general consensus that enabled an increasing inflow of economic resources. The growth of tax revenue generated some resources for the public sector. This brought about many difficulties in the relationship between the ITPF and the political authorities due to the well-known mistrust between the newly appointed personnel and the already-operating staff. The first measure taken by the new director of the ITNO was to appoint a reliable team. The environment generated by the new team produced a distance between the ITPF and these authorities, who perceived the ITPF to be a powerful as well as an amorphous group of manage.

The new administration soon noticed that the ITPF had a power of its own. This was owing to the fact that it had reached a strong identity among its members, obtained through the sharing of common goals.

On the other hand, many of its participants held significant positions whether in the IT arena or in their own organizations. It is worthwhile bearing in mind that due to the cross-agency nature of the ITPF, many IT representatives from different agencies attended the forum. Some of these agencies have, even nowadays, a higher rank than the ITNO in terms of political and economic relevance. The ITPF continued growing and generating projects and innovations.[19]

In time, certain politicians became aware of the ITPF's importance as a problem-solving resource. In this respect, the present ITNO director and chief officer of the e-government plan claims that in view of the weak state of the ITNO as opposed to the powerful position that the ITPF has achieved, it is necessary to balance both organizations by means of human resources, infrastructure, and suitable policies developed by the ITNO itself. According to the director, only a strong ITNO could standardize the innovation taking place in the ITPF.[20]

However, the ITPF is likely to be included in further plans in charge of certain tasks.

On the other hand, as time goes by, the usual turn of events, as far as management occurs, mainly, the new officials get to know the old ones

and a bond of trust is established between them.[21,22] Besides, ITNO has fount it hard to consolidate due to the following factors:

1. ICTs are not relevant in the public agenda, despite the efforts made by certain ITNO directors.
2. The ITNO was left in a weakened position (such as in the state in general) as a consequence of applying new public management.

Therefore, the expected balance between the ITNO and the ITPF has not yet been achieved.

The authorities lack a strong support to implement the projects they announce. As a consquence of this, the ITPF keeps generating IT solutions and recommendations that the government does not apply immediately. Nevertheless, they are stored and may become available for the political authorities to be used when they encounter difficulties in carrying out plans that need sound results. The suitability of many of these solutions could bring forth closer bonds between the government and the ITPF as long as a technical rationality is enforced as regards political decisions.[23]

A second issue is the political authorities' indifference toward the networks.

Actually, regarding underlying networks, CoPs, and political authorities, there are different logical ways of thinking as well as different foci of interest.

As far as networks and CoPs are concerned, their goal is to solve daily issues associated with their needs or professional practices. In the case of networks, they solve these by means of complementary actions. In the case of CoPs, issues are solved by means of KM and innovation (Cohendet et al., 2001).

The networks and CoPs within the state are driven by a technical rationality aimed at solving difficulties in management. In contrast, for most political authorities, their main interest lies in their party relationships, political commitments, and state agenda. Many issues are not included in this agenda. In view of the present crisis Argentina is going through, with its resulting poverty, hunger, and unemployment, it would seem politically incorrect to develop technological policies in order to improve the state's performance. This is the case with the E-Government National Plan because it would mean an expense in hardware and software, which is not a priority. The ITNO falls under this context, making it hard to fulfill its goals.

With respect to the informal structure of networks and CoPs, governmental control is limited, causing certain uneasiness in political authorities. This situation could be reverted if the government became familiar with their functioning.

In other countries, there are also misunderstandings. Snyder and Souza Briggs (2003, p. 51) state that:

there are several ways to address these concerns: by seeing the emergence of CoPs as an evolutionary process, not a cataclysmic revolution; by distinguishing the knowledge-building and knowledge-sharing functions of these communities with the primarily transactional focus of product- and service-delivery units; and by understanding that collaborative, boundary-crossing networks need not mark the loss of government's public-service identity and influence, but rather serve as an expansion of both.

Another interesting topic has to do with the possibilities to develop free software in a context of scarcity of resources.

Indeed, it is a hard task to develop software without the necessary resources. However, it should be remembered that the ITPF is made up of several organizations that may be working on software developments with their own resources (for example, the AFIP, the Argentinean tax agency; ANSES, the pension funds administrator, and the Central Bank). This software is usually made available in order to test its applicability in other sectors.

It goes without saying that every agency where the software is applied will need its own resources so that the software can be implemented and the necessary training supplied. In some cases, directives from the ITNO are required.

I have mentioned earlier some ways in which it has been possible to generate a network for the creation of LINUX training courses. I should add that the group of tutors is made up of IT experts who share their knowledge. Their tutoring is almost free. Moreover, they have designed courses for public officials. It should be noticed that it would have been hard to find enough LINUX teachers for this task, and the few available ones would have charged very high fees. If this had been the case, the courses would not have started.

The fourth challenge I would like to refer to is how the ITPF can broaden the professional competencies of IT experts.

The ITPF has come a long way. At its inception, the members were against interacting with other systems, actors, or forums. Nowadays, they are starting to change this attitude of isolation, interacting with legislators, scholars, lawyers, human-resources directors, and front-desk chiefs.

The evolution of the ITPF is also reflected in the language its members have been adopting. Rather than just using IT jargon, they have integrated IT terms into an interlinguistic field. This attitude helps to include the addressees' needs by letting them have a say in their decisions. Broadly speaking, IT experts are responsible for showing the way in which technology can be used to improve decision-making processes. Thus, they should be familiar with public-administration rules and the specific needs of public officials. The ITPF has contributed to collective knowledge about the culture of organizations in connection with information and technology, the rules of the game, as well as the implicit hierarchies and their informal structure.

Through their own experience at the ITPF, its members have also learned to work in networks to perceive the environment, communicate skills, and so forth. They confront the challenge of bridging the gaps with non-IT areas, taking into account that the latter are constantly producing data. This data needs to be standardized in order to be included in IT systems and to feed new developments. This compatibility should be the priority of the back office. Yet, it proves difficult to achieve given that IT and non-IT experts are used to working based on different disciplinary logics. Therefore, the job of IT experts is to match these differences.[24]

It is also interesting to know the processes that have led to interdisciplinary relationships with non-IT expert customers. These interchanges took place due to the following:

1. The gradual awareness by IT experts of the customers' needs
2. The gradual incorporation of basic IT logics by non-IT experts

The massive use of ICT together with its inadvertently growing daily use led customers to become more participative. Moreover, users have started to demand solutions tailored to their needs as they rely increasingly on ICT tools. These practices are being developed through daily routines that are giving way to a certain familiarity. Needless to say, the ITPF is involved in these processes. Although at first the forum rejected any kind of interchange with other actors, little by little it abandoned such reluctance. [25]

As regards the incoporation of basic IT logic by non IT experts, and viceversa, we should remember that interaction among CoPs may take the shape of border meetings where some of the members of two or more CoPs get together in order to foster an interchange of practices and to trigger thinking processes into the community itself or in the border practices. For example, the ITPF needed to acquire competencies developed by librarians in order to be able to classify the developments spotted by the Free Software Group. The Forum of Documents Center, in turn, needed

to incorporate competencies from the former in order to work with digital documents and to be able to deal with them. It was necessary to learn, among other issues, how to keep these documents from disappearing from the Internet.

This phenomenon also takes place with non-IT actors in general as they try to become familiar with the use of ICT (Falivene & Kaufman, 2005).

Finally, a last question remains: Why are IT public officials more likely to work in networks, incorporating IT, therefore becoming the main support of the e-government back office?

The ITPF experience, as well as other empirical cases, shows a trend of many IT experts to develop systems that enable a horizontal flow of information. This behaviour is a strong core identity mechanism in their CoPs.[26] Needless to say, it forms part of the development of an IT professional. It is as obvious as mentioning the physician's predisposition to heal. The fact is that such behaviour concerning the horizontal flow of information is not neutral as regards public-administration practices. That is to say, it generates a conflict when confronted with political and bureaucratic points of view. Usually, the hierarchies in these CoPs are synonymous with professional pride and know-how. So, these different perspectives constitute dissociated worlds sharing common environments.

On the other hand, many IT experts do not conceive institutional or personal power as isolated compartments. This fragmented view of power has always existed within the Argentine government, preventing the consolidation of a strong and efficient state.

Nevertheless, ICTs are in a way becoming a dangerous-enough weapon to injure the Achilles heel of fragmentation. Many IT experts understand the crucial importance of these tools and are willing to generate positive changes. To make this happen, they are building other institutional architectures (usually informal ones) that enable the inflow of information to legitimate addressees.

IT experts may not be the champions of transparent processes or of participation through ICT. They may just be good professionals.

OTHER EXPERIENCES

Some current government policies encourage CoPs as strategic lines of action, such as in Canada,[27] the United States, Australia,[28] and other countries. These lines of action are oriented toward reinforcing federal policies as well as supporting government

structures in complex processes. This is the case of e-government plans when a government wants to change and integrate the institutional, cultural, and technological systems.

The developments implemented by the above-mentioned administrations have key government authorities as their sponsors. Such was the case with Al Gore in the United States when he was the vice president of that country ("Reinventing Government," 1998). Conversely in Argentina, as far as IT areas, this initiative stems from the public-management undersecretariat and the ITNO (which depends on the former). In view of this categorization, it is difficult to undertake a political strategy as strong as those from the previously mentioned countries.

This emerging complementary relationship between CoPs and the bureaucratic structures is an interesting strategy given that CoPs constitute an effective way of solving unusual problems, sharing knowledge beyond traditional structural borders through the coexistence of informal integration models and bureaucratic models. Within these interrelationships, formal structures can be fed by the production generated in turn by CoP members. The different CoPs intertwine in a blurred way and cut across the organizational arena (Tuomi, 1999). These CoPs also contribute the improvement of teams that are set up for specific government projects (such as e-government), recognizing that formally managed projects work best when the following are true:

1. Problems can be clearly defined.
2. Reliable, quantifiable measurements are established.
3. An authority structure is in place to ensure that project results get implemented.

Additionally, communities are most effective when they follow certain criteria, as follows:

1. Problems are complex and dynamic or very situation specific.
2. Measures require stories to link cause and effect.
3. Authority is decentralized and depends more on professionals' intrinsic commitment to getting results (vs. extrinsic appraisals and incentives).

In the United States, the IBM Center for the Business of Government has performed case studies, led by Snyder and Souza Briggs (2003), that reveal the strategic relevance the U.S. federal government has placed on the development of CoPs to support a variety of state-related issues, such as children's health, highway controls, antiterrorism, e-government, and so forth. Specifically, the federal e-government encourage the development of CoPs to generate a cross-agency pilot community because it addressed a strategic concern that aligned with a new government-wide legislative mandate, the Government Paperwork Elimination Act, which required agencies to streamline processes and reduce paperwork by October 2003 (Snyder & Wenger, 2003).

The Australian government has also included CoPs in its experience of e-government. The Australian Government Information Management Office (AGIMO) states:

CoPs are practical vehicles for sharing and building knowledge and promoting better practice... In this spirit, AGIMO's role is that of a catalyst and facilitator, providing initial structure, while encouraging ownership and engagement by community of practice members. Facilitation of the CoPs is shared with other government agencies.[29]

As mentioned before,[30] the Australian CIO Forum is an alternative version of the ITPF.[31]

On the Web page of the AGIMO, it is possible to find the following excerpt:

The CIO Forum has been established to provide a mechanism for CIOs across the Australian Government to share information and enhance linkages to the Chief Information Officer Committee (CIOC) and the Information Management Strategy Committee (IMSC). The objectives of the CIO Forum are to:

1. *Share information about better practice approaches and key strategic issues being faced by agencies in their use of ICT to facilitate better government.*

2. *Provide a mechanism for CIOs across government to hear about Chief Information Officer Committee (CIOC) and Information Management Strategy Committee (IMSC) activities.*

3. *Explore opportunities to contribute to CIOC activities and provide CIOC with non CIOC perspectives.*

4. *Explore and pursue collaborative and cooperative opportunities.*

CONCLUSION

Some Thoughts about International Experiences

Since the creation of the ITPF, I have been researching the process of building the back office. I always thought I was witnessing a new practice and my belief was confirmed by all the practitioners who attended the events where I put forward this experience.

At the same time, I was devoted to relaying a bibliography on the following subjects: CoPs, epistemic communities, and networks, and their relationship with KM. In this respect, I found mainly theoretical approaches with some practical references to private environments.

At first, the subjects bore no relationship in my mind. But little by little, they began to fit a certain pattern. I could integrate CoPs and e-government. Therefore, I changed my theoretical outlook toward the ITPF experience.

I considered this approach a very innovative one. On finishing my first draft of this chapter, some workmates[32] discovered that in several countries, this model of relationships was put into practice as a political strategy for e-government programs. CoPs were becoming an essential tool. This realization became a shared joy for the ITPF and the ITNO authorities since they felt less lonely in their initiative.

However, I found no detailed descriptions of how these relationships (formal-informal) operated within the framework of the back office. Therefore, I consider it useful to state the specific experience of the ITPF, giving more accurate information and detailed reflections.

Final Thoughts

Historically, the traditional structures of government have failed to provide integral answers to e-government plans, above all in third-world countries such as Argentina (Kaufman, 2005). This seems also to be the case in first-world countries, as seen from the examples of Canada, the United States, and Australia, even though they have support policies regarding CoPs. Traditional structures have very sharp internal boundaries marking isolated compartments. Therefore, it is hard for them to incorporate functions and actors to interact within different contexts, even when a strong political environment encourages this. Informal institutions, such as CoPs, should support such goals as the production of information and services within a network tissue model with the understanding that e-government has a main function to perform in the information society.

Manuel Castells (1997) has defined the information society as a society where the central processes of knowledge generation, economic productivity, political and military power, and media have been deeply transformed by an informational paradigm. This paradigm has been shaped by the new technological medium that follows the logic of interconnection among systems (networks morphology). The development of a society bearing these characteristics depends on the capacity of its agents to generate processes and efficiently apply information based on knowledge and to organize itself on a global scale.

It can be said that the function of e-government consists of being a trigger for the integration of networks, permitting their articulation through information and services that e-government produces (alone or with other partners within networks). This should also facilitate the articulation of private actors on a global scale in order to permit adequate insertion in the new economy.[33]

This scenario is light years away from e-government conceived by Latin American politicians, although the region needs the economic development that would be made possible by efficient articulation. This region needs all its available resources to strengthen its states: the maximum effort (public and private) at a minimum cost. There is a big difference between this region and the first world, which can encourage these developments with a lot of funding. Latin America has only been receiving foreign money to pay consultancies that work in a superficial, nonsystematic and nonintegrative way. Most government, university, nonprofit, and business actors should integrate resources to support key policies leading to a way out of economic stagnation. For this reason, the tasks of integration into networks and CoPs (public and private) are fundamental. An important part of these tasks is carried out in the back office of a type of e-government that I call

associative, in which the back office has already become back networks.

With reference to associative e-governments, it is worth mentioning that technology enables society and government to interact. Furthermore, it can transform the players or stakeholders into partners together with the government. If this is the case, on entering the e-government portal, users are at the same time entering the digital city where they can find all the services, whether public or private, that each society or government chooses. In an associative model, many segments of society can participate in the decision making about the kind of services that the government and each social and economic segment have to provide through the Internet. Also, each particular segment, stakeholder, or partner decides on the implementation and evaluation of such services and can monitor them. Each and every part is essential to build up the back networks where users can find unions, small and medium enterprises, civil and cultural organizations, universities, ICT enterprises, and so on. Some of the Net workers could work interconnected with others. For instance, the enterprises could work with schools, universities, and unions in order to develop the kind of workers and professionals that the market needs. In this kind of relationship, the government is not self-centered. It works as a strong coordinator, although it is not the only one (Kaufman, 2003a).

Most Latin American governments are not in a position to carry out the necessary tasks of integration of the back networks, nor are they interested in them (Kaufman, 2003b). The ambitions of those in power within the state have weakened the state itself in a swamp of corruption and spurious special interests. This weakness of the state might be corrected through networks and CoPs, allowing the weaving of a fabric that had never been finished. Such new interventions may also function as controls. Furthermore, networking in itself makes it possible to demand participation in political decision making.

It is my belief that these networks promote the common good because, together with an increasing use of ICT, they can sharpen a watchful gaze on matters that until recently were kept in the dark. The ICT put into effect mechanisms that impede total control over information.[34]

The profound transformations brought about by the information society often occur in a disorganized and chaotic fashion. They can never be entirely taken into account by public policies precisely because many are the fruit of forms of self-organization that exceed the responsibility of the state.

However, some specific courses of action may help or hinder these transformations, such as the ones developed by the ITPF. It is essential to achieve a cross-technological alignment of the different public agencies so that they become interoperable in order to build a networks system (or back networks) in accordance with the morphological model of the information society. The courses of action adopted by the ITPF present a different perspective to the fixed e-government models that satisfy mainly technology suppliers and associated consultants. CoPs, such as the ITPF, are key structures to counteract special interests and poor models of e-government. These should allow accessing more ambitious projects that address the common good, such as the associative e-government. In Argentina, no other mechanisms have as yet paved the way for these processes.[37]

Yet these mechanisms are not enough. Needless to say, specific e-government and information-society policies, as well as a strong political will, are missing. Some decisions should be made within the framework of a strategic e-government plan. They should address issues such as the following:

1. Who does the plan target?
2. Who are its stakeholders?
3. What are the available resources?
4. What methodology is to be used?
5. What are the priorities?
6. What are the expected results?

The belief that CoPs and networks may make the above decisions would mean continuing with the assumption of the "magic" role of IT professionals, though they may have contributed their knowledge as in the case of the ITPF.

REFERENCES

Castells, M. (1997). *La era de la información: Economía, sociedad y cultura* (Vol. 1). Madrid, Spain: Alianza Editorial.

Cohendet, P., Creplet, F., & Dupouët, O. (2001). *CoPs and epistemic communities: A renewed approach of organisational learning within the firm.* Retrieved November 22, 2004, from http://www.marsouin.org/IMG/pdf/dupouet.pdf

Community Intelligence. (2003). *Innovation and CoPs: The "great symphony" paradox. The innovation potential of bridging structural holes.* Retrieved April 2, 2004, from http://www.communityintelligence.com/pdf/Communities_&_Innovation.pdf

Danish Technological Institute. (2004). *Reorganisation of government back offices for better electronic public services: European good practices (Back-office reorganisation). Final report to the European Commission.* Retrieved March 3, 2004, from http://www.cio.gv.at/news/files/Back_office.pdf & http://hw.oeaw.ac.at/0xc1aa500d_0x0010b255

Falivene, G., & Kaufman, E. (2005). The potential of CoPs in Argentina to articulate public organizations and training through knowledge management approach. In E. Coakes & S. Clarke (Eds.), *Encyclopedia of communities of practice in information and knowledge management.* Hershey, PA: Idea Group Reference.

Falivene, G., Silva, G., & Gurmendi, L. (2003). *El e-learning como mecanismo articulador de procesos de gestión del conocimiento y formación continua en las organizaciones públicas: El caso del Sistema de Información Universitaria.* Retrieved September 19, 2004, from http://www.clad.org.ve/fulltext/0048201.pdf

Gascó, M., & Equiza, F. (2002). Formulación de políticas públicas de transición a la sociedad del conocimiento: El caso argentino. *Desarrollo Humano e Institucional en América Latina (DHIAL), 36.* Retrieved December 20, 2002, from http://www.iigov.org/dhial/?p=36_04_

Gualtieri, R. (1998). *Impact of the emerging information society on the policy development process and democratic quality.* Paris OECD Public Management Service. Retrieved November 14, 1998, from http://www.alfa-redi.com//apc-aa-alfaredi/img_upload/a63473ef6aa82c7a2b2cc688d7e635dd/12E81094.doc

Herzog, R. (2002). Internet und politik in Lateinamerika: Argentinien. In R. Herzog, B. Hoffman, & M. Schulz (Eds.), *Internet und politik in Lateinamerika: Regulierung und nutzung der neuen informationsund kommunikationstechnologien im kontext der politischen und wirtschaftlichen transformationen* (pp. 100-112). Frankfurt, Germany: Vervuert Verlag. Retrieved September 12, 2002, from http://www1.uni-hamburg.de/IIK/nikt/Argentinien.pdf

Kaufman, E. (2003a). *Associative model for e-gov including digital cities.* Retrieved December 5, 2003, from http://www.cities-lyon.org/es/articles/203

Kaufman, E. (2003b, November). *Panorama latinoamericano de gobiernos electrónicos: Modelos existentes.* Paper presented at the Second Argentinean Conference on Public Administration, Córdoba, Argentina. Retrieved March 1, 2004, from http://www.aaeap.org.ar/ponencias/congreso2/Kaufman_Ester.pdf

Kaufman, E. (2004). E-gobierno en Argentina: Crisis, burocracia y redes. In R. Araya & M. Porrúa (Eds.), *América Latina puntogob* (pp. 151-187). Santiago, Chile: FLACSO Chile & Organization of American States.

Kaufman, E. (2005). E-government and e-democracy in Latin America: Stages of development. In S. Marshall, W. Taylor, & X. Yu (Eds.), *The encyclopedia of developing regional communities with information and communication technology.* Hershey, PA: Idea Group Reference.

Klijn, E., & Coppenhan, J. (2000). Public management and policy networks: Foundations of a network approach to governance. *Public Management, an International Journal of Research and Theory, 2*(2), 135-158. Retrieved February 3, 2001, from http://www.inlogov.bham.ac.uk/pdfs/readinglists/Klijn%20and%20Koppenjan%20on%20policy%20network%20theory.pdf

Lave, J., & Wenger, E. (1991). *Situated learning: Legitimate peripheral participation.* New York: Cambridge University Press.

Nonaka, I., & Takeuchi, H. (1995). *The knowledge-creating company: How the Japanese companies create the dynamic of innovation.* New York: Oxford University Press.

Rocheleau, B. (1997). Governmental information system problems and failures: A preliminary review. *Public Administration and Management: An Interactive Journal, 2*(3). Retrieved May 25, 1999, from http://www.pamij.com/roche.html

Snyder, W. M., & Souza Briggs, X. (2003). Communities of practice: A new tool for government managers. *Collaboration series of the IBM Center for the business of government.* Retrieved December 22, 2004, from http://www.businessofgovernment.org/pdfs/Snyder_report.pdf

Snyder, W. M., & Wenger, E. (2003). *Communities of practice in government: The case for sponsorship.* Retrieved December 30, 2004, from http://www.ewenger.com/pub/pubusfedcioreport.doc

Tuomi, I. (1999). *Corporate knowledge: Theory and practice of intelligent organizations.* Helsinki, Finland: Metaxis.

Weber, M. (1992). *Economía y sociedad.* Mexico: Fondo de Cultura Económica.

Wenger, E. (1998). *Communities of practice: Learning, meaning and identity.* New York: Cambridge University Press.

Wenger, E. (2000). Communities of practice and social learning systems. *Organization, 7*(2), 225-246.

ENDNOTES

1   A debt of gratitude goes to the IT Directors Forum coordinator, José Carllinni, for his help in developing this chapter. I also wish to acknowledge the help of Julie Taylor (Department of Anthropology, Rice University, Texas, USA) and Diana Stalman, who assisted me in translating and editing this chapter.

2   In some English-speaking countries, this kind of forum is referred to as a CIO (chief information officer) forum. I have chosen to use ITPF because CIO indicates the participation mainly of upper level IT areas. By contrast, ITPF also includes its broader membership.

3   See http://www.sgp.gov.ar/sitio/foros/foro_rrii.html.

4   See http://www.ewenger.com.

5   In its complete version, NPM consists of (a) privatizations of public enterprises, (b) a downsizing of government agencies, (c) a trend toward an increase of middle-management skills through the requirement of professionals, (d) the setting of performance standards, (e) an emphasis on outcomes, (f) the decentralizing of areas of competence in government agencies, (g) the advance-ment of competences and rivalry among participants, and (h) more control in the use of resources.

6   According to Gascó and Equiza (2002), digitalizing the government is not synonymous with having a few computers installed. Nor does it mean to design a Web site offering information. Rather, it aims at transforming the fundamental relationship between the government and the citizens.

7   See the ITPF methodology in the previous section.

8   This term was coined by José Luis Tesoro.

9   These improvements obviously depend on public politics. In this respect, the ITPF can only help by widening its CoPs and networks since it faces some limitations, such as (a) the voluntary nature of its members, (b) its limited scope, since it functions mainly within the national government, and (c) its independence from public-policy agendas (an issue associated with politician authorities).

10   The IT National Office (Oficina Nacional de Tecnología Informática, ONTI) has as its main objective to assist the public-management undersecretary to design politics and implement the process of development and IT innovation for the transformation and modernization of the state. It is the state regulating office in charge of furthering the integration of new technologies and their compatibility and interoperability, as well as promoting technological standardization. Among its projects are digital signatures, IT security, a government portal, as well as the e-government program. Each project is managed by a special team. Every IT area of the national government falls under the coordination of this regulating office, which sets norms and functioning standards related to IT. Its relationship with the ITPF and the state's bureaucratic structure may be seen in the annex at the end of this chapter. For

more information, see http://www.sgp.gov.
ar/sitio/institucional/oficinas/onti.html.

[11] The first year of this experience has been analyzed by Kaufman (2004).

[12] These kinds of difficulties are still present throughout the state.

[13] The ITPF coordinator has his office at the ITNO. Meetings are held in public-management undersecretariat offices. The support team as well as the ITPF coordinator is within the government payroll in order to run the ITPF. This shows that this forum is not a totally self-organized CoP, but it was set up by the government, which provides it with resources. Regarding the ITPF activities, they are mainly self-organized.

[14] The work groups are organized in the plenary meetings by the consensus of all the attendees. See more details in the previous section.

[15] These courses have a very low cost ($0.30 per student). A further project proposes a team of LINUX coaches and tutors.

[16] This subgroup is made up of lawyers from different public organizations together with software chambers, universities, and IT experts.

[17] Anonymity was the chosen course of action in this task in the face of the offers made by private firms to ITPF members, siphoning them away from the public sphere.

[18] See Endnote 2.

[19] At this stage, the ITPF widened its variety of members to include IT experts with no specific hierarchy within the government, for instance, young programmers who worked in the free-software area.

[20] The present director is Carlos Achiary, and his opinion has especially been recorded for this research.

[21] Concurring this particular point, Mr. Achiary explained that he decided not to include the ITPF as a relevant actor in the E-Government National Plan because this degree of institutionalization would take away the ITPF's innovation force, caused by its informal style of bringing different participants together. The ITPF was meant to be an informal source of solutions for the e-government plan.

[22] Notice that Mr. Achiary has been actively participating in the lastest plenary meeting ("Criteria for Recommendations for the Implementation of Free Software"an "Interoperability") as a member.

[23] Up to the present, the collaboration between the ITPF and ITNO has increased. Some ITPF solutions have been carried out by the ITNO. This is the case of Web services and also the one-stop-shop file system follow-up.

[24] This issue is neglected by the political authorities. In Argentinean public agencies, acquired technologies could have triggered an upgrading of the processes. Nevertheless, this upgrading never took place due to the existing gap between technology data administration, workflows, and management.

[25] If these interchanges were regarded from a CoP approach, a border area could be identified since belonging to a community establishes a difference between the outside and the inside. It also reminds us of a bridge. The CoPs are connected to other collective subjects, their shared undertakings are linked, their members are in turn members of other communities, and their artifacts and tools are usually available to several groups. These bridges have a high potential. They offer the communities the possibility of confronting difference, experimenting with a cognitive dissonance between their own practice and others; of counteracting the risk of group thinking trapped at the community boundaries, incorporating new resources, themes, languages, and behaviours; and of meeting the challenge of building a language

26   to accomplish meaningful interchanges among the communities (Falivene & Kaufman, 2005).

26   This tendency is stressed by some youngsters who have made an ideological issue out of free software; their culture is a culture of gift giving and reputation.

27   http://www.communities-collectivites. gc.ca

28   http://www.agimo.gov.au

29   See http://www.agimo.gov.au/resources/ cop.

30   See Endnote 2.

31   See http://www.agimo.gov.au/government/ cio_forum.

32   They were José Carllinni (the ITPF coordinator) and Graciela Silva (an expert in CoPs).

33   To make all this possible, the government must also generate orchestrated policies for digital access that guarantee skillful and informed use of ICT. These functions must be applied for the successful integration into the information society.

34   In fact, this may lead to a trivialization of politics (suffice it to watch the superficial level of the media and political speeches). To read further on this matter, see Gualtieri (1998).

APPENDIX

Figure 1. The Argentine national authorities, the ITNO, the ITPF, network, CoPs and other public organisations

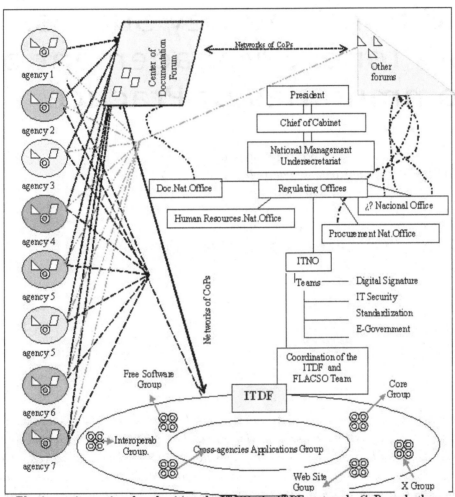

The Argentine national authorities, the ITNO, the ITPF, network, CoPs and other public organizations

⊚ CIO and IT expert from different public agencies

▱ Documental Directors from different public agencies

◿ Directors from other agencies (in charge of: human resources, budgetary, procurement, training, etc.

This work was previously published in Latin America Online: Cases, Successes and Pitfalls, edited by M. Gascó-Hernandez, pp. 1-33, copyright 2007 by IRM Press (an imprint of IGI Global).

Chapter 20
Conditions and Key Success Factors for the Management of Communities of Practice

Edurne Loyarte
VICOMTech Visual Communication Interaction Technologies Centre
San Sebastian, Spain

Olga Rivera
University of Deusto, San Sebastian, Spain

ABSTRACT

Communities of practice (CoPs) have been taken into account by both practitioners and academics during the last ten years. From a strategic point of view, CoPs have shown their importance for the management of organizational knowledge by offering repositories of knowledge, improved capacity of making knowledge actionable and operational (Brown & Duguid, 1998) and by facilitating mainte-nance, reproduction, and extension of knowledge (Brown and Durguid, 2001). CoPs are also reported to achieve value creation and competitive advantages (Davenport and Prusak, 1998), learning at work (Swan et alt., 2002) that promotes organizational competitiveness (Furlong and Johnson, 2003), in-novation, even a radical type (Swan et alt., 2002), responsiveness, improved staff skills and reduced duplication (du Plessis, 2008). This impressive list of achievements is not for free; some authors have pointed out the limits of CoP's (Duguid, 2005; Roberts, 2006; Amin & Roberts, 2008) from diverse points of view, including diversity of working environments, size, spatial or relational proximity, but mainly emphasizing the specificity of CoPs as a social practice paradigm, as it was defined by Wenger (1999, 2000) credited as the "inventor" of the term "CoP" (Lave and Wenger, 1991). This chapter focuses on the consideration of CoPs as an organizational reality than can be managed (Thompson, 2005), the contradictions that the idea of managing them generates, and how these controversial points can be overcome in a sound and honest way. To do so, we review different cases of CoP's within organizations intended for the managerial team to achieve important organizational goals. Our analysis provides: (a) a reflection regarding the Key Success Factors in the process of integrating communities of practice, (b) insight to the structure of a model of cultivation, intended as a guideline for new experiences in this area, and (c) an informative account of this model's adaptation to the studied organizations.

IS THE IDEA OF MANAGING COP'S AN OXYMORON?

Communities of Practice (CoPs) are activity systems that include individuals who are united in action and in the meaning that action has for them and for the larger collective (Lave and Wenger, 1991). CoPs are not part of formal structures; they are informal entities that exist in the mind of each member. When people participate in problem-solving and share the knowledge necessary to solve problems, it is possible to speak about the generation of knowledge in CoPs (Wenger, 1998). Therefore, CoPs are groups whose members regularly engage in sharing and learning based on common interests, and can improve organizational performance (Lesser & Storck, 2001). CoPs can (and are more likely to) extend beyond the boundaries of the firm (Malone, 2002), and they are about content (about learning as a living experience of negotiating meaning) not about form. In this sense, they cannot be legislated into existence or defined by order. They can be recognized, supported, encouraged, and nurtured, but they are not reified, designable units (Lesser and Storck, 2001). All these arguments can lead managers to question if it's possible to consider CoP as a managerial initiative oriented to achieve organizational goals.

On the other hand some other authors, considering the epistemic components and theoretical background of CoP's have pointed out that CoP's may not always contribute to business settings, due to their self managed character (Kimble & Hildreth, 2004; Roberts, 2006). Others have shown that CoP's contribution to innovation is not always

clear, while it only happens in some specific situations (Swan et al., 2002; Mutch, 2003), and even the negative impact that structure can exert over practice (Thompson, 2005) if the nature of the interrelations is not dressed in a sound way.

All this evidence makes the previous question even more complex: even if CoPs can be managed, it is not evident in which conditions or situation it should be the best option, or when the risks undertaken can exceed the potential gains.

In this chapter, the authors approach CoPs from a management perspective and practice. Although CoPs are organic and spontaneous, the purpose of the study is to analyse the CoPs promotion and cultivation from the organizational management point of view, therefore, as organizational management instrument. This framework can generate incoherencies between the situated and social learning theory and the consideration of a CoP's system as a management tool (CoP). For the purposes of advancing our understanding in this path, we have summarized the main contradictions between the epistemic component of CoPs (theoretical point of view) and its expected managerial use (management tool point of view) in the following questions:

- Should CoPs always be organic or could they be promoted by the organizations?
- Are CoPs designable units by the organizations?
- The cultivation of CoPs should be motivated by individuals or by organizations?
- How is it possible to achieve the sharing of knowledge? Is it necessary a tangible motivation or can it be intangible?

- Regarding knowledge management, should it be inside or outside the organizational culture?
- Should technology be a support or a purpose for the creation of CoPs?

Trying to find answers to those questions is the main purpose of this chapter that also will point out some apparent incoherence between the theory and practice related to CoPs. More specifically, key theoretical notions will be contrasted and linked to actual experiences based on a qualitative case study design, with main units of analysis being CoPs. The objective is achieved by analyzing the accomplishment of organisational results obtained in very different cases of promoted CoPs considering its epistemic components with a model based on the key dimensions created by R. McDermott (1999) and tested by the authors in previous research (Loyarte, 2006; Loyarte & Rivera, 2007). The reported research project involves analysing documented experiences of CoPs in more than 20 different kinds of organizations with a unique evaluation methodology developed for Loyarte's doctoral dissertation and inspired by the work of Mc Dermmott (McDermott, 2000). This methodology addresses the ten Critical Success Factors in building CoPs and the four challenges for building CoPs.

The chapter is structured as follows. The next section reviews the concept of CoP from a managerial point of view, which facilitates contrasting the theory of CoPs with actual experiences and clarifying what CoPs are and how they can be integrated in organizations. We then offer insights to avoiding the contradictory elements that emerge when we try to maintain the CoP's specificity as situated and social learning system, and also explore all its potential as an instrument to achieve organizational goals. Then, the next section analyzes cases of organizationally promoted CoP's, presenting the conditions of promotion and the results achieved, crossing these results with the previously identified paths. In the discussion

section we revisit our research questions providing answers based on our study and the analysis of its results. The chapter is wrapped up with conclusions and future work.

BACKGROUND

This section concentrates on reviewing, from a theoretical perspective, the concept of CoP and its organic nature. Although this review implies some important limitations of management-sponsored CoP, as the authors reveal in the first subsection, it also illuminates both the conditions for implementing CoP to achieve organizational goals and the kind of managerial intervention likely to have a positive effect.

CoP Within the Context of Social Learning Theory

The concept of Community of Practice (Lave & Wegner, 1991; Brown & Durguid, 1991; Wenger, 1998) is part of the social learning theory, which is based on the following premises:

- We are social beings – which is considered an essential aspect of learning
- Knowledge is a matter of competence in respect to certain valued practices, such as singing in tune, discovering scientific facts, fixing machines, writing poetry, being convivial, growing up, etc
- Knowing is a matter of participating in the achievement of these practices, engaging oneself actively in the world
- Meaning is what learning must ultimately produce

The main core of interest of this theory, which is based on the assumptions quoted above, rests on learning as social participation. Participation within this context does not refer to mere engagement, but rather to a process of greater reach that consists of actively participating in the practices of social communities and of building identities within them. As a result, the social learning theory developed here must integrate the necessary components in order to characterize social participation as a learning and knowing process. These components are listed below:

- **Meaning**, understood as a way of talking about our ability, both individually and collectively; of experiencing our lives and the world as something meaningful.
- **Practice**, understood as a way of talking about shared historical and social resources, frameworks, and perspectives that can sustain mutual engagement in action.
- **Community**, understood as a way of talking about social configurations in which the pursuit of enterprises is defined as valuable and participating in them is recognized as competence.
- **Identity**, understood as a way of talking about the change that learning effects on who we are and of how it creates personal histories within the context of communities.

These elements are deeply interconnected and define each other mutually, as shown in Figure 1.

CoP in Organizational Contexts

According to Davenport and Prusak (1998), communities of practice are a sign of the knowledge market. They are self-organized groups that share work practices, interests, or common objectives. They constitute a common body of experience and of joint problem solving. The community of practice is also defined by Lave and Wenger (1991) as an active system in which its participants share knowledge based on their daily tasks. They share the meaning of this knowledge in their life within the community. Therefore, it can be said that the participants of the community are united in the community's practice and in the meaning of said practice, both at the community level and at broader levels (Lave and Wenger, 1991:98).

One of the characteristics that define communities of practice is the fact that they emerge spontaneously among people who have similar interests or work activities (Lesser and Everest 2001; Lave and Wenger 1991; Wenger, 1998)[1]. Organizations are embracing various heterogeneous types of communities of practice that help

Figure 1. Inventory of social learning theory components (Adapted from Wenger, 1998)

them to develop (Saint-Onge and Wallace, 2003). However, there are different kinds of groups which exhibit characteristics similar to CoPs (Thompsom, 2005; Bogenreider and Nooteboom, 2004; Lindkvist, 2005, Klein et al., 2005; Klein, 2008) and, in this sense, the term "CoP" has been recognized as somewhat problematic (Malone, 2002; Contu and Willmott, 2003; Thomson 2005; Handley, Sturdy Fincham and Clarke, 2006; Lindkvist, 2005; Roberts, 2006; Amin & Roberts, 2008). Moreover, some authors claim that in certain contexts, CoPs cannot be usefully identified (Engerstrom, 2001) or are may not be useful "per se" (Roberts, 2006).

In spite of the critiques, CoPs characteristics such as spontaneity and freedom that overcome organizational restrictions are precisely what allows authors to establish a relationship between communities of practice and the learning of knowledge flows, or even between communities of practice and innovation (Brown and Duguid, 2001; Orr, 1996)[2]. Wenger (1998) defines three important characteristics for communities of practice:

- **Mutual engagement:** Comes from the interaction of their members, since members are motivated to share their experiences as a result of said interaction
- **Negotiation of common initiatives:** This characteristic provides the community with a sense of coherence and a raison d'être
- **Shared repertoire:** Is the group of resources that members share: Stories, theories, etc. This repertoire is what shapes understandable information that is manageable for the community's components

The combination of these is what generates the theoretical value of the communities of practice to the organizational knowledge.

Since communities of practice are dynamic, interactive, and fluid, their management cannot be carried out with established control mechanisms.

In fact, Thompson (2005) demonstrated that when CoP's are heavily structured and controlled, they loose most of their potential. Instead each organization's management must understand that communities need an environment in which they can prosper, including features such as having time and resources at their disposal. The organization must promote participation, reduce barriers, give their members a voice in decision-making, and develop internal processes in order to manage the value created by communities (Wenger et al., 2002)[3].

Communities of practice contribute to promoting an environment in which knowledge can be created and shared in such a way that their members can carry out their work with the help of other people (Wagner, 2000)[4] and, even more importantly, knowledge can be used to improve efficiency, effectiveness, and innovation (Lesser and Everest, 2001:41)[5.] Brown and Duguid (1991) argue that these communities are an important space for local inventions, since they are constantly improving and adapting their behavior in order to face the formal limitations of organizations and canonical practices. Results of experiments carried out and important knowledge that organizations should bear in mind in their innovation management systems can emerge from communities of practice (Brown and Duguid, 1991).

Communities of practice are normally created in an informal manner to share experiences jointly. Contributions from members flow freely, which does not necessarily mean that this intangibility represents a failure in knowledge management, since this is the very reason why communities of practice develop creative ways of solving organizational problems, generating new business or product lines, and even managing new strategies (Wenger and Snyder, 2000). They do not tend to have an explicit mission either, but are able to make enormous achievements.

Communities of practice exist in many more places than each individual thinks. According to Wenger (1998), there are communities of practice everywhere, and every single person has undoubtedly been part of one at school, at home, when involved in a hobby, etc. Some are named and some aren't. In fact, there are many examples of communities of practice within organizations that are named differently, such as "learning communities" at Hewlett-Packard, "family groups" at Xerox Corporation, "thematic groups" at the World Bank, "peer groups" at British Petroleum, and "knowledge networks" at IBM. Regardless of their name, once they have been detected, it is obvious that all communities of practice have features in common (Gongla and Rizzuto, 2001).

Communities of practice constitute an opportunity to stimulate the process of socialization in organizations. One of the main reasons for the spontaneous action of cultivating a community of practice is the common interest of members (Orr, 1996; Wenger, 1998)[6]. In practice, it is people who build knowledge in a social manner, which helps members learn or share different points of view on technical or social problems and to exchange solutions - or even to create them (Orr, 1996[7]; Stewart, 2001[8]).

A community of practice has three important parts: An area where knowledge unfolds, the community (people), and the practice (group of ideas and points of view to be shared) (Wenger, McDermott, and Snyder, 2002). Communities of practice emerge from the moment in which people work together, and their identity is based on how their members structure and organize themselves. Through the engagement of the people belonging to the communities, these, as a group, are able to negotiate their identity and meaning within companies, and can eventually act as communication nodes in organizational learning. Communities, in turn, are the foothold for the identity of each component (Smeds and Alvesalo, 2003)). Each member develops their individual identity within the community, which contributes their personal meaning and interest in the development of their work and of the community. As a result, the negotiation of the identities of each member is an important principle both at an individual level and at a community level (Wenger, 1998) and, therefore, learning can become a transformation of identity for each member in which the experience of learning per se is profound and difficult not to experience. As a result, the people who integrate the group find an important meaning in their work and individually (Schwen, 2003).

Within the context of communities of practice, learning is thought of as a path in which those who learn move from the group's periphery towards its core (while they contribute and learn, they become increasingly interested in the community and end up being active and important members of it), where, apart from sharing knowledge, members can also share beliefs and practices (Barab and Duffy, 2000)[9]. According to Barab and Duffy (2000), communities of practice have four characteristics:

- Shared knowledge, values, and beliefs
- Similar member histories
- Mutual interdependency
- Reproduction mechanisms

Barab (2001)[10], based on Wenger (1998), also includes the following characteristics:

- Common practices and initiatives
- Opportunities of interaction and participation
- Significant personal relationships
- Respect towards the diversity of perspectives and minority points of view

Therefore, considering the analysis carried out on the concept of the community of practice, it could be said that this concept goes beyond the organization as such, since it is based on the creation of an identity, a commitment for the group, and its members' continuous learning. This will end up creating value for the organization, which is the reason why it is so relevant to identify ways of promoting its use in firms and trying to move them to achieve organizational goals strategically defined.

Implementing and Operating CoPs

In this section authors tries to identify the factors that the theory of CoP's gives, in order to emphasize its importanceduring the process of cultivation of communities of practice, as well as the strategies that can be adopted for the integration of communities into organizations. Authors thinks that only the fundamentals provide a sound basis to do so, and that a honest use of CoPs requires coherence with its basis. Not considering the previous concepts, or using them opportunistly or only formally will lead to a failure.

Considerations for the Cultivation of Communities of Practice

The fact that communities of practice are created in a neutral manner does not mean that organizations should not influence their development (Wenger, 1998b). In fact, the existence of some communities of practice depends on the recognition that the organization awards them. A lot of communities, some more than others, require the attention of the organization for their development, even though no interference should be made in the community's management or organization per se.

Normally, the development of communities of practice depends fundamentally on internal leadership. Depending on the actual case, there are various types of leadership, such as:

- **Inspiring leadership:** Tries to lead to reflection and to gratify experts.
- **Everyday leadership:** Tries to organize the community's activities.
- **Interpersonal leadership:** Balances the community's social web.
- **Leadership based on limits:** Interrelates its own community with others.

- **Institutional leadership:** Tries to maintain uniting ties to other organizational instances, and to the hierarchy in particular.
- **Vanguard leadership:** Tries to promote original initiatives.

These types of leadership can emerge in a community either naturally or in a chosen manner, and can be concentrated in the community's main group or extended throughout the entire community. Regardless of these characteristics, however, leadership must be legitimate and intrinsic in the community. As a result, and in order to be effective, managers must work on communities of practice from the inside, rather than manipulating them from outside.

The creation of communities of practice within an organization includes the following aspects:

- **Legitimizing participation:** The introduction of the term "community of practice" into an organization's vocabulary can have a positive effect if the people who work in it are given the opportunity of commenting and sharing on how each of them contributes to the organization through participation in the communities.
- **Negotiating the strategic context:** Organizations must be capable of developing the way in which knowledge is linked to the organizational strategy and therefore help communities of practice articulate their own strategies of value for the company.
- **Becoming aware of the community's real practices:** Knowledge that is necessary for the organization is normally found within the organization itself, which is why promoting communities of practice that are able to identify and use the company's potential is an option worth pursuing.
- **Reciprocating the community's efforts (from the organization):** There are several elements within an organizational environ-

ment that have an influence on the promotion or inhibition of communities, including the interest of managers, compensation systems, work processes, corporate cultures, and organizational policies. These factors do not determine the participation of members in communities, but can make it easier or hinder it. As a result, directors should make sure that compensation systems in the company environment do not penalize work involved in developing communities.

- **Providing support:** Communities of practice are practically self-sufficient, even though they can benefit from organizational resources such as external experts, trips, facilities for meetings, and technological tools.

If there is a team of people selected for the creation of communities of practice, they would be in charge of the following tasks:

- Provide communities with advice and resources when they need them.
- Help communities adjust their agenda to the existing organizational strategies.
- Promote original initiatives in communities and community engagement.
- Make sure that the rights of each member are upheld.
- Help communities associate with other communities.

This team could also help identify and eliminate the barriers that hinder the development of communities within a corporate structure or culture.

Summarizing, communities of practice do not require large institutional infrastructures, but their participants need time and space to collaborate. An external manager is not required, but internal leadership is. They are self-organized groups, but prosper when they learn how to adapt to the organizational environment. Therefore, the key

element is to help communities find resources and ways of communicating among themselves and with the organization, as well as to achieve a balance between communities and the organization that takes into account the fact that communities are not able to design others' learning or their own learning by themselves.

An important aspect to take into account in communities of practice is the fact that they do not exist as a formal structure, but rather inside the mind of each member - in members' relationships among themselves and with the organization per se (Liedtka, 1999). Another element to bear in mind is the fact that communities are as varied as the organizational situations behind them. As a result, people from communities of practice with different objectives and interests, as well as due to diverse situations (Wenger and Snyder, 2000).

Alignment of Interests Between the Organization & CoP Members

Communities of practice prosper when both the employees and the organization perceive benefits for each one of them. In order to achieve this, the interest of both parties must be aligned in order to generate joint value. According to a study by Van Winkelen and Ramsell (2003), the individual motivations of people who are members of communities of practice are:

- **Intellectual motivations:** Search of opportunities within the organization, exploration of various perspectives, improvement in professional position, generation of influences, comprehension, and ways of sharing diverse interests.
- **Emotional motivations:** Satisfaction of helping other people, recognition, increase in confidences, building new relationships, feeling of identification with groups.
- **Result-based motivations:** Financial recognition through improvement in performance.

Therefore, in order for the organization to get its employees to share their knowledge so that they cam improve their competitiveness and maintain existing communities, it should take the employees' interests into account[11]. The organization could then align its interests with those of people in the following manner (Lee, 2003):

- **Initial recognition:** By definition, communities of practice consist of people with similar interests, but the actual level of knowledge and experience can vary, depending on the people that form them. The organization can use a plan to effect formalized recognition by notifying members of communities of acknowledgments based on the contributions that they make to the organization. This recognition can initially consist of appreciation for people who sustain the community's base and its knowledge. If the organization abstains from this recognition, it is possible for contributors to the community's generation to end up feeling frustrated, since they could think that the work done is not useful for the community.
- **Subsequent recognitions and rewards:** Once communities have been consolidated, the organization must ensure that there are subsequent recognitions and rewards. Contributors of knowledge that is important for the community and the organization must be recognized for their contributions both within the community itself and within the organization.
- **Inclusion in action and revision plans:** Another important incentive can be acknowledgment on behalf of the organization by including the members of communities in action plans in order to have them share different points of view and knowledge, which can lead to the creation of new knowledge and its spreading, which, in turn, can lead to innovation.

- **Participation in feedback on the organization's actions:** Requesting an evaluation of the organization's actions from communities' means closing the loop that is necessary for maintaining communities in the long term by means of (necessary) recognition.

This way, both the organization and the members of communities perceive the benefits of the creation and maintenance of communities of practice, cushioning the drain of intellectual capital and creating an environment that allows people to share their knowledge in order to carry out tasks efficiently. This increase in efficiency, in turn, provides the organization with a significant advantage over other competitors.

Key Success Factors in the Cultivation of CoP

McDermott (2000) makes a valuable contribution regarding the main challenges in the cultivation and nourishing of communities of practice. He highlights 4 challenges, listed as follows:

- **The management challenge:** In order to show that communities of practice are truly important for business management, it is essential to make sure that they are formed around subjects that are important to the organization, so that the development of knowledge regarding these subjects will have an important impact on the company. If it's not the case, of course the CoP can continue existing, but will not be a priority for the organization and so, it would not receive organizational support. It is also necessary to take into account the fact that the success of a community of practice depends on the coordinator of it, as well as on its members. Therefore, and as far as the steward is concerned, it is necessary to make sure that the leader has the experience and prestige enough, as well as the social skills to motivate people and communicate with them. Regarding members, it is necessary to bear in mind that they themselves assume a commitment to participate in the community and that they must have enough time to do so. In addition, the community cannot go against the organizational culture in question, since the latter will always be stronger than the former. Because of this, it is preferable for the community to be created with a sense of respect for the organizational culture and, as a result, for it to deal with subjects that agree with the organizational values in question.

- **The community challenge:** The worst that can happen to a community is the loss of energy due to apathetic behavior on behalf of its members, leaving the coordinator with the entire responsibility for the community. This stage will always occur when it exist an organization goal but it does not match with any existing community goals. If it's not the case, it can be prevented by involving leaders from other networks, with forums that pursue the maintenance of contact among the members of the community. In fact, the members of the community's core are also its pillars; the people who contribute to the community living energetically.

- **The personal challenge:** One of the greatest values of CoP's is their space and artifacts for their members thinking and solving problems as a group. However, discussions, contributions, and sharing ideas, knowledge, and experience is not something that is revealed naturally, unless people are motivated

Figure 2. Key success factors in the cultivation of CoP (Adapted from McDermott, 1999b)

CRITICAL SUCCESS FACTORS IN BUILDING CoPs

Management Challenge

    1. Focus on topics important to the business and community members.

    2. Find a well-respected community member to coordinate the community.

    3. Make sure people have time and encouragement to participate.

    4. Build on the core values of the organization.

Community Challenge

    5. Get key thought leaders involved.

    6. Build personal relationships among community members.

    7. Develop an active passionate core group.

    8. Create forums for thinking together as well as systems for sharing information.

Technical Challenge

    9. Make it easy to contribute and access the community's knowledge and practices.

Personal Challenge

    10. Create real dialogue about cutting edge issues.

and engaged, and this last element is where the challenge resides.

- **The technical challenge:** Technology must be at the service of the community and strengthen its social part. It must help people to communicate and to get along with each other. Therefore, the community's technological development must be focused on people, i.e., on the social usefulness of the technology in question.

These four groups of challenges can be subdivided into ten factors that are critical for the success of communities of practice. Without them, communities are deemed to fail. These ten factors, which are grouped under the aforementioned challenges, are shown in Figure 2.

ANALYZING MANAGEMENT-PROMOTED CoP

In this section we will present an in depth analysis of the results of CoPs promoted and cultivated

from the management team of the firm. We will try to know if they have been able to overcome the possible contradictions and if they have done so accomplishing the key success factors identified above.

Case Study Methodology

According to McDermott (1999b) in his three dimensions cultivation model, and the concepts of practice and community (Wenger, 1998), the authors developed a model (see Figure 3) for the analysis of CoP's (Loyarte and Rivera 2007) that has been used for an in depth case analysis of management-promoted CoP's.

The analysis of compared experiences is based on this framework, through which the following information is analyzed in each experience:

- Company, location, year of implementation of communities of practice.
- Manner of creation of the communities of practice: Promoted or organic.

Figure 3. Analysis of the creation of CoPs within organizations (Adapted from Loyarte and Rivera, 2007)

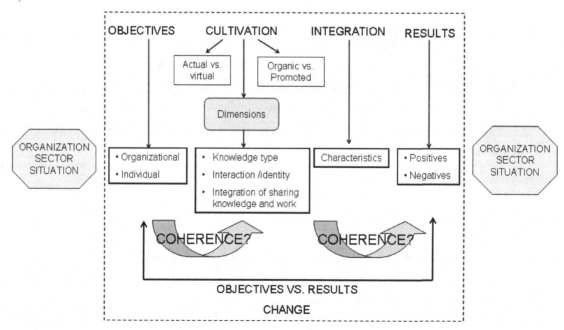

- Type of community of practice: Real or virtual.
- Primary Objective when creating the communities: Organizational, community, individual.
- Analysis of the cultivation of communities: According to McDermott (1999b), the result of experiences in organizations can be satisfactory only if the community of practice is the most suitable system to achieve the expected results. To do so, it's important to take into account the following issues:
- What is the type of knowledge that needs to be shared
- What is the type of link that unites the community's members and how strong it is
- What is the need for the new knowledge generated in the community to be transferred to the daily work of people in the organization

These questions, and their dichotomic answers, are shown in Figure 4, which constitutes the Three Dimensions Model of McDermott (2001). It is worth noticing that the closer our needs would be to the right, the CoP's will appear as being a more adequate learning and sharing system.

This model has been used to analyze the differences in the cultivation process of Communities of Practices followed by diverse organizations. The selection was made among specific published case studies that contain the required information to our research purposes.

Case Selection

Table 1 shows some of the companies that were studied, and some of their basic features, such as their respective profiles, the year of implementation of CoPs in them, and the main results derived from their experience. The authors are also integrating in this framework other documented experiences, such as (Thompson 2005) (called WorldSystem- largest global IT hardware and services organization), (Mutch 2003) (Pubs Managers), (du Plessis 2008) (SME's), (Wisker, Robinson et al. 2007) (Anglia Ruskin University), (Venters and Wood 2007) (British Council), (Sandrock and Tobin 2007) (AngloAmericanCorporation- Mining Company) and others. Therefore, the study is growing with the purpose of finding experiences of cultivation of CoPs when the organizations do not achieve their goals, as it happens in (Ferlie E 2005). It must be mentioned here that the selection of cases has not been an easy task, mainly because the authors have had to define for this

Figure 4. Three dimensions model (Adapted from McDermott, 1999b)

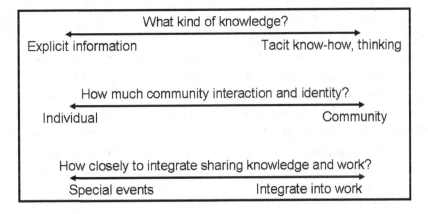

Table 1. Main features of the experiences analyzed

ORGANIZATION	SECTOR	COUNTRY	SIZE	CASE PUBLISHED BY
IBM Global Services	Telecomunication	USA	big	Gongla, P. & Rizutto. C. R. (2001)
World Bank	Bank	USA	big	
Andersen Consulting Education	Consultancy	USA	big	Graham, W. & Osgood, D. (1998)
Cap Gemini Ernest & Young	Consultancy	France	big	American productivity and quality center (2000)
DaimlerChrysler	Automotion	Germany	big	American productivity and quality center (2000)
Ford Motor Company	Automotion	USA	big	American productivity and quality center (2000)
Schumberger	Technological Services	USA	big	American productivity and quality center (2000)
Xerox Corporation	Technology and Services	USA	big	American productivity and quality center (2000)
Watson Wyatt	International consultancy	England	big	Hildreth, P. & Kimble, C. (2000)
International company	Distributor/Commercial company	England	small	Hildreth, P. & Kimble, C. (2000)
Defence Department	Civil Sevice	USA	big	Defense Department of USA (2004)
Medico	Bioscience	UK	big	Swan, Scarbrough, & Robertson (2002)
University of Indiana	Education	USA	big	Liedtka, J. (1999)
Open source software	open source software	All over the world	big	Mas, J. (2005)
Basque Company	Automotion	Basque Country	small	Calzada, I. (2004)

purpose which are the conditions that distinguish a CoP from just a group or a network. This is not an issue of being purists, but in order to advance in any field – and this one is no exception – concepts should be used with rigor. There is a certain respect that must be afforded to the term "community of practice," and the fact is that not every group is one, as some other authors have indicated (Roberts 2006)[12] (Lindkvist 2005)[13] and more recently (Amin and Roberts 2008)[14].

The three dimensions model established by McDermott (1999b) helps us to understand the diversity of CoP's that can emerge, and the diversity of mechanisms, artifacts and operating systems they can use, depending on the knowledge objec-

tives they pursue and the contextual variables in which they operate. However, McDermott's model also gives the possibility of getting conscious that cultivating communities can be a failure option, depending on the chosen combination of dimensions. For instance, if the group shares explicit knowledge through e-mails and sporadically without any type of identity regarding the group, it is better to consider the promotion of an informal network, rather than a community of practice.

To include an experience in our study of CoP's we have gone to the origins, and analyzed the meaning of each word according to Wenger (1998), establishing that the critical characteristics in a community are those that make it possible for the group to be called a community of practice in a strict manner. This entails the following:

- **Community:** Refers to members with a group identity that share experiences. Therefore, groups in which the motivation and identity of each member is exclusively individual and no common experiences are shared would be excluded.
- **Practice:** Is the uniting subject within the group. A subject that excites members so much that it leads them to share their experiences, problems, findings, etc. with the rest of their colleagues and to listen to, help, or discuss the experiences of other members. Therefore, the need for the transfer of experiences and of explicit and tacit knowledge can be perceived in this case. Tacit knowledge can be made explicit due to which not all communities oriented to share documents or reports (explicit knowledge) are excluded, as long as this functioning can be understood working under the terms of experience mentioned in this section. Perceiving the exchange of explicit knowledge in a community is easy, but perceiving the fact that tacit knowledge is being shared is not as easy, since this requires experiencing an encounter with the members of the community or examining the results at the level of knowledge of involved members (if it is perceived that they know more things with time).

Regarding the necessary dimensions, the dimension of group identity takes precedence, since it is the dimension that can guarantee the community's long-term continuity the most. If individual identity prevails, there are more risks of members abandoning the group, since any change or movement within the group can affect said people. However, with a group objective and identity, members will work jointly and for the

group, which allows the community to follow its course.

The dimensions that are sufficient, however, in our work, have been established by the analysis of the objectives set by community cultivators. For example, it has been sufficient for being part of our sample of cases if the knowledge that is shared is directly related and linked to the work of the communities' members, even if only explicit knowledge is shared. In other contexts, the interaction of knowledge with work does not have to occur in a direct manner.

RESULTS AND DISCUSSION

The relevant features that can affect the configuration of communities of practice have been identified in each one of the cases studied and also the results obtained have been stated. This analysis is summarized in Table 2. It is now useful to discuss these results in relation to the questions formulated in the introductory section of this chapter and to each potential contradiction related to management-promoted CoP's.

The Creation of Communities: Organic or Promoted?

According to the background theory of communities of practice one of the requirements for these groups to be named as such is the fact that they must be born spontaneously or organically. Our research, however, shows that it's possible to promote the appearance of these groups to achieve organizational goals. In some of the cases studied, the way of promotion is an organizational culture in which staff is informed of the existence of this type of groups in order to encourage them to form communities within the organization (The World Bank, IBM); in others, CoP are born organically and the organization supports the initiative (Andersen Consulting Education); in others, CoP are implemented as a research project

Table 2. Comparative study of Communities of Practice

ORGANIZATION	CULTIVATION		DESIGN		KNOWLEDGE		INTERACTION & IDENTITY		KNOWLEDGE INTERACTION		OBJECTIVES	WERE THE OBJECTIVES ACHIEVED?
	PROM.	ORG.	VIRT.	REAL.	EXP.	TÁC.	INDIV.	COMUN.	EVENTS	WORK		
IBM Global Services		X		X	X	X	X	X		X	IBM's main objective when supporting CoPs is to relate knowledge management with the organizational strategy, where they create a value system in which people improve the organization by sharing knowledge.	YES
World Bank	X		X		X	X	X		X	X	The main objective is the effectiveness: access to information and knowledge (explicit and tacit) had to be easy and available when needed.	YES
Andersen Consulting Education		X		X	X		X			X	The main objective of the Programme is that CoPs are created in an organical ways since nobody better than themselves know which of the skills they need they develop.	YES
Cap Gemini Ernest & Young	X			X		X		X		X	The main objective is to increase its profit and effectiveness by increaseing individual and organizational competencies	YES
DaimlerChrysler	X	X		X		X	X			X	The company begins to establish knowledge management and CoPs in order to get people's tacit knowledge, since most of the staff are nearing their retirement.	YES
Ford Motor Company	X			X	X	X		X		X	The organization visualized a strategy to achieve low cost and value added worldwide excellence in the product. It was also visualized the strategy that would confer power to employees so that their colleagues would share their knowledge and it would be spread all over the organization.	YES
Schumberger		X		X		X	X			X	The organization is intensive in knowledge and this contributes a competitive advantage of the same through a better customer service. This is the key point that drives the company to emphasize the long-term importance of knowledge management and CoPs.	YES
Xerox Corporation		X		X		X		X		X	Knowledge is part of VICOMTech's strategy aand CoPs are created for the achievement of product innovation and the creation of practicals that improve the company's results. CoPs accelerate organizational learning and create competitive advantages.	YES
Watson Wyatt	X		X			X		X		X	International business organizations are undergoing staff loss and they face the challenge of managing their business internationally spread.	YES
International company	X		X		X	X		X		X	The main objective is to evaluate if the CoPs are valid for knowledge-sharing in spread environments (geographically separated) and allow its members to meet.	YES
Defence Department	X		X			X	X	X		X	To achive corporate knowledge remains within the organization even though experts retire, keeping basic organization compentences.	YES
Medico	X			X	X	X		X		X	The main objective is to evaluate if the CoPs are valid for radical innovation	NO
University of Indiana	X		X		X	X	X	X		X	The main objective of this investigation (creation of a virtual CoP) is the creation of a means of discussion for daily educational practices and the creation of an advanced community that allows the professional development of its members.	YES
Open source software		X	X			X		X		X	The main objective is the development of open source software	YES
Basque Company	X			X		X		X		X	Redesign of the organization with a big reaction capacity because of the unstable market conditions. People must be able to manage one own's knowledge in order to answer flexibly and soon.	NO

or as a pilot project in order to assess staff reaction (Indiana University); and in others, such as Cap Gemini Ernst & Young, CoP are created and their staff is forced to become a part of them. In this last case, both the spontaneity of creation of communities and the voluntary participation of their members comes into question, which may justify why they should probably be referred to by another name. However, the implementation of these community forms has been a success for the company, since it has achieved the objectives originally set. So is it really indispensable for the creation of communities to be spontaneous and led by members?

It is also true that any change today (especially in small and medium-sized enterprises) towards knowledge management or towards the creation of value-based on individual competencies entails important organization restructuring (as can be seen in the case of the Basque Country automotive company). Communities of practice can facilitate these goals as they are based on the transfer of knowledge in order to create value. So, even if CoPs are promoted, it's important to consider that achieving success requires respecting the identity basis, generating the truth between members and considering also the individual goals. This is in line with what Thompson (2005), based on a single case study, identified as the distinction between a Seeding and a Controlling Structure. In the case in which communities are formed due to an organizational initiative and attendance is mandatory, it would most likely evolve to some other knowledge mechanism, possibly more focused to transferring explicit knowledge, which can be interesting in order to save costs, mostly at the beginning, but does not yield the results that a community sharing tacit knowledge yields.

Can Communities of Practice be Structurally Designed?

Following along the lines of the previous argumentation, there is another controversy that is important to clarify. According to CoP's theoretical background, communities of practice are not units that can be designed – in this context design is understood as a systematic, planned, and reflexive colonization of time and space in the service of a task, while it may not only include the production of artifacts, but also the design of social processes such as organizations or education. Authors reiterate in any discussion on the design of learning—which cannot be designed because it belongs to the environment of experience and practice—that communities of practice have already existed for a long time and are not a new fashion in design or a type of pedagogical organization or device to be implemented. Communities are about content, about learning as a live experience of negotiating meaning, not about forms. Therefore, they can be recognized, encouraged, supported, and nourished, but not designed. Learning cannot be designed either, it can only be facilitated or thwarted.

The important and critical fact for our management-based perspective is that infrastructures, systems, resources, and connections can be chosen and reinforced in order to nourish communities of practice. As a matter of fact, the reflection on which type of community could be interesting at an organizational level through the dimensions studied in this research encourages organizations to create communities of practice, but not to design them. However, it is possible for an organization to understand the type of communication needed at an organizational level, the type of community that can make an impression on potential members, and the type of knowledge that must be shared in everyday work. With this information, the organization in question should have the ability to develop communities.

In short, the process of developing communities of practice is closer to agriculture (cultivation) than to architecture (design). Nevertheless, based on the experiences analyzed previously, it would seem that the role of organizations is to be sensitive to the importance of the communities of practice, thus identifying existing ones, extracting results from previous experience and fostering new ones, as needed. However, as mentioned earlier, the cornerstone of communities is people and their willingness to share knowledge. Therefore, the real organizational challenge is to strengthen, develop, cultivate, and support these organic groups and try to translate their energy and results to an organizational level. Moreover, although their creation and maintenance must be monitored, it must also be clear that the objective should not to design, implement, and analyze results, but rather to build on a day-to-day basis, even if it seems otherwise.

Interest in the Creation of Communities of Practice: Individual or Organizational?

Following our answers to the previous questions, another difference in how communities are created is where the idea originates from. According to theory, it could be said that communities are an individual (or group) initiative, but organizational initiatives were also documented in the experiences studied in our case analysis.

The initiative of implementing knowledge management programs can be at an organizational level and it may include the implementation of communities of practice (U.S. Department of Defense, for instance). If the initiative is taken at an individual level, at least there will be an important motivation at the beginning, even if members do not manage to sustain the community due to lack of organizational support (Andersen Consulting Education).

There are also companies that compensate participation in communities in order to motivate their staff (DaimlerChrysler). In this case, individual motivation could depend on the recognition and not on the interest in the practice or in the members of the community and, as a result, it may disappear when the recognition ceases to satisfy the compensation objectives of the staff. Furthermore,

it is possible that competition between personnel is being encouraged by detecting who contributes the most to the community, etc. This does not mean that members' motivation will assure by itself more sustainable CoP's just because the interest is in the practice or in the members, al least, emphasizing organizational purposes and goals. There could be members who leave the community, or the practice and customs could change along time, thus influencing the members as well. The fact of having an organizational support could help to overcome these necessaries and frequent changes in corporate evolution. Also, if a firm tries to achieve a broad scope of staff committed with the project, it should be considered that each individual shall be taken into account. The point is that it is not the same for motivations to be financial or to be intangible, and that there will be people who will not work without being compensated and others who will.

In our research, the experiences studied are coherent with McDermott's (2000) earlier analysis and conclusions. The long-term operation of a community requires an important commitment from the leader but it would never exist without the commitment from its members, since their contributions sustain the community. This commitment of each member to the community is part of the Community challenge, but our research also suggest that it should be useful to integrate as a community challenge getting the organization support to the CoP so that their members can obtain the resources (flexibility, financing, and infrastructure) necessary to continue its activities.

We don't under value the importance of community identity and trust that are also important and relevant issues related to this challenge. If members do not feel that they are part of the group and do not trust other members, it will be difficult for them to contribute to the transfer of knowledge.

We have also proved that the content and even process of knowledge sharing are very different if it's motivated by group reasons (Schlumberger) or by individual reasons (DaimlerChrysler), When motivations are exclusively individual, the participation in the community can be limited to what the community contributes to the member considered attending their own criteria; in the other case the motivation of each member will be aligned with the community, which will provide the group and the person with more integrity.

Is it Necessary a Tangible Motivation for Individuals or is the Most Powerful Motivation Intangible?

Nobody would deny the contribution of value that people achieve when they share their knowledge – which occurs when they are motivated and engaged-. However, the following questions arise: Why does a person share their knowledge? What leads them to do that? What motivations could they have to do so?

According to Davenport and Prusak (1998), there is a market of knowledge on which knowledge can be bought and sold. It doesn't have to be through financial transactions, since it is possible to give knowledge without receiving any compensation for it, but there must be some other motivation, such as trust between the giver and the receiver of knowledge, the practice of the community or interests, the engagement and group identity of people, etc.

Based on this idea, one of the premises for communities at the World Bank was that trust had to be built through group participation and that mutual recognition among professionals who valued contributions made in communities had to exist. This fact results in people feeling valuable, and encourages them to keep participating and sharing what they know. There was a similar environment at Andersen Consulting Education, where professionals perceived an important advantage in the transfer of knowledge.

Other cases showed that a lack of motivation can constitute a barrier in the implementation of communities, i.e. Medico or even the Basque Country automotive company, where the fear of losing a position of power (on behalf of certain people) in relation to others constituted an organizational problem to overcome in the implementation of communities. At Medico, this subject was considerably more prominent, since urologists did not want to participate in the implementation of new communities of practice when they saw their status, and their resulting organizational power in relation to other doctors, endangered.

Therefore, the individual challenge can be difficult to overcome if the organizational hierarchy in question is altered, since those who are bound to lose power or status will be reluctant to participate in the change. It is also important to consider what the motivations that could move people to share what they know are, and the leader of the community should be a key element in detecting said interests.

The most relevant contribution along these lines is the experiences resulting from communities of practice without organizational limits. These communities show not only that people share their knowledge for reasons that have nothing to do with financial ones, but also that intangible motivations are a key element for a community to work and work well. Regarding the 10 KSFs contributed by McDermott (2000), and explained earlier, it is worth mentioning that all of them are pretty much necessary for communities of practice to be successful and viable in the long run. Depending on the organization and environment in question, some KSFs will be fulfilled more than others, but our experience reveals that what companies' value in the success of the implementation of communities is always constituted by some of the KSFs established by McDermott (2000).

Knowledge Management: Within or Outside the Organizational Culture?

Within the organizational challenge, McDermott (2000) suggests focusing on knowledge due to its importance for both the organization and for people, but also suggests not imposing knowledge management within an organizational culture. In several of the analyzed experiences, companies developed a program of knowledge management including the implementation of communities in it. Other companies, on the other hand, decided to implement communities directly, without any previous knowledge management program. Neither one of the two systems can be considered wrong attending the results analyzed and their performance. Anyway, authors consider hat the process of cultivating CoPs is much easier to implement in communities that include a key practice for the company and therefore entail knowledge management implicitly, than trying to make people understand what knowledge management is without first implementing something tangible. The latter option makes people feel lost and start questioning what knowledge really is and if it can really be managed. As a result, it is easier for staff to perceive the benefits of knowledge transfer by experiencing it through a community, for instance, than by listening to the importance of knowledge management within the organization in informative sessions.

Should Technology be a Support or a Purpose for the Creation of CoPs?

In the cases studied in this research, some communities are completely dependent upon technology, either due to them being virtual communities or due to their reliance on an important technological platform (Indiana University, US Department of Defense, Watson Wyatt). In all cases, their creators felt that a key element in the development of platforms was for technology never to take precedence, but rather to be a support tool

that also guaranteed the community members' participation rather than their rejection due to the lack of technical knowledge or to the use of user-unfriendly technologies.

This is consistent with McDermott (2000), who states that technology must be at the service of the community, strengthening its social element. It is obvious that the important element in communities is people, not technology, and that if they do not perceive ease of using the technical support, and ability for building confidence and trust in an intuitive way (as Soto and alt, 2007 pointed out) they will reject it instead of using it, which can even lead to the community's existence being thrown into doubt.

In the experiences analyzed by this study, the design and creation of technological platforms implied the investment of many resources, including financial, technology expert personnel as well personnel in charge of promoting communities, while it built upon earlier analysis as to whether or not potential members would be willing to use the technology that was going to be developed in order to enable participation in the community. As a result, technological support can either be a facilitator or a terrible enemy, depending on how it is introduced into communities, which is why spending time on its design is well worth it. We also think that the recent work of Amin and Roberts (2008) can help managers to understand when the use of a technical support is more appropriate for the expected "knowing in action" objectives.

FUTURE WORK

Our research shows fairly the strengths of the CoP for achieving organizational goals, and also the real possibility of managing their process of creation and development, but also emphasizes the importance of people and their motivation in making CoP work. We have shown some potential signs of agreement between the management-promoted perspective and the emergent approach, and also some interesting reinforcement links between them. But also we are conscious that this approach can motivate some important contradictions, such as imposing formal structures upon existing CoPs, or treating as CoP structures which are not. This is why, in order to advance a future research on the topic of management-promoted CoP we would suggest a more detailed analysis of the specific dimensions of the cultivation process undertaken and comparisons with the dimensions followed by organic ones to assess differences in the development process and goal achievement.

It would also be extremely interesting to sum up the opinions of entrepreneurs regarding their vision on the strengths and weaknesses of the process of cultivating CoP in organizations and also the experience of community members receiving organizational support so as to compare the perceived pros and cons. Likewise, it would be a good idea to evaluate which is the present general situation in the industry regarding the existence of CoP in organizations, and the way they have been originated and developed.

Finally, the study of the alignment between individual and community interests is also an important issue, not only for our research focus, but also for CoP area in general. In fact, analyzing open-source software communities it is possible to note that they are effective communities, very often more effective than communities cultivated within organizations. This example can thus be extended to organizations themselves, in which it is obvious that it would be necessary to understand what CoP already exists and which kind of interest and goals are they serving.

CONCLUSION

Contributions

The main contribution of our study is demonstrating that CoP's can be promoted and led by man-

agement teams to achieve organizational goals, and this will not be an obstacle for their right development if they are honest with the means used for that purpose. To be honest means accept the four elements that constitute a CoP and working to develop them and not weaken them.

As we have seen, some of the measures that can weaken the development of the community, can have accelerate its emergence, so it's important to be conscious of the evolutionary process that the CoP will continue in case of success.

This study offers interesting insights for the implementation of communities of practice understood as a tool for knowledge management and for improving competitiveness in organizations.

The reflection made on the challenges of the creation of communities of practice clarifies possible uncertainties or incoherencies that could appear after reading the theory on these communities, as well as their applicability on a practical level. It also analyzes the various documented real experiences, which can contribute to better understand concepts such as design, cultivation of communities, promotion of communities, organic communities, etc.

Limitations of the Study

The most important limitation of this investigation projects are the following:

- All the cases of CoP studied are established within organizations, except for the free-software community experience. The important knowledge connection with clients, procurers, public bodies, universities and other actors of the innovation system and the role that CoP's can play on it, has been out of question.
- Most of the experiences were successful, no failure. This is the reason why these experiences allow the detection of Success Key Factors. Nevertheless, failure could occur during CoPs' cultivation process, even if the

Success Key Factors shown in this analysis were taken into account. Should there have been further failure cases, there could have been more details for those cases where CoPs are a valid knowledge management tool in companies.

- The sample is constituted by experiences documented and published by other authors, which of course prevent authors from having access to the information and knowledge needed to go deeper in their analysis. Authors hope that the variables analyzed could be considered for other researchers in future case studies to develop a more consistent
- research avenue.

General Interest

This chapter has been written having in mind a broad public, ranging from academics and researchers (MSc and PhD students) to professionals in industry, interested in the Knowledge Management field and the Communities of Practice from a pragmatic point of view, oriented to identify practices that had shown increased performance.

Authors have prioritized a managerial point of view, looking at case studies, and emphasizing results over firms in a challenging environment, considering its contribution on some key subjects such as innovation, knowledge management, learning, technology, and motivational approach, that are studied from this additional point of view.

Authors expect that academics and researchers will find the chapter useful in incorporating the Management approach to their advanced postgraduate and PhD materials on communities of practices. Industry professionals would obtain useful insight for re-considering management strategies, personnel relationship management and learning organizations.

REFERENCES

American productivity and quality center (2000). *Building and sustaining communities of practice.* Final Report. APQC, USA.

Amin, A., & Roberts, J. (2008). Knowing in action: Beyond communities of practice. *Research Policy, 37*(2), 353-369.

Barab, S. A., Mackinster, J. G., & Scheckler, R. (2003). Designing system dualities: Characterizing a Web-supported professional development community. *Information Society, 19*(3), 237-257.

Brown, J. S., & Durguid, P. (1991). Organizational Learning and communities of practice: Toward a unified view of working, learning and innovation. *Management Science.*

Brown, J. S., & Gray, E. S. (1995, November). The people are the company. *Fast Company Magazine.*

Calzada, I. (2004). Una forma organizativa para intervenir en las organizaciones: comunidad de prácticas (CoP). *MIK, S. Coop.*

Davenport, T. H., & Prusak, L. (1998). *Working knowledge: How organizations manage what they know.* Boston: Harvard Business School Press.

Defense Department of USA (2004). Information technology (IT) community of practice. *Defense & AT-L, 33*(5), 79-80.

du Plessis, M. (2008). The strategic drivers and objectives of communities of practice as vehicles for knowledge management in small and medium enterprises. *International Journal of Information* Management, *28*(1), 61-67.

Engestrom, Y. (2001). Expansive learning at work: Toward an activity theory reconceptualization. *Journal od Eduaction and Work, 14*, 133-156.

Ferlie, E. F. L., Wood, M., & Hawkins, C. (2005). The nonspread of innovations: The mediating role of professionals. *Academy of Management Journal 48*(1), 117-134.

Finchman, R., & Clark, T. (2006). Within and beyond communities of practice: Making sense of learning through participation, identity and practice. *Journal of Management Studies, 43*(3), 641-53.

Gongla, P., & Rizutto, C. R. (2001). Evolving communities of practice: IBM Global Services experience. *IBM Systems Journal, 40*(4), 842-853.

Graham, W., & Osgood, D. (1998). A real-life community of practice. *Training & Development,* 52(5), 34-38.

Handley, K., Sturdy, A., Fincham, R., & Clark, T. (2006). Within and beyond communities of practice: making sense of learning through participation, identity and practice. *Journal of Management Studies, 43*(3), 641-53.

Hildreth, P., & Kimble, C. (2000). Communities of practice in the international distributed environment. *Journal of Knowledge Management,* 4(1), 27-38.

Iverson, J. O. (2003). *Knowing volunteers through communities of practice.* Arizona State University. Arizona, USA.

Kakadadse, N. K., Kakadadse, A., & Kouzmin, A. (2003). Reviewing the knowledge management literature: Towards a taxonomy. *Journal of Knowledge Management, 7*(4), 75-91.

Klein, J. H., Connell, N., & Meyer, E. (2005). Knowledge characteristics of communities of practice. *Knowledge Management Research and Practice, 3,* 106-114.

Klein, J. H. (2008). Some directions for research in Knowledge Sharing. *Knowledge Management Research and Practice, 6,* 41-46.

Lave, J., & Wenger, E. (1991). *Situated learning: Legitimate peripheral participation.* New York: Cambridge University Press.

Lee, J. (2003). Building successful communities of practice: CoPs are networks of activities. *Information Outlook.*

Lesser, E., & Everest, K. (2001). Using communities of practice to manage intellectual capital. *Ivey Business Journal, 65*(4), 37-42.

Liedtka, J. (1999). Linking competitive advantage with communities of practice. *Journal of Management Inquiry, 8*(1), 5-17.

Lindkvist, L. (2005). Knowledge communities and knowledge collectivities: A typology of knowledge work in groups. *Journal of Management Review, 42*(6), 1189-1210.

Loyarte, E., & Rivera, O. (2007). Communities of practice: A model for their cultivation. *Journal: Journal of Knowledge Management, 113,* 67-77.

Malone, D. (2002). Knowledge management: A model for organizational learning. *International Journal of Accounting Information Systems,* 3(2), 111-124.

Mas, J. (2005). *Software libre: técnicamente viable, económicamente sostenible y socialmente justo.* Zero Factory, S.L. Barcelona.

McDermott, R. (2000). Critical success factors in building communities of practice. *Knowledge Management Review, 3*(2), 5.

McDermott, R. (1999). Learning across teams: How to build communities of practice in team organizations. *Knowledge Management Review,* 2(2), 32.

McDermott, R. (1999b). Nurturing three dimensional communities of practice: How to get the most out of human networks. *Knowledge Management Review, 2*(5), 26.

Mutch, A. (2003). Communities of practice and habitus: A critique. *Organization Studies, 24*(3), 383-401.

Roberts, J. (2006). Limits of communities of practice. *Journal of Management Studies, 43*(3), 623-639.

Saint-Onge, H., & Wallace, D. (2003). *Leveraging communities of practice for strategic advance.* Butterworth & Heinemann, USA.

Sandrock, J., & Tobin, P. (2007). *Critical success factors for communities of practice in a global mining company.* Nr Reading, Academic Conferences Ltd.

Schewen, T. M. & Hara, N. (2003). Community of practice: A metaphor for online design? *Information Society, 19*(3), 257-271.

Smeds, R., & Alvesalo, J. (2003). Global business process development in a virtual community of practice. *Production Planning & Control, 14*(4), 361-372.

Soto, J. P., Vizcaino, A., Portillo-Rodriguez, J., & Piattini, M. (2007). Applying trust, reputation and intuition aspects to support virtual communities of practice. In *Knowledge-Based Intelligent Information and Engineering Systems*: Kes 2007 - Wirn 2007, Pt Ii, Proceedings, (pp. 353-360).

Swan, J. A., Scarbrough, H., & Robertson, M. (2002). The construction of communities of practice in the management of innovation. *Management Learning, 33*(4), 477-497.

Thompson, M. (2005). Structural and epistemic parameters in communities of practices. *Organizational Science, 16*(2), 151-164.

Urquhart, C., Yeoman, A., & Sharp, S. (2002). *NeLH communities of practice evaluation report.* University of Wales Aberystwyth, England.

Van Zolinger, S. L., Sreumer, J. N., & Stooker, M. (2001). Problems in knowledge management: A case study of a knowledge-intensive company.

International Journal of Training & Development, 5(3), 168-185.

Venters, W., & Wood, B. (2007). Degenerative structures that inhibit the emergence of communities of practice: A case study of knowledge management in the British Council. *Information Systems Journal, 17*(4), 349-368.

Wenger, E., McDermott, R., & Snyder, W. M. (2002). *Cultivating communities of practice.* Boston: Harvard Business School.

Wenger, E., & Snyder, W. M. (2000). Communities of practice: The organizational frontier. *Harvard Business Review, 78*(1), 139-146.

Wenger, E. (1998). *Communities of practice: Learning, meaning and identity.* Boston: Cambridge University Press.

Wenger, E. (1998b). Communities of practice: Learning as a social system. *Systems Thinker.*

Wisker, G., Robinson, G., et al. (2007). Postgraduate research success: Communities of practice involving cohorts, guardian supervisors and online communities. *Innovations in Education and Teaching International, 44*, 301-320.

KEY TERMS

Case Studies: A detailed intensive study of a unit, such as a corporation or a corporate division that stresses factors contributing to its success or failure.

Communities of Practice: An active system in which its participants share knowledge based on their daily tasks. They share the meaning of this knowledge in their life within the community. The participants of the community are united in the community's practice and in the meaning of said practice, both at the community level and at broader levels (Wenger, 1998).

Cultivation Model: A model of evaluation for communities of practice in the process of cultivation that makes it possible to estimate the probabilities of success for the proposal of creating communities at a specific moment and under a specific situation is included. The cultivation and integration of communities is a continuous process, due to which its evaluation must be performed periodically.

Knowledge Management: Managing the corporation's knowledge through a systematically and organizationally specified process for acquiring, organizing, sustaining, applying, sharing and renewing both the tacit and explicit knowledge of employees to enhance organizational performance and create value (Davenport, 1998).

ENDNOTES

[1]   Lesser and Everest 2001, quoted by Swan, Scarbrough, and Robertson, 2002.

[2]   Brown and Duguid, 2001; Orr, 1996, quoted by Swan, Scarbrough, and Robertson, 2002.

[3]   Wenger et al., 2002, quoted by Iverson and McPhee, 2002.

[4]   Wagner, 2000 quoted by Kakadadse, Kakadadse, and Kouzmin, 2003.

[5]   Lesser and Everest 2001:41, quoted by Swan, Scarbrough, and Robertson, 2002.

[6]   Orr, 1996, quoted by van Zolingen, Streumer, and M. Stooker, 2001.

[7]   Orr, 1996, quoted by van Zolingen, Streumer, and Stooker, 2001.

[8]   Stewart, 2001, quoted by Urquhart, Yerman, and Sharp, 2002.

[9]   Barab and Duffy, 2000, quoted by Barab; MaKinster and Scheckler, 2003.

[10]   Barab, 2001, quoted by Barab; MaKinster and Scheckler, 2003.

[11]   Heald, 2004.

[12]   Roberts identifies also collectivities and constellations of practice

[13]   This author differentiate collectivity-of-practice from Community of practice

[14]   Those authors identified different varieties of knowing in action. The paper notes the differences - in organisation, spatial dynamics, innovation outcomes, and knowledge processes - between four modes: craft or task-based knowing; epistemic or high creativity knowing; professional knowing; and virtual knowing.

This work was previously published in Virtual Community Practices and Social Interactive Media: Technology Lifecycle and Workflow Analysis, edited by D. Akoumianakis, pp. 18-41, copyright 2009 by Information Science Reference (an imprint of IGI Global).

Compilation of References

Abdul-Rahman, A. and Hailes, S., (2000), "Supporting Trust in Virtual Communities". Proceedings of the 33rd Hawaii International Conference on Systems Sciences (HICSS'00), Vol. 6.

Abiteboul, S., Buneman, P., & Suciu, D. (2000). *Data on the Web: From relations to semistructured data and XML*. San Francisco: Morgan Kaufmann Publishers.

Ackerman, M. S. (1998). Augmenting organizational memory: A field study of answer garden. [TOIS]. *ACM Transactions on Information Systems, 16*(3), 203–224. doi:10.1145/290159.290160

Ackoff, R., (1989), "From Data to Wisdom". Journal of Applies Systems Analysis. Vol. 16, pp. 3-9.

ADL Technical Team. (2004). *Sharable content object reference model (SCORM) 2004* (2nd ed.). Alexandria, VA: Advanced Distributed Learning.

Akhavan, P., Jafari, M., & Fathian, M. (2005). Exploring failure-factors of implementing knowledge management systems in organizations. *Journal of Knowledge Management Practice*.

Alavi, M., & Leidner, D. (2001). Review: Knowledge management and knowledge management systems: Conceptual foundations and research issues. *MIS Quarterly, 25*(1), 107-136.

Alavi, M., & Leidner, D. E. (1999). Knowledge management systems: Issues, challenges, and benefits. *Communications of the AIS, 1*(7).

Alberts, B. (2009). Making a science of education. *Science, 323*(2), 15. doi:10.1126/science.1169941

Allen, I. E., & Seaman, J. (2004). *Entering the mainstream: The quality and extent of online education in the United States, 2003 and 2004*. Newburyport, MA: The Sloan Consortium.

Allen, I. E., & Seaman, J. (2006). *Online nation: Five years of growth in online learning*. Newburyport, MA: The Sloan Consortium.

Allen, S., Evans, S., & Ure, D. (2005). Virtual communities of practices: Vehicles for organisational learning and improved job performance. *International Journal of Learning Technology, 1*(3), 252-272.

Allen, T., (1984), "Managing the Flow of Technology: Technology Transfer and the Dissemination of Technological Information within the R&D Organization", Cambridge, MA: MIT Press.

American productivity and quality center (2000). *Building and sustaining communities of practice.* Final Report. APQC, USA.

Amin, A., & Roberts, J. (2008). Knowing in action: Beyond communities of practice. *Research Policy, 37*(2), 353-369.

Anderberg, M. R. (1973). *Cluster analysis for applications.* New York: Academic Press, Inc.

Anderson, R. (2007). What is Web 2.0? Ideas, technologies and implications for education (Tech. Rep.). *JISC Technology and Standards Watch.*

Anderson, T., Rourke, L., Garrison, D. R., & Archer, W. (2001). Assessing teaching presence in a computer conferencing context. *Journal of Asynchronous Learning Networks, 5*(2).

Andrews, N., & Tyson, L. D. (2004). *The upwardly global MBA.* Retrieved from http://www.strategy-business.com

Andriessen, J., Baker, M., & Suthers, D. (2003). Argumentation, computer support, and the educational context of confronting cognitions. In J. Andriessen, M. Baker, & D. Suthers (Eds.), *Arguing to learn: Confronting cognitions in computer-supported collaborative learning environments* (pp. 1-25). Amsterdam, The Netherlands: Kluwer.

Anma, F., Ninomiya, T., & Okamoto, T. (2007). A development of learning management system for interactive e-learning in higher education. In *Proceedings of the World Conference on E-Learning in Corporate, Government, Healthcare & Higher Education,* Quebec, Canada (pp. 1956-1963).

Anthonisse, J. M. (1971). *The rush in a directed graph* (Tech. Rep. BN 9/71). Amsterdam, The Netherlands: Stichting Mathematisch Centrum.

Appelt, W., & Mambrey, P. (1999), Experiences with the BSCW Shared Workspace System as the Backbone of a Virtual Learning Environment for Students. *In Proceedings of ED Media '99.'* Charlottesville, (pp. 1710-1715).

Arbaugh, J. B., & Hwang, A. (2006). Does "teaching presence" exist in online MBA courses? *The Internet and Higher Education, 9*(1), 9–21. doi:10.1016/j.iheduc.2005.12.001

Ardichvili, A. (2003). Motivation and barriers to participation in virtual knowledge-sharing communities of practice. *Journal of Knowledge Management, 7*(1), 64-77.

Argote, L., & Ingram, P. (2000). Knowledge transfer: A basis for competitive advantage in firms. *Organizational Behavior and Human Decision Processes, 82*(1), 150-169.

Aristotle. (1996). *Poetics* (M. Heath, Trans.). New York: Penguin Books.

ASTC. (2008). *Sourcebook of statistics & analysis.* Washington, DC: Association of Science-Technology Centers (ASTC).

Atkins, H., Moore, D., Sharpe, S., & Hobbs, D. (2001). Learning style theory and computer mediated communication. In *Proceedings of the ED-MEDIA 2001 World Conference on Educational Multimedia, Hypermedia & Telecommunications,* Tampere, Finland (pp. 71-75).

Backbase. (2008). *AJAX in enterprise* [white paper].

Backingham Shum, S., MacLean, A., Forder, J., & Hammond, N. (1993). Summarising the evolution of design concepts within a design rationale framework. In *Adjunct Proceedings of the InterCHI'93: ACM/IFIP Conference on Human Factors in Computing Systems,* Amsterdam, The Netherlands (pp. 43-44).

Baets, W., & Van der Linden, G. (2003). *Virtual corporate universities: A matrix of knowledge and learning for the new digital dawn.* Kluwer Academic Publisher.

Balasubramanian, S., & Mahajan, V. (2001). The economic leverage of the virtual community. *International Journal of Electronic Commerce, 5*(3), 103-138.

Balasubramanian, S., Brennan, R., Norrie, D., (2001), "An Architecture for Metamorphic Control of Holonic Manufacturing Systems". Computers in Industry, Vol. 46(1), pp. 13-31.

Bandura, A. (1977). *Social learning theory.* New York: General Learning Press. Bandura, A. (n.d.). *Social learning theory.*

Banner, G., & Rayner, S. (2000). Learning language and learning style: Principles, process and practice. *Language Learning Journal, 21,* 37–44. doi:10.1080/09571730085200091

Barab, S. A., Mackinster, J. G., & Scheckler, R. (2003). Designing system dualities: Characterizing a Web-supported professional development community. *Information Society, 19*(3), 237-257.

Barab, S. A., MaKinster, J. G., & Scheckler, R. (2003). Designing system dualities: Characterizing a web-supported professional development community. *The Information Society, 19,* 237-256.

Barabási, A. L., Jeong, H., Néda, Z., Ravasz, E., Schubert, A., & Vicsek, T. (2002). Evolution of the social network of scientific collaborations. *Physica A, 311*(3-4), 590–614. doi:10.1016/S0378-4371(02)00736-7

Barber, K. and Kim, J., (2004), "Belief Revision Process Based on Trust: Simulation Experiments". 4th Workshop on Deception, Fraud and Trust in Agent Societies, Montreal Canada, pp. 1-12.

Barlow, D. H. (2002). *Anxiety and its disorders: The nature and treatment of anxiety and panic* (2nd ed.). New York: The Guilford Press.

Barrows, H. S., & Tamblyn, R. M. (1980). *Problem-based learning: An approach to medical education.* New York: Springer Publishing Co.

Bateman, C. (2008). *Story, plot & narrative.*

Bateson, G. (1942). *Social planning and the concept of deutero-learning: Conference on science, philosophy and religion, second symposium.* New York: Harper.

Bateson, G. (1956). Toward a theory of schizophrenia. *Behavioral Science, 1,* 251–264.

Bateson, G. (2000). *Step to an ecology of mind.* Chicago, IL: The University of Chicago Press.

Beldarrain, Y. (2006). Distance education trends: Integrating new technologies to foster student interaction and collaboration. *Distance Education, 27*(2), 139–153. doi:10.1080/01587910600789498

Belotti, V., Ducheneaut, N., Howard, M., & Smith, I. (2003). Taking email to task: The design and evaluation of a task management centered email tool. In *Proceedings of the SIGCHI Conference on Human Factors in Computing Systems* (pp. 345-352).

Bergeron, F., & Raymond, L. (1992). The advantages of electronic data interchange. *SIGMIS Database, 23*(4), 19–31. doi:10.1145/146553.146556

Berne, E. (1996). *Games people play: The basic handbook of transactional analysis.* New York: Penguin Books.

Berners-Lee, T. (1999). *Weaving the Web.* London: Orion Business Books.

Berners-Lee, T. (2007). *Giant global graph.*

Bernhard, E., Fischer, F., & Mandl, H. (2006). Conceptual and socio-cognitive support for collaborative learning in videoconferencing environments. *Computers & Education, 47,* 298–315. doi:10.1016/j.compedu.2004.11.001

Bieber, M., D., Engelbart, D., Furuta, R., Hiltz, S. R., Noll, J., Preece, J. et al.(2002). Toward virtual community knowledge evolution. *Journal of Management Information Systems, 18*(4), 11-35.

Blanchard, A. L., & Markus, M. L. (2004). The experienced 'sense' of a virtual community: Characteristics and processes. *Database for Advances in Information Systems, 35*(1), 65-79.

Blau, J. R., & Goodman, N. (Eds.). (1995). *Social roles & social institutions*. New Brunswick, NJ: Transaction Publishers.

Bock, G. W., Zmud, R. W., Kim, Y. G., & Lee, J. N. (2005). Behavioral intention formation in knowledge sharing: Examining the roles of extrinsic motivators, social-psychological forces, and organizational climate. *MIS Quarterly, 29*(1), 87-111.

Bock, H. H. (1989). Probabilistic aspects in cluster analysis. In *Conceptual and numerical analysis of data*. Berlin, Germany: Springer-Verlag.

Bonk, C., & Zhang, K. (2006). Introducing the R2D2 model: Online learning for the diverse learners of this world. *Distance Education, 27*(2), 249–264. doi:10.1080/01587910600789670

Boukottaya, A. (2004). *Schema matching for structured document transformations* (Doctoral dissertation). Lausanne, Switzerland: École Polytechnique Fédérale de Lausanne.

Boukottaya, A., & Vanoirbeek, C. (2005). Schema matching for transforming structured documents. In *Proceedings of the 2005 ACM symposium on Document engineering*, Bristol, United Kingdom (pp. 101-110). New York: ACM Press.

Boyle, M., & Greenberg, S. (2005). The language of privacy: Learning from video media space analysis and design. *Journal of ACM Transactions on Human Computer Interaction, 12*(2), 328–370. doi:10.1145/1067860.1067868

Brandenburg, D. C., & Binder, C.V. (1999). Emerging trends in human performance interventions. In H. D. Stolovitch & E. J. Keeps (Eds.), *Handbook of human performance technology: Improving individual and organizational performance worldwide (pp.* 843866). San Francisco: Jossey-Bass.

Bransford, J., Brown, A. L., & Cocking, R. R. (Eds.). (1999). *How people learn*. Washington, DC: National Academy Press.

Branting, L. K., & Lester, J. C. (1996). Justification structures for document reuse. In I. Smith & B. Faltings (Eds.), *Proceedings of the Third European Workshop on Case-Based Reasoning*, Lausanne, Switzerland (pp. 76-90). Berlin, Germany: Springer-Verlag.

Bretl, R., Maier, D., Otis, A., Penney, J., Schuchardt, B., Stein, J., et al. (1989). The GemStone data management system. In W. Kim & F. Lochovsky (Eds.), *Object-oriented concepts, databases and applications* (pp. 283-308). New York: ACM Press.

Brower, H. H. (2003). On emulating classroom discussion in a distance-delivered OBHR course: Creating an on-line learning community. *Academy of Management Learning & Education, 2*(1), 22–37.

Brown, H., & Cole, F. C. (1992). Editing structured documents: Problems and solutions. *Electronic Publishing -- Origination . Dissemination and Design, 5*(4), 209–216.

Brown, J. S. & Duguid, P. (1999). Organizing knowledge. *The society for organizational learning, 1*(2), 28-44.

Brown, J. S. & Duguid, P. (2000). Balancing act: How to capture knowledge without killing it. *Harvard Business Review, 73-80.*

Brown, J. S. & Gray, E. S. (1995). The people are the company. *FastCompany*. Retrieved from http://www.fastcompany.com/online/01/people.html

Brown, J. S., & Duguid, P. (2000). *The social life of Information.* Boston. Harvard Business School Press.

Brown, J. S., & Durguid, P. (1991). Organizational Learning and communities of practice: Toward a unified view of working, learning and innovation. *Management Science.*

Buckingham Shum, S. (1996). Design argumentation as design rationale. In *The encyclopedia of computer science and technology* (pp. 95-128). New York: Marcel Dekker, Inc.

Buckingham Shum, S. (2007). Hypermedia discourse: Contesting networks of ideas and arguments. In *Conceptual structures: Knowledge architectures for smart applications*, (LNAI 4604, pp. 29-44).

Buckingham Shum, S. (2008). Cohere: Towards Web 2.0 argumentation. In . *Proceedings of COMMA, 2008*, 97–108.

Bull, S., & McCalla, G. (2002). Modeling cognitive style in a peer help network. *Instructional Science, 30*(6). doi:10.1023/A:1020570928993

Burk, M. (1999). *Knowledge management: Everyone benefits by sharing information.*

Burke, R. (2002). Hybrid recommender systems: Survey and experiments. *User Modeling and User-Adapted Interaction, 12*(4), 331–370. doi:10.1023/A:1021240730564

Butler, B. (1999) *The dynamics of electronic communities.* Unpublished PhD dissertation, Graduate School of Industrial Administration, Carnegie Mellon University.

Butler, B. S. (2001). Membership size, communication activity and sustainability: A resource-based model of online social structures. *Information Systems Research, 12*(4), 346-362.

Buxton, W. (1992). Telepresence: Integrating shared task and person spaces. In R. Baecker (Ed.), *Readings in groupware and computer-supported cooperative work* (pp. 816-822). San Francisco: Morgan Kaufman.

Cali, A., Calvanese, D., Giacomo, G., & Lenzerini, M. (2002). On the expressive power of data integration systems. In S. Spaccapietra, S. T. March, & Y. Kambayashi (Eds.), *Proceedings of 21st International Conference on Conceptual Modeling*, Tampere, Finland (pp. 338-350). Berlin, Germany: Springer-Verlag.

Callon, M. (1986). Some elements of a sociology of translation: Domestication of the scallops and the fishermen of St. Brieuc Bay. In J. Law (Ed.), *Power, action and belief* (pp. 196-233). London: Routledge & Kegan Paul.

Calzada, I. (2004). Una forma organizativa para intervenir en las organizaciones: comunidad de prácticas (CoP). *MIK, S. Coop.*

Campbell, F., & Deakin, M. (2005). Cities as leading examples of digitally-inclusive knowledge societies: the e-citizenship course, representative users, pedagogy and engagement matrix. In M. Osborne & B. Wilson (Eds.), *Making Knowledge Work.* Stirling: Stirling University.

Carbó, J., Molina, M., Dávila, J., (2003), "Trust Management through Fuzzy Reputation". International Journal of Cooperative Information Systems. Vol. 12(1), pp. 135-155.

Carver, C. A., Howard, R. A., & Lane, W. D. (1999). Addressing different learning styles through course hypermedia. *IEEE Transactions on Education, 42*(1), 33–38. doi:10.1109/13.746332

Cassidy, S. (2004). Learning styles: An overview of theories, models, and measures. *Educational Psychology, 24*(4), 419–444. doi:10.1080/0144341042000228834

Castells, M. (1997). *La era de la información: Economía, sociedad y cultura* (Vol. 1). Madrid, Spain: Alianza Editorial.

Chae, B., Koch, H., Paradice, D., & Huy, V. (2005). Exploring knowledge management using network theories: Questions, paradoxes and prospects. *Journal of Computer Information Systems 45*(4), 62-74.

Chakrabarti, S., Dom, B. E., Gibson, D., Kumar, R., Raghavan, P., Rajagopalan, S., & Tomkins, A. (1998). *Spectral filtering for resource discovery.* In *Proceedings of the ACM SIGIR workshop on Hypertext Information Retrieval on the Web.*

Chen, D., & Gellersen, H. W. (1999). Recognition and reasoning in an awareness support system for generation of storyboard-like views of recent activity. In *Proceedings of the International SIGGROUP Conference on Supporting Group Work*, Phoenix, AZ.

Cheuk, B. W. (2006). Using social networking analysis to facilitate knowledge sharing in the British Council. *International Journal of Knowledge Management, 2*(4), 67-76.

Chou, C. (2003). Interactivity and interactive functions in Web-based learning systems: A technical framework for designers. *British Journal of Educational Technology, 34*(3), 265–279. doi:10.1111/1467-8535.00326

Claypool, K. T., Jin, J., & Rundensteiner, E. A. (1998). OQL SERF: An ODMG implementation of the template-based schema evolution framework. In S. A. MacKay & J. H. Johnson (Eds.), *Proceedings of the 1998 conference of the Centre for Advanced Studies on Collaborative research*, Toronto, Canada (pp. 108-122). Armonk, NY: IBM Press.

Cleveland-Innes, M., Garrison, R., & Kinsel, E. (2007). Role adjustment for learners in an online community of inquiry: Identifying the needs of novice online learners. *International Journal of Web-Based Learning and Teaching Technologies, 2*(1), 1–16.

Cohen, D. (2006). What's your return on knowledge? *Harvard Business Review, 84*(12), 28-28.

Cohen, D., & Prusak, L. (2001). *In good company: How social capital makes organizations work.* Boston: Harvard Business School Press.

Cohendet, P., Creplet, F., & Dupouët, O. (2001). *CoPs and epistemic communities: A renewed approach of organisational learning within the firm.* Retrieved November 22, 2004, from http://www.marsouin.org/IMG/pdf/dupouet.pdf

Cole, M., & Engestrom, Y. (1993). A cultural-historical approach to distributed cognition. In G. Salomon (Ed.), *Distributed cognitions: Psychological and educational considerations.* New York: Cambridge University Press.

Collier, P. (2001). A differentiated model of role identity acquisition. *Symbolic Interaction, 24*(2), 217–235. doi:10.1525/si.2001.24.2.217

Community Intelligence. (2003). *Innovation and CoPs: The "great symphony" paradox. The innovation potential of bridging structural holes.* Retrieved April 2, 2004, from http://www.communityintelligence.com/pdf/Communities_&_Innovation.pdf

Conklin, J. (2005). *Dialogue mapping: Building shared understanding of wicked problems.* New York: John Wiley & Sons.

Conklin, J., & Begeman, M. (1989). gIBIS: A tool for all reasons. *Journal of the American Society for Information Science American Society for Information Science, 40*(3), 200–213. doi:10.1002/(SICI)1097-4571(198905)40:3<200::AID-ASI11>3.0.CO;2-U

Conklin, J., Selvin, A., Shum, S. B., & Sierhuis, M. (2001). Facilitated hypertext for collective sensemaking: 15 years on from gIBIS. In *Proceedings of the Twelfth ACM Conference on Hypertext and Hypermedia*, Aarhus, Denmark (pp. 123-124).

Connect. (2005). *Designing the classroom of tomorrow by using advanced technologies to connect formal and informal learning. The implementation guide.* Ellinogermaniki Agogi. EPINOIA S.A.

Connect. (2006). *D2.1 (Pedagogical report).*

Conrad, D. (2008). From community to community of practice: Exploring the connection of online learners to informal learning in the workplace. *American Journal of Distance Education, 22*(1), 3–23. doi:10.1080/08923640701713414

Constant, D., Keisler, S., & Sproull, L. (1994). What's mine is ours, or is it? A study of attitudes about information sharing. *Information Systems Research, 5*(4), 400-421.

Cox, D., & Greenberg, S. (2000). Supporting collaborative interpretation in distributed Groupware. In *Proceedings of the ACM Conference on Computer Supported Cooperative Work (CSCW '00)* (pp. 289-298).

Cross, R., Laseter, T., Parker, A., & Velasquez, G. (2006). Using social network analysis to improve communities of practice. *California Management Review, 49*(1), 32-60.

Curry, L. (1983). An organization of learning styles theory and constructs. In L. Curry (Ed.), *Learning style in continuing education* (pp. 115-131). Dalhousie University.

Curwell, S., Deakin, M., Cooper, I., Paskaleva-Shapira, K., Ravetz, J., & Babicki, D. (2005). Citizens expectations of information cities: implications for urban planning and design. *Building Research and Information, 22*(1), 55-66.

Daconta, M., Orbst, L., & Smith, K. (2003). *The semantic web*. Indianapolis: Wiley Publishing.

Daele, A., Erpicum, M., Esnault, L., Pironet, F., Platteaux, H., Vandeput, E., & Wiele, N. (2006). An example of participatory design methodology in a project which aims at developing individual and organisational learning in communities of practice. In *Proceedings of the first European Conference on Technology Enhanced Learning (EC-TEL'06)*, Greece.

Damiani, E., Corallo, A., Elia, G., & Ceravolo, P. (2002). *Standard per i learning objects: Interoperabilità ed integrazione nella didattica a distanza*. Convegno internazionale: eLearning. Una sfida per l'Universita: Strategie metodi prospettive.

Damodaran, L., & Olphert, W. (2000). Barriers and facilitators to the use of knowledge management systems. *Behavior and Information Technology, 19*(6), 405-413.

Daniel, B., Schwier, R. A., & McCalla, G. (2003). Social capital in virtual learning communities and distributed communities of practice. *Canadian Journal of Learning and Technology, 29*(3), 113-139.

Danish Technological Institute. (2004). *Reorganisation of government back offices for better electronic public services: European good practices (Back-office reorganisation). Final report to the European Commission*. Retrieved March 3, 2004, from http://www.cio.gv.at/news/files/Back_office.pdf & http://hw.oeaw.ac.at/0xc1aa500d_0x0010b255

Darabi, A. A., Sikorski, E. G., & Harvey, R. B. (2006). Validated competencies for distance teaching. *Distance Education, 27*(1), 105–122. doi:10.1080/01587910600654809

Davenport , P., (1998), "Working Knowledge: How Organizations Manage What They Know". Boston, MA, Project Management Institute, Harvard Business School Press.

Davenport T. H., De Long, D. W., & Beers, M. C. (1998). Successful knowledge management projects. *MIT Sloan Management Review, 39*(2), 43-57.

Davenport, T. H., & Prusak, L. (1997). *Working knowledge: How organizations manage what they know*. Cambridge, MA: Harvard Business School Press.

Davenport, T. H., De Long, D. W., & Beers, M. C. (1997). *Building successful knowledge management projects*. Center for Business Innovation Working Paper, Ernst and Young.

Davis, F. D. (1989). Perceived usefulness, perceived ease of use, and user acceptance of information technology. *MIS Quarterly, 13*(3), 319-341.

De Liddo, A., & Buckingham Shum, S. (2007). Capturing, mapping and integrating argumentation as project memory in participatory urban planning. In *Proceedings of the Workshop on Argumentation Support Systems for eParticipation, EU-IST DEMO-net Network of Excellence*, Berlin, Germany.

de Moor, A., & Aakhus, M. (2006). Argumentation support: From technologies to tools. *Communications of the ACM, 49*(3), 93–98. doi:10.1145/1118178.1118182

de Moor, A., & van den Heuvel, W. J. (2004). Web service selection in virtual communities. In *Proceedings of the 37th Annual Hawaii International Conference on System Sciences (HICSS'04)*, Big Island, Hawaii.

Deakin, M & Allwinkle, S. (2007). e-Topia, SUD and ICTs: the post-human nature, embedded intelligence, cyborg-self and agency of digitally-inclusive regeneration platforms. *International Journal of the Humanities, 5*(2),199-208.

Deakin, M. & Allwinkle, S. (2006). The IntelCities community of practice: the e-learning platform, knowledge management system and digital library for semantically-interoperable e-governance services, *International Journal of Knowledge, Culture and Change Management, 6*(3),155-162.

Deakin, M. & Allwinkle, S. (2007). Urban regeneration and sustainable communities: the role of networks, innovation and creativity in building successful partnerships. *Journal of Urban Technology, 14*(1), 77-91.

Deakin, M. (2007). e-Topia, SUD and ICTs: taking the digitally-inclusive urban regeneration thesis full circle. *Journal of Urban Technology, 14*(3), 131-139.

Deakin, M., Van Isacker, K. & Wong. A. (2004) *Review of the IntelCities Knowledge Capture Requirements Using a S.W.O.T. Analysis.* Edinburgh: Napier University.

Deakins, D., & Freel, M. (1998). Entrepreneurial learning and the growth process in SMEs. *Learning Organisation*, pp. 144-155.

Dede, C. (2009). Immersive interfaces for engagement and learning. *Science, 323*, 66–68. doi:10.1126/science.1167311

Defense Department of USA (2004). Information technology (IT) community of practice. *Defense & AT-L, 33*(5), 79-80.

Desouza, K., Awazu, Y., Baloh, P., (2006), "Managing Knowledge in Global Software Development Efforts: Issues and Practices". IEEE Software, pp. 30-37.

Dewey, J. (1933). *How we think* (rev. ed.). Boston, MA: D.C. Heath.

Dewey, J. (1938). *Experience and education.* New York: Collier.

Diaz, D., & Cartnal, R. (1999). Comparing student learning styles in an online distance learning class and an equivalent on-campus class. *College Teaching, 47*(4), 130–135.

Dickey, M. (2004). The impact of Web-logs (blogs) on student perceptions of isolation and alienation in a Web-based distance-learning environment. *Open Learning, 19*(3), 279–291. doi:10.1080/0268051042000280138

Dillenbourg, P., (1999), "Introduction: What Do You Mean By 'Collaborative Learning'?." Collaborative Learning Cognitive and Computational Approaches. Dillenbourg (Ed.). Elsevier Science.

Ding, C., & He, X. *(2002).* Cluster merging and splitting in hierarchical clustering algorithms. *In* Proceedings of the IEEE International Conference on Data Mining (ICDM'02).

Ding, C., He, X., Zha, H., Gu, M., & Simon, H. (2001). A min-max cut algorithm for graph partitioning and data clustering. In *Proceedings of the IEEE Int'l Conf. Data Mining* (pp. 107-114).

Doering, A. (2006). Adventure learning: Transformative hybrid online education. *Distance Education, 27*(2), 197–215. doi:10.1080/01587910600789571

Donath, J. S. (1999). Identity and deception in the virtual community. In M. A. S. a. P. Kollock (Ed.), *Communities in cyberspace* (pp. 29-59).. London, Routledge.

Douglas, K. M., & McGarty, C. (2001). Identifiability and self-presentation: Computer-mediated communication and intergroup interaction. *British Journal of Social Psychology, 40*, 399-416.

Dourish, P. (2006). Re-space-ing place: "Place" and "space" ten years on. In *Proceedings of the ACM conference on Computer-supported cooperative work*, Banff, Canada, Edigo, C. (1988). Videoconferencing as a technology to support group work: A review of its failure. In *Proceedings of the ACM conf. on Computer-Supported Cooperative Work.*

Dredze, M., Lau, T., & Kushmerick, N. (2006). Automatically classifying emails into activities. In *Proceedings of the 11th International Conference on Intelligent User Interfaces*, Australia.

Dretske, F. (1991). *Explaining behavior: Reasons in a world of causes.* Cambridge, MA: MIT Press.

Driscoll, M. P. (2000). *Psychology of learning for instruction.* Boston: Allyn & Bacon.

du Plessis, M. (2008). The strategic drivers and objectives of communities of practice as vehicles for knowledge management in small and medium enterprises. *International Journal of Information* Management, *28*(1), 61-67.

Duffy, T., & Jonassen, D. H. (1992). Constructivism: New implications for instructional technology. In T. Duffy & D. H. Jonassen (Eds.), *Constructivism and the technology of instruction: A conversation.* Hillsdale, NJ: Erlbaum.

Edelstein, H. A. (2001, March 12). Pinning for gold in the Clickstream. *Information Week.*

Edmonds, E., Moran, T., & Do, E. (1998). Interactive systems for supporting the emergence of concepts and ideas. *SIGCHI Bulletin, 30*(1), 62–76. doi:10.1145/280571.280581

Egan, K. (2004). *Teaching as story telling.* London, Canada: The Althouse Press.

Eisen, M. J. (2001). Peer-based professional development viewed through the lens of transformative learning. *Holistic Nursing Practice, 16*(1), 30–42.

El Helou, S., Gillet, D., Salzmann, C., & Rekik, Y. (2007). Feed-oriented awareness services for eLogbook mobile users. In *Proceedings of the 2nd International Conference on Interactive Mobile and Computer aided Learning (IMCL 2007),* Jordan.

Ellis, D., Oldridge, R., & Vasconcelos, A. (2004) Community and Virtual Community. *Annual Review of Information Sciences and Technology, 38,* 146–186.

Engestrom, Y. (2001). Expansive learning at work: Toward an activity theory reconceptualization. *Journal od Eduaction and Work, 14,* 133-156.

Epple, D. & Argote, L. (1996). An empirical investigation of the microstructure of knowledge acquisition and transfer through learning by doing. *Operations Research, 44*(1), 77-86.

Erdem, F., & Ozen, J. (2003). Cognitive and affective dimensions of trust in developing team performance. *Team Performance Management: An International Journal, 9,* 131–135. doi:10.1108/13527590310493846

Ester, M., Kriegel, H., Sander, J., & Xu, X. (1996). A Density-Based Algorithm for Discovering Clusters in Large Spatial Databases with Noise. In *Proceedings of 2nd International Conference on KDD.*

Evans, T., & Lockwood, F. (1994). *Understanding learners in open and distance education.* London: Koggan Page Ltd.

Falivene, G., & Kaufman, E. (2005). The potential of CoPs in Argentina to articulate public organizations and training through knowledge management approach. In E. Coakes & S. Clarke (Eds.), *Encyclopedia of communities of practice in information and knowledge management.* Hershey, PA: Idea Group Reference.

Falivene, G., Silva, G., & Gurmendi, L. (2003). *El e-learning como mecanismo articulador de procesos de gestión del conocimiento y formación continua en las organizaciones públicas: El caso del Sistema de Información Universitaria.* Retrieved September 19, 2004, from http://www.clad.org.ve/fulltext/0048201.pdf

Faraj, S., & Wasko, M. M. (Forthcoming). The web of knowledge: An investigation of knowledge exchange in networks of practice. AMR.

Farrell, J., & Nezlek, G. S. (2007). Rich Internet applications the next stage of application development. In *Proceedings of the 29th International Conference on Information Technology Interfaces, ITI 2007* (pp. 413-418).

Feist, J., & Feist, G. J. (2006). *Theories of personality* (6th ed.). New York: McGraw-Hill.

Felder, R. M. (1996). "Matters of Style". ASEE Prism. Vol. 6(4), pp. 18-23.

Felder, R. M., & Silverman, L. K. (1988). Learning and teaching styles in engineering education. *English Education, 78*, 674–681.

Ferlie, E. F. L., Wood, M., & Hawkins, C. (2005). The non-spread of innovations: The mediating role of professionals. *Academy of Management Journal 48*(1), 117-134.

Finchman, R., & Clark, T. (2006). Within and beyond communities of practice: Making sense of learning through participation, identity and practice. *Journal of Management Studies, 43*(3), 641-53.

Fink, J., & Kobsa, A. (2001). A review and analysis of commercial user modeling servers for personalization on the World Wide Web. *User Modeling and User-Adapted Interaction, Special Issue on Deployed User Modeling, 10*(3-4).

Freeman, L. C. (1977). A set of measures of centrality based on betweenness. *Sociometry, 40*, 35–41. doi:10.2307/3033543

Fuentes, R., Gómez-Sanz, J., Pavón, J. (2004). "A Social Framework for Multi-agent Systems Validation and Verification". Wang, S. et al Eds. ER Workshops, Springer Verlag, LNCS 3289, pp. 458-469.

Furuta, R., Quint, V., & André, J. (1988). Interactively editing structured documents. *Electronic Publishing -- Origination, Dissemination and Design, 1*(1), 19-44.

GAO (United States Government Accountability Office). (2007). *HIGHER EDUCATION: Challenges in attracting international students to the united states and implications for global competitiveness*

Garrison, D. R. (2006). *Online community of inquiry review: Understanding social, cognitive and teaching presence.* Paper presented at the Sloan Consortium Asynchronous Learning Network Invitational Workshop, Baltimore, MD.

Garrison, D. R., & Anderson, T. (2003). *E-learning in the 21ˢᵗ century: A framework for research and practice.* London: Routledge/Falmer.

Garrison, D. R., & Arbaugh, J. B. (2007). Researching the community of inquiry framework: Review, issues, and future directions. *The Internet and Higher Education, 10*(3), 157–172. doi:10.1016/j.iheduc.2007.04.001

Garrison, D. R., & Archer, W. (2000). *A transactional perspective on teaching-learning: A framework for adult and higher education.* Oxford, UK: Pergamon.

Garrison, D. R., & Cleveland-Innes, M. (2003). Critical factors in student satisfaction and success: Facilitating student role adjustment in online communities of inquiry. In J. Bourne & J. Moore (Eds.), *Elements of quality online education: Into the mainstream* (pp. 29-38). Needham, MA: Sloan-C.

Garrison, D. R., Anderson, T., & Archer, W. (2000). Critical inquiry in a text-based environment: Computer conferencing in higher education. *The Internet and Higher Education, 11*(2), 1–14.

Garrison, D. R., Anderson, T., & Archer, W. (2001). Critical thinking, cognitive presence and computer conferencing in distance education. *American Journal of Distance Education, 15*(1), 7–23.

Garrison, R., & Cleveland-Innes, M. (2005). Facilitating cognitive presence in online learning: Interaction is not enough. *American Journal of Distance Education, 19*(3), 133–148. doi:10.1207/s15389286ajde1903_2

Garrison, R., Cleveland-Innes, M., & Fung, T. (2004). Student role adjustment in online communities of inquiry: Model and instrument validation. *Journal of Asynchronous Learning Networks, 8*(2), 61-74.

Garton, L., Haythornthwaite, C., & Wellman, B. (1997). Studying online social networks. *Journal of Computer-Mediated Communication, 3*(1), 75-105.

Gascó, M., & Equiza, F. (2002). Formulación de políticas públicas de transición a la sociedad del conocimiento: El caso argentino. *Desarrollo Humano e Institucional en América Latina (DHIAL), 36*. Retrieved December 20, 2002, from http://www.iigov.org/dhial/?p=36_04

Gebert, H., Geib, M., Kolbe, L., Brenner, W., (2003), "Knowledge-enabled Customer Relationship Management - Integrating Customer Relationship Management and Knowledge Management Concepts". Journal of Knowledge Management. Vol. 7(5), pp. 107-123.

Gee, D. (1990). *The impact of students' preferred learning style variables in a distance education course: A case study.* Portales, NM: Eastern New Mexico University. (ERIC Document Reproduction Service No. ED 358 836)

Geib, M., Braun, C., Kolbe, L., Brenner, W., (2004). Measuring the Utilization of Collaboration Technology for Knowledge Development and Exchange in Virtual Communities. 37th Hawaii International Conference on System Sciences 2004 (HICSS-37), Big Island, Hawaii, IEEE Computer Society, Vol. 1, pp. 1-10.

Germanakos, P., Tsianos, N., Lekkas, Z., Mourlas, C., Belk, M., & Samaras, G. (2007). An adaptive Web system for integrating human factors in personalization of Web content. In *Proceedings of the 11th International Conference on User Modeling (UM 2007)*, Corfu, Greece.

Germanakos, P., Tsianos, N., Mourlas, C., & Samaras, G. (2005). New fundamental profiling characteristics for designing adaptive Web-based educational systems. In *Proceedings of the IADIS International Conference on Cognition and Exploratory Learning in Digital Age (CELDA2005)*, Porto, Portugal (pp. 10-17).

Geroimenko, V. & Chen, C. (2003). *Visualizing the semantic web.* London: Springer.

Gibb, A. (1997). Small firms training and competitiveness: Building up the small business as a learning organisation. *International Small Business Journal, 3*, 13-29.

Gilbert, J. E., & Han, C. Y. (1999). Arthur: Adapting instruction to accommodate learning style. In *Proceedings of the WebNet 99 World Conference on the WWW and Internet* (pp. 433-438).

Gillet, D., El Helou, S., Rekik, Y., & Salzmann, C. (2007). Context-sensitive awareness services for communities of practice. In *Proceedings of the 12th International Conference on Human-Computer Interaction (HCI2007)*, Beijing.

Girgensohn, A., Lee, A., & Turner, T. (1999). Being in public and reciprocity: Design for portholes and user preference. In [Amsterdam, The Netherlands: IOS Press.]. *Proceedings of the Human-Computer Interaction INTERACT, 99*, 458–465.

Glass, R. L. (2007). What's with this blog thing? *IEEE Software, 24*(5), 103–104. doi:10.1109/MS.2007.151

Goel, L. & Mousavidin, E. (2007). vCRM: Virtual customer relationship management. forthcoming in DATABASE Special Issue on Virtual Worlds, November 2007.

Goleman, D. (1995). *Emotional intelligence: Why it can matter more than IQ.* New York: Bantam Books.

Goleman, D. (1998). *Working with emotional intelligence.* New York: Bantam.

Gongla, P., & Rizutto, C. R. (2001). Evolving communities of practice: IBM Global Services experience. *IBM Systems Journal, 40*(4), 842-853.

Goodhue, D. L. & Thompson, R. L. (1995). Task-technology fit and individual performance. *MIS Quarterly, 19*(2), 213-236.

Gordon, D., & Bull, G. (2004). The nexus explored: A generalised model of learning styles. In *Proceedings of the 15th International Conference of Society of Information Technology & Teacher Education*, Atlanta, Georgia, USA.

Gordon, R. & Grant, D. (2005). Knowledge management or management of knowledge? Why people interested in knowledge management need to consider foucault and the construct of power. *Journal of Critical Postmodern Organization Science, 3*(2), 27-38.

Gorman, G., Hanlon, D., & King, W. (1997). Some research perspectives on entrepreneurship education, enterprise education and education for small business management: A ten year literature review. *International Small Business Journal, 3*, 56-77.

Graff, M. (2003). Learning from Web-based instructional systems and cognitive style. *British Journal of Educational Technology, 34*(4), 407–418. doi:10.1111/1467-8535.00338

Graham, S. and Marvin, S. (1996). *Telecommunications and the City*. London: Routledge.

Graham, W., & Osgood, D. (1998). A real-life community of practice. *Training & Development, 52*(5), 34-38.

Granovetter, M. (1973). The strength of weak ties. *American Journal of Sociology, 78*, 1360-1380.

Grant, R. M. (1996). Toward a knowledge-based theory of the firm. *Strategic Management Journal 17(Winter Special Issue)*, 109-122.

Greenfield, P. M. (2009). Technology and informal education: What Is taught, what is learned. *Science, 323*, 69–72. doi:10.1126/science.1167190

Gregorc, A. F. (1982). *An adult's guide to style*. Maynard, MA: Gabriel Systems.

Grippin, P., & Peters, S. (1984). *Learning theory and learning outcomes*. Landham, MD: University Press of America.

Grudin, J. (1996). Evaluating opportunities for design capture. In T. P. Moran & J. M. Carroll (Eds.), *Design rationale: Concepts, techniques and use*. Mahwah, NJ: Lawrence Erlbaum Associates.

Gualtieri, R. (1998). *Impact of the emerging information society on the policy development process and democratic quality*. Paris OECD Public Management Service. Retrieved November 14, 1998, from http://www.alfa-redi.com//apc-aa-alfaredi/img_upload/a63473ef6aa82c7a2b2cc688d7e635dd/12E81094.doc

Gueddana, S., & Roussel, N. (2006). Pêle-Mêle, a video communication system supporting a variable degree of engagement. In *Proceedings of the ACM conference on Computer Supported cooperative work*, Banff, Alberta, Canada.

Guerrini, G., Mesiti, M., & Rossi, D. (2006). *XML schema evolution* (Tech. Rep.). Genova, Italy: Universita di Genova.

Guha, S., Rastogi, R., & Shim, K. (1998). CURE: An efficient clustering algorithm for large databases. In *Proceedings of ACM SIGMOD International Conference on Management of Data* (pp. 73-84). New York: ACM Press.

Guizzardi, R., Perini, A., Dignum, V., (2004), «Providing Knowledge Management Support to Communities of Practice through Agent-Oriented Analysis». Proceedings of the 4th International Conference on Knowledge Management (I-KNOW), Granz, Austria.

Gunawardena, C. N., Ortegano-Layne, L., Carabajal, K., Frechette, C., Lindemann, K., & Jennings, B. (2006). New model, new strategies: Instructional design for building online wisdom communities. *Distance Education, 27*(2), 217–232. doi:10.1080/01587910600789613

Haake, A., Lukosch, S., & Schummer, T. (2005). Wikitemplates: Adding structure support to Wikis on demand. In *Proceedings of the 2005 international symposium on Wikis*, New York, USA (pp. 41-51). New York: ACM Press.

Habermas, J. (1984). *The theory of communicative action*. Boston: Beacon Press.

Hammer, M., Leonard, D., & **Davenport,** T. H. (2004). Why don't we know more about knowledge? *MIT Sloan Management Review, 45*(4), 14-18.

Hampel, T., & Keil-Slawik, R. (2001, Summer). sTeam: Structuring information in team–distributed knowledge management in cooperative learning environments. *Journal of Educational Resources in Computing, 1*(2), 1–27. doi:10.1145/384055.384058

Han, J., & Kamber, M. (2001). *Data mining: Concepts and techniques.* San Francisco: Morgan Kaufmann Publishers.

Hand, D. J., Mannila, H., & Smyth, P. (2000). *Principles of data mining.* Cambridge, MA: MIT Press.

Handley, K., Sturdy, A., Fincham, R., & Clark, T. (2006). Within and beyond communities of practice: making sense of learning through participation, identity and practice. *Journal of Management Studies, 43*(3), 641-53.

Hansen, M. T. (1999). The search-transfer problem: The role of weak ties in sharing knowledge across organizational subunits. *ASQ, 44,* 82-111.

Hardwig, J. (1991). The role of trust in knowledge. *The Journal of Philosophy, 88*(12), 693-708.

Hart, D., & Warne, L. (2006). Comparing cultural and political perspectives of data, information, and knowledge sharing in organisations. *International Journal of Knowledge Management, 2*(2), 1-15.

Haythornthwaite, C., Kazmer, M. M., Robins, J., & Shoemaker, S. (2000). Community development among distance learners: Temporal and technological dimensions. *Journal of Computer-Mediated Communication, 6*(1), 1–26.

Heck, J. (2009). State, national universities see spike in distance-learning enrollment. *Dallas Business Journal.*

Hedberg, J. G. (2003). Ensuring quality e-learning: Creating engaging tasks. *Educational Media International, 40*(3), 175–187. doi:10.1080/0952398032000113095

Hedberg, J. G. (2006). E-learning futures? Speculations for a time yet to come. *Studies in Continuing Education, 28*(2), 171–183. doi:10.1080/01580370600751187

Henry, G. (2004, September). Connexions: An alternative approach to publishing. In *Proceedings of the European Conference on Digital Libraries,* Bath, UK.

Heo, H. (2004). Story telling and retelling as narrative inquiry in cyber learning environments. In R. Atkinson, C. McBeath, D. Jonas-Dwyer, & R. Phillips (Eds.), *Beyond the comfort zone: Proceedings of the 21st ASCILITE Conference,* Perth, Australia (pp. 374-378).

Hergenhahn, B. R. (1988). *An introduction to theories of learning* (3rd ed.). Englewood Cliffs, NJ: Prentice Hall.

Hermant, C. (2003). *Does mastery of ICT really improve pupil performance?* eLearning Programme, Directorate General for Education and Culture, European Commission.

Herzog, R. (2002). Internet und politik in Lateinamerika: Argentinien. In R. Herzog, B. Hoffman, & M. Schulz (Eds.), *Internet und politik in Lateinamerika: Regulierung und nutzung der neuen informationsund kommunikationstechnologien im kontext der politischen und wirtschaftlichen transformationen* (pp. 100-112). Frankfurt, Germany: Vervuert Verlag. Retrieved September 12, 2002, from http://www1.uni-hamburg.de/IIK/nikt/Argentinien.pdf

Hildreth, P., & Kimble, C. (2000). Communities of practice in the international distributed environment. *Journal of Knowledge Management, 4*(1), 27-38.

Hill, W., Stead, L., Rosenstein, M., & Furnas, G. (1995). Recommending and evaluating choices in a virtual community of use. *SIGCHI Conference on Human factors in Computing systems,* Denver, Colorado.

Hillery, G., (1955), «Definitions of Community: Areas of Agreement», Rural Sociology, Vol. 20, pp. 118-125.

Hin, L., Subramaniam, R., & Meng, D. (2005). Use of log analysis and text mining for simple knowledge extraction. In L. Tan & R. Subramaniam (Eds.), *E-learning and virtual science centre* (pp. 347-365). Hershey, PA: Information Science Publishing.

Hippel, E. V. (1994). Sticky information and the locus of problem solving: Implications for innovation. *Management Science, 40*(4), 429-440.

Holmes, G., & McElwee, G. (1995). Total quality management in higher education how to approach human resource management. *Total Quality Management, 7*(6), 5.

Honey, P., & Mumford, A. (1986). *A manual of learning styles*. Maidenhead, UK: Peter Honey.

Höök, K., Benyon, D., & Munro, A. (2003). *Designing information spaces: The social navigation approach*. London: Springer.

Hounsell, D. (2003). Student feedback, learning and development. In M. Slowey & D. Watson (Eds.), *Higher education and the lifecourse* (pp. 67-78). Buckingham, UK: SRHE and Open University Press.

Hounsell, D., McCune, V., Hounsell, J., & Litjens, J. (2008). The quality of guidance and feedback to students. *Higher Education Research & Development, 27*(1), 55–67. doi:10.1080/07294360701658765

Huber, G. (2001). Transfer of knowledge in knowledge management systems: unexplored issues and suggested studies. *European Journal of Information Systems (EJIS), 10*, 72-79.

Hudson, S. E., & Smith, I. (1996). Techniques for addressing fundamental privacy and disruption tradeoffs in awareness support systems. In *Proceedings of the ACM Conference on Computer-Supported Cooperative Work*, Cambridge MA, USA.

Hung, D., & Der-Thanq, C. (2001). Situated cognition, Vygotskian thought and learning from the communities of practice perspective: Implications for the design of Web-based e-learning. *Educational Media International, 38*(1), 3–12. doi:10.1080/09523980110037525

Hurwitz, R., & Mallery, J. C. (1995). The open meeting: A Web-based system for conferencing and collaboration. In *Proceedings of the 4ᵗʰ International World Wide Web Conference*, Boston, MA.

Husted, K., & Michailova, S. (2002). Diagnosing and fighting knowledge-sharing hostility. *Organizational Dyanmics, 31*(1), 60-73.

Huynh, T., Jennings, N., Shadbolt, N., (2004), «FIRE: An Integrated Trust and Reputation Model for Open Multi-agent Systems». Proceedings of the 16th European Conference on Artificial Intelligence (ECAI).

Ice, P., Arbaugh, B., Diaz, S., Garrison, D. R., Richardson, J., Shea, P., & Swan, K. (2007). Community of inquiry framework: Validation and instrument development. In *Proceedings of the 13ᵗʰ Annual Sloan-C International Conference on Online Learning*, Orlando, FL.

Ilola, L. (2008). *The effects of ICT on school: Teacher's and students' perspectives* (Ser. B. 314). Finland: Turun yliopisto.

Ilola, L., Lakkala, M., & Paavola, S. (2006). Case studies of learning objects used in school settings. *Learning, Media and Technology, 31*(3), 249–267. doi:10.1080/17439880600893291

Imbert, R., and de Antonio, A., (2005), «When emotion does not mean loss of control». Lecture Notes in Computer Science, T. Panayiotopoulos, J. Gratch, R. Aylett, D. Ballin, P. Olivier, and T. Rist (Eds.), Springer-Verlag, London, pp.152-165.

IMS Global Learning Consortium. (2003). *IMS learning design information model, revision: 20 January 2003*.

INI-GraphicsNet. (2006). *Augmented reality. New fields of application through innovative technologies*. The International of Institutions for Advanced Education, Training and R&D in Computer Graphics technology, system and applications.

Inkpen, A. C. (2005). *Learning through alliances: General motors and NUMMI. California Management Review, 47(4), 114-136*.

Isaacs, E., Walendowski, A., Whittaker, S., Schiano, D. J., & Kamm, C. (2002). The character, functions and styles of instant messaging in the workplace. In *Proceedings of the ACM CSCW*, New Orleans, Louisiana, USA.

Iverson, J. O. (2003). *Knowing volunteers through communities of practice*. Arizona State University. Arizona, USA.

Jain, A. K., & Dubes, R. C. (1988). *Algorithms for clustering data.* Upper Saddle River, NJ: Prentice-Hall, Inc.

Jarvenpaa, S. L., & Staples, D. S. (2000). The Use of Collaborative Electronic Media for Information Sharing: An Exploratory Study of Determinants. Journal of Strategic Information Systems 9(2/3): 129-154.

Jennex, M. & Olfman, L. (2000). Development recommendations for knowledge management/ organizational memory systems. In *Proceedings of the Information Systems Development Conference.*

Jennex, M., & Olfman, L. (2004). Assessing Knowledge Management success/Effectiveness Models. *Proceedings of the 37th Hawaii International Conference on System Sciences.*

Jennex, M., &Olfman, L. (2005). Assessing knowledge management success. *International Journal of Knowledge Management, 1*(2), 33-49.

Jennex, M., Smolnik, S. & Croasdell, D. (2007). Knowledge management success. *International Journal of Knowledge Management, 3*(2), i-vi.

Jennex, M.E. (2005). What is knowledge management? *International Journal of Knowledge Management, 1*(4), i-iv.

Jennex, M.E., & Olfman, L. (2006). A model of knowledge management success. *International Journal of Knowledge Management, 2*(3), 51-68.

John, D., & Boucouvalas, A. C. (2002). Multimedia tasks and user cognitive style. In *Proceedings of the International Symposium on CSNDSP 2002.*

Johnson, C. (2001). A survey of current research on online communities of practice. *The Internet and Higher Education, 4*(1), 45–60. doi:10.1016/S1096-7516(01)00047-1

Johnson, S. C. (1967). Hierarchical clustering schemes. *Psychometrika, 2,* 241–254. doi:10.1007/BF02289588

Jonassen, D., Davidson, M., Collins, M., Campbell, J., & Hag, B. (1995). Constructivism and computer-mediated communication in distance education. *American Journal of Distance Education, 9*(2), 7-26.

Jones, B. (2005). Establishing identification in virtual science museums: Creating connections and community. In L. Tan & R. Subramaniam (Eds.), *E-learning and virtual science centre* (pp. 1-27). Hershey, PA: Information Science Publishing.

Jones, Q. (1997). Virtual-communities, virtual settlements and cyber archeology: A theoretical outline. *Journal of Computer Mediated Communication, 3*(3).

Jones, Q., & Rafaeli, S. (2000). Time to split, virtually: 'Discourse architecture' and 'community building' create vibrant virtual publics. *Electronic Markets, 10*(4), 214-223.

Jones, Q., Ravid, G., & Rafaeli, S. (2004). Information overload and the message dynamics of online interaction spaces: A theoretical model and empirical exploration. *Information Systems Research, 15*(2), 194-210.

Josefsson, U. (2005). Coping with illness online: the case of patients online communities. *The Information Society, 21,* 143–153.

Kakabadse, N., Kouzmin, A., Kakabadse, A., (2001), «From Tacit Knowledge to Knowledge Management: Leveraging Invisible Assets». Journal of Knowledge and Process Management, Vol. 8(3), pp. 137-154.

Kakadadse, N. K., Kakadadse, A., & Kouzmin, A. (2003). Reviewing the knowledge management literature: Towards a taxonomy. *Journal of Knowledge Management, 7*(4), 75-91.

Kankanhalli, A., Tan, B. C. Y., & Kwok-Kei, W. (2005). Contributing knowledge to electronic knowledge repositories: An empirical investigation. *MIS Quarterly, 29*(1), 113-143.

Kanwar, M., & Swenson, D. (2000). *Canadian sociology.* IA: Kendall/Hunt Publishing Company.

Karacapilidis, N., & Papadias, D. (2001). Computer supported argumentation and collaborative decision making: The HERMES system. *Information Systems, 26*(4), 259–277. doi:10.1016/S0306-4379(01)00020-5

Karacapilidis, N., & Tzagarakis, M. (2007). Supporting incremental formalization in collaborative learning environments. In E. Duval, R. Klamma, & M. Wolpers (Eds.), *Proceedings of the 2nd European Conference on Technology Enhanced Learning (EC-TEL 2007)* (LNCS 4753, pp. 127-142). Berlin: Springer-Verlag.

Karypis, G., Han, E. H., & Kumar, V. (1999). Chameleon: A hierarchical clustering algorithm using dynamic modeling. *IEEE Computer, 32*, 68–75.

Katz, D., & Kahn, R. (1978). *The social psychology of organizations.* New York: John Wiley & Sons.

Kaufman, E. (2003). *Associative model for e-gov including digital cities.* Retrieved December 5, 2003, from http://www.cities-lyon.org/es/articles/203

Kaufman, E. (2003, November). *Panorama latinoamericano de gobiernos electrónicos: Modelos existentes.* Paper presented at the Second Argentinean Conference on Public Administration, Córdoba, Argentina. Retrieved March 1, 2004, from http://www.aaeap.org.ar/ponencias/congreso2/Kaufman_Ester.pdf

Kaufman, E. (2004). E-gobierno en Argentina: Crisis, burocracia y redes. In R. Araya & M. Porrúa (Eds.), *América Latina puntogob* (pp. 151-187). Santiago, Chile: FLACSO Chile & Organization of American States.

Kaufman, E. (2005). E-government and e-democracy in Latin America: Stages of development. In S. Marshall, W. Taylor, & X. Yu (Eds.), *The encyclopedia of developing regional communities with information and communication technology.* Hershey, PA: Idea Group Reference.

Kaufman, L., & Rousseeuw, P. J. (1990). *Finding groups in data.* New York: John Wiley & Sons.

Kautz, H. (2004), «Knowledge Mapping: A Technique for Identifying Knowledge Flows in Software Organizations», EuroSPI, pp. 126-137.

Kellogg, W., Erickson, T., Vetting Wolf, T., Leevy, S., Christensen, J., Sussman, J., & Bennett, W. E. (2006). Leveraging Digital bakchannels to enhance user experience in electronically mediated communication. In *Proceedings of the ACM CSCW*, Banff, Alberta, Canada.

Kendall, D., Murray, J., & Linden, R. (2000). *Sociology in our times.* (2nd ed.). Ontario, Canada: Nelson Thompson Learning.

Kerlin, C. A. (2000). *Measuring student satisfaction with the service processes of selected student educational support services at Everett Community College* (Doctoral dissertation, Oregon State University).

Kim, J., & Gorman, J. (2005). The psychobiology of anxiety. *Clinical Neuroscience Research, 4*, 335–347. doi:10.1016/j.cnr.2005.03.008

Kim, Y., & Baylor, A. (2006). A social-cognitive framework for pedagogical agents as learning companions. *ETR & D, 54*(6), 569–596. doi:10.1007/s11423-006-0637-3

Kimble, C., & Hildreth, P. (2005). *Communities of practice: Going one step too far?* EconWPA, Industrial Organization 0504008.

Kimble, C., Hildreth, P., & Wright, P. (2001). Communities of practice: Going virtual. In Y. Malhotra (Ed.), *Knowledge management and business model innovation* (pp. 220-234). Hershey, PA: IGI Global.

Kimble, C., Li, F., & Barlow, A. (2000). *Effective virtual teams through communities of practice* (Paper No. 00/9). University of Strathclyde, Management Science Research.

King, W. R. (2006). The critical role of information processing in creating an effective knowledge organization. *Journal of Database Management, 17*(1), 1-15.

Klein, J. H. (2008). Some directions for research in Knowledge Sharing. *Knowledge Management Research and Practice, 6*, 41-46.

Klein, J. H., Connell, N., & Meyer, E. (2005). Knowledge characteristics of communities of practice. *Knowledge Management Research and Practice, 3*, 106-114.

Kleinberg, J. (1999). Authoritative sources in a hyperlinked environment. *Journal of the ACM, 46*(5), 604–632. doi:10.1145/324133.324140

Klijn, E., & Coppenhan, J. (2000). Public management and policy networks: Foundations of a network approach to governance. *Public Management, an International Journal of Research and Theory, 2*(2), 135-158. Retrieved February 3, 2001, from http://www.inlogov.bham.ac.uk/pdfs/readinglists/Klijn%20and%20Koppenjan%20on%20policy%20network%20theory.pdf

Knuttila, M. (2002) *Introducing sociology: A critical perspective.* Don Mills, Ontario, Canada: Oxford University Press.

Koeglreiter, G., Smith, R., & Torlina, L. (2006). The role of informal groups in organisational knowledge work: Understanding an emerging community of practice. *International Journal of Knowledge Management, 2*(1), 6-23.

Kohlhase, M., & Anghelache, R. (2004). Towards collaborative content management and version control for structured mathematical knowledge. *In Proceedings Mathematical Knowledge Management: 2nd International Conference, MKM 2003*, Bertinoro, Italy,.

Kolb, A. (1984). *Experiential learning: Experience as the source of learning and development.* Boston: McBer & Company.

Kolb, A. Y., & Kolb, D. A. (2005). *The Kolb learning style inventory – version 3.1 2005 technical specifications.* Experience Based Learning Systems Inc.

Kopp, S. F. (2000). The role of self-esteem. *LukeNotes, 4*(2).

Kort, B., & Reilly, R. (2002). Analytical models of emotions, learning and relationships: Towards an affect-sensitive cognitive machine. In *Proceedings of the Conference on Virtual Worlds and Simulation (VWSim 2002).*

Koschmann, T. D. (1999). Toward a dialogic theory of learning: Bakhtin's contribution to understanding learning in settings of collaboration. In C. M. Hoadley & J. Roschelle (Eds.), *Proceedings of the CSCL'99 Conference* (pp. 308-313). Mahwah, NJ: Lawrence Erlbaum Associates.

Kowch, E. G., & Schwier, R. A. (1997). *Characteristics of technology-based virtual learning communities.* Retrieved September 27, 2003, from http://www.usak.ca/education/coursework/802papers/communities/community

Kramer, D. K., & Rundensteiner, E. A. (2001). Xem: XML evolution management. In K. Aberer & L. Liu (Eds.), *Proceedings of the Eleventh International Workshop on Research Issues in Data Engineering: Document Management for Data Intensive Business and Scientific Applications,* Heidelberg, Germany (pp. 103-110). Washington, DC: IEEE Computer Society.

Krause, K., Hartley, R., James, R., & McInnis, C. (2005). *The first year experience in Australian universities: Findings from a decade of national studies.*

Kreijns, K., Kirschner, P., & Jochems, W. (2002). The sociability of computer-supported collaborative learning environments. *Educational Technology & Society, 5*(1), 8–22.

Kuikka, E. (1996). *Transformation of structured documents. Processing of structured documents using a syntax-directed approach* (Doctoral dissertation). Kuopio, Finland: University of Kuopio, Computer Science and Applied Mathematics.

Kushmerick, N., & Lau, T. (2005). Automated email activity management: An unsupervised learning approach. In *Proceedings of the 10th International Conference on Intelligent User Interfaces* (pp. 67-74).

Lagoze, C., Payette, S., Shin, E., & Wilper, C. (2006). Fedora: An architecture for complex objects and their relationships. [special issue on Complex Objects]. *Journal of Digital Libraries, 6*(2), 124–138. doi:10.1007/s00799-005-0130-3

Langley, A. (2000). Emotional intelligence - a new evaluation for management development? *Career Development International, 5,* 177–183. doi:10.1108/13620430010371937

Lapre, M. A., & Van Wassenhove, L. N. (2003). Managing learning curves in factories by creating and transferring knowledge. *California Management Review, 46*(1), 53-71.

Lave, J., & Wenger, E. (1991). *Situated learning: Legitimate peripheral participation.* Cambridge, UK: Cambridge University Press.

Lee, A., Girgensohn, A., & Schlueter, K. (1997). NYNEX portholes: Initial user reactions and redesign implications. In *Proceedings of the International ACM SIGGROUP Conference on Supporting Group Work*, New York, (pp. 385-394).

Lee, J. (2003). Building successful communities of practice: CoPs are networks of activities. *Information Outlook*.

Lee, J. Cho., H., Gay, G., Davidosn, B., & Ingraffea, T. (2003). *Technology acceptance and social networking in distance education.*

Leimeister, J. M., Ebner, W., & Krcmar, H. (2005). Design, implementation, and evaluation of trust-supporting components in virtual communities for patients. *Journal of Management Information Systems, 21*(4), 101-135.

Lekkas, Z., Tsianos, N., Germanakos, P., & Mourlas, C. (2007). Integrating cognitive and emotional parameters into designing adaptive hypermedia environments. In *Proceedings of the Second European Cognitive Science Conference (EuroCogSci'07)*, Delphi, Hellas, (pp. 705-709).

Leont'ev, A. N. (1981). The problem of activity in psychology. In J. V. Wertsch (Eds.), *The concept of activity in soviet psychology (pp.* 37-71). Armonk, NY: Sharpe.

Lerner, B. S. (1996). *A model for compound type changes encountered in schema evolution* (Tech. Rep. UM-CS-96-044). Amherst: University of Massachusetts, Computer Science Department.

Lesser, E., & Everest, K. (2001). Using communities of practice to manage intellectual capital. *Ivey Business Journal, 65*(4), 37-42.

Lesser, E., & Prusak, L. (2000). Communities of practices social capital and organisational knowledge. In E. Lesser, M. Fontaine, & J. Slusher(Eds.), *Knowledge and communities.* Butterworth-Heinemann.

Lesser, E., & Storck, J. (2001). Communities of practice and organizational performance. *IBM Systems Journal, 40*(4), 831–842.

Lévi-Strauss, C. (1995). *Myth and meaning: Cracking the code of culture.* New York: Schocken Books.

Levy, D. M. (1993). Document reuse and document systems. *Electronic publishing, 6*(4), 339-348.

Lewin, K. (1935). *A dynamic theory of personality.* New York: McGraw-Hill.

Lewin, K. (1943). Forces behind food habits and methods of change. *Bulletin of the National Research Council, 108*, 35–65.

Licklider, J., & Taylor, R. (1968). The computer as a communication device. Sci. Tech.

Liedtka, J. (1999). Linking competitive advantage with communities of practice. *Journal of Management Inquiry, 8*(1), 5-17.

Lindkvist, L. (2005). Knowledge communities and knowledge collectivities: A typology of knowledge work in groups. *Journal of Management Review, 42*(6), 1189-1210.

Lippman, S. A., & Rumelt, R. P. (1982). Uncertain imitability: An analysis of interfirm differences in efficiency under competition. *Bell Journal of Economics, 13*, 418-438.

Liu, Y., & Ginther, D. (1999). Cognitive styles and distance education. *Online Journal of Distance Learning Administration, 2*(3).

Lombardi, P. and Curwell. S. (2005). INTELCITY Scenarios for the City of the Future. In D. Miller & D. Patassini (Eds.), *Beyond Benefit Cost Analysis.* Aldershot: Ashgate.

Loyarte, E., & Rivera, O. (2007). Communities of practice: A model for their cultivation. *Journal: Journal of Knowledge Management, 113*, 67-77.

Lueg, C. (2000, September). Where is the action in virtual communities of practice? In *Proceedings of the German Computer-Supported Cooperative Work Conference (D-CSCW), Workshop on Communication and Cooperation in Knowledge Communities*, Munich, Germany.

Luria, A. R. (1976). *Cognitive development: Its cultural and social foundations*. Cambridge, MA: Harvard University Press.

Malhotra, A., Gosain, S., & Hars, A. (1997). Evolution of a virtual community: Understanding design issues through a longitudinal study. *International Conference on Information Systems (ICIS), AIS*.

Malhotra, Y. (2000), «Knowledge Management and Virtual Organizations», IDEA Group publishing, Hershey.

Malone, D. (2002). Knowledge management: A model for organizational learning. *International Journal of Accounting Information Systems, 3*(2), 111-124.

Markham, S. (2004). *Learning styles measurement: A cause for concern* (Tech. Rep.). Computing Educational Research Group.

Markus, L. M. (1987). Towards a critical mass theory of interactive media: Universal access, interdependence and diffusion. *Comm. Res., 14*, 491-511.

Markus, L. M. (2001). Towards a theory of knowledge reuse: Types of knowledge reuse situations and factors in reuse success. *Journal of Management Information Systems, 18*(1), 57-94.

Markus, L. M., Majchrzak, A., & Gasser, L. (2002). A design theory for systems that support emergent knowledge processes. *MIS Quarterly, 26*(3), 179-212.

Marquardt, C. G., Becker, K., & Ruiz, D. D. (2004). A pre-processing tool for Web usage mining in the distance education domain. In *Proceedings of the International Database Engineering and Applications Symposium*.

Marshall, C., & Shipman, F. (1995). Spatial hypertext: Designing for change. *Communications of the ACM, 38*(8), 88–97. doi:10.1145/208344.208350

Marshall, C., & Shipman, F. (1997). Spatial hypertext and the practice of information triage. In *Proceedings of the 8th ACM Conference on Hypertext*, Southampton, UK (pp. 124-133).

Martinez, R. (2004). Online education: Designing for the future in appraiser education. *The Appraisal Journal, 72*(3), 266–184.

Mas, J. (2005). *Software libre: técnicamente viable, económicamente sostenible y socialmente justo*. Zero Factory, S.L. Barcelona.

Maslow, A. H. (1970). *Motivation and personality* (2nd ed.). New York: Harper-Collins.

Mayadas, A. (2009). Online education today. *Science, 323*, 85–88. doi:10.1126/science.1168874

Mc Lean, N. (2004, September). The ecology of repository services: A cosmic view. In *Proceedings of the European Conference on Digital Libraries*, Bath, UK.

McCarthy, B. (1990). Using the 4MAT system to bring learning styles to schools. *Educational Leadership, 48*(2), 31–37.

McDermott, R. (1999). Learning across teams: How to build communities of practice in team organizations. *Knowledge Management Review, 2*(2), 32.

McDermott, R. (1999). How to get the most out of human networks: Nurturing three-dimensional communities of practice. *Knowledge Management Review, 2*(5), 26-29.

McDermott, R. (1999). Why information inspired but cannot deliver knowledge management. *California Management Review, 41*(4), 103-117.

McDermott, R. (2000). Critical success factors in building communities of practice. *Knowledge Management Review, 3*(2), 5.

McKee, R. (1998). *Story: Substance, structure, style and the principles of screenwriting*. London: Methuen.

McLuhan, M. (1995). *Understanding media: The extensions of man*. Cambridge, MA: The MIT Press.

Mehlhorn, K., & Näher, S. (1999). *The LEDA platform of combinatorial and geometric computing*. Cambridge, UK: Cambridge University Press.

Meila, M., & Pentney, W. (2007). Clustering by weighted cuts in directed graphs. In *Proceedings of the SDM 07*.

Merriam, S. B., & Caffarella, R. S. (1999). *Learning in adulthood*. San Francisco: Jossey-Bass.

Meyer, K. A. (2003). Face-to-face versus threaded discussions: The role of time and higher-order thinking. *Journal of Asynchronous Learning Networks, 7*(3), 55–65.

Mika, P. (2005). Flink: Semantic Web technology for the extraction and analysis of social networks. *Journal of Web Semantics, 3*(2), 211–223. doi:10.1016/j.websem.2005.05.006

Millen, D. R., Fontaine, M. A., & Muller, M. J. (2002). Understanding the benefit and costs of communities of practice. *Communications of the ACM, 45*(4), 69–73. doi:10.1145/505248.505276

Millen, D., Fontaine, M., Muller, M., (2002), "Understanding the benefits and costs of communities of practice". Communications of the ACM., Vol. 45(4), pp. 69-73.

Mitchell. W. (2000). *e-Topia: Urban Life, Jim But Not as You Know It*. Cambridge Massachusetts: MIT Press.

Moran, T. P., Chiu, P., & van Melle, W. (1997). Pen-based interaction techniques for organizing material on an electronic whiteboard. In *Proceedings of the 10th Annual ACM Symposium on User interface Software and Technology UIST '97*, Banff, Alberta, Canada (pp. 45-54).

Mui, L., Halberstadt, A., Mohtashemi, M., (2002), "Notions of Reputation in Multi-Agents Systems: A Review". International Conference on Autonomous Agents and Multi-Agents Systems (AAMAS), pp. 280-287.

Murphy, E. (2004). Identifying and measuring ill-structured problem formulation and resolution in online asynchronous discussions. *Canadian Journal of Learning and Technology, 30*(1), 5–20.

Mutch, A. (2003). Communities of practice and habitus: A critique. *Organization Studies, 24*(3), 383-401.

Myers-Briggs, I., McCaulley, M. H., Quenk, N. L., & Hammer, A. L. (1998). *MBTI manual (A guide to the development and use of the Myers Briggs type indicator)*. Mountain View, CA: Consulting Psychologists Press.

Nam, K., & Ackerman, M. S. (2007). Arkose: Reusing informal information from online discussions. In *Proceedings of the 2007 international ACM conference on Supporting Group Work*, Sanibel Island, Florida, USA.

Nanopoulos, A., Theodoridis, Y., & Manolopoulos, Y. (2001). C2P: Clustering based on closest pairs. In *Proceedings of the 27th International Conference on Very Large Data Bases* (pp. 331-340).

Neurath, M., & Cohen, R. (1973). *Empiricism and sociology: The life and work of Otto Neurath*. Boston, MA: Reidel.

Newhart, R. L., & Joyce, C. (2005). Free radicals of innovation [videorecording]. Innovation Center, Star Thrower Distribution.

Nickols, F. (2003). *Communities of practice: An overview*.

Nidumolu, S. R., Subramani, M., & Aldrich, A. (2001). Situated learning and the situated knowledge web: Exploring the ground beneath knowledge management. *Journal of Management Information Systems (JMIS), 18*(1), 115-150.

Ninomiya, T., Taira, H., & Okamoto, T. (2007). A personalised learning environment architecture for e-learning. In *Proceedings of the 6th IASTED International Conference on Web-based Education*, Chamonix, France (pp. 517-521).

Nonaka, I. (1994). A dynamic theory of organizational knowledge creation. *Organization Science, 5*(1), 14-37.

Nonaka, I., & Takeuchi, H. (1995). *The knowledge-creating company: How the Japanese companies create the dynamic of innovation*. New York: Oxford University Press.

O'Reilly, T. (2005). *What is Web 2.0: Design patterns and business models for the next generation of software.*

Ohl, R. (2007). *Compendium used to map Queensland public consultation.* Retrieved January 18, 2007 from http://news.kmi.open.ac.uk/rostra/news.php?r=55&t=2&id=26

Okamoto, T., & Ninomiya, T. (2007). Organisational knowledge management system for e-learning practice in universities. In *Proceedings of the 6th IASTED International Conference on Web-based Education*, Chamonix, France (pp. 528-536).

Okamoto, T., & Sato, K. (1978). A study of the decision making model on the design and evaluation for a CAI program. *Japan Journal of Educational Technology*, *3*(1), 25–37.

Okamoto, T., Nagata, N., Anma, F., & Ninomiya, T. (2008). The knowledge circulated-organisational management for e-learning practice. In *Proceedings of the IADIAS Multi Conference on Computer Science and Information Systems*, Amsterdam, The Netherlands (pp. 121-128).

Orlikowski, W. J. (2002). Knowing in practice: Enacting a collective capability in distributed organizing. *Organization Science, 13*(3), 249-273.

Ormrod, J. E. (1995). *Human learning* (2nd ed.). Englewood Cliffs, NJ: Merrill.

Orr, J. E. (1989). Sharing knowledge, celebrating identity: War stories and community memory among service technicians. In D.S. Middleton, & D. Edwards (Eds.), *Collective remembering: memory in society.* Newbury Park, CA: Sage Publications.

Palloff, R. M., & Pratt, K. (1999). *Building learning communities in cyberspace.* San Francisco: Jossey-Bass Publishers.

Pan, S. L., & Leidner, D. E. (2003). Bridging communities of practice with information technology in the pursuit of global knowledge sharing. *Journal of Strategic Information Systems, 12*, 71-88.

Pan, Z., Cheok, A., Yang, H., Zhu, J., & Shi, J. (2006). Virtual reality and mixed reality for virtual learning environments. *Computers & Graphics*, *30*(1), 20–28. doi:10.1016/j.cag.2005.10.004

Paolillo, J. C., & Wright, E. (2004). The challenges of FOAF characterization. In *Proceedings of the 1st Workshop on Friend of a Friend, Social Networking and the Semantic Web.*

Papanikolaou, K. A., Grigoriadou, M., Kornilakis, H., & Magoulas, G. D. (2003). Personalising the interaction in a Web-based educational hypermedia system: The case of INSPIRE. *User Modeling and User-Adapted Interaction*, *13*(3), 213–267. doi:10.1023/A:1024746731130

Pascarella, E. T., & Terenzini, P. T. (2005). How college affects students: A third decade of research. San Francisco: Jossey-Bass.

Paulson, L. D. (2005). Building rich Web applications with AJAX. *IEEE Computer*, *38*(10), 14–17.

Perkowitz, M., & Etzioni, O. (2000). Adaptive Web sites . *Communications of the ACM*, *43*(8). doi:10.1145/345124.345171

Peterson, E. R., Deary, I. J., & Austin, E. J. (2003). On the assessment of cognitive style: Four red herrings. *Personality and Individual Differences*, *34*(5), 899–904. doi:10.1016/S0191-8869(02)00118-6

Piazzalunga, R., & Barretto, S. (2005). Challenges in virtual environment design: An architectural approach to virtual spaces. In L. Tan & R. Subramaniam (Eds.), *E-learning and virtual science centre* (pp. 251-271). Hershey, PA: Information Science Centre Publishing.

Pierrakos, D., Paliouras, G., Papatheodorou, C., & Spyropoulos, C. D. (2003). Web usage mining as a tool for personalization: A survey. *User Modeling and User-Adapted Interaction*, *14*(4).

Polanyi, M. (1958). *Personal knowledge, towards a post-critical philosophy.* Chicago, IL: University of Chicago Press.

Popa, L., Velegrakis, Y., Miller, R. J., Hernandez, M. A., & Fagin, R. (2002). Translating Web data. In P. A. Bernstein, Y. E. Loannidis, R. Ramakrishnan, & D. Papadias, *Proceedings of the International Conference of Very Large Databases*, Hong Kong, China (pp. 598-609). Very Large Data Base Endowment Inc.

Porra, J., & Goel, L. (2006, November 18-21). Importance of Power in the Implementation Process of a Successful KMS: A Case Study. *In 37th Annual Meeting of the Decision Sciences Institute,* San Antonio, TX..

Porra, J., & Parks, M.S. (2006). Sustaining virtual communities: Suggestions from the colonial model. *Information Systems and e-Business Management, 4*(4), 309-341.

Postmes, T., Spears, R., & Lea, M. (2000). The formation of group norms in computer-mediated communication. *Human Communication Research, 26*(3), 341-371.

Prandelli, E., Verona, G. & Raccagni, D. (2006). Diffusion of web-based product innovation. *California Management Review, 48*(4), 109-135.

Preece, J., Nonnecke, B., & Andrews, D. (2003). The top five reasons for lurking: improving community experiences for everyone. *Computers in Human Behavior* In Press.

Prusak, L. (2001). Where did knowledge management come from? *IBM Systems Journal, 40*(4), 1002-1007.

Puntambekar, S. (2006). Analyzing collaborative interactions: Divergence, shared understanding and construction of knowledge. *Computers & Education, 47*, 332–351. doi:10.1016/j.compedu.2004.10.012

Rafaeli, S., Barak, M., Dan-Gur, Y., & Toch, E. (2004). QSIA – a Web-based environment for learning, assessing and knowledge sharing in communities. *Computers & Education, 43*(3), 273–289. doi:10.1016/j.compedu.2003.10.008

Rahm, E., & Bernstein, P. A. (2001). *On matching schemas automatically* (Tech. Rep. 1/2001). Leipzig, Germany: University of Leipzig, Department of Computer Science.

Raven, J., Raven, J. C., & Court, J. H. (2003). *Manual for Raven's progressive matrices and vocabulary scales.* Oxford, UK: OPP Limited.

Rayner, S., & Riding, R. (1997). Towards a categorisation of cognitive styles and learning styles. *Educational Psychology, 17*(1&2), 5–27. doi:10.1080/0144341970170101

Redden, E. (2009). Blackboard 9.0. *Inside Higher Ed.*

Redmond, J. A., Walsh, C., & Parkinson, A. (2003). Equilibrating instructional media for cognitive styles. In *Proceedings of the 8th annual conference on Innovation and technology in computer science*, Thessaloniki, Greece (pp. 55-59).

Reichelt, L. (2007). *Design consequences: A fun workshop technique for brainstorming & consensus building.*

Rekik, Y., Gillet, D., El Helou, S., & Salzmann, C. (2007). The eLogBook framework: Sustaining interaction, collaboration, and learning in laboratory-oriented CoPs. *The International Journal of Web-Based Learning and Teaching, 2*(3).

Renton, A., & Macintosh, A. (2007). Computer supported argument maps as a policy memory. *The Information Society, 23*(2), 125–133. doi:10.1080/01972240701209300

Rice, M., Mousley, I., & Davis, R. (1994). Improving student feedback in distance education: A research report. In T. Evans & D. Murphy (Eds.), *Research in distance education 3: Revised papers from the third research in distance education conference.* Geelong, Australia: Deakin University Press.

Riedel, C. (2009). *Immersive gameplay: The future of education?*

Rigou, M., Sirmakessis, S., & Tsakalidas, A. (2004). Integrating personalization in e-learning communities. *Journal of Distance Learning Technologies, 2*(3), 47–58.

Ritter, S. (2008). *Social networking in higher education. Penn State World Campus.*

Roberts, D. (1996). Feedback on assignments. *Distance Education, 17*(1), 95–116. doi:10.1080/0158791960170107

Roberts, J. (2006). Limits of communities of practice. *Journal of Management Studies*, *43*(3), 623-639.

Robey, D., Khoo, H. M., & Powers, C. (2000). Situated-learning in cross-functional virtual teams. *IEEE Transactions on Professional Communication*, *43*(1), 51–66. doi:10.1109/47.826416

Robinson, P. (Director), & Kinsella, W. (Writer). (1989). *Field of dreams* [Motion picture]. USA: Gordon Company.

Robinson, W. N., & Volkov, S. (1997). A meta-model for restructuring stakeholder requirements. In *Proceedings of the 19th International Conference on Software Engineering*, Boston, MA (pp. 140-149). Washington, DC: IEEE Computer Society Press.

Roblyer, M. D., Davis, L., Mills, S. C., Marshall, J., & Pape, L. (2008). Toward practical procedures for predicting and promoting success in virtual school students'. *American Journal of Distance Education*, *22*(2), 90–109. doi:10.1080/08923640802039040

Rocard-report. (2006). *Science education now: A renewed pedagogy for the future of Europe*. European Commission, Directorate-General for Research, Information and Communication Unit. Brussels.

Rocheleau, B. (1997). Governmental information system problems and failures: A preliminary review. *Public Administration and Management: An Interactive Journal*, *2*(3). Retrieved May 25, 1999, from http://www.pamij.com/roche.html

Rogers, C. R. (1983). *Freedom to learn for the 80s*. Columbus, OH: Merrill.

Rogers, E. M., & Agarwala-Rogers, R. (1975). Organizational communication. G. L. Hanneman, & W. J. McEwen, (Eds.), Communication behaviour (pp. 218–236). Reading, MA: Addision Wesley.

Rogers, P., & Lea, M. (2005). Social presence in distributed group environments: The role of social identity. *Behaviour & Information Technology*, *24*(2), 151–158. doi:10.1080/01449290410001723472

Rogoff, B., & Wertsch, J. (1984). *Children's learning in the zone of proximal development*. San Francisco: Jossey-Bass.

Romano, A., Elia, V., & Passiante, G. (2001). *Creating business innovation leadership: An ongoing experiment. The E-Business Management School at ISUFI*. Naples, Italy: Edizioni Scientifiche Italiane.

Rosenberg, M. J. (2001). *E-learning: Strategies for delivering knowledge in the digital age*. New York: McGraw-Hill.

Rourke, L., Anderson, T., Garrison, D. R., & Archer, W. (1999). Assessing social presence in asynchronous text-based computer conferencing. *The Journal of Distance Education / Revue de l'Education à Distance*, *14*(2), 50-71.

Ryle, G. (1949/1984). *The concept of mind*. Chicago, IL: University of Chicago Press.

Sabater, J. and Sierra, C., (2002), "Social REGRET, a Reputation Model based on social relations", Proceedings of the Fifth International Conference on Autonomous Agents. Vol. 3(1), pp. 44-56.

Sabidussi, G. (1966). The centrality index of a graph. *Psychometrika*, *31*, 581–603. doi:10.1007/BF02289527

Sadler-Smith, E., & Riding, R. (1999). Cognitive style and instructional preferences. *Instructional Science*, *27*(5), 355–371.

Saint-Onge, H., & Wallace, D. (2003). *Leveraging communities of practice for strategic advance*. Butterworth & Heinemann, USA.

Sakai, S., Mashita, N., Yoshimitsu, Y., Shingeno, H., & Okada, K. (2004). An efficient method of supporting interactions for an integrated learning system. *Journal of Distance Education Technologies*, *2*(3), 1–10.

Salmi, H. (2005). Open learning environments: Combining Web-based virtual and hands-on science centre learning. In L. Tan & R. Subramaniam (Eds.), *E-learning and virtual science centre* (pp. 327-344). Hershey, PA: Information Science Publishing.

Salomon, G., & Perkins, D. N. (1998). Individual and social aspects of learning. In P. D. Pearson & A. Iran-Nejad (Eds.), *Review of research in education* (Vol. 23, pp. 1-24). Washington, DC: American Educational Research Association.

Salovey, P., & Mayer, J. D. (1990). Emotional intelligence. *Imagination, Cognition and Personality, 9*, 185–211.

Sandrock, J., & Tobin, P. (2007). *Critical success factors for communities of practice in a global mining company.* Nr Reading, Academic Conferences Ltd.

Sariola, J. (1998). The planning of an open learning environment and didactic media choice in teacher education. In T. Nummi, A. Rönkä, & J. Sariola (Eds.), *Virtuality and digital nomadism: An introduction to the LIVE project (1997-2000).* Finland: MediaEducation Centre. Department of Teacher Education. University of Helsinki. Media Education Publications 6.

Schafer, B. J., Konstan, A., J., Riedl, J. (1999). "Recommender Systems in E-Commerce", 1st ACM Conference on Electronic Conference (EC), pp. 158-166.

Schewen, T. M. & Hara, N. (2003). Community of practice: A metaphor for online design? *Information Society, 19*(3), 257-271.

Schullo, S., Hilbelink, A., Venable, M., & Barron, A. (2009). Selecting a virtual classroom system: Elluminate live vs. macromedia breeze (Adobe Acrobat Connect Professional). *Journal of Online Learning and Teaching.*

Schultze, U., & Leidner, D. (2002). Studying knowledge management in information systems research: Discourses and theoretical assumptions. *MISQ, 26*(3), 213-242.

Schultze, U., & Stabell, C. (2004). Knowing what you don't know? Discourses and contradictions in knowledge management research. *Journal of Management Studies, 41*(4), 549–573.

Schunk, D. H. (1989). Self-efficacy and cognitive skill learning. In C. Ames & R. Ames (Eds.), *Research on motivation in education. Vol. 3: Goals and cognitions* (pp. 13-44). San Diego, CA: Academic Press.

Schunk, D. H., & Lilly, M. W. (1984). Sex differences in self-efficacy and attributions: Influence of performance feedback. *The Journal of Early Adolescence, 4*, 203–213. doi:10.1177/0272431684043004

Scott, P. J., Quick, K. A., Tomadaki, E., & Linney, J. (2006). Ambient video awareness: It's great, but i still don't want it. In E. Tomadaki & P. Scott (Eds.), *Proceedings of the innovative approaches for learning and knowledge sharing, EC-TEL Workshops* (pp. 207- 214).

Scott, P. J., Tomadaki, E., & Quick, K. A. (2007). Using live virtual technologies to support communities of practice: The impact of extended events. In *Proceedings of the EC-TEL Workshop on Technology-Enhanced Learning Communities of Practice.*

Scott, P. J., Tomadaki, E., & Quick, K. A.(2007). The shape of live online meetings. *International Journal of Technology, Knowledge and Society, 3.*

Scribner, S. (1985). Vygotsky's uses of history. In J. V. Wertsch (Eds.), *Culture, communication, and cognition: Vygotskian perspectives* (pp. 119-145). Cambridge, United Kingdom: Cambridge University Press.

Seashore, N. C., Whitfield-Seashore, E., & Weinberg, G. M. (1999). *What did you say? The art of giving and receiving Feedback.* Columbia, MD: Bingham House Books.

Selvin, A. M. & Sierhuis, M. (1999). Case studies of project compendium in different organizations. In *Proceedings of the Workshop on Computer-Supported Collaborative Argumentation for Learning Communities, CSCL '99,* Stanford, CA. Retrieved from http://d3e.open.ac.uk/cscl99/Selvin-CaseStudies/Selvin-CaseStudies-paper.html

Selvin, A. M., & Buckingham Shum, S. J. (2005). Hypermedia as a productivity tool for doctoral research. [Special Issue on Scholarly Hypermedia]. *New Review of Hypermedia and Multimedia, 11*(1), 91–101. doi:10.1080/13614560500191303

Sharda, N. (2005). Movement oriented design: A new paradigm for multimedia design. *International Journal of Lateral Computing, 1*(1), 7–14.

Sharda, N. (2006). Applying movement oriented design to create educational stories. *International Journal of Learning, 13*(12), 177–184.

Sharda, N. (2007). Authoring educational multimedia content using learning styles and story telling principles. In *Proceedings of the ACM Workshop on Educational Multimedia and Multimedia Education in conjunction with ACM Multimedia 2007*, Augsburg, Germany (pp. 93-102).

Sharda, R., Romano, N., Lucca, J., Weiser, M., Scheets, G., Chung, J., & Sleezer, C. (2004). Foundation for the study of computer-supported collaborative learning requiring immersive presence. *Journal of Management Information Systems, 20*(4), 31–63.

Sharp, J. E. (1997). Applying Kolb learning style theory in the communication classroom. *Business Communication Quarterly, 60*(2), 129–134. doi:10.1177/108056999706000214

Shea, P., Li, C., Swan, K., & Pickett, A. (2005). Developing learning community in online asynchronous college courses: The role of teaching presence. *Journal of Asynchronous Learning Networks, 9*(4).

Shea, P., Pickett, A., & Pelz, W. (2004). Enhancing student satisfaction through faculty development: The importance of teaching presence. In *Elements of quality online education: Into the mainsteam*. Needham, MA: SCOLE.

Sheikholeslami, G., Chatterjee, S., & Zhang, A. (1998). WaveCluster - a multi-resolution clustering approach for very large spatial databases. In *Proceedings of the 24th VLDB conference* (pp. 428-439).

Sherif, K., & Xing, B. (2006). Adaptive processes for knowledge creation in complex systems: the case of a global IT consulting firm, *Information and Management, 43*(4), 530 - 540

Shin, M. (2004). A framework for evaluating economics of knowledge management systems. *Information & Management, 42*, 179-196.

Shipman, F. M. III, & Marshall, C. C. (1999). Formality considered harmful: Experiences, emerging themes, and directions on the use of formal representations in interactive systems. *Computer Supported Cooperative Work, 8*(4), 333–352. doi:10.1023/A:1008716330212

Shipman, F. M., & Marshall, C. C. (1999). Formality considered harmful: Experiences, emerging themes, and directions on the use of formal representations in interactive systems. *Computer Supported Cooperative Work, 8*(4), 333–352. doi:10.1023/A:1008716330212

Shipman, F. M., & McCall, R. (1994). Supporting knowledge-base evolution with incremental formalization. In *Proceedings of the CHI'94 Conference*, Boston, MA (pp. 285-291).

Silva, L., Mousavidin, E., & Goel, L. (2006). Weblogging: Implementing Communities of Practice. *In Social Inclusion: Societal and Organizational Implications for Information Systems: IFIP TC8 WG 8.2*, Limirick, Ireland.

Simpson, O. (2000). *Supporting students in online open and distance education*. London: Koggan Page Ltd.

Sire, S., Chatty, S., Gaspard Boulinc, H., & Colin, F.-R. (1999). How can groupware preserve our coordination skills? Designing for direct collaboration. In A. Sasse * C. Johnson (Eds.), *Proceedings of the Human-Computer Interaction - INTERACT'99*. Amsterdam, The Netherlands: IOS Press.

Siu, N., Iverson, L., & Tang, A. (2006). Going with the flow: Email awareness and task management. In *Proceedings of the 2006 20th Anniversary Conference on Computer Supported Cooperative Work* (pp. 441-450).

Smeds, R., & Alvesalo, J. (2003). Global business process development in a virtual community of practice. *Production Planning & Control, 14*(4), 361-372.

Smith, M., Rodgers, R., Walker, J., & Tansley, R. (2004, September). DSpace: A year in the life of an open source digital repository. In *Proceedings of the European Conference on Digital Libraries*, Bath, UK.

Smyth, K. (2004). The benefits of students learning about critical evaluation rather than being summatively judged. *Assessment & Evaluation in Higher Education, 29*(3), 370–378. doi:10.1080/0260293042000197609

Snyder, W. M., & Souza Briggs, X. (2003). Communities of practice: A new tool for government managers. *Collaboration series of the IBM Center for the business of government*. Retrieved December 22, 2004, from http://www.businessofgovernment.org/pdfs/Snyder_report.pdf

Snyder, W. M., & Wenger, E. (2003). *Communities of practice in government: The case for sponsorship*. Retrieved December 30, 2004, from http://www.ewenger.com/pub/pubusfedcioreport.doc

Sorohan, E. G. (1993). We do; therefore we learn. *Training and Development, 47*(10), 47-55.

Sotiriou, S., et al. (2007). *Proceedings of the Symposium Designing the Science Laboratory for the School of Tomorrow. Advantaged technologies in education*, Athens, Greece. Ellinogermaniki Agogi.

Soto, J. P., Vizcaino, A., Portillo-Rodriguez, J., & Piattini, M. (2007). Applying trust, reputation and intuition aspects to support virtual communities of practice. In *Knowledge-Based Intelligent Information and Engineering Systems*: Kes 2007 - Wirn 2007, Pt Ii, Proceedings, (pp. 353-360).

Spielberger, C. D. (1972). Conceptual and methodological issues in anxiety research. In C. D. Spielberger (Ed.), *Anxiety. Current trends in theory and research* (Vol. 2). New York: Academic Press.

Spielberger, C. D., & Vagg, P. R. (1995). Test anxiety: A transactional process model. In C. D. Spielberger & P. R. Vagg (Eds.), *Test anxiety: Theory, assessment, and treatment* (pp. 3-14). Washington, DC: Taylor & Francis.

Srivastava, J., Cooley, R., Deshpande, M., & Tan, P.-N. (2000). Web usage mining: Discovery and applications of usage patterns from Web data. *SIGKDD Explorations, 1*(2).

Stearn, B. (2007). XULRunner: A new approach for developing rich Internet applications. *IEEE Internet Computing, 11*(3), 67–73. doi:10.1109/MIC.2007.75

Stein, E. W (2006). A qualitative study of the characteristics of a community of practice for knowledge management and its success factors *International Journal of Knowledge Management, 1*(4), 1-24

Sternberg, R. J., & Grigorenko, E. L. (1997). Are cognitive styles still in style? *The American Psychologist, 52*(7), 700–712. doi:10.1037/0003-066X.52.7.700

Stevens, C. D. (2007). *Coming to insight, eventually. Screenhub.*

Stevenson, K., Sander, P., & Naylor, P. (1996). Student perceptions of the tutor's role in distance learning. *Open Learning, 11*(1), 22–30. doi:10.1080/0268051960110103

Swan, J. A., Scarbrough, H., & Robertson, M. (2002). The construction of communities of practice in the management of innovation. *Management Learning, 33*(4), 477-497.

Swan, K. (2003). Developing social presence in online discussions. In S. Naidu (Ed.), *Learning and teaching with technology: Principles and practices* (pp. 147-164). London: Kogan Page.

Swan, K. (in press). Teaching and learning in post-industrial distance education. In M. Cleveland-Innes & D. R. Garrison (Eds.), *An introduction to distance education: Understanding teaching and learning in a new era.* New York: Routledge.

Swan, K. P., Richardson, J. P., Ice, P., Garrison, R. D., Cleveland-Innes, M., & Arbaugh, J. B. (2008). Validating a measurement tool of presence in online communities of inquiry. *e-Mentor, 2*(24).

Swan, K., & Shih, L.-F. (2005). On the nature and development of social presence in online course discussions. *Journal of Asynchronous Learning Networks, 9*(3), 115–136.

Tailby, R., Dean, R., Milnerm, B., & Smith, D. (2006). Email classification for automated service handling. In *Proceedings of the 2006 ACM Symposium on Applied Computing* (pp. 1073-1077).

Tajfel, H., & Turner, J. C. (1986). The *social* identity theory of intergroup behavior. In S.Worchel & W. G.Austin (Eds.), *Psychology of intergroup relations* (pp. 7–24). Chicago: Nelson-Hall.

Thompson, M. (2005). Structural and epistemic parameters in communities of practices. *Organizational Science, 16*(2), 151-164.

Timmer, J. (2009). College courses: even "offline" classes are online now. *Science.*

Triantafillou, E., Pomportsis, A., & Georgiadou, E. (2002). AES-CS: Adaptive educational system based on cognitive styles. In *Proceedings of the AH2002 Workshop, Second International Conference on Adaptive Hypermedia and Adaptive Web-based Systems*, Spain.

Trindade, A. R., Carmo, H., & Bidarra, J. (2000). Current developments and best practice in open and distance learning. *International Review of Research in Open and Distance Learning, 1*(1).

Tsianos, N., Germanakos, P., & Mourlas, C. (2006). Assessing the importance of cognitive learning styles over performance in multimedia educational environments. In *Proceedings of the 2nd International Conference on Interdisciplinarity in Education (ICIE2006)*, Athens, Greece (pp. 123-130).

Tsianos, N., Lekkas, Z., Germanakos, P., Mourlas, C., & Samaras, G. (2008). User-centered profiling on the basis of cognitive and emotional characteristics: An empirical study. In *Proceedings of the 5th International Conference on Adaptive Hypermedia and Adaptive Web-based Systems (AH 2008)*, Hannover, Germany (LNCS 5149, pp. 214-223). Berlin, Germany: Springer-Verlag.

Tuomi, I. (1999). *Corporate knowledge: Theory and practice of intelligent organizations.* Helsinki, Finland: Metaxis.

Turner, J. (1990). Role change. *Annual Review of Sociology, 16*, 87–110. doi:10.1146/annurev.so.16.080190.000511

Ullrich, C., Borau, K., Luo, H., Tan, X., Shen, L., & Shen, R. (2008). Why Web 2.0 is good for learning and for research: Principles and prototypes. In Proceeding of the 17th international Conference on World Wide Web, Beijing, China (pp. 705-714).

Urquhart, C., Yeoman, A., & Sharp, S. (2002). *NeLH communities of practice evaluation report.* University of Wales Aberystwyth, England.

Ushida, H., Hirayama, Y., Nakajima, H., (1998), "Emotion Model for Life like Agent and its Evaluation". Proceedings of the Fifteenth National Conference on Artificial Intelligence and Tenth Innovative Applications of Artificial Intelligence Conference (AAAI / IAAI), Madison, Wisconsin, USA, pp. 8-37.

Usoro, A., & Kuofie, M. H. S (2006). Conceptualisation of cultural dimensions as a major influence on knowledge sharing. *International Journal of Knowledge Management, 2*(2), 16-25.

Valenta, A., et al. (2001). Identifying Student Attitudes and Learning Styles in Distance Education. *Journal of Asynchronous Learning Networks, 5*(2).

Van Zolinger, S. L., Sreumer, J. N., & Stooker, M. (2001). Problems in knowledge management: A case study of a knowledge-intensive company. *International Journal of Training & Development, 5*(3), 168-185.

van-Elst, L., Dignum, V., Abecker, A., (2003), "Agent-Mediated Knowledge Management". International Simposium AMKM, Stanford, CA, USA, Springer, pp. 1-30.

Vaughan, N., & Garrison, D. R. (2006). How blended learning can support a faculty development community of inquiry. *Journal of Asynchronous Learning Networks, 10*(4), 139–152.

Vélez, I. P., & Vélez, B. (2006). Lynx: An open architecture for catalyzing the deployment of interactive digital government workflow-based systems. In *Proceedings of the 2006 International Conference on Digital Government Research* (pp. 309-318).

Venters, W., & Wood, B. (2007). Degenerative structures that inhibit the emergence of communities of practice: A case study of knowledge management in the British Council. *Information Systems Journal, 17*(4), 349-368.

Vygotsky, L. S. (1978). *Mind in society.* Cambridge, MA: Harvard University Press.

Vygotsky, L. S. (1985). *Vygotsky and the social formation of mind* (J. Wertsch, Ed.). Cambridge, MA: Harvard University Press.

Vygotsky, L. S. (Ed.). (1987). *The collected works of Vygotsky.* New York: Plenum Press.

Waddill, D. D., Milter, R., & Stinson, J. (2006). Innovative action-based e-learning strategies. In *Proceedings of the AHRD Scholar-Practitioner Track* (pp. 603-608).

Wang, Y., Vassileva, J., (2003), "Trust and Reputation Model in Peer-to-Peer Networks". Proceedings of the 3rd International Conference on Peer-to-Peer Computing.

Wasko, M. M., & Faraj, S. (2005). Why should I share? Examining knowledge contribution in networks of practice. *MIS Quarterly, 29*(1), 35-57.

Wasko, M. M., &Faraj, S. (2000). 'It is what one does:' Why people participate and help others in electronic communities of practice. *JSIS, 9*(2/3), 155-173.

Wasko, M. M., Faraj, S., & Teigland, R. (2004). Collective action and knowledge contribution in electronic networks of practice. *JAIS, 5*(11-12), 493-513.

Wasserman, S. and Glaskiewics, J., (1994), "Advances in Social Networks Analysis". Sage Publications.

Wasserman, S., & Faust, K. (1994). *Social network analysis: Methods and applications.* Cambridge, UK: Cambridge University Press.

Weber, M. (1992). *Economía y sociedad.* Mexico: Fondo de Cultura Económica.

Weinberger, A., & Mandl, H. (2003). *Computer-mediated knowledge communication* (Research Rep.). Institute for Empirical Pedagogy and Pedagogical Psychology, University of Munich.

Weintraub, R. (1995). Transforming mental models through formal and informal learning: A guide for workplace educators. In S. Chawla & J. Renesch (Eds.), *Learning organizations: Developing cultures for tomorrow's workplace (pp.* 417-429). Portland, OR: Productivity Press.

Wellman, B. (1996). For a Social Network Analysis of Computer Networks: A Sociological Perspective on Collaborative Work and Virtual Community. *SIGCPR/ SIGMIS*, Denver, Colorado.

Wellman, B., & Gulia, M. (1997). *Net surfers don't ride alone: Virtual communities as communities. Communities and cyberspace.* New York: Routledge.

Wellman, B., Salaff, J., Dimitrova, D. Garton, L, Gulia, M., & Haythornthwaite, C. (1996). Computer networks as social networks: Collaborative work, telework, and virtual community. *Annual Review of Sociology, 22,* 213-238.

Wenger, E. (1998). *Communities of practice: Learning, meaning and identity.* New York: Cambridge University Press.

Wenger, E. (1998). Communities of practice: Learning as a social system. *Systems Thinker.*

Wenger, E. (2000). Communities of practice and social learning systems. *Organization, 7*(2), 225-246.

Wenger, E. (2004). Knowledge management as a doughnut: Shaping your knowledge strategy through communities of practice. *Ivey Business Journal Online.*

Wenger, E., & Snyder, W. M. (2000). Communities of practice: The organizational frontier. *Harvard Business Review, 78*(1), 139-146.

Wenger, E., McDermott, R., Snyder, W., (2002), "Cultivating Communities of Practice", Harvard Business School Press.

Wenger, E., White, N., Smith, J., & Rowe, K. (2005). *Technology for communities, CEFRIO book chapter v 5.2.*

Whitehead, A. N., & Russell, B. (1910-1913). *Principia mathematica, 3 vols* (2nd ed.). Cambridge, UK: Cambridge University Press.

Whittaker, S., Bellotti, V., & Gwiydka, J. (2006). Email in personal information management. *Communications of the ACM, 49*(1), 68–73. doi:10.1145/1107458.1107494

Wild, R. H., Griggs, K. A., & Li, E. Y. (2005). An architecture for distributed scenario building and evaluation. *Communications of the ACM, 48*(11), 80–86. doi:10.1145/1096000.1096009

Wilson, D., Varnhagen, S., Krupa, E., Kasprzak, S., Hunting, V., & Taylor, A. (2003). Instructors' adaptation to online graduate education in health promotion: A qualitative study. *Journal of Distance Education, 18*(2), 1–15.

Wisker, G., Robinson, G., et al. (2007). Postgraduate research success: Communities of practice involving cohorts, guardian supervisors and online communities. *Innovations in Education and Teaching International, 44*, 301-320.

Witkin, H. A., Moore, C. A., Goodenough, D. R., & Cox, P. W. (1977). Field-dependent and field-independent cognitive styles and their implications. *Review of Educational Research, 47*, 1–64.

Wolf, K. D. (1995). The implementation of an open learning environment under World Wide Web. In H. Maurer (Ed.), *Educational multimedia and hypermedia, 1995. Proceedings of EdMedia 95*. Charlottsville, VA: Advancement of Computing in Education (AACE).

Wooldridge, M., Ciancarini, P., (2001), Agent-Oriented Software Engineering: The State of the Art.

World Wide Web Consortium. (1999). *XSL transformations (XSLT) version 1.0* (W3C recommendation).

World Wide Web Consortium. (2001). *XML schema part 0: Primer* (W3C recommendation).

World Wide Web Consortium. (2008). *Extensible markup language (XML) 1.0 (fifth edition)* (W3C recommendation).

Wu, D., & Hiltz, S. R. (2004). Predicting learning from asynchronous online discussions. *Journal of Asynchronous Learning Networks, 8*(2), 139–152.

Yin, R. K. (1994). *Case study research: Design and methods*. CA: Sage.

Yue Wah, C., Menkhoff, T., Loh, B., & Evers, H. D. (2007). Social capital and knowledge sharing in knowledge-based organizations: An empirical study. *International Journal of Knowledge Management, 3*(1), 29-38.

Zacharia, G., Moukas, A., Maes, P. (1999). "Collaborative Reputation Mechanisms in Electronic Marketplaces". In *32nd Annual Hawaii International Conference on System Science (HICSS-32)*.

Zhang, L., Wu, X., & Yu, Y. (2006). Emergent semantics from folksonomies: A quantitative study. In *Journal on Data Semantics VI* (LNCS 4090, pp. 168-186). Berlin, Germany: Springer.

Zhang, T., Ramakrishnan, R., & Livny, M. (1996). BIRCH: An efficient data clustering method for very large databases. In *Proceedings of the 1996 ACM SIGMOD International Conference on Management of Data*, Montreal, Canada (pp. 103-114).

Zhang, W., & Storck, J. (2001). Peripheral members in online communities. In *Proceedings of the Americas Conference on Information Systems*, Boston, MA.

About the Contributors

Nikos Karacapilidis holds a professor position at the University of Patras, Greece (field: Management Information Systems). His research interests lie in the areas of Intelligent Web-Based Information Systems, Technology-Enhanced Learning, e-Collaboration, Knowledge Management Systems, Group Decision Support Systems, Computer-Supported Argumentation, Enterprise Information Systems and Semantic Web. He has been appointed as Editor-in-Chief of the Advances in Web-based Learning (AWBL) Book Series (http://www.igi-pub.com/bookseries/details.asp?id=432), as well as Co-Editor-in-Chief of the International Journal of Web-based Learning and Teaching Technologies (IJWLTT - http://www.igi-pub.com/journals/details.asp?ID=4286). More detailed information about his publications list, research projects involved and professional activities can be found at http://www.mech.upatras.gr/~nikos/.

* * *

Fumihiko ANMA received his B.E. from Tokyo Institute of Technology in 2000 and his Master Degree and PhD Degree from Shizuoka University, Japan in 2002 and 2005 respectively. His Ph. D thesis theme was a research for an educational system for supporting novice programming language learners by explaining the domain-oriented functions of programs, and describe its experimental evaluation. Presently he is an assistant professor with the Graduate school of Information Systems, the University of Electro Communications. His research interests include Knowledge Computing, Intelligent Educational System, e-learning, Artificial Intelligence, and Software Agent and so on. He is researching in a learning management system based on SNS (Social Networking Service). His system has functions to encourage learner interaction by the "the architecture of participation". This phrase "the architecture of participation", defined by O'Reilly describes the nature of systems that are designed for user contribution. He is a member of Japanese Society for Information and Systems in Education (JSiSE), Japanese Society for Artificial Intelligence (JSAI), and Japan Society for Educational Technology (JSET).

Franz X. Bogner is full professor, head of the Institute of Biology Didactics and the director of the Z-MNU (Centre of Math & Science Education). Involved in pre-service teacher education and in-service teacher enhancement, his main research includes learning processes within cognitive achievement approaches as well as attitudes and value involvement in such processes. Media assisted learning in science education and informal learning environments are major research questions within this context. Altogether, a balance is provided between the development of innovative educational programs and its empirical evaluation on the basis of valid and reliable measurement instruments. Prof.Bogner's research projects consistently included cognitive (and emotional and attitudinal) assessment. A recently published empirical study sophistically described that hands-on approaches sometimes even decrease a learning success due to additional cognitive (over-) loads caused by experimental environments; this points to potential strategies to overcome this specific dilemma in educational hands-on activities.

Aida Boukottaya has been involved in several projects related to information systems interoperability at EPFL, UNIL (University of Lausanne) and UNIFR (University of Fribourg). She participates in several European projects as senior researcher. Her main interests are reuse of structured documents and semantic Web services. She also ensured several courses and trainings around multimedia documents, semantic Web and databases engineering and has several publications related to schema matching techniques and structured document reuse. She is currently working on the IST/IP/Palette project as senior researcher and Workpackage leader.

Bernadette Charlier is the leader of the Did@cTIC center and head of the department of Educational Sciences of the University of Fribourg. Her main interests in research and teaching relate to educational technology and adult learning. For many years, a special care has been given on the design and implementation of educational environments for teacher's professional development. She is currently the Deputy Scientific Coordinator of the IST/IP/Palette project.

Spyros Christodoulou is a computer engineer and member of Research Academic Computer Technology Institute in Patras, Greece since 2004. He is a graduate of Computer Engineering and Informatics Department, Patras, Greece (2001) and received his master degree in Signal Processing and Telecommunications from the same department (2003). Since 2000, he has been with CTI, published papers in a number of conferences and participated in national and European research projects.

M. Cleveland-Innes is a faculty member and program director in the Center for Distance Education at Athabasca University in Alberta, Canada. She teaches Research Methods and Leadership in the graduate programs of this department. Martha has received awards for her work on the student experience in online environments and held a major research grant through the Canadian Social Sciences and Humanities Research Council. In 2009 she received the President's Award for Research and Scholarly Excellence from Athabasca University. Her work is well published in academic journals in North America and Europe. Current research interests are in the area of leadership in open and distance higher education, teaching across the disciplines in online higher education and emotional presence in online communities of inquiry.

Grazia Concilio (MSc, PhD) is a civil engineer, took her PhD in 'Evaluation Methods for the Integrated Conservation of Environmental, Urban and Architectural Heritage' at the Università degli Studi di Napoli Federico II, and is currently assistant professor at the Polytechnic of Milan. Her research has been mainly focussed on the implementation of methodologies and techniques of knowledge representation for decision making in spatial planning. She is recently working on methods and ICT systems to support the production and the acquisition of action-oriented knowledge.

Anna De Liddo (MSc, PhD) has a background in Civil Engineering, a Master in Environmental Policy and Management and a PhD in Environmental and Urban Planning. Research interests focus on new technologies supporting knowledge representation, structuring and management, particularly with regards to collaborative decision-making processes in Environmental and Urban Planning domain. Her PhD centred on tracing the "memory" of a collaborative process of design. She is now Research Associate at KMi (Knowledge Media Institute) of The Open University, in Milton Keynes (UK). Current research plans aim at investigating how new media can shape the development of collective intelligence to cope with complex environmental matters such as global warming and climate change.

Sandy El Helou is a PhD student and research assistant at the School of Engineering, EPFL, since August 2006. She received her Bachelor degree in Computer Engineering from the Lebanese American University in June 2006. Her research interests lie in the field of computer supported cooperative work (CSCW) and focus on the modeling, development and evaluation of social software applications and personalized awareness services for sustaining collaboration for online communities. She is currently involved in PALETTE, an European project aiming at developing interoperable Web services to sustain individual as well as organizational learning in Communities of Practice.

D.R. Garrison is currently the director of the Teaching & Learning Centre and a full professor in the Faculty of Education at the University of Calgary. Dr. Garrison has co-authored a book titled "E-Learning in the 21st Century" where he provides a framework and core elements for online learning. He has most recently co-authored a book titled "Blended Learning in Higher Education" that uses the Community of Inquiry Framework to organize the book. Dr. Garrison won the 2004 Canadian Society for Studies in Higher Education Award for distinguished contribution to research in higher education and the 2005 Canadian Association for Distance Education Excellence in Research Award.

Panagiotis Germanakos, PhD, is a research scientist, in the Semantic and Cognitive Research Adaptivity Technologies (SCRAT) research group of the Department of Computer Science, University of Cyprus and in the Laboratory of New Technologies of the Faculty of Communication & Media Studies, National & Kapodistrian University of Athens. He obtained his PhD from the University of Athens in 2008 and his MSc in International Marketing Management from the Leeds University Business School in 1999. His BSc was in Computer Science and also holds a HND Diploma of Technician Engineer in the field of Computer Studies. His research interest is in Web Adaptation and Personalization Environments and Systems based on user profiling / filters encompassing amongst others visual, mental and affective processes, implemented on desktop and mobile / wireless platforms. He has several publications, including co-edited books, chapters, articles in journals, and conference contributions. Furthermore, he actively participates in numerous national and EU funded projects that mainly focus on the analysis, design and development of open interoperable integrated wireless/mobile and personalized technological infrastructures and systems in the ICT research areas of e Government, e-Health and e-Learning and has an extensive experience in the provision of consultancy of large scaled IT solutions and implementations in the business sector.

Denis Gillet received the Diploma (MS) in Electrical Engineering from the Swiss Federal Institute of Technology in Lausanne (EPFL) in 1988, and the PhD degree in Information Systems also from the EPFL in 1995. During 1992 he was appointed as research fellow at the Information Systems Laboratory of Stanford University in the United States. He is currently associate professor (MER) at EPFL where he leads a multi-disciplinary research group. His current research interests include new learning technologies, sustainable interaction and collaboration systems, as well as real-time Internet services. He is also a core partner of the PALETTE European integrated project (http://palette.ercim.org/) in charge of investigating innovative Web 2.0 social software to support collaborative learning and of the new STELLAR Network of Excellence on Technology Enhanced Learning.

George Gkotsis is a PhD student at the Mechanical Engineering and Aeronautics Department, University of Patras. He works as a research collaborator at the E-learning Sector of the Research Academic Computer Technology Institute, Patras, Greece. He holds a M.Sc. from the Computer Engineering and Informatics Department, University of Patras (2005), where he got his Diploma (2002). His research interests are on collaboration, argumentation systems, knowledge management and visualization, Web engineering and hypertext.

Evelyn Gullett previously taught at the Department of Business and Technology, Webster University, St. Louis, Missouri in the U.S. She combines her teaching experience with more than 23 years of international work experience in areas such as human resources management and recruitment, training and development, account management, sales and customer service support, marketing, research analysis, strategic planning, project management and consulting. Her research interests include e-learning, organisational behaviour, change and development, work relationships, leadership application, coaching, cultural diversity, training and development as well as qualitative research. Dr. Gullett has worked on projects in various industries ranging from international hotel and tourism management, airline services, retail, call centers, hospital administration, education and the federal government. Dr. Gullett received her PhD in Human and Organizational Systems, a business behavioural science degree, from The Fielding Graduate University, Santa Barbara, California. She holds an MA in Organizational Development and earned her MBA with a concentration in Human Resource Management (focus on M&A) and BA in Human Resource Development from Hawaii Pacific University.

Thanasis Hadzilacos, 55, is a professor of Information Systems at the Open University of Cyprus where he directs the graduate program in Information Systems. Until September 2007 he was Dean of Science and Technology at the Hellenic Open University where he served as associate professor of software engineering, directed the Open and Distance Laboratory for Educational Material and Educational Methodology, the graduate course on Information Systems and the undergraduate Computer Science course. Educated at Harvard, USA, he had substantial industrial experience before joining Computer Technology Institute in 1986, where he continues as a researcher with the responsibility of the Educational Technology and the e-Learning Sectors and R&D Unit III "Applied Information Systems". During 1996-2001 he designed and managed the Greek national project "Odysseia" for the utilization of Information and Communication Technologies in secondary education. He has served as a member of the Council of Europe working group for Teaching and Learning in the Communication Society and the Greek national representative to E.U. DG Education and Culture for building the European portal on educational opportunities.

Nory B. Jones (PhD), is an associate professor of Management Information Systems and Director of Graduate Programs at the University of Maine Business School. She received her PhD in Information Systems from the University of Missouri-Columbia. Her research interests include knowledge management, collaborative technologies, and organizational learning.

Dimitris Kalles (born 1969) was educated in Greece (Diploma) and in the UK (MSc, PhD). He is a researcher and tutor with the Hellenic Open University and the Open University of Cyprus. He has also worked as a research manager for a research institute and as an expert evaluator for the European Commission and as a technical director for a software development company. He has been teaching courses, authoring coursework and supervising diploma theses on AI, complexity, programming and software engineering for several years, at an undergraduate and postgraduate level. He has co-developed several systems and he has published about 40 papers in journals and conferences on the above subjects.

Vasilis Kallistros is a computer engineer and member of Research Academic Computer Technology Institute in Patras, Greece since 1997. He is a graduate of Computer Engineering and Informatics Department of the University of Patras, Greece (1987). He holds a masters degree from Stanford University (1989). His research interests include computer supported collaboration systems, educational software, Web-based information systems, role-based access control models.

Dionysis Karaiskakis (born 1967) graduated University of Patras (Department of Physics, 1989) and received MSc degree in Computer Science (Department of Computer Engineering & Informatics, (University of Patras, 2000). Currently he is a candidate PhD at the Hellenic Open University (HOU), School of Sciences and Technology. Since 1994 has been working in Research Academic Computer Technology Institute (CTI) and in the HOU in Greece as technical responsible for major IT R&D projects, in the field of e-learning and network technologies. Research interest focus on knowledge discovery and data mining on networked communities in e-learning environments. He has published 3 papers in conferences and one Journal on the above subjects.

Nikos Karousos holds a Diploma (1998) and a M.Sc. (2000) from the Dept. of Computer Engineering and Informatics University of Patras, Greece. He is currently a PhD student in the provision of hypertext services. He works in the E-Learning Sector of the Research Academic Computer Technology Institute, Patras, Greece. His research is focused on the areas of Hypertext/Hypermedia, Web Services, Web-based Information Systems and Knowledge Management.

Omar J. Khan, (PhD) Dr. Khan is an assistant professor of Marketing at the University of Maine Business School. He received his PhD in International Business and Marketing from Saint Louis University. His research interests are knowledge management, social networks, online consumer behavior, regionalization of firms and countries and emerging markets

Zacharias Lekkas is a research assistant and doctoral candidate at the New Technologies Laboratory of the Faculty of Communication and Media Studies of the University of Athens. He holds an Msc in Occupational Psychology from the University of Nottingham. He is interested in the role of emotions in web-based educational systems, and has conducted empirical research on the effect of human factors such as anxiety, emotional moderation, emotional intelligence, self efficacy etc. Additionally, his research interests include the field of decision making support in Adaptive Hypermedia and the design of personalized training systems. His work has been published in conferences, journals and edited books, whilst he is one of the awarded authors (best student paper award) at the Adaptive Hypermedia 2008 conference.

Loïc Merz is a software engineer. He has worked on implementation of several platforms related to structuring web documents and has participated to the IST/IP/Palette project, especially on automatic querying of structured documents. He is currently working for MTI Management as business analyst and consultant.

Christos G. Mettouris is a graduate of the Computer Engineering & Informatics Department in the University of Patras. He holds a masters degree of the same department. He is a member of the e-Learning sector of the Research Academic Computer Technology Institute (RACTI). He has published award-winning papers in national conferences and participated in national and European research projects. His research interests include Human Computer Interaction, Web-Based Information Systems, Wireless technologies and Mobile Networks.

Costas Mourlas is assistant professor in the National and Kapodistrian University of Athens (Greece), Department of Communication and Media Studies since 2002. He obtained his PhD from the Department of Informatics, University of Athens in 1995 and graduated from the University of Crete in 1988 with a Diploma in Computer Science. In 1998 was an ERCIM fellow for post-doctoral studies through research in STFC, UK. He was employed as Lecturer at the Univeristy of Cyprus, Department of Computer Science from 1999 till 2002. His previous research work focused on distributed multimedia systems with adaptive behaviour, Quality of Service issues, streaming media and the Internet. His current main research interest is in the design and the development of intelligent environments that provide adaptive and personalized context to the users according to their preferences, cognitive characteristics and emotional state. He has several publications including edited books, chapters, articles in journals and conference contributions. Dr. C. Mourlas has taught various undergraduate as well as postgraduate courses in the Dept. of Computer Science of the University of Cyprus and the Dept. of Communication and Media Studies of the University of Athens. Furthermore, he has coordinated and actively participated in numerous national and EU funded projects.

Toshie Ninomiya graduated from Department of Administration Engineering, Faculty of Science and Technology, Keio University in 1993. After graduation, she worked in Toyota Motor Corporation as an engineer of industrial technology, and developed a system for coating with colleagues and got a patent with the system. As her interest went forward human cognition, she worked in Counselling Room of Keio University as an intake-counsellor, and searched genes related to cognition at Social, Genetics and Developmental Psychiatry Research Centre, Institute of London, the UK. After coming back to Japan, she worked in Department of Education, Ibaraki University as an assistant professor. She is currently an assistant professor at the University of Electro-Communications, Graduate School of Information Systems. Her research interests are in Human Cognition, Human Development, and Learning Design. Her new research plans are in Infrastructure for Ubiquitous Society with Distributed Computers, and ICT Skill Standards between companies.

Dora Nousia is a senior computer engineer educated at the University of Patras, and currently, director of the eLearning Sector of Research Academic Computer Technology Institute(CTI), Greece. She has designed and managed large pilot projects on the utilization of ICT in schools in Greece and abroad, and she is a consultant for various aspects of the application of eLearning into the entire educational system. She leads projects related to innovative software development for communities, collaboration and distance learning.

Toshio Okamoto graduated from Kyoto University of Education in 1973, obtained Master of educational psychology from Tokyo Gakugei University in 1975, PhD from Tokyo institute of Technology in 1989. He worked at Kanazawa Institute of Technology as lecturer and at Tokyo Gakugei University as an associate professor. He is currently a professor at the University of Electro-Communications, Graduate School of Information Systems from 1992 and a director of the Center for e-Learning Research and Promotion. His research interests include artificial intelligence, knowledge computing, educational technology and learning science, theoretical and application studies/design of e-Learning, computer-supported collaborative learning systems and curriculum development in Information Education. He standardizes collaborative technology in learning technology as a convener of WG2 (Collaborative Technology) of LTSC/ISO SC36 (Learning Technologies Standards Committee). He is a president of Japanese Society for Information and Systems in Education, and also a president of Japanese Association for Education of Information Studies.

Kiriakou Panagiotis is a graduate of the Computer Engineering & Informatics Department in the University of Patras. He is a member of the e-Learning sector of the Research Academic Computer Technology Institute (RACTI). He has published award-winning papers in national conferences and participated in national and European research projects. His research interests include knowledge management systems, human computer interaction and Web-based information systems.

Micaël Paquier is a software engineer. He has worked on implementation of several platforms related to information systems and webservices interoperability, including widgets. He is also interested in the problematic of structured documents production and reuse. He is currently working on the IST/IP/Palette project as scientific assistant. He is responsible for the platform of DocReuse Evolution and Portal.

Maria Pouliopoulou has graduated at 2003 from the department of Computer Engineering and Informatics at the University of Patras. Since then she has been working at the Hellenic Open University as a computer engineer, supporting and administering the university's portal, developing web courses and engaging in research work about e-learning. At 2007 she received her MSc in Informatics from Edinburgh University with specialism in Knowledge Representation and Reasoning, having received an EPSRC (Engineering and Physical Sciences Research Council) scholarship. She is currently working as a computer engineer and a researcher at the Research Academic Computer Technology Institute in Patras, Greece.

Kevin Quick is a research fellow in the Knowledge Media Institute at the Open University (UK). His work focuses on the development and research into new collaborative multimedia tools, and their application into various types of online communities. His current works forms part of the ProLearn European Network of Excellence. Current areas of investigation include the FlashMeeting video conferencing tool, FlashVlog video blogging tool and Hexagon video presence tool. In addition to his knowledge in new media systems Kevin also has a background in electronics and a PhD in new material technologies from Imperial College, London.

Hannu Salmi works currently as a professor of science centre pedagogy in Finland at the University of Helsinki, Department of Applied Sciences in Education. Before that he held a position of Professor of Science Communication in Sweden at the University of Dalarna. For more than two decades (since

1984) he has been working as the Manager of Research and Development in Heureka, the Finnish Science Centre developing the hands-on science learning. He has been also coordinating many EU-funded science education projects like Hands-on & Brains-on, Open Science Info, and PENCIL. The main interest of the research of professor Salmi is open learning environments, informal education, intrinsic motivation, career choices, and teacher training.

Christophe Salzmann is a senior research associate at the Swiss Federal Institute of Technology in Lausanne (EPFL). He received his MS degree in computer Science from the University of Florida in 1999 and his PhD degree from the EPFL in 2005. His research interests include Web technologies, real-time control, real-time interaction over the Internet with an emphasis on Quality of Service and bandwidth adaptation.

Peter Scott is the director of the Knowledge Media Institute of the Open University (UK). Peter's research group prototypes the application of new technologies and media to learning at all levels. Peter's current research interests range widely across knowledge and media research. Three key threads at the moment are: tele-presence; streaming media systems; and ubiquity. He has a BA (1983) and PhD (1987) in Psychology. Peter Scott lectured in Psychology and Cognitive Science at the University of Sheffield. He then joined the OU to help launch the innovative Knowledge Media research agenda. In this new field he has over 15 recent major research grants from the UK EPSRC. Recent EU grants include the successful EU Network of Excellence, Prolearn, where he serves on the executive board. The Prolearn network also supports two of Peter's hottest current technology developments: Hexagon and FlashMeeting. The FlashMeeting research into effective live and online events is also now a core element of the Open University's OpenLearn LabSpace which was launched in October 2006. He has a strong portfolio of over 40 conventional research publications in this field.

Nalin Sharda gained B.Tech. and PhD degrees from the Indian Institute of Technology, Delhi. Presently he teaches and leads research in Multimedia and Internet Communications at the School of Computer Science and Mathematics, Victoria University, Australia. Dr. Sharda publications include the Multimedia Information Networking textbook, and around 100 papers and handbook chapters. Nalin has invented Movement Oriented Design (MOD) paradigm for the creation of effective multimedia content based experience, and applied it to e-Learning and other applications. Dr, Sharda is has led projects for the Australian Sustainable Tourism CRC, to develop e-Tourism systems using Semantic Web technologies, and innovative visualisation methodologies. Nalin has been invited to present lectures and seminars in the Distinguished Lecturer series of the European Union's Prolearn program. He has presented over fifty seminars, lectures, and Key Note addresses in Austria, Australia, Canada, Finland, Germany, Hong Kong, India, Malaysia, Pakistan, Japan, Singapore, Sweden, Switzerland, UAE, and USA.

Stéphane Sire has 10 years of experience in human computer interaction. He has developed languages and tools for user interface (UI) programming, designed UI for collaborative environments, and conducted usability evaluations. He has been involved in numerous projects while at CENA (French Air Traffic Control R&D centre), CWI (Centre for Mathematics and Computer Science in Amsterdam), IntuiLab (a French startup company doing innovative UI design) and EPFL/MEDIA. He is currently working on interaction styles and software techniques for integrating Web applications and services to improve group collaboration.

Sofoklis Sotiriou got his PhD in Physics in 1996 at the University of Athens, Greece. He joined postgraduate courses at CERN in Geneva. Since 1998 he is the Head of R&D of Ellinogermaniki Agogi foundation. He has been active in co-ordination and development of research project on implementation and teachers training within the framework of several EU funded programmes. He is member of the European Academy of science and the member of the Board of the ECSITE – European network for science centres and museums. The main research interests are the ict-based new technologies in science education.

Eleftheria Tomadaki has worked as a research fellow in the Knowledge Media Institute (Open University, UK), in the context of the UK Open Learning initiative, while she is currently involved in numerous industrial projects as an e-Learning specialist. Her research interests focus on the study of large-scale synchronous collaborative media, e-Learning and social software. She received her PhD in Information Extraction by the University of Surrey. Her PhD research investigated the merging of information from texts describing video content for video annotation by employing cross-document coreference techniques and introduced a new and challenging scenario - film and the variety of collateral text genres narrating its content, including unrestricted sets of events.

Nikos Tsianos is a research assistant and doctoral candidate at the New Technologies Laboratory of the Faculty of Communication and Media Studies of the University of Athens. He holds an Msc in Political Communication and a bachelor degree in Communication and Mass Media from the University of Athens. His main research area is the incorporation of theories from the Psychology of Individual Differences into Adaptive Educational Hypermedia, the development of corresponding systems and the empirical evaluation of such systems in the context of an experimental psychology methodology. He has published several articles in conferences and journals regarding this field of research, while he has been credited with the best student paper award at the Adaptive Hypermedia 2008 conference. He is currently editing a book about cognitive and emotional human factors in web-learning.

Nikos Tsirakis is a PhD candidate in the Computer Engineering and Informatics Department in the University of Patras (Advisor Assis. Prof. Christos Makris). In September 1999 he entered the Department of Computer Engineering and Informatics, School of Engineering, University of Patras and he received his Diploma, as a Computer Engineer, in December 2004. In October 2006 he received his Master in Computer Science in the same Department. His research interests are the Design and Analysis of Data Mining Algorithms and Applications (specially for huge data manipulation ex. Data Bases, Data Streams, XML Data), Hypertext, Software Quality Assessment and finally Web Technologies.

Manolis Tzagarakis holds a PhD in Computer Engineering & Informatics and is currently a researcher at the Research Academic Computer Technology Institute in Patras, Greece. He has published papers in international conferences and journals. His research interests are in the areas of hypertext and hypermedia, knowledge management, collaboration support systems, Web-based information systems, technology-enhanced learning, and group decision support systems. He has served the program committees of several conferences and workshops.

367

Christine Vanoirbeek is the leader of the MEDIA (Models and Environments for Document related Interaction and Authoring) research group at the School of Computer and Communication Sciences at EPFL. Her main interests in research and teaching relate to structured dynamic documents and Web based information systems. For many years, a special care has been given on the design and implementation of Web-based environments in educational purposes. She is currently the scientific coordinator of the IST/IP/Palette project. She has been acting for 10 years as the Swiss delegate in the executive committee of ERCIM. She is also the EPFL contact at W3C.

Chiu-Man Yu received his B.Eng (Hons) in Computer Engineering in July 2000, and M.Phil. in Computer Science and Engineering in August 2002, both from the Chinese University of Hong Kong. In September 2002 to July 2003, he worked as research assistant in the same University to research on Mobile agents for mobile devices. From August 2003 to April 2007, he was a PhD student and research on Grid computing and authorization systems. He received my PhD in Computer Science and Engineering in May 2007 from the Chinese University of Hong Kong. During May 2007 to July 2008, he worked in EPFL as a research associate to participate into the Palette project.

Index